# Rock Slope Engineering

# Rock Slope Engineering

## Civil and mining
## 4th edition

Duncan C. Wyllie and
Christopher W. Mah

Spon Press
Taylor & Francis Group

LONDON AND NEW YORK

First published 1974 by the Institute of Mining and Metallurgy
Second edition published 1977
Third edition published 1981

Reprinted 1991, 1994 (twice), 1996, 1997, 1999, 2001
© The Institute of Mining and Metallurgy and E. Hoek and J. W. Bray
2 Park Square, Milton Park, Abingdon, Oxon OX14 4RN

Simultaneously published in the USA and Canada
by Spon Press
270 Madison Ave, New York, NY 10016

*Spon Press is an imprint of the Taylor & Francis Group*

© 2004 Duncan C. Wyllie and Christopher W. Mah

Reprinted 2007 (twice)

Typeset in Sabon by
Newgen Imaging Systems (P) Ltd, Chennai, India
Printed and bound in Great Britain by
St Edmundsbury Press Ltd, Bury St Edmunds, Suffolk

*British Library Cataloguing in Publication Data*
A catalogue record for this book is available from the British Library

*Library of Congress Cataloging in Publication Data*
    Rock slope engineering : civil and mining / Duncan C. Wyllie,
Christopher W. Mah—4th ed.
      p. cm.
   "Based on Rock Slope Engineering (third edition, 1981) by
Dr Evert Hoek and Dr John Bray."
   1. Rock slopes. I. Mah, Christopher W. II. Wyllie, Duncan C.,
1933—Rock slope engineering. III. Title.
TA706.W98 2004
624.1'51363–dc22                    2003014937

ISBN 978–0–415–28001–3

# Contents

# Introduction

Readers will undoubtedly recognize the similarity of this book to *Rock Slope Engineering* by Dr Evert Hoek and Dr John Bray. We hope the following discussion of the origin and evolution of the current book will help to demonstrate the relationship between the two.

*Rock Slope Engineering* was published in three editions (1974, 1977 and 1981) by the Institute of Mining and Metallurgy in London. The original research for the book at the University of London was sponsored by the mining industry in response to a need to develop design methods for increasingly deep open pits. The 1960s and 1970s had seen the development of a new generation of high production drills, shovels and trucks that made low grade ore deposits economical to mine, and there was a consequent significant increase in the size of open pits. The investigation and design techniques originally developed in *Rock Slope Engineering* for mines were soon adopted in civil engineering where the slopes' heights are usually less than those in open pits, but there is a need for a high level of reliability in terms of both rock falls and overall stability. In response to the demand for a book that clearly presents well-proven methods to design rock slopes, Hoek and Bray's book has continued to sell steadily around the world, and has been translated into a number of languages.

In 1980, one of the authors of this book (DCW) was awarded a contract by the Federal Highway Administration (FHWA) in Washington to prepare a manual on rock slope design and construction specifically applicable to highways. At that time, I was working with Dr Hoek and he generously agreed that his manuscript of *Rock Slope Engineering* could be adapted for this purpose. The manual closely followed the original book, apart from chapters on slope stabilization and movement monitoring. A second FHWA contract was awarded in 1996 as part of an eleven module series on highway geotechnical engineering, and this opportunity was taken to embark on a major updating of the manual. The manuals have been used primarily as teaching material for a series of courses sponsored by the National Highway Institute for highway engineers in the United States; to date over 40 courses have been presented.

It was realized that a limitation of the FHWA manuals was their focus on highway engineering, and that their availability was generally limited to course participants. Therefore, in 2001 it was decided that it would be worthwhile to produce another update that would cover the wider field of rock slope engineering, including civil and mining applications. In order to take this step, it was necessary to obtain the permission and co-operation of a number of organizations and individuals—Mr Jerry DiMaggio of the Federal Highway Administration, Dr G. P. Jayaprakash of the Transportation Research Board, both in Washington, and Dr George Munfakh of Parsons Brinckerhoff Quade and Douglas (PBQD) in New York. We are most grateful for their assistance and encouragement.

Of course, the most important participant in this work has been Dr Evert Hoek who generously agreed that we could use *Rock Slope Engineering* as the basis for the new work. Since Dr Hoek lives in the same neighborhood, it has been possible to have a series of meetings to discuss both the overall approach and details of the contents and methods. We express our gratitude for the valuable assistance that we have received from Dr Hoek over the two years, as well as his pioneering work with Dr Bray in establishing the fundamental procedures for rock slope engineering.

Dr Lorin Lorig and Mr Pedro Varona of Itasca Corporation and Mr Alan Stewart and his colleagues at Piteau Associates Engineering have also made important contributions. Dr Lorig and Mr Varona wrote Chapter 10 on numerical analysis methods, and the personnel from Piteau wrote Chapter 15 on case studies on open pit mining. We decided these two chapters were best written by persons working in these specialist fields, and we appreciate their hard work and dedication.

One of our objectives in writing this book has been to maintain much of the original content of *Rock Slope Engineering*, because the basic slope design methods that were developed for the 1974 edition are still valid to this day. Our approach has been to incorporate, within the original framework, technical advances and experience in rock slope design and construction projects over the past 30 years. This has allowed us to maintain the structure of *Rock Slope Engineering* so that those who are familiar with Hoek and Bray can readily find their way around this book. In addition to generally updating the book, the following is a list of the major topics that have been added:

- *Geological data collection*—The International Society of Rock Mechanics nomenclature for structural geology is included in Chapter 3 and Appendix II.
- *Rock mass strength*—The 2002 version of the Hoek–Brown rock mass strength criterion is included in Chapter 4.
- *Earthquakes*—The effects of earthquakes on slope stability and design methods for slopes in seismic areas are described in Chapter 6.
- *Probabilistic, and Load and Resistance Factor design methods*—The basic principles of probabilistic and LRFD design are discussed in Chapter 1; an example of probabilistic design is included in Chapter 6.
- *Numerical analysis*—Chapter 10 is a new chapter describing the use of numerical analysis methods in slope design.
- *Production blasting*—Updated methods of designing production blasts have been added to Chapter 11, which covers in addition, blasting methods for final walls and control of damage outside the blast area.
- *Slope stabilization and rock fall protection*—Chapter 12 is a new chapter describing rock slope hazard assessment, slope reinforcement and rock fall protection such as ditches, fences and sheds.
- *Slope movement monitoring*—Surface and sub-surface movement monitoring methods, and data interpretation are described in Chapter 13.
- *Case studies in civil engineering*—Case studies of plane, wedge, circular and toppling failures are described in Chapter 14.
- *Case studies in open pit mining*—Four case studies demonstrating pit slope design in a variety of geologic environments are described in Chapter 15.

It may be noticed that some material is very similar to that in the books *Foundations on Rock* and *Landslides: Investigation and Stabilization*. This duplication is inevitable when discussing fundamentals of rock mechanics that do not change significantly over time.

We would like to express our gratitude to a number of people, in addition to Dr Hoek who have assisted us with this work. In particular, Ms Sonia Skermer and Mr George Gorczynski prepared the illustrations, and Ms Glenda Gurtina prepared the original FHWA manual and has worked on many of the complex portions of the text. We also appreciate the valuable input on seismic design by Dr Randy Jibson and Dr Upul Atukorala, the photographs supplied by Rio Tinto Ltd and acknowledge our long associations with the Federal Highway Administration in Washington DC, the Canadian Pacific Railway, and the British Columbia Ministry of Transportation.

Finally, we are most grateful to our colleagues, fellow geotechnical engineers and contractors with whom we have worked over many years on a wide range of projects. This book attempts to distill our collectively acquired experience.

Duncan C. Wyllie
www.wnrockeng.com

Christopher W. Mah
www.cmrockeng.com
Vancouver, Canada, 2003

# Foreword

My work on rock slope engineering started more than thirty years ago while I was Professor of Rock Mechanics at the Imperial College of Science and Technology in London, England. A four-year research project on this topic was sponsored by 23 mining companies around the world, and was motivated by the need to develop design methods for the rock slopes in large open pit mines which were becoming increasingly important in the exploitation of low-grade mineral deposits. *Rock Slope Engineering*, co-authored with my colleague Dr John Bray, was first published in 1974 and then revised in 1977 and again in 1981.

While rock slope engineering remains an important subject, my own interests have shifted towards tunnelling and underground excavations. Consequently, when Duncan Wyllie suggested that he and Christopher Mah were willing to prepare a new book on rock slopes I felt that this would be an excellent move. They have had a long involvement in practical rock slope engineering, mainly for civil engineering construction projects, and are familiar with recent developments in methods of analysis and stabilization. The evolution of their text, from *Rock Slope Engineering* to a manual on rock slope design for the US Federal Highway Administration, is described in their introduction and need not be repeated here.

The text that follows is a comprehensive reference work on all aspects of rock slope engineering and, while it embodies all the original concepts of my work, it expands on these and introduces a significant amount of new material, for both mining and civil engineering and several new case studies. As such, I believe that it will be an important source of fundamental and practical information for both students and designers for many years to come.

I commend the authors for their efforts in producing this volume and I look forward to having a copy on my own bookshelf.

Evert Hoek
Vancouver, 2003

# Notation

| | |
|---|---|
| $A$ | Area of plane (m$^2$) |
| a | Material constant for rock mass strength; ground acceleration (m/s$^2$) |
| $B$ | Burden distance for blast holes (m) |
| $b$ | Distance of tension crack behind crest of face (m); joint spacing (m) |
| $C_d$ | Dispersion coefficient |
| $c$ | Cohesion (kPa) |
| $D$ | Disturbance factor for rock mass strength; depth (m) |
| d | Diameter (mm) |
| $E_m$ | Deformation modulus for rock mass |
| $e$ | Joint aperture (mm) |
| F | Shape factor |
| FS | Factor of safety |
| $G$ | Shear modulus (GPa) |
| GSI | Geological Strength Index |
| $g$ | Acceleration due to gravity (m/s$^2$) |
| $H$ | Height of slope, face (m) |
| $h$ | Water level head above datum (m) |
| $i$ | Roughness angle of asperities (degrees) |
| JRC | Joint roughness coefficient |
| $K$ | Bulk modulus (GPa); hydraulic conductivity (cm/s$^{-1}$); corrosion service life constant ($\mu$m), rate of slope movement constant |
| $k$ | Seismic coefficient; attenuation constant for blast vibrations |
| $L$ | Length of scan line, face, borehole (m) |
| $l$ | Persistence of discontinuity (m); unit vector |
| $m$ | Unit vector |
| $m_b$ | Material constant for rock mass strength |
| $m_i$ | material constant for intact rock |
| $N$ | Number of joints, readings |
| $n$ | Unit vector, number of toppling blocks |
| $P$ | Probability |
| $p$ | Pressure (kPa) |
| $Q$ | External load (kN) |
| $R$ | Resultant vector; hole radius (mm) |
| $r$ | radius of piezometer (mm) |

| | |
|---|---|
| $S$ | Shape factor; spacing distance for blast holes (m) |
| SD | Standard deviation |
| $s$ | Spacing of discontinuity (m); material constant for rock mass strength |
| $T$ | Rock bolt tension force (kN) |
| $t$ | Time (s, yr) |
| $U$ | Uplift force on sliding plane due to water pressure (kN) |
| $V$ | Thrust force in tension crack due to water pressure (kN); velocity of seismic waves (m/s), velocity of slope movement |
| $W$ | Weight of sliding block (kN); explosive weight per delay (kg) |
| $X$ | Loss of element thickness, corrosion ($\mu$m) |
| $z$ | Depth of tension crack (m) |
| $z_w$ | Depth of water in tension crack (m) |
| $\alpha$ | Dip direction of plane (degrees) |
| $\beta$ | Attenuation constant for blast vibrations |
| $\Delta x$ | Width of toppling slab, slice in circular failure (m) |
| $\delta$ | Displacement (mm) |
| $\varepsilon$ | Coefficient of thermal expansion (per °C) |
| $\phi$ | Friction angle (degrees) |
| $\gamma$ | Unit weight (kN/m$^3$) |
| $\mu$ | Poisson's ratio |
| $\sigma$ | Normal stress (kPa) |
| $\sigma_{cm}$ | Compressive strength of rock mass (kPa) |
| $\sigma_{ci}$ | Compressive strength of intact rock (kPa) |
| $\sigma'_1$ | Major principal effective stress (kPa) |
| $\sigma'_3$ | Minor principal effective stress (kPa) |
| $\tau$ | Shear stress (kPa) |
| $\psi$ | Dip of plane (degrees) |
| $\upsilon$ | Viscosity of water (m$^2$/s) |

# Note

The recommendations and procedures contained herein are intended as a general guide, and prior to their use in connection with any design, report, specification or construction procedure, they should be reviewed with regard to the full circumstances of such use. Accordingly, although every care has been taken in the preparation of this book, no liability for negligence or otherwise can be accepted by the authors or the publisher.

# Chapter 1

# Principles of rock slope design

## 1.1 Introduction

A variety of engineering activities require excavation of rock cuts. In civil engineering, projects include transportation systems such as highways and railways, dams for power production and water supply, and industrial and urban development. In mining, open pits account for the major portion of the world's mineral production. The dimensions of open pits range from areas of a few hectares and depths of less than 100 m, for some high grade mineral deposits and quarries in urban areas, to areas of hundreds of hectares and depths as great as 800 m, for low grade ore deposits. The overall slope angles for these pits range from near vertical for shallow pits in good quality rock to flatter than 30° for those in very poor quality rock.

Figure 1.1 shows two typical rock slopes. Figure 1.1(a) is a rock cut, with a face angle of about 60°, supported with tensioned anchors incorporating reinforced concrete bearing pads about 1 m$^2$ that distribute the anchor load on the face. The face is also covered with shotcrete to prevent weathering and loosening between the bolts. Water control measures include drain holes through the shotcrete and drainage channels on the benches and down the face to collect surface run-off. The support is designed to both ensure long-term stability of the overall slope, and minimize rock falls that could be a hazard to traffic. Figure 1.1(b) shows the Palabora open pit in South Africa that is 830 m deep and an overall slope angle of 45–50°; this is one of the steepest and deepest pits in the world (Stewart *et al.*, 2000).

The upper part of the pit is accessed via a dual ramp system, which reduces to a single ramp in the lower part of the pit.

In addition to these man-made excavations, in mountainous terrain the stability of natural rock slopes may also be of concern. For example, highways and railways located in river valleys may be located below such slopes, or cut into the toe, which may be detrimental to stability. One of the factors that may influence the stability of natural rock slopes is the regional tectonic setting. Factors of safety may be only slightly greater than unity where there is rapid uplift of the land mass and corresponding down-cutting of the watercourses, together with earthquakes that loosen and displace the slope. Such conditions exist in seismically active areas such as the Pacific Rim, the Himalayas and central Asia.

The required stability conditions of rock slopes will vary depending on the type of project and the consequence of failure. For example, for cuts above a highway carrying high traffic volumes it will be important that the overall slope be stable, and that there be few if any rock falls that reach the traffic lanes. This will often require both careful blasting during construction, and the installation of stabilization measures such as rock anchors. Because the useful life of such stabilization measures may only be 10–30 years, depending on the climate and rate of rock degradation, periodic maintenance may be required for long-term safety. In contrast, slopes for open pit mines are usually designed with factors of safety

*Figure 1.1* Examples of rock slopes: (a) rock slope in Hong Kong supported with tensioned rock anchors and reinforced concrete reaction blocks, and shotcrete (photograph by Gary Fu); and (b) 830 m deep Palabora open pit copper mine, South Africa. (Photograph courtesy: Rio Tinto Ltd.)

in the range of 1.2–1.4, and it is accepted that movement of the slope and possibly some partial slope failures will occur during the life of the mine. In fact, an optimum slope design is one that fails soon after the end of operations.

In the design of cut slopes, there is usually little flexibility to adjust the orientation of the slope to suit the geological conditions encountered in the excavation. For example, in the design of a highway, the alignment is primarily governed by such factors as available right-of-way, grades and vertical and horizontal curvature. Therefore, the slope design must accommodate the particular geological conditions that are encountered along the highway. Circumstances where geological conditions may dictate modifications to the slope design include the need for relocation where the alignment intersects a major landslide that could be activated by construction. With respect to open pit slope design, the pit must obviously be located on the ore body, and the design must accommodate the geological conditions that exist within the area of the pit. This may require different slope designs around the pit.

The common design requirement for rock cuts is to determine the maximum safe cut face angle compatible with the planned maximum height.

The design process is a trade-off between stability and economics. That is, steep cuts are usually less expensive to construct than flat cuts because there is less volume of excavated rock, less acquisition of right-of-way and smaller cut face areas. However, with steep slopes it may be necessary to install extensive stabilization measures such as rock bolts and shotcrete in order to minimize both the risk of overall slope instability and rock falls during the operational life of the project.

### 1.1.1  Scope of book

The design of rock cuts involves the collection of geotechnical data, the use of appropriate design methods, and the implementation of excavation methods and stabilization/protection measures suitable for the particular site conditions. In order to address all these issues, the book is divided into three distinct sections that cover respectively design data, design methods and excavation/support procedures. Details of the main topics covered in each section are as follows:

(a)  *Design data*

- *Geological data* of which structural geology is usually the most important. This information includes the orientation of discontinuities and their characteristics such as length, spacing, roughness and infilling. Chapter 2 discusses interpretation of these data, while Chapter 3 describes methods of data collection.

- *Rock strength* with the most important parameter being the shear strength of discontinuity surfaces or rock masses, and to a lesser extent the compressive strength of the intact rock (Chapter 4).
- *Ground water* conditions comprise the likely ground water level within the slope, and procedures to drain the slope, if necessary (Chapters 5 and 12).

(b) *Design methods*

- Design methods for rock slopes fall into two groups—*limit equilibrium analysis* and *numerical analysis*. Limit equilibrium analyses calculates the factor of safety of the slope and different procedures are used for plane, wedge, circular and toppling failures; the type of failure is defined by the geology of the slope (Chapters 6–9). Numerical analysis examines the stresses and strains developed in the slope, and stability is assessed by comparing the stresses in the slope with the rock strength (Chapter 10).

(c) *Excavation and stabilization*

- *Blasting* issues relevant to slope stability include production blasting, controlled blasting on final faces, and in urban areas the control of damage from ground vibrations, flyrock and noise (Chapter 11).
- *Stabilization* methods include rock reinforcement with rock anchors and dowels, rock removal involving scaling and trim blasting, and rock fall protection measures comprising ditches, fences and sheds (Chapter 12).
- *Monitoring* of slope movement is often an important part of slope management in open pit mines. Surface and sub-surface monitoring methods are discussed, as well as interpretation of the data (Chapter 13).
- *Civil and mining applications* are discussed in Chapters 14 and 15, respectively, which describe examples of slope design, including stabilization methods and movement monitoring programs. The examples illustrate the design procedures discussed in the earlier chapters.

Also included in the book are a series of example problems demonstrating both data analysis and design methods.

### 1.1.2 Socioeconomic consequences of slope failures

Failures of rock slopes, both man-made and natural, include rock falls, overall slope instability and landslides, as well as slope failures in open pit mines. The consequence of such failures can range from direct costs of removing the failed rock and stabilizing the slope to possibly a wide variety of indirect costs. Examples of indirect costs include damage to vehicles and injury to passengers on highways and railways, traffic delays, business disruptions, loss of tax revenue due to decreased land values, and flooding and disruption to water supplies where rivers are blocked by slides. In the case of mines, slope failures can result in loss of production together with the cost of removal of the failed material, and possible loss of ore reserves if it is not possible to mine the pit to its full depth.

The cost of slope failures is greatest in urbanized areas with high population densities where even small slides may destroy houses and block transportation routes (Transportation Research Board, 1996). In contrast, slides in rural areas may have few indirect costs, except perhaps the costs due to the loss of agricultural land. An example of a landslide that resulted in severe economic costs is the 1983 Thistle Slide in Utah that resulted in losses of about $200 million when the landslide dammed the Spanish Fork River severing railways and highways, and flooding the town

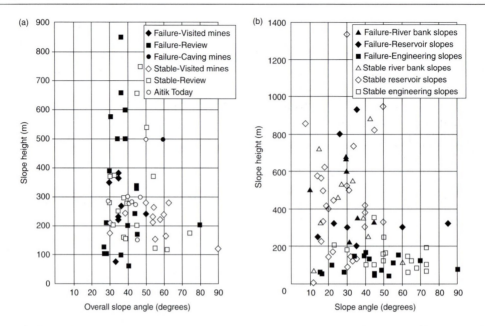

*Figure 1.2* Relationship between slope height and slope angle for open pits, and natural and engineered slopes: (a) pit slopes and caving mines (Sjöberg, 1999); and (b) natural and engineered slopes in China (data from Chen (1995a,b)).

of Thistle (University of Utah, 1985). An example of a landslide that resulted in both loss of life and economic costs is the Vaiont Slide in Italy in 1963. The slide inundated a reservoir sending a wave over the crest of the dam that destroyed five villages and took about 2000 lives (Kiersch, 1963; Hendron and Patton, 1985).

A country that experiences high costs of rock falls and landslides is Japan. This country has both highly developed infrastructure and steep mountainous terrain, and in addition, there are frequent triggering events such as high rainfall, freeze–thaw cycles and ground shaking due to earthquakes. Documentation of major landslides between 1938 and 1981 recorded total losses of 4834 lives and 188,681 homes (Ministry of Construction, Japan, 1983).

## 1.2   Principles of rock slope engineering

This section describes the primary issues that need to be considered in rock slope design for civil projects and open pit mines. The basic difference between these two types of project are that in civil engineering a high degree of reliability is required because slope failure, or even rock falls, can rarely be tolerated. In contrast, some movement of open pit slopes is accepted if production is not interrupted, and rock falls are of little consequence.

As a frame of reference for rock slope design, Figure 1.2 shows the results of surveys of the slope height and angle and stability conditions for natural, engineered and open pit mine slopes (Chen, 1995a,b; Sjöberg, 1999). It is of interest to note that there is some correspondence between the steepest and highest stable slopes for both natural and man-made slopes. The graphs also show that there are many unstable slopes at flatter angles and lower heights than the maximum values because weak rock or adverse structure can result in instability of even low slopes.

### 1.2.1   Civil engineering

The design of rock cuts for civil projects such as highways and railways is usually concerned with details of the structural geology. That is,

*Figure 1.3* Cut face coincident with continuous, low friction bedding planes in shale on Trans Canada Highway near Lake Louise, Alberta. (Photograph by A. J. Morris.)

the orientation and characteristics (such as length, roughness and infilling materials) of the joints, bedding and faults that occur behind the rock face. For example, Figure 1.3 shows a cut slope in shale containing smooth bedding planes that are continuous over the full height of the cut and dip at an angle of about 50° towards the highway. Since the friction angle of these discontinuities is about 20–25°, any attempt to excavate this cut at a steeper angle than the dip of the beds would result in blocks of rock sliding from the face on the beds; the steepest unsupported cut that can be made is equal to the dip of the beds. However, as the alignment of the road changes so that the strike of the beds is at right angles to the cut face (right side of photograph), it is not possible for sliding to occur on the beds, and a steeper face can be excavated.

For many rock cuts on civil projects, the stresses in the rock are much less than the rock strength so there is little concern that fracturing of intact rock will occur. Therefore, slope design is primarily concerned with the stability of blocks of rock formed by the discontinuities. Intact rock strength, which is used indirectly in slope design, relates to the shear strength of discontinuities and rock masses, as well as excavation methods and costs.

Figure 1.4 shows a range of geological conditions and their influence on stability, and illustrates the types of information that are important to design. Slopes (a) and (b) show typical conditions for sedimentary rock, such as sandstone and limestone containing continuous beds, on which sliding can occur if the dip of the beds is steeper than the friction angle of the discontinuity surface. In (a) the beds "daylight" on the steep cut face and blocks may slide on the bedding, while in (b) the face is coincident with the bedding and the face is stable. In (c) the overall face is also stable because the main discontinuity set dips into the face. However, there is some risk of instability of surficial blocks of rock formed by the conjugate joint set that dips out of the face, particularly if there has been blast damage during construction. In (d) the main joint set also dips into the face but at a steep angle to form a series of thin slabs that can fail by toppling where the center of gravity of the block lies outside the base. Slope (e) shows a typical horizontally bedded sandstone–shale sequence in which the shale weathers considerably faster than the sandstone to form a series of overhangs that can fail suddenly along vertical stress relief joints. Slope (f) is cut in weak rock containing closely spaced but low persistence joints that do not form a continuous sliding surface. A steep slope cut in this weak rock mass may fail along a shallow circular surface, partially along joints and partially through intact rock.

### 1.2.2 Open pit mining slope stability

The three main components of an open pit slope design are as follows (Figure 1.5). First, the overall pit slope angle from crest to toe, incorporates all ramps and benches. This may be a composite slope with a flatter slope in weaker, surficial materials, and a steeper slope in more competent rock at depth. In addition, the slope angle may vary around the pit to accommodate both differing geology and the layout of the ramp. Second, the inter-ramp angle is the slope, or slopes, lying between each ramp that will depend on the number of ramps and their widths. Third,

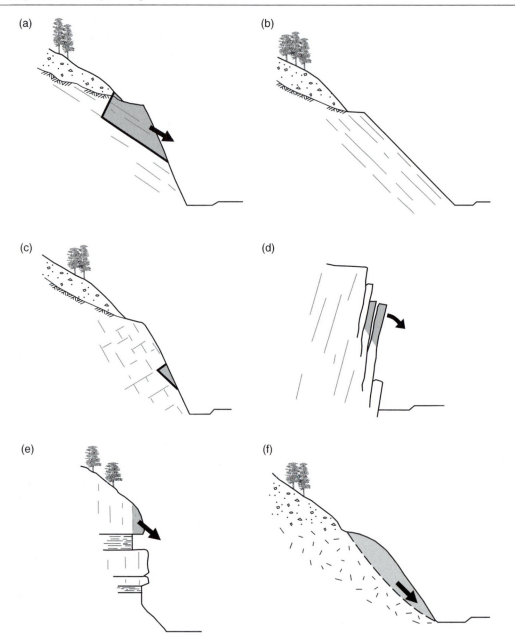

*Figure 1.4* Influence of geological conditions on stability of rock cuts: (a) potentially unstable—discontinuities "daylight" in face; (b) stable slope—face excavated parallel to discontinuities; (c) stable slope—discontinuities dip into face; (d) toppling failure of thin beds dipping steeply into face; (e) weathering of shale beds undercuts strong sandstone beds to form overhangs; (f) potentially shallow circular failure in closely fractured, weak rock.

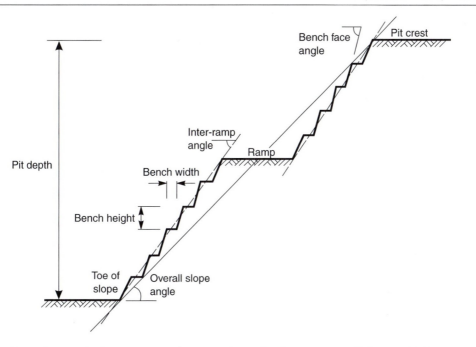

*Figure 1.5* Typical open pit slope geometry showing relationship between overall slope angle, inter-ramp angle and bench geometry.

the face angle of individual benches depends on vertical spacing between benches, or combined multiple benches, and the width of the benches required to contain minor rock falls.

Some of the factors that may influence slope design are the slope height, geology, rock strength, ground water pressures and damage to the face by blasting. For example, with each successive push-back of a slope, the depth of the pit will increase and there may need to be a corresponding decrease in the overall slope angle. Also, for slopes on which the ramp is located, the slope angle may be flatter to limit the risk of failures that take out the ramp, compared to slopes with no ramp where some instability may be tolerated. Where there is significant water pressure in the slope, consideration may be given to installing a drainage system if it can be shown that a reduction in water pressure will allow the slope angle to be increased. For deep pits where an increase in slope angle of one or two degrees will result in a saving of several million cubic meters of rock excavation, an extensive drainage system may be

justified. Such drainage systems could comprise fans of holes with lengths of hundreds of meters drilled from the slope face, or a drainage adit with holes drilled into the rock above the tunnel.

With respect to the bench face angle, this may be governed by the orientation of a predominant joint set if there are joints that dip out of the face at a steep angle. If this situation does not exist, then the bench angle will be related to the overall slope geometry, and whether single benches are combined into multiple benches. One factor that may influence the maximum height of individual benches is the vertical reach of excavating equipment, to limit the risk accidents due to collapse of the face.

In order to provide a guideline on stable pit slope angles, a number of studies have been carried out showing the relationship between slope angle, slope height and geology; the records also distinguished whether the slopes were stable or unstable (see Figure 1.2). These studies have been made for both open pit mine slopes (Sjöberg, 1999), and natural and engineered slopes in

China (Chen, 1995a,b). As would be expected, if the slopes were not selected according to geology, there is little correlation between slope height and angle for stable slopes. However, sorting of the data according to rock type and rock strength shows a reasonable correlation between slope height and angle for each classification.

## 1.3   Slope features and dimensions

The International Association of Engineering Geology has prepared definitions of landslide features and dimensions as shown in Figures 1.6 and 1.7 (IAEG, 1990; TRB, 1996). Although the diagrams depicting the landslides show soil-type slides with circular sliding surfaces, many of these landslide features are applicable to both rock slides and slope failures in weak and weathered rock. The value of the definitions shown in

Figures 1.6 and 1.7 is to encourage the use of consistent terminology that can be clearly understood by others in the profession when investigating and reporting on rock slopes and landslides.

## 1.4   Rock slope design methods

This section summarizes four different procedures for designing rock slopes, and shows the basic data that is required for analyzing slope stability. The design methods and the design data are common to both mining and civil engineering.

### 1.4.1   Summary of design methods

A basic feature of all slope design methods is that shear takes place along either a discrete sliding surface, or within a zone, behind the face. If the shear force (displacing force) is greater than

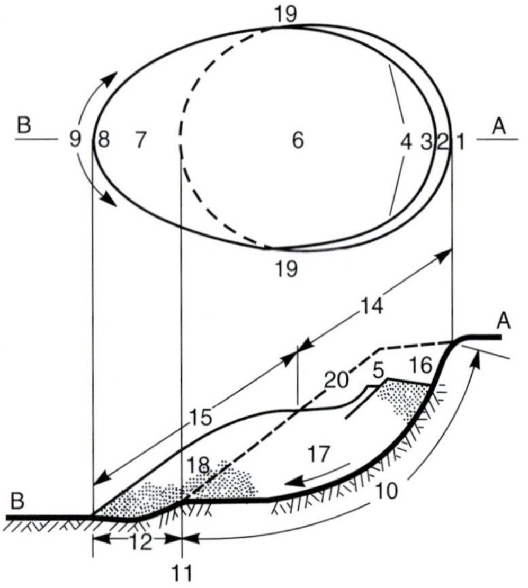

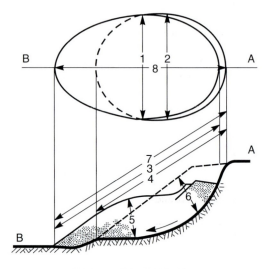

*Figure 1.6* Definitions of landslide features: *upper portion*, plan of typical landslide in which dashed line indicates trace of rupture surface on original ground surface; *lower portion*, section in which hatching indicates undisturbed ground and stippling shows extent of displaced material. Numbers refer to dimensions defined in Table 1.1 (IAEG Commission on Landslides, 1990).

*Figure 1.7* Definitions of landslide dimensions: *upper portion*, plan of typical landslide in which dashed line is trace of rupture surface on original ground surface; *lower portion*, section in which hatching indicates undisturbed ground, stippling shows extent of displaced material, and broken line is original ground surface. Numbers refer to dimensions defined in Table 1.2 (IAEG Commission on Landslides, 1990).

*Table 1.1* Definition of landslide features

| No. | Name | Definition |
|---|---|---|
| 1 | Crown | Practically undisplaced material adjacent to highest parts of main scarp |
| 2 | Main scarp | Steep surface on undisturbed ground at upper edge of landslide caused by movement of displaced material (13, stippled area) away from undisturbed ground; it is visible part of surface rupture (10) |
| 3 | Top | Highest point of contact between displaced material (13) and main scarp (2) |
| 4 | Head | Upper parts of landslide along contact between displaced material and main scarp (2) |
| 5 | Minor scarp | Steep surface on displaced material of landslide produced by differential movements within displaced material |
| 6 | Main body | Part of displaced material of landslide that overlies surface of rupture between main scarp (2) and toe of surface of rupture (11) |
| 7 | Foot | Portion of landslide that has moved beyond toe of surface of rupture (11) and overlies original ground surface (20) |
| 8 | Tip | Point on toe (9) farthest from top (3) of landslide |
| 9 | Toe | Lower, usually curved margin of displaced material of a landslide, most distant from main scarp (2) |
| 10 | Surface of rupture | Surface that forms (or that has formed) lower boundary of displaced material (13) below original ground surface (20); mechanical idealization of surface of rupture is called *sliding surface* in stability analysis |
| 11 | Toe of surface of rupture | Intersection (usually buried) between lower part of surface of rupture (10) of a landslide and original ground surface (20) |
| 12 | Surface of separation | Part of original ground surface (20) now overlain by foot (7) of landslide |
| 13 | Displaced material | Material displaced from its original position on slope by movement in landslide; forms both depleted mass (17) and accumulation (18); it is stippled in Figure 1.6 |
| 14 | Zone of depletion | Area of landslide within which displaced material (13) lies below original ground surface (20) |
| 15 | Zone of accumulation | Area of landslide within which displaced material lies above original ground surface (20) |
| 16 | Depletion | Volume bounded by main scarp (2), depleted mass (17), and original ground surface (20) |
| 17 | Depleted mass | Volume of displaced material that overlies surface of rupture (10) but underlies original ground surface (20) |
| 18 | Accumulation | Volume of displaced material (13) that lies above original ground surface (20) |
| 19 | Flank | Undisplaced material adjacent to sides of surface of rupture; compass directions are preferable in describing flanks, but if left and right are used, they refer to flanks as viewed from crown |
| 20 | Original ground surface | Surface of slope that existed before landslide took place |

the shear strength of the rock (resisting force) on this surface, then the slope will be unstable. Instability could take the form of displacement that may or may not be tolerable, or the slope may collapse either suddenly or progressively. The definition of instability will depend on the application. For example, an open pit slope may undergo several meters of displacement without effecting operations, while a slope supporting a bridge abutment would have little tolerance for movement. Also, a single rock fall from a slope above a highway may be of little consequence if there is an adequate ditch to contain the fall, but failure of a significant portion of the slope that

*Table 1.2* Definitions of landslide dimensions

| No. | Name | Definition |
|---|---|---|
| 1 | Width of displaced mass, $W_d$ | Maximum breadth of displaced mass perpendicular to length, $L_d$ |
| 2 | Width of surface of rupture, $W_r$ | Maximum width between flanks of landslide perpendicular to length, $L_r$ |
| 3 | Length of displaced mass, $L_d$ | Minimum distance from tip to top |
| 4 | Length of surface of rupture, $L_r$ | Minimum distance from toe of surface of rupture to crown |
| 5 | Depth of displaced mass, $D_d$ | Maximum depth of surface of rupture below original ground surface measured perpendicular to plane containing $W_d$ and $L_d$ |
| 6 | Depth of surface of rupture, $D_r$ | Maximum depth of surface of rupture below original ground surface measured perpendicular to plane containing $W_r$ and $L_r$ |
| 7 | Total length, $L$ | Minimum distance from tip of landslide to crown |
| 8 | Length of center line, $L_{cl}$ | Distance from crown to tip of landslide through points on original ground surface equidistant from lateral margins of surface of rupture and displaced material |

reaches the traveled surface could have serious consequences.

Based upon these concepts of slope stability, the stability of a slope can be expressed in one or more of the following terms:

(a) *Factor of safety, FS*—Stability quantified by limit equilibrium of the slope, which is stable if FS > 1.
(b) *Strain*—Failure defined by onset of strains great enough to prevent safe operation of the slope, or that the rate of movement exceeds the rate of mining in an open pit.
(c) *Probability of failure*—Stability quantified by probability distribution of difference between resisting and displacing forces, which are each expressed as probability distributions.
(d) *LRFD (load and resistance factor design)*—Stability defined by the factored resistance being greater than or equal to the sum of the factored loads.

At this time (2003), the factor of safety is the most common method of slope design, and there is wide experience in its application to all types of geological conditions, for both rock and soil. Furthermore, there are generally accepted factor of safety values for slopes excavated for different purposes, which promotes the preparation of reasonably consistent designs. The

*Table 1.3* Values of minimum total safety factors

| Failure type | Category | Safety factor |
|---|---|---|
| Shearing | Earthworks | 1.3–1.5 |
| | Earth retaining structures, excavations | 1.5–2.0 |
| | Foundations | 2–3 |

ranges of minimum total factors of safety as proposed by Terzaghi and Peck (1967) and the Canadian Geotechnical Society (1992) are given in Table 1.3.

In Table 1.3, the upper values of the total factors of safety apply to usual loads and service conditions, while the lower values apply to maximum loads and the worst expected geological conditions. For open pit mines the factor of safety generally used is in the range of 1.2–1.4, using either limit equilibrium analysis to calculate directly the factor of safety, or numerical analysis to calculate the onset of excessive strains in the slope.

Although probabilistic design methods for rock slopes were first developed in the 1970s (Harr, 1977; Canada DEMR, 1978), they are not widely used (as of 2003). A possible reason for this lack of acceptance is that terms such as "5% probability of failure" and "consequence of failure expressed as lives lost" are not well understood, and there is limited experience on acceptable probabilities to use in design (see Section 1.4.4).

The calculation of strain in slopes is the most recent advance in slope design. The technique has resulted from the development of numerical analysis methods, and particularly those that can incorporate discontinuities (Starfield and Cundall, 1988). It is most widely used in the mining field where movement is tolerated, and the slope contains a variety of geological conditions (see Chapter 10).

The load and resistance factor design method (LRFD) has been developed for structural design, and is now being extended to geotechnical systems such as foundations and retaining structures. Further details of this design method are discussed in Section 1.4.5.

The actual factor of safety, probability of failure or allowable strain that is used in design should be appropriate for each site. The design process requires a considerable amount of judgment because of the variety of geological and construction factors that must be considered. Conditions that would require the use of factors of safety at the high end of the ranges quoted in Table 1.3 include the following:

- A limited drilling program that does not adequately sample conditions at the site, or drill core in which there is extensive mechanical breakage or core loss.
- Absence of rock outcrops so that mapping of geological structure is not possible, and there is no history of local stability conditions.
- Inability to obtain undisturbed samples for strength testing, or difficulty in extrapolating laboratory test results to *in situ* conditions.
- Absence of information on ground water conditions, and significant seasonal fluctuations in ground water levels.
- Uncertainty in failure mechanisms of the slope and the reliability of the analysis method. For example, plane type failures can be analyzed with considerable confidence, while the detailed mechanism of toppling failures is less well understood.

- Concern regarding the quality of construction, including materials, inspection and weather conditions.
- The consequence of instability, with higher factors of safety being used for dams and major transportation routes, and lower values for temporary structures or industrial roads for logging and mining operations.

This book does not cover the use of rock mass rating systems (Haines and Terbrugge, 1991; Durn and Douglas, 1999) for slope design. At this time (2003), it is considered that the frequent influence of discrete discontinuities on stability should, and can be, incorporated directly into stability analyses. In the rock mass rating, the geological structure is only one component of the rating and may not be given an appropriate weight in the rating.

A vital aspect of all rock slope design is the quality of the blasting used in excavation. Design assumes that the rock mass comprises intact blocks, the shape and size of which are defined by naturally occurring discontinuities. Furthermore, the properties of these discontinuities should be predictable from observations of surface outcrops and drill core. However, if excessively heavy blasting is used which results in damage to the rock behind the face, stability could be dependent on the condition of the fractured rock. Since the properties of the fractured rock are unpredictable, stability conditions will also be unpredictable. Blasting and the control of blast damage are discussed in Chapter 11.

### 1.4.2  *Limit equilibrium analysis (deterministic)*

The stability of rock slopes for the geological conditions shown in Figure 1.4(a) and (f) depends on the shear strength generated along the sliding surface. For all shear type failures, the rock can be assumed to be a Mohr–Coulomb material in which the shear strength is expressed in terms of the cohesion $c$ and friction angle $\phi$. For a sliding surface on which there is an effective normal stress $\sigma'$ acting, the shear strength $\tau$ developed on

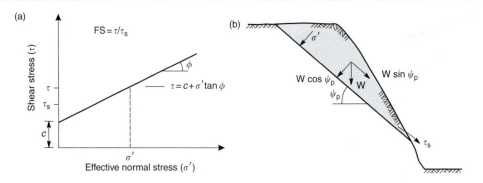

*Figure 1.8* Method of calculating factor of safety of sliding block: (a) Mohr diagram showing shear strength defined by cohesion $c$ and friction angle $\phi$; (b) resolution of force $W$ due to weight of block into components parallel and perpendicular to sliding plane (dip $\psi_p$).

this surface is given by

$$\tau = c + \sigma' \tan\phi \qquad (1.1)$$

Equation (1.1) is expressed as a straight line on a normal stress—shear stress plot (Figure 1.8(a)), in which the cohesion is defined by the intercept on the shear stress axis, and the friction angle is defined by the slope of the line. The effective normal stress is the difference between the stress due to the weight of the rock lying above the sliding plane and the uplift due to any water pressure acting on this surface.

Figure 1.8(b) shows a slope containing a continuous joint dipping out of the face and forming a sliding block. Calculation of the factor of safety for the block shown in Figure 1.8(b) involves the resolution of the force acting on the sliding surface into components acting perpendicular and parallel to this surface. That is, if the dip of the sliding surface is $\psi_p$, its area is $A$, and the weight of the block lying above the sliding surface is $W$, then the normal and shear stresses on the sliding plane are

$$\text{Normal stress, } \sigma = \frac{W \cos\psi_p}{A} \quad \text{and}$$

$$\text{shear stress, } \tau_s = \frac{W \sin\psi_p}{A} \qquad (1.2)$$

and equation (1.1) can be expressed as

$$\tau = c + \frac{W \cos\psi_p \tan\phi}{A} \qquad (1.3)$$

or

$$\tau_s A = W \sin\psi_p \quad \text{and}$$

$$\tau A = cA + W \cos\psi_p \tan\phi \qquad (1.4)$$

In equations (1.4), the term $[W \sin\psi_p]$ defines the resultant force acting down the sliding plane and is termed the "driving force" $(\tau_s A)$, while the term $[cA + W \cos\psi_p \tan\phi]$ defines the shear strength forces acting up the plane that resist sliding and are termed the "resisting forces" $(\tau A)$. The stability of the block in Figure 1.8(b) can be quantified by the ratio of the resisting and driving forces, which is termed the factor of safety, FS. Therefore, the expression for the factor of safety is

$$FS = \frac{\text{resisting forces}}{\text{driving forces}} \qquad (1.5)$$

$$FS = \frac{cA + W \cos\psi_p \tan\phi}{W \sin\psi_p} \qquad (1.6)$$

The displacing shear stress $\tau_s$ and the resisting shear stress $\tau$ defined by equations (1.4) are plotted on Figure 1.8(a). On Figure 1.8(a) it is shown that the resisting stress exceeds the displacing stress, so the factor of safety is greater than one and the slope is stable.

If the sliding surface is clean and contains no infilling then the cohesion is likely to be zero and

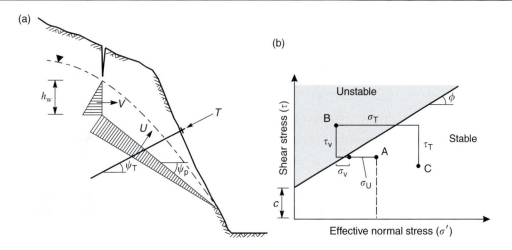

*Figure 1.9* The effect of ground water and bolt forces on factor of safety of rock slope: (a) ground water and bolting forces acting on sliding surface; (b) Mohr diagram of stresses acting on sliding surface showing stable and unstable stability conditions.

equation (1.6) reduces to

$$FS = \frac{\cos \psi_p \cdot \tan \phi}{\sin \psi_p} \qquad (1.7)$$

or

$$FS = 1 \quad \text{when } \psi_p = \phi \qquad (1.8)$$

Equations (1.7) and (1.8) show that for a dry, clean surface with no support installed, the block of rock will slide when the dip angle of the sliding surface equals the friction angle of this surface, and that stability is independent of the size of the sliding block. That is, the block is at a condition of "limiting equilibrium" when the driving forces are exactly equal to the resisting forces and the factor of safety is equal to 1.0. Therefore, the method of slope stability analysis described in this section is termed *limit equilibrium analysis*.

Limit equilibrium analysis can be applied to a wide range of conditions and can incorporate forces such as water forces acting on the sliding surface, as well as external reinforcing forces supplied by tensioned rock anchors. Figure 1.9(a) shows a slope containing a sliding surface with area $A$ and dip $\psi_p$, and a vertical tension crack. The slope is partially saturated such that the tension crack is half-filled with water, and the water

table exits where the sliding surface daylights on the slope face. The water pressures that are generated in the tension crack and on the sliding surface can be approximated by triangular force diagrams where the maximum pressure, $p$ at the base of the tension crack and the upper end of the sliding surface is given by

$$p = \gamma_w \, h_w \qquad (1.9)$$

where $\gamma_w$ is the unit weight of water and $h_w$ is the vertical height of water in the tension crack. Based on this assumption, the water forces acting in the tension crack, $V$, and on the sliding plane, $U$, are as follows:

$$V = \frac{1}{2}\gamma_w \, h_w^2 \quad \text{and} \quad U = \frac{1}{2}\gamma_w \, h_w A \qquad (1.10)$$

and the factor of safety of the slope is calculated by modifying equation (1.6) as follows:

$$FS = \frac{cA + (W \cos \psi_p - U - V \sin \psi_p)\tan \phi}{W \sin \psi_p + V \cos \psi_p}$$

$$(1.11)$$

Similarly, an equation can be developed for a reinforced slope in which a tensioned rock anchor has been installed with the anchor below the sliding plane. If the tension in the anchor is $T$ and it is installed at an angle $\psi_T$ below the horizontal, then the normal and shear forces acting on the sliding plane due to the anchor tension are respectively:

$$N_T = T \sin(\psi_T + \psi_p) \quad \text{and}$$
$$S_T = T \cos(\psi_T + \psi_p) \tag{1.12}$$

and the equation defining the factor of safety of the anchored, partially saturated slope is

$$FS = \frac{cA + (W \cos \psi_p - U - V \sin \psi_p + T \sin(\psi_T + \psi_p)) \tan \phi}{W \sin \psi_p + V \cos \psi_p - T \cos(\psi_T + \psi_p)} \tag{1.13}$$

Figure 1.9(b) shows on a Mohr diagram the magnitude of the normal and shear stresses on the sliding surface developed by the water and bolting forces, and their influence on the factor of safety. That is, destabilizing forces (e.g. water) decrease the normal stress and increase the shear stress, and tend to cause the resultant of the forces to be above the limiting strength line, indicating instability (Point B). In contrast, stabilizing forces (bolting and drainage) increase the normal stress and decrease the shear stress, and cause the resultant to be below the line, indicating stability (Point C).

The force diagram in Figure 1.9(b) can also be used to show that the optimum dip angle for the bolts, that is, the dip that produces the greatest factor of safety for a given rock anchor force is

$$\psi_{T(opt)} = (\phi - \psi_p) \quad \text{or} \quad \phi = \psi_p + \psi_{T(opt)} \tag{1.14}$$

Strict application of equation (1.14) may show that the anchor should be installed above the horizontal, that is, $\psi_T$ is negative. However, in practice, it is usually preferable to install anchors below the horizontal because this facilitates drilling and grouting, and provides a more reliable installation.

These examples of limit equilibrium analysis to calculate the stability of rock slopes show that

this is a versatile method that can be applied to a wide range of conditions. One limitation of the limit equilibrium method is that all the forces are assumed to act through the center of gravity of the block, and that no moments are generated.

This analysis described in this section is applicable to a block sliding on a plane. However, under certain geometric conditions the block may topple rather than slide, in which case a different form of limit equilibrium analysis must be used. Figure 1.10 shows the conditions that differentiate stable, sliding and toppling blocks in relation to the width $\Delta x$ and height $y$ of the block, the dip $\psi_p$ of the plane on which it lies and the friction angle $\phi$ of this surface. Sliding blocks are analyzed either as plane or wedge failures (see Chapters 6 and 7 respectively), while the analysis of toppling failures is discussed in Chapter 9. Figure 1.10(b) shows that there are only limited conditions under which toppling occurs, and in fact this is a less common type of failure compared with sliding failures.

### 1.4.3  Sensitivity analysis

The factor of safety analysis described above involves selection of a single value for each of the parameters that define the driving and resisting forces in the slope. In reality, each parameter has a range of values, and a method of examining the effect of this variability on the factor of safety is to carry out sensitivity analyses using upper and lower bound values for those parameters considered critical to design. However, to carry out sensitivity analyses for more than three parameters is cumbersome, and it is difficult to examine the relationship between each of the parameters. Consequently, the usual design procedure involves a combination of analysis and judgment in assessing the influence on stability of variability in the design parameters, and then selecting an appropriate factor of safety.

An example of sensitivity analysis is shown in Section 4.4 in Chapter 4 that describes the stability analysis of a quarry slope in which sensitivity analyses were carried out for both the friction

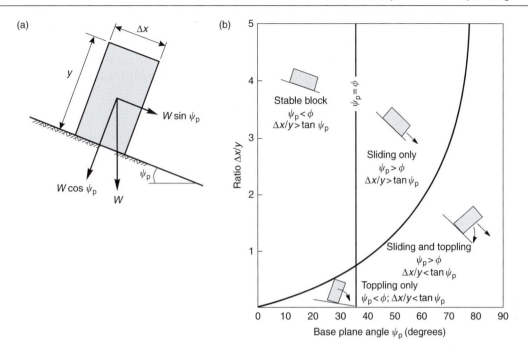

*Figure 1.10* Identification of sliding and toppling blocks: (a) geometry of block on inclined plane; (b) conditions for sliding and toppling of block on an inclined plane.

angle (range 15–25°) and the water pressure—fully drained to fully saturated (Figure 4.20). This plot shows that water pressures have more influence on stability than the friction angle. That is, a fully drained, vertical slope is stable for a friction angle as low as 15°, while a fully saturated slope is unstable at an angle of 60°, even if the friction angle is 25°.

The value of sensitivity analysis is to assess which parameters have the greatest influence on stability. This information can then be used in planning investigation programs to collect data that will define this parameter(s) more precisely. Alternatively, if there is uncertainty in the value of an important design parameter, this can be accounted for in design by using an appropriate factor of safety.

### 1.4.4  Probabilistic design methods

Probabilistic design is a systematic procedure for examining the effect of the variability of each parameter on slope stability. A probability distribution of the factor of safety is calculated, from which the probability of failure (PF) of the slope is determined.

Probability analysis was first developed in the 1940s and is used in the structural and aeronautical engineering fields to examine the reliability of complex systems. Among its early uses in geotechnical engineering was in open pit mine slope design where a certain risk of failure is acceptable, and this type of analysis could be readily incorporated into the economic planning of the mine (Canada DEMR, 1978; Pentz, 1981; Savely, 1987). Examples of its use in civil engineering are in the planning of slope stabilization programs for transportation systems (Wyllie *et al.*, 1979; McGuffey *et al.*, 1980), landslide hazards (Fell, 1994; Cruden, 1997) and in design of storage facilities for hazardous waste (Roberds, 1984, 1986).

There is sometimes reluctance to use probabilistic design when there is a limited amount

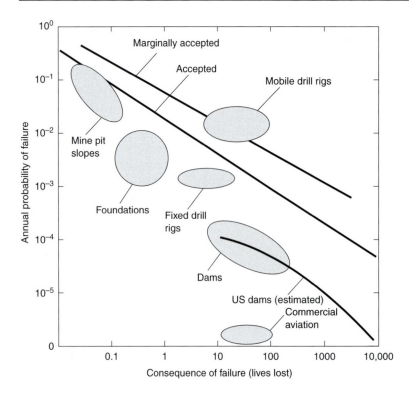

*Figure 1.11* Risks for selected engineering projects (Whitman, 1984).

of design data that may not be representative of the population. In these circumstances, it is possible to use subjective assessment techniques that provide reasonably reliable probability values from small samples (Roberds, 1990). The basis of these techniques is the assessment and analysis of available data, by an expert or group of experts in the field, in order to arrive at a consensus on the probability distributions that represent the opinions of these individuals. The degree of defensibility of the results tends to increase with the time and cost that is expended in the analysis. For example, the assessment techniques range from, most simply, informal expert opinion to more reliable and defensible techniques such as Delphi panels (Rohrbaugh, 1979). A Delphi panel comprises a group of experts who are each provided with the same set of data and are required to produce a written assessment of these data. These documents are then provided anonymously to each of the other assessors who are encouraged to adjust their

assessments in light of their peer's results. After several iterations of this process, it should be possible to arrive at a consensus that maintains anonymity and independence of thought.

The use of probability analysis in design requires that there be generally accepted ranges of probability of failure for different types of structure, as there are for factors of safety. To assist in selecting appropriate probability of failure values, Athanasiou-Grivas (1979) provides charts relating factor of safety to the probability of failure. Also, Figure 1.11 gives a relationship between levels of annual probability of failure for a variety of engineering projects, and the consequence of failure in terms of lives lost. For example, for open pit mine slopes for which slope performance is closely managed and there is little risk to life in the event of a failure, the acceptable range of annual probability of failure can be about $10^{-1}$ to $10^{-2}$. In comparison, for dams where failure could result in the loss of several hundred lives, annual probability of failure should not exceed about

(a)

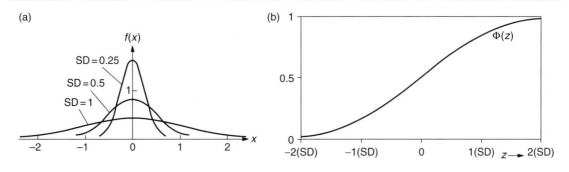

(b)

Figure 1.12 Properties of the normal distribution: (a) density of the normal distribution with mean $\bar{x} = 0$ and standard deviations (SD) of 0.25, 0.5 and 1.0; (b) distribution function $\Phi(z)$ of the normal distribution with mean 0 and standard deviation 1.0 (Kreyszig, 1976).

$10^{-4}$ to $10^{-5}$. Despite the wide range of values shown in Figure 1.11, this approach provides a useful benchmark for the ongoing development of probabilistic design (Salmon and Hartford, 1995).

## (a) Distribution functions

In probability analysis, each parameter for which there is some uncertainty is assigned a range of values that is defined by a probability density function. Some types of distribution functions that are appropriate for geotechnical data include normal, beta, negative exponential and triangular distributions. The most common type of function is the normal distribution in which the mean value is the most frequently occurring value (Figure 1.12(a)). The density of the normal distribution is defined by

$$f(x) = \frac{1}{\text{SD}\sqrt{2\pi}} e^{-\frac{1}{2}[(x-\bar{x})/\text{SD}]^2} \qquad (1.15)$$

where $\bar{x}$ is the mean value given by

$$\bar{x} = \frac{\sum_{x=1}^{n} x}{n} \qquad (1.16)$$

and SD is the standard deviation given by

$$\text{SD} = \left[ \frac{\sum_{x=1}^{n}(x - \bar{x})^2}{n} \right]^{1/2} \qquad (1.17)$$

As shown in Figure 1.12(a), the scatter in the data, as represented by the width of the curve, is measured by the standard deviation. Important properties of the normal distribution are that the total area under the curve is equal to 1.0. That is, there is a probability of unity that all values of the parameter fall within the bounds of the curve. Also, 68% of the values will lie within a range of one standard deviation either side of the mean, and 95% will lie within two standard deviations either side of the mean.

Conversely, it is possible to determine the value of a parameter defined by a normal distribution by stating the probability of its occurrence. This is shown graphically in Figure 1.12(b) where $\Phi(z)$ is the distribution function with mean 0 and standard deviation 1.0. For example, a value which has a probability of being greater than 50% of all values is equal to the mean, and a value which has a probability of being greater than 16% of all values is equal to the mean plus one standard deviation.

The normal distribution extends to infinity in both directions, but this is often not a realistic expression of geotechnical data for which the likely upper and lower bounds of a parameter can be defined. For these conditions, it is appropriate to use the beta distribution which has finite maximum and minimum points, and can be uniform, skewed to the left or right, U-shaped or J-shaped (Harr, 1977). However, where there is little information on the distribution of the data, a simple triangular distribution can be used which are defined by three values: the most likely, and the minimum and maximum values. Examples of probability distributions are shown in the worked example in Section 6.6.

### (b) Probability of failure

The probability of failure is calculated in a similar manner to that of the factor of safety in that the relative magnitude of the displacing and resisting forces in the slope is examined (see Section 1.4.2). Two common methods of calculating the coefficient of reliability are the margin of safety method, and the Monte Carlo method as discussed later.

The *margin of safety* is the difference between the resisting and displacing forces, with the slope being unstable if the margin of safety is negative. If the resisting and displacing forces are mathematically defined probability distributions—$f_D(r)$ and $f_D(d)$ respectively in Figure 1.13(a)—then it is possible to calculate a third probability distribution for the margin of safety. As shown in Figure 1.13(a), there is a probability of failure if the lower limit of the resisting force distribution $f_D(r)$ is less than the upper limit of the displacing force distribution $f_D(d)$. This is shown as the shaded area on Figure 1.13(a), with the probability of failure being proportional to the area of the shaded zone. The method of calculating the area of the shaded zone is to calculate the probability density function of the margin of safety:

the area of the negative portion of this function is the probability of failure (Figure 1.13(b)). If the resisting and displacing forces are defined by normal distributions, the margin of safety is also a normal distribution, the mean and standard deviation of which are calculated as follows (Canada DEMR, 1978):

$$\text{Mean, margin of safety} = \bar{f}_r - \bar{f}_d \qquad (1.18)$$

$$\text{Standard deviation, margin of safety}$$
$$= (SD_r^2 + SD_d^2)^{1/2} \qquad (1.19)$$

where $\bar{f}_r$ and $\bar{f}_d$ are the mean values, and $SD_r$ and $SD_d$ are the standard deviations of the distributions of the resisting and displacing forces respectively. Note that the definition of the deterministic factor of safety is given by $\bar{f}_r/\bar{f}_d$.

Having determined the mean and standard deviation of the margin of safety, the probability of failure can be calculated from the properties of the normal distribution. For example, if the mean margin of safety is 2000 MN and the standard deviation is 1200 MN, then the margin of safety is zero at (2000 – 0)/1200, or 1.67 standard deviations. From Figure 1.12(b), where the margin of safety distribution is represented by $\Phi(z)$, the probability of failure is 5%.

Note that the margin of safety concept discussed in this section can only be used where the resisting and displacing forces are independent variables. This condition would apply where the displacing force is the weight of the sliding mass,

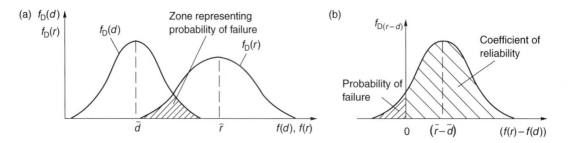

*Figure 1.13* Calculation of probability of failure using normal distributions: (a) probability density functions of the resisting force $f_R$ and the displacing force $f_D$ in a slope; and (b) probability density function of difference between resisting and displacing force distributions $f_{D(r-d)}$.

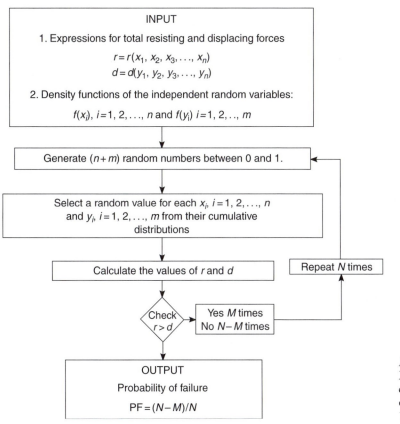

*Figure 1.14* Flow chart for Monte Carlo simulation to calculate probability of failure of a slope (Athanasiou-Grivas, 1980).

and the resisting force is the installed reinforcement. However, where the resisting force is the shear strength of the rock, then this force and the displacing force are both functions of the weight of the slope, and are not independent variables. Under these circumstances, it is necessary to use Monte Carlo analysis as described next.

*Monte Carlo* analysis is an alternative method of calculating the probability of failure which is more versatile than the margin of safety method described earlier. Monte Carlo analysis avoids the integration operations that can become quite complex, and in the case of the beta distribution cannot be solved explicitly. The particular value of Monte Carlo analysis is the ability to work with any mixture of distribution types, and any number of variables, which may or may not be independent of each other (Harr, 1977; Athanasiou-Grivas, 1980).

The Monte Carlo technique is an iterative procedure comprising the following four steps (Figure 1.14):

1   Estimate probability distributions for each of the variable input parameters.
2   Generate random values for each parameter; Figure 1.12(b) illustrates the relationship for a normal distribution between a random number between 0 and 1 and the corresponding value of the parameter.
3   Calculate values for the displacing and resisting forces and determine if the resisting force is greater than the displacing force.
4   Repeat the process $N$ times ($N > 100$) and then determine probability of failure $P_f$ from the ratio:

$$P_f = \frac{N - M}{N} \tag{1.20}$$

where $M$ is the number of times the resisting force exceeded the displacing force (i.e. the factor of safety is greater than 1.0).

An example of the use of Monte Carlo analysis to calculate the coefficient of reliability of a slope against sliding is given in Section 6.6 in Chapter 6 on "Plane failure." This example shows the relationship between the deterministic and probabilistic analyses. The factor of safety is calculated from the mean or most likely values of the input variables, while the probabilistic analysis calculates the distribution of the factor of safety when selected input variables are expressed as probability density functions. For the unsupported slope, the deterministic factor of safety has a value of 1.4, while the probabilistic analysis shows that the factor of safety can range from a minimum value of 0.69 to a maximum value of 2.52. The proportion of this distribution with a value less than 1.0 is 7.2%, which represents the probability of failure of the slope.

### 1.4.5   Load and Resistance Factor Design

This design method is based on the use of probability theory to develop a rational design basis for structural design that accounts for variability in both loads and resistance. The objective is to produce a uniform margin of safety for steel and concrete structures such as bridges, and geotechnical structures such as foundations under different loading conditions. The LRFD method has been developed in structural engineering and is becoming widely used in the design of major structures such as bridges (CSA, 1988; Eurocode, 1995; AASHTO, 1996). In order that foundations design is consistent with structural design, the LRFD method has been extended to include geotechnical engineering (Transportation Research Board, 1999).

Some of the early LRFD work in geotechnical engineering was carried out by Myerhoff (1984) who used the term Limit States Design, and defined the two limit states as follows. First, the structure and its components must have, during the intended service life, an adequate margin of safety against collapse under the maximum loads that might reasonably occur. Second, the structure and its components must serve the designed functions without excessive deformations and deterioration. These two service levels are the ultimate and serviceability limit states respectively and are defined as follows:

- *Ultimate limit state*—Collapse of the structure and slope failure including instability due to sliding, toppling and excessive weathering.
- *Serviceability limit state*—Onset of excessive deformation and unacceptable deterioration.

The basis of LRFD design is the multiplication of loads and resistances by factors that reflect the degree of uncertainty and variability in the parameters. The requirement of the design is that the factored resistance is equal to, or greater than, the factored loads. This is stated in mathematical terms as follows:

$$\phi_k R_{nk} \geq \sum \eta_{ij} \gamma_{ij} Q_{ij} \qquad (1.21)$$

where $\phi_k$ is the resistance factor and $R_{nk}$ is the nominal strength for the $k$th failure mode or serviceability limit state, $\eta_{ij}$ is the factor to account for the ductility, redundancy and operational importance of the element or system, $\gamma_{ij}$ is the load factor and $Q_{ij}$ the member load effect for the $i$th load type in the $j$th load combination under consideration.

In the application of equation (1.21), the load factors are greater than unity unless the load is beneficial to stability, and the resistance factors are less than unity. On this basis, the Mohr–Coulomb equation for the shear resistance of a sliding surface is expressed as follows:

$$\tau = f_c c + (\sigma - f_U U) f_\phi \tan \phi \qquad (1.22)$$

The cohesion $c$, friction coefficient $\tan \phi$ and water pressure $U$ are all multiplied by partial factors with values less than unity, while the normal stress $\sigma$ on the sliding surface is calculated using a partial load factor greater than unity applied to the slope weight and any applied loads. Actual values for the resistance factors will vary depending on such factors as the extent of testing during construction and ratio of the live load to the dead load.

LRFD would usually only be used for slope design where the slope was a component of a bridge foundation, for example. For slopes that are not part of any structure, the design methods described in Sections 1.4.2–1.4.4 would be more commonly used.

# Chapter 2

# Structural geology and data interpretation

## 2.1 Objectives of geological investigations

The stability of rock slopes is often significantly influenced by the structural geology of the rock in which the slope is excavated. Structural geology refers to naturally occurring breaks in the rock such as bedding planes, joints and faults, which are generally termed *discontinuities*. The properties of discontinuities relative to stability include orientation, persistence, roughness and infilling. The significance of discontinuities is that they are planes of weakness in the much stronger, intact rock so failure tends to occur preferentially along these surfaces. The discontinuities may directly influence stability such as the slopes shown in Figure 2.1. In Figure 2.1(a) the face is formed by the bedding planes that are continuous over the full height of the cut—this condition is termed a *plane* failure and is discussed in detail in Chapter 6. Alternatively, slope failure may occur on two discontinuities that intersect behind the face (Figure 2.1(b))—this condition is termed a *wedge* failure and is discussed in detail in Chapter 7.

Alternatively, discontinuities may only indirectly influence stability where their length is much shorter than the slope dimensions, such as an open pit mine slope where no single discontinuity controls stability. However, the properties of the discontinuities will affect the strength of the rock mass in which the slope is mined.

Almost all rock slope stability studies should address the structural geology of the site, and such studies involve two steps as follows. First, determine the properties of the discontinuities, which involves mapping outcrops and existing cuts, if any, and examining diamond drill core, as appropriate for the site conditions. Second, determine the influence of the discontinuities on stability, which involves studying the relationship between the orientation of the discontinuity and the face. The objective of this study, which is termed *kinematic analysis*, is to identify possible modes of slope failure.

The overall purpose of a geological mapping program is to define a set or sets of discontinuities, or a single feature such as a fault, which will control stability on a particular slope. For example, the bedding may dip out of the face and form a plane failure, or a pair of joint sets may intersect to form a series of wedges. It is common that the discontinuities will occur in three orthogonal sets (mutually at right angles), with possibly one additional set. It is suggested that four sets is the maximum that can be incorporated into a slope design, and that any additional sets that may appear to be present are more likely to represent scatter in the orientation of the sets. Discontinuities that occur infrequently in the rock mass are not likely to have a significant influence on stability of the overall slope and so can be discounted in design. However, it is important to identify a single feature such as a through-going, adversely orientated fault that may be a controlling feature for stability.

There are certain geological conditions where the discontinuities may be randomly orientated. For example, basalt that has cooled rapidly while still flowing may have a "crackled" structure in which the joints are not persistent, curved and have no preferred orientation. Also, some volcanic rocks exhibit sets that only extend over a few meters on the face, and then different sets occur in an adjacent area.

In the design of rock slopes on civil projects, it is usually advisable that the full length of each slope be designed with a uniform slope angle; it is not practical to excavate a slope with varying slope angles because this will complicate surveying and the lay out of blast holes. This will require that in applying geological data to slope design, the dominant geological structure, such as bedding or orthogonal joint sets, be used for the design. An exception to this guideline may be where there is a significant change in rock type within the cut, and it may be appropriate to prepare a separate design for each. However, even in these circumstances, it may be more economical in terms of construction costs to cut the entire slope at the flatter of the two slope designs, or to install support in the less stable material.

Another issue in planning a geological mapping program is to decide how many discontinuities should be mapped in order to define the design sets. It is usually possible, by inspection of a natural face or existing cut, to ascertain whether the structure occurs in sets or is randomly oriented. For locations where there is good rock exposure and the structure is uniform, as few as 20 measurements should provide information on the orientation of the sets, with a further 50–100 measurements required to define typical properties such as persistence, spacing and infilling. Conditions in which a greater number of discontinuities should be mapped include faulted or folded structure, or contacts between different rock types. In these cases, several hundred features may need to be mapped in order to define the properties of each unit. A detailed procedure for determining the number of joints to be mapped is described by Stauffer (1966).

Structural geology is specifically addressed in two chapters in the book. Chapter 2 describes the properties of discontinuities and how they are used in kinematic analysis, and Chapter 3

(a)

(b)

*Figure 2.1* Rock faces formed by persistent discontinuities: (a) plane failure formed by bedding planes parallel to face with continuous lengths over the full height of the slope (shale on Route 19 near Robbinsville, North Carolina); (b) wedge failure formed by two intersecting planes dipping out of the face (sedimentary formation on Route 60 near Phoenix, Arizona).

discusses methods of collecting structural geological data, including mapping and drilling.

## 2.2   Mechanism of joint formation

All the rocks observed in outcrops and excavations have undergone a long history of modification over a time of hundreds of millions, or even billions of years. The sequence of modification that a sedimentary rock, for example, typically undergoes is deposition at the surface, gradual burial to depths of up to several kilometers with imposition of heat and pressure, and then uplift to the surface (Figure 2.2). Throughout this sequence, the rock may also be subject to deformation comprising folding and faulting. These processes usually result in the stresses in the rock exceeding its strength a number of times,

causing the rock to fracture and form joints and faults. In sedimentary rock, bedding planes that are coincident with breaks in the continuity of sedimentation will also form.

Figure 2.2(a) shows how the stresses in rock increase with burial, assuming that there are no water, thermal or tectonic pressures acting in the rock (Davis and Reynolds, 1996). The vertical stress, which is the major principal stress $\sigma_1$, is equal to the weight of the overlying rock and is given by

$$\sigma_1 = \gamma_r H \tag{2.1}$$

where $\gamma_r$ is the unit weight of the rock and $H$ is the depth of burial. The horizontal stress, which is the minor principal stress $\sigma_3$, also increases with the depth of burial due to the effect of the

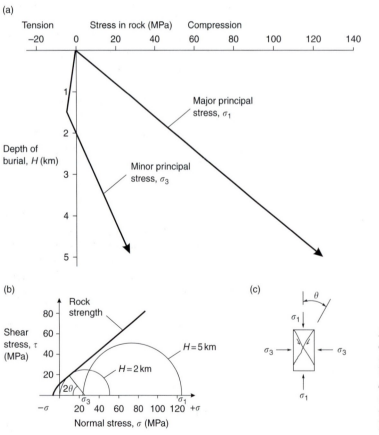

Figure 2.2 Development of jointing due to burial and uplift of rock: (a) stress changes in rock during burial; (b) Mohr diagram showing conditions for rock fracture; (c) inclination of joints with respect to stress direction (adapted from Davis and Reynolds (1996)).

Poisson's Ratio $\mu$, and any temperature increase that occurs. In ideal conditions $\sigma_3$ is related to $\sigma_1$ as follows:

$$\sigma_3 = \left(\frac{\mu}{1-\mu}\sigma_1\right) + \left(\frac{E}{1-\mu}\varepsilon\Delta T\right) \qquad (2.2)$$

where $E$ is the modulus of deformation of the rock, $\varepsilon$ is the coefficient of thermal expansion and $\Delta T$ is the temperature rise. The first component of equation (2.2) shows the value of the horizontal stress due to gravitational loading; if the Poisson's ratio is 0.25, for example, then $\sigma_3 = 0.33\sigma_1$. If the rock were not free to expand, and a temperature rise of 100°C occurs in a rock with a modulus value of 50 GPa and an $\varepsilon$ value of $15 \times 10^{-6}/°C$, then a thermal stress of 100 GPa will be generated. In reality, the values of the principal stresses will be modified by tectonic action resulting in deformation such as folding and faulting.

On Figure 2.2(a), the value of $\sigma_1$ is defined by equation (2.1), and the value of $\sigma_3$ varies with depth as follows. The value of $\sigma_3$ is tensile at depths less than 1.5 km where the sediments have not been consolidated into rock, and below this depth, $\sigma_3$ increases as defined by equation (2.2), assuming no temperature change.

The formation of joints in rock during the burial–uplift process shown in Figure 2.2(a) will depend on the rock strength in comparison to the applied stresses. A method of identifying conditions that will cause the rock to fracture is to use a Mohr diagram (Figure 2.2(b)). In Figure 2.2(b) the rock strength is shown as a straight line under compressive stress, and curved under tensile stress because micro-fractures within the rock act as stress concentrators that diminish the strength when a tensile stress is applied. On the Mohr diagram, circles represent the $\sigma_1$ and $\sigma_3$ stresses at different depths, and where the circle intersects the strength line, failure will occur. The stress conditions show that fracture will occur at a depth of 2 km ($\sigma_1 = 52$ MPa; $\sigma_3 = 0$ MPa) because there is no horizontal confining stress acting. However, at a depth of 5 km where the rock is highly confined ($\sigma_1 = 130$ MPa; $\sigma_3 = 25$ MPa) the rock will not fracture because the strength

exceeds the stress. For conditions where $\sigma_3$ is low or tensile (negative), failure occurs more readily compared to conditions at greater depth where both $\sigma_1$ and $\sigma_3$ are compressive (positive).

The Mohr diagram also shows the orientation of the fracture with respect to the stress direction (Figure 2.2(c)). Since principal stresses are oriented mutually at right angles, sets of joints tend to form in orthogonal directions.

## 2.3   Effects of discontinuities on slope stability

While the orientation of discontinuities is the prime geological factor influencing stability, and is the subject of this chapter, other properties such as persistence and spacing are significant in design. For example, Figure 2.3 shows three slopes excavated in a rock mass containing two joint sets: set J1 dips at 45° out of the face, and set J2 dips at 60° into the face. The stability of these slopes differs as follows. In Figure 2.3(a), set J1, which is widely spaced and has a persistence greater than the slope height, forms a potentially unstable plane failure over the full height of the cut. In Figure 2.3(b) both sets J1 and J2 have low persistence and are closely spaced so that while small blocks ravel from the face, there is no overall slope failure. In Figure 2.3(c), set J2 is persistent and closely spaced, and forms a series of thin slabs dipping into the face that create a toppling failure.

The significance of Figure 2.3 is that, while an analysis of the orientation of joint sets J1 and J2 would show identical conditions on a stereonet, there are other characteristics of these discontinuities that must also be considered in design. These characteristics, which are discussed further in Chapter 3, should be described in detail as part of the geological data collection program for rock slope design.

## 2.4   Orientation of discontinuities

The first step in the investigation of discontinuities in a slope is to analyze their orientation and

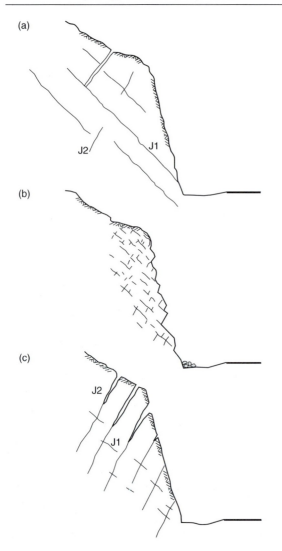

*Figure 2.3* Effects of joint properties on slope stability: (a) persistent J1 joints dipping out of face forms potentially unstable sliding blocks; (b) closely spaced, low persistence joints cause raveling of small blocks; (c) persistent J2 joints dipping into face form potential toppling slabs.

identify sets of discontinuities, or single discontinuities that could form potentially unstable blocks of rock. Information on discontinuity orientation may be obtained from such sources as surface and underground mapping, diamond drill core and geophysics, and it is necessary to

combine these data using a procedure that is readily amenable to analysis. This analysis is facilitated by the use of a simple and unambiguous method of expressing the orientation of a discontinuity. The recommended terminology for orientation is the *dip* and *dip direction* which are defined as follows, and shown schematically in Figure 2.4(a) and (b).

1   *Dip* is the maximum inclination of a discontinuity to the horizontal (angle $\psi$).
2   *Dip direction* or *dip azimuth* is the direction of the horizontal trace of the line of dip, measured clockwise from north (angle $\alpha$).

As will be demonstrated in Section 2.5, the dip/dip direction system facilitates field mapping, plotting stereonets, and analysis of discontinuity orientation data. *Strike*, which is an alternative means of defining the orientation of a plane, is the trace of the intersection of an inclined plane with a horizontal reference plane.

The strike is at right angles to the dip direction, and the relationship between the strike and the dip direction is illustrated in Figure 2.4(b) where the plane has a strike of N45E and a dip of 50SE. In terms of dip and dip direction, the orientation of the plane is 50/135, which is considered to be a simpler nomenclature that also facilitates the use of stereographic analysis. By always writing the dip as two digits and the dip direction as three digits, for example, 090 for 90°, there can be no confusion as to which set of figures refers to which measurement. Strike and dip measurements can be readily converted into dip and dip direction measurements, if this mapping system is preferred.

In defining the orientation of a line, the terms *plunge* and *trend* are used (Figure 2.4(c)). The plunge is the dip of the line, with a positive plunge being below the horizontal and a negative plunge being above the horizontal. The trend is the direction of the horizontal projection of the line measured clockwise from north, and corresponds to the dip direction of a plane.

When mapping geological structure in the field, it is necessary to distinguish between the true and

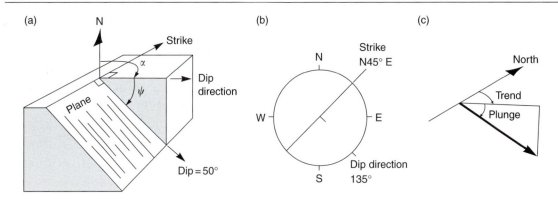

*Figure 2.4* Terminology defining discontinuity orientation: (a) isometric view of plane (dip and dip direction); (b) plan view of plane; (c) isometric view of line (plunge and trend).

apparent dip of a plane. True dip is the steepest dip of the plane, and is always steeper than the apparent dip. The true dip can be found as follows. If a pebble or a stream of water is run down the plane, it will always fall in a direction that corresponds to the dip direction; the dip of this line is the true dip.

## 2.5 Stereographic analysis of structural geology

Previous sections describe structural geological features that influence rock slope stability. This data often occurs in three dimensions with a degree of natural scatter, and in order to be able to use the data in design, it is necessary to have available an analysis technique that can address these matters. It has been found that the stereographic projection is an ideal tool for this application.

This section describes methods of analyzing structural geology data using the stereonet to identify discontinuity sets, and examine their influence on slope stability.

### 2.5.1 Stereographic projection

The stereographic projection allows the three-dimensional orientation data to be represented and analyzed in two dimensions. Stereographic presentations remove one dimension from consideration so that lines or points can represent

planes, and points can represent lines. An important limitation of stereographic projections is that they consider only angular relationships between lines and planes, and do not represent the position or size of the feature.

The stereographic projection consists of a reference sphere in which its equatorial plane is horizontal, and its orientation is fixed relative to north (Figure 2.5). Planes and lines with a specific plunge and trend are positioned in an imaginary sense so that the axis of the feature passes through the center of the reference sphere. The intersection of the feature with the lower half of the reference sphere defines a unique line on the surface of the reference hemisphere. For a plane, this intersection with the reference sphere is a circular arc called a great circle, while for a line, the intersection with the reference sphere is a point. In order to develop a stereographic projection of a plane or line, the intersection with the reference sphere is rotated down to a horizontal surface at the base of the sphere (Figure 2.6). The rotated lines and points are unique locations on the stereonet that represent the dip (plunge) and dip direction (trend) of the feature. In slope stability analysis using stereonets, planes are used to represent both discontinuities and slope faces.

An alternative means of representing the orientation of a plane is the pole to the plane (Figure 2.6(a)). The pole is the point on the surface of the reference sphere that is pierced by a radial line in a direction normal to the plane. The

(a)

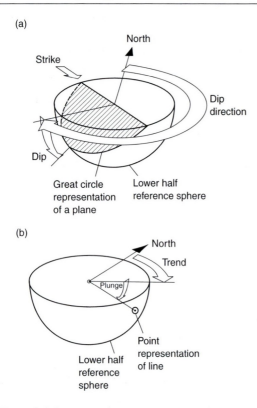

(b)

*Figure 2.5* Stereographic representation of plane and line on lower hemisphere of reference sphere: (a) plane projected as great circle; (b) isometric view of line (plunge and trend).

(a)

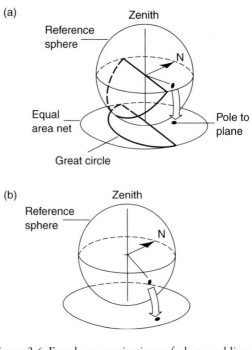

(b)

*Figure 2.6* Equal area projections of plane and line: (a) plane projected as great circle and corresponding pole; (b) line projected as pole.

value of the pole projection is that a single point can represent the complete orientation of a plane. As described in Section 2.5.2, the use of poles facilitates the analysis of a large number of planes compared with the use of great circles.

As an aid to interpreting the information shown on stereonets, it can be seen from Figures 2.5 and 2.6 that planes and lines with shallow dips have great circles and points that plot near the circumference of the stereonet, and those with steep dips plot near the center. In contrast, the pole of a shallow dipping plane plots close to the center of the circle, and the pole of a steep plane plots close to the perimeter.

The two types of stereographic projections used in structural geology are the polar and equatorial projections as shown in Figure 2.7. The polar

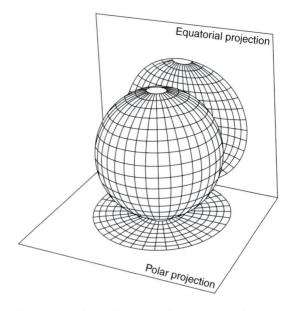

*Figure 2.7* Polar and equatorial projections of a sphere.

net can only be used to plot poles, while the equatorial net can be used to plot both planes and poles as described later. In the case of the equatorial projection, the most common type of stereonet projection is the equal area or Lambert (Schmidt) net. On this net, any area on the surface of the reference sphere is projected as an equal area on the stereonet. This property of the net is used in the contouring of pole plots to find concentrations of poles that represent preferred orientations, or sets of discontinuities. The other type of equatorial projection is the equal angle or Wulff net; both the Wulff and Lambert nets can be used to examine angular relationships, but only the Lambert net can be used to develop contours of pole concentrations.

These two nets are included in Appendix I in a size that is convenient for plotting and analyzing structural data. For hand plotting of structural data, the usual procedure is to place tracing paper on the nets and then draw poles and planes on the tracing paper as shown in Figure 2.8. Since plotting of great circles requires that the tracing paper be rotated on the net, as described below, a thumbtack is placed at the

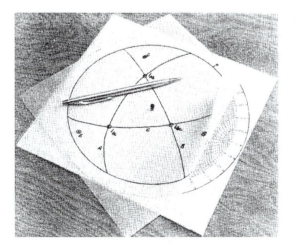

*Figure 2.8* Geological data plotted and analyzed on a piece of tracing paper that is located over the center of the stereonet with a pin to allow the paper to be rotated.

center point so that the curves can be plotted without distortion.[1]

Further details on stereographic projections are described by Phillips (1971) who discusses the theoretical background to this technique, and Leyshon and Lisle (1996) who demonstrated applications of this technique to geological mapping. Goodman and Shi (1985) demonstrate stereographic techniques for identifying wedges of rock that can slide from the face, or are "removable"; this technique is termed *key block theory*.

### 2.5.2  Pole plots and contour plots

The pole to a plane, as shown in Figure 2.6, allows a point to represent the orientation of the plane. Pole plots, in which each plane is represented by a single point, are the most convenient means of examining the orientation of a large number of discontinuities. The plot provides an immediate visual depiction of concentrations of poles representing the orientations of sets of discontinuities, and the analysis is facilitated by the use of different symbols for different types of discontinuities.

Poles can be plotted by hand on a polar net as shown in Figure 2.9. On the net, the dip direction scale (0–360°) around the periphery has the zero mark at the bottom of the vertical axis and the 180° mark is at the top of the net. This is a convenience for plotting such that poles can be plotted directly without the need for rotating the tracing paper; it can be demonstrated that poles plotted on both the polar and equatorial nets are in identical positions.

Pole plots are commonly generated by stereographic computer programs, an example of which is shown in Figure 2.10. This is a lower hemisphere, equal angle projection of 421 original

---

1 For occasions in remote hotel rooms when a computer or light table is not available for preparing stereonets, it has been found that a television screen provides an adequate substitute. If the set is tuned to "snow," the static electricity holds the papers to the screen and allows the tracing sheet to be rotated on the stereonet.

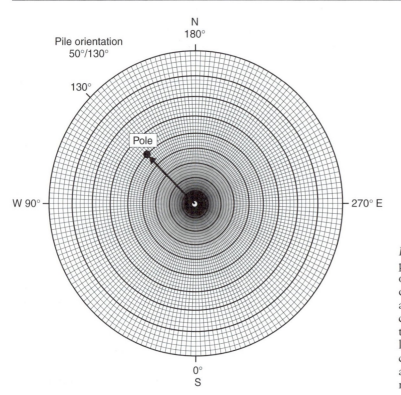

*Figure 2.9* Plotting poles on a polar net. Plot pole of plane oriented at 50/130—locate dip direction of 130° clockwise around the circumference of a circle starting at the lower end of the vertical axis. At 130° radial line, count 50° out from the center of the net, and plot a point at the intersection between 130° radial line and 50° circle.

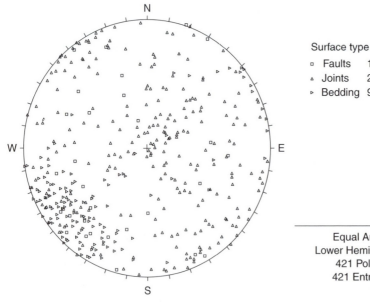

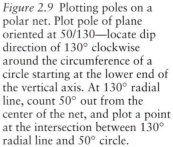

Surface type

- □  Faults      1 [33]
- ▵  Joints      2 [253]
- ▷  Bedding   9 [135]

Equal Area
Lower Hemisphere
421 Poles
421 Entries

*Figure 2.10* Example of pole plot of 421 planes comprising bedding, joints and faults.

poles mapped over an area of about a square kilometer, at a site where the rock is a bedded limestone. The rock contains discontinuity sets comprising the bedding and two sets of joints, together with a number of faults that are generally coincident with the bedding. On Figure 2.10, there is a different symbol for each of the three types of discontinuity. While there is considerable scatter in the pole orientations, careful examination of this plot shows that there is some clustering particularly in the southwest quadrant. In order to identify discontinuity sets on pole plots with considerable scatter, it is necessary to prepare contours of the pole density, as described in the next section.

### 2.5.3  Pole density

All natural discontinuities have a certain amount of variation in their orientations that results in scatter of the pole plots. If the plot contains poles from a number of discontinuity sets, it can be difficult to distinguish between the poles from the different sets, and to find the most likely orientation of each set. However, by contouring the plot, the most highly concentrated areas of poles can be more readily identified. The usual method

of generating contours is to use the contouring package contained with most stereographic projection computer programs. Contouring can also be carried out by hand using a counting net such as the Kalsbeek net that consists of mutually overlapping hexagons, each with an area of 1/100 of the total area stereonet (Leyshon and Lisle, 1996); a Kalsbeek counting net is shown in Appendix I. Contouring is carried out by overlaying the counting net on the pole plot and counting the number of poles in each square. For example, if there are eight poles out of a total of 421 poles in one square, then the concentration in that square is 2%. Once the percent concentration in each square has been determined, contours can be drawn.

Figure 2.11 shows a contour plot of the poles plotted in Figure 2.10. The contour plot shows that the orientation of the bedding has relatively little scatter—the maximum concentration is 5–6%, and that the mean orientation of the bedding has a dip of 74° and a dip direction of 050°. In contrast, the joint orientations show more scatter, and on the pole plot it is difficult to identify discontinuity sets. However, on the contoured plot, it is possible to distinguish clearly two sets of orthogonal joints. Set A has a shallow dip of about 26°, and a dip direction of about 219°, that is in a direction at 180° to the bedding.

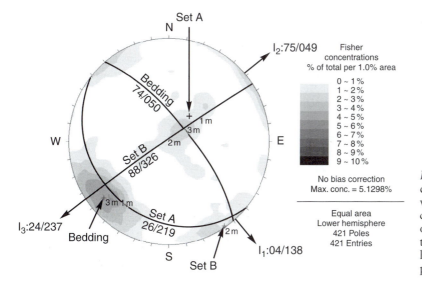

*Figure 2.11* Contoured plot of data shown in Figure 2.10, with great circles corresponding to mean orientation of bedding and two orthogonal joint sets, and lines of intersection between planes.

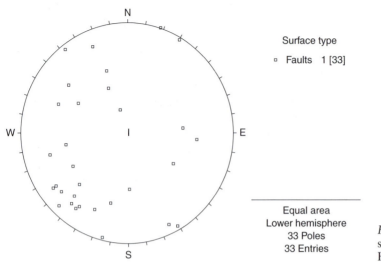

Surface type

□ Faults   1 [33]

Equal area
Lower hemisphere
33 Poles
33 Entries

*Figure 2.12* Pole plot of faults selected from data plotted in Figure 2.10.

Set B has a near vertical dip and a dip direction of 326°, approximately at right angles to Set A. The poles for set B occur in two concentrations on opposite sides of the contour plot because some dip steeply to the north-west and others steeply to the south-east.

In Figure 2.11, the different pole concentrations are shown by symbols for each 1% contour interval. The percentage concentration refers to the number of poles in each 1% area of the surface of the lower hemisphere.

A further use of the stereographic projection program in analyzing structural data is to prepare plots of data selected from the total data collected. For example, joints with lengths that are only a small fraction of the slope dimensions are unlikely to have a significant influence on stability. However, faults usually have greater persistence and lower friction angle than joints. Therefore, it would facilitate design to prepare a stereographic plot showing only faults (Figure 2.12). This plot shows that only 33 discontinuities are faults, and that their orientations are similar to those of the bedding. Selections can also be made, for example, of discontinuities that have a certain type of infilling, or are slickensided, or show evidence of seepage, provided that the mapping identifies this level of detail for each surface.

Appendix II contains field mapping sheets for recording details of discontinuity properties by the use of codes that are input directly into the stereographic analysis program.

The assignment of poles into discontinuity sets is usually achieved by a combination of contouring, visual examination of the stereonet, and knowledge of geological conditions at the site, which will frequently show trends in orientation of the sets. It is also possible to identify discontinuity sets by rigorous and less subjective analysis of clusters in orientation data. A technique presented by Mahtab and Yegulalp (1982) identifies clusters from random distributions of orientations using the Poisson's distribution. However, in applying such techniques, a result that identifies more than about four concentrations should be carefully examined before being used in design.

### 2.5.4   Great circles

Once the orientation of the discontinuity sets, as well as important single discontinuities such as faults, have been identified on the pole plots, the next step in the analysis is to determine if these discontinuities form potentially unstable blocks in the slope face. This analysis is carried out by plotting great circles of each of the discontinuity set orientations, as well as the orientation of the face. In this way the orientation of all the surfaces that have an influence on stability are represented on a single diagram. Figure 2.11 shows the great circles of the three discontinuity sets identified by contouring the pole plot in Figure 2.10. It is usually only possible to have a maximum of about five or six great circles on a plot, because with a greater number, it is difficult to identify all the intersection points of the circles.

While computer generated great circles are convenient, hand plotting is of value in developing an understanding of stereographic projections. Figure 2.13 illustrates the procedure for drawing great circles on an equal area net. As shown in Figure 2.8, the procedure involves overlaying the stereonet with tracing paper on which the great circles are plotted.

The primary purpose of plotting great circles of discontinuity sets in a slope is to determine the shape of blocks formed by intersecting discontinuities, and the direction in which they may slide. For example, in Figure 2.1 the slope failures only occurred for conditions where single

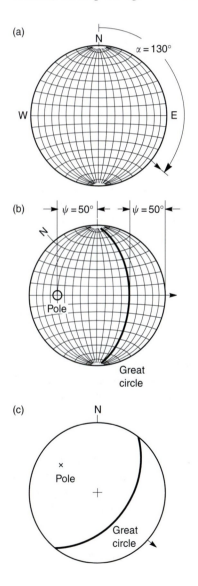

*Figure 2.13* Construction of great circles and a pole representing a plane with orientation 50 (dip)/130 (dip direction) on an equal area net: (a) with the tracing paper located over the stereonet by means of the center pin, trace the circumference of the net and mark the north point. Measure off the dip direction of 130° clockwise from north and mark this position on the circumference of the net; (b) rotate the net about the center pin until the dip direction mark lies on the W–E axis of the net, that is, the net is rotated through 40° counterclockwise. Measure 50° from the outer circle of the net and trace the great circle that corresponds to a plane dipping at this angle. The position of the pole, which has a dip of (90–50), is found by measuring 50° from the center of the net as shown, or alternatively 40° from the outside of the net. The pole lies on the projection of the dip direction line which, at this stage of the construction, is coincident with the W–E axis of the net; (c) the tracing is now rotated back to its original position so that the north mark on the tracing coincides with the north mark of the net. The final appearance of the great circle and the pole representing a plane dipping at 50° in a dip direction of 130° is as illustrated.

discontinuities (Figure 2.1(a)), or pairs of intersecting discontinuities (Figure 2.1(b)), dip out of
the face. It is, of course, important to identify
such potential failures before movement and collapse occurs. This requires an ability to visu-
alize the three-dimensional shape of the wedge
from the traces of the discontinuities on the face
of the original slope. The stereographic projection is a convenient means of carrying out
the required three-dimensional analysis, keeping
in mind that this procedure examines only the
orientation of the discontinuities and not their
position or dimensions. If the stereonet shows
the possible occurrence of a potentially unstable

block, examination of the location of the discontinuities on the geological map would help to
determine if they intersect the slope.

### 2.5.5  Lines of intersection

The intersection of two planes defines a line in
space that is characterized by a trend (0–360°)
and plunge (0–90°). In the stereographic projection, this line of intersection is defined as the point
where the two great circles cross (Figure 2.14).
The two intersecting planes may form a wedge-
shaped block as shown in Figure 2.1(b), and
the direction in which this block may slide is

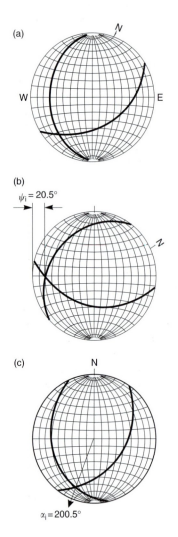

*Figure 2.14* Determination of orientation
(plunge and trend) of line intersection between
two planes with orientations 50/130 and
30/250: (a) the first of these planes has already
been drawn in Figure 2.13. The great circle
defining the second plane is obtained by
marking the 250° dip direction on the
circumference of the net, rotating the tracing
until the mark lies on the W–E axis and
tracing the great circle corresponding to a dip
of 30°; (b) the tracing is rotated until the
intersection of the two great circles lies along
the W–E axis of the stereonet, and the plunge
of the line of intersection is measured as
20.5°; (c) the tracing is now rotated until the
north mark coincides the north point on the
stereonet and the trend of the line of
intersection is found to be 200.5°.

determined by the trend of the line of intersection. However, the existence of two intersecting great circles on the stereonet does not necessarily mean that a wedge failure will occur. The factors that influence the stability of the wedge include the direction of sliding relative to the slope face, the dip of the planes relative to the friction angle, external forces such as ground water, and whether the planes are located so that they actually intersect behind the face. These factors are discussed further in Section 2.6.3.

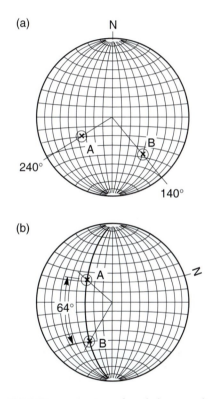

240°

140°

64°

*Figure 2.15* Determination of angle between lines with orientations 54/240 and 40/140: (a) the points A and B that define the poles of these two lines are marked on the stereonet as described in Figure 2.13 for locating the pole; (b) the tracing is rotated until the two poles lie on the same great circle on the stereonet. The angle between the lines is determined by counting the small circle divisions between A and B, along the great circle; this angle is found to be 64°. The great circle on which A and B lie defines the plane that contains these two lines. The dip and direction of this plane are 60° and 200° respectively.

Figure 2.14 shows the procedure for measuring the trend and plunge of the line of intersection of two planes on the equal area stereonet, while Figure 2.15 shows the procedure for measuring the angle between two planes. The value of these two measurements is that the orientation of the line of intersection shows the direction of sliding, and the angle between the planes gives an indication of the wedging action where two planes intersect. If the angle between the planes is small, a narrow, tight wedge will be formed with a higher factor of safety compared to a wide, open wedge in which the angle between the planes is large.

For the data shown on Figures 2.10 and 2.11, intersections occur between the bedding and joint set A ($I_1$) and joint set B ($I_2$), and between joint sets A and B ($I_3$). The orientations of the three lines of intersection are also shown on Figure 2.11. Intersection line $I_3$ has a trend of 237° and a plunge of 24°, and joint sets A and B could together form a wedge failure that would slide in the direction of the trend. Intersection line $I_1$ is almost horizontal so the wedge formed by the bedding and joint set A is unlikely to slide, while intersection line $I_2$ is near vertical and would form a thin wedge in the face.

## 2.6 Identification of modes of slope instability

Different types of slope failure are associated with different geological structures and it is important that the slope designer be able to recognize potential stability problems during the early stages of a project. Some of the structural patterns that should be identified when examining pole plots are outlined on the following pages.

Figure 2.16 shows the four types of failure considered in this book, and typical pole plots of geological conditions likely to lead to such failures. Note that in assessing stability, the cut face of the slope must be included in the stereo plot since sliding can only occur as the result of movement towards the free face created by the cut. The importance of distinguishing between these four types of slope failure is that there is a specific type of stability analysis for each as shown

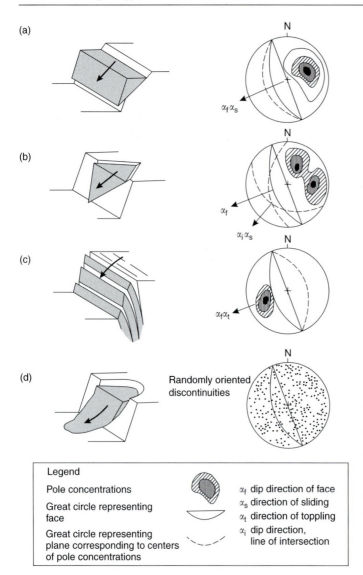

(a)

(b)

(c)

(d)

Randomly oriented
discontinuities

Legend

Pole concentrations

Great circle representing
face

Great circle representing
plane corresponding to centers
of pole concentrations

$\alpha_f$ dip direction of face
$\alpha_s$ direction of sliding
$\alpha_t$ direction of toppling
$\alpha_i$ dip direction,
  line of intersection

*Figure 2.16* Main types of block failures
in slopes, and structural geology
conditions likely to cause these failures:
(a) plane failure in rock containing
persistent joints dipping out of the slope
face, and striking parallel to the face;
(b) wedge failure on two intersecting
discontinuities; (c) toppling failure in
strong rock containing discontinuities
dipping steeply into the face; and
(d) circular failure in rock fill, very weak
rock or closely fractured rock with
randomly oriented discontinuities.

in Chapters 6–9, and it is essential that the correct analysis method be used in design.

The diagrams given in Figure 2.16 have been simplified for the sake of clarity. In an actual rock slope, several types of geological structures may be present, and this may give rise to additional types of failure. For example, in Figure 2.11, a plane failure could occur on joint set A, while the bedding could form a toppling failure on the same slope.

In a typical field study in which structural data have been plotted on stereonets, a number of significant pole concentrations may be present. It is useful to be able to identify those that represent potential failure planes, and to eliminate those that represent structures that are unlikely to be involved in slope failures. Tests for identifying important pole concentrations have been developed by Markland (1972) and Hocking (1976). These tests establish the possibility of a wedge failure in which sliding takes place along the line of intersection of two planar discontinuities as illustrated in Figure 2.16(b). Plane failure shown in Figure 2.16(a) is also covered by this test since it is a special case of wedge failure. For a wedge failure, contact is maintained on both planes and sliding occurs along the line of intersection between the two planes. For either plane or wedge failure to take place, it is fundamental that the dip of the sliding plane in the case of plane failure, or the plunge of the line of intersection in the case of wedge failure, be less than the dip of the slope face (i.e. $\psi_i < \psi_f$) (Figure 2.17(a)). That is, the sliding surface "daylights" in the slope face.

The test can also differentiate between sliding of a wedge on two planes along the line of intersection, or along only one of the planes such that a plane failure occurs. If the dip directions of the two planes lie outside the included angle between $\alpha_i$ (trend of intersection line) and $\alpha_f$ (dip direction of face), the wedge will slide on both planes (Figure 2.17(b)). If the dip direction of one plane (A) lies within the included angle between $\alpha_i$ and $\alpha_f$, the wedge will slide on only that plane (Figure 2.17(c)).

### 2.6.1   Kinematic analysis

Once the type of block failure has been identified on the stereonet, the same diagram can also be used to examine the direction in which a block will slide and give an indication of stability conditions. This procedure is known as kinematic analysis. An application of kinematic analysis is the rock face shown in Figure 2.1(b) where two joint planes form a wedge which has slid out of the face and towards the photographer. If the slope face had been less steep than the line of intersection between the two planes, or had a strike at 90° to the actual strike, then although the two planes form a wedge, it would not have been able to slide from the face. This relationship between the direction in which the block of rock will slide and the orientation of the face is readily apparent on the stereonet. However, while analysis of the stereonet gives a good indication of stability conditions, it does

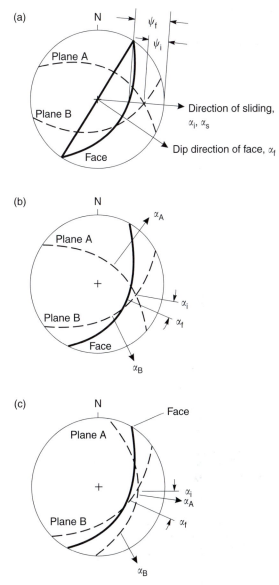

Figure 2.17 Identification of plane and wedge failures on stereonet: (a) sliding along line of intersection of planes A and B is possible where the plunge of this line is less than the dip of the slope face, measured in the direction of sliding, that is, $\psi_i < \psi_f$; (b) wedge failure occurs along line of intersection (dip direction $\alpha_i$) on slope with dip direction $\alpha_f$ because dip directions of planes A and B ($\alpha_A$ and $\alpha_B$) lie outside included angle between $\alpha_i$ and $\alpha_f$; (c) plane failure occurs on plane A (dip direction $\alpha_A$) on slope with dip direction $\alpha_f$ because dip direction of planes A lies inside included angle between $\alpha_i$ and $\alpha_f$.

not account for external forces such as water pressures or reinforcement comprising tensioned rock bolts, which can have a significant effect on stability. The usual design procedure is to use kinematic analysis to identify potentially unstable blocks, followed by detailed stability analysis of these blocks using the procedures described in Chapters 6–9.

An example of kinematic analysis is shown in Figure 2.18 where a rock slope contains three sets of discontinuities. The potential for these discontinuities to result in slope failures depends on their dip and dip direction relative to the face; stability conditions can be studied on the stereonet as described in the next section.

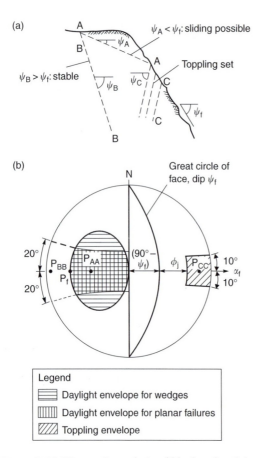

### 2.6.2 Plane failure

In Figure 2.18(a), a potentially unstable planar block is formed by plane AA, which dips at a flatter angle than the face ($\psi_A < \psi_f$) and is said to "daylight" on the face. However, sliding is not possible on plane BB which dips steeper than the face ($\psi_B > \psi_f$) and does not daylight. Similarly, discontinuity set CC dips into the face and sliding cannot occur on these planes, although toppling is possible. The poles of the slope face and the discontinuity sets (symbol $P$) are plotted on the stereonet in Figure 2.18(b), assuming that all the discontinuities strike parallel to the face. The position of these poles in relation to the slope face shows that the poles of all planes that daylight and are potentially unstable, lie inside the pole of the slope face. This area is termed the *daylight envelope* and can be used to identify quickly potentially unstable blocks.

The dip direction of the discontinuity sets will also influence stability. Plane sliding is not possible if the dip direction of the discontinuity differs from the dip direction of the face by more than about 20°. That is, the block will be stable if $|\alpha_A - \alpha_f| > 20°$, because under these conditions there will be an increasing thickness of intact rock at one end of the block which will have sufficient strength to resist failure. On the stereonet this restriction on the dip direction of the planes is shown by two lines defining dip directions of $(\alpha_f + 20°)$ and $(\alpha_f - 20°)$. These two lines designate the lateral limits of the daylight envelope on Figure 2.18(b).

### 2.6.3 Wedge failure

Kinematic analysis of wedge failures (Figure 2.16(b)) can be carried out in a similar manner to that of plane failures. In this case the pole of the line of intersection of the two discontinuities is plotted on the stereonet and sliding is possible if the pole daylights on the face, that is ($\psi_i < \psi_f$). The direction of sliding of kinematically permissible wedges is less restrictive than that of plane failures because there are two planes to form release surfaces. A daylighting envelope for the

*Figure 2.18* Kinematic analysis of blocks of rock in slope: (a) discontinuity sets in slope; and (b) daylight envelopes on equal area stereonet.

line of intersection, as shown on Figure 2.18(b), is wider than the envelope for plane failures. The wedge daylight envelope is the locus of all poles representing lines of intersection whose dip directions lie in the plane of the slope face.

### 2.6.4  Toppling failure

For a toppling failure to occur, the dip direction of the discontinuities dipping into the face must be within about 10° of the dip direction of the face so that a series of slabs are formed parallel to the face. Also, the dip of the planes must be steep enough for interlayer slip to occur. If the faces of the layers have a friction angle $\phi_j$, then slip will only occur if the direction of the applied compressive stress is at angle greater than $\phi_j$ with the normal to the layers. The direction of the major principal stress in the cut is parallel to the face of the cut (dip angle $\psi_f$), so interlayer slip and toppling failure will occur on planes with dip $\psi_p$ when the following conditions are met (Goodman and Bray, 1976):

$$(90° - \psi_f) + \phi_j < \psi_p \qquad (2.3)$$

These conditions on the dip and dip direction of planes that can develop toppling failures are defined on Figure 2.18(b). The envelope defining the orientation of these planes lies at the opposite side of the stereonet from the sliding envelopes.

### 2.6.5  Friction cone

Having determined from the daylight envelopes whether a block in the slope is kinematically permissible, it is also possible to examine stability conditions on the same stereonet. This analysis is carried out assuming that the shear strength of the sliding surface comprises only friction and the cohesion is zero. Consider a block at rest on an inclined plane with a friction angle of $\phi$ between the block and the plane (Figure 2.19(a)). For an at-rest condition, the force vector normal to the plane must lie within the friction cone. When the only force acting on the block is gravity, the pole to the plane is in the same direction as the normal

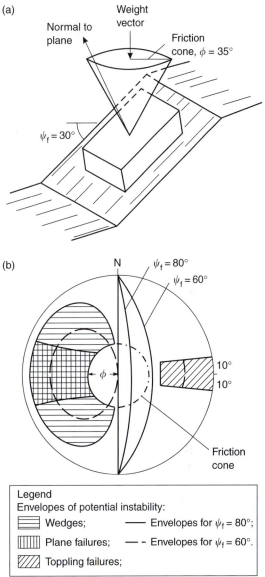

Figure 2.19 Combined kinematics and simple stability analysis using friction cone concept: (a) friction cone in relation to block at rest on an inclined plane (i.e. $\phi > \psi_p$); and (b) stereographic projection of friction cone superimposed on "daylighting" envelopes.

force, so the block will be stable when the pole lies within the friction circle.

The envelopes on Figure 2.19(b) show the possible positions of poles that may form unstable blocks. Envelopes have been drawn for slope face angles of 60° and 80°, which show that the risk of instability increases as the slope becomes steeper as indicated by the larger envelopes for the steeper slope. Also, the envelopes become larger as the friction angle diminishes. The envelopes also indicate that, for the simple gravity loading condition, instability will only occur in a limited range of geometric conditions.

### 2.6.6   *Applications of kinematic analysis*

The techniques demonstrated on Figures 2.16–2.19 to identify both potentially unstable blocks of rock on the slope and the type of instability can readily be applied to the preliminary stages of slope design. This is illustrated in the two examples that follow.

*Highway*: A proposed highway on a north–south alignment passes through a ridge of rock in which a through-cut is required to keep the highway on grade (Figure 2.20(a)). Diamond drilling and mapping shows that the geological conditions in the ridge are consistent so that the same structure will be exposed in each face. The predominant geological structure is the bedding that strikes north–south, parallel to the highway alignment and dips to the east at angles of between 70° and 80° (i.e. dip and dip direction of 70–80/090).

The stereonets in Figure 2.20(b) show poles representing the dip and dip direction of the bedding, and great circles representing the orientations of the left and right cut faces. Also plotted on the stereonets is a friction cone representing a friction angle of 35° on the bedding. These stereonets show that on the left (west) face, the bedding dips towards the excavation at a steeper angle than the friction angle so sliding can occur on the bedding. The cut face has been made along the bedding to create a stable face.

On the right (east) face the bedding dips steeply into the face and there is a possibility that the slabs formed by these joints will fail by toppling. According to equation (2.3), toppling is possible if $(90° - \psi_f) + \phi_j < \psi_p$. If the face is cut at 76° (0.25V:1H) and the friction angle is 35°, then the

left side of this equation equals 49°, which is less than the dip of the bedding (70°–80°). The potential for toppling is indicated by the poles to the bedding planes lying inside the toppling envelope.

This preliminary analysis shows that the right (east) cut slope has potential stability problems and that more detailed investigation of structural geology conditions would be required before finalizing the design. The first step in this investigation would be to examine the spacing of the bedding planes and determine if the center of gravity of the slabs will lie outside the base, in which case toppling is likely. Note that it is rarely possible to change the alignment sufficiently to overcome a stability problem, so it may be necessary to either reduce the slope angle on the right side, or stabilize the 76° face.

*Open pit slopes*: During the feasibility studies on a proposed open pit mine, an estimate of the safe slope is required for the calculation of ore-to-waste ratios and the preliminary pit layout. The only structural information that may be available at this stage is that which has been obtained from diamond drill cores drilled for mineral evaluation purposes, and from the mapping of surface outcrops. Scanty as this information is, it does provide a basis for preliminary slope design.

A contour plan of the proposed open pit mine is presented in Figure 2.21 and contoured stereo plots of available structural data are superimposed on this plan. Two distinct structural regions, denoted by A and B, have been identified and the boundary between these regions has been marked on the plan. For the sake of simplicity, major faults have not been shown. However, it is essential that any information on faults should be included on large-scale plans of this sort and that the potential stability problems associated with these faults should be evaluated.

Overlaid on the stereonets are great circles representing the orientations of the east and west pit faces, assuming an overall slope angle of 45°. Also shown on the stereonets is a friction cone of 30°, which is assumed to be the average friction angles of the discontinuity surfaces. The stereonets show that the western and southern portions of the pit

(a)

(b)

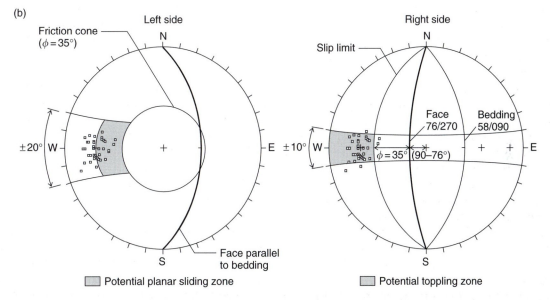

*Figure 2.20* Relationship between structural geology and stability conditions on slope faces in through-cut: (a) photograph of through-cut showing two failure mechanisms—plane sliding on left side (west), and toppling on right side (east) on Route 60 near Globe AZ; (b) stereographic plots showing kinematics analysis of left and right cut slopes.

are likely to be stable at the proposed slope of 45°. This suggests that, if the rock is strong and free of major faults, these slopes could probably be steepened or, alternately, this portion of the pit

wall could be used as a haul road location with steep faces above and below the haul road.

On the other hand, the northeastern portion of the pit contains a number of potential slope

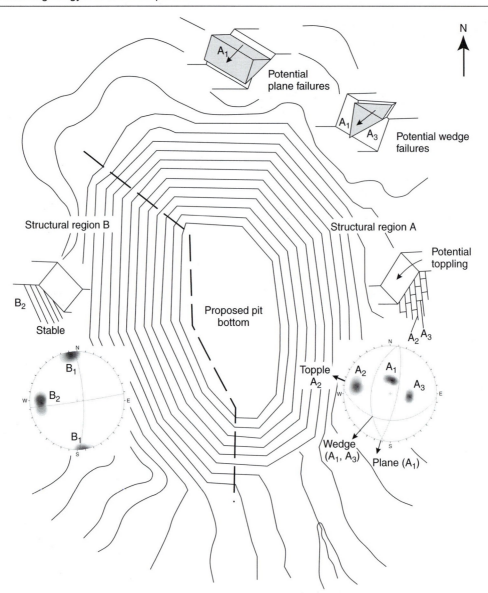

*Figure 2.21* Presentation of structural geology on stereonets, and preliminary evaluation of slope stability of proposed open pit mine.

problems. The northern face is likely to suffer from plane sliding on discontinuity set A1, since this set will daylight in the face at an angle steeper than the friction angle. Wedge failures on the intersection of sets A1 and A3 are possible in the northeastern corner of the pit, and toppling failure on set A2 may occur in the eastern slopes.

Indications of potential instability would suggest that consideration be given to flattening the slopes in the northeastern part of the proposed pit.

It is interesting to note that three types of structurally controlled slope failure can occur in the same structural region, depending upon the orientation of the slope face.

## 2.7 Example Problem 2.1: stereo plots of structural geology data

### Statement

A structural geology mapping program for a proposed highway produced the following results for the orientation of the discontinuities (format-dip/dip direction).

| 40/080 | 45/090 | 20/160 | 80/310 | 83/312 | 82/305 |
| 23/175 | 43/078 | 37/083 | 20/150 | 21/151 | 39/074 |
| 70/300 | 75/305 | 15/180 | 80/010 | 31/081 | |

### Required

(a) Plot the orientation of each discontinuity as a pole on a stereonet using the equal area polar net and tracing paper.

(b) Estimate and plot the position of the mean pole of each of the three sets of discontinuities.

(c) Determine the angle between the mean poles with the steepest and shallowest dips.

(d) Plot the great circles of the mean pole of each set on the equal area equatorial net.

(e) Determine the plunge and trend of the line of intersection between the joint sets with the steepest and intermediate dip angles.

### Solution

(a) The poles of the 17 planes are plotted on Figure 2.22, which shows that there are three sets of discontinuities.

(b) The mean pole of each discontinuity set is as follows:

*Set 1* : 78/305;   *Set 2* : 40/081;

*Set 3* : 20/163

There is one pole (80/010) that does not belong to any of the three discontinuity sets.

(c) The angle between the mean poles of joint sets 1 and 3 is determined by rotating the stereonet until both mean poles lie on the same

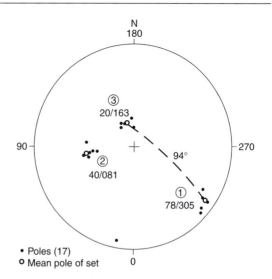

Figure 2.22 Example problem 2.1—plot of poles of structural mapping data (lower hemisphere projection).

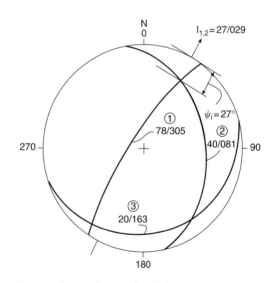

Figure 2.23 Example problem 2.1—great circles of mean poles plotted using equatorial net.

great circle. The number of divisions on this great circle is 94° as shown by the dotted line on Figure 2.22. The actual included angle is 86° (180 − 94).

(d) The great circles of the three mean poles are plotted on Figure 2.23.

(e) The plunge and trend of the line of intersection of joint sets 1 and 2 are also shown on Figure 2.23. The values are as follows:

Dip, $\psi_i = 27$;   dip direction, $\psi_i = 029$

## 2.8   Example Problem 2.2: slope stability evaluation related to structural geology

### Statement

In order to make a 90° curve in a highway, a rock cut has been excavated that follows the curve of the highway, the face is cut at an angle of 50°.

The joints in the rock at the site form three sets with the following orientations:

*Set 1* : 78/305;   *Set 2* : 40/081;

*Set 3* : 20/163

Figure 2.24 shows the alignment of the highway and the orientation of the three sets in the slope. The friction angle of the joint surfaces is 25°.

### Required

(a) On a piece of tracing paper draw a great circle representing the 50° slope face and a 25° friction circle.
(b) Determine the most likely mode of failure, that is, plane, wedge or toppling, on the following slopes:

- East dipping slope.
- North dipping slopes.

(c) State the joint set or sets on which sliding would occur on each slope.
(d) Determine the steepest possible slope angle for these two slopes assuming that only the orientation of the discontinuities and the

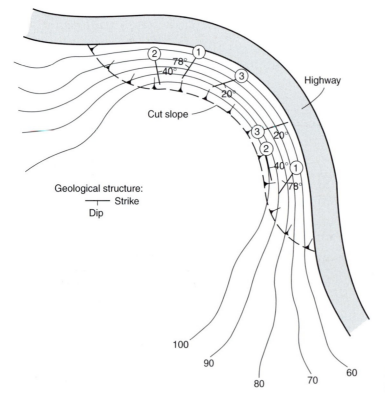

*Figure 2.24* Cut slope and geological structures in cut face.

friction angle of the surfaces have to be considered.

### Solution

(a)  Figure 2.25 shows the great circle of the slope dipping to the east at a face angle of 50°; and a 25° friction circle plotted as a small circle.

(b)  The stability evaluation is carried out by placing first the tracing of the great circles (Figure 2.23) and then the tracing of the slope face and friction circle (Figure 2.25) on the equal area net. The tracing of the slope great circle is rotated to the corresponding orientation of the slope face to give the following results:

*East dipping slope*: Plane failure possible on joint set 2 (Figure 2.26). Sliding could be prevented by cutting the slope at 40° coincident with the joint surfaces. If the friction angle had been greater than 40°, then sliding may not occur on these planes.

*North dipping slope*: Wedge failure possible on joint sets 1 and 2 (Figure 2.27). Sliding

could be prevented by cutting the slope at an angle of 27° so that the wedges are not undercut by the slope.

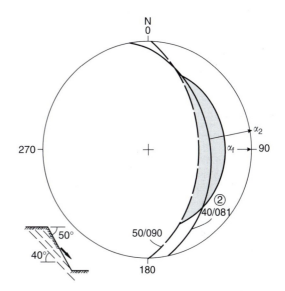

*Figure 2.26* Stability conditions on east dipping slope—plane failure on joint set 2.

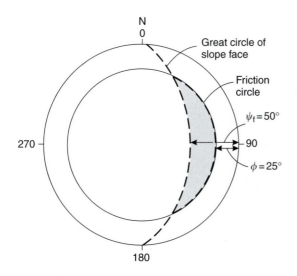

*Figure 2.25* Great circle of slope dipping at 50°, and 25° friction circle.

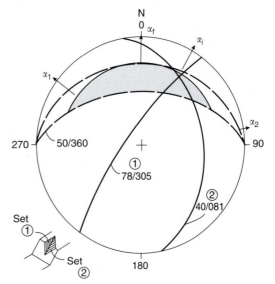

*Figure 2.27* Stability conditions on north dipping slope—wedge failure on joint set 1 and joint set 2.

# Chapter 3

# Site investigation and geological data collection

## 3.1 Planning an investigation program

The design of rock cuts is often an iterative process that proceeds from initial reconnaissance, through preliminary and final design followed by construction. This process involves progressively collecting more detailed design data, specific to the site conditions and needs of the project. Typically, the three stages of a complete investigation are as follows:

- *Reconnaissance*: examination of published geological maps and reports, study of air photographs, gathering of local experience, field visits to examine, if possible, the performance of existing slopes in similar geological conditions, and geophysics studies if outcrops are limited.
- *Route selection/preliminary pit slope design*: if the project involves the evaluation of alternative routes, limited investigations could be carried out of each route comprising outcrop mapping, geophysics to find overburden thickness and index tests of rock properties. For an open pit mine, there will usually be considerable geological information on the property generated during the exploration program. This will often include mapping, geophysics and drilling from which geotechnical data can be obtained. It is beneficial to the design of the pit slopes if geotechnical data can be collected as part of the exploration program.
- *Detailed investigations*: final design would usually require detailed mapping of outcrops

and existing cuts to study structural geology, test pits to obtain information on overburden thickness and properties, and diamond drilling to investigate rock conditions at depth. Components of the drilling could include core orientation to obtain structural geology information, and installation of piezometers to measure ground water levels, and possibly measure permeability. Rock strength testing could comprise laboratory testing of drill core to determine the friction angle of discontinuities, uniaxial compression strength tests and slake durability tests. Figure 3.1 shows a diamond drilling program in progress where an inclined hole and triple tube core barrel are being used to investigate targeted geological structure and collect high quality core in closely fractured rock. Some of the current (2003) requirements for drilling and sampling programs may include collection of all circulation water ("zero discharge drilling"), and complete restoration of the drill site and access roads.

Because of the wide variety of both site conditions and slope designs, it is not considered appropriate to draw up any rules on the types and quantity of investigation programs. That is, every investigation is unique. The only general rule that applies to investigation for rock slope design is that information is required on geology, rock strength and ground water. These three sets of design parameters are discussed in the following sections.

*Figure 3.1* Photograph of typical diamond drilling equipment for hole depths up to about 300 m.

### 3.1.1 *Geology*

A distinguishing feature of many investigations for rock slopes is that it is particularly important to focus on the details of the structural geology. For example, the orientation of one clay-filled fault that dips out of the face can make the difference between stability and instability. Structural geology data provided by surface mapping, where available, is usually more reliable than that obtained by diamond drilling because outcrops and cuts show larger scale features and undisturbed *in situ* conditions compared to the very small volume of a drill core. Furthermore, the orientation of discontinuities in core is not known unless the core is oriented.

It is recommended wherever possible, that the mapping be carried out by the same person or engineering group who will carry out the design so that the objectives of the mapping program are clearly identified and the data collected is relevant to the design. For example, a large number of short, non-persistent joints that have little influence on the rock mass strength or stability should be given less attention during mapping than a limited number of shears with continuous lengths equal to that of the slope height. A design engineer who is analyzing the data and is not familiar with the site, may be unable to distinguish on a contoured stereonet the relative importance between the many non-persistent joints and the shears.

Alternative approaches to geological investigations are as follows. First, there may be a number of existing slopes, either natural or excavated, near the site where the geological conditions are similar to those on the project. In this case, strong reliance could be placed on extrapolating the performance of these slopes to the new design. In these circumstances, it may not be necessary to collect additional data, except to carefully document existing slope performance and assessing how this may be applied to the proposed design. Alternatively, where there is little local experience in cut slope stability, it may be necessary to conduct an extensive investigation program involving mapping, drilling, and laboratory testing. As this program develops, it should be modified to suit particular conditions at the site. For example, the drilling and mapping may show that although the rock is strong and the jointing is favorable to stability, there are a number of faults that could control stability conditions. The investigation program would then concentrate on determining the location and orientation of these faults, and their shear strength properties. This chapter describes geological investigation methods.

### 3.1.2 Rock strength

The rock strength parameters that are used in slope design are primarily the shear strength of discontinuities and the rock mass, the weathering characteristics of the rock where applicable, and to a lesser extent the compressive strength of intact rock. The shear strength of discontinuities can be measured in the laboratory on samples obtained from drill core, or samples cut from lumps of rock that are intersected by a discontinuity. The shear strength of the rock mass can either be determined by back-analysis of slope failures, or calculated by an empirical method that requires information on the intact rock strength, the rock type and the degree of fracturing. The compressive strength of rock can be measured on core samples, or from index tests applied to outcrops in the field. The susceptibility of rock to weathering can also be measured in the laboratory, or assessed by field index tests. Details of rock testing methods are described in Chapter 4.

### 3.1.3 Ground water

The investigation of ground water plays an important part in any slope design program. In climates with high precipitation levels, water pressures should always be included in the design. The design water pressures should account for likely peak pressures that may develop during intense rainfall events or snow melt periods, rather than the pressure due to the average seasonal water table. Furthermore, if drainage measures are installed, the design may account for the possible degradation of these systems due to lack of maintenance.

Similarly to geological investigations, the extent of the ground water investigation will also depend on site conditions. In most cases, it is sufficient to install piezometers to measure the position and variation in the water table so that realistic values of water pressure can be used in design. However, if it is planned to install extensive drainage measures such as a drainage adit, then measurements of permeability are beneficial to assess whether the adit will be successful in draining the slope, and then to determine the optimum location and layout of the adit and drain holes. Details of ground water investigations are described in Chapter 5.

## 3.2 Site reconnaissance

The following is a discussion on some of the reconnaissance techniques that may be used early in a project, mainly for the purpose of project evaluation. It is rare that the information gathered at this stage of a project would be adequate for use in final design, so these studies would be followed by more detailed investigations such as surface mapping and drilling once the overall project layout has been finalized.

Part of any site reconnaissance is the collection of all relevant existing data on the site, ranging from published data from both government and private sources to observations of the performance of existing natural slopes and cut faces. These sources will provide such information as rock types, depth of weathering, likely slope failure modes and the frequency and size of rock falls.

An important first step in the reconnaissance stage of a project is to define *zones*, in each of which the geological properties are uniform with regards to the requirements of the project (ISRM, 1981a). Typical boundaries between zones include rock type contacts, faults or major folds. The zoning of the rock mass should provide information on the location, orientation and type of boundary between zones, as well as some information on the engineering properties of the rock mass in each. By defining the boundaries of each zone, it is possible to determine the extent to which stability conditions will vary along the alignment or around the pit, and plan more detailed investigations in those zones in which there is potential for instability.

Figure 3.2 shows an example of a reconnaissance-level geologic map for a highway project. This map shows basic location features such as universal transverse Mercator (UTM) co-ordinates, a river, the existing highway and rail-way, and the proposed new alignment. Note that ground contours have been left off the map for the sake of clarity. The geologic data includes the rock type, a landslide, thrust faults, and the strike and dip orientation of discontinuities mapped on outcrops. The numbers such as "10-3" are references linked to a table that provides more information on the characteristics of each discon-tinuity; the locations of the discontinuities were determined using a GPS (geographical position-ing system) unit. Orientations of the bedding and two primary orthogonal joint sets are shown on the stereonets on Figures 2.11–2.13.

### 3.2.1 Aerial and terrestrial photography

The study of stereographic pairs of vertical aerial photographs or oblique terrestrial photographs provides much useful information on the larger-scale geological conditions at a site (Peterson *et al.*, 1982). Often these large features will be difficult to identify in surface mapping because they are obscured by vegetation, rock falls or more closely spaced discontinuities. Photographs most commonly used in geotechnical engineer-ing are black and white, vertical photographs taken at heights of between 500 and 3000 m with scales ranging from 1:10,000 to 1:30,000. On some projects, it is necessary to have both high and low level photographs, with the high level photographs being used to identify landslides for example, while the low level photographs provide more detailed information on geological structure.

One of the most important uses of aerial photo-graphs is the identification of landslides that have the potential for causing movement, or even destruction of facilities. Landslide features that are often readily apparent on vertical aerial photographs are scarps along the crest of the slide, hummocky terrain in the body of the slide and areas of fresh disturbance in the toe, including sudden changes in river direction. By compar-ing photographs taken over a number of years, it may be possible to determine the rate of move-ment of a slide, and whether it is growing in size. Figure 3.3 shows stereo pair aerial photographs of the Hope Slide in British Columbia that occurred in 1965. The volume of rock that failed was about 47 million $m^3$; a 3.2 km length of the highway was buried to a depth of about 80 m. The slide mass failed on a continuous foliation plane dipping at about 30° out of the slope face.

Other features that may be evident on aerial photographs are major geological structures such as faults, bedding planes and continuous joint sets. The photographs may provide information on the position, length and continuity of these features (Goodman, 1976).

### 3.2.2 Geophysics

Geophysical methods are often used in the recon-naissance or preliminary stages of a site invest-igation program to provide such information as the depth of weathering, the bedrock profile, contacts between rock types of significantly dif-ferent density, the location of major faults, and the degree of fracturing of the rock (Griffiths and King, 1988). The results obtained from geo-physical measurements are usually not sufficiently accurate to be used in final design and should preferably be calibrated by putting down a num-ber of test pits or drill holes to spot check actual properties and contact elevations. However, geo-physical surveys provide a continuous profile of subsurface conditions and this information can be used as a fill-in between drill holes. For rock slope engineering purposes the most common geophy-sical investigation method is seismic refraction as described next.

*Seismic methods.* Seismic surveys are used to determine the approximate location and density of layers of soil and rock, a well-defined water

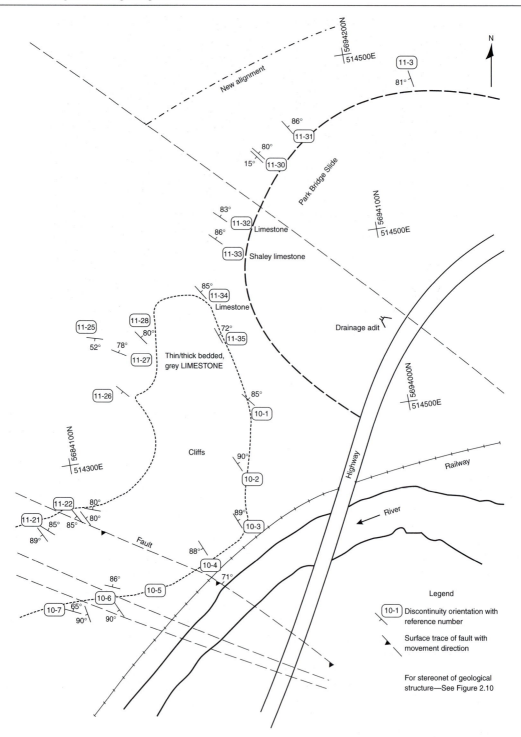

*Figure 3.2* Typical reconnaissance-level geological map showing structural geology features (mapping by Dr C. H. B. Leitch).

*Figure 3.3* Stereo pair aerial photographs of Hope Slide, British Columbia; slide had volume of 47 million m$^3$ of rock and buried a 3.2 km length of highway.

table, or the degree of fracturing, porosity and saturation of the rock. Seismic velocities of a variety of rock types have also been correlated with their rippability, which is a useful guideline in the selection of rock excavation methods (Caterpillar, 2001). The seismic method is effective to depths in the range of tens of meters to a maximum of a few hundred meters. Discontinuities will not be detected by seismic methods unless there is shear displacement and a distinct elevation change of a layer with a particular density as a result of fault movement.

Seismic surveys measure the relative arrival times, and thus the velocity of propagation, of elastic waves traveling between a shallow energy source and a number of transducers set out in a straight line along the required profile. The energy source may be a hammer blow, an explosion of a propane–oxygen mixture in a heavy chamber (gas-gun), or a light explosive charge. In elastically homogeneous ground subject to a sudden stress near its surface, three elastic pulses travel outward at different speeds. Two are body waves that are propagated as spherical fronts affected to only a minor extent by the free surface of the ground. The third wave is a surface wave (Raleigh wave) that is confined to the region near the surface; its amplitude falling off rapidly with depth. The two body waves, namely the primary or "$P$" wave and the secondary or "$S$" wave, differ in both their direction of motion and speed. The $P$ wave is a longitudinal compressive wave in the direction of propagation, while the $S$ wave induces shear stresses in the medium. The velocities of the primary ($V_p$) and secondary ($V_s$) waves are related to the elastic constants and density of the medium by the equations:

$$V_p = \left( \frac{(K + 4G/3)}{\gamma_r} \right)^{1/2} \qquad (3.1)$$

$$V_s = \left( \frac{G}{\gamma_r} \right)^{1/2} \qquad (3.2)$$

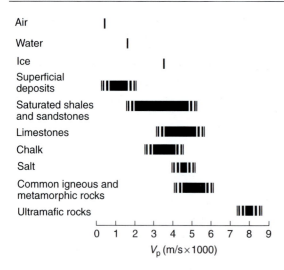

*Figure 3.4* Approximate range of *P* wave velocities (*V*$_p$) for some common geological materials (Griffiths and King, 1988).

where *K* is the bulk modulus, *G* is the shear modulus and $\gamma_r$ is the rock density. The velocity of the *S* wave in most rocks is about one half that of the *P* wave, and the *S* wave is not propagated at all in fluids. The ratio $V_p/V_s$ depends only on the Poisson's ratio of the medium. Figure 3.4 shows typical values of the *P* wave for a variety of rock types.

Some of the rock properties that can be assessed from the behavior waves include the strength (or consolidation), the density and degree of fracturing. For example, the amplitude of the waves decreases with distance from their source because the energy wave spreads over the increasing wave front area. Earth materials are imperfectly elastic leading to energy loss and attenuation of the seismic waves that is greater than would be expected from geometric spreading alone. This reduction in amplitude is more pronounced for less consolidated rocks.

The sonic velocity of the elastic wave will be greater in higher density material, and in more massive rock compared to low density, closely fractured rock; this information is used to assess the rippability of rock. Where a layer of low density material overlies a denser layer, such as soil overlying bedrock, then the elastic wave velocity will be greater in the bedrock and the contact between the layers will act as a refracting surface. In a specific range of distances from the shot point, the times of first arrival at different distances from the shot point will represent waves traveling along this surface. This information can be used to plot the contact profile between the two layers.

## 3.3  Geologic mapping

Geological mapping of surface outcrops or existing cuts, in similar geological formations to that in which the excavation will be made, usually furnishes the fundamental information on site conditions required for slope design. While mapping is a vital part of the investigation program, it is also an inexact process because a certain amount of judgment is usually required to extrapolate the small amount of information available from surface outcrops to the overall cut slope (McClay, 1987).

In order to produce geological maps and descriptions of the engineering properties of the rock mass that can be used with confidence in design, it is important to have a well-defined process that produces comparable results obtained by different personnel working at several sites. To meet these requirements, standard mapping procedures have been drawn up which have the following objectives:

- Provide a language that enables observers to transmit their general impression of a rock mass, particularly with regard to its anticipated mechanical behavior. The language of the geological description must be unambiguous so that different observers of a given rock mass describe the rock mass in the same way.
- Contain as far as possible quantitative data of interest to the solution of definite practical problems.
- Whenever possible, use simple measurements rather than visual observations alone.
- Provide a complete specification of the rock mass for engineering purposes.

### 3.3.1 Line and window mapping

Methods of structural mapping that will systematically examine all significant geological features are "line" and "window" mapping (see also Appendix II).

Line mapping comprises stretching a tape along the face and mapping every discontinuity that intersects the line; line lengths are normally between 50 and 100 m. If the ends of the line are surveyed, then the location of all the discontinuities can be determined. Window mapping comprises mapping all discontinuities within a representative segment or "window" of fixed size, spaced at regular intervals along the exposure. The intervening areas are examined for similarity of structure. The dimensions of a window would normally be about 10 m. Either of these mapping techniques may be used in both the reconnaissance and final design stages of a project, depending on the extent of the face available for mapping. If the initial investigations identify a particular feature that is likely to have a significant effect on stability, then more detailed mapping, such as roughness and persistence measurements, could be carried out on these structures.

### 3.3.2 Stereogrammetric mapping of discontinuities

There are circumstances where it is not possible to directly access a rock face for mapping because, for example, there is a hazard to the geologists of rock falls or the face is overhanging in places. Under these conditions, there are available indirect methods of geological mapping using terrestrial photography. The basic principle involves obtaining the co-ordinates of at least three points on each surface from which its orientation can be calculated.

One system that provides this facility is SIRO-JOINT (CSIRO, 2001). A digital image of the slope face taken by a camera at a known location, and the image is converted into three-dimensional spatial data defining the surface of the rock face. Each spatial point has a position ($x$, $y$, $z$ co-ordinates) in space, and each local set of three spatial points defines a triangle. From these co-ordinates, the orientation of the triangles can be defined in terms of the dip and dip direction, together with the co-ordinates of the centroid. The software allows a mouse to be used to outline the surface to be analyzed, and the calculated dip and dip direction can then be imported directly to a stereonet.

### 3.3.3 Types of discontinuity

Geological investigations usually categorize discontinuities according to the manner in which they were formed. This is useful for geotechnical engineering because discontinuities within each category usually have similar properties as regards both dimensions and shear strength properties that can be used in the initial review of stability conditions of a site. The following are standard definitions of the most common types of discontinuities:

(a) *Fault*—Discontinuity along which there has been an observable amount of displacement. Faults are rarely single planar units; normally they occur as parallel or sub-parallel sets of discontinuities along which movement has taken place to a greater or less extent.

(b) *Bedding*—Surface parallel to the surface of deposition, which may or may not have a physical expression. Note that the original attitude of the bedding plane should not be assumed to be horizontal.

(c) *Foliation*—Parallel orientation of platy minerals, or mineral banding in metamorphic rocks.

(d) *Joint*—Discontinuity in which there has been no observable relative movement. In general, joints intersect primary surfaces such as bedding, cleavage and schistosity. A series of parallel joints is called a *joint set*; two or more intersecting sets produce a *joint system*; two sets of joints approximately at right angles to one another are said to be *orthogonal*.

(e)  *Cleavage*—Parallel discontinuities formed in incompetent layers in a series of beds of varying degrees of competency are known as cleavages. In general, the term implies that the cleavage planes are not controlled by mineral particles in parallel orientation.

(f)  *Schistosity*—Foliation in schist or other coarse grained crystalline rock due to the parallel arrangement of mineral grains of the platy or prismatic type, such as mica.

### 3.3.4   *Definition of geological terms*

The following is a summary of information that may be collected to provide a complete description of the rock mass, and comments on how these properties influence the performance of the rock mass. This information is based primarily on procedures developed by the International Society of Rock Mechanics (ISRM, 1981b), with some additional information from the Geological Society Engineering Group (1977). More details of the mapping data is provided in Appendix II, which includes mapping field sheets and tables relating descriptions of rock mass properties to quantitative measurements.

Figure 3.5(a) illustrates the 12 essential features of geological structure, each of which is described in more detail in this section. The diagram and photograph in Figure 3.5 show that sets of discontinuities often occur in orthogonal sets (mutually at right angles) in response to the stress field that has deformed the rock; the photograph shows three orthogonal joints in massive granite. Orthogonal structure is also illustrated in the stereonet in Figure 2.11. The value of recognizing orthogonal structure on an outcrop or in a stereonet is that these features are often the most prevalent in a cut and are likely to control stability.

The following is a list, and a description of the parameters that define the characteristics of the rock mass.

A  *Rock type*—The rock type is defined by the origin of the rock (i.e. sedimentary, metamorphic or igneous), the mineralogy, the color and grain size (Deere and Miller, 1966).

The importance of defining the rock type is that there is wide experience in the performance of different rock types (e.g. granite is usually stronger and more massive than shale), and this information provides a useful guideline on the likely behavior of the rock.

B  *Discontinuity type*—Discontinuity types range from clean tension joints of limited length to faults containing several meters thickness of clay gouge and lengths of many kilometers; obviously the shear strength of such discontinuities will be very different. Section 3.3.3 provides a definition of the six most common types of discontinuity.

C  *Discontinuity orientation*—The orientation of discontinuities is expressed as the dip and dip direction (or strike) of the surface. The dip of the plane is the maximum angle of the plane to the horizontal (angle $\psi$), while the dip direction is the direction of the horizontal trace of the line of dip, measured clockwise from north, angle $\alpha$ (see Figure 2.4). For the plane shown in Figure 3.5 that dips to the northeast, the orientation of the plane can be completely defined by five digits: 30/045, where the dip is 30° and the dip direction is 45°. This method of defining discontinuity orientation facilitates mapping because the dip and dip direction can be read from a single compass reading (Figure 3.6). Also, the results can be plotted directly on a stereonet to analyze the structural geology (see Section 2.5). In using the compass shown in Figure 3.6, the dip is read off a graduated scale on the lid hinge, while the dip direction is read off the compass scale that is graduated from 0° to 360°.

Some compasses allow the graduated circle to be rotated to account for the magnetic declination at the site so that measured dip directions are relative to true north. If the compass does not have this feature, then the magnetic readings can be adjusted accordingly: for a magnetic declination of *20° east*, for example, *20° is added to the magnetic readings* to obtain true north readings.

D  *Spacing*—Discontinuity spacing can be mapped in rock faces and in drill core, with

(a)

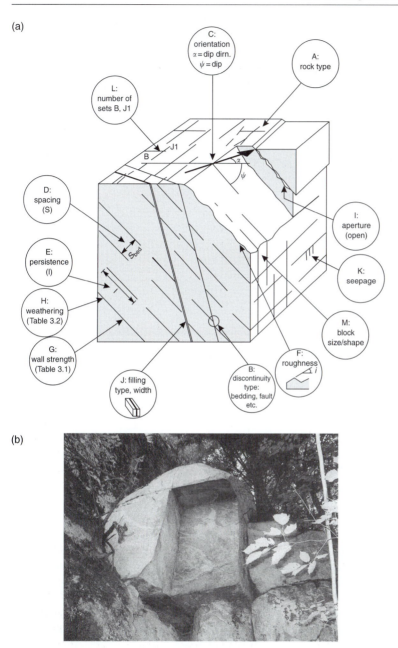

(b)

*Figure 3.5* Characteristics of discontinuities in rock masses: (a) parameters describing the rock mass; letters ("A" etc.) refer to description of parameter in text (Wyllie, 1999); (b) photograph of blocky granitic rock containing three joints orientated in orthogonal directions (near Hope, British Columbia).

the true spacing being calculated from the apparent spacing for discontinuities inclined to the face (see also Section 3.4.1); spacing categories range from extremely wide (>2 m) to very narrow (<6 mm). Measurement of discontinuity spacing of each set of discontinuities will define the size and shape of blocks and give an indication of stability modes such as toppling failure. Also, the rock mass strength is related to spacing because in closely fractured rock the individual discontinuities will more readily join

*Figure 3.6* Geological compass (Clar type) used to directly measure dip and dip direction of surfaces. Lid is placed on surface and body is rotated until it is level, as indicated by the spirit level; the needle is released to indicate dip direction, and the dip is read off scale on the hinge. (The Brunton Co., Riverton, WY.)

to form a continuous zone of weakness. A method of calculating the strength of fractured rock masses taking into account discontinuity spacing is discussed in Section 4.5.

E   *Persistence*—Persistence is the measure of the continuous length or area of the discontinuity; persistence categories range from very high (>20 m) to very low (<1 m). This parameter defines the size of blocks and the length of potential sliding surfaces, so the mapping should concentrate on measuring the persistence of the set of discontinuities that will have the greatest influence on stability. Where it is not possible to measure the length of discontinuities directly on the face, the procedure described in Section 3.4.2 can be used to estimate the average length of fractures that extend beyond the dimensions of the face.

F   *Roughness*—The roughness of a discontinuity surface is often an important component

of the shear strength, especially where the discontinuity is undisplaced and interlocked. Roughness becomes less important where the discontinuity is infilled, or displaced and interlock is lost. Roughness should be measured in the field on exposed surfaces with lengths of at least 2 m, if possible, in the anticipated direction of sliding, and can be described in terms of a combination of both the large- and small-scale features:

Shape: stepped        Roughness: rough
       undulating                smooth
       planar                    slickensided

The degree of roughness can be quantified in terms of the $i°$ value, which is a measure of the inclination of the irregularities (or *asperities*) on the surface (see inset F, Figure 3.5(a)). The total friction angle of a rough surface is $(\phi + i)$. Values for $i$ can be determined either by direct measurement of the surface, or by comparing the surface with standard profiles of irregular joint surfaces. These techniques are described in Section 3.4.3. Usual practice would be to use the standard roughness profiles during the preliminary mapping. If there is a critical discontinuity that will control stability, then the values estimated from the profiles could be calibrated with a limited number of detailed measurements of roughness.

G  *Wall strength*—The strength of the rock forming the walls of discontinuities will influence the shear strength of rough surfaces. Where high stresses, compared to the wall strength, are generated at local contact points during shearing, the asperities will be sheared off resulting in a reduction of the roughness component of the friction angle. In the initial stages of weathering, there is often a reduction in rock strength on the discontinuity surfaces that may result in a diminished roughness value. It is usually adequate to estimate the compressive strength from the simple field tests as shown in Table 3.1 (ISRM, 1981b), or if core or lump samples are available, by carrying out point load tests. The Schmidt hammer test is also a method of estimating the compressive strength of rock at discontinuity surfaces.

*Table 3.1* Classification of rock and soil strengths (ISRM, 1981b)

| Grade | Description | Field identification | Approx. range of uniaxial compressive strength (MPa) |
|---|---|---|---|
| R6 | Extremely strong rock | Specimen can only be chipped with geological hammer. | >250 |
| R5 | Very strong rock | Specimen requires many blows of geological hammer to fracture it. | 100–250 |
| R4 | Strong rock | Specimen requires more than one blow of geological hammer to fracture it. | 50–100 |
| R3 | Medium strong rock | Cannot be scraped or peeled with a pocket knife, specimen can be fractured with single firm blow of geological hammer. | 25–50 |
| R2 | Weak rock | Can be peeled by a pocket knife with difficulty, shallow indentations made by firm blow with point of geological hammer. | 5.0–25 |
| R1 | Very weak rock | Crumbles under firm blows with point of geological hammer and can be peeled by a pocket knife. | 1.0–5.0 |
| R0 | Extremely weak rock | Indented by thumbnail. | 0.25–1.0 |
| S6 | Hard clay | Indented with difficulty by thumbnail. | >0.5 |
| S5 | Very stiff clay | Readily indented by thumbnail. | 0.25–0.5 |
| S4 | Stiff clay | Readily indented by thumb but penetrated only with great difficulty. | 0.1–0.25 |
| S3 | Firm clay | Can be penetrated several inches by thumb with moderate effort. | 0.05–0.1 |
| S2 | Soft clay | Easily penetrated several inches by thumb. | 0.025–0.05 |
| S1 | Very soft clay | Easily penetrated several inches by fist. | <0.025 |

Notes
Discontinuity wall strength will generally be characterized by grades R0–R6 (rock). Some rounding of strength values has been made when converting to SI units (ISRM, 1981b).

The strength of the intact rock is also one of the parameters used to calculate rock mass strength as discussed in Section 4.5.

H   *Weathering*—Reduction of rock strength due to weathering will reduce the shear strength of discontinuities as described in (G). Weathering will also reduce the shear strength of the rock mass due to the diminished strength of the intact rock. Weathering categories range from fresh rock to residual soil. Weathering of rock takes the form of both disintegration and decomposition. Disintegration is the result of environmental conditions such as wetting and drying, freezing and thawing that break down the exposed surface layer. Disintegration is most prevalent in sedimentary rocks such as sandstones and shales, particularly if they contain swelling clays, and in metamorphic rocks with a high mica content. Decomposition weathering refers to changes in rock produced by chemical agents such as oxidation (e.g. yellow discoloration in rock containing iron), hydration (e.g. decomposition of feldspar in granite to kaolinite clay) and carbonation (e.g. solution of limestone). Table 3.2 (ISRM, 1981b) lists weathering grades that categorize the rock mass according to the degree of disintegration and decomposition.

I   *Aperture*—Aperture is the perpendicular distance separating the adjacent rock walls of an open discontinuity, in which the intervening space is air or water filled; categories of aperture range from cavernous (>1 m), to very tight (<0.1 mm). Aperture is thereby distinguished from the "width" of a filled discontinuity. It is important in predicting the likely behavior of the rock mass, such as hydraulic conductivity and deformation under stress changes, to understand the reason that open discontinuities develop. Possible causes include scouring of infillings, solution of the rock forming the walls of a discontinuity, shear displacement and dilation of rough discontinuities, tension features at the head of landslides and relaxation of steep valley walls following glacial retreat or erosion. Aperture may be measured in outcrops or tunnels provided that extreme care is taken to discount any blast-induced open discontinuities, in drill core if recovery is excellent, and in boreholes using a borehole camera if the walls of the hole are clean.

*Table 3.2* Weathering grades

| Term | Description | Grade |
|---|---|---|
| Fresh | No visible sign of rock material weathering; perhaps slight discoloration on major discontinuity surfaces. | I |
| Slightly weathered | Discoloration indicates weathering of rock material and discontinuity surfaces. All the rock material may be discolored by weathering and may be somewhat weaker externally than in its fresh condition. | II |
| Moderately weathered | Less than half of the rock material is decomposed and/or disintegrated to a soil. Fresh or discolored rock is present either as a continuous framework or as corestones. | III |
| Highly weathered | More than half of the rock material is decomposed and/or disintegrated to a soil. Fresh or discolored rock is present either as a discontinuous framework or as corestones. | IV |
| Completely weathered | All rock material is decomposed and/or disintegrated to soil. The original mass structure is still largely intact. | V |
| Residual soil | All rock material is converted to soil. The mass structure and material fabric are destroyed. There is a large change in volume, but the soil has not been significantly transported. | VI |

J  *Infilling/width*—Infilling is the term for material separating the adjacent walls of discontinuities, such as calcite or fault gouge; the perpendicular distance between the adjacent rock walls is termed the *width* of the filled discontinuity. A complete description of filling material is required to predict the behavior of the discontinuity include the following: mineralogy, particle size, over-consolidation ratio, water content/conductivity, wall roughness, width and fracturing/crushing of the wall rock. If the filling is likely to be a potential sliding surface in the slope, samples of the material (undisturbed if possible) should be collected for shear testing.

K  *Seepage*—The location of seepage from discontinuities provides information on aperture because ground water flow is confined almost entirely in the discontinuities (secondary permeability); seepage categories range from very tight and dry to continuous flow that can scour infillings. These observations will also indicate the position of the water table, or water tables in the case of rock masses containing alternating layers of low and high conductivity rock such as shale and sandstone respectively. In dry climates, the evaporation rate may exceed the seepage rate and it may be difficult to observe seepage locations. In cold weather, icicles provide a good indication of even very low seepage rates. The flow quantities will also help anticipate conditions during construction such as flooding and pumping requirements of excavations.

L  *Number of sets*—The number of sets of discontinuities that intersect one another will influence the extent to which the rock mass can deform without failure of the intact rock. As the number of discontinuity sets increases and the block size diminishes, the greater the opportunity for blocks to rotate, translate and crush under applied loads. Mapping should distinguish between systematic discontinuities that are members of a set and random discontinuities, the orientation of which are less predictable.

M  *Block size/shape*—The block size and shape are determined by the discontinuity spacing and persistence, and the number of sets. Block shapes include blocky, tabular, shattered and columnar, while block size ranges from very large ($>8\,m^3$) to very small ($<0.0002\,m^3$). The block size can be estimated by selecting several typical blocks and measuring their average dimensions.

Using the terms outlined in this section, a typical description for a *rock material* would be as follows:

*Moderately weathered, weak, fine grained, dark gray to black carbonaceous shale.*

Note that the rock name comes last since this is less important than the engineering properties of the rock.

An example of a *rock mass* description is as follows:

*Interbedded sequence of shale and sandstone; typically the shale units are 200–400 mm thick and the sandstone units are 1000–5000 mm thick. In the shale, the bedding spacing is 100–200 mm and many contain a soft clay infilling with width up to 20 mm; the bedding is planar and often slickensided. The sandstone is blocky with the spacing of the beds and two conjugate joint sets in the range of 500–1000 mm; the bedding and joint surfaces are smooth and undulating, and contain no infilling. The upper contacts of the shale beds are wet with some dripping; the sandstone is dry.*

## 3.4  Spacing, persistence and roughness measurements

A component of the geological mapping of rock exposures may involve detailed measurements of surface roughness, and discontinuity spacing and persistence. Usually these detailed measurements would only be carried out on discontinuity sets or specific features that have been identified to have a significant influence on stability because, for example, they are persistent and dip out the face.

### 3.4.1  Spacing of discontinuities

The spacing of discontinuities will determine the dimensions of blocks in the slope, which will influence the size of rock falls and the design of bolting patterns. A factor to consider in the interpretation of spacing measurements from surface mapping is the relative orientation between the face and the discontinuities. That is, the relative orientation introduces a bias to the number and spacing of discontinuities in which the actual spacing is less than the apparent spacing, and the actual number of discontinuities is greater than the number mapped. The bias arises because all discontinuities oriented at right angles to the face will be visible on the face at their true spacing, while few apparently widely spaced discontinuities, oriented sub-parallel to the face will be visible (Figures 3.5 and 3.7). The bias in spacing can be corrected as follows (Terzaghi, 1965):

$$S = S_{\text{app}} \sin \theta \qquad (3.3)$$

where $S$ is the true spacing between discontinuities of the same set, $S_{\text{app}}$ is the measured (apparent) spacing, and $\theta$ is the angle between face and strike of discontinuities.

The number of discontinuities in a set can be adjusted to account for the relative orientation between the face and the strike of the discontinuity as follows:

$$N = \frac{N_{\text{app}}}{\sin \theta} \qquad (3.4)$$

where $N$ is the adjusted number of discontinuities and $N_{\text{app}}$ is the measured number of discontinuities. For example, a vertical drill hole will intersect few steeply dipping discontinuities, and a vertical face will intersect few discontinuities parallel to this face; the Terzaghi correction will calculate an appropriate increase in the number of these surfaces. Some stereonet programs can apply the Terzaghi correction to increase the number of discontinuities to allow for the bias in sampling orientation, and more accurately represent the population of discontinuities.

In rock outcrops, the spacing between discontinuities in a set will be variable, and the following is a discussion on methods of calculating the average spacing of a joint set, and the application of the Terzaghi correction. Figure 3.8 shows a rock outcrop in which it is planned to make a steep cut; the rock contains a set of joints that dip out of the face at angle $\psi$. The characteristics of

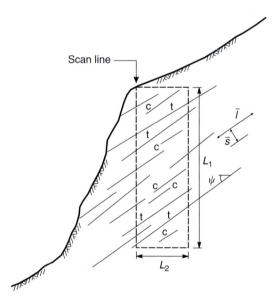

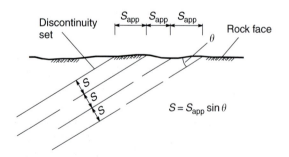

*Figure 3.7* Relationship between apparent and true spacing for a set of discontinuities.

*Figure 3.8* Measurement of average spacing and persistence of a set of discontinuities in an outcrop.

this joint set can be determined using line mapping by hanging a tape vertically down the face and recording the characteristics of each joint that intersects the tape. The tape can be termed a *scan line*, which in this case has a length of 15 m.

The average true spacing ($\bar{s}$) of joint set in Figure 3.8 is calculated using equation (3.5), for the conditions where the scan line is vertical and is not at right angles to the joints. If there are $N'$ joints with dip $\psi$ intersecting a scan line of length $L_1$, then the value of $\bar{s}$ is given by

$$\bar{s} = L_1 \cos \psi / N' \tag{3.5}$$

On Figure 3.8 there are nine joints ($N' = 9$) with an average dip of 35° intersecting the scan line, which has a length of 15 m ($L_1 = 15$). The average spacing of these joints is 1.5 m; this average spacing is plotted to scale on Figure 3.8.

One approach that may be taken to study the spacings of different sets of discontinuities is to make measurements along scan lines with different orientations; it is preferable that the scan lines are at right angles to each set (Hudson and Priest, 1979, 1983).

The Terzaghi correction can be applied to the joints measured on the scan line as follows. There are nine joints intersecting the scan line ($N_{app} = 9$), and the average angle between the joints dipping at 35° and the vertical scan line is 55°. Therefore, equation (3.4) shows that approximately 11 joints would have been intersected by a 15 m long scan line orientated at right angles to the joints.

### 3.4.2   Persistence of discontinuity sets

Persistence of discontinuities is one of the most important rock mass parameters because it defines, together with spacing, the size of blocks that can slide from the face. Furthermore, a small area of intact rock between low persistence discontinuities can have a positive influence on stability because the strength of the rock will often be much higher than the shear stress acting in the slope. Unfortunately, persistence is one of the more difficult parameters to measure because

often only a small part of the discontinuity is visible in the face. In the case of drill core, no information on persistence is available.

A number of procedures have been developed to calculate the approximate average persistence of a set of discontinuities by measuring their exposed trace lengths on a specified area of the face (Pahl, 1981; Priest and Hudson, 1981; Kulatilake and Wu, 1984).

The procedure developed by Pahl (1981) comprises first, defining a mapping area on a face with dimensions $L_1$ and $L_2$ (Figure 3.8). Then the total number of discontinuities ($N''$) of a particular set (with dip $\psi$) in this area is counted, and the numbers of these discontinuities that are either contained within ($N_c$), or transect ($N_t$) the mapping area are identified. Contained discontinuities are short and have both ends visible within the area, while transecting discontinuities are relatively long and have neither end visible. The approximate average length ($\bar{l}$) of a set of discontinuities is calculated from equations (3.6) to (3.8) that are independent of the assumed form of the statistical distribution of the lengths.

$$\bar{l} = H' \frac{(1 + m)}{(1 - m)} \tag{3.6}$$

where

$$H' = \frac{L_1 \cdot L_2}{(L_1 \cdot \cos \psi + L_2 \cdot \sin \psi)} \tag{3.7}$$

and

$$m = \frac{(N_t - N_c)}{(N'' + 1)} \tag{3.8}$$

As demonstrated by these equations, the basis of this method of estimating the average length of discontinuities is to count discontinuities on a face with a known area, and does not involve measuring the length of individual discontinuities which can be a much more time-consuming task.

For the joints depicted on Figure 3.8, the average persistence can be calculated as follows. The total number of joints ($\psi \sim 35°$) within the scan area is 14 ($N'' = 14$), of which five are contained within the scan area ($N_c = 5$), and four transect the scan area ($N_t = 4$). If the dimensions of the scan area are $L_1 = 15$ and $L_2 = 5$, then the value of $m$ is $-0.07$ and the value of $H'$ is 4.95. From equation (3.6), the average length of the joints in this set is 4.3 m. This average persistence is plotted to scale on Figure 3.8.

If there was a second set of discontinuities in the scan area that would influence stability, then these could be counted seperately using the same procedure to determine their average spacing and persistence.

### 3.4.3 Roughness of rock surfaces

The friction angle of a rough surface comprises two components—the friction of the rock material ($\phi$), plus interlocking produced by the irregularities (asperities) of the surface ($i$). Because roughness can be a significant component of the total friction angle, measurement of roughness is often an important part of a mapping program.

During the preliminary stages of an investigation it is usually satisfactory to make a visual assessment of the roughness as defined by the Joint Roughness Coefficient (JRC) (Barton, 1973). JRC varies from zero for smooth, planar and particularly slickensided surfaces to as much as 20 for rough, undulating surfaces. The value of

JRC can be estimated by visually comparing the surface condition with standard profiles based on a combination of surface irregularities (at a scale of several centimeters) and waviness (at a scale of a several meters) as shown in Figure 3.9.

JRC is related to the roughness of the surface, $i$ value by the following equation:

$$i = \text{JRC} \log_{10}\left(\frac{\text{JCS}}{\sigma'}\right) \tag{3.9}$$

where JCS (Joint Compressive Strength) is the compressive strength of the rock on the discontinuity surface (see Table 3.1), and $\sigma'$ is the effective normal stress on the surface due to the weight of the overlying rock less any uplift water pressure on the surface. Equation (3.9) shows that $i$ diminishes as the asperities are ground off when the rock strength is low compared to the applied normal stress. The application of equation (3.9) to determine the shear strength of rock surfaces is discussed in more detail in Section 4.2.

In the final design stage of a project, a few discontinuities having a significant effect on stability may be identified, and there are a number of methods of accurately measuring the surface roughness of these critical surfaces. A method developed by Fecker and Rengers (1971) consists of measuring the orientation of the discontinuity using a geological compass with a series of plates of different

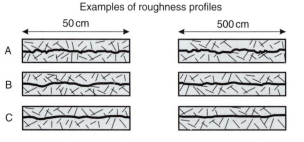

Examples of roughness profiles

A   Rough undulating—tension joints, rough sheeting,   JRC = 20
    rough bedding

B   Smooth undulating—smooth sheeting, non-planar foliation,   JRC = 10
    undulating bedding

C   Smooth nearly planar—planar shear joints, planar foliation,   JRC = 5
    planar bedding

Figure 3.9 Standard profiles defining joint roughness coefficient, JRC (Barton, 1973).

diameters attached to the lid. If the diameter of the larger plates is about the same dimensions as the wavelength of the roughness, then the measured orientation will be approximately equal to the average orientation of the surface. However, the smaller diameter plates will show a scatter in the orientation measurements as the plates lie on irregularities with shorter wavelengths. If the orientation measurements are plotted on a stereonet, the degree of scatter in the poles about the mean orientation is a measure of the roughness.

Quantitative methods of profile measurement have been established by Tse and Cruden (1979) using a mechanical profilometer, and Mearz et al. (1990) have developed a shadow profilometer that records the shape of the surface with a video camera and image analyzer.

The method developed by Tse and Cruden is illustrated in Figure 3.10(a). The profile is defined by measuring the distance ($y_i$) of the surface from a fixed reference line at specified equal intervals ($\Delta x$) over a length of $M$ intervals. From these measurements the coefficient Z2 is defined as

$$Z2 = \left[ \frac{1}{M(\Delta x)^2} \sum_{i=1}^{M} (y_{i+1} + y_i)^2 \right]^{1/2} \quad (3.10)$$

A study has also been carried out to assess the effect of the size of the sampling interval ($\Delta x$) along the profile on the calculated value of JRC (Yu and Vayssade, 1991). This study found that the calculated value of JRC was dependent on the size of $\Delta x$, and that the most accurate results were obtained with small sampling intervals. The value of JRC can be calculated from the coefficient Z2 using one of the following equations for the appropriate sampling interval:

$$JRC = 60.32(Z2) - 4.51 \quad \text{for } \Delta x = 0.25 \, \text{mm} \quad (3.11a)$$

$$JRC = 61.79(Z2) - 3.47 \quad \text{for } \Delta x = 0.5 \, \text{mm} \quad (3.11b)$$

$$JRC = 64.22(Z2) - 2.31 \quad \text{for } \Delta x = 1 \, \text{mm} \quad (3.11c)$$

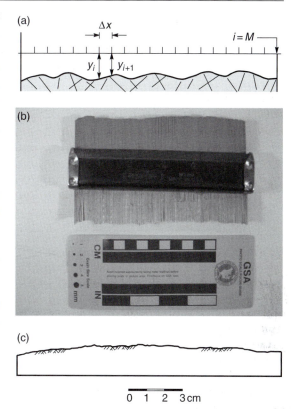

Figure 3.10 Measurement of joint roughness: (a) procedure for measuring roughness with mechanical profilometer (modified from Tse and Cruden (1979); reprinted with kind permission from Elsevier Science Ltd. The Boulevard, Langford Lane, Kidlington, UK); (b) photograph of profilometer; (c) profile of joint with JRC of 11.4.

One means of making profile measurements is to use a carpenter's comb that consists of a series of metal rods, positioned in a frame, such that they can slide relative to each other (Figure 3.10(b)). If the comb is pressed against a rock face, the rods will slide to conform to the shape of the surface. This profile can then be traced on to a piece of paper and the shape of the rock surface quantified by measuring the distance of each rod from a reference line.

Figure 3.10(c) shows the results of a profile measurement with a carpenter's comb of a rough, planar joint in granite. The profile of the surface was digitized, with 145 measurements made on a 1 mm interval ($M = 145; \Delta x = 1$), from which Z2 was calculated from equation (3.11c) to be 0.214 with a corresponding JRC value of 11.4.

## 3.5 Probabilistic analysis of structural geology

As discussed in Section 1.4.4, a measure of the stability of a slope is the probability of failure. Calculation of the probability of failure involves expressing the design parameters in terms of probability distributions that give the most likely value of each parameter (e.g. average), as well as the probability of its occurrence within a range of possible values (e.g. standard deviation).

This section demonstrates techniques to determine the probability distributions of structural geology data. The distribution in orientation can be calculated from the stereonet, while the distributions of persistence and spacing are calculated from field measurements.

### 3.5.1 Discontinuity orientation

The natural variation in orientation of discontinuities results in there being scatter of the poles when plotted on the stereonet. It can be useful to incorporate this scatter into the stability analysis of the slope because, for example, a wedge analysis using the mean values of pair of discontinuity sets may show that the line of intersection of the wedge does not daylight in the face and that the slope is stable. However, an analysis using orientations other than the mean values may show that some unstable wedges can be formed. The risk of occurrence of this condition would be quantified by calculating the mean and standard deviation of the dip and dip direction as described next.

A measure of the dispersion, and from this the standard deviation, of a discontinuity set can be calculated from the direction cosines as follows (Goodman, 1980). The direction cosines of any plane with dip $\psi$ and dip direction $\alpha$ are the unit vectors l, m and n, where

$$\left. \begin{array}{l} \mathbf{l} = \sin \psi \cdot \cos \alpha \\ \mathbf{m} = \sin \psi \cdot \sin \alpha \\ \mathbf{n} = \cos \psi \end{array} \right\} \quad (3.12)$$

For a number of poles, the direction cosines ($l_R$, $m_R$ and $n_R$) of the mean orientation of the discontinuity set is the sum of the individual direction cosines, as follows:

$$l_R = \frac{\sum \mathbf{l}_i}{|R|}; \quad m_R = \frac{\sum \mathbf{m}_i}{|R|}; \quad n_R = \frac{\sum \mathbf{n}_i}{|R|} \quad (3.13)$$

where $|R|$ is the magnitude of the resultant vector given by

$$|R| = \left[ \left( \sum \mathbf{l}_i \right)^2 + \left( \sum \mathbf{m}_i \right)^2 + \left( \sum \mathbf{n}_i \right)^2 \right]^{1/2} \quad (3.14)$$

The dip $\psi_R$ and dip direction $\alpha_R$ of the mean orientation are

$$\left. \begin{array}{ll} \psi_R = \cos^{-1}(n_R) & \\ \alpha_R = +\cos^{-1}(l_R/\sin \psi_R) & \text{for } m_R \geq 0 \\ \alpha_R = -\cos^{-1}(l_R/\sin \psi_R) & \text{for } m_R < 0 \end{array} \right\} \quad (3.15)$$

A measure of the scatter of a set of discontinuities comprising $N$ poles can be obtained from the dispersion coefficient $C_d$, which is calculated as follows:

$$C_d = \frac{N}{(N - |R|)} \quad (3.16)$$

If there is little scatter in the orientation of the discontinuities, the value of $C_d$ is large, and its value diminishes as the scatter increases.

From the dispersion coefficient, it is possible to calculate from equation (3.17) the probability, $P$, that a pole will make an angle $\theta°$ or less than the mean orientation.

$$\theta = \cos^{-1}[1 + (1/C_d)\ln(1 - P)] \qquad (3.17)$$

For example, the angle from the mean defined by one standard deviation occurs at a probability $P$ of 0.16 (refer to Figure 1.12). If the dispersion is 20, one standard deviation lies at 7.6° from the mean.

Equation (3.17) is applicable when the dispersion in the scatter is approximately uniform about the mean orientation, which is the case in joint set $A$ in Figure 2.11. However, in the case of the bedding in Figure 2.11, there is less scatter in the dip than in the dip direction. The standard deviations in the two directions can be calculated approximately from the stereonet as follows. First, two great circles are drawn at right angles corresponding to the directions of dip and dip direction respectively. Then the angles corresponding to the 7% and 93% levels, $P_7$, and $P_{93}$ respectively, are determined by counting the number of poles in the set and removing the poles outside these percentiles. The equation for the standard deviation along either of the great circles is as follows (Morriss, 1984):

$$\text{SD} = \tan^{-1}\{0.34[\tan(P_{93}) - \tan(P_7)]\} \qquad (3.18)$$

More precise methods of determining the standard deviation are described by McMahon (1982), but the approximate method given by equation (3.18) may be sufficiently accurate considering the difficulty in obtaining a representative sample of the discontinuities in the set. An important aspect of accurate geological investigations is to account for bias when mapping a single face or logging a single borehole when few of the discontinuities aligned parallel to the line of mapping are measured. This bias in the data can be corrected by applying the Terzaghi correction as described in Section 3.4.1.

### 3.5.2  Discontinuity length and spacing

The length and spacing of discontinuities determines the size of blocks that will be formed in the slope. Designs are usually concerned with persistent discontinuities that could form blocks with dimensions great enough to influence overall slope stability. However, discontinuity dimensions have a range of values and it is useful to have an understanding of the distribution of these values in order to predict how the extreme values may be compared to values obtained from a small sample. This section discusses probability distributions for the length and spacing of discontinuities, and discusses the limitations of making accurate predictions over a wide range of dimensions.

The primary purpose of making length and spacing measurements of discontinuities is to estimate the dimensions of blocks of rock formed by these surfaces (Priest and Hudson 1976; Cruden, 1977; Kikuchi et al., 1987; Dershowitz and Einstein, 1988; Kulatilake, 1988; Einstein, 1993). This information can then be used, if necessary, to design appropriate stabilization measures such as rock bolts and rock fall barriers. Attempts have also been made to use this data to calculate the shear strength of "stepped" surfaces comprising joints separated by portions of intact rock (Jennings, 1970; Einstein et al., 1983). However, it has since been found that the Hoek–Brown method of calculating the shear strength of rock masses is more reliable (see Section 4.5).

#### Probability distributions

Discontinuities are usually mapped along a scan line, such as drill core, slope face or wall of a tunnel. Individual measurements are made of the properties of each fracture, including its visible length and the spacing between discontinuities in each set (Appendix II). The properties of discontinuities typically vary over a wide range and it is possible to describe the distribution of these properties by means of probability distributions. A normal distribution is applicable if a particular property has values in which the mean value is the most commonly occurring. This condition would indicate that the property of each discontinuity, such as its orientation, is related to the property of the adjacent discontinuities reflecting that the discontinuities were formed by stress relief. For properties that are normally distributed, the mean and standard deviation are given by equations (1.16) and (1.17).

A negative exponential distribution is applicable for properties of discontinuities, such as their length and spacing, which are randomly distributed indicating that the discontinuities are mutually independent. A negative exponential distribution would show that the most commonly occurring discontinuities are short and closely spaced, while persistent, widely spaced discontinuities are less common. The general form of a probability density function $f(x)$ of a negative exponential distribution is (Priest and Hudson, 1981)

$$f(x) = \frac{1}{\bar{x}} (e^{-x/\bar{x}}) \qquad (3.19)$$

and the associated cumulative probability $F(x)$ that a given spacing or length value will be less than dimension $x$ is given by

$$F(x) = (1 - e^{-x/\bar{x}}) \qquad (3.20)$$

where $x$ is a measured value of length or spacing and $\bar{x}$ is the mean value of that parameter. A property of the negative exponential distribution is that the standard deviation is equal to the mean value.

From equation (3.20) for a set of discontinuities in which the mean spacing is 2 m, the probabilities that the spacing will be less than 1 m and 5 m,

respectively, are

$$F(x) = (1 - e^{-1/2}) = 40\%$$

and

$$F(x) = (1 - e^{-5/2}) = 92\%$$

Equation (3.20) could be used to estimate the probability of occurrence of discontinuities with a specified length. This result could be used, for example, to determine the likelihood of a plane being continuous through a slope.

Another distribution that can often be used to describe the dimensions of discontinuities is the lognormal distribution which is applicable where the variable $x = \ln y$ is normally distributed (Baecher et al., 1977). The probability density function for a lognormal distribution is (Harr, 1977)

$$f(x) = \frac{1}{y\,SD_x\sqrt{2\pi}} \exp\left[ -\frac{1}{2} \left( \frac{\ln y - \bar{x}}{SD_x} \right)^2 \right] \qquad (3.21)$$

where $\bar{x}$ is the mean value and SD is the standard deviation.

Figure 3.11 shows the measured lengths of 122 joints in a Cambrian sandstone for lengths of less than 4 m; the mean length $\bar{l}$ is 1.2 m (Priest

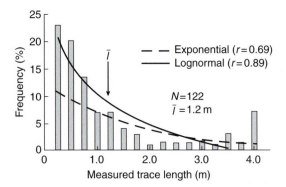

*Figure 3.11* Histogram of joint trace lengths, with best fit exponential and lognormal curves (Priest and Hudson, 1981).

and Hudson, 1981). To these data have been fitted both exponential and lognormal curves for which the correlation coefficients $r$ are 0.69 and 0.89, respectively. While the lognormal curve has a higher correlation coefficient, the exponential curve has a better fit at the longer discontinuity lengths. This demonstrates that for each set of data the most appropriate distribution should be determined.

## 3.6  Diamond drilling

On many projects, surface mapping is supplemented by diamond drilling to obtain core samples of the subsurface rock. The extent of the drilling will depend on such factors as the soil cover, the availability of rock outcrops and the confidence with which surface data can be extrapolated over the full depth of the cut. For example, if the rock at the surface is weathered or disturbed by blasting, then drilling may be required to find rock conditions at depth.

The type of information that can be obtained by diamond drilling may be somewhat different from surface mapping information. While surface mapping is the primary means of obtaining information on geological structure, in drill core there is no information on persistence, and the orientation of discontinuities can only be obtained if the core is oriented (see Section 3.6.4). The types of information that are provided by drill core are *in situ* rock strength, fracture frequency and the characteristics of shear zones. The core can also be used for laboratory strength testing (Chapter 4), and instrumentation such as piezometers can be installed in the holes (Chapter 5).

### 3.6.1  Diamond drilling equipment

Figure 3.1 shows a typical diamond drill. The major components of the drill comprise a motor, usually gasoline or diesel powered, a head to generate torque and thrust to the drill rods, a mast to support the wire line equipment, and a string of drill rods at the end of which is a core barrel and a diamond impregnated bit. Drill rods are flush coupled, usually in 3 m lengths, and the diameters available for common North American equipment are listed on Table 3.3, together with the corresponding hole and core sizes. The rod diameters are designated by four letters (e.g. BQTT)—the first letter indicates the diameter, the second that it is used with wire line

*Table 3.3* Dimensions of diamond drilling equipment (Christensen Boyles Corp.) triple tube core barrels

| Drill size | AQTT | BQTT | NQTT | HQTT | PQTT |
|---|---|---|---|---|---|
| Hole diameter, mm (in.) | 48.0 (1.89) | 60 (2-23/64) | 75.7 (2-63/64) | 96 (3-25/32) | 122.6 (4-53/64) |
| Core diameter, mm (in.) | 26.9 (1.06) | 33.5 (1-5/16) | 45 (1-25/32) | 61.1 (2-13/32) | 83 (3-9/32) |
| Hole volume, l/100 m (Usgal/100 ft) | 181 (14.6) | 282 (22.7) | 451 (36.3) | 724 (58.3) | 1180 (95.1) |
| Casing ID, mm (in.) | 48.4 (1-29/32) | 60.3 (2-3/8) | 76.2 (3.0) | 101.6 (4.0) | 127 (5.0) |
| Casing OD, mm (in.) | 57.1 (2-1/4) | 73 (2-7/8) | 88.9 (3-1/2) | 114.3 (4-1/2) | 139.7 (5-1/2) |
| Casing weight, kg/3 m (lb/10 ft) | 17 (38) | 31.3 (70) | 38.4 (86) | 50.5 (113) | 64.3 (144) |
| Drill rod ID, mm (in.) | 34.9 (1-3/8) | 46 (1-13/16) | 60.3 (2-3/8) | 77.8 (3-1/16) | 103.2 (4-1/16) |
| Drill rod OD, mm (in.) | 44.5 (1-3/4) | 55.6 (2-3/16) | 69.9 (2-3/4) | 88.9 (3-1/2) | 117.5 (4-5/8) |
| Drill rod weight, kg/3 m (lb/10 ft) | 14 (31) | 18 (40) | 23.4 (52) | 34.4 (77) | 47.2 (106) |

equipment and TT indicates a triple tube core barrel. Also listed on the table are casing diameters; casing is used in the upper part of holes, in soil or weathered rock, to prevent caving. The casing and rod diameters are arranged such that N rods fit inside N casing, and that B rods fit inside B casing, for example. This allows holes to be "telescoped" down to a smaller diameter, if necessary, as the hole is advanced. It is usual in geotechnical drilling to use NQTT rods, or HQTT if the rock is highly broken because better core recovery is achieved with the larger diameter.

For geotechnical drilling where one of the objectives is to recover the weakest portion of the rock, recommended practice is to use a triple tube core barrel. The triple tube barrel comprises an outer tube coupled to the drill rods and bit, which turns with the rods while drilling. The middle tube locks into a roller bearing at the top of the core barrel such that it remains stationary while the drill rods rotate. The inner tube is split into two pieces longitudinally, and also remains stationary during drilling.

The drilling procedure involves rotating the rods and bit at high speed (up to about 1000 rpm), while applying a steady thrust to the bit and pumping water down the center of the drill rods. In this way the bit is advanced into the rock while the water cools the bit, and removes the cuttings in the annular space outside the rods. The core fills the core barrel as the bit advances, and the drilling is stopped when the core barrel is full—the core barrel is usually 3 m long. In holes with depths less than about 20 m, it is possible to recover the core at the end of each run by removing the rods from the hole. For deeper holes the usual practice is to lower a wireline down the hole with a core catcher on the end which locks into the core barrel and releases it from the drill rods. The core barrel is lifted from the hole without moving the rods. The core is extracted from the core barrel by pumping the inner split tube out of the barrel and then removing the upper half of the tube. The core can then be logged in the core barrel with minimal disturbance. In contrast, if a double tube barrel is used, the core has to be pumped or hammered out of the tube, which inevitably results in some damage and disturbance, especially to the weaker portions of the rock that are the most important to recover.

In very poor quality rock, it is possible to modify the triple tube by inserting a clear plastic liner inside the split inner tube. The core is contained in the plastic tube so that it can be logged and then stored with minimal disturbance.

### 3.6.2 Diamond drilling operations

The following are some of the factors that may need to be considered in a diamond drilling operation. First, the drill rig should be set up on level ground, or on a level platform if the ground surface is irregular. Furthermore, the platform should be robust and the rig should be securely attached to the ground or platform. If the rig is able to move during drilling, vibration in the rods will diminish core quality and may damage the rods.

It is essential that the drill bit be continuously flushed with a fluid, usually water, to cool the bit and remove the cuttings. The circulating water also lubricates the drill string to reduce the torque required to turn the rods, and reduces vibration of the rods. Water is usually supplied to the site by pumping from a nearby river, or by a tanker truck. Factors to consider in the supply of water include the pumping head between the supply and the site, freezing of the pipeline, and available road access. It is usual that the return drill water is collected in a settling tank at the site to remove the cuttings, and is then recirculated down the hole. This reduces the quantity of supplied water, and eliminates environmental contamination by silt-laden water.

The addition of certain chemicals and solids to the drilling water can improve the properties of the circulating fluid, and can be essential for successfully drilling highly permeable or unstable formations (Australian Drilling Industry, 1996). The most common additive in diamond drilling is organic, long chain polymers that have thixotropic properties. That is, they have low viscosity when they are stirred or pumped, but gel when allowed to stand. The effect of these properties is that the mud can be readily circulated in the hole to remove the cuttings in the narrow annular space around the rods, but will gel to form a cake to seal and stabilize the walls of the hole.

The correct application of these dual properties of mud will greatly enhance diamond drilling operations. For example, if the hole intersects a zone of broken and weak rock, the mud can stabilize the walls, and there will be no need to extend the casing down to this level. Similarly, if the circulation fluid is lost in permeable zones, these can be sealed with a mud cake. Ideally, the mud cake should be thin and have low permeability, and should penetrate the formation so that it is not broken up by the rotation of the drill rods. The fluid pressure in the hole then helps to keep the cake in place. Where the polymer muds are not sufficiently viscous to form a mud cake, possible additives to the mud include fine flakes of mica or paper to help seal fine openings in the rock on the wall of the hole. In the case of artesian flows, the density of the mud can be increased by bentonite–barytes mixtures, so that the mud weight balances the upward pressure of the water in the artesian formation.

For holes that are to be used for hydrologic testing, such as permeability measurements and the installation of piezometers, it is necessary that there be no mud cake on the walls. For these conditions, there are biodegradable muds that break down with time to leave the walls of the hole clean.

At the completion of the hole and any associated down-hole testing, there is often a requirement to fill the hole completely with cement grout to prevent changes to the hydrological conditions after the hole is completed.

### 3.6.3  Core logging

Recording the properties of the recovered drill core involves making a detailed and complete log of the rock; an example of a diamond drill core log is shown in Figure 3.12. The log should be prepared using the same properties and descriptions of the rock mass discussed in Section 3.3 so that there is consistency between the surface and sub-surface data. This data will include the

rock description, the properties of the discontinuities and their orientation with respect to the core axis. Measurements can also be made of the Rock Quality Designation (RQD), fracture index and core recovery, which are indicative of the rock mass quality, as described. Also, the log records all testing carried out in the hole such as permeability measurements, the results of strength tests on core samples and the position of instrumentation such as piezometers. Finally, the core is photographed, complete with a color reference and dimension scale.

Where rock types such as shales are recovered that are highly susceptible to degradation when exposed to the atmosphere, it may be necessary to preserve the rock as soon as it has been logged. Preservation of core samples would be necessary where they are to be transported to the laboratory for strength testing and it is necessary that they be tested close to their *in situ* state. Often the lowest strength rock will influence slope design, and these samples should not be allowed to break down and loose strength, or bake in the sun and gain strength.

One method of preservation is to wrap the core in plastic film and then dip it in molten wax to create a barrier to moisture loss. Finally, the sealed core can be embedded in a rigid foam so that it can be transported without damage. A further precaution that may be necessary is to prevent the sample from freezing because the formation of ice can fracture weak rock.

The following are measurements of the core that are routinely made to assess the intact rock strength and the degree of fracturing.

(a)  *RQD* (rock quality index) is an index related to the degree of fracturing of the core. The RQD is calculated by measuring the total length of all pieces of core in a drill run with lengths greater than 100 mm (4 in.), discounting fractures due to drilling. These lengths are then added together, and the total length is expressed as a percentage of the length of the drill run. A low RQD value would be indicative of a closely fractured rock, while an RQD of 100% means that all pieces of core are longer than 100 mm. RQD is calculated as follows.

$$RQD = \frac{\sum(\text{lengths of core pieces with lengths} > 100 \text{ mm})}{\text{Total length of core run}} \times 100\%$$

(3.22)

(b) *Fracture index* is a count of the number of natural fractures in the core measured over a fixed length of say 0.5 m. This parameter is related to the RQD value but is standardized to a fixed length so is not influenced by the

(a)

## RECORD OF ROCK CORE DRILLING AND TESTING - BOREHOLE NO. __DH03-2__

**WN Rock**

Project No. _031-106_    Name _Left Bank Stability Investigation_    Sheet _3_ of _3_   Date _March 3, 2003_

Borehole Location _Refer to Figure 2_    Logged by _SDW_

Elevation _6.94 m_   Ref. Point _Top of Structure_   Datum _Hub 34-01_   Drillrig _HT500_

Inclination _90°_   Azimuth _N/A_   Bit Type _HQ/NQ_   Flush _Water_   Feed _Hydraulic_

| Core Dia. :Depth | Casing Dia. :Depth | Water Notes | Flush Return (%) | ROCK TYPE | | | Symbolic | Depth Scale feet | CORE RECOV. DATA | | | | | DISCONTINUITY DATA | | | STRENGTH DATA | | | ADDITIONAL TESTING |
|---|---|---|---|---|---|---|---|---|---|---|---|---|---|---|---|---|---|---|---|---|
| | | | | Depth Elev | Description | | | | Run No. (from – to) | T.C.R. (Length – %) | S.C.R. (Length – %) | R.Q.D. (Length – %) | Fractures Per foot | Angle W.R.T Core Axis | Symbolic Log | Type and Surface Description | Weathering Index | Strength Index | Point Load Index | |
| NQ | CASED | All return lost at 64 ft.; no return to end of hole | 100% return – light grey    0 % return |   64    71 ft. -14.7 m | Fresh, massive granite, with rounded sand and gravel in discontinuities    EOH | | | 58<br>59<br>60<br>61<br>62<br>63<br>64<br>65<br>66<br>67<br>68<br>69<br>70<br>71 | 5<br><br>**23**<br>61.5<br>4.5<br><br>**24**<br><br>66<br>3<br>**25**<br>69<br>2<br>**26**<br>71 | 96<br><br><br>89<br><br><br>83<br><br>90 | 83<br><br><br>78<br><br><br>64<br><br>70 | 0<br>0<br>1<br>2<br>1<br>5<br>1<br>1<br>3<br>5<br>10<br>3<br>2 | 70-80<br><br><br><br>5-10<br>75-85 | | Joints generally oriented at right angle to core axis with one joint parallel to axis. Joint surfaces clean and rough. Fractured zone at 68 to 69 ft. | I<br><br>I<br><br><br>I<br><br>I | R4<br><br><br><br><br>R4 | 3100 kPa<br><br><br>2900 kPa | Piezo-meter 62.5 to 70.5 ft. K = 4×10⁻⁶ m/s |

(b)

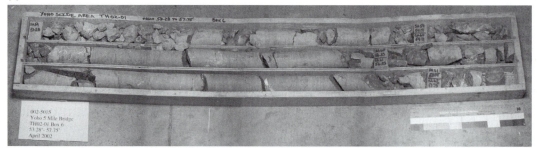

*Figure 3.12* Diamond drill records: (a) typical core log with histograms indicating values for recovery and RQD; (b) photograph of drill core with length scale and color reference chart.

length of the core runs.

$$\text{Fracture index} = \frac{\text{number of natural discontinuities}}{0.5\,\text{m length of core}}$$
(3.23)

(c) *Core recovery* is a measure of how much rock has been lost during drilling. Core loss may result from weak zones being washed out by the drilling water, or grinding of the core during drilling, or the presence of an open cavity. Drillers can often detect areas of very weak rock or cavities where there is a sudden increase in the advance rate; these zones should be noted on the log. The core recovery value is determined by measuring the length of recovered core compared to the total length drilled. If a length of lost core is identified when logging the core, it is good practice to install a wooden spacer at the location of the lost core.

$$\text{Recovery} = \frac{\text{total length of recovered core}}{\text{length of drill run}} \times 100$$
(3.24)

On Figure 3.12, values for these three parameters are shown graphically so that areas of weak or broken rock can be readily identified when scanning down the log. When making RQD and fracture index measurements it is important that drilling breaks in the core are identified and not included in the reported values.

### 3.6.4   Core orientation

For conditions where there is insufficient design data on discontinuity orientation from surface mapping, it may be necessary to obtain this data from drill core. This will require that the core be oriented.

The first step in orienting core is to determine the plunge and trend of the drill hole using a down-hole survey tool. One such tool comprises an aluminum (non-magnetic) drill rod that contains a dip meter and a compass, both of which can be photographed at specified time intervals. The orientation tool is lowered down the hole on the end of the drill string, and is held stationary at the times specified for the camera operation. At each time interval a photograph is taken of the dip meter and compass, and the depth is recorded. When the tool is recovered from the hole, the film is developed to show the hole orientation at the recorded depths. Other hole orientation tools include the Tropari single shot instrument, and gyroscopes for use in magnetic environments (Australian Drilling Industry, 1996).

Most methods of orienting core involve marking a line down the core representing the top of the hole. Since the orientation of this line is known from the hole survey, the orientation of all discontinuities in the core can be measured relative to this line, from which their dip and strike can be calculated (Figure 3.13). Figure 3.13 shows that a plane intersected by the core has the shape of an ellipse, and the first step in the calculation process is to mark the down-hole end major axis of this ellipse. The dip ($\delta$) of this plane is then measured relative to the core axis, and a reference angle ($\alpha$) is measured clockwise (looking down-hole) around the circumference of the core from the top-of-core line to the major axis of the ellipse. The dip and dip direction of the plane is calculated from the plunge and trend of the hole and the measured angles $\delta$ and $\alpha$. The true dip and dip direction of a discontinuity in the core can be determined by stereographic methods (Goodman, 1976), or by spherical/analytical geometry methods (Lau, 1983).

In a few cases, the core may contain a distinct and consistent marker of known orientation,

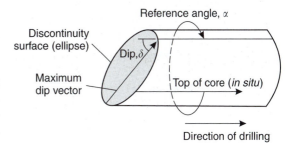

*Figure 3.13* Measurement of orientation of discontinuity in oriented drill core.

such as bedding, which can be used to orient the core and measure the orientation of the other discontinuities. However, minor, and unknown variations in the orientation of the marker bed are likely to lead to errors. Therefore, it is usually preferable to use one of the following three methods to determine the top-of-the-core.

The clay impression method to orient core involves fabricating a wireline core barrel with one side weighted so that the barrel can rotate and position the weight at the bottom of the hole (Figure 3.14) (Call *et al.*, 1982). A piece

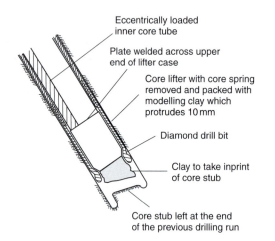

*Figure 3.14* Clay impression core barrel to orient drill core in an inclined hole (Call *et al.*, 1982).

of clay is placed at the lower end of the barrel such that it protrudes past the drill bit when the core barrel is lowered down the rods and locked into place. A light pressure is then applied to the rods so that the clay takes an impression of the rock surface at the end of the hole. The core barrel is then removed and the clay impression, with top-of-core reference line, is retrieved. The next drill run proceeds normally. When this length of core is removed, the top-of-the-core is matched with the clay impression and the top-of-core line is transferred from the clay to the core run. The discontinuities in the core run are then oriented relative to the top-of-core line using the method shown in Figure 3.13.

The advantages of the clay impression core orientation method are its simplicity and low equipment cost. However, the time required to take an impression on each drill run slows drilling, and the method can only be used in holes inclined at angles flatter than about 70°. Also, the orientation line will be lost at any place where the core is broken and it is not possible to extend the top-of-the-core line past the break.

A more sophisticated core orientation tool is the Christiensen–Hugel device that scribes a continuous line down the core during drilling; the orientation of the scribed line is determined by taking photographs of a compass in the head of the core barrel. The advantage of this method

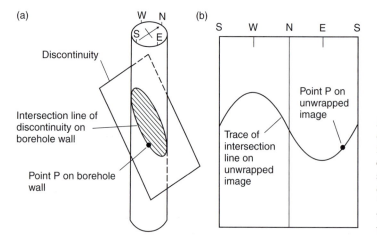

*Figure 3.15* Orientation of discontinuity in borehole using image from 360° scanning video camera: (a) core-like image of drill hole wall showing elliptical intersection between discontinuity and core; (b) "unwrapped" view of borehole wall with discontinuity displayed as a sine wave (Colog Inc., 1999).

is that a continuous reference line is scribed so there is no loss of the line in zones of broken core. However, this is a more expensive and sophisticated piece of equipment than the clay impression tool.

The most recent advance in core orientation is the use of the scanning borehole camera. A camera developed by Colog Inc. takes a continuous 360° image of the wall of the hole as the camera is lowered down the hole. The image can then be processed to have the appearance of a piece of core that can be rotated and viewed from any direction, or can be "unwrapped" (Figure 3.15). In the core view, planes intersecting the core have an elliptical shape, while in the unwrapped view the trace of each discontinuity has the form of a sine wave. The dip and dip direction of planes intersecting the core can be determined from the plunge and trend of the hole, and the orientation of the image from the compass incorporated in the camera. The dip direction of the plane is found from the position of the sine wave with respect to the compass reading, and the dip of the plane with respect to the core axis can be determined by the amplitude of the sine wave. The software with the camera system allows orientation data indicated by the sine waves to be plotted directly on a stereonet.

The significant advantages of Colog camera system are that the camera is run down the hole at the completion of the hole so there is no interruption to drilling. Also, the image provides a continuous record of rock conditions, including cavities and zones of broken rock that may be lost in the recovered core. The disadvantage of the system is the cost and the need for a stable hole with clean walls, that is either dry or is filled with clean water.

# Chapter 4

# Rock strength properties and their measurement

## 4.1  Introduction

In analyzing the stability of a rock slope, the most important factor to be considered is the geometry of the rock mass behind the face. As discussed in Chapter 3, the relationship between the orientation of the discontinuities and of the excavated face will determine whether parts of the rock mass are free to slide or topple. After geology, the next most important factor governing stability is the shear strength of the potential sliding surface, which is the subject of this chapter.

### 4.1.1  Scale effects and rock strength

The sliding surface in a slope may consist of a single plane continuous over the full area of the surface, or a complex surface made up of both discontinuities and fractures through intact rock. Determination of reliable shear strength values is a critical part of slope design because, as will be shown in later chapters, small changes in shear strength can result in significant changes in the safe height or angle of a slope. The choice of appropriate shear strength values depends not only on the availability of test data, but also on a careful interpretation of these data in light of the behavior of the rock mass that makes up the full-scale slope. For example, it may be possible to use the results obtained from a shear test on a joint in designing a slope in which failure is likely to occur along a single joint similar to the one being tested. However, these shear test results could not be used directly in designing a slope in which a complex failure process involving several

joints and some failure of intact rock is expected. In this book the term *rock mass* is used for rock materials in which this complex failure process occurs.

This discussion demonstrates that the selection of an appropriate shear strength of a slope depends to a great extent on the relative scale between the sliding surface and structural geology. For example, in the open pit mine slope illustrated in Figure 4.1, the dimensions of the overall slope are much greater than the discontinuity length so any failure surface will pass through the jointed rock mass, and the appropriate rock strength to use in design of the pit slope

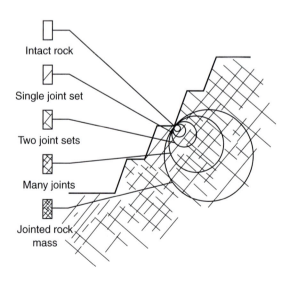

*Figure 4.1* Idealized diagram showing transition from intact rock to jointed rock mass with increasing sample size.

is that of the rock mass. In contrast, the bench height is about equal to the joint length so stability could be controlled by a single joint, and the appropriate rock strength to use in design of the benches is that of the joints set that dips out of the face. Finally, at a scale of less than the joint spacing, blocks of intact rock occur and the appropriate rock strength to use in the assessment of drilling and blasting methods, for example, would be primarily that of the intact rock.

Based on this relationship between sample size and rock strength characteristics, this chapter examines methods of determining the strength of the following three classes of rock:

(i) *Discontinuities*—Single bedding planes, joints or faults. The properties of discontinuities that influence shear strength include the shape and roughness of the surfaces, the rock on the surface which may be fresh or weathered, and infillings that may be low strength or cohesive.

(ii) *Rock mass*—The factors that influence the shear strength of a jointed rock mass include the compressive strength and friction angle of the intact rock, and the spacing of the discontinuities and the condition of their surfaces.

(iii) *Intact rock*—A factor to consider in measuring the strength of the intact rock is that

the strength could diminish over the design life of the slope due to weathering.

In this book, the subscript "i" is used to designate intact rock, and the subscript "m" to designate the rock mass, for example, the respective compressive strengths are $\sigma_{ci}$ and $\sigma_{cm}$.

### 4.1.2 Examples of rock masses

Figures 4.2–4.5 show four different geological conditions that are commonly encountered in the design and analysis of rock slopes. These are typical examples of rock masses in which the strength of laboratory-size samples may differ significantly from the shear strength along the overall sliding surface. In all four cases, instability occurs because of shear movement along a sliding surface that either lies along an existing fracture, or passes partially or entirely through intact rock. Figures 4.2–4.5 also show that, in fractured rock, the shape of the sliding surface is influenced by the orientation and length of the discontinuities.

Figure 4.2 shows a strong, massive limestone containing a set of continuous bedding surfaces that dip out of the slope face. Because the near vertical cut face is steeper than the dip of the bedding, the bedding surfaces are exposed, or "daylight" on the face and sliding has occurred with a tension

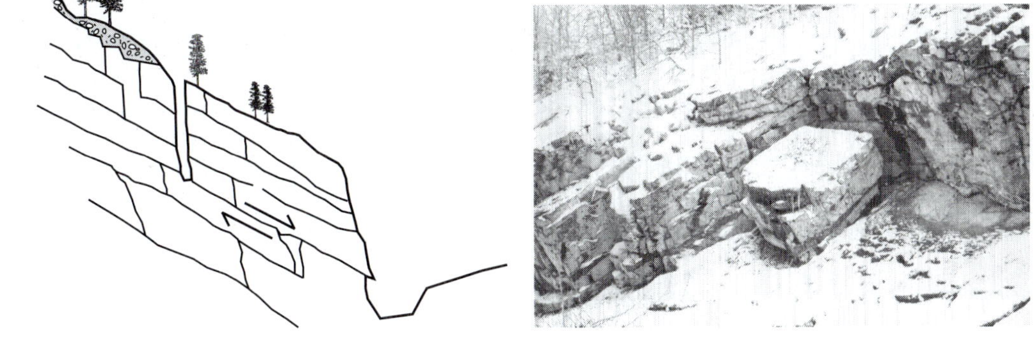

*Figure 4.2* Plane failure on continuous bedding plane dipping out of the slope (strong, blocky limestone, Crowsnest Pass, Alberta, Canada).

(a)

(b)

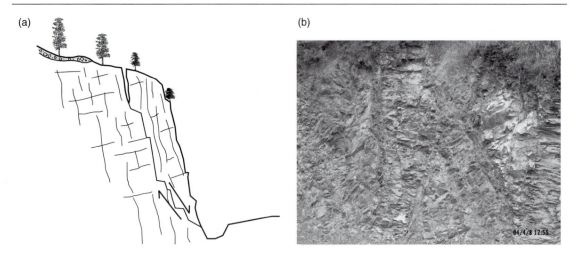

*Figure 4.3* Shallow circular failure in closely jointed rock mass (closely jointed, slightly weathered basalt, Island of Oahu, HI).

(a)

(b)

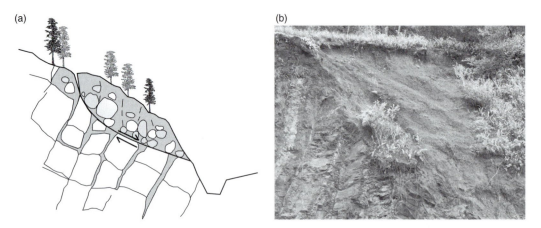

*Figure 4.4* Circular failure in residual soil and weathered rock (weathered basalt, Island of Oahu, HI).

crack opening along the sub-vertical, orthogonal joint set. Under these circumstances, the shear strength used in stability analysis is that of the bedding surfaces. Section 4.2 of this chapter discusses the strength properties of discontinuity surfaces, and Section 4.3 describes methods of measuring the friction angle in the laboratory.

Figure 4.3 shows a slope cut in a slightly weathered, medium weak basalt containing low persistence, closely spaced joints that occur in a wide variety of orientations. Because the joints are discontinuous, no single joint controls stability of

the slope. However, if a sliding surface was to develop in this slope it would follow a stepped path, which would partly lie along joint surfaces and partly pass through intact rock. The shear strength of this complex sliding surface cannot be determined analytically, so a set of empirical equations has been developed from which the cohesion and friction angle can be calculated with respect to the degree of fracturing and the rock strength. This procedure is described in Section 4.5.

Figure 4.4 shows a slope cut in a weathered rock in which the degree of weathering varies

(a)

(b)

*Figure 4.5* Shallow failure in very weak, massive rock containing no discontinuities (volcanic tuff, Trans European Highway, near Ankara, Turkey).

from residual soil in the upper part (right) of the slope to slightly weathered rock at greater depth. For these conditions, the sliding surface will lie predominantly in the weaker materials in the upper part of the slope, and in the stability analysis it is necessary to use different strength parameters for the upper and lower portions of the sliding surface. Because the degree of degradation of weathered rock tends to be highly variable, the strength of the rock mass will also be variable and can be difficult to measure. Consequently, a means of determining the strength of weathered rock is to carry out a back analysis of slopes in similar material; this approach is described in Section 4.4.

A fourth geological condition that may be encountered is that of a very weak but intact rock containing essentially no discontinuities. Figure 4.5 shows a cut face in tuff, a rock formed by the consolidation of volcanic ash. A geological hammer could be embedded in the face with a few blows, indicating the low strength of this rock. However, because this rock contains no discontinuities, it has a significant cohesive strength in addition to a moderate friction angle. Therefore, it was possible to cut a stable, vertical face to a height of tens of meters in this material, provided water pressures and erosion were controlled.

### 4.1.3   Classes of rock strength

Based on the scale effects and geological conditions discussed in the previous sections, it can be seen that sliding surfaces can form either along discontinuity surfaces, or through the rock mass, as illustrated in Figure 4.6. The importance of the classification shown in Figure 4.6 is that in essentially all slope stability analysis it is necessary to use the shear strength properties of either the discontinuities or of the rock mass, and there are different procedures for determining the strength properties as follows:

- *Discontinuity shear strength* can be measured in the field and the laboratory as described in Sections 4.2 and 4.3.
- *Rock mass shear strength* is determined by empirical methods involving either back analysis of slopes cut in similar geological conditions, or by calculation involving rock strength indices as described in Sections 4.4 and 4.5.

As a further illustration of the effects of geology on shear strength, relative strength parameters for three types of discontinuity and two types of rock mass are shown on the Mohr diagram in Figure 4.7. The slope of these lines represents the friction angle, and the intercept with

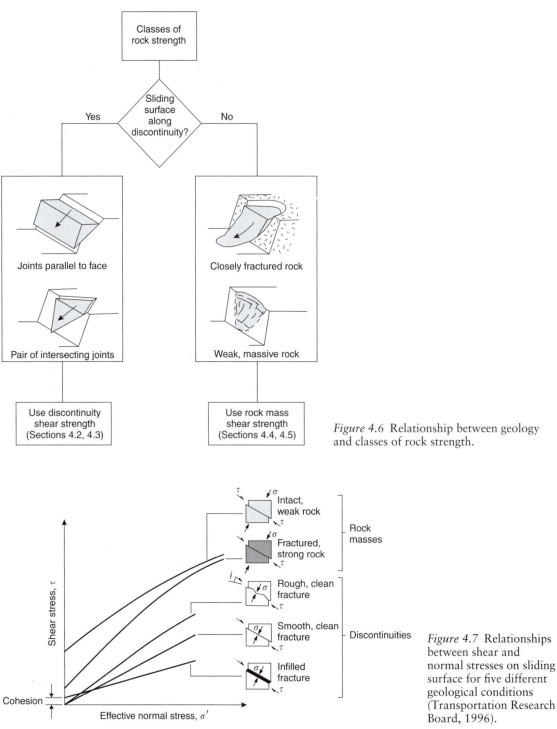

*Figure 4.6* Relationship between geology and classes of rock strength.

*Figure 4.7* Relationships between shear and normal stresses on sliding surface for five different geological conditions (Transportation Research Board, 1996).

the shear stress axis represents the cohesion (see Figure 1.8(a)). A description of these conditions on Figure 4.7 is as follows:

*Curve 1 Infilled discontinuity:*   If the infilling is a weak clay or fault gouge, the infilling friction angle ($\phi_{\text{inf}}$) is likely to be low, but there may be some cohesion if the infilling is undisturbed. Alternatively, if the infilling is a strong calcite for example, which produces a healed surface, then the cohesive strength may be significant (see Section 4.2.5).

*Curve 2 Smooth discontinuity:*   A smooth, clean discontinuity will have zero cohesion, and the friction angle will be that of the rock surfaces ($\phi_{\text{r}}$). The friction angle of rock is related to the grain size, and is generally lower in fine-grained rocks than in coarse-grained rocks (see Section 4.2.2).

*Curve 3 Rough discontinuity:*   Clean, rough discontinuity surfaces will have zero cohesion, and the friction angle will be made up of two components. First, the rock material friction angle ($\phi_{\text{r}}$), and second, a component ($i$) related to the roughness (asperities) of the surface and the ratio between the rock strength and the normal stress. As the normal stress increases, the asperities are progressively sheared off and the total friction angle diminishes (see Section 4.2.4).

*Curve 4 Fractured rock mass:*   The shear strength of a fractured rock mass, in which the sliding surface lies partially on discontinuity surfaces and partially passes through intact rock, can be expressed as a curved envelope. At low normal stresses where there is little confinement of the fractured rock and the individual fragments may move and rotate, the cohesion is low but the friction angle is high. At higher normal stresses, crushing of the rock fragments begins to take place with the result that the friction angle diminishes. The shape of the strength envelope is related to the degree of fracturing, and the strength of the intact rock (see Section 4.5).

*Curve 5 Weak intact rock:*   Rock such as the tuff shown in Figure 4.5 is composed of fine-grained material that has a low friction angle. However, because it contains no discontinuities,

the cohesion can be higher than that of a strong intact rock that is closely fractured.

The range of shear strength conditions that may be encountered in rock slopes as illustrated in Figures 4.2–4.5 clearly demonstrates the importance of examining both the characteristics of the discontinuities and the rock strength during the site investigation.

## 4.2   Shear strength of discontinuities

If geological mapping and/or diamond drilling identify discontinuities on which shear failure could take place, it will be necessary to determine the friction angle and cohesion of the sliding surface in order to carry out stability analyses. The investigation program should also obtain information on characteristics of the sliding surface that may modify the shear strength parameters. Important discontinuity characteristics include continuous length, surface roughness, and the thickness and characteristics of any infilling, as well as the effect of water on the properties of the infilling.

The following sections describe the relationship between the shear strength and the properties of the discontinuities.

### 4.2.1   Definition of cohesion and friction

In rock slope design, rock is assumed to be a Coulomb material in which the shear strength of the sliding surface is expressed in terms of the cohesion ($c$) and the friction angle ($\phi$) (Coulomb, 1773). The application of these two strength parameters to rock is discussed in the following paragraphs.

Assume a number of test samples were cut from a block of rock containing a smooth, planar discontinuity. Furthermore, the discontinuity contains a cemented infilling material such that a tensile force would have to be applied to the two halves of the sample in order to separate them. Each sample is subjected to a force at right angles to the discontinuity surface (normal stress, $\sigma$), and a force is applied in the direction parallel to

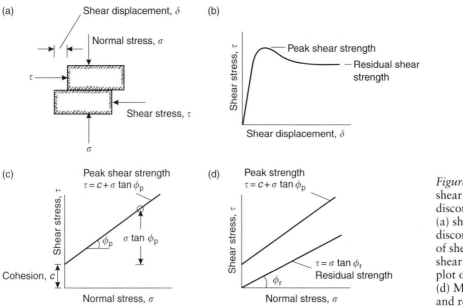

*Figure 4.8* Definition of shear strength of discontinuity surface; (a) shear test of discontinuity; (b) plot of shear displacement vs shear stress; (c) Mohr plot of peak strength; (d) Mohr plot of peak and residual strength.

the discontinuity (shear stress, $\tau$) while the shear displacement ($\delta_s$) is measured (Figure 4.8(a)).

For a test carried out at a constant normal stress, a typical plot of the shear stress against the shear displacement is shown in Figure 4.8(b)). At small displacements, the specimen behaves elastically and the shear stress increases linearly with displacement. As the force resisting movement is overcome, the curve become non-linear and then reaches a maximum that represents the *peak* shear strength of the discontinuity. Thereafter, the stress required to cause displacement decreases and eventually reaches a constant value termed the *residual* shear strength.

If the peak shear strength values from tests carried out at different normal stress levels are plotted, a relationship shown in Figure 4.8(c) is obtained; this is termed a Mohr diagram (Mohr, 1900). The features of this plot are first, that it is approximately linear and the slope of the line is equal to the peak friction angle $\phi_p$ of the rock surface. Second, the intercept of the line with the shear stress axis represents the cohesive strength $c$ of the cementing material. This cohesive component of the total shear strength is independent of the normal stress, but the frictional component increases with increasing normal stress. Based on the relationship illustrated on Figure 4.8(c), the peak shear strength is defined by the equation:

$$\tau = c + \sigma \tan \phi_p \qquad (4.1)$$

If the residual shear stress values at each applied normal stress are plotted on the Mohr diagram, the residual shear strength line is obtained as shown on Figure 4.8(d), and is defined by the equation:

$$\tau = \sigma \tan \phi_r \qquad (4.2)$$

where $\phi_r$ is the residual friction angle. For the residual strength condition, the cohesion is lost once displacement has broken the cementing action; on the Mohr diagram this is represented by the strength line passing through the origin of the graph. Also, the residual friction angle is less than the peak friction angle because the shear displacement grinds the minor irregularities on the rock surface and produces a smoother, lower friction surface.

*Table 4.1* Typical ranges of friction angles for a variety of rock types

| Rock class | Friction angle range | Typical rock types |
|---|---|---|
| Low friction | 20–27° | Schists (high mica content), shale, marl |
| Medium friction | 27–34° | Sandstone, siltstone, chalk, gneiss, slate |
| High friction | 34–40° | Basalt, granite, limestone, conglomerate |

### 4.2.2 Friction angle of rock surfaces

For a planar, clean (no infilling) discontinuity, the cohesion will be zero and the shear strength will be defined solely by the friction angle. The friction angle of the rock material is related to the size and shape of the grains exposed on the fracture surface. Thus, a fine-grained rock, and rock with a high mica content aligned parallel to the surface, such as a phyllite, will tend to have a low friction angle, while a coarse-grained rock such as granite, will have a high friction angle. Table 4.1 shows typical ranges of friction angles for a variety of rock types (Barton, 1973; Jaegar and Cook, 1976).

The friction angles listed in Table 4.1 should be used as a guideline only because actual values will vary widely with site conditions. Laboratory testing procedures to determine friction angle are described in Section 4.3.

### 4.2.3 Shearing on an inclined plane

In the previous section, it was assumed that the discontinuity surface along which shearing occurs is exactly parallel to the direction of the shear stress, $\tau$. Consider now a discontinuity surface inclined at an angle $i$ to the shear stress direction (Figure 4.9). In this case, the shear and normal stresses acting on the sliding surface, $\tau_i$ and $\sigma_i$ respectively are given by

$$\tau_i = \tau \cos^2 i - \sigma \sin i \cos i \quad (4.3)$$

$$\sigma_i = \sigma \cos^2 i + \tau \sin i \cos i \quad (4.4)$$

If it is assumed that the discontinuity surface has zero cohesion and that its shear strength is

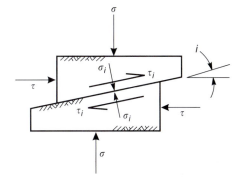

*Figure 4.9* Shear displacement on an inclined plane.

given by

$$\tau_i = \sigma_i \tan \phi \quad (4.5)$$

then equations (4.3) and (4.4) can be substituted in equation (4.5) to give the relationship between the applied shear stress and the normal stress as

$$\tau = \sigma \tan (\phi + i) \quad (4.6)$$

This equation was confirmed in a series of tests on models with regular surface projections carried out by Patton (1966) who must be credited with having emphasized the importance of this simple relationship in the analysis of rock slope stability.

Patton convincingly demonstrated the particular significance of this relationship by measuring the average value of the angle $i$ from photographs of bedding plane traces in unstable limestone slopes. Three of these are reproduced in Figure 4.10 and it will be seen that the rougher the bedding plane trace, the steeper the slope angle. Patton found that the inclination of the bedding plane trace was approximately equal to the sum of

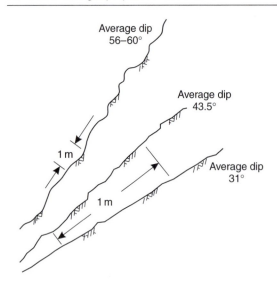

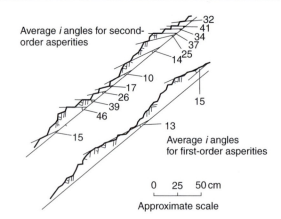

*Figure 4.11* Measurement of roughness angles *i* for first- and second-order asperities on rough rock surfaces (Patton, 1966).

*Figure 4.10* Patton's observations of bedding plane traces in unstable limestone slopes (Patton, 1966).

the friction angle of the rock $\phi$ found from laboratory tests on planar surfaces, and the average roughness *i* angle.

### 4.2.4   Surface roughness

All natural discontinuity surfaces exhibit some degree of roughness, varying from polished and slickensided sheared surfaces with very low roughness, to rough and irregular tension joints with considerable roughness. These surface irregularities are given the general term *asperities*, and because they can have a significant effect on the stability of a slope, they should be accounted for appropriately in design as discussed in this section.

The discussion in Section 4.2.3 has been simplified because Patton found that asperities can be divided into two classes: first- and second-order asperities as shown in Figure 4.11. The first-order asperities are those that correspond to the major undulations on the bedding surfaces, while the second-order asperities are small bumps and ripples on the surface and have higher *i* values. In order to obtain reasonable agreement between field observations of the dip of the

unstable bedding planes shown in Figure 4.10 and the $(\phi+i)$ values, it was necessary to measure only the first-order asperities.

Later studies by Barton (1973) showed that Patton's results were related to the normal stress acting across the bedding planes in the slopes that he observed. At low normal stresses, the second-order projections come into play and Barton quotes $(\phi + i)$ values in the range of 69–80° for tests conducted at low normal stresses ranging from 20 to 670 kPa (Goodman, 1970; Paulding, 1970; Rengers, 1971). Assuming a friction angle for the rock of 30°, these results show that the effective roughness angle *i* varies between 40 and 50° for these low normal stress levels.

The actual shear performance of discontinuity surfaces in rock slopes depends on the combined effects of the surface roughness, the rock strength at the surface, the applied normal stress and the amount of shear displacement. This is illustrated in Figure 4.12 where the asperities are sheared off, with a consequent reduction in the friction angle with increasing normal stress. That is, there is a transition from dilation to shearing of the rock. The degree to which the asperities are sheared will depend on both the magnitude of the normal force in relation to the compressive strength of the rock on the fracture surface, and the displacement

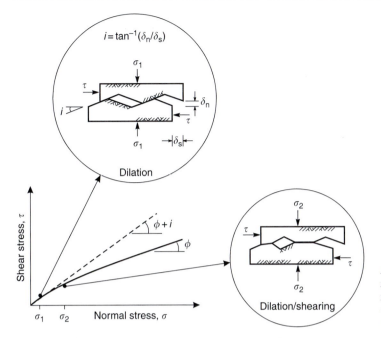

*Figure 4.12* Effect of surface roughness and normal stress on friction angle of discontinuity surface (Transportation Research Board, 1996).

distance. A rough surface that is initially undisturbed and interlocked will have a peak friction angle of $(\phi+i)$. With increasing normal stress and displacement, the asperities will be sheared off, and the friction angle will progressively diminish to a minimum value of the basic, or residual, friction angle of the rock. This dilation–shearing condition is represented on the Mohr diagram as a curved strength envelope with an initial slope equal to $(\phi + i)$, reducing to $\phi_r$ at higher normal stresses.

The shear stress–normal stress relationship shown in Figure 4.12 can be quantified using a technique developed by Barton (1973) based on the shear strength behavior of artificially produced rough, clean "joints." The study showed that the shear strength of a rough rock surface depends on the relationship between the roughness, the rock strength and the normal stress, and can be defined by the following empirical equation

$$\tau = \sigma' \tan\left(\phi + \text{JRC}\,\log_{10}\left(\frac{\text{JCS}}{\sigma'}\right)\right) \qquad (4.7)$$

where JRC is the joint roughness coefficient, JCS is the compressive strength of the rock at the fracture surface and $\sigma'$ is the effective normal stress. The value of JRC is determined using the techniques discussed in Section 3.4.3 that involve either comparing the roughness of the surface with standard roughness profiles, or making measurements of the surface. The compressive strength of the rock (JCS) can be estimated using the simple field observations described in Table 3.1, or with a Schmidt hammer to measure the rock on the joint surface. The normal stress acting on the surface is the component acting normal to the surface, of the product of the depth of rock above the sliding surface and the unit weight of the rock.

In equation (4.7), the term $[\text{JRC}\,\log_{10}(\text{JCS}/\sigma')]$ is equivalent to the roughness angle $i$ in equation (4.6). At high stress levels, relative to the rock strength, when $(\text{JCS}/\sigma') = 1$ and the asperities are sheared off, the term $[\text{JRC}\,\log_{10}(\text{JCS}/\sigma')]$ equals zero. At low stress levels the ratio $(\text{JCS}/\sigma')$ tends to approach infinity and the roughness component of the shear strength becomes very large. In order that realistic values of the roughness component are used in design, the term $(\phi + i)$ should not exceed about $50°$ and the useful range for the ratio $(JCS/\sigma')$ is between about 3 and 100.

It is found that both JRC and JCS values are influenced by scale effects, that is, as the discontinuity size increases, there is a corresponding decrease in JRC and JCS values. The reason for this relationship is that small-scale roughness of a surface becomes less significant compared to the dimensions of the discontinuity, and eventually large-scale undulations have more significance than the roughness (Barton and Bandis, 1983; Bandis, 1993). These effects are consistent with properties of first- and second-order asperities shown in Figure 4.11. The scale effect can be quantified by the following two equations:

$$JRC_n = JRC_0 \left( \frac{L_n}{L_0} \right)^{-0.02JRC_0}$$

and

$$JCS_n = JCS_0 \left( \frac{L_n}{L_0} \right)^{-0.03JRC_0} \qquad (4.8)$$

where $L_0$ is the dimension of the surface used to measure JRC such as the wire comb (Figure 3.10), and $L_n$ is the dimension of the sliding surface.

An example of the application of equations (4.7) and (4.8) is as follows. Consider a discontinuity dipping $(\psi_p)$ at $35°$ and the dimension of this surface is 10 m $(L_n)$. If the average depth $(H)$ of the discontinuity is 20 m below the crest of the slope, and the rock unit weight $(\gamma_r)$ is $26 \, kN/m^3$, then the effective normal stress $(\sigma')$ for a dry slope is

$$\sigma' = \gamma_r H \cos(\psi_p) = 26 \times 20 \times \cos(35)$$
$$= 426 \, kPa$$

If the $JRC_0$ value measured with a wire comb $(L_0 = 0.2 \, m)$ is 15, and the rock is strong with a $JCS_0$ value of 50,000 kPa, then the scaled values

are

$$JRC_n = 15 \left( \frac{10}{0.2} \right)^{-0.02 \times 15} \approx 5$$

and

$$JCS_n = 50,000 \left( \frac{10}{0.2} \right)^{-0.03 \times 15} \approx 8600 \, kPa$$

and the roughness angle is

$$JRC \log_{10}(JCS/\sigma') = 5 \times \log_{10}(8600/426)$$
$$\approx 7°$$

The concepts of shear strength of rough joints and scale effects discussed in this section can be applied to rock slope design as illustrated in Figure 4.13. For example, stress relief, and possibly blast damage during construction, can cause shear movement along discontinuities and dilation of the rock at the face. Also, the stress levels on the sliding surface may be high enough to cause some shearing of the asperities (Figure 4.13(a)). For these conditions, the first effect is that any cohesion existing on the undisturbed surface is diminished. The second effect is loss of interlock on the rough surface so that the second-order asperities have a diminished effect on the shear strength. The consequence of this dilation is that the roughness angle corresponding to undulating first-order asperities would be used in design.

In contrast to the displaced block shown in Figure 4.13(a), the rock mass can be prevented from movement and dilation by the use of careful blasting (see Chapter 11), and installation of tensioned rock anchors or passive support such as dowels and buttresses (see Chapter 12). Under these conditions, interlock along the sliding surface is maintained and the second-order asperities contribute to the shear strength of the potential sliding surface.

The difference in the total friction angle between the displaced and undisturbed rock will have a significant effect on stability and

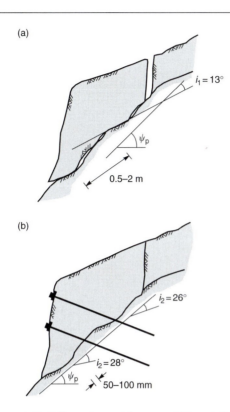

*Figure 4.13* Effect of asperities on stability of sliding blocks: (a) shear strength of displaced block controlled by first-order asperities ($i_1$); (b) tensioned rock bolts prevent dilation along potential sliding surface and produce interlock along second-order asperities ($i_2$).

design of stabilization measures. This demonstrates the value of using construction measures that minimize relaxation and dilation of rock masses.

### 4.2.5 Discontinuity infilling

The preceding section discussed rough, clean discontinuity surfaces with rock-to-rock contact and no infilling, in which the shear strength is derived solely from the friction angle of the rock material. However, if the discontinuity contains an infilling, the shear strength properties of the fracture are often modified, with both the cohesion and friction angle of the surface being influenced by the thickness and properties of the infilling. For example, for a clay-filled fault zone in granite, it would be assumed that the shear strength of the discontinuity would be that of the clay and not the granite. In the case of a healed, calcite-filled fracture, a high cohesion would be used in design, but only if it were certain that the discontinuity would remain healed after any disturbance caused by blasting when excavating the slope.

The presence of infillings along discontinuity surfaces can have a significant effect on stability. It is important that infillings be identified in the investigation program, and that appropriate strength parameters be used in design. For example, one of the contributing factors to the massive landslide into the Vaiont Reservoir in Italy that resulted in the death of about 3000 people was the presence of low shear strength clay along the bedding surfaces of the shale (Trollope, 1980).

The effect of the infilling on shear strength will depend on both the thickness and strength properties of the infilling material. With respect to the thickness, if it is more than about 25–50% of the amplitude of the asperities, there will be little or no rock-to-rock contact, and the shear strength properties of the fracture will be the properties of the infilling (Goodman, 1970).

Figure 4.14 is a plot of the results of direct shear tests carried out to determine the peak friction angle and cohesion of filled discontinuities (Barton, 1974). Examination of the test results shows that the infillings can be divided approximately into two groups, as follows:

- *Clays*: montmorillonite and bentonitic clays, and clays associated with coal measures have friction angles ranging from about 8 to 20° and cohesion values ranging from 0 to about 200 kPa. Some cohesion values were measured as high as 380 kPa, which would probably be associated with very stiff clays.
- *Faults, shears and breccias*: the material formed in fault zones and shears in rocks such as granite, diorite, basalt, and limestone may contain clay in addition to granular fragments. These materials have friction angles

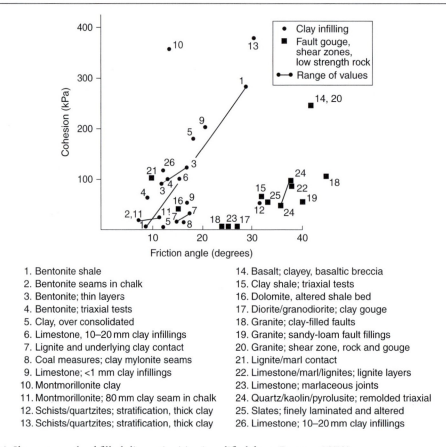

1. Bentonite shale
2. Bentonite seams in chalk
3. Bentonite; thin layers
4. Bentonite; triaxial tests
5. Clay, over consolidated
6. Limestone, 10–20 mm clay infillings
7. Lignite and underlying clay contact
8. Coal measures; clay mylonite seams
9. Limestone; <1 mm clay infillings
10. Montmorillonite clay
11. Montmorillonite; 80 mm clay seam in chalk
12. Schists/quartzites; stratification, thick clay
13. Schists/quartzites; stratification, thick clay

14. Basalt; clayey, basaltic breccia
15. Clay shale; triaxial tests
16. Dolomite, altered shale bed
17. Diorite/granodiorite; clay gouge
18. Granite; clay-filled faults
19. Granite; sandy-loam fault fillings
20. Granite; shear zone, rock and gouge
21. Lignite/marl contact
22. Limestone/marl/lignites; lignite layers
23. Limestone; marlaceous joints
24. Quartz/kaolin/pyrolusite; remolded triaxial
25. Slates; finely laminated and altered
26. Limestone; 10–20 mm clay infillings

*Figure 4.14* Shear strength of filled discontinuities (modified from Barton, 1970).

ranging from about 25 to 45°, and cohesion values ranging from 0 to about 100 kPa. Fault gouge derived from coarse-grained rocks such as granites tend to have higher friction angles than those from fine-grained rocks such as limestones.

Some of the tests shown in Figure 4.14 also determined residual shear strength values. It was found that the residual friction angle was only about 2–4° less than the peak friction angle, while the residual cohesion was essentially zero.

Shear strength–displacement behavior is an additional factor to consider regarding the shear strength of filled discontinuities. In analyzing the stability of slopes, this behavior will indicate whether there is likely to be a reduction in

shear strength with displacement. In conditions where there is a significant decrease in shear strength with displacement, slope failure can occur suddenly following a small amount of movement.

Filled discontinuities can be divided into two general categories, depending on whether there has been previous displacement of the discontinuity (Barton, 1974). These categories are further subdivided into either normally consolidated (NC) or over-consolidated (OC) materials (Figure 4.15):

- *Recently displaced discontinuities*—These discontinuities include faults, shear zones, clay mylonites and bedding-surface slips. In faults and shear zones, the infilling is formed by

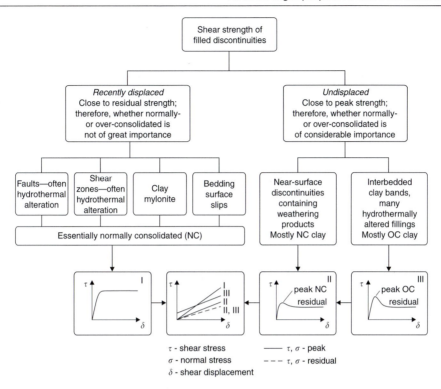

*Figure 4.15* Simplified division of filled discontinuities into displaced and undisplaced, and NC and OC categories (modified from Barton, 1974).

the shearing process that may have occurred many times and produced considerable displacement. The gouge formed in this process may include both clay-size particles, and breccia with the particle orientation and striations of the breccia aligned parallel to the direction of shearing. In contrast, the mylonites and bedding-surface slips are discontinuities that were originally clay bearing, and along which sliding occurred during folding or sliding.

For these types of discontinuities their shear strength will be at, or close to, the residual strength (Figure 4.15, graph I). Any cohesive bonds that existed in the clay due to previous over-consolidation will have been destroyed by shearing and the infilling will be equivalent to the normally consolidated state. In addition, strain softening may occur, with any increase in water content resulting in a further strength reduction.

- *Undisplaced discontinuities*—Infilled discontinuities that have undergone no previous displacement include igneous and metamorphic rocks that have weathered along the discontinuity to form a clay layer. For example, diabase weathers to amphibolite and eventually to clay. Other undisplaced discontinuities include thin beds of clay and weak shales that are found with sandstone in interbedded sedimentary formations. Hydrothermal alteration is another process that forms infillings that can include low strength materials such as montmorillonite, and high strength materials such as quartz and calcite.

The infillings of undisplaced discontinuities can be divided into normally-consolidated (NC) and over-consolidated (OC) materials that have significant differences in peak strength values. This strength difference is illustrated on Figure 4.15, graphs II and III.

While the peak shear strength of over-consolidated clay infillings may be high, there can be a significant loss of strength due to softening, swelling and pore pressure changes on unloading. Unloading occurs when rock is excavated for a slope or foundation, for example. Strength loss also occurs on displacement in brittle materials such as calcite.

### 4.2.6 *Influence of water on shear strength of discontinuities*

The most important influence of water in a discontinuity is the diminished shear strength resulting from the reduction of the effective normal shear stress acting on the surface. The effective normal stress is the difference between the weight of the overlying rock and the uplift pressure produced by the water pressure. The effect of water pressure, $u$ on the shear strength can be incorporated into the shear strength equation as follows:

$$\tau = c + (\sigma - u) \tan \phi_p - \text{peak strength}$$
(4.9a)

or

$$\tau = (\sigma - u) \tan \phi_r - \text{residual strength}$$
(4.9b)

These equations assume that the cohesion and friction angle are not changed by the presence of water on the surface. In most hard rock and in many sandy soils and gravels, the strength properties are not significantly altered by water. However, many clays, shales and mudstones, and similar materials will exhibit significant reduction in strength with changes in moisture content. It is important, therefore, that the moisture content of the test samples be as close as possible to that of the *in situ* rock (see Section 3.6.3 regarding the preservation of rock samples).

## 4.3 Laboratory testing of shear strength

The friction angle of a discontinuity surface can be determined in the laboratory using a direct shear box of the type shown in Figure 4.16. This is portable equipment that can be used in the field if required, and is suited to testing samples with dimensions up to about 75 mm, such as NQ

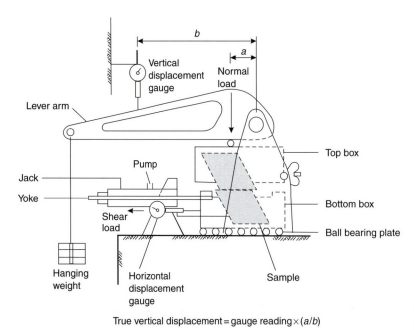

True vertical displacement = gauge reading × (a/b)

*Figure 4.16* Simple equipment for performing direct shear tests on rock samples up to about 75 mm dimensions.

and HQ drill core. The most reliable values are obtained if a sample with a smooth, planar surface is used because it is found that, with an irregular surface, the effect of surface roughness can make the test results difficult to interpret.

The test procedure consists of using plaster of paris or molten sulphur to set the two halves of the sample in a pair of steel boxes (ISRM, 1981b). Particular care is taken to ensure that the two pieces of core are in their original, matched position, and the discontinuity surface is exactly parallel to the direction of the shear force. A constant normal load is then applied using the cantilever, and the shear load gradually increased until sliding failure occurs. Measurement of the vertical and horizontal displacement of the upper block relative to the lower block can be made most simply with dial gauges, while more precise, continuous displacement measurements can

be made with linear variable differential transformers (LVDT's) (Hencher and Richards, 1989).

Each sample is usually tested three or four times, at progressively higher normal loads. That is, when the residual shear stress has been established for a normal load, the sample is reset, the normal load increased, and another shear test conducted. The test results are expressed as plots of shear displacement against shear stress from which the peak and residual shear stress values are determined. Each test will produce a pair of shear stress–normal stress values, which are plotted to determine the peak and residual friction angles of the surface.

Figure 4.17 shows a typical result of a direct shear test on a surface with a 4 mm thick sandy silt infilling. The curves on the upper right are shear stress–shear displacement plots showing an approximate peak shear stress, as well as a

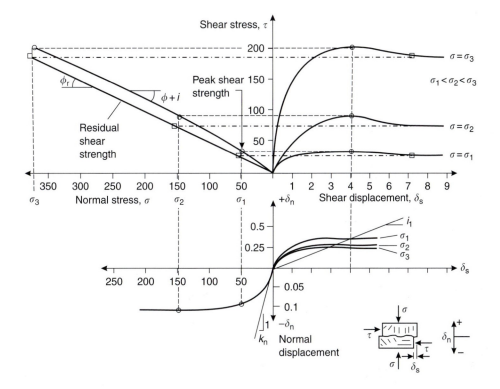

*Figure 4.17* Results of direct shear test of filled discontinuity showing measurements of shear strength, roughness ($i$), and normal stiffness ($k_n$) (modified from Erban and Gill, 1988).

slightly lower, residual shear stress. The sample was initially undisplaced, so exhibited a difference between peak and residual strengths (see Figure 4.8). The normal stresses at the peak and residual shear stress values are calculated from the applied normal load and the contact area. When calculating the contact area, an allowance is made for the decrease in area as shear displacement takes place. For diamond drill core in an inclined hole, the fracture surface is in the shape of an ellipse, and the formula for calculating the contact area is as follows (Hencher and Richards, 1989):

$$A = \pi a b - \left[ \frac{\delta_s b (4a^2 - \delta_s^2)}{2a} \right]^{1/2}$$

$$- 2ab \sin^{-1} \left( \frac{\delta_s}{2a} \right) \tag{4.10}$$

where A is the gross area of contact, $2a$ is the major axis of ellipse, $2b$ is the minor axis of ellipse and $\delta_s$ is the relative shear displacement.

The increase in the normal stress with displacement for a constant normal load is shown in the upper left diagram of Figure 4.17 where the normal stress for the residual shear stress is greater than that for the peak shear stress.

The measured friction angle is the sum of the friction angle of the rock ($\phi_r$), and the roughness of the surface ($i$). The roughness of the surface is calculated from the plots of shear and normal displacement ($\delta_s$ and $\delta_n$, respectively, on the lower right side of Figure 4.17) as follows:

$$i = \tan^{-1} \left( \frac{\delta_n}{\delta_s} \right) \tag{4.11}$$

This value of $i$ is then subtracted from the friction angle calculated from the plot of shear and normal stresses at failure to obtain the friction angle of the rock. While the shear test can be conducted on a sawed sample on which there is no roughness component, the saw may polish the surface resulting in a low value of the friction angle compared to a natural surface.

As shown in Figure 4.17, it is usual to test each sample at a minimum of three normal stress levels, with the sample being reset to its original position between tests. When the tests are run at progressively higher normal stress levels, the total friction angle of the surface will diminish with each test if the asperities are progressively sheared. This produces a concave upwards normal stress–shear stress plot as shown in the upper left plot of Figure 4.17. The degree to which the asperities are sheared off will depend on the level of the normal stress in comparison to the rock strength, that is, the ratio JCS/$\sigma$ in equation (4.7). The maximum normal stress that is used in the test is usually the maximum stress level that is likely to develop in the slope.

It is also possible to measure the normal stiffness of the discontinuity infilling during the direct shear test as shown in the lower left plot in Figure 4.17. Normal stiffness $k_n$ is the ratio of the normal stress $\sigma$ to normal displacement $\delta_n$, or

$$k_n = \left( \frac{\sigma}{\delta_n} \right) \tag{4.12}$$

The plot of $\sigma$ against $\delta_n$ is highly non-linear and the value of $k_n$ is the slope of the initial portion of the curve. The normal stiffness of a fracture is not usually an issue in rock slope design, and is more often used in the estimation of the deformation modulus of a rock mass (Wyllie, 1999), and in numerical analysis (see Chapter 10).

It can be difficult to measure the cohesion of a surface with the direct shear test because, if the cohesion is very low, it may not be possible to obtain an undisturbed sample. If the cohesion is high and the sample is intact, the material holding the sample in the test equipment will have to be stronger than the infilling if the sample is to shear. Where it is important that the cohesion of a weak infilling be measured, an *in situ* test of the undisturbed material may be required.

## 4.4   Shear strength of rock masses by back analysis of slope failures

For the geological conditions shown in Figure 4.3 where a cut has been made in fractured rock,

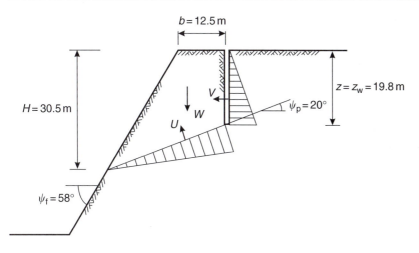

$b = 12.5\,\mathrm{m}$

$z = z_w = 19.8\,\mathrm{m}$

$H = 30.5\,\mathrm{m}$

$V$

$W$

$U$

$\psi_p = 20°$

$\psi_f = 58°$

*Figure 4.18* Cross-section of quarry slope failure showing geometry and water forces.

there is no distinct discontinuity surface on which sliding can take place. A sliding surface in this rock mass will comprise both natural discontinuities aligned on the sliding surface, together with some shear failure through intact rock. It is generally difficult and expensive to sample and test large samples (~1 m diameter) of fractured rock. Consequently, two empirical methods of determining the friction angle and cohesion of rock masses have been developed—back analysis that is described in this section, and the Hoek–Brown strength criterion that is discussed in Section 4.5. In both methods, it is necessary to categorize the rock mass in terms of both the intact rock strength and the characteristics of the discontinuities. This may require some judgment and it is advisable, where possible, to compare the strength values obtained by both methods to improve the reliability of values used in design.

Probably the most reliable method of determining the strength of a rock mass is to back analyze a failed, or failing slope. This involves carrying out a stability analysis using available information on the position of the sliding surface, the ground water conditions at the time of failure and any external forces such as foundation loads and earthquake motion, if applicable. With the factor of safety set at 1.0, the stability analysis is used to calculate the friction angle and cohesion. This section describes the back analysis of a failed slope in a limestone quarry, and the use of

the calculated shear strength values to design an appropriate slope angle for a deeper pit (Roberts and Hoek, 1972).

Figure 4.18 shows the geometry of the slope failure in which sliding occurred on bedding planes striking parallel to the face, and dipping out of the face at an angle of 20°. These conditions are applicable to plane failure conditions as shown in Figure 2.16 and described in more detail in Chapter 6.

At the time of failure, there was an open tension crack on the upper, horizontal bench of the quarry and the dimensions of the failed mass were defined by the dimensions $H$, $b$, $\psi_f$ and $\psi_p$. From these dimensions and a rock unit weight of $25.1\,\mathrm{kN/m^3}$, the weight of the sliding mass was calculated to be $12.3\,\mathrm{MN/m}$. Immediately prior to failure, a heavy rainstorm flooded the upper bench so that the tension crack was full of water ($z_w = z$). It was assumed that water forces acting in the tension crack and on the bedding plane could be represented by triangular distributions with magnitudes of $V = 1.92\,\mathrm{MN/m}$ and $U = 3.26\,\mathrm{MN/m}$ respectively.

In back analysis, both the friction angle and the cohesion of the sliding surface are unknown, and their values can be estimated by the following method. The likely range of the friction angle can usually be estimated by inspection (see Table 4.1), or by laboratory testing if samples containing bedding planes are available. In this case where

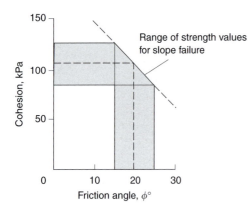

*Figure 4.19* Shear strength mobilized on bedding plane for slope failure shown in Figure 4.18.

the limestone was fine-grained and the bedding planes smooth, it was estimated that the friction angle was in the range of 15–25°. The next step was to carry out a number of stability analyses with a range of cohesion values and a factor of safety of 1.0. The results of this analysis show that, at a friction angle of 20° the corresponding cohesion value is about 110 kPa, and that for higher friction angles the required cohesion is reduced (Figure 4.19).

The shear strength values calculated in this manner can be used to design slopes excavated in this limestone, provided that careful blasting is used to maintain the cohesion on the bedding planes. Figure 4.20 shows the relationship between the factor of safety and the face angle for a 64 m high cut, assuming plane failure on a bedding plane dipping at 20° out of the face. If the slope is drained, the shear strength is sufficient for the face to stand vertically, but if the slope is saturated, the steepest stable slope is about 50°.

In many cases it may not be feasible to carry out a back analysis of a slope in similar geological conditions to that in which the new slope is to be excavated. In these circumstances, published results of rock mass shear strength can be used in design. Figure 4.21 shows the results of back analyses of slope failures in a variety of geological conditions (as described in Table 4.2), and the shear strength parameters ($\phi/c$ values) calculated at failure. By adding additional points to

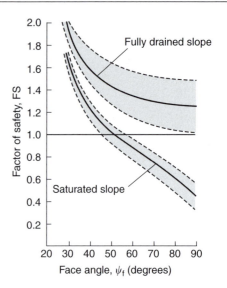

*Figure 4.20* Relationship between factor of safety and face angle of dry and saturated slope for slope shown in Figure 4.18.

Figure 4.21 for local geological conditions, it is possible to draw up a readily applicable rock mass strength chart for shear failures. Point 6 is for the slope shown in Figure 4.18.

## 4.5   Hoek–Brown strength criterion for fractured rock masses

As an alternative to back analysis to determine the strength of fractured rock masses, an empirical method has been developed by Hoek and Brown (1980a,b) in which the shear strength is represented as a curved Mohr envelope. This strength criterion was derived from the Griffith crack theory of fracture in brittle rock (Hoek, 1968), as well as from observations of the behavior of rock masses in the laboratory and the field (Marsal, 1967, 1973; Brown, 1970; Jaeger, 1970).

Hoek and Brown introduced their failure criterion to provide input data for the analyses required for the design of underground excavations in hard rock. The criterion started from the properties of intact rock, and then introduced factors to reduce these properties based on the characteristics of joints in a rock mass. The

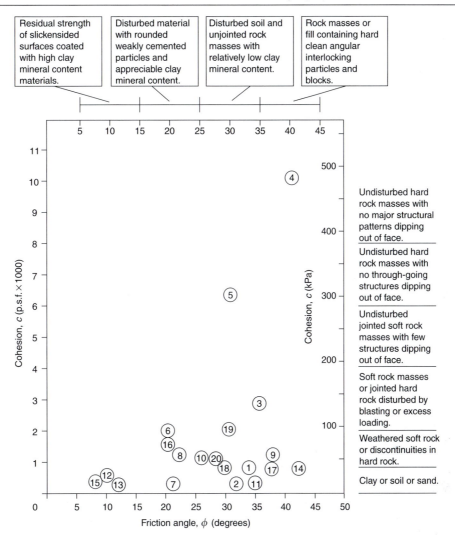

*Figure 4.21* Relationship between friction angles and cohesive strength mobilized at failure for slopes analyzed in Table 4.2.

authors sought to link the empirical criterion to geological observations by means of one of the available rock mass classification schemes and, for this purpose, they chose the Rock Mass Rating proposed by Bieniawski (1976).

Because of the lack of suitable alternatives, the criterion was soon adopted by the rock mechanics community and its use quickly spread beyond the original limits used in deriving the strength reduction relationships. Consequently, it became necessary to re-examine these relationships and introduce new elements from time to time to account for the wide range of practical problems to which the criterion was being applied (Hoek *et al.*, 2002). Typical of these enhancements were the introduction of the idea of "undisturbed" and "disturbed" rock masses Hoek and Brown (1988), and of a modified criterion to force the rock mass tensile strength to zero for very poor quality rock masses (Hoek *et al.*, 1992).

*Table 4.2* Sources of shear strength data plotted in Figure 4.21

| Point number | Material | Location | Slope height (m) | Reference |
|---|---|---|---|---|
| 1 | Disturbed slates and quartzite's | Knob Lake, Canada | — | Coates *et al.* (1965) |
| 2 | Soil | Any location | — | Whitman and Bailey (1967) |
| 3 | Jointed porphyry | Rio Tinto, Spain | 50–110 | Hoek (1970) |
| 4 | Ore body hanging wall in granite rocks | Grangesberg, Sweden | 60–240 | Hoek (1974) |
| 5 | Rock slopes with slope angles of 50–60° | Any location | 300 | Ross–Brown (1973) |
| 6 | Bedding planes in limestone | Somerset, England | 60 | Roberts and Hoek (1972) |
| 7 | London clay, stiff | England | — | Skempton and Hutchinson (1969) |
| 8 | Gravelly alluvium | Pima, Arizona | — | Hamel (1970) |
| 9 | Faulted rhyolite | Ruth, Nevada | — | Hamel (1971a) |
| 10 | Sedimentary series | Pittsburgh, Pennsylvania | — | Hamel (1971b) |
| 11 | Kaolinized granite | Cornwall, England | 75 | Ley (1972) |
| 12 | Clay shale | Fort Peck Dam, Montana | — | Middlebrook (1942) |
| 13 | Clay shale | Gardiner Dam, Canada | — | Fleming *et al.* (1970) |
| 14 | Chalk | Chalk Cliffs, England | 15 | Hutchinson (1970) |
| 15 | Bentonite/clay | Oahe Dam, South Dakota | — | Fleming *et al.* (1970) |
| 16 | Clay | Garrison Dam, North Dakota | — | Fleming *et al.* (1970) |
| 17 | Weathered granites | Hong Kong | 13–30 | Hoek and Richards (1974) |
| 18 | Weathered volcanics | Hong Kong | 30–100 | Hoek and Richards (1974) |
| 19 | Sandstone, siltstone | Alberta, Canada | 240 | Wyllie and Munn (1979) |
| 20 | Argillite | Yukon, Canada | 100 | Wyllie (project files) |

One of the early difficulties arose because many geotechnical problems, particularly regarding slope stability analysis, are more conveniently dealt with in terms of shear and normal stresses rather than the principal stress relationships of the original Hoek–Brown criterion, defined by the equation:

$$\sigma_1' = \sigma_3' + \sigma_{ci}\left(m\frac{\sigma_3'}{\sigma_{ci}} + s\right)^{0.5} \qquad (4.13)$$

where $\sigma_1'$ and $\sigma_3'$ are respectively the major and minor effective principal stresses at failure, $\sigma_{ci}$

is the uniaxial compressive strength of the intact rock material and $m$ and $s$ are material constants; $s = 1$ for intact rock.

An exact relationship between equation (4.13) and the normal and shear stresses at failure was derived by J. W. Bray (reported by Hoek, 1983) and later by Ucar (1986).

Hoek (1990) discussed the derivation of equivalent friction angles and cohesive strengths for various practical situations. These derivations were based upon tangents to the Mohr envelope derived by Bray. Hoek (1994) suggested that the cohesive strength determined by fitting a tangent to the curvilinear Mohr envelope is an upper bound value and may give optimistic results in stability calculations. Consequently, an average value, determined by fitting a linear Mohr–Coulomb relationship by least squares methods, may be more appropriate. In the 1994 paper, Hoek also introduced the concept of the Generalized Hoek–Brown criterion in which the shape of the principal stress plot or the Mohr envelope could be adjusted by means of a variable coefficient *a* in place of the 0.5 power term in equation (4.13).

Hoek and Brown (1997) attempted to consolidate all the previous enhancements into a comprehensive presentation of the failure criterion and they gave a number of worked examples to illustrate its practical application.

In addition to the changes in the equations, it was also recognized that the Rock Mass Rating of Bieniawski was no longer adequate as a vehicle for relating the failure criterion to geological observations in the field, particularly for very weak rock masses. This resulted in the introduction of the Geological Strength Index (GSI) by Hoek *et al.* (1992), Hoek (1994) and Hoek, Kaiser and Bawden (1995). This index was subsequently extended for weak rock masses in a series of papers by Hoek *et al.* (1998), Marinos and Hoek (2000, 2001) and Hoek and Marinos (2000).

The GSI provides a system for estimating the reduction in rock mass strength for different geological conditions. Values of GSI are related to both the degree of fracturing and the condition of fracture surfaces, as shown in Tables 4.3 and 4.4 respectively for blocky rock masses and schistose metamorphic rock masses. The strength of a jointed rock mass depends on the properties of the intact rock pieces, as well as the freedom of the rock pieces to slide and rotate under different stress conditions. This freedom is controlled by the geometrical shape of the intact rock pieces and the condition of the surfaces separating the pieces. Angular rock pieces with clean, rough surfaces will result in a much stronger rock mass than one that contains rounded particles surrounded by weathered and altered material.

The description of the Hoek–Brown strength criterion in this section includes all the data in this work up to 2002.

### 4.5.1 Generalized Hoek–Brown strength criterion

The generalized Hoek–Brown strength criterion is expressed in terms of the major and minor principal stresses, and is modified from equation (4.13) as follows (Figure 4.22)

$$\sigma_1' = \sigma_3' + \sigma_{ci}\left(m_b\frac{\sigma_3'}{\sigma_{ci}} + s\right)^a \quad (4.14)$$

where $m_b$ is a reduced value of the material constant $m_i$ for intact rock and is given by

$$m_b = m_i \exp\left(\frac{\text{GSI} - 100}{28 - 14D}\right) \quad (4.15)$$

Table 4.5 gives values of $m_i$ for a wide variety of rock types, and $s$ and $a$ are constants for the rock mass given by

$$s = \exp\left(\frac{\text{GSI} - 100}{9 - 3D}\right) \quad (4.16)$$

$$a = \frac{1}{2} + \frac{1}{6}(e^{-\text{GSI}/15} - e^{-20/3}) \quad (4.17)$$

$D$ is a factor that depends upon the degree of disturbance to which the rock mass has been subjected by blast damage and stress relaxation. It varies from 0 for undisturbed *in situ* rock masses to 1 for very disturbed rock masses; guidelines for the selection of appropriate values for $D$ are discussed in Section 4.5.6.

The uniaxial compressive strength of the rock mass is obtained by setting $\sigma_3' = 0$ in equation (4.14), giving

$$\sigma_c = \sigma_{ci} \cdot s^a \quad (4.18)$$

and, the tensile strength is

$$\sigma_t = -\frac{s\sigma_{ci}}{m_b} \quad (4.19)$$

*Table 4.3* GSI values characterizing blocky rock masses on the basis of particle interlocking and discontinuity condition

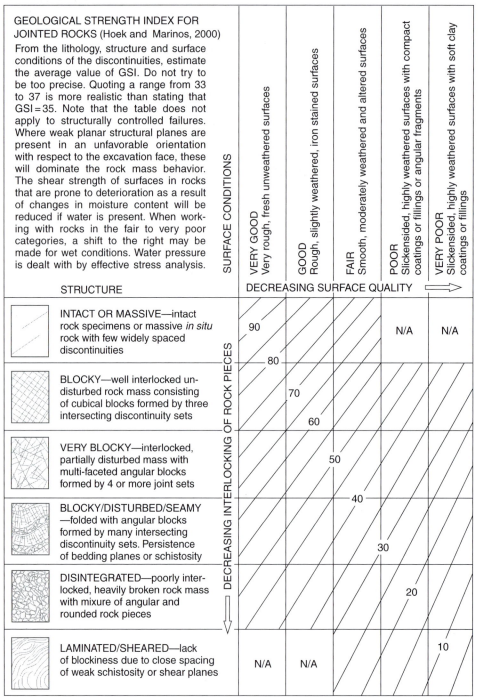

*Table 4.4*  GSI values characterizing schistose metamorphic rock masses on the basis of foliation and discontinuity condition

| GSI FOR HETEROGENEOUS ROCK MASSES SUCH AS FLYSCH (Marinos P. and Hoek E., 2000) | VERY GOOD—Very rough, fresh unweathered surfaces | GOOD—Rough, slightly weathered surfaces | FAIR—Smooth, moderately weathered and altered surfaces | POOR—Very smooth, occasionally slickensided surfaces with compact coatings or fillings with angular fragments | VERY POOR—Very smooth slicken-sided or highly weathered surfaces with soft clay coatings or fillings |
|---|---|---|---|---|---|

From a description of the lithology, structure and surface conditions (particularly of the bedding planes), choose a box in the chart. Locate the position in the box that corresponds to the condition of the discontinuities and estimate the average value of GSI from the contours. Do not attempt to be too precise. Quoting a range from 33 to 37 is more realistic than giving GSI = 35. Note that the Hoek-Brown criterion does not apply to structurally controlled failures. Where unfavourably oriented continuous weak planar discontinuities are present, these will dominate the behaviour of the rock mass. The strength of some rock masses is reduced by the presence of groundwater and this can be allowed for by a slight shift to the right in the columns for fair, poor and very poor conditions. Water pressure does not change the value of GSI and it is dealt with by using effective stress analysis.

**COMPOSITION AND STRUCTURE**

Contours: 70, 60, 50, 40, 30, 20, 10

Categories in chart: A, B, C, D, E, F, G, H

A. Thick bedded, very blocky sandstone
The effect of pelitic coatings on the bedding planes is minimized by the confinement of the rock mass. In shallow tunnels or slopes these bedding planes may cause structurally controlled instability.

B. Sand-stone with thin inter-layers of siltstone

C. Sand-stone and siltstone in similar amounts

D. Siltstone or silty shale with sand-stone layers

E. Weak siltstone or clayey shale with sandstone layers

C,D,E and G—may be more or less folded than illustrated but this does not change the strength. Tectonic deformation, faulting and loss of continuity moves these categories to F and H.

F. Tectonically deformed, intensively folded/faulted, sheared clayey shale or siltstone with broken and deformed sandstone layers forming an almost chaotic structure

G. Undisturbed silty or clayey shale with or without a few very thin sandstone layers

H. Tectonically deformed silty or clayey shale forming a chaotic structure with pockets of clay. Thin layers of sandstone are transformed into small rock pieces.

⇢ : Means deformation after tectonic disturbance

*Table 4.5* Values of constant $m_i$ for intact rock by rock Group (values in parenthesis are estimates)

| Rock type | Class | Group | Texture | | | |
|---|---|---|---|---|---|---|
| | | | Coarse | Medium | Fine | Very fine |
| SEDIMENTARY | Clastic | | Conglomerates (21±3)  Breccias (19±5) | Sandstones 17±4 | Siltstones 7±2  Greywackes (18±3) | Claystones 4±2  Shales (6±2)  Marls (7±2) |
| | Non-Clastic | Carbonates | Crystalline Limestone (12±3) | Sparitic Limestones (10±2) | Micritic Limestones (9±2) | Dolomites (9±3) |
| | | Evaporites | | Gypsum 8±2 | Anhydrite 12±2 | |
| | | Organic | | | | Chalk 7±2 |
| METAMORPHIC | Non foliated | | Marble 9±3 | Hornfels (19±4)  Metasandstone (19±3) | Quartzites 20±3 | |
| | Slightly foliated | | Migmatite (29±3) | Amphibolites 26±6 | Gneiss 28±5 | |
| | Foliated* | | | Schists 12±3 | Phyllites (7±3) | Slates 7±4 |
| IGNEOUS | Plutonic | Light | Granite 32±3    Diorite 25±5  Granodiorite (29±3) | | | |
| | | Dark | Gabbro 27±3  Norite 20±5 | Dolerite (16±5) | | |
| | Hypabyssal | | Porphyries (20±5) | | Diabase (15±5) | Peridotite (25±5) |
| | Volcanic | Lava | | Rhyolite (25±5)  Andesite 25±5 | Dacite (25±3)  Basalt (25±5) | Obsidian (19±3) |
| | | Pyroclastic | Agglomerate (19±3) | Breccia (19±5) | Tuff (13±5) | |

* These values are for intact rock specimens tested normal to bedding or foliation. The value of $m_i$ will be significantly different if failure occurs along a weakness plane.

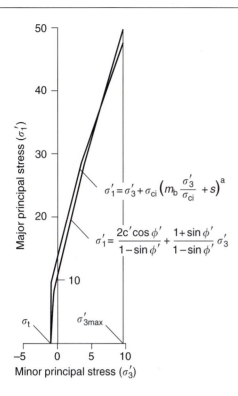

*Figure 4.22* Relationships between major and minor principal stresses for Hoek–Brown and equivalent Mohr–Coulomb criteria.

Equation (4.19) is obtained by setting $\sigma_1' = \sigma_3' = \sigma_t$ in equation (4.14). This represents a condition of biaxial tension. Hoek (1983) showed that, for brittle materials, the uniaxial tensile strength is equal to the biaxial tensile strength.

Note that the "switch" at GSI = 25 for the coefficients $s$ and $a$ (Hoek and Brown, 1997) has been eliminated in equations (4.16) and (4.17) which give smooth continuous transitions for the entire range of *GSI* values.[1]

Normal and shear stresses are related to principal stresses by the equations published by

Balmer[2] (1952):

$$\sigma_n' = \frac{\sigma_1' + \sigma_3'}{2} - \frac{\sigma_1' - \sigma_3'}{2}\left(\frac{d\sigma_1'/d\sigma_3' - 1}{d\sigma_1'/d\sigma_3' + 1}\right)$$
(4.20)

$$\tau = (\sigma_1' - \sigma_3')\frac{\sqrt{d\sigma_1'/d\sigma_3'}}{d\sigma_1'/d\sigma_3' + 1}$$
(4.21)

where

$$d\sigma_1'/d\sigma_3' = 1 + am_b(m_b\sigma_3'/\sigma_{ci} + s)^{a-1}$$
(4.22)

### 4.5.2 Modulus of deformation

The Hoek–Brown failure criterion also allows the rock mass modulus of deformation to be calculated as follows:

$$E_m = \left(1 - \frac{D}{2}\right)\sqrt{\frac{\sigma_{ci}}{100}}\, 10^{((GSI-10)/40)}$$

(units: GPa)  (4.23)

Note that the original equation proposed by Hoek and Brown (1997) has been modified, by the inclusion of the factor $D$, to allow for the effects of blast damage and stress relaxation.

The principal use of the rock mass modulus of deformation is in numerical analysis to calculate strain in rock slopes (see Chapter 10).

### 4.5.3 Mohr–Coulomb criterion

The analysis of slope stability involves examination of the shear strength of the rock mass on the sliding surface expressed by the Mohr–Coulomb failure criterion. Therefore, it is necessary to determine friction angles and cohesive strengths that are equivalent between the Hoek–Brown and Mohr–Coulomb criteria. These strengths are required for each rock mass and stress range along the sliding surface. This is done by fitting an average linear relationship to the curve generated by

---

1 Note that the numerical values of $s$ and $a$, given by equations (4.16) and (4.17), are very close to those given by the previous equations in Hoek and Brown (1997) and it is not necessary to revisit and make corrections to old calculations.

2 The original equations derived by Balmer contained errors that have been corrected in equations (4.20) and (4.21).

solving equation (4.14) for a range of minor principal stress values defined by $\sigma_t < \sigma_3 < \sigma_{3\,max}$, as illustrated in Figure 4.22. The fitting process involves balancing the areas above and below the Mohr–Coulomb plot. This results in the following equations for the angle of friction $\phi'$ and cohesive strength $c'$ (Figure 4.23):

$$\phi' = \sin^{-1}\left[\frac{6am_b(s + m_b\sigma'_{3n})^{a-1}}{2(1 + a)(2 + a) + 6am_b(s + m_b\sigma'_{3n})^{a-1}}\right]$$

(4.24)

$$c' = (\sigma_{ci}\left[(1 + 2a)s + (1 - a)m_b\sigma'_{3n}\right](s + m_b\sigma'_{3n})^{a-1})$$

$$/\left[(1 + a)(2 + a)\right.$$

$$\left.\times\sqrt{1 + (6am_b(s + m_b\sigma'_{3n})^{a-1})/((1 + a)(2 + a))}\right]$$

(4.25)

where $\sigma_{3n} = \sigma'_{3\,max}/\sigma_{ci}$.

Note that the value of $\sigma_{3\,max}$, the upper limit of confining stress over which the relationship between the Hoek–Brown and the Mohr–Coulomb criteria is considered, has to be determined for each individual case. Guidelines for selecting these values for slopes are presented in Section 4.5.5.

The Mohr–Coulomb shear strength $\tau$, for a given normal stress $\sigma$, is found by substitution of these values of $c'$ and $\phi'$ into the following equation:

$$\tau = c' + \sigma\tan\phi'$$

(4.26)

The equivalent plot, in terms of the major and minor principal stresses, is defined by

$$\sigma'_1 = \frac{2c'\cos\phi'}{1 - \sin\phi'} + \frac{1 + \sin\phi'}{1 - \sin\phi'}\sigma'_3$$

(4.27)

### 4.5.4  Rock mass strength

The uniaxial compressive strength of the rock mass $\sigma_c$ is given by equation (4.18). For underground excavations, instability initiates at the boundary of the excavation when the compressive strength $\sigma_c$ is exceeded by the stress induced on

that boundary. The failure propagates from this initiation point into the biaxial stress field and it eventually stabilizes when the local strength, defined by equation (4.14), is higher than the induced stresses $\sigma'_1$ and $\sigma'_3$. Most numerical models can follow this process of fracture propagation and this level of detailed analysis is very important when considering the stability of excavations in rock and designing support systems.

However, for slope stability, failure is initiated along a sliding surface within the slope where the rock is subject to a biaxial stress field and it is useful to consider the overall behavior of a rock mass rather than the detailed failure propagation process described earlier. This leads to the concept of a global "rock mass strength" and Hoek and Brown (1997) proposed that this could be estimated from the Mohr–Coulomb relationship:

$$\sigma'_{cm} = \frac{2c'\cos\phi'}{1 - \sin\phi'}$$

(4.28)

with $c'$ and $\phi'$ determined for the stress range $\sigma_t < \sigma'_3 < \sigma_{ci}/4$ giving the following value for the rock mass strength $\sigma'_{cm}$:

$$\sigma'_{cm} = \sigma_{ci}\frac{(m_b + 4s - a(m_b - 8s))(m_b/4 + s)^{a-1}}{2(1 + a)(2 + a)}$$

(4.29)

### 4.5.5  Determination of $\sigma'_{3\,max}$

The issue of determining the appropriate value of $\sigma'_{3\,max}$ for use in equations (4.24) and (4.25) depends upon the specific application. For the case of slopes, it is necessary that the calculated factor of safety and the shape and location of the failure surface be equivalent. Stability studies of rock slopes using Bishop's circular failure analysis for a wide range of slope geometries and rock mass properties have been carried out for both Generalized Hoek–Brown and Mohr–Coulomb criteria to find the value of $\sigma'_{3\,max}$ that gives equivalent characteristic curves. These analyses gave the following relationship between $\sigma'_{3\,max}$ the rock mass strength

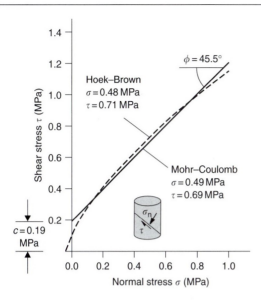

*Figure 4.23* Non-linear Mohr envelope for fractured rock mass defined by equations (4.24) and (4.25); best fit line shows cohesion and friction angle for applicable slope height. Rock mass parameters: $\sigma_c = 30\,\text{MPa}$, GSI = 50, $m_i = 10$, $D = 0.7$, $H = 20\,\text{m}$, $\gamma = 0.026\,\text{MN/m}^3$.

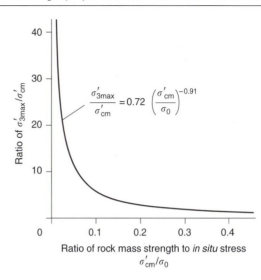

*Figure 4.24* Relationship for the calculation of $\sigma'_{3\,\text{max}}$ for equivalent Mohr–Coulomb and Hoek–Brown parameters for slopes.

$\sigma'_{cm}$ and the stress level on the sliding surface, $\sigma_0$ (Figure 4.24):

$$\frac{\sigma'_{3\,\text{max}}}{\sigma'_{cm}} = 0.72 \left(\frac{\sigma'_{cm}}{\sigma_0}\right)^{-0.91} \qquad (4.30)$$

The stress level on the sliding surface is related to the slope height $H$ and the unit weight of the rock $\gamma_r$ is given by

$$\sigma_0 = H \cdot \gamma_r \qquad (4.31)$$

### 4.5.6 *Estimation of disturbance factor D*

Experience in the design of slopes in very large open pit mines has shown that the Hoek–Brown criterion for undisturbed *in situ* rock masses ($D = 0$) results in rock mass properties that are too optimistic (Pierce *et al.*, 2001; Sjöberg *et al.*, 2001). The effects of heavy blast damage as well as stress relief due to removal of the overburden

result in disturbance of the rock mass (Hoek and Brown, 1988). It is considered that the "disturbed" rock mass properties using $D = 1$ in equations (4.14) and (4.15) are more appropriate for these rock masses.

A number of other studies to assess the degree of disturbance of the rock mass have been carried out by observing the performance of surface and underground excavations. For example, Lorig and Varona (2001) showed that factors such as the lateral confinement produced by different radii of curvature of slopes (in plan) as compared with their height also have an influence on the degree of disturbance. Also, Sonmez and Ulusay (1999) back-analyzed five slope failures in open pit coal mines in Turkey and attempted to assign disturbance factors to each rock mass based upon their assessment of the rock mass properties predicted by the Hoek–Brown criterion. Unfortunately, one of the slope failures appears to be structurally controlled while another consists of a transported waste pile. Hoek considers that the Hoek–Brown criterion is not applicable to these two cases. In addition, Cheng and Liu (1990) report the results of very careful back analysis of deformation measurements, from extensometers placed before the commencement of excavation, in the Mingtan power cavern in Taiwan. It was found that a zone of blast damage extended for a distance of approximately 2 m around all large excavations. The back-calculated strength and deformation properties of the damaged rock mass give an equivalent disturbance factor $D = 0.7$.

From these references it is clear that a large number of factors can influence the degree of disturbance in the rock mass surrounding an excavation, and that it may never be possible to quantify these factors precisely. However, based on experience and on the analysis of the details contained in these papers, Hoek *et al.* (2002) have drawn up a set of guidelines for estimating the factor $D$ (Table 4.6).

The influence of this disturbance factor can be large. This is illustrated by a typical example in which $\sigma_{ci} = 50$ MPa, $m_i = 10$ and GSI $= 45$. For an undisturbed *in situ* rock mass surrounding a tunnel at a depth of 100 m, with a disturbance factor $D = 0$, the equivalent friction angle is $\phi' = 47.16°$ while the cohesive strength is $c' = 0.58$ MPa. A rock mass with the same basic parameters but in highly disturbed slope of 100 m height, with a disturbance factor of $D = 1$, has an equivalent friction angle of $\phi' = 27.61°$ and a cohesive strength of $c' = 0.35$ MPa.

Note that these are guidelines only, and the reader would be well advised to apply the values given with caution, and to compare the calculated results with those obtained by back analysis as shown in Figure 4.21. It is considered that the Hoek–Brown calculations can be used to provide a realistic starting point for any design and, if the observed or measured performance of the excavation turns out to be better than predicted, the disturbance factors can be adjusted downwards.

These methods have all been implemented in a Windows program called "RocLab" that can be downloaded (free) from www.rocscience.com. This program includes tables and charts for estimating the uniaxial compressive strength of the intact rock elements ($\sigma_{ci}$), the material constant $m_i$, the Geological Strength Index (GSI) and Disturbance Factor (D).

## 4.6   Rock durability and compressive strength

The strength parameters that are usually of most significance to the analysis of slope stability are the cohesion and friction angle on the sliding surface, as discussed previously in this chapter. However, both the durability and compressive strength of the rock may be of importance depending on the geological and stress conditions at the site, as discussed later. The durability and compressive strength test procedures are index tests best used to classify and compare one rock with another; if necessary, the index measurements can be calibrated by more precise laboratory tests.

### 4.6.1   Slake durability

Widely occurring rock materials are prone to degradation when exposed to weathering processes such as wetting and drying, and freezing and thawing cycles. Rock types that are particularly susceptible to degradation are shale and mudstone, which usually have a high clay content. The degradation can take the form of swelling, and the time over which weakening and disintegration can occur after exposure may range from minutes to years. The effect of degradation on slope stability can range from surficial sloughing and gradual retreat of the face to slope failures resulting from the loss of strength with time (Wu *et al.*, 1981). In sedimentary formations comprising alternating beds of resistant sandstone and relatively degradable shale, the weathering process can develop overhangs in the sandstone and produce a rock fall hazard due to sudden failure of the sandstone (see Figure 1.4(e)).

A simple index test of the tendency of rock to weather and degrade is the slake durability test (ISRM, 1981a) (Figure 4.25). It is important that undisturbed samples are used that have not been excessively broken in the sampling procedure, or allowed to freeze. The test procedure comprises placing the sample in the wire mesh drum, drying it in an oven at 105° for 2–6 hours, and then weighing the dry sample. The drum is then partially submerged in water and rotated

*Table 4.6* Guidelines for estimating disturbance factor *D*

| Appearance of rock mass | Description of rock mass | Suggested value of D |
| --- | --- | --- |
| | Excellent quality controlled blasting or excavation by Tunnel Boring Machine results in minimal disturbance to the confined rock mass surrounding a tunnel. | $D = 0$ |
| | Mechanical or hand excavation in poor quality rock masses (no blasting) results in minimal disturbance to the surrounding rock mass. | $D = 0$ |
|  | Where squeezing problems result in significant floor heave, disturbance can be severe unless a temporary invert, as shown in the photograph, is placed. | $D = 0.5$ No invert |
| | Very poor quality blasting in a hard rock tunnel results in severe local damage, extending 2 or 3 m, in the surrounding rock mass. | $D = 0.8$ |

*(Table 4.6 continued)*

*Table 4.6* Continued

| Appearance of rock mass | Description of rock mass | Suggested value of D |
|---|---|---|
|  | Small-scale blasting in civil engineering slopes results in modest rock mass damage, particularly if controlled blasting is used as shown on the left hand side of the photograph. However, stress relief results in some disturbance. | $D = 0.7$ Good blasting $D = 1.0$ Poor blasting |
| | Very large open pit mine slopes suffer significant disturbance due to heavy production blasting, and also due to stress relief from overburden removal. | $D = 1.0$ Production blasting |
| | In some softer rocks, excavation can be carried out by ripping and dozing, and the degree of damage to the slopes is less. | $D = 0.7$ Mechanical excavation |

at 20 revolutions per minute for a period of 10 minutes. The drum is then dried a second time and the loss of weight recorded. The test cycle is then repeated and the slake durability index is calculated as the percentage ratio of final to initial dry sample masses. A low slake durability index will indicate that the rock is susceptible to degradation when exposed. For highly degradable rocks, it is useful to carry out soil classification tests such as Atterberg limits, as well as X-ray diffraction tests to identify clay mineral types and determine if swelling clays such as bentonites and montmorillonites are present.

### 4.6.2 *Compressive strength*

In many slopes in moderately strong to strong rock, the stress level due to gravity loads will be less than the strength of the rock. Therefore, there will be little tendency for intact rock within the slope to fracture, and consequently compressive strength is a less important design parameter than shear strength. The compressive strength of the rock on the sliding surface is only used indirectly in stability analysis when determining the roughness of a fracture (JCS term in equation (4.7)), and in the application of the Hoek–Brown strength criteria (Section 4.5). For both these applications, it is satisfactory to use an estimate of the compressive strength because the results are not particularly sensitive to the value of this parameter. The compressive strength is also used in evaluating excavation methods and costs. For example, the progress rate for blast hole drilling and excavation by ripping, as well as selection of explosive types and design of blasts

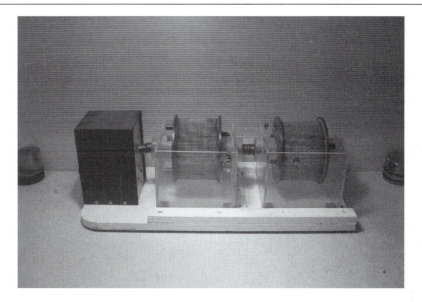

*Figure 4.25* Slake durability testing equipment.

are all influenced by the compressive strength of the rock.

The point load test is an appropriate method to estimate the compressive strength for rock slope design (Figure 4.26(a)). The equipment is portable, and tests can be carried out quickly and inexpensively in the field on both core and lump samples (ISRM, 1985). Because the point load test provides an index value for the strength, usual practice is to calibrate the results with a limited number of uniaxial compressive tests on prepared core samples.

The test procedure involves placing the sample between the platens and applying a load with the hydraulic jack to break the sample in tension. If $P$ is the point load breaking strength, then the point load index, $I_s$ is given by

$$I_s = \frac{P}{D_e^2} \tag{4.32}$$

where $D_e$ is the equivalent core diameter, defined as

$$D_e^2 = D^2 \text{ (diametral tests where } D \text{ is the core diameter)}$$

or

$$D_e^2 = \frac{4WD}{\pi} \text{ (axial, block or lump tests)}$$

where $W$ is the specimen width and $D$ is the distance between the platens. The term $(WD)$ is the minimum cross-sectional area of a lump sample for the plane through the platen contact points.

The size-corrected point load strength index $I_{s(50)}$ of a rock specimen is defined as the value of $I_s$ that would have been measured by a diametral test with $D = 50\,\text{mm}$. For tests conducted on samples with dimensions different from 50 mm, the results can be standardized to a size-corrected point load strength index by applying a correction factor $k_{PLT}$ as follows:

$$I_{s(50)} = I_s k_{PLT} \tag{4.33}$$

The value of the size-correction factor $k_{PLT}$ is shown in Figure 4.26(b) and is given by

$$k_{PLT} = \left(\frac{D_e}{50}\right)^{0.45} \tag{4.34}$$

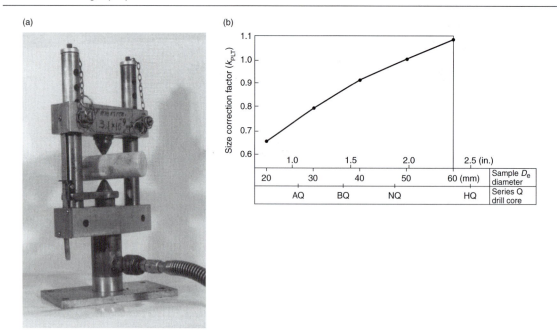

*Figure 4.26* Point load testing: (a) point load test equipment; and (b) relationship between sample equivalent core diameter $D_e$, and size correction factor $k_{PLT}$.

It has been found, on average, that the uniaxial compressive strength is about 20–25 times the point load strength index. However, tests on many different types of rock show that the ratio can vary between 15 and 50, especially for anisotropic rocks. Consequently, the most reliable results are obtained if uniaxial calibration tests are carried out.

Point load test results are not acceptable if the failure plane lies partially along a pre-existing fracture in the rock, or is not coincident with the line between the platens. For tests in weak rock where the platens indent the rock, the test results should be adjusted by measuring the amount of indentation and correcting the distance $D$.

If no equipment is available to measure the compressive strength, simple field observations can be used to estimate the strength with sufficient accuracy for most purposes. Table 3.1 describes a series of field index tests and observations of rock behavior, and gives the corresponding range of approximate compressive strengths.

## 4.7  Example Problem 4.1: analysis of direct shear strength test results

*Statement*

The following table of results was obtained from a direct shear box test on a planar discontinuity in a sample of weathered granite. The average normal pressure on the sample was 200 kPa.

| Shear stress (kPa) | Shear displacement (mm) |
|---|---|
| 159 | 0.05 |
| 200 | 1.19 |
| 241 | 3.61 |
| 228 | 4.50 |
| 214 | 8.51 |
| 207 | 9.40 |
| 200 | 11.61 |
| 193 | 12.60 |
| 179 | 17.09 |
| 179 | 19.81 |

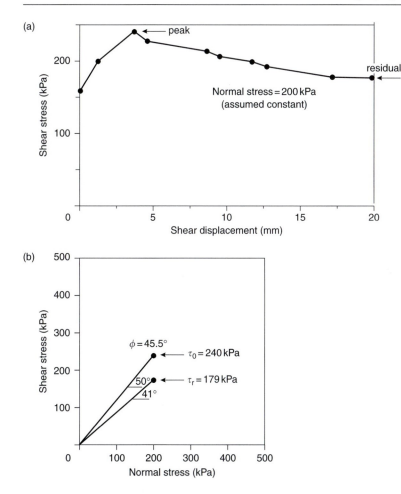

*Figure 4.27* Analysis of direct shear strength tests, Example Problem 4.1: (a) plot of shear stress against shear displacement; (b) plot of shear stress against normal stress.

*Required*

(a) Plot a graph of shear stress against shear displacement with shear stress on the vertical axis; from the graph determine the peak and residual shear strengths of the surface.

(b) Plot a graph of the peak and residual shear strengths (on the vertical axis) against the average normal stress on the surface; from the graph determine the peak and residual friction angles of the surface.

*Solution*

(a) The graph of shear stress against shear displacement is shown on Figure 4.27(a); the

peak strength is 241 kPa and the residual strength is 179 kPa.

(b) The graph of shear stress against normal stress is shown in Figure 4.27(b); the peak friction angle is 50.3° and the residual friction angle is 41.8°.

## 4.8  Example Problem 4.2: analysis of point load test results

*Statement*

A series of point load tests on pieces of NQ core 48 mm in diameter gave an average point load breaking strength ($P$) of 17.76 kN when the core was loaded diametrically.

*Required*

Determine the approximate average uniaxial compressive strength of the samples.

*Solution*

The point load strength index ($I_s$) is calculated from the point load breaking strength by

$$I_s = P/D^2$$

where $D$ is the core diameter of 48 mm.

$$I_s = 17.76\text{E}3/(0.048)^2 = 7.71\,\text{MPa}$$

Correction factor,

$$k_{PLT} = (48/50)^{0.48} = 0.98$$

The size-corrected point load strength,

$$I_{s(50)} = I_s k_{PLT} = 7.71 \cdot 0.98 = 7.56\,\text{MPa}$$

The approximate compressive strength of the rock samples,

$$\sigma_{ci} \approx 24 \cdot 7.56 \approx 180\,\text{MPa}$$

# Chapter 5

# Ground water

## 5.1 Introduction

The presence of ground water in a rock slope can have a detrimental effect upon stability for the following reasons:

- *Water pressure* reduces the stability of the slopes by diminishing the shear strength of potential failure surfaces as described in Chapter 1. Water pressure in tension cracks or similar near vertical fissures reduces stability by increasing the forces that induce sliding.
- Changes in *moisture content* of some rock, particularly shales, can cause accelerated weathering and a decrease in shear strength.
- *Freezing* of ground water can cause wedging in water-filled fissures due to temperature-dependent volume changes in the ice. Also, freezing of surface water on slopes can block drainage paths resulting in a build-up of water pressure in the slope with a consequent decrease in stability.
- *Erosion* of weathered rock by surface water, and of low strength infillings by ground water can result in local instability where the toe of a slope is undermined, or a block of rock is loosened.
- *Excavation costs* can be increased when working below the water table. For example, wet blast holes require the use of water-resistant explosives that are more expensive than non-water-resistant ANFO. Also, flow of ground water into the excavation or pit will require pumping and possibly treatment of the discharge water, and equipment trafficability may be poor on wet haul roads.

By far the most important effect of ground water in a rock mass is the reduction in stability resulting from water pressures within the discontinuities. Methods for including these water pressures in stability calculations and designing drainage systems are dealt with in later chapters of this book. This chapter describes the hydrologic cycle (Section 5.2), methods that are used to analyze the flow of water through fractured rock, and the pressures developed by this flow (Sections 5.3 and 5.4). Sections 5.5 and 5.6 discuss, respectively methods of making hydraulic conductivity and pressure measurements in the field.

In examining rock or soil slopes, it may be a mistake to assume that ground water is not present if no seepage appears on the slope face. The seepage rate may be lower than the evaporation rate, and hence the slope surface may appear dry and yet there may be water at significant pressure within the rock mass. It is water pressure, and not rate of flow, which is responsible for instability in slopes and it is essential that measurement or calculation of this water pressure forms part of site investigations for stability studies. Drainage, which is discussed in Chapter 12, is one of the most effective and economical means available for improving the stability of rock slopes. Rational design of drainage systems is only possible if the water flow pattern within the rock mass is understood, and measurement of hydraulic conductivity and water pressure provides the key to this understanding.

A useful means of assessing ground water conditions in a slope is to make observations during periods of below freezing temperatures. At these times even minor seeps on the face may form icicles that can show both the location of the water tables, and the set(s) of discontinuities in which flow is occurring.

## 5.2   The hydrologic cycle

A simplified hydrologic cycle illustrated in Figure 5.1 shows some typical sources of ground water, and emphasizes that ground water can travel considerable distances through a rock mass. It is important, therefore, to consider the regional geology of an area when starting a rock slope design program. In general, ground water flows from recharge areas to discharge areas. A recharge area is one in which the net saturated flow of ground water is directed away from the water table, while in a discharge area the net saturated flow is directed towards the water table. In Figure 5.1, discharge areas occur at the rock cut, tailings dam and open pit, and there is a recharge area from the ocean to the pit.

Clearly, precipitation in the catchment area is the most important source of ground water, and Figure 5.2 illustrates the typical relationship between the precipitation and ground water levels in three climatic regions. In tropical and desert climates the ground water table is usually more predictable and consistent than temperate climates where the precipitation levels are more variable. In assessing the relationship between climate and ground water levels in the slope, both the average precipitation and the peak events should be considered because the peak events are those that usually cause instability. Examples of peak precipitation events that can lead to high infiltration rates include typhoons, intense rainstorms and rapid snowmelt. If these climatic conditions exist at the site, then it is advisable to use correspondingly high water pressures in design, or to design high-capacity drainage systems.

Sources of ground water in addition to precipitation may include recharge from adjacent rivers, tailings dams, reservoirs or the ocean as shown in Figure 5.1. There are several instances of substantial quarries and open pit mines (e.g. Dutra Minerals in California, and

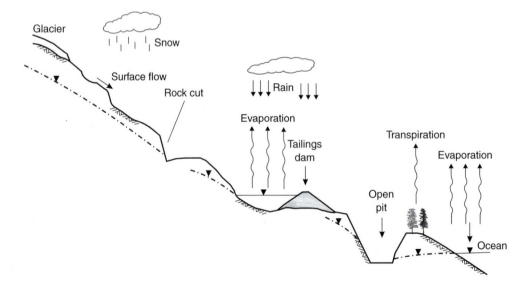

*Figure 5.1* Simplified representation of a hydrologic cycle showing some typical sources of ground water (modified from Davis and de Wiest (1966)).

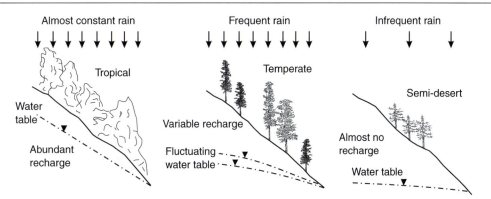

*Figure 5.2* Relationship between water table level and precipitation (modified from Davis and de Wiest (1966)).

Granisle Copper and Island Copper in Canada) that successfully operated below, and close to, substantial bodies of water. However, in such operations significant seepage may develop into the pit, as well as instability resulting from high water pressures.

Another important factor influencing ground water within a slope is distribution of rock types, and details of the structural geology such as fault infillings, persistence of joint sets and the presence of solution cavities. These features can result in regions of low and high hydraulic conductivity within the slope that are termed aquitards and aquifers, respectively. These matters are discussed in more detail in Section 5.4 later in this chapter.

## 5.3   Hydraulic conductivity and flow nets

Where ground water effects are to be included in slope design, there are two possible approaches to obtaining data on distributions of the water pressures within a rock mass:

(a) Deduction of the ground water flow pattern from consideration of the hydraulic conductivity of the rock mass and sources of ground water.

(b) Direct measurement of water levels in boreholes or wells, or of water pressure by means of piezometers installed in boreholes.

Because of the important influence of water pressure on slope stability, it is essential that the best possible estimates of the likely range of pressures should be available before a detailed stability analysis is attempted. There are a large number of factors that control ground water flow in jointed rock masses, and it is only possible in this book to highlight the general principles that may apply. If detailed studies of ground water conditions are required, it is advisable to obtain additional data from such sources as Freeze and Cherry (1979) and Cedergren (1989) on ground water flow analysis, and Dunnicliff (1993) on instrumentation.

### 5.3.1   Hydraulic conductivity

The basic parameter defining the flow of ground water, and the distribution of water pressure, in geologic media is hydraulic conductivity. This parameter relates the flow rate of water through the material to the pressure gradient applied across it (Scheidegger, 1960; Morgenstern, 1971).

Consider a cylindrical sample of soil or rock beneath the water table in a slope as illustrated in Figure 5.3. The sample has a cross-sectional area of $A$ and length $l$. Water levels in boreholes at either end of this sample are at heights $h_1$ and $h_2$ above a reference datum and the quantity of water flowing through the sample in a unit of time is $Q$. According to Darcy's law, the coefficient of hydraulic conductivity $K$ of this sample is defined as

$$K = \frac{Ql}{A(h_1 - h_2)} = \frac{Vl}{(h_1 - h_2)} \qquad (5.1)$$

where $V$ is the discharge velocity. Substitution of dimensions for the terms in equation (5.1) shows that the hydraulic conductivity $K$ has the same dimensions as the discharge velocity $V$, that is length per unit time. The units most commonly used in ground water studies is centimeters per second, and a number of hydraulic conductivity conversion factors are given in Table 5.1.

Equation (5.1) can be rearranged to show the volume of water, $Q$ flowing through the sample shown in Figure 5.3 under a specified

head, as follows:

$$Q = \frac{KA(h_1 - h_2)}{l} \qquad (5.2)$$

In most rock types flow through intact rock is negligible (defined by $K_{primary}$), and essentially all flow occurs along the discontinuities (defined by $K_{secondary}$). For example, the primary hydraulic conductivity for intact granite and basalt is about $10^{-10}$ cm/sec, while for some coarse grained, poorly indurated sandstones the primary hydraulic conductivity may be as high as $10^{-4}$ cm/sec. The term secondary hydraulic conductivity refers to flow in the rock mass and encompasses flow in both the intact rock and any discontinuities that are present. These conditions result in secondary hydraulic conductivities having a wide range of values depending on the persistence, width and infilling characteristics of the discontinuities. For example, granite that has a very low primary hydraulic conductivity usually contains tight, clean, low persistence joints, so the secondary hydraulic conductivity is also low. In contrast, sandstone may have some primary conductivity, and the presence of persistent bedding planes may result in high secondary conductivity in the direction parallel to the bedding. For further discussion on flow in fractured rock see Section 5.4.

*Table 5.1* Hydraulic conductivity conversion table

| To convert cm/s to | Multiply by |
| --- | --- |
| m/s | $1.00 \times 10^{-2}$ |
| ft/s | $3.28 \times 10^{-2}$ |
| US gal/day/ft$^2$ | $2.12 \times 10^{4}$ |
| ft/year | $1.03 \times 10^{6}$ |
| m/year | $3.14 \times 10^{5}$ |

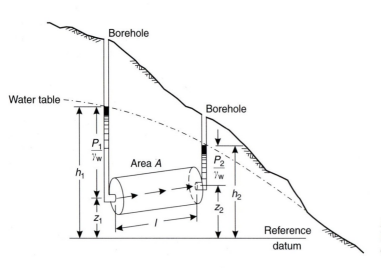

*Figure 5.3* Illustration of Darcy's Law for definition of hydraulic conductivity.

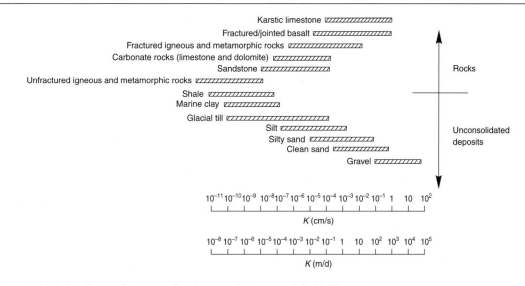

*Figure 5.4* Hydraulic conductivity of various geologic materials (Atkinson, 2000).

Typical ranges of secondary hydraulic conductivity for a variety rock types, as well as unconsolidated deposits, are shown in Figure 5.4. The range of hydraulic conductivities for geological materials covers 13 orders of magnitude, and for any single rock type the range can be four orders of magnitude. This shows the difficulty in predicting water inflow quantities and pressures within slopes.

Figure 5.3 also shows that the total head $h$ at any point can be expressed in terms of the pressure $P$ and the height $z$ above a reference datum. The relationship between these parameters is

$$h = \frac{P}{\gamma_w} + z \qquad (5.3)$$

where $\gamma_w$ is the density of water. The total head $h$ represents the level to which water will rise in a borehole standpipe.

Darcy's law is applicable to porous media and so can be used to study ground water flow in both intact rock, and rock masses on a macroscopic scale. However, it is required that the flow be laminar, so Darcy's law is not applicable in the event of non-linear or turbulent flow in an individual fracture.

### 5.3.2  Porosity

The total volume $V_T$ of a rock or soil is made up of the volume of solid portion $V_s$ and the volume of the voids $V_v$. The porosity, $n$, of a geologic material is defined as the ratio:

$$n = \frac{V_v}{V_T} \qquad (5.4)$$

In general, rocks have lower porosities than soil. For example, the porosities of sand and clay are in the range of 25–50% respectively. In comparison, fractured basalt and karstic limestone may have porosities in the range of 5–50%, while the porosity of dense crystalline rock is usually in the range of 0–5%.

The significance of the porosity to rock slopes is in the design of drainage systems. For example, drains installed in a low porosity granite need only discharge a small amount of water to lower the water pressures, while drains in karstic limestone may discharge large volumes of water with little effect on the ground water table.

### 5.3.3  Flow nets

The graphical representation of ground water flow in a rock or soil mass is known as a flow net

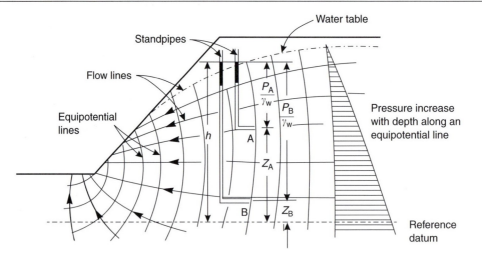

*Figure 5.5* Two-dimensional flow net in a slope.

and a typical example is illustrated in Figure 5.5. A flow net comprises two sets of intersecting lines as follows:

(i) *Flow lines* are paths followed by the water in flowing through the saturated rock or soil.
(ii) *Equipotential lines* are lines joining points at which the total head $h$ is the same. As shown in Figure 5.5, the water level is the same in standpipes that terminate at points $A$ and $B$ on the same equipotential line. Water pressures at points $A$ and $B$ are not the same since, according to equation (5.3), the total head $h$ is given by the sum of the pressure head $P/\gamma_w$, and the elevation $z$ of the measuring point above the reference datum. The water pressure increases with depth along an equipotential line.

There are characteristics of flow nets that are applicable under all conditions and must be used in drawing flow nets. First, equipotential lines must meet impermeable boundaries at right angles and be parallel to constant head boundaries. Second, there is a uniform head loss between adjacent equipotential lines. Third, equipotential and flow lines intersect at right angles to form curve-linear squares in rock with isotropic hydraulic conductivity. For a flow net such as that

shown in Figure 5.5, the equipotential lines illustrate how the ground water pressure varies within the slope, and that flow quantity is equal between the adjacent flow lines.

An example of the application of flow nets to study the distribution of pressures in rock slopes is illustrated in Figure 5.6. If the pit is located in a recharge area, flow occurs towards the pit, and artesian pressures can be developed below the pit floor (a, b). In contrast, for pits in discharge areas, flow is away from the pit and there will be low pressures below the pit floor (c, d).

A complete discussion on the construction or computation of flow nets exceeds the scope of this book and the interested reader is referred to the comprehensive texts by Cedergren (1989), Haar (1962) and Freeze and Cherry (1979) for further details. The use of graphical methods for constructing flow nets is often an important step in understanding how geology and drainage systems influence possible ground water conditions within a slope.

## 5.4 Ground water flow in fractured rock

As discussed in Section 5.2 on hydraulic conductivity, ground water flow in fractured rock masses occurs predominately along the discontinuities

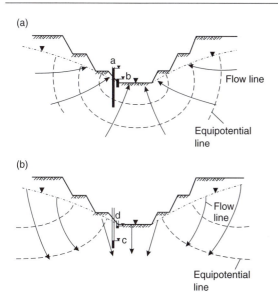

(a)

a

b

Flow line

Equipotential
line

(b)

d

c

Flow
line

Equipotential
line

*Figure 5.6* Ground water conditions for pit slopes in regional (a) discharge and (b) recharge areas (Patton and Deere, 1971).

*Figure 5.7* Rock mass with persistent vertical joints and relatively high vertical hydraulic conductivity (modified from Atkinson (2000)).

because of the very low primary hydraulic conductivity of most intact rock. Therefore, the conductivity of rock masses will be influenced by the characteristics of the discontinuities, with a necessary condition required for flow being that the persistence of the discontinuities is greater than the spacing. Figure 5.7 shows a rock mass containing two vertical joint sets and one horizontal set in which the persistence of the vertical joints is much greater than the spacing, but the persistence of the horizontal set is less than the spacing. For these conditions, the hydraulic conductivity would be significantly greater in the vertical direction than that in the horizontal direction.

The analysis of flow in fractured rock can be carried out either assuming that the rock is a *continuum*, as has been assumed in the derivation of Darcy's equation and drawing flow nets, or that the rock is a *non-continuum* in which laminar flow occurs in individual discontinuities. Rock can be assumed a continuum if the discontinuities spacing is sufficiently close that the fractured rock acts hydraulically as a granular porous media so that the flow occurs through a number of discontinuities.

### 5.4.1 *Flow in clean, smooth discontinuities*

The flow of water through fissures in rock has been studied in detail by Huitt (1956), Snow (1968), Louis (1969), Sharp (1970), Maini (1971) andothers. Subsequent to this, extensive research has been carried out on this topic in relation to the design of underground nuclear waste storage facilities; this work has provided much additional information on fluid flow in fractured rock. However, for the purpose of this discussion, the problem is simplified to that of the determination of the equivalent hydraulic conductivity of an array of parallel, smooth, clean discontinuities (Davis, 1969). The hydraulic conductivity parallel to this array is given by

$$K \approx \frac{ge^3}{12vb} \tag{5.5}$$

where $g$ is the gravitational acceleration (9.81 m/s$^2$), $e$ and $b$ are respectively the discontinuity aperture and spacing, and $v$ is

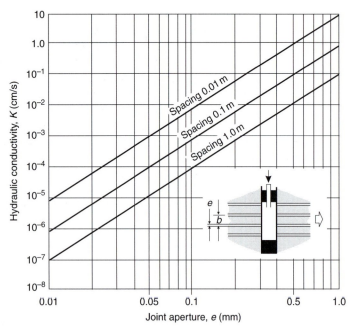

*Figure 5.8* Influence of joint aperture $e$ and spacing $b$ on hydraulic conductivity $K$ in the direction of a set of smooth parallel joints in a rock mass.

the coefficient of kinematic viscosity ($1.01 \times 10^{-6}$ m²/s for pure water at 20°C).

The equivalent conductivity of a parallel array of discontinuities in relation to aperture and spacing is shown in Figure 5.8. Since the hydraulic conductivity is proportional to the third power of the aperture, small changes in the aperture due, for example, to increasing stress in the rock will significantly decrease the conductivity. This condition could develop at the toe of a steep slope where high stresses decrease the aperture and result in a build up of water pressure in the slope.

Figures 5.4 and 5.8 demonstrate the application of equation (5.5) to the actual hydraulic conductivities of rock masses. For example, the conductivity of sandstone is about $10^{-6}$ cm/s, while that of fractured and jointed basalt is about $10^{-2}$ cm/s. This difference in conductivity of four orders of magnitude can be attributed to the joint spacing decreasing from 1 to 0.1 m, and the aperture increasing by a small amount from 0.02 to 0.2 mm.

The relationship between discontinuity aperture and hydraulic conductivity was studied for the construction of the ship locks at the Three Gorges Project in China, which involved making parallel excavations with depths up to 170 m in strong, jointed granite (Zhang *et al.*, 1999). The excavations caused relaxation of the rock in the walls of the locks and the opening of the joints, which resulted in the hydraulic conductivity increasing by a factor of 18. The application of a support pressure of 2 MPa on the vertical walls of the excavation resulted in the hydraulic conductivity only increasing by a factor of 6 from the *in situ* condition.

### 5.4.2 *Flow in filled discontinuities*

Equation (5.5) applies only to laminar flow in planar, smooth, parallel discontinuities and represents the highest equivalent hydraulic conductivity for fracture systems. The lowest equivalent hydraulic conductivity occurs for infilled discontinuities, and is given by

$$K = \frac{eK_f}{b} + K_r \qquad (5.6)$$

where $K_f$ is the hydraulic conductivity of the filling and $K_r$ is that of the intact rock. The term $K_r$ is included in equation (5.6) to account for the condition where there is flow in both the intact rock and along the discontinuities.

While equations (5.5) and (5.6) illustrate the principles of water flow along discontinuity planes, this simple model cannot be used to calculate hydraulic conductivity of actual fractured rock masses. Methods of modeling ground water flow in rock have been developed using probabilistic techniques to simulate, in three dimensions, the likely ranges of discontinuity characteristics that may occur. One such modeling technique is termed FRACMAN (Dershowitz *et al.*, 1994; Wei *et al.*, 1995).

### 5.4.3   Heterogeneous rock

Figure 5.9 shows a shallow dipping sequence of sandstone and shale beds. The shale, which is a fine-grained rock with few persistent discontinuities, has low hydraulic conductivity and is termed an *aquitard*. In contrast, the sandstone, which is coarse grained, has a relatively high hydraulic conductivity and is termed an *aquifer*. Because of the significant difference between the hydraulic properties of the shale and sandstone, this is a heterogeneous rock mass. Flow nets in heterogeneous rock are modified from the simple net shown in Figure 5.5 because flowlines preferentially use the high conductivity formations as conduits and traverse the low conductivity formations by the shortest possible route. The equipotentials tend to loose a greater proportion of the head in the low conductivity formation than in the higher conductivity formation. This behavior results in refraction of flow lines at the formation boundary, depending on the relative conductivities, according to the following relationship:

$$\frac{K_{sandstone}}{K_{shale}} = \frac{\tan \theta_1}{\tan \theta_2} \qquad (5.7)$$

The refraction angles $\theta_1$ and $\theta_2$ are defined on Figure 5.9 for a conductivity ratio of $K_1/K_2 = 10$.

Features of the flow conditions shown in Figure 5.9 are as follows. First, flow in the upper, unconfined aquifer tends to flow down-dip

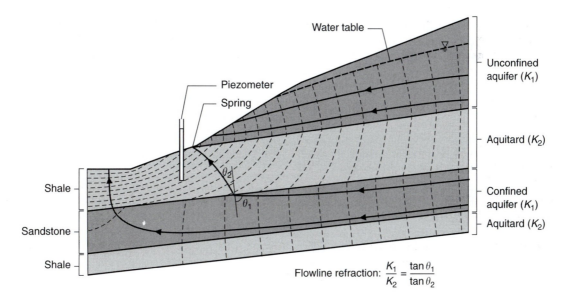

*Figure 5.9* Water flow and pressure distribution in aquifers and aquitards formed by dipping sandstone and shale beds (Dr P. Ward, plots by W. Zawadzki).

in the sandstone and exits the slope at the sandstone/shale contact. This seepage line on the valley wall would be an indication of the location of the contact. Second, flow in the lower, confined aquifer is recharged from a source up-dip from the valley that develops artesian pressure in the sandstone. This condition could be demonstrated by completing a piezometer in the lower sandstone, in which the water would rise above the ground surface to the level of the equipotential in which it is sealed. Third, flow in the confined aquifer is refracted at the boundary and flows upwards in the shale to exit in the valley floor.

### 5.4.4  Anisotropic rock

In formations such as that shown in Figure 5.7, in which the conductivity of one set or sets of discontinuities is higher than another set, the rock mass will exhibit *anisotropic* hydraulic conductivity. For the rock shown in Figure 5.7, the vertical hydraulic conductivity will be considerably more than that in the horizontal direction. On the flow net, anisotropic hydraulic conductivity is depicted by squares formed by the flow lines and equipotentials being elongated in the direction of the higher hydraulic conductivity. In general, the aspect ratio of the flow line/equipotential squares is equal to $(K_1/K_2)^{1/2}$.

Examples of flow nets in isotropic and anisotropic rock are shown in Figure 5.10. The significance of these conditions to slope stability is as follows. First, in rock with high hydraulic conductivity in the horizontal direction, such as horizontally bedded sandstone, the ground water can readily drain from the slope (Figure 5.10(b)). For these conditions there will be relatively low water pressures on potential sliding surfaces compared to the isotropic case. Second, in rock with high hydraulic conductivity parallel to the face such as a slope cut parallel to bedding, flow to the face will be inhibited and high water pressures will develop in the slope. For the slope shown in Figure 5.10(c), the use of horizontal drains that connect the high conductivity bedding planes to the face would be effective in lowering water pressures within the slope.

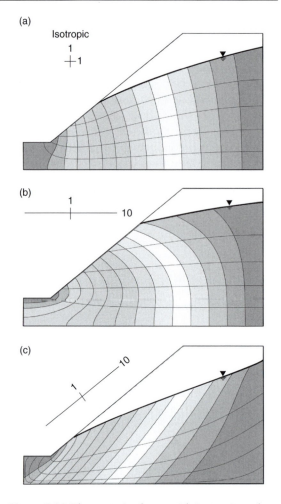

*Figure 5.10* Flow nets in slopes with isotropic and anisotropic hydraulic conductivity: (a) isotropic rock; (b) $K_{horizontal} = 10 \times K_{vertical}$; (c) $K_{parallel\ to\ slope} = 10 \times K_{perpendicular\ to\ slope}$ (plots by W. Zawadzki).

### 5.4.5  Ground water in rock slopes

The discussion on ground water flow in rock masses shows that details of the geology can have a significant effect on water pressures and seepage quantities in rock slopes. In addition to the conditions shown in Figures 5.9 and 5.10 that relate to heterogeneous and anisotropic rock, a variety of other possible ground water conditions

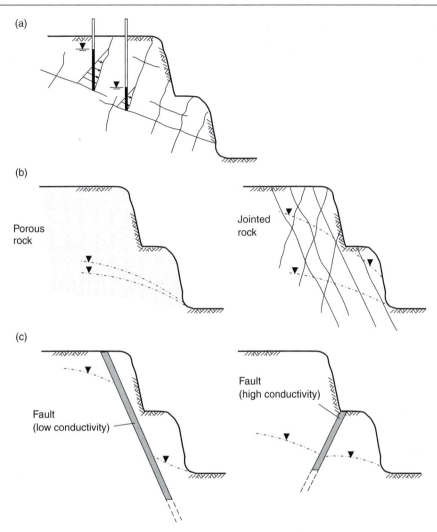

*Figure 5.11* Relationship between geology and ground water in slopes: (a) variation in water pressure in joints related to persistence; (b) comparison of water tables in slopes excavated in porous and jointed rock; (c) faults as low conductivity ground water barrier, and high conductivity sub-surface drain (Patton and Deere, 1971).

are related to geology as follows:

(a)  Low persistence joints that are not connected to the slope face may develop high transient water pressures, compared to joints with greater persistence that are connected to the face and allow water to drain at the face (Figure 5.11(a)). It should be noted that blast damage is one of the causes of persistent joints and fractures close to the face.

However, any improvement in slope stability due to the increase in conductivity is probably out-weighed by the decrease in stability resulting from blast damage to the rock.

(b)  The porosity of the rock mass will affect the level of the transient water table in response to the same precipitation event (Figure 5.11(b)). In a porous rock mass the infiltrating water will be contained within the rock with the result that there will be little increase in the water table. In contrast, a strong rock with widely spaced joints will have low porosity so ground water flow will rapidly fill the joints and increase the water pressure within the slope. It is commonly found that rock falls on steep rock faces occur soon after heavy rainfalls, particularly if the water freezes and expands behind the face.

(c) Faults comprising clay and weathered rock may have low conductivity and act as ground water barriers behind which high water pressures could develop. In contrast, faults comprising crushed and broken rock may have high conductivity and act as a drain (Figure 5.11(c)). Measurement of water pressures on either side of the fault will indicate the hydraulic properties of these features.

## 5.5   Measurement of water pressure

The importance of water pressure to the stability of slopes has been emphasized in previous chapters. If a reliable estimate of stability is to be obtained or if the stability of a slope is to be controlled by drainage, it is essential that water pressures within the slope be measured. Such measurements are most conveniently carried out by piezometers. Piezometers are devices sealed within the ground, generally in boreholes, which respond only to ground water pressure in the immediate vicinity, and not to ground water pressures at other locations. Piezometers can also be used to measure the *in situ* hydraulic conductivity of rock masses using variable head tests as described in Section 5.6.

The following are a number of factors that may be considered when planning a piezometer installation to measure water pressures in a rock slope:

(a) The drill hole should be oriented such that it will intersect the discontinuities in which the ground water is likely to be flowing. For example, in a sedimentary rock containing persistent beds but low persistence joints, the hole should intersect the beds.

(b) The completion zone of the piezometer should be positioned where the rock mass contains discontinuities. For example, if drill core is available, it should be studied to locate zones of fractured or sheared rock where ground water flow is likely to be concentrated. Positioning the completion zone in massive rock with few discontinuities may provide limited information on ground water pressures. The length of the completion zone in rock is usually longer than that in soil because of the need to intersect discontinuities.

(c) Other geological features that may be considered in piezometer installations are fault zones. These may act as conduits for ground water if they contain crushed rock, or they may be barriers to ground water flow if they contain clay gouge. In the case of high hydraulic conductivity faults, the completion zone may be located in the fault, and for low hydraulic conductivity faults, the completion zones may be located either side of the fault to determine any pressure differential.

(d) The number of piezometers, or the number of completion zones in a single piezometer, may be determined by the geology. For example, in a sedimentary deposit containing low hydraulic conductivity shale and relatively high hydraulic conductivity sandstone, it may be necessary to install completion zones in each rock unit.

(e) The hydrodynamic time lag is the volume of water required to register a head fluctuation in a piezometer standpipe. The time lag is dependent primarily on the type and dimensions of the piezometer and can be significant in rock with low hydraulic conductivity. Standpipe piezometers have a greater hydrodynamic time lag than diaphragm piezometers because a greater movement of pore or joint water is required to register. The term slow response time is used to describe a long hydrodynamic time lag.

(f) In rock slopes where the piezometer is being used to measure joint water pressure in which pressure fluctuations are not likely to be significant, a standpipe piezometer is likely to be suitable. However, if the purpose of the piezometer is to measure the response of the ground water pressures to a drainage system such as a series of horizontal drains, or to detect transient water pressures in response to precipitation, then a diaphragm piezometer with a much shorter time lag would be more appropriate.

(g) The filter material in the completion zone should be suited to the rock type. Installations in clay shales or weathered micaceous rocks should use fine grained filter material that will not be clogged by rock weathering products washed in from the walls of the hole.

(h) Cost and reliability are other factors to consider in selecting piezometer types. Standpipe piezometers are simple to install and can be read with inexpensive well sounders, while pneumatic and vibrating wire piezometers are expensive and require more costly readout units. In situations where the slope is moving and piezometers may be lost, it would be preferable to install standpipe piezometers for reasons of economy.

The following is a brief description of piezometer types and the conditions in which they may be used (Dunnicliff, 1993).

• *Observation wells*—Ground water pressures may be monitored in open holes if the permeability of the rock mass is greater than about $10^{-4}$ cm/s, such as coarse-grained sandstones and highly fractured rock. The major limitation of observation wells is that they create a vertical connection between strata so their only application is in consistently permeable rock in which the ground water pressure increases continuously with depth. Observation wells are rarely utilized in monitoring ground water pressures in rock.

• *Standpipe piezometers*—A standpipe piezometer consists of a length of plastic pipe, with a perforated or porous section at the lower

end, which is encased in clean gravel or sand to provide a good hydraulic connection with the rock (Figure 5.12). This perforated section of the piezometer, which is the point

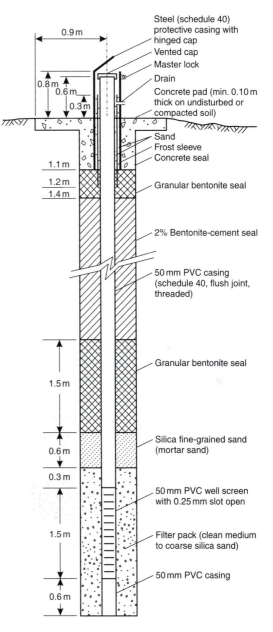

*Figure 5.12* Typical standpipe piezometer installation.

where the water pressure is measured, is isolated from the rest of the hole with a bentonite seal and a filter layer to prevent contamination of the clean sand around the perforated section. The bentonite is usually placed in the form of compacted pellets that will fall a considerable depth down a water-filled hole before they expand. In very deep holes, the balls can be first soaked in oil to form a protective layer that delays their expansion. However, cement is preferred as a seal for holes with depths greater than about 300 m.

The water level in a standpipe piezometer can be measured with a well sounder consisting of a graduated electrical cable, with two bared ends, connected to an electrical circuit consisting of a battery and an ammeter. When the bared ends contact water, the circuit is closed and a current is registered on the ammeter. The advantages of this type of piezometer are that it is simple and reliable, but the disadvantages are that there must be access to the top of the hole, and there can be significant time lag in low conductivity rock.

- *Pneumatic piezometers*—A rapid response time can be achieved using pneumatic piezometers that comprise a valve assembly and a pair of air lines that connect the valve to the surface. The valve is placed in the sealed section of the piezometer to measure the water pressure at that point. The operating principle is to pump air down the supply line until the air pressure equals the water pressure acting on a diaphragm in the sealed section and the valve opens to start air flowing in the return tube. The pressure required to open the valve is recorded on a pressure gauge at the surface.

Pneumatic piezometers are suitable for low conductivity rock installations, and are particularly useful where there is no access to the collar of the hole since readings can be made at a remote location. The disadvantages of this type of piezometer are the risk of damage to the lines either during construction or operation, and the need to maintain a calibrated readout unit.

- *Electronic transducers*—Water pressure measurements with electrical transducers allow very rapid response time and the opportunity to record and process the results at a considerable distance from the slope. Common types of electrical transducers include strain gauges and vibrating wire gauges that measure pressure with a high degree of accuracy. It is recommended that all transducers be thoroughly tested and calibrated before installation. It should also be kept in mind that the long-term reliability of these sensitive electrical instruments may not equal the design life of the slope and provision should be made for their maintenance and possible replacement.

- *Multi-completion piezometers*—For slopes excavated in rock types with differing hydraulic conductivities, it is possible that zones of high ground water pressure exist within a generally depressurized area. In such circumstances, it may be desirable to measure the ground water pressure at a number of points in a drill hole. This can be achieved by installing multiple standpipe piezometers in a single drill hole with bentonite or cement seals between each section of perforated pipe. The maximum number of such standpipes that can be installed in an NX borehole is three; with more pipes, placement of filter and effective seals becomes very difficult.

An alternative method of measuring water pressures at a number of different points in a drill hole is to use a Multi-port (MP) system which also allows measurement of hydraulic conductivity and retrieval of water samples (Black *et al.*, 1986) (Figure 5.13). The MP system is a modular multiple-level monitoring device employing a single, closed access tube with valved ports. The valved ports provide access to several different levels of a drill hole in a single well casing, and the modular design permits as many monitoring zones as desired to be established in a drill hole. The system consists of casing components that are permanently installed in the drill hole, and pressure transducers, sampling probes and specialized tools that are lowered down

(a)

(b)

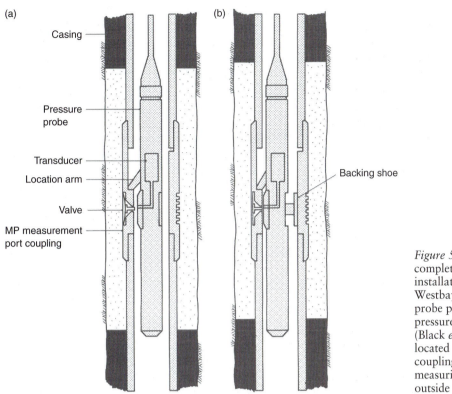

Casing

Pressure probe

Transducer

Location arm

Valve

MP measurement port coupling

Backing shoe

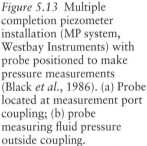

*Figure 5.13* Multiple completion piezometer installation (MP system, Westbay Instruments) with probe positioned to make pressure measurements (Black *et al.*, 1986). (a) Probe located at measurement port coupling; (b) probe measuring fluid pressure outside coupling.

the hole. The casing components include casing sections of various lengths, two types of valved port couplings with capabilities to either measure pressure or take samples. The port assemblies can be isolated in the drill hole by sealing the annulus between the monitoring zones using either pairs of packers, or by filling the annulus with a cement grout or bentonite seal. The MP system has been used in drill holes up to 1200 m deep.

## 5.6   Field measurement of hydraulic conductivity

Determination of the hydraulic conductivity of a rock mass is necessary if estimates are required of ground water discharge from a slope, or in the design of a drainage system.

For evaluation of the stability of the slopes, it is the water pressure rather than the volume of ground water flow in the rock mass that is important. The water pressure at any point is independent of the hydraulic conductivity of the rock mass at that point, but it does depend upon the path followed by the ground water in arriving at the point (Figures 5.9 and 5.10). Hence, the heterogeneity and anisotropy of the rock mass with respect to the distribution of hydraulic conductivity is of interest in estimating the water pressure distribution in a slope.

Because ground water flow in fractured rock takes place predominately in the discontinuities, it is necessary that hydraulic conductivity measurements be made *in situ*; it is not possible to simulate water flow in a fractured rock mass in the laboratory. The following is a brief description of the two most common methods of *in situ* conductivity testing, namely variable head tests and pumping tests. Detailed procedures for hydraulic conductivity tests are described in the literature, and the tests themselves are usually conducted by specialists in the field of hydrogeology.

## 5.6.1 Variable head tests

In order to measure the hydraulic conductivity at a "point" in a rock mass, it is necessary to change the ground water conditions at that point and to measure the time taken for the original conditions to be re-established. These tests are most conveniently carried out in a borehole, and the test length may represent the general rock mass properties in the slope, or the test may be located in a specific geologic feature such as a fault. An essential requirement of the test is that the borehole wall is clean and there is no clogging of the discontinuities by drill cuttings or drilling mud. This will require flushing of the hole and the use of polymer muds that break down some time after drilling to leave a clean hole (see Section 3.6.2).

*Test configurations.* A number of borehole test configurations are possible. A piezometer installed in a drill hole will isolate a section at the end of the hole (Figure 5.14(a)), or at some point up the hole. It is also possible to conduct hydraulic conductivity measurements in open holes (Figure 5.14(b)), although it is necessary that the geologic conditions are consistent over the test length.

*Test procedure.* The procedure for the variable head test is first to establish the rest water level, which is the static equilibrium level of the water table at the drill hole location (Figure 5.14(a) and (b)). Pumping of circulation water during drilling will disturb this equilibrium and the permeability results will be in error if insufficient time is allowed for equilibrium to be re-established. Once equilibrium has been established, water can either be removed from (*bail test*) or added to (*slug test*) the standpipe (piezometer test) or hole to change the water level. If the test is conducted above the water table it is necessary to perform a slug test, while for a test below the water table, a bail test is preferred because the flow of water out of the formation minimizes clogging of the fractures.

Water is added or removed from the hole to change the water level by about 1–2 m and the rate at which the water level recovers to the equilibrium level is measured. For the test shown in Figure 5.14(a), the hydraulic conductivity $K$ is calculated from the following general relationship:

$$K = \frac{A}{F(t_2 - t_1)} \ln\left(\frac{h_1}{h_2}\right) \quad \text{for} \quad \frac{L}{R} > 8 \quad (5.8)$$

where $F$ is the shape factor. For a drill hole with radius $R$ and a test zone of length $L$, the shape factor is given by

$$F = \frac{2\pi L}{\ln(L/R)} \quad (5.9)$$

In equation (5.8), $A$ is the cross-section area of the standpipe ($A = \pi r^2$) and $r$ is the internal radius of the standpipe. For a bail test, $t_1$ and $t_2$ are the times at which the water levels are at depths $h_1$ and $h_2$ respectively below the equilibrium water level. The differential heads $h_1$ and $h_2$, as well as the initial equilibrium head $h_0$, are defined in Figure 5.14(a), while a typical semilog plot of the rise in water level in the casing with time is shown in Figure 5.14(c).

The types of test shown in Figure 5.14 are suitable for measurement of the hydraulic conductivity of reasonably uniform rock. Anisotropic hydraulic conductivity coefficients cannot be measured directly in these tests but allowance can be made for this anisotropy in the calculations as follows. If an estimate of the ratio of vertical and horizontal hydraulic conductivities $K_v$ and $K_h$ respectively is made, the ratio $m$ is given by

$$m = \sqrt{\frac{K_h}{K_v}} \quad (5.10)$$

and the shape factor $F$ given by equation (5.9) is modified as follows:

$$F = \frac{2\pi L}{\ln(L(m/R))} \quad (5.11)$$

When this value of $F$ is substituted in equation (5.8), then the calculated value of the

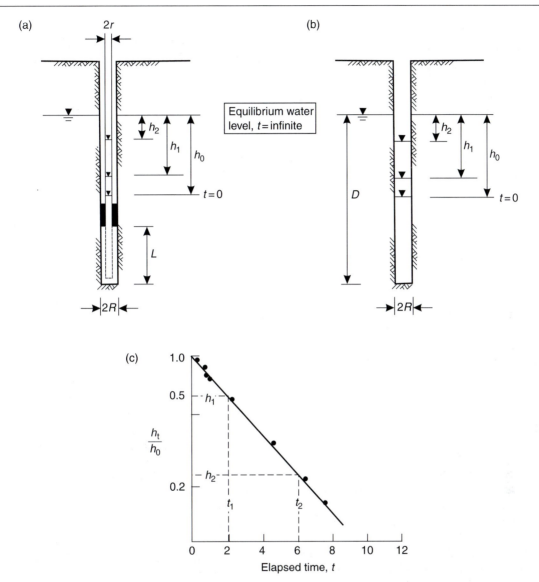

*Figure 5.14* Method of calculating hydraulic conductivity for variable head test: (a) piezometer with completion length $L$; (b) open hole to depth $D$ below water table; (c) typical plot of head increase (recovery) against time.

hydraulic conductivity, $K$, is the mean hydraulic conductivity given by $\sqrt{(K_v \times K_h)}$.

*Packer tests.* Where conductivity tests are required at specific locations within a drill hole, a test zone can be isolated using packers positioned at any location in the hole, and over any required

length (Figure 5.15). Packer tests can be made during diamond drilling using a triple packer system that is lowered through the rods so that the test is conducted in a portion of the hole below the drill bit. The packer system consists of three inflatable rubber packers, each 1 m long that is

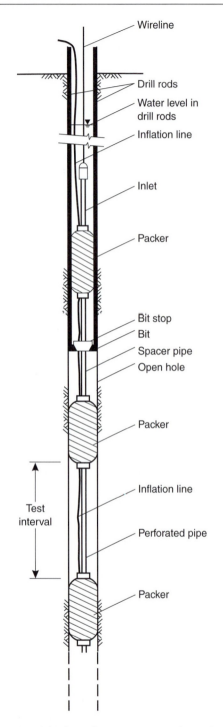

Wireline

Drill rods

Water level in
drill rods

Inflation line

Inlet

Packer

Bit stop

Bit

Spacer pipe

Open hole

Packer

Inflation line

Test
interval

Perforated pipe

Packer

*Figure 5.15* Triple packer arrangement for making
variable head hydraulic conductivity tests in
conjunction with diamond drilling (Wyllie, 1999).

sufficient to minimize the risk of leakage past the
packer. The lower two packers are joined by a
perforated steel pipe, the length of which depends
on the required test length, while the top and
middle packers are joined by a solid pipe. The
whole packer assembly is lowered down the drill
hole on the wire line through the drill rods and the
lower two packers extend through the bit into the
open hole, while the upper packer is located in
the lower end of the core barrel. The three packers are then inflated with nitrogen through a small
diameter plastic tube that runs down the hole.
The inflated packers seal the packer assembly into
the rods, and isolate a length of drill hole below
the bit. If water is removed from the drill rods,
formation water will flow from the rock, over
the test interval isolated by the two lower packers, and through the perforated pipe to restore
the water level in the rods. This flow of water
is measured by monitoring the change of water
level in the drill rods with time. A plot of the results is head recovery plot such as that shown in
Figure 5.14(c). Cedergren (1989) provides a comprehensive discussion of variable head hydraulic
conductivity testing.

### 5.6.2  Pumping test

The main limitations of conductivity tests carried
out in drill holes are that only a small volume of
rock in the vicinity of the hole is tested, and it
is not possible to determine the anisotropy of the
rock mass. Both these limitations are overcome by
conducting pump tests, as described briefly in the
next paragraph.

A pump test arrangement consists of a vertical well equipped with a pump, and an array
of piezometers in which the water table elevation
can be measured in the rock mass surrounding the
well. The piezometers can be arranged so that the
influence of various geologic features on ground
water conditions can be determined. For instance,
piezometers could be installed on either side of
a fault, or in directions parallel and perpendicular to sets of persistent discontinuities such as
bedding planes. Selection of the best location for
both the pumped well and the observation wells

requires considerable experience and judgment, and should only be carried out after thorough geological investigations have been carried out.

The test procedure consists of pumping water at a steady rate from the well and measuring the drop in water level in both the pumped well and the observation wells. The duration of the test can range from as short as eight hours to as long as several weeks, depending on the permeability of the rock mass. When the pumping is stopped, the water levels in all the wells are measured until a static water level is determined—this is known as the recovery stage of the test. Plots of draw down (or recovery) against time can be used to calculate permeability values using methods described by Cedergren (1989), Todd (1959), Jacob (1950) and Theis (1935).

Because of the cost and time required for conducting a pump test, they are rarely carried out for rock slope engineering. An example of a situation where a pump test may be justified would be to assess the feasibility of driving a drainage adit for stabilization of a landslide. Generally, installation of piezometers to measure the ground water table and conduct variable head tests to measure hydraulic conductivity in boreholes provide sufficient information on ground water conditions for slope design purposes.

## 5.7   Example Problem 5.1: Influence of geology and weather conditions on ground water levels

### Statement

Figure 5.16 shows a slope, cut in isotropic, fractured rock, under a variety of operational and climatic conditions; in all cases ground water is infiltrating the horizontal ground surface behind the crest of the slope (Terzaghi, 1962). In Figure 5.16(a) the slope has been recently excavated, and prior to excavation, the water table was horizontal and at a shallow depth below the ground surface. In Figure 5.16(b) and (c) the slope has been open for a sufficiently long time for ground water equilibrium conditions to be established, but the climatic conditions vary. The

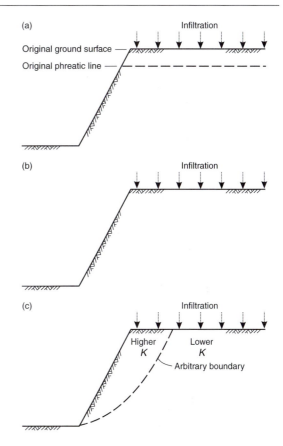

*Figure 5.16* Cut slope in rock with water infiltration on ground surface behind crest for Example 5.1: (a) position of the ground water surface before excavation; (b) slope with variety of surface infiltration and rock conductivity conditions; (c) slope with higher conductivity rock close to face, and various climatic conditions.

objective of the exercise is to sketch in the ground water table on each slope based on the general behavior of ground water in slopes as governed by Darcy's Law.

### Required

A   On the cross-section in Figure 5.16(a), draw the approximate position of the ground water table after excavation of the slope.

B   On the cross-section in Figure 5.16(b), draw the approximate positions of the ground

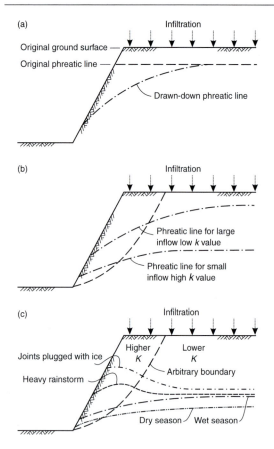

*Figure 5.17* Positions of ground water surface for conditions shown in Figure 5.16 for Example 5.1: (a) position of the ground water surface before and after excavation; (b) relative positions of ground water table for variations of inflow and conductivity; (c) hypothetical positions of the ground water surface in jointed rock for variety of climatic conditions.

water table for the following conditions:

- large infiltration, low hydraulic conductivity; and
- small infiltration, high hydraulic conductivity.

C   On the cross-section in Figure 5.16(c) draw the approximate positions of the ground water table for the following conditions:

- joints on slope face plugged with ice;
- immediately following a heavy rainstorm;
- wet season; and
- dry season.

### Solution

Figure 5.17(a), (b) and (c) show the positions of the ground water table under the various conditions shown in Figure 5.16.

In general, the rock near the slope face has been disturbed by blasting and has undergone stress relief so it will have a higher hydraulic conductivity than the undisturbed rock. When the hydraulic conductivity is high, the rock drains readily and the ground water table has a relatively flat gradient.

If the face freezes and the water cannot drain from the slope, the ground water surface will rise behind the face. The same situation arises when heavy infiltration exceeds the rate at which the rock will drain.

# Chapter 6

# Plane failure

## 6.1 Introduction

A plane failure is a comparatively rare sight in rock slopes because it is only occasionally that all the geometric conditions required to produce such a failure occur in an actual slope. However, it would not be right to ignore the two-dimensional case because there are many valuable lessons to be learned from a consideration of the mechanics of this simple failure mode. Plane failure is particularly useful for demonstrating the sensitivity of the slope to changes in shear strength and ground water conditions—changes that are less obvious when dealing with the more complex mechanics of a three-dimensional slope failure. This chapter describes the method of analysis for plane failure (Sections 6.2 and 6.3), and demonstrates its application to the design of reinforced slopes (Section 6.4), analysis methods for slopes subject to seismic ground motion (Section 6.5), and probabilistic design methods (Section 6.6). Two case studies describing the stabilization of plane failures are described in Chapter 14.

## 6.2 General conditions for plane failure

Figure 6.1 shows a typical plane failure in a rock slope where a block of rock has slid on a single plane dipping out of the face. In order for this type of failure to occur, the following geometrical conditions must be satisfied (Figure 6.2(a)):

(a) The plane on which sliding occurs must strike parallel or nearly parallel (within approximately ±20°) to the slope face.

(b) The sliding plane must "daylight" in the slope face, which means that the dip of the plane must be less than the dip of the slope face, that is, $\psi_p < \psi_f$.

(c) The dip of the sliding plane must be greater than the angle of friction of this plane, that is, $\psi_p > \phi$.

(d) The upper end of the sliding surface either intersects the upper slope, or terminates in a tension crack.

(e) Release surfaces that provide negligible resistance to sliding must be present in the rock mass to define the lateral boundaries of the slide. Alternatively, failure can occur on a sliding plane passing through the convex "nose" of a slope.

## 6.3 Plane failure analysis

The slope geometries and ground water conditions considered in this analysis are defined in Figure 6.3, which shows two geometries as follows:

(a) slopes having a tension crack in the upper surface; and

(b) slopes with a tension crack in the face.

When the upper surface is horizontal ($\psi_s = 0$), the transition from one condition to another occurs when the tension crack coincides with the slope crest, that is when

$$\frac{z}{H} = (1 - \cot \psi_f \tan \psi_p) \qquad (6.1)$$

*Figure 6.1* Plane failure on smooth, persistent bedding planes in shale (Interstate 40, near Newport, Tennessee).

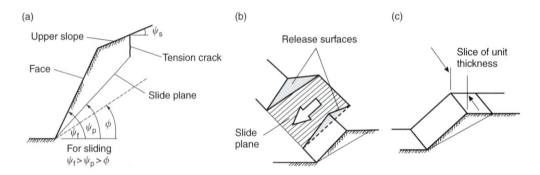

*Figure 6.2* Geometry of slope exhibiting plane failure: (a) cross-section showing planes forming a plane failure; (b) release surfaces at ends of plane failure; (c) unit thickness slide used in stability analysis.

where $z$ is the depth of the tension crack, $H$ is the slope height, $\psi_f$ is the slope face angle and $\psi_p$ is the dip of the sliding plane.

The following assumptions are made in plane failure analysis:

(a) Both sliding surface and tension crack strike parallel to the slope.
(b) The tension crack is vertical and is filled with water to a depth $z_w$.
(c) Water enters the sliding surface along the base of the tension crack and seeps along the sliding surface, escaping at atmospheric pressure where the sliding surface daylights in the slope face. The pressure distributions induced by the presence of water in the tension crack and along the sliding surface are illustrated in Figure 6.3.

(d) The forces $W$ (the weight of the sliding block), $U$ (uplift force due to water pressure on the sliding surface) and $V$ (force due to water pressure in the tension crack) all act through the centroid of the sliding mass. In other words, it is assumed that there are no

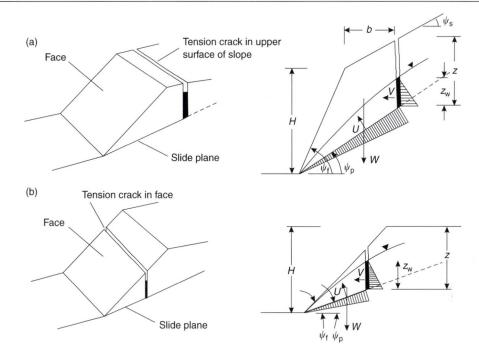

*Figure 6.3* Geometries of plane slope failure: (a) tension crack in the upper slope; (b) tension crack in the face.

moments that would tend to cause rotation of the block, and hence failure is by sliding only. While this assumption may not be strictly true for actual slopes, the errors introduced by ignoring moments are small enough to neglect. However, in steep slopes with steeply dipping discontinuities, the possibility of toppling failure should be kept in mind (see Chapter 9).

(e) The shear strength $\tau$ of the sliding surface is defined by cohesion $c$ and friction angle $\phi$ that are related by the equation $\tau = c + \sigma \tan \phi$, as discussed in Chapter 4. In the case of a rough surface or a rock mass having a curvilinear shear strength envelope, the apparent cohesion and apparent friction angle are defined by a tangent that takes into account the normal stress acting on the sliding surface. The normal stress $\sigma$ acting on a sliding surface can be determined from the curves given in Figure 6.4.

(f) It is assumed that release surfaces are present so that there is no resistance to sliding at the lateral boundaries of the failing rock mass (Figure 6.2(b)).

(g) In analyzing two-dimensional slope problems, it is usual to consider a slice of unit thickness taken at right angles to the slope face. This means that on a vertical section through the slope, the area of the sliding surface can be represented by the length of the surface, and the volume of the sliding block is represented by the cross-section area of the block (Figure 6.2(c)).

The factor of safety for plane failure is calculated by resolving all forces acting on the slope into components parallel and normal to the sliding plane. The vector sum of the shear forces, $\sum S$ acting down the plane is termed the *driving force*. The product of the total normal forces, $\sum N$ and the tangent of the friction angle $\phi$, plus the cohesive force is termed the *resisting force* (see Section 1.4.2). The factor of safety FS of the sliding block is the ratio of the resisting forces to

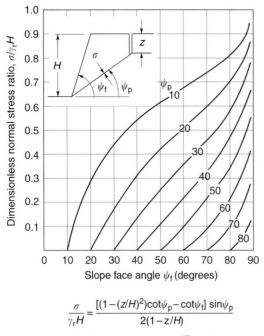

$$\frac{\sigma}{\gamma_r H} = \frac{[(1-(z/H)^2)\cot\psi_p - \cot\psi_f]\sin\psi_p}{2(1-z/H)}$$

where $z/H = 1 - (\cot\psi_f \tan\psi_p)^{1/2}$, and $\psi_s = 0$

*Figure 6.4* Normal stress acting on the slide plane in a rock slope.

the driving forces, and is calculated as follows:

$$FS = \frac{\text{Resisting force}}{\text{Driving force}} \quad (6.2)$$

$$= \frac{cA + \sum N \tan\phi}{\sum S} \quad (6.3)$$

where $c$ is the cohesion and $A$ is the area of the sliding plane.

Based on the concept illustrated in equations (6.2) and (6.3), the factor of safety for the slope configurations shown in Figure 6.3 is given by

$$FS = \frac{cA + (W\cos\psi_p - U - V\sin\psi_p)\tan\phi}{W\sin\psi_p + V\cos\psi_p}$$

$$(6.4)$$

where $A$ is given by

$$A = (H + b\tan\psi_s - z)\,\text{cosec}\,\psi_p \quad (6.5)$$

The slope height is $H$, the tension crack depth is $z$ and it is located a distance $b$ behind the slope crest. The dip of the slope above the crest is $\psi_s$. When the depth of the water in the tension crack is $z_w$, the water forces acting on the sliding plane $U$ and in the tension crack $V$ are given by

$$U = \tfrac{1}{2}\gamma_w z_w (H + b\tan\psi_s - z)\,\text{cosec}\,\psi_p$$

$$(6.6)$$

$$V = \tfrac{1}{2}\gamma_w z_w^2 \quad (6.7)$$

where $\gamma_w$ is the unit weight of water.

The weights of the sliding block $W$ for the two geometries shown in Figure 6.3 are given by equations (6.8) and (6.9). For the tension crack in the inclined upper slope surface (Figure 6.3(a)),

$$W = \gamma_r \left[ (1 - \cot\psi_f \tan\psi_p)\left(bH + \tfrac{1}{2}H^2\cot\psi_f\right) \right.$$
$$\left. + \tfrac{1}{2}b^2(\tan\psi_s - \tan\psi_p) \right] \quad (6.8)$$

and, for the tension crack in the slope face (Figure 6.3(b)).

$$W = \frac{1}{2}\gamma_r H^2 \left[ \left(1 - \frac{z}{H}\right)^2 \cot\psi_p \right.$$
$$\left. \times (\cot\psi_p \tan\psi_f - 1) \right] \quad (6.9)$$

where $\gamma_r$ is the unit weight of the rock.

Figure 6.3 and equations (6.4)–(6.9) illustrate that the geometry of a plane failure and the ground water conditions can be completely defined by four dimensions ($H$, $b$, $z$ and $z_w$) and by three angles ($\psi_f$, $\psi_p$ and $\psi_s$). These simple models, together with the ground water, rock bolting and seismic ground motion concepts discussed in the following sections allow stability calculations to be carried out for a wide variety of conditions.

### 6.3.1 *Influence of ground water on stability*

In the preceding discussion, it has been assumed that it is only the water present in the tension crack and along the sliding surface that influences the stability of the slope. This is equivalent to assuming that the rest of the rock mass is impermeable, an assumption that is certainly not always justified. Therefore, consideration must be given to water pressure distributions other than those presented in this chapter. Under some conditions, it may be possible to construct a flow net from which the ground water pressure distribution can be determined from the intersection of the equipotentials with the sliding surface (see Figure 5.10). Information that would assist in developing flow nets includes the rock mass permeability (and its anisotropy), the locations of seepage on the face and recharge above the slope, and any piezometric measurements.

In the absence of actual ground water pressure measurements within a slope, the current state of knowledge in rock engineering does not permit a precise definition of the ground water flow patterns in a rock mass. Consequently, slope design should assess the sensitivity of the factor of safety to a range of realistic ground water pressures, and particularly the effects of transient pressures due to rapid recharge (see Figure 5.11(b)).

The following are four possible ground water conditions that may occur in rock slopes, and the equations that can be used to calculate the water forces $U$ and $V$. In these examples, the pressure distributions in the tension crack and along the sliding plane are idealized and judgment is required to determine the most suitable condition for any particular slope.

(a)    Ground water level is above the base of tension crack so water pressures act both in the tension crack and on the sliding plane. If the water discharges to the atmosphere where the sliding place daylights on the slope face, then it is assumed that the pressure decreases linearly from the base of the tension crack to zero at the face. This condition is illustrated in Figure 6.3 and the method of calculating

forces $U$ and $V$ is given by equations (6.6) and (6.7), respectively.

(b)    Water pressure may develop in the tension crack only, in conditions for example, where a heavy rainstorm after a long dry spell results in surface water flowing directly into the crack. If the remainder of the rock mass is relatively impermeable, or the sliding surface contains a low permeability clay filling, then the uplift force $U$ could also be zero or nearly zero. In either case, the factor of safety of the slope for these transient conditions is given by equation (6.4) with $U = 0$ and $V$ given by equation (6.7).

(c)    Ground water discharge at the face may be blocked by freezing (Figure 6.5(a)). Where the frost penetrates only a few meters behind the face, water pressures can build up

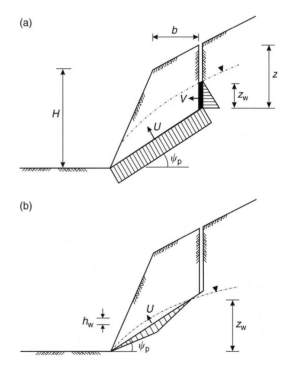

*Figure 6.5* Possible ground water pressures in plane failures: (a) uniform pressure on slide plane for drainage blocked at toe; (b) triangular pressure on slide plane for water table below the base of tension crack.

in the slope and the uplift pressure $U$ can exceed that shown in Figure 6.3. For the idealized rectangular pressure distribution shown in Figure 6.5(a), the uplift force $U$ is given by

$$U = Ap \qquad (6.10)$$

where $A$ is the area of the sliding plane given by equation (6.5) and $p$ is the pressure in the plane (and at the base of the tension crack) given by

$$p = \gamma_w z_w \qquad (6.11)$$

The condition shown in Figure 6.5(a) may only occur rarely, but could result in a low factor of safety; a system of horizontal drains may help to limit the water pressure in the slope.

(d) Ground water level in the slope is below the base of the tension crack so water pressure acts only on the sliding plane (Figure 6.5(b)). If the water discharges to the atmosphere where the sliding plane daylights on the face, then the water pressure can be approximated by a triangular distribution, from which the uplift force $U$ is given by

$$U = \frac{1}{2}\frac{z_w}{\sin \psi_p} h_w \gamma_w \qquad (6.12)$$

where $h_w$ is the estimated depth of water at the mid-point of the saturated portion of the sliding plane.

## 6.3.2  *Critical tension crack depth and location*

In the analysis, it has been assumed that the position of the tension crack is known from its visible trace on the upper surface or on the face of the slope, and that its depth can be established by constructing an accurate cross-section of the slope. However, the tension crack position may be unknown, due for example, to the presence

of soil above the slope crest, or an assumed location may be required for design. Under these circumstances, it becomes necessary to consider the most probable position of a tension crack.

When the slope is dry or nearly dry ($z_w/z = 0$), equation (6.4) for the factor of safety can be modified as follows:

$$FS = \frac{c \cdot A}{W \sin \psi_p} + \cot \psi_p \tan \phi \qquad (6.13)$$

The critical tension crack depth $z_c$ for a dry slope can be found by minimizing the right-hand side of equation (6.13) with respect to $z/H$. This gives the critical tension crack depth as

$$\frac{z_c}{H} = 1 - \sqrt{\cot \psi_f \tan \psi_p} \qquad (6.14)$$

and the corresponding position of the critical tension crack $b_c$ behind the crest is

$$\frac{b_c}{H} = \sqrt{\cot \psi_f \cot \psi_p} - \cot \psi_f \qquad (6.15)$$

Critical tension crack depths and locations for a range of dimensions for dry slopes are plotted in Figure 6.6(a) and (b). However, if the tension crack forms during heavy rain or if it is located on a pre-existing geological feature such as a vertical joint, equations (6.14) and (6.15) no longer apply.

## 6.3.3  *The tension crack as an indicator of instability*

Anyone who has examined excavated rock slopes cannot have failed to notice the occasional tension cracks behind the crest (Figure 6.7). Some of these cracks have been visible for tens of years and, in many cases, do not appear to have had any adverse influence upon the stability of the slope. It is interesting, therefore, to consider how such cracks are formed and whether they can give any indication of slope instability.

In a series of very detailed model studies on the failure of slopes in jointed rocks, Barton (1971)

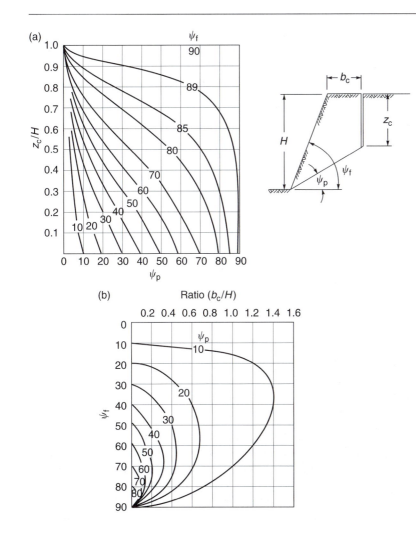

*Figure 6.6* Critical tension crack locations for a dry slope: (a) critical tension crack depth relative to crest of cut; (b) critical tension crack location behind crest of cut.

found that the tension crack resulted from small shear movements within the rock mass. Although these individual movements were very small, their cumulative effect was that there was a significant displacement of the slope surfaces—sufficient to cause separation of vertical joints behind the slope crest and to form "tension" cracks. The fact that the tension crack is caused by shear movements in the slope is important because it suggests that, when a tension crack becomes visible in the surface of a slope, it must be assumed that shear failure has initiated within the rock mass.

It is impossible to quantify the significance of tension cracks since their formation is only the start of a complex progressive failure process within the rock mass, about which little is known. It is quite probable that, in some cases, the improved drainage resulting from dilation of the rock structure, combined with the interlocking of individual blocks within the rock mass, could give rise to an increase in stability. However, where the failure surface comprises a single discontinuity surface such as a bedding plane daylighting in the slope face, initial movement could be followed by a very rapid decrease in stability because a small amount of movement could result in a reduction in the shear strength from the peak to the residual value.

*Figure 6.7* A tension crack behind a sliding rock mass in which significant horizontal displacement has occurred (above Kooteney Lake, British Columbia).

In summary, the presence of a tension crack should be taken as an indication of potential instability and that, in the case of an important slope, this should signal the need for a detailed investigation of stability.

### 6.3.4  *Critical slide plane inclination*

When a persistent discontinuity such as a bedding plane exists in a slope and the inclination of this discontinuity is such that it satisfies the conditions for plane failure defined in Figure 6.2, stability of the slope will be controlled by this feature. However, where no such feature exists and a sliding surface, if it were to occur, would follow minor geological features and, in some places, pass through intact material, how can the inclination of such a failure path be determined?

The first assumption that must be made concerns the shape of the slide surface. In a weak rock slope or a soil slope with a face angle less than about 45°, the slide surface would have a circular shape. The analysis of such a failure surface is discussed in Chapter 8.

In steep rock slopes, the slide surface is approximately planar and the inclination of such a plane can be found by partial differentiation of equation (6.4) with respect to $\psi_p$ and by equating the resulting differential to zero. For dry slopes this gives the critical slide plane inclination $\psi_{pc}$ as

$$\psi_{pc} = \tfrac{1}{2}(\psi_f + \phi) \qquad (6.16)$$

The presence of water in the tension crack will cause the slide plane inclination to be reduced by as much as 10%, but in view of the uncertainties associated with the inclination of this slide surface, the added complication of including the influence of ground water is not considered to be justified. Consequently, equation (6.16) can be used to obtain an estimate of the critical slide plane inclination in steep slopes that do not contain through-going discontinuities.

### 6.3.5   Analysis of failure on a rough plane

The stability analyses discussed so far in this section have used shear strength parameters that are constant throughout the slope. However, as discussed in Section 4.2.4 on the shear strength of rough rock surfaces, the friction angle that will be mobilized in the slope may depend on the normal stress acting on the surface. That is, the friction angle will decrease with increasing normal stress as the asperities on the surface are ground off, as defined by equation (4.7). The significance of this relationship between friction angle and normal stress is illustrated in this section.

Consider a plane slope failure with the geometry as shown in Figure 6.3(a). For a dry slope $(U = V = 0)$, the normal stress $\sigma$ acting on the sliding surface is given by

$$\sigma = \frac{W \cos \psi_p}{A} \qquad (6.17)$$

where $W$ is the weight of the sliding block, $\psi_p$ is the dip of the sliding surface and $A$ is the area of this surface. If the sliding plane contains no cohesive infilling so that the shear strength comprises only friction, then the factor of safety can be calculated using equations (1.2)–(1.6) for limit equilibrium analysis, equation (4.7) to define the shear strength of the rough surface, and equation (6.17) to define the normal stress on this

surface. For these conditions the factor of safety is given by

$$\text{FS} = \frac{\tau A}{W \sin \psi_p} \qquad (6.18)$$

$$= \frac{\sigma \tan(\phi + \text{JRC} \log_{10}(\text{JCS}/\sigma))A}{W \sin \psi_p} \qquad (6.19)$$

$$= \frac{\tan(\phi + \text{JRC} \log_{10}(\text{JCS}/\sigma))}{\tan \psi_p} \qquad (6.20)$$

$$= \frac{\tan(\phi + i)}{\tan \psi_p} \qquad (6.21)$$

The application of these equations and the effect of a rough surface on the factor of safety can be illustrated by the following example. Consider a slope with dimensions $H = 30\,\text{m}$, $z = 15\,\text{m}$, $\psi_p = 30°$ and $\psi_f = 60°$, in which the properties of the clean rough joint forming the sliding surface are $\phi = 25°$, $\text{JRC} = 15$ and $\text{JCS} = 5000\,\text{kPa}$. From Figure 6.4, the normal stress ratio $\sigma/\gamma_r H$ is 0.36, and the value of $\sigma$ is 281 kPa if the rock density $\gamma_r$ is $26\,\text{kN/m}^3$. The value of the $\sigma$ calculated from Figure 6.4 is the average normal stress acting on the sliding surface. However, the maximum stress acting on this surface is below the crest of the slope where the depth of rock is 20 m. The calculated maximum stress is

$$\sigma_{max} = 20 \cdot 26 \cdot \cos(30)$$
$$= 450\,\text{kPa}$$

Using equation (4.7) and the roughness properties quoted in the previous paragraph, the shear strength of the sliding surface and the corresponding factors of safety at the average and maximum normal stresses can be calculated as

$$\sigma = 281\,\text{kPa} \quad \tau = 269\,\text{kPa}; \quad (\phi + i) = 44°$$
$$\text{and} \quad \text{FS} = 1.66$$
$$\sigma = 450\,\text{kPa} \quad \tau = 387\,\text{kPa}; \quad (\phi + i) = 41°$$
$$\text{and} \quad \text{FS} = 1.49$$

These results indicate that the effect of increasing normal stress level on the sliding surface is to diminish the friction angle (due to the asperities being ground off) and there is a corresponding decrease in the factor of safety (10% in this case).

## 6.4   Reinforcement of a slope

When it has been established that a slope is potentially unstable, reinforcement may be an effective method of improving the factor of safety. Methods of reinforcement include the installation of tensioned anchors or fully grouted, untensioned dowels, or the construction of a toe buttress. Factors that will influence the selection of an appropriate system for the site include the site geology, the required capacity of the reinforcement force, drilling equipment availability and access, and time required for construction. This section describes the design methods for slope reinforcement, while Section 12.4.2 discusses construction aspects of slope reinforcement, and Section 14.3 discusses a case study where a plane failure was reinforced with tensioned cables.

If rock anchors are to be installed, it is necessary to decide if they should be anchored at the distal end and tensioned, or fully grouted and untensioned. Untensioned dowels are less costly to install, but they will provide less reinforcement than tensioned anchors of the same dimensions, and their capacity cannot be tested. One technical factor influencing the selection is that if a slope has relaxed and loss of interlock has occurred on the sliding plane, then it is advisable to install tensioned anchors to apply normal and shear forces on the sliding plane. However, if the reinforcement can be installed before the excavation takes place, then fully grouted dowels are effective in reinforcing the slope by preventing relaxation on potential sliding surfaces (see Figure 12.5). Untensioned dowels can also be used where the rock is randomly jointed and there is a need to reinforce the overall slope, rather than a particular plane.

### 6.4.1   Reinforcement with tensioned anchors

A tensioned anchor installation involves drilling a hole extending below the sliding plane, installing a rock bolt or strand cable that is bonded into

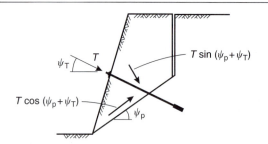

*Figure 6.8* Reinforcement of a slope with tensioned rock bolt.

the stable portion of the slope, and then tensioning the anchor against the face (Figure 6.8). The tension in the anchor $T$ modifies the normal and shear forces acting on the sliding plane, and the factor of safety of the anchored slope is given by

$$FS = \frac{cA + (W\cos\psi_p - U - V\sin\psi_p + T\sin(\psi_T + \psi_p))\tan\phi}{W\sin\psi_p + V\cos\psi_p - T\cos(\psi_T + \psi_p)}$$

(6.22)

where $T$ is the tension in the anchor inclined at an angle $\psi_T$ below the horizontal. Equation (6.22) shows that the normal component of the anchor tension ($T\sin(\psi_p + \psi_T)$) is added to the normal force acting on the sliding plane, which has the effect of increasing the shear resistance to sliding. Also, the shear component of the anchor tension ($T\cos(\psi_p + \psi_T)$) acting up the sliding plane is subtracted from the driving forces, so the combined effect of the anchor force is to improve the factor of safety (if ($\psi_p + \psi_T$) < 90°).

The factor of safety of a slope reinforced with tensioned rock anchors varies with the inclination of the bolt. It can be shown that the most efficient angle ($\psi_{T(opt)}$) for a tensioned rock is when

$$\phi = (\psi_{T(opt)} + \psi_p) \quad \text{or} \quad \psi_{T(opt)} = (\phi - \psi_p)$$

(6.23)

This relationship shows that the optimum installation angle for a tensioned bolt is flatter than the normal to the sliding plane. In practice, cement grouted anchors are installed at about 10–15° below the horizontal to facilitate grouting, while resin grouted anchors may be installed in up-holes. It should be noted that bolts installed at an angle steeper than the normal to the sliding plane (i.e. $(\psi_p + \psi_T) > 90°$) can be detrimental to stability because the shear component of the tension, acting down the plane, increases the magnitude of the displacing force.

Since the stability analysis of plane failures is carried out on a 1 m thick slice of the slope, the calculated value of $T$ for a specified factor of safety has the units kN/m. The procedure for designing a bolting pattern using the calculated value of $T$ is as follows. For example, if the tension in the each anchor is $T_B$, and a pattern of bolts is installed so that there are $n$ bolts in each vertical row, then the total bolting force in each vertical row is $(T_B \cdot n)$. Since the required bolting force is $T$, then the horizontal spacing $S$ between each vertical row is given by

$$S = \frac{T_B n}{T} \left( \frac{kN}{kN/m} \right) \qquad (6.24)$$

This design method is illustrated in the worked example at the end of this chapter.

### 6.4.2 Reinforcement with fully grouted untensioned dowels

Fully grouted, untensioned dowels comprise steel bars installed in holes drilled across the potential sliding plane, which are then encapsulated in cement or resin grout. The steel acts as a rigid shear pin across any plane of weakness in the rock. A method of calculating the reinforcement provided by dowels, developed by Spang and Egger (1990), is discussed here.

Figure 6.9 shows the results of a finite element analysis of a steel bar grouted into a drill hole in a rock containing a joint surface; the angle $\alpha$ between the axis of the bolt and the normal to the joint is 30°. Shear displacement on the joint causes deformation of the bolt that takes place in three stages as follows:

(a) *Elastic stage*—After overcoming the cohesion of the joint, the blocks begin to slide relative

to each other. The shear resistance of the doweled joint comprises the shear strength due to friction on the joint, and the elastic response of the steel dowel, grout and rock.

(b) *Yield stage*—At displacements of less than about 1 mm in installations where the rock is deformable and the grout thickness is at least equal to the dowel radius, the steel is deformed in order to mobilize shear resistance. As a result of the deformation, the yield strengths of the steel and grout are reached in bending and compression respectively.

(c) *Plastic stage*—All the materials in the grouted dowel installation yield at an early stage of shear displacement and at low shear forces. Therefore, the shear resistance of the doweled joint depends on the shear force–displacement relationship of the plasticized materials. The contribution of the dowel to the total shear strength of the joint is a function of the friction angle $(\phi)$ and roughness $(i)$ of the joint, the dowel inclination $(\alpha)$, the compressive strength of the rock and grout $(\sigma_{ci})$ and the tensile strength of the steel bar $(\sigma_{t(s)})$. In general, the shear resistance is enhanced where the joint has a high friction angle and is rough so there is some dilation during shearing, the inclination angle $\alpha$ is between about 30° and 45°, and the rock is deformable but not so soft that the dowel cuts into the rock.

Based on the tests conducted by Spang and Egger, the shear resistance $R_b$ (kN) of a dowelled joint is given by

$$R_b = \sigma_{t(s)}[1.55 + 0.011\sigma_{ci}^{1.07} \sin^2(\alpha + i)]$$
$$\times \sigma_{ci}^{-0.14}(0.85 + 0.45 \tan \phi) \qquad (6.25)$$

where the units of $\sigma_{ci}$ are MPa and of $\sigma_{t(s)}$ are kN. The corresponding displacement $\delta_s$ of a dowelled joint is given by

$$\delta_s = (15.2 - 55.2\sigma_{ci}^{-0.14} + 56.2\sigma_{ci}^{-0.28})$$
$$\times (1 - \tan \alpha(70/\sigma_c)^{0.125}(\cos \alpha)^{-0.5}) \qquad (6.26)$$

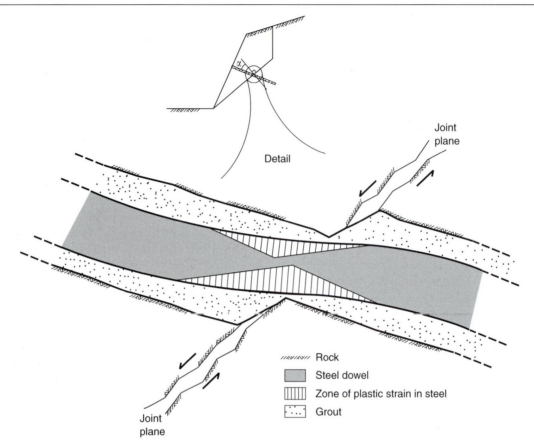

*Figure 6.9* Strain in fully grouted steel dowel due to shear movement along joint (modified from Spang and Egger (1990)).

In the stability analysis of a plane failure in which fully grouted dowels have been installed across the sliding plane, equation (6.4) for the factor of safety is modified as follows to account for the increased shear resistance to sliding:

$$FS = \frac{cA + N \tan \phi + R_b}{S} \qquad (6.27)$$

### 6.4.3   *Reinforcement with buttresses*

The two previous sections discussed reinforcement by installing anchors across the potential sliding surface. An alternate method is to construct a buttress at the toe to provide external support to the slope, using the methods shown on Figure 6.10. In both cases, the factor of safety is calculated using equation (6.27) using the appropriate value for $R_b$ for the system installed.

Near the crest of the slope where the bedding forms a series of slabs, steel bars can be grouted into holes drilled into the rock and then encased in shotcrete or concrete. The steel provides shear resistance to movement, while the concrete provides continuous support between the dowels and keeps small fragments of rock in place. These buttresses are particularly applicable where the rock along the crest is slightly weathered, and if rock anchors were installed, the on-going weathering would eventually expose the bolts. It is likely that the maximum thickness

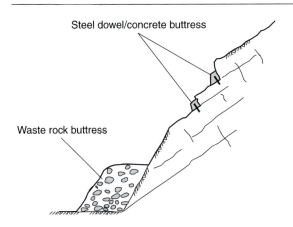

*Figure 6.10* Reinforcement of slope with buttresses.

of slab that can be supported in this manner is about 2 m.

Larger scale support can be provided by placing a waste rock buttress at the toe of the slope. The support provided by such a buttress depends on the buttress weight, and the shear resistance generated along the base of the buttress that is a function of the weight of the rock, and the roughness and inclination of the base. This method can only be used, of course, if there is sufficient space at the toe to accommodate the required volume of rock. It is also important that the waste rock be free draining so that water pressures do not build up behind the buttress.

## 6.5 Seismic analysis of rock slopes

In seismically active areas of the world, the design of rock slopes should take into account the effects on stability of earthquake-induced ground motions. This section describes the influence of ground motions on stability, and design procedures that incorporate seismic acceleration.

### 6.5.1 Performance of rock slopes during earthquakes

There are numerous records of rock falls and landslides being induced by seismic ground motions (Youd, 1978; Van Velsor and Walkinshaw, 1992; Harp and Noble, 1993; Ling and Cheng,

1997). For example, in 1980 a magnitude 6.0–6.1 earthquake at Mammoth Lakes, California dislodged a 21.4 ton boulder that bounced and rolled a horizontal distance of 421 m from its source, and in 1983 in an earthquake in Idaho, a 20.5 ton boulder traveled a distance of about 95 m (Kobayashi, 1990). With respect to landslides, a detailed inventory of landslides induced by the magnitude 6.7 Northridge earthquake in Los Angeles identified about 11,000 landslides in an area of approximately 10,000 km$^2$. (Jibson and Harp, 1995). These slides occurred primarily in the Santa Susana Mountains where the slopes comprise Late Miocene through Pleistocene clastic sediments that have little or no cementation, and that have been folded and uplifted by rapid tectonic deformation (Jibson *et al.*, 1998). For these three events, the maximum epicentral distance to the landslide limit was about 70 km, which is about the average in relation to historical worldwide earthquakes of this magnitude (Keefer, 1984). Another example of seismically induced landslides was the occurrence of slides in strong rock with volumes of millions of cubic meters during the Denali, Alaska event in 2002 (Harp *et al.*, 2003).

Studies of the number and distribution of landslides and rock falls near earthquakes has shown that the concentrations of landslides can be as high as 50 events per square kilometer. These data have been used to assess the geological and topographical conditions for which the landslide and rock fall hazard is high (Keefer, 1992). It has also been found that the following five slope parameters have the greatest influence on stability during earthquakes:

- *Slope angle*—Rock falls and slides rarely occur on slopes with angles less than about 25°.
- *Weathering*—Highly weathered rock comprising core stones in a fine soil matrix, and residual soil are more likely to fail than fresh rock.
- *Induration*—Poorly indurated rock in which the particles are weakly bonded is more likely to fail than stronger, well-indurated rock.

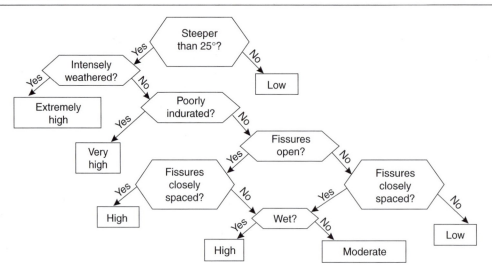

*Figure 6.11* Decision tree for susceptibility of rock slopes to earthquake-induced failure (Keefer, 1992).

- *Discontinuity characteristics*—Rock containing closely spaced, open discontinuities are more susceptible to failure than massive rock in which the discontinuities are closed and healed.
- *Water*—Slopes in which the water table is high, or where there has been recent rainfall, are susceptible to failure.

The relationship between these five conditions and the slope failure hazard is illustrated in the decision tree in Figure 6.11. It is also of interest that the hazard is high for pre-existing landslides with slopes flatter than 25°. Furthermore, there is a hazard for slopes with local relief greater than about 2000 m, probably because seismic shaking is amplified by the topography (Harp and Jibson, 2002), and possible freeze–thaw action at high altitude that loosens the surficial rock.

The decision tree shown in Figure 6.11 can be used, for example, as a screening tool in assessing rock fall and slide hazards along transportation and pipeline corridors. If a more rigorous hazard assessment of a specific site is required, it is possible to use a technique developed by Harp and Wilson (1995) that involves calculating the Arias intensity of the ground motion at the location of interest. The Arias intensity $I_a$ is a measure

of the total energy of the ground motion, and is defined as

$$I_a = \frac{\pi}{2} g \int_0^{T_d} [a(t)]^2 \, dt \quad \text{(units: m/s)} \quad (6.28)$$

where $a(t)$ is a single component acceleration–time series for a strong-motion record with total duration $T_d$ (seconds), $t$ is the time in seconds, and $g$ is the acceleration of gravity. The occurrence of rock falls and slides has been correlated with the Arias intensity of the recorded strong-motion records for the Whittier and Superstition earthquakes in California. The study showed that the Arias intensity threshold for slides in Miocene and Pliocene deposits was in the range of 0.08–0.6 m/s, and the threshold for Precambrian and Mesozoic rocks, where the discontinuities were open, was in the range of 0.01–0.07 m/s. Note that this method is restricted to sites where acceleration-time histories are available, or can be estimated.

### 6.5.2  Seismic hazard analysis

The design of slopes that may be subjected to seismic ground motion requires quantitative information on the magnitude of the motion

(Abrahamson, 2000). This information may be either the peak ground acceleration (PGA) or the acceleration–time history of the motions, depending on the method of stability analysis that is to be used. The process by which the design motion parameters are established is termed "seismic hazard" analysis, which involves the following three steps (NHI, 1998; Glass, 2000):

(a) Identification of seismic sources capable of producing strong ground motions at the site.
(b) Evaluation of seismic potential for each capable source.
(c) Evaluation of the intensity of design ground motions at the site.

Implementation of these three steps involves the following activities.

*Seismic sources.* Earthquakes are the result of fault movement, so identification of seismic sources includes establishing the types of faults and their geographic location, depth, size and orientation. This information is usually available from publications such as geological maps and reports prepared by government geological survey groups and universities, and any previous projects that have been undertaken in the area. Also, the identification of faults can be made from the study of aerial photographs, geological mapping, geophysical surveys and trenching. On aerial photographs, such features as fault scarplets, rifts, fault slide ridges, shutter ridges and fault saddles, and off-sets in such features as fence lines and road curbs (Cluff *et al.*, 1972) may identify active faults. In addition, records of seismic monitoring stations provide information on the location and magnitude of recent earthquakes that can be correlated to fault activity.

*Seismic potential.* Movement of faults within the Holocene Epoch (approximately the last 11,000 years) is generally regarded as the criterion for establishing that the fault is active (USEPA, 1993). Although the occurrence interval of some major earthquakes may be greater than 11,000 years, and not all faults rupture to the surface, lack of evidence that movement has occurred in the Holocene is generally sufficient evidence to dismiss the potential for ground surface rupture. Most Holocene fault activity in North America has occurred west of the Rocky Mountains, and may be identified by detailed mapping, followed by trenching, geophysics or drilling. In regions where there is no surface expression of fault rupture, seismic source characterization depends primarily on micro-seismic studies and the historic record of felt earthquakes.

*Ground motion intensity.* Once the seismic sources capable of generating strong ground motions at a site have been identified and characterized, the intensity of the ground motions can be evaluated either from published codes and standards, or from seismic hazard analysis as discussed in Section 6.5.3. The building codes of countries with seismic areas publish maps in which the country is divided into zones showing, for example, the effective peak acceleration levels (as a fraction of gravity acceleration) with a 10% probability of being exceeded in a 50-year period (Frankel *et al.*, 1996). The information on these maps may also be available on the internet. For example, in the United States it is possible to find acceleration levels for postal zip codes (http:/geohazards.cr.usgs.gov/eq/). These published accelerations can be used in geotechnical design and have the value of promoting standard designs within each zone.

### 6.5.3   *Ground motion characterization*

As a complement to the published maps, a seismic hazard analysis for a specific site can be conducted by evaluating the magnitude of ground motions from all capable sources with the potential for generating strong ground motions at the site. The value of seismic analysis, in contrast to the use of published codes as discussed in the previous paragraph, is the ability to incorporate the latest developments in local seismicity. Furthermore, it is possible to develop site-specific ground motions compared with the regional seismicity on which the codes are based.

The three steps in this analysis are first, to establish the location and style of faulting of all potential sources, and assign each a representative earthquake magnitude. Second, an appropriate attenuation relationship is selected as a function of magnitude, fault mechanism, site-to-source distance and site conditions. Third, the capable sources are screened based on magnitude and ground motion intensity at the site to determine the governing source.

*Attenuation.* Attenuation equations, discussed in the previous paragraph, define the relationship between the source moment magnitude ($M_w$) and peak ground acceleration (PGA) at the site. The equations are based upon either statistical analysis of values observed in previous earthquakes, or from theoretical models of the propagation of strong ground motions, depending on the amount of observed data available. For example, for subduction zones and in the eastern United States the PGA on rock at a hypocentral distance $R$ is given by (Youngs *et al.*, 1988):

$$\ln(\text{PGA}) = 19.16 + 1.045 M_w - 4.738 \ln[R + 154.7 \exp(0.1323 M_w)] \quad (6.29)$$

for $20 < R \leq 40\,\text{km}$, and $M_w > 8$. The moment magnitude is a measure of the kinetic energy released by the earthquake, and the hypocenter is the point from which the seismic waves first emanate.

*Time histories.* If deformation analyses are to be carried out, it is necessary to use a representative time history of the ground motions. Time histories can be selected from previously recorded motions, or by simulation techniques to generate a project-specific synthetic time history. In selecting a representative time history from the catalogue of available records, the relevant characteristics of the project and source sites should be matched as closely as possible. Some of the characteristics that are important in matching time histories include magnitude, source mechanism, focal depth, site-to-source distance, site

geology, PGA, frequency content, duration and energy content.

### 6.5.4  Pseudo-static stability analysis

The limit equilibrium method of determining the factor of safety of a sliding block as described in Section 6.3 can be modified to incorporate the effect on stability of seismic ground motions. The analysis procedure, known as the pseudo-static method, involves simulating the ground motions as a static horizontal force acting in a direction out of the face. The magnitude of this force is the product of a seismic coefficient $k_H$ (dimensionless) and the weight of the sliding block $W$. The value of $k_H$ may be taken as equal to the design PGA, which is expressed as a fraction of the gravity acceleration (i.e. $k_H = 0.1$ if the PGA is 10% of gravity). However, this is a conservative assumption since the actual transient ground motion with a duration of a few seconds is being replaced by a constant force acting over the entire design life of the slope.

In the design of soil slopes and earth dams, it is common that $k_H$ is fraction of the PGA, provided that there is no loss of shear strength during cyclic loading (Seed, 1979; Pyke, 1999). Study of slopes using Newmark analysis (see Section 6.5.5) with a yield acceleration $k_y$ equal to 50% of the PGA (i.e. $k_y = 0.5 \cdot a_{max}/g$) showed that permanent seismic displacement would be less than 1 m (Hynes and Franklin, 1984). Based on these studies, the California Department of Mines and Geology (CDMG, 1997) suggests that it is reasonable to use a value of $k_H$ equal to 50% of the design PGA, in combination with a pseudo-static factor of safety of 1.0–1.2. With respect to soil slopes, and rock slopes where the rock mass contains no distinct sliding surface and some movement can be tolerated, it may be reasonable to use the CDMG procedure to determine a value for $k_H$. However, for rock slopes there are two conditions for which it may be advisable to use $k_H$ values somewhat greater than 0.5 times the PGA. First, where the slope contains a distinct sliding surface for which there is likely to be a significant decrease in shear strength with limited displacement; sliding planes on which the strength would be sensitive to movement include smooth, planar joints or bedding planes with no infilling. Second, where the slope is a topographic high point and some amplification of the ground motions may be expected. In critical situations, it may also be advisable to check the sensitivity of the slope to seismic deformations using Newmark analysis as discussed in Section 6.5.5.

The factor of safety of a plane failure using the pseudo-static method is given by modifying equation (6.4) as follows (assuming the slope is drained, $U = V = 0$):

$$FS = \frac{cA + (W(\cos \psi_p - k_H \sin \psi_p)) \tan \phi}{W(\sin \psi_p + k_H \cos \psi_p)}$$

(6.30)

The equation demonstrates that the effect of the horizontal force is to diminish the factor of safety because the shear resistance is reduced and the displacing force is increased.

Under circumstances where it is considered that the vertical component of the ground motion will be in phase with, and have the same frequency, as the horizontal component, it may be appropriate to use both horizontal and vertical seismic coefficients in stability analysis. If the vertical coefficient is $k_V$ and the ratio of the vertical to the horizontal components is $r_k$ (i.e. $r_k = k_V/k_H$), then the resultant seismic coefficient $k_T$ is

$$k_T = k_H(1 + r_k^2)^{1/2}$$

(6.31)

acting at an angle $\psi_k = \text{atn}(k_V/k_H)$ above the horizontal, and factor of safety is given by

$$FS = \frac{cA + (W(\cos \psi_p - k_T \sin(\psi_p + \psi_k))) \tan \phi}{W(\sin \psi_p + k_T \cos(\psi_p + \psi_k))}$$

(6.32)

Study of the effect of the vertical component on the factor of safety has shown that incorporating the vertical component will not change the factor of safety by more than about 10%,

provided that $k_V < k_H$ (NHI, 1998). Furthermore, equation (6.32) will only apply when the vertical and horizontal components are exactly in phase. Based on these results, it may be acceptable to ignore the vertical component of the ground motion.

### 6.5.5  Newmark analysis

When a rock slope is subject to seismic shaking, failure does not necessarily occur when the dynamic transient stress reaches the shear strength of the rock. Furthermore, if the factor of safety on a potential sliding surface drops below 1.0 at some time during the ground motion it does not necessarily imply a serious problem. What really matters is the magnitude of permanent displacement caused at the times that the factor of safety is less than 1.0 (Lin and Whitman, 1986). The permanent displacement of rock and soil slopes as the result of earthquake motions can be calculated using a method developed by Newmark (1965). This is a more realistic method of analyzing seismic effects on rock slopes than the pseudo-static method of analysis.

The principle of Newmark's method is illustrated in Figure 6.12 in which it is assumed that the potential sliding block is a rigid body on a yielding base. Displacement of a block occurs when the base is subjected to a uniform horizontal acceleration pulse of magnitude $ag$ and duration $t_0$. The velocity of the block is a function of the time $t$ and is designated $y(t)$, and its velocity at time $t$ is $y$. Assuming a frictional contact between the block and the base, the velocity of the block will be $x$, and the relative velocity between the block and the base will be $u$ where

$$u = x - y$$

(6.33)

The resistance to motion is accounted for by the inertia of the block. The maximum force that can be used to accelerate the block is the shearing resistance on the base of the block, which has a friction angle of $\phi°$. This limiting force is proportional to the weight of the block ($W$)

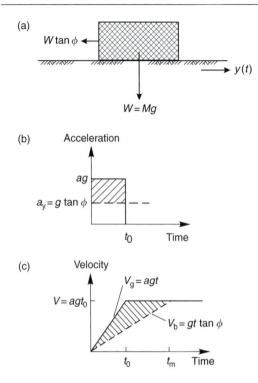

*Figure 6.12* Displacement of rigid block on rigid base (Newmark, 1965): (a) block on moving base; (b) acceleration plot; (c) velocity plot (Newmark, 1965).

and is of magnitude ($W \tan \phi$), corresponding to a yield acceleration $a_y$ of ($g \tan \phi$), as shown by the dashed line on the acceleration plot (Figure 6.12(b)). The shaded area shows that the ground acceleration pulse exceeds the acceleration of the block, resulting in slippage.

Figure 6.12(c) shows the velocities as a function of time for both the ground and the block accelerating forces. The maximum velocity for the ground accelerating force has a magnitude $v$ which remains constant after an elapsed time of $t_0$. The magnitude of the ground velocity $v_g$ is given by

$$v_g = agt_0 \qquad (6.34)$$

while the velocity of the block $v_b$ is

$$v_b = gt \tan \phi \qquad (6.35)$$

After time $t_m$, the two velocities are equal and the block comes to rest with respect to the base, that is, the relative velocity, $u = 0$. The value of $t_m$ is calculated by equating the ground velocity to the velocity of the block to give the following expression for the time $t_m$:

$$t_m = \frac{v_b}{g \tan \phi} \qquad (6.36)$$

The displacement $\delta_m$ of the block relative to the ground at time $t_m$ is obtained by computing the area of the shaded region on Figure. 6.12(c) as follows:

$$
\begin{aligned}
\delta_m &= \tfrac{1}{2} v t_m - \tfrac{1}{2} v t_0 \\
&= \frac{v^2}{2g \tan \phi} - \frac{v^2}{2ag} \\
&= \frac{v^2}{2g \tan \phi} \left( 1 - \frac{\tan \phi}{a} \right) \qquad (6.37)
\end{aligned}
$$

Equation (6.37) gives the displacement of the block in response to a single acceleration pulse (duration $t_0$, magnitude $ag$) that exceeds the yield acceleration ($g \tan \phi$), assuming infinite ground displacement. The equation shows that the displacement is proportional to the square of the ground velocity.

While equation (6.37) applies to a block on a horizontal plane, a block on a sloping plane will slip at a lower yield acceleration and show greater displacement, depending on the direction of the acceleration pulse. For a cohesionless surface where the factor of safety of the block FS is equal to ($\tan \phi / \tan \psi_p$) and the applied acceleration is horizontal, Newmark shows that the yield acceleration $a_y$, is given by

$$a_y = (FS - 1)g \sin \psi_p \qquad (6.38)$$

where $\phi$ is the friction angle of sliding surface, and $\psi_p$ is the dip angle of this surface. Note that for $\psi_p = 0$, $a_y = g \tan \phi$. Also equation (6.38) shows that for a block on a sloping surface, the yield acceleration is higher when the acceleration pulse is in the down-dip direction compared to the pulse in the up-dip direction.

The displacement of a block on an inclined plane can be calculated by combining equations (6.37) and (6.38) as follows:

$$\delta_m = \frac{(agt)^2}{2ga_y}\left(1 - \frac{a_y}{a}\right) \qquad (6.39)$$

In an actual earthquake, the pulse would be followed by a number of pulses of varying magnitude, some positive and some negative, which will produce a series of displacement pulses. This method of displacement analysis can be applied to the case of a transient sinusoidal acceleration $(a(t)g)$ illustrated in Figure 6.13 (Goodman and Seed, 1966). If during some period of the acceleration pulse the shear stress on the sliding surface exceeds the shear strength, displacement will take place. Displacement will take place more readily in a downslope direction; this is illustrated in Figure 6.13 where the shaded areas are the portion of each pulse in which movement takes place. For the conditions illustrated in Figure 6.13, it is assumed that the yield acceleration diminishes with displacement, that is, $a_{y1} > a_{y2} > a_{y3}$ due to shearing of the asperities in the manner described in Section 4.2.4.

Integration of the yield portions of the acceleration pulses gives the velocity of the block. It will start to move at time $t_1$ when the yield acceleration is exceeded, and the velocity will increase up to time $t_2$ when the acceleration drops below the yield acceleration. The velocity drops to zero at time $t_3$ as the acceleration direction begins to change from down slope to up slope. Integration of the velocity pulses gives the displacement of the block, with the duration of each displacement pulse being $(t_3 - t_1)$.

The simple displacement models shown in Figures 6.12 and 6.13 have since been developed to more accurate model displacement due to actual earthquake motions, with much of this work being related to earth dams (Sarma, 1975; Franklin and Chan, 1977). With respect to slope stability, and Jibson (1993) and Jibson *et al.* (1998) have developed procedures for estimating the probability of landslide occurrence as a function of Newmark displacement based on observations of landslides caused by the 1994 Northridge earthquake in California.

Newmark displacement analysis is useful for design if there are guidelines on the relationship between slope stability and the calculated displacement. While the Newmark method of analysis is highly idealized and the calculated

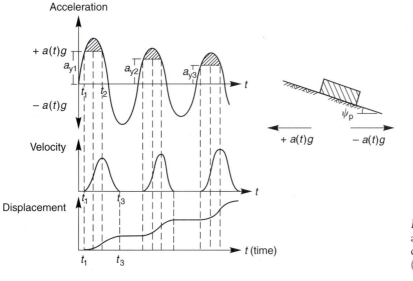

*Figure 6.13* Integration of accelerograms to determine downslope movement (Goodman and Seed, 1966).

displacements should be considered order-of-magnitude estimates of actual field behavior, CDMG (1997) has developed the following guidelines on likely slope behavior:

- 0–100 mm displacement—unlikely to correspond to serious landslide movement;
- 100–1000 mm—slope deformations may be sufficient to cause serious ground cracking or enough strength loss to result in continuing post-seismic failure; and
- >1000 mm displacement—damaging landslide movement and slopes should be considered unstable.

When applying these displacement criteria in rock slope design, consideration should be given to the amount of displacement that will have to occur before the residual shear strength is reached. For example, if the sliding surface is a single discontinuity surface containing a weak infilling, a few centimeters of movement may be sufficient for the strength to be reduced to the residual value. In contrast, a fractured rock mass may undergo several meters of displacement with little reduction in shear strength.

## 6.6   Example of probabilistic design

The design procedures discussed so far in this chapter all use, for each design parameter, single values that are assumed to be the average or best estimate values. In reality, each parameter has a range of values that may represent natural variability, changes over time, and the degree of uncertainty in measuring their values. Therefore, the factor of safety can be realistically expressed as a probability distribution, rather than a single value. In design, this uncertainty can be accounted for by applying judgment in using a factor of safety consistent with the variability/uncertainty in the data. That is, a high factor of safety would be used where the values of the parameters are not well known. Alternatively, the uncertainty can be quantified using probabilistic analysis, such as Monte Carlo analysis, to calculate the probability of failure (see Section 1.4.4).

Examples of variability in design parameters are as follows. The orientation of a discontinuity may vary across the slope due to surface irregularities or folding. This variation will be evident from scatter in the pole locations on the stereonet, and can be quantified in terms of means and standard deviations of the dip and dip direction using the procedure shown in Section 3.5. Also, the shear strength may vary over the sliding surface because of variations in surface roughness and infilling, and can be quantified by testing a number of drill core or lump samples in the laboratory. The water pressure is likely to vary with time in response to precipitation events such as heavy rain storms or melting snow.

Figure 6.14 shows the results of a probabilistic stability analysis of the slope described in Section 4.4 (see Figures 4.18 and 4.19). Section 4.4 describes the calculation of the shear strength properties of the bedding planes, assuming that the factor of safety was 1.0 when the tension crack filled with water and the slope failed. The purpose of the probabilistic analysis described in this section is to show the range in factor of safety that is likely to exist in practice due to the variability in the slope parameters. Figure 6.14(b)–(c) show the probability distributions of the following parameters:

- *Dip of the sliding plane,* $\psi_p$—Normal distribution with a mean value of 20° and a standard deviation of 2.4°.
- *Cohesion, c*—Skewed triangular distribution with most likely value of 80 kPa and maximum and minimum values of 40 and 130 kPa, respectively (4–13.3 ton/m$^2$).
- *Friction angle,* $\phi$—Normal distribution with a mean value of 20° and a standard deviation of 2.7°.
- *Water pressure expressed as percent filling of tension crack*—Triangular distribution ranging from dry (0%) to full (100%), with the most likely value being 50%.

The triangular distribution is used where the most likely value and the upper and lower bounds can only be estimated, whereas the normal distribution is used where there is sufficient data

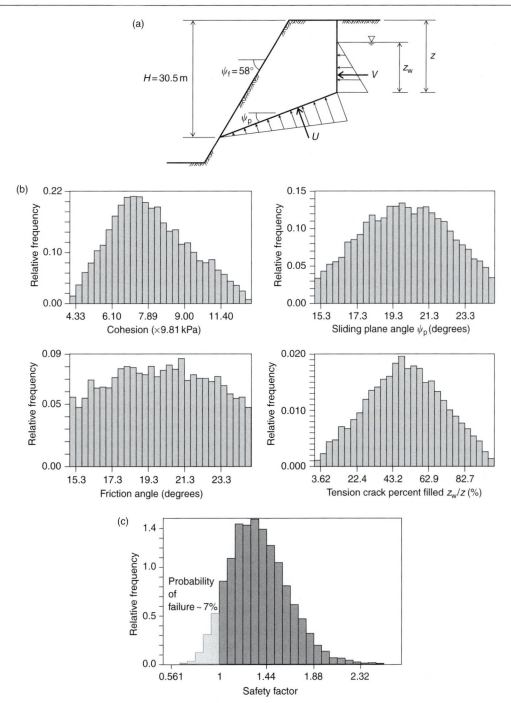

*Figure 6.14* Probabilistic analysis of plane failure: (a) slope model showing water pressures $U$ and $V$; (b) probability distributions of cohesion, friction angle, sliding plane angle and depth of water in tension crack; (c) probability distribution of factor of safety showing 7% of probability of failure (refer to Figures 4.18–4.20).

available to calculate the mean and standard deviation. Other distributions can be used as applicable.

Figure 6.14(c) shows the distribution of the factor of safety generated, using the Monte Carlo method (see Section 1.4.4(b)), as the result of 10,000 iterations with values randomly selected from the input parameter distributions. The histogram shows that the mean, maximum and minimum factors of safety are 1.36, 2.52 and 0.69 respectively. Also, the factor of safety was less than 1.0 for 720 iterations, so the probability of failure is 7.2%. If the mean values of all the input parameters are used in the stability analysis, the calculated deterministic factor of safety is 1.4. The sensitivity analysis associated with these calculations shows that the factor of safety is most strongly influenced by the dip of the slide plane, and least influence by the depth of water in the tension crack. This analysis was performed using the computer program ROCPLANE (Rocscience, 2003).

## 6.7   Example Problem 6.1: plane failure—analysis and stabilization

### Statement

A 12-m high rock slope has been excavated at a face angle of 60°. The rock in which this cut has been made contains persistent bedding planes that dip at an angle of 35° into the excavation. The 4.35-m deep tension crack is 4 m behind the crest, and is filled with water to a height of 3 m above the sliding surface (Figure 6.15). The strength parameters of the sliding surface are as follows:

$$\text{Cohesion, } c = 25\,\text{kPa}$$
$$\text{Friction angle, } \phi = 37°$$

The unit weight of the rock is $26\,\text{kN/m}^3$, and the unit weight of the water is $9.81\,\text{kN/m}^3$.

### Required

Assuming that a plane slope failure is the most likely type of instability, analyze the following stability conditions.

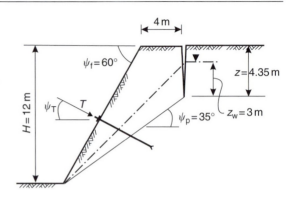

*Figure 6.15* Plane failure geometry for Example Problem 6.1.

### Factor of safety calculations

(a)   Calculate the factor of safety of the slope for the conditions given in Figure 6.15.
(b)   Determine the factor of safety if the tension crack were completely filled with water due to run-off collecting on the crest of the slope.
(c)   Determine the factor of safety if the slope were completely drained.
(d)   Determine the factor of safety if the cohesion were to be reduced to zero due to excessive vibrations from nearby blasting operations, assuming that the slope was still completely drained.
(e)   Determine whether the 4.35-m deep tension crack is the critical depth (use Figure 6.6).

### Slope reinforcement using rock bolts

(a)   It is proposed that the drained slope with zero cohesion be reinforced by installing tensioned rock bolts anchored into sound rock beneath the sliding plane. If the rock bolts are installed at right angles to the sliding plane, that is, $\psi_T = 55°$, and the total load on the anchors per lineal meter of slope is 400 kN, calculate the factor of safety.
(b)   Calculate the factor of safety if the bolts are installed at a flatter angle so that the $\psi_T$ is decreased from 55° to 20°.
(c)   If the working load for each bolt is 250 kN, suggest a bolt layout, that is, the number of bolts per vertical row, and the horizontal and

vertical spacing between bolts to achieve a bolt load of 400 kN/m of slope length.

## Solution

*Factor of safety calculations*

(a)  The factor of safety is calculated using equations (6.4)–(6.10).

The weight $W$ of the block is 1241 kN/m (equation 6.8), and the area $A$ of the sliding plane is 13.34 m$^2$/m (Equation 6.5). For water in the tension crack to depth, $z_w = 4.35$ m, the values of the water forces $U$ and $V$ acting on the block are 196.31 kN/m and 44.15 kN/m (equations (6.6) and (6.7)).

$$FS = \{cA + (W \cos \psi_p - U - V \sin \psi_p) \tan \phi\}$$
$$/ \{W \sin \psi_p + V \cos \psi_p\}$$
$$= \{25(13.34) + (1241.70 \cos 35 - 196.31$$
$$-44.15 \sin 35) \tan 37\}$$
$$/ \{1241.70 \sin 35 + 44.15 \cos 35\}$$
$$= 1.25$$

(In civil applications, this is usually a marginal factor of safety for a permanent slope with a high consequence of failure.)

(b)  If the tension crack is completely filled with water, that is, $z_w = 4.35$ m, and the new factor of safety is

$$FS = \{333.50 + (1017.14 - 284.57 - 53.23)$$
$$\times \tan 37\} / \{712.21 + 76.02\}$$
$$= 1.07$$

(This indicates that the slope is close to failure.)

(c)  If the slope were drained so that there was no water in the tension crack, that is, $z_w = 0$, then the new factor of safety is

$$FS = \frac{333.50 + 1017.14 \tan 37}{712.21}$$
$$= 1.54$$

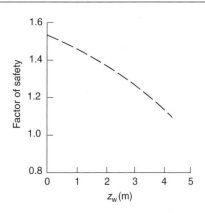

*Figure 6.16* Plot of factor of safety against depth of water in tension crack for example Problem 6.1.

(This is usually an adequate factor of safety). The factor of safety values are plotted on Figure 6.16.

(d)  If the slope is drained and the cohesion on the sliding plane is reduced from 25 kPa to zero by blast vibrations, then the new factor of safety is

$$FS = \frac{0 + 1017.14 \tan 37}{712.21}$$
$$= 1.08$$

The loss of cohesion reduces the factor of safety from 1.54 to 1.08 which illustrates the sensitivity of the slope to the cohesion on the sliding plane.

(e)  Figure 6.6(a) shows that the critical tension crack depth is 4.32 m (i.e. $z/H = 0.36$) which is close to the position of the tension crack (i.e. $4.35/12 = 0.36$).

*Slope reinforcement with rock bolts*

(a)  The factor of safety of plane slope failure reinforced with rock bolts is calculated using equation (6.22). In this case, the slope is drained and the cohesion is zero, that is

$$c = U = V = 0 \qquad (6.40)$$

Therefore, for a reinforcement force of $T$ of 400 kN/m installed at a dip angle $\psi_T$ of 55°, the factor of safety is

$$FS = \frac{[W \cos \psi_p + T \sin(\psi_T + \psi_p)] \tan \phi}{W \sin \psi_p - T \cos(\psi_T + \psi_p)}$$

$$= \frac{[1241.70 \cos 35 + 400 \sin(55 + 35)] \tan 37}{1241.70 \sin 35 - 400 \cos(55 + 35)}$$

$$= \frac{1067.90}{712.21}$$

$$= 1.5$$

(b)  If the bolts are installed at a flatter angle, $\psi_T = 20°$, then the factor of safety is

$$FS = \frac{[1241.70 \cos 35 + 400 \sin(20 + 35)] \tan 37}{1241.70 \sin 35 - 400 \cos(20 + 35)}$$

$$= \frac{1013.38}{482.78}$$

$$= 2.10$$

This shows the significant improvement that can be achieved by installing bolts at an angle flatter than the normal to the sliding surface. The optimum angle is when

$$\psi_{Topt} = (\phi - \psi_p) \quad \text{(see equation (6.23))}$$

$$= (37° - 35°)$$

$$= 2°, \text{ and factor of safety } = 2.41$$

(c)  The rock bolt pattern should be laid out so that the distribution of bolts on the slope is as even as possible. If four bolts are installed in each vertical row, the horizontal spacing $S$ of the vertical rows is calculated as follows:

$$S = \frac{T_B n}{T} \left( \frac{\text{kN}}{\text{kN/m}} \right) \qquad (6.24)$$

$$= \frac{240.4}{400}$$

$$\approx 2.5 \text{ m}$$

# Chapter 7

# Wedge failure

## 7.1 Introduction

The previous chapter was concerned with slope failure resulting from sliding on a single planar surface dipping into the excavation, and striking parallel or nearly parallel to the slope face. It was stated that the plane failure analysis is valid if the strike of the failure plane is within $\pm 20°$ of the strike of the slope face. This chapter is concerned with the failure of slopes containing discontinuities striking obliquely to the slope face where sliding of a wedge of rock takes place along the line of intersection of two such planes (Figure 7.1). Wedge failures can occur over a much wider range of geologic and geometric conditions than plane failures, so the study of wedge stability is an important component of rock slope engineering. The analysis of wedges has been extensively discussed in geotechnical literature, and the manual draws heavily upon the work of Goodman (1964), Wittke (1965), Londe (1965), Londe *et al.* (1969, 1970), John (1970).

In this chapter, the structural geological conditions that result in the formation of a wedge formed by two intersecting planes are defined, and the method of identifying wedges on the stereonet is illustrated. The stereonet defines the shape of the wedge, the orientation of the line of intersection and the direction of sliding. This information can be used to assess the potential for the wedge to slide from the cut face. The procedure is termed *kinematic analysis*, the purpose of which is to identify potentially unstable wedges, although it does not provide precise information on their factor of safety.

*Figure 7.1* Typical wedge failure involving sliding on two persistent joints with line of intersection of joints daylighting at toe of rock face, and an upper plane that formed a tension crack (strong, volcanic rock on Interstate 5, near Grants Pass, Oregon).

The chapter presents design charts that can be used to find the factor of safety of wedges for which friction is the only component of the shear strength, and there are no external forces such as water pressures or bolting acting on the wedge.

In addition, equations are presented that can be used to calculate the factor of safety of wedges where the shear strength on the two slide planes is defined by cohesion and friction angle, and each plane can have different shear strengths. The analysis can also incorporate water pressure.

The presence of a tension crack, and the influence of external forces due to water pressures, tensioned anchors, seismic accelerations or bridge foundations results in a significant increase in the complexity of the equations. Appendix III presents the complete solution for the wedge analysis.

## 7.2  Definition of wedge geometry

Typical wedge failures illustrated in Figures 7.1 and 7.2 show the conditions that are normally assumed for the analytical treatment of wedges. Figure 7.1 shows a cut slope where a wedge is formed by two continuous, planar discontinuities and the line of intersection of these two planes daylights just at the toe of the rock face. That is, the trend of the line of intersection and the dip direction of the face are approximately equal. Furthermore, the plunge of the line of intersection is about 50–55°, while the friction angle of these joints is in the range of 35–40°. That is, the line of intersection dips steeper than the friction angle. These conditions meet the kinematic requirements for failure of the wedge. Figure 7.1 also illustrates how a slight change in the site conditions would result in a stable slope. For example, if the line of intersection had been slightly behind the face, or just one of the joints had been discontinuous, then no failure would have occurred.

The wedge in Figure 7.2 is formed by bedding on the left and a conjugate joint set on the right. As in Figure 7.1, the line of intersection daylights in the slope face and failure occurred. However, in this wedge, sliding occurred almost entirely on the bedding with the joint acting as a release surface. Therefore, the shear strength of the joint has little effect on stability.

The geometry of the wedge for analyzing the basic mechanics of sliding is defined in Figure 7.3. Based on this geometry, the general conditions for wedge failure are as follows:

1  Two planes will always intersect in a line (Figure 7.3(a)). On the stereonet, the line of

*Figure 7.2* Wedge formed by bedding (left) and a conjugate joint set (right); sliding occurred on bedding with joints acting as a release surface (bedded shale, near Helena, Montana).

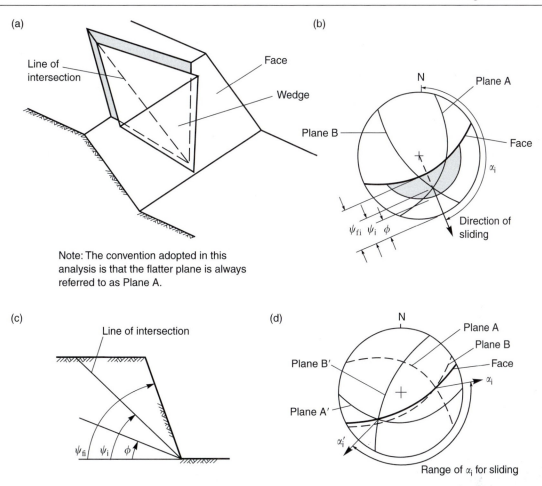

*Figure 7.3* Geometric conditions for wedge failure: (a) pictorial view of wedge failure; (b) stereoplot showing the orientation of the line of intersection, and the range of the plunge of the line of intersection $\psi_i$ where failure is feasible; (c) view of slope at right angles to the line of intersection; (d) stereonet showing the range in the trend of the line of intersection $\alpha_i$ where wedge failure is feasible.

intersection is represented by the point where the two great circles of the planes intersect, and the orientation of the line is defined by its trend ($\alpha_i$) and its plunge ($\psi_i$) (Figure 7.3(b)).

2   The plunge of the line of intersection must be flatter than the dip of the face, and steeper than the average friction angle of the two slide planes, that is $\psi_{fi} > \psi_i > \phi$ (Figure 7.3(b) and (c)). The inclination of the slope face $\psi_{fi}$ is measured in the view at right angles to the line of intersection. Note the $\psi_{fi}$ would only be the same as $\psi_f$, the true dip of the slope face, if the

dip direction of the line of intersection were the same as the dip direction of the slope face.

3   The line of intersection must dip in a direction out of the face for sliding to be feasible; the possible range in the trend of the line of intersection is between $\alpha_i$ and $\alpha_i'$ (Figure 7.3(d)).

In general, sliding may occur if the intersection point between the two great circles of the sliding planes lies within the shaded area on Figure 7.3(b). That is, the stereonet will show if wedge failure is kinematically feasible. However, the actual factor of safety of the wedge cannot be determined from the stereonet, because it depends on the details of the geometry of the wedge, the shear strength of each plane and water pressure, as described in the following sections.

The trend $\alpha_i$ and plunge $\psi_i$ of the line of intersection of planes $A$ and $B$ can be determined on the stereonet, or calculated using equations (7.1) and (7.2) as follows:

$$\alpha_i = \tan^{-1}\left(\frac{\tan \psi_A \cos \alpha_A - \tan \psi_B \cos \alpha_B}{\tan \psi_B \sin \alpha_B - \tan \psi_A \sin \alpha_A}\right) \tag{7.1}$$

$$\psi_i = \tan \psi_A \cos(\alpha_A - \alpha_i) = \tan \psi_B \cos(\alpha_B - \alpha_i) \tag{7.2}$$

where $\alpha_A$ and $\alpha_B$ are the dip directions, and $\psi_A$ and $\psi_B$ are the dips of the two planes. Equation (7.1) gives two solutions 180° apart; the correct value lies between $\alpha_A$ and $\alpha_B$.

## 7.3  Analysis of wedge failure

The factor of safety of the wedge defined in Figure 7.3, assuming that sliding is resisted only by friction and that the friction angle $\phi$ is the same for both planes, is given by

$$FS = \frac{(R_A + R_B)\tan\phi}{W\sin\psi_i} \tag{7.3}$$

where $R_A$ and $R_B$ are the normal reactions provided by planes A and B as illustrated in Figure 7.4, and the component of the weight acting down the line of intersection is $(W\sin\psi_i)$. The forces $R_A$ and $R_B$ are found by resolving them into components normal and parallel to the direction along the line of intersection as follows:

$$R_A\sin\left(\beta - \tfrac{1}{2}\xi\right) = R_B\sin\left(\beta + \tfrac{1}{2}\xi\right) \tag{7.4}$$

$$R_A\cos\left(\beta - \tfrac{1}{2}\xi\right) + R_B\cos\left(\beta + \tfrac{1}{2}\xi\right)$$
$$= W\cos\psi_i \tag{7.5}$$

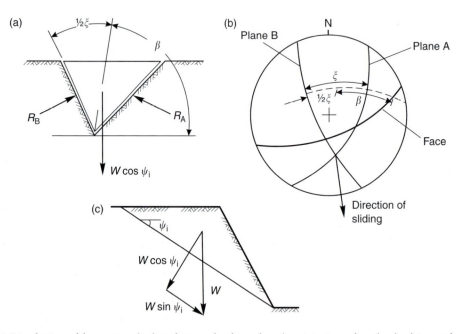

*Figure 7.4* Resolution of forces to calculate factor of safety of wedge: (a) view of wedge looking at face showing definition of angles $\beta$ and $\xi$, and reactions on sliding planes $R_A$ and $R_B$; (b) stereonet showing measurement of angles $\beta$ and $\xi$; (c) cross-section of wedge showing resolution of wedge weight $W$.

where the angles $\xi$ and $\beta$ are defined in Figure 7.4(a). Angles $\xi$ and $\beta$ are measured on the great circle containing the pole to the line of intersection and the poles of the two slide planes. In order to meet the conditions for equilibrium, the normal components of the reactions are equal (equation (7.4)), and the sum of the parallel components equals the component of the weight acting down the line of intersection (equation (7.5)).

The values of $R_A$ and $R_B$ are found from equations (7.4) and (7.5) by solving and adding as follows:

$$R_A + R_B = \frac{W \cos \psi_i \sin \beta}{\sin(\xi/2)} \tag{7.6}$$

Hence

$$FS = \frac{\sin \beta}{\sin(\xi/2)} \cdot \frac{\tan \phi}{\tan \psi_i} \tag{7.7}$$

In other words,

$$FS_W = K \, FS_P \tag{7.8}$$

where $FS_W$ is the factor of safety of a wedge supported by friction only, and $FS_P$ is the factor of safety of a plane failure in which the slide plane, with friction angle $\phi$, dips at the same angle as the line of intersection $\psi_i$.

$K$ is the wedge factor that, as shown by equation (7.7), depends upon the included angle of the wedge $\xi$ and the angle of tilt $\beta$ of the wedge. Values for the wedge factor $K$, for a range of values of $\xi$ and $\beta$ are plotted in Figure 7.5.

The method of calculating the factor of safety of wedges as discussed in this section is, of course, simplistic because it does not incorporate different friction angles and cohesions on the two slide planes, or ground water pressures. When these factors are included in the analysis, the equations become more complex. Rather than develop these equations in terms of the angles $\xi$ and $\beta$, which cannot be measured directly in the field, the more complete analysis is presented in terms of directly measurable dips and dip directions. The following section gives equations for the factor of safety

of a wedge with cohesion and friction acting on the slide planes and water pressure. The complete set of equations for stability analysis of a wedge is shown in Appendix III; this analysis includes parameters to define the shape and dimensions of the wedge, different shear strengths on each slide surface, water pressures and two external loads.

This section shows the important influence of the wedging action as the included angle of the wedge decreases below 90°. The increase by a factor of 2 or 3 on the factor of safety determined by plane failure analysis is of great practical importance because, as shown in Figure 7.5, the factor of safety of a wedge can be significantly greater than that of a plane failure. Therefore, where the structural features that are likely to control the stability of a rock slope do not strike parallel to the slope face, the stability analysis should be carried out by means of three-dimensional methods discussed in this chapter.

## 7.4    Wedge analysis including cohesion, friction and water pressure

Section 7.3 discussed the geometric conditions that could result in a wedge failure, but this kinematic analysis provides limited information of the factor of safety because the dimensions of the wedge were not considered. This section describes a method to calculate the factor of safety of a wedge that incorporates the slope geometry, different shear strengths of the two slide planes and ground water (Hoek et al., 1973). However, the limitations of this analysis are that there is no tension crack, and no external forces such as bolting can be included.

Figure 7.6(a) shows the geometry and dimensions of the wedge that will be considered in the following analysis. Note that the upper slope surface in this analysis can be obliquely inclined with respect to the slope face, thereby removing a restriction that has been present in the stability analyses that have been discussed so far in the book. The total height of the slope $H$ is the difference in vertical elevation between the upper and lower extremities of the line of intersection along which sliding is assumed to occur. The water

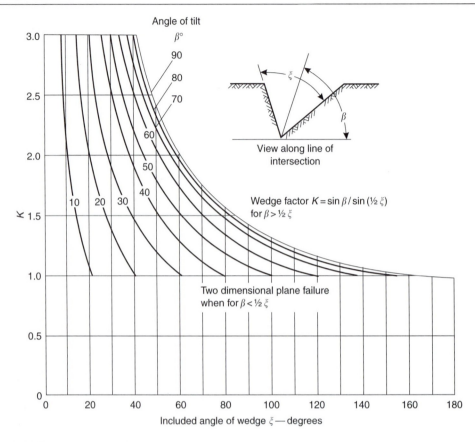

*Figure 7.5* Wedge factor $K$ as a function of wedge geometry.

pressure distribution assumed for this analysis is based upon the hypothesis that the wedge itself is impermeable and that water enters the top of the wedge along lines of intersection 3 and 4 and leaks from the slope face along lines of intersection 1 and 2. The resulting pressure distribution is shown in Figure 7.6(b)—the maximum pressure occurring along the line of intersection 5 and the pressure being zero along lines 1, 2, 3 and 4. This is a triangular pressure distribution with the maximum value occurring at the mid-height of the slope, with the estimated maximum pressure being equal to $(\frac{1}{2}\gamma_w H)$. This water pressure distribution is believed to be representative of the extreme conditions that could occur during very heavy rain and the slope is saturated.

The two planes on which sliding occurs are designated A and B, with plane A having the

shallower dip. The numbering of the five lines of intersection of the four planes defining the wedge is as follows:

Line 1   Intersection of plane A with the slope face

Line 2   Intersection of plane B with the slope face

Line 3   Intersection of plane A with upper slope surface

Line 4   Intersection of plane B with upper slope surface

Line 5   Intersection of planes A and B

It is assumed that sliding of the wedge always takes place along the line of intersection numbered 5, and its factor of safety is given by

(a)

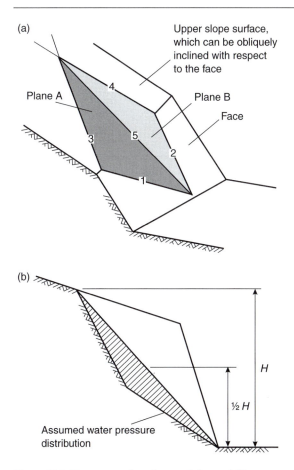

Upper slope surface, which can be obliquely inclined with respect to the face

Plane A

Plane B

Face

(b)

$H$

½ $H$

Assumed water pressure distribution

*Figure 7.6* Geometry of wedge used for stability analysis including the influence of friction and cohesion, and of water pressure on the slide surfaces: (a) pictorial view of wedge showing the numbering of the intersection lines and planes; (b) view normal to the line of intersection (5) showing wedge height and water pressure distribution.

(Hoek *et al.*, 1973):

$$FS = \frac{3}{\gamma_r H}(c_A X + c_B Y) + \left(A - \frac{\gamma_w}{2\gamma_r}X\right)\tan\phi_A$$
$$+ \left(B - \frac{\gamma_w}{2\gamma_r}Y\right)\tan\phi_B \qquad (7.9)$$

where $c_A$ and $c_B$ are the cohesive strengths, and $\phi_A$ and $\phi_B$ are the angles of friction respectively on planes A and B, $\gamma_r$ is the unit weight of the rock,

$\gamma_w$ is the unit weight of the water, $H$ is the total height of the wedge. The dimensionless factors $X, Y, A$ and $B$ depend upon the geometry of the wedge.

The values of parameters $X, Y, A$ and $B$ are given in equations (7.10)–(7.13):

$$X = \frac{\sin\theta_{24}}{\sin\theta_{45}\cos\theta_{2.na}} \qquad (7.10)$$

$$Y = \frac{\sin\theta_{13}}{\sin\theta_{35}\cos\theta_{1.nb}} \qquad (7.11)$$

$$A = \frac{\cos\psi_a - \cos\psi_b\cos\theta_{na.nb}}{\sin\psi_5\sin^2\theta_{na.nb}} \qquad (7.12)$$

$$B = \frac{\cos\psi_b - \cos\psi_a\cos\theta_{na.nb}}{\sin\psi_5\sin^2\theta_{na.nb}} \qquad (7.13)$$

where $\psi_a$ and $\psi_b$ are the dips of planes A and B respectively and $\psi_5$ is the dip of the line of intersection, line 5. The angles required for the solution of these equations can be measured most conveniently on a stereoplot that defines the geometry of the wedge and the slope (Figure 7.7).

The application of the equations discussed in this section is illustrated in the following example, using the parameters shown in Table 7.1.

The total height of the wedge $H$ is 40 m, the unit weight of the rock is 25 kN/m$^3$, and the unit weight of the water 9.81 kN/m$^3$.

The stereoplot of the great circles representing the four planes involved in this example is presented in Figure 7.7, and all the angles required for the solution of equations (7.10)–(7.13) are marked in this figure.

Determination of the factor of safety is most conveniently carried out on a calculation sheet such as that presented on Table 7.2. Setting the calculations out in this manner not only enables the user to check all the data, but it also shows how each variable contributes to the overall factor of safety. Hence, if it is required to check the influence of the cohesion on both planes falling to zero, this can be done by setting the two groups containing the cohesion values $c_A$ and $c_B$ to zero, giving a factor of safety of 0.62. Alternatively, the effect of drainage can be checked by

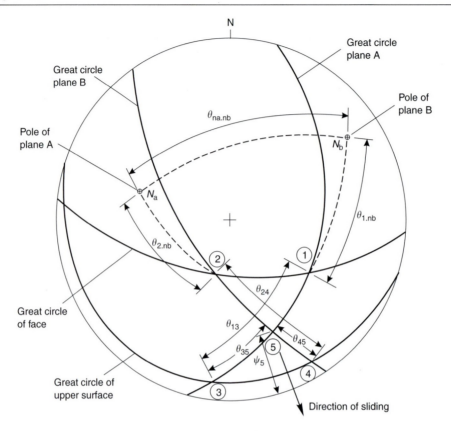

*Figure 7.7* Stereoplot of data required for wedge stability analysis.

*Table 7.1* Parameters defining properties of wedge

| Plane | Dip | Dip direction | Properties |
|-------|-----|---------------|------------|
| A | 45 | 105 | $\phi_A = 20°$, $c_A = 24\,\text{kPa}$ |
| B | 70 | 235 | $\phi_B = 30°$, $c_B = 48\,\text{kPa}$ |
| Slope face | 65 | 185 | |
| Upper surface | 12 | 195 | |

varying the water density to simulate the effect of reducing the water pressure. In this example, the factor of safety is 1.98 when the slope is completely drained.

As has been emphasized in previous chapters, this ability to check the sensitivity of the factor of safety to changes in material properties or water

pressures is important because the value of these parameters are difficult to define precisely.

## 7.5   Wedge stability charts for friction only

A rapid check of the stability of a wedge can be made if the slope is drained and there is zero cohesion on both the slide planes A and B. Under these conditions, equation (7.9) reduces to

$$FS = A \tan \phi_A + B \tan \phi_B \qquad (7.14)$$

The dimensionless factors $A$ and $B$ are found to depend upon the dips and dip directions of the two planes. The values of these two factors have been computed for a range of wedge geometries, and the results are presented as a series of charts (Figures 7.8–7.15).

*Table 7.2* Wedge stability calculation sheet

| Input data | Function value | Calculated values | | |
|---|---|---|---|---|
| $\psi_a = 45°$ | $\cos \psi_a = 0.707$ | | | |
| $\psi_b = 70°$ | $\cos \psi_b = 0.342$ | $A = \dfrac{\cos \psi_a - \cos \psi_b \cos \theta_{na.nb}}{\sin \psi_5 \sin^2 \theta_{na.nb}} = \dfrac{0.707 + 0.342 \times 0.191}{0.518 \times 0.964} = 1.548$ | | |
| $\psi_5 = 31.2°$ | $\sin \psi_5 = 0.518$ | | | |
| $\psi_{na.nb} = 101°$ | $\cos \psi_{na.nb} = -0.191$ | | | |
| | $\sin \psi_{na.nb} = 0.982$ | $B = \dfrac{\cos \psi_b - \cos \psi_a \cos \theta_{na.nb}}{\sin \psi_5 \sin^2 \theta_{na.nb}} = \dfrac{0.342 + 0.707 \times 0.191}{0.518 \times 0.964} = 0.956$ | | |
| $\theta_{24} = 65°$ | $\sin \theta_{24} = 0.906$ | | | |
| $\theta_{45} = 25°$ | $\sin \theta_{45} = 0.423$ | $X = \dfrac{\sin \theta_{24}}{\sin \theta_{45} \cos \theta_{2.na}} = \dfrac{0.906}{0.423 \times 0.643} = 3.336$ | | |
| $\theta_{2.na} = 50°$ | $\cos \theta_{2.na} = 0.643$ | | | |
| $\theta_{13} = 62°$ | $\sin \theta_{13} = 0.883$ | | | |
| $\theta_{35} = 31°$ | $\sin \theta_{35} = 0.515$ | $Y = \dfrac{\sin \theta_{13}}{\sin \theta_{35} \cos \theta_{1.nb}} = \dfrac{0.883}{0.515 \times 0.5} = 3.429$ | | |
| $\theta_{1.nb} = 60°$ | $\cos \theta_{1.nb} = 0.500$ | | | |
| $\phi_A = 30°$ | $\tan \phi_A = 0.577$ | | | |
| $\phi_B = 20°$ | $\tan \phi_B = 0.364$ | $FS = \dfrac{3}{\gamma_r H}(c_A X + c_B Y) + \left(A - \dfrac{\gamma_w}{2\gamma_r}X\right)\tan \phi_A + \left(B - \dfrac{\gamma_w}{2\gamma_r}Y\right)\tan \phi_B$ | | |
| $\gamma_r = 25\,\text{kN/m}^3$ | $\gamma_w/2\gamma_r = 0.196$ | | | |
| $\gamma_w = 9.81\,\text{kN/m}^3$ | $3c_A/\gamma H = 0.072$ | $FS = 0.241 + 0.494 + 0.893 - 0.376 + 0.348 - 0.244 = 1.36$ | | |
| $c_A = 24\,\text{kPa}$ | $3c_B/\gamma H = 0.144$ | | | |
| $c_B = 48\,\text{kPa}$ | | | | |
| $H = 40\,\text{m}$ | | | | |

Note that the factor of safety calculated from equation (7.14) is independent of the slope height, the angle of the slope face and the inclination of the upper slope surface. This rather surprising result arises because the weight of the wedge occurs in both the numerator and denominator of the factor of safety equation and, for the friction only case, this term cancels out, leaving a dimensionless ratio which defines the factor of safety. As discussed in Section 1.4, the factor of safety of a plane failure is also independent of the slope dimensions if the slope is drained and the cohesion is zero. This simplification is very useful in that it enables the user of these charts to carry out a quick check on the stability of a slope based on the dips and dip directions of the two discontinuities that form the slide planes of the wedge. An example of such an analysis is presented later in this chapter.

Many trial calculations have shown that a wedge having a factor of safety in excess of 2.0, as obtained from the friction-only stability charts, is unlikely to fail under even the most severe combination of conditions to which the slope is likely to be subjected. Consider the example discussed in Section 7.4 in which the factor of safety for the worst conditions (zero cohesion and maximum water pressure) is 0.62. This is 50% of the factor of safety of 1.24 for the friction only case. Hence, had the factor of safety for the friction only case been 2.0, the factor of safety for the worst conditions would have been 1.0, assuming that the ratio of the factors of safety for the two cases remains constant.

Based on such trial calculations, it is suggested that the friction-only stability charts can be used to define those slopes that are adequately stable and can be ignored in subsequent analyses. That is, slopes having a factor of safety in excess of 2.0. Slopes with a factor of safety, based upon friction only, of less than 2.0 must be regarded as potentially unstable and require further detailed examination as discussed in Section 7.6 and Appendix III.

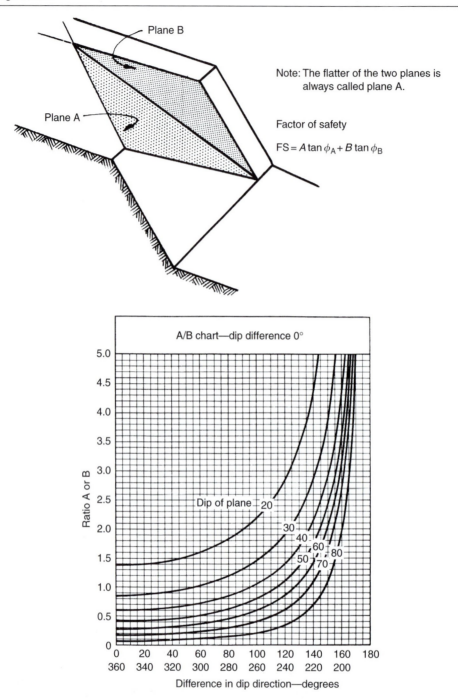

*Figure 7.8* Wedge stability charts for friction only: A and B charts for a dip difference of 0°.

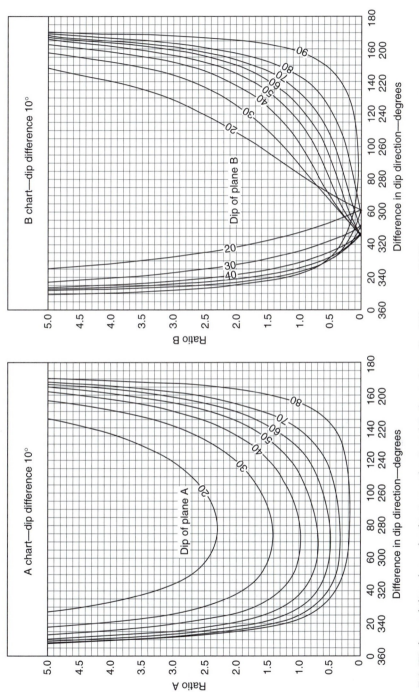

*Figure 7.9* Wedge stability charts for friction only: A and B charts for a dip difference of 10°.

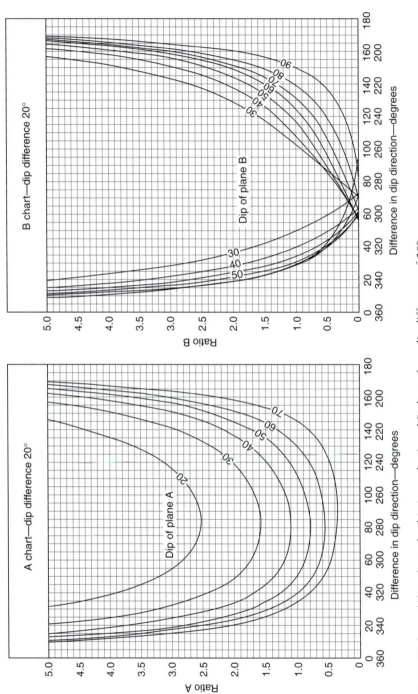

*Figure 7.10* Wedge stability charts for friction only: A and B charts for a dip difference of 20°.

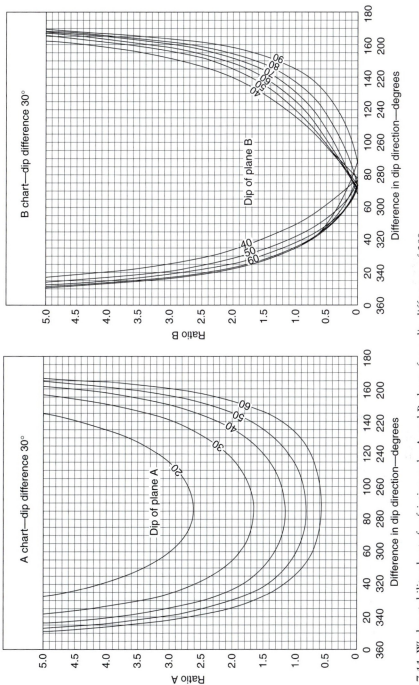

*Figure 7.11* Wedge stability charts for friction only: A and B charts for a dip difference of 30°.

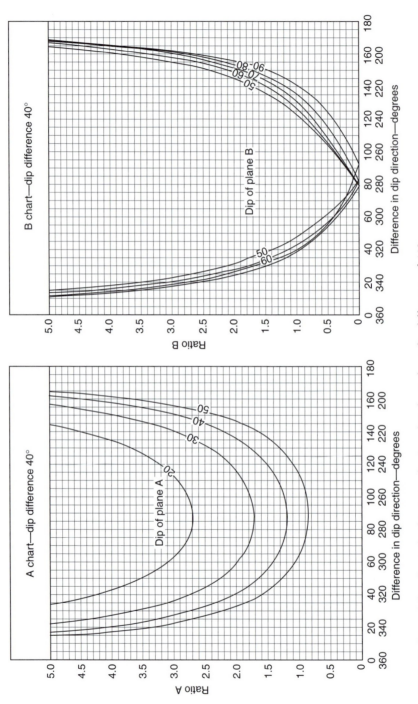

*Figure 7.12* Wedge stability charts for friction only: A and B charts for a dip difference of 40°.

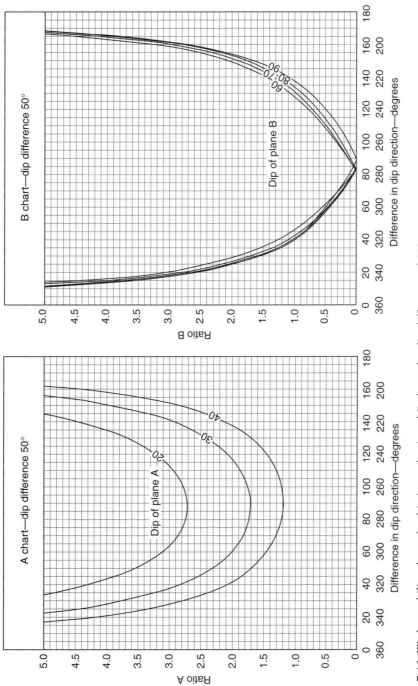

*Figure 7.13* Wedge stability charts for friction only: A and B charts for dip difference of 50°.

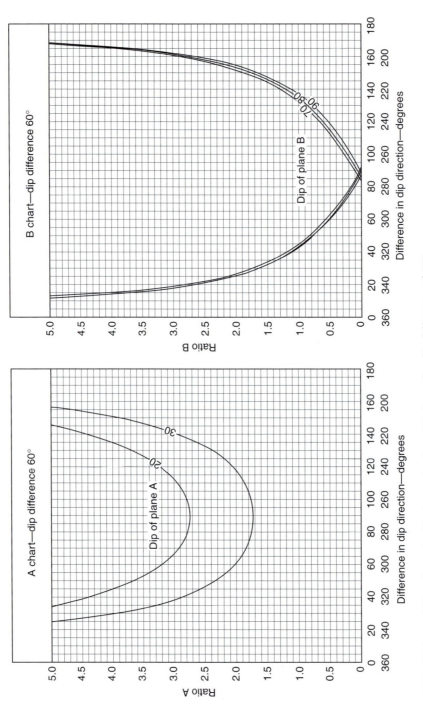

*Figure 7.14* Wedge stability charts for friction only: A and B charts for dip difference of 60°.

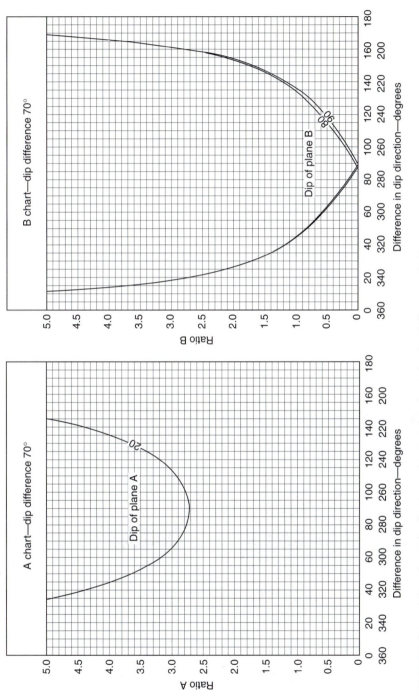

Figure 7.15 Wedge stability charts for friction only: A and B charts for dip difference of 70°.

*Table 7.3* Wedge stability analysis for friction only

|  | Dip (degrees) | Dip direction | Friction angle |
|---|---|---|---|
| Plane A | 40 | 165 | 35 |
| Plane B | 70 | 285 | 20 |
| Differences | 30 | 120 |  |

*Table 7.4* Orientations of discontinuity sets in wedge analysis example

| Discontinuity set | Dip | Dip direction |
|---|---|---|
| 1 | $66 \pm 2$ | $298 \pm 2$ |
| 2 | $68 \pm 6$ | $320 \pm 15$ |
| 3 | $60 \pm 16$ | $360 \pm 10$ |
| 4 | $58 \pm 6$ | $76 \pm 6$ |
| 5 | $54 \pm 4$ | $118 \pm 2$ |

In the design of the cut slopes on many projects, it will be found that these friction-only stability charts provide all the information that is required for preliminary design and planning stages of a slope project. This information will help identify potentially unstable wedges before excavation of the slope is started. During construction, the charts can be used to make a rapid check of stability conditions when, for example, faces are being mapped as the excavation is proceeding and decisions are required on the need for support. If the factor of safety is less than 2.0, the detailed analysis can be used to design a bolting pattern (see Appendix III).

The following example illustrates the use of the friction-only charts, in which Plane A has the flatter dip (Table 7.3).

The first step in the analysis is to calculate the absolute values of the difference in the dip angles, and the difference in the dip direction angles (third line in Table 7.3). For a dip difference of 30°, the values of ratios *A* and *B* and determined from the two charts on Figure 7.11 for a difference in dip direction of 120°. The values of *A* and *B* are 1.5 and 0.7 respectively, and substitution in equation (7.14) gives the factor of safety of 1.30.

The values of *A* and *B* give a direct indication of the contribution which each of the planes makes to the total factor of safety.

### 7.5.1 *Example of wedge analysis using friction-only charts*

During the route location study for a proposed highway, the layout engineer has requested guidance on the maximum safe angles that may be used for the design of the slopes. Extensive geological mapping of outcrops, together with core logging, identified five sets of discontinuities in the rock mass through which the road will pass. The dips and dip directions of these discontinuities are shown in Table 7.4, together with the measured variation in these measurements.

Note that, because the mapping covers the entire alignment that extends over several kilometers, the scatter in the dip and dip direction measurements can be taken into account in the analysis.

Figure 7.16 shows the pole locations for these five sets of discontinuities. Also shown on this figure are the extent of the scatter in the pole measurements, and the great circles corresponding to the average pole positions. The dashed figure surrounding the great circle intersections is obtained by rotating the stereoplot to find the extent to which the intersection point is influenced by the scatter around the pole points. The intersection of great circles 2 and 5 has been excluded from the dashed figure because it defines a line of intersection dipping flatter than 20°, which is less than the estimated angle of friction.

The factors of safety for each of the discontinuity intersections is determined from the wedge charts, assuming a friction angle of 30° (some interpolation is necessary), and the values are given in the circles over the intersection points. Because all of the planes are steep, some of the factors of safety are dangerously low. Since it is likely that slopes with a factor of safety of less than 1.0 will fail as the slope is excavated, the only practical solution is to cut the slopes at an angle that is coincident with the dip of the line of intersection. For marginally stable wedges with factors of safety between 1.0 and 2.0, a detailed

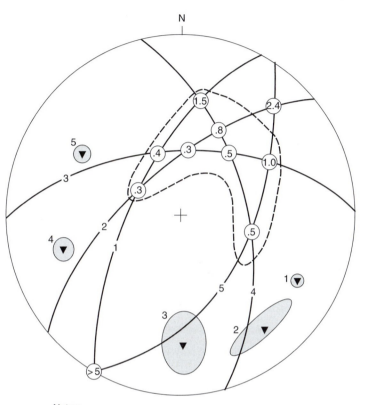

Notes:
a. Black triangles mark most likely position of poles of five sets
   of discontinuities present in rock mass.
b. Shaded area surrounding pole position defines extent of
   scatter in measurements.
c. Factors of safety for each combination of discontinuities are
   shown in circle over corresponding intersection of great circles.
d. Dashed line surrounds area of potential instability (FS < 2).

*Figure 7.16* Stereoplot of geological
data for the preliminary design of
highway slopes.

analysis can be carried out to determine the bolting force required to increase the factor of safety
to an acceptable level.

The stereoplot in Figure 7.17(a) can be used to
find the maximum safe slope angle for the slopes
of any dip direction. This stereographic analysis
involves positioning the great circle representing
the slope face for a particular dip direction in
such a way that the unstable region (shaded)
is avoided. The maximum safe slope angles are
marked around the perimeter of this figure and
their positions correspond to the orientation of
the slope face (Figure 7.17(a)). For example, if a
through-cut for a highway is planned in this rock,

the slope on the south side of the cut would be an
angle of 30° and the slope on the north side would
be at 85° (Figure 7.17(b)).

## 7.6  Comprehensive wedge analysis

### 7.6.1  *Data for comprehensive analysis*

If the friction-only wedge stability charts show
that the factor of safety is less than 2.0, then a
comprehensive stability analysis may be required
to calculate, for example, the bolting force to
achieve a required factor of safety. This analysis
takes into account the dimensions and shape of

(a)

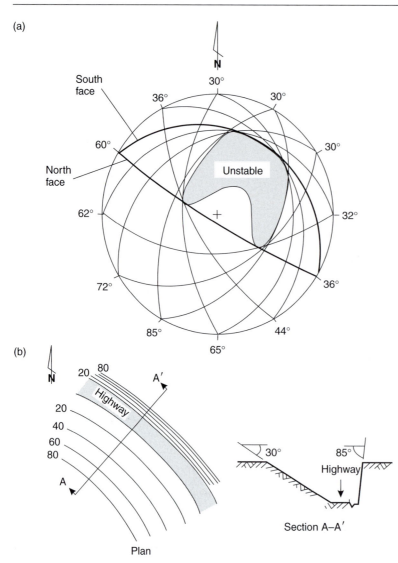

(b)

*Figure 7.17* Slope design based on wedge stability analysis: (a) stereoplot of great circles representing stable slopes in a rock mass containing the five sets of discontinuities defined in Figure 7.16; (b) stable cut slope angles based on wedge stability analysis shown in (a).

the wedge, different cohesion and friction angles on each slide plane, water pressure and a number of external forces. The external forces that may act on the wedge include earthquake ground motion, tensioned bolts and possible loads generated by structures that may include a bridge footing or building located on the wedge.

Figure 7.18 shows the features of the slope involved in the comprehensive wedge analysis, and a complete list of the equations used in the analysis is included Appendix III. A fundamental

assumption in the analysis is that all the forces act through the center of gravity of the wedge so no moments are generated. The following is a description of the components of the analysis:

• *Wedge shape*—the shape of the wedge is defined by five surfaces: the two slide planes (1 and 2) with their line of intersection daylighting in the face, the upper slope (3) and face (4), and a tension crack (5) (Figure 7.18(a)). The orientations of these

(a)

(b)

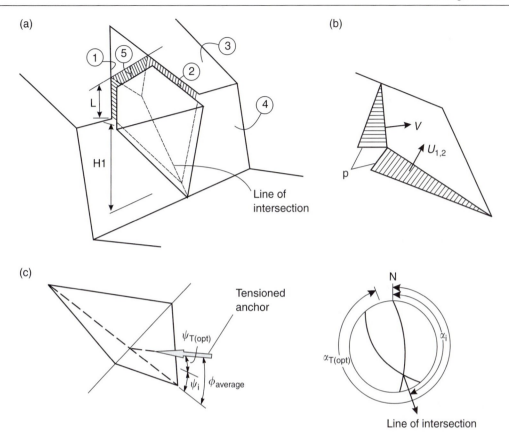

(c)

*Figure 7.18* Comprehensive wedge analysis: (a) dimensions and surfaces defining size and shape of wedge; (b) water pressures acting in tension crack and along line of intersection; (c) optimum anchor orientation for reinforcement of a wedge.

surfaces are each defined by their dip and dip direction. The range of orientations that the analysis can accommodate include an overhanging face, different dip directions for the upper slope and the face, and a tension crack dipping either towards or away from the face.

• *Wedge dimensions*—the dimensions of the wedge are defined by the two dimensions $H$ and $L$ (Figure 7.18(a)). $H$ is the vertical height between the point where the line of intersection daylights on the face and the intersection of plane 1 with the crest of the slope, $L$ is the distance measured along plane 1 between the crest of the slope face (4) and the tension crack (5).

• *Wedge weight*—the orientations of the five planes, and the two dimensions can be used to calculate the volume of the wedge, and the weight is determined from the unit weight of the rock ($\gamma_r$).

• *Water pressures*—if it is assumed that the tension crack (5) is filled with water and that the water discharges to the atmosphere where planes 1 and 2 intersect the face (plane 4), then triangular water pressures act on planes 1, 2 and 5 (Figure 7.18(b)). The water pressure $p$ at the base of the tension crack (and the top of the line of intersection) is equal to ($h_5 \gamma_w$), where $h_5$ is the average vertical depth below the top of the tension crack. The water forces

$U_1$, $U_2$ and $V$ are calculated by integrating the pressures over the areas of planes 1, 2 and 5, respectively.

- *Shear strengths*—the slide planes (1 and 2) can have different shear strengths defined by the cohesion ($c$) and friction angle ($\phi$). The shear resistance is calculated by multiplying the cohesion by the area of slide plane, and adding the product of the effective normal stress and the friction angle. The normal stresses are found by resolving the wedge weight in directions normal to the each slide plane (see equations (7.3)–(7.5)).
- *External forces*—external forces acting on the wedge are defined by their magnitude and orientation (plunge $\psi$ and trend $\alpha$). The equations listed in Appendix III can accommodate a total of two external forces; if there are three or more forces, the vectors are added as necessary. One external force that may be included in the analysis is the pseudo-static force used to simulate seismic ground motion (see Section 6.5.4). The horizontal component of this force would act in the same direction as the line of intersection of planes 1 and 2.
- *Bolting forces*—if tensioned anchors are installed to stabilize the wedge, they are considered to be an external force. The orient-ation of the anchors can be optimized to minimize the anchor force required to produce a specified factor of safety. The optimum anchor plunge $\psi_{T(opt)}$ and trend $\alpha_{T(opt)}$, with respect to the line of intersection ($\psi_i/\alpha_i$), are as follows (Figure 7.18(c)):

$$\psi_{T(opt)} = (\phi_{average} - \psi_i) \qquad (7.15)$$

and

$$\alpha_{T(opt)} = (180 + \alpha_i) \quad \text{for } \alpha_{T(opt)} \leq 360 \qquad (7.16)$$

where $\phi_{average}$ is the average friction angle of the two slide planes.

### 7.6.2 Computer programs for comprehensive analysis

Appendix III lists equations that can be used to carry out a comprehensive stability analysis of a wedge using the input parameters discussed in Section 7.6.1. These equations were originally developed by Dr John Bray and are included in the third edition of *Rock Slope Engineering* (1981). This method of analysis has been used in a number of computer programs that allow rapid and reliable analysis of wedge stability. However, there is a limitation to this analysis that should be noted:

*Wedge geometry.* The analysis procedure is to calculate the dimensions of a wedge that extends from the face to the point where planes 1, 2 and 3 intersect. The next step is to calculate the dimensions of a second wedge formed by sliding planes 1 and 2, the upper slope (plane 3) and the tension crack (plane 5). The dimensions of the wedge in front of the tension crack are then found by subtracting the dimensions of the wedge in front of the tension crack from the overall wedge (see equations (III.54) to (III.57), Appendix III). Prior to performing the subtractions, the program tests to see if a wedge is formed and a tension crack is valid (equations (III.48) to (III.53), Appendix III). The program will terminate if the dip of the upper slope (plane 3) is greater than the dip of the line of intersection of planes 1 and 2, or if the tension crack is located beyond the point where the point where planes 1, 2 and 3 intersect.

While these tests are mathematically valid, they do not allow for a common geometric condition that may exist in steep mountainous terrain. That is, if plane 3 is steeper than the line of intersection of planes 1 and 2, a wedge made up of five planes can still be formed if a tension crack is located behind the slope face to create a valid plane 5. Where this physical condition exists in the field, an alternative method of analysis is to use Key Block Theory in which the shape and stability condition of removal wedges can be completely defined (Goodman and Shi, 1985; Kielhorn, 1999; PanTechnica, 2002).

## 7.6.3  Example of comprehensive wedge analysis

The following is an example of the comprehensive stability analysis of a wedge (Rocscience, 2001). Consider the wedge formed by joint sets 3 and 5 in Figure 7.16. This has a friction-only factor of safety of 1.0, so water pressures and seismic ground motion may result in instability, depending on the cohesions on the slide surfaces. This analysis shows the bolting force required to raise the factor of safety to 1.5, based on the input parameters shown in Table 7.5.

The other input parameters are as follows:

| | |
|---|---|
| Wedge height, $H1$ | $= 28$ m; |
| Distance of tension crack from crest measured along plane 3, $L$ | $= 9$ m; |
| Rock density, $\gamma_r$ | $= 26$ kN/m$^3$; |
| Water density, $\gamma_w$ | $= 10.0$ kN/m$^3$; and |
| Seismic coefficient (horizontal), $k_H$ | $= 0.1$. |

The stability analysis of the wedge using these parameters gave the following results:

(i) Dry, static, $c_3 = c_5 = 0$ kPa, FS = 1.05
   $T = 0$,
(ii) $z_w = 50\%$, static, FS = 0.93
   $c_3 = c_5 = 0$ kPa, $T = 0$
(iii) $z_w = 50\%$, $k_H = 0.1$, FS = 0.76
   $c_3 = c_5 = 0$ kPa, $T = 0$
(iv) $T = 27.2$ MN, $\psi_T = -8°$, FS = 1.5
   $\alpha_T = 242°$, $z_w = 50\%$,
   $k_H = 0.1$, $c_3 = c_5 = 0$ kPa
(v) $T = 38.3$ MN, $\psi_T = 10°$, FS = 1.5
   $\alpha_T = 200°$
(vi) $z_w = 50\%$, $k_H = 0.1$, FS = 1.49
   $c_3 = c_5 = 50$ kPa, $T = 0$

Table 7.5  Orientation of planes forming wedge

| Plane | Dip | Dip direction | Shear strength |
|---|---|---|---|
| 3 | 60 | 360 | $\phi_3 = 30°$, $c_3 = 50$ kPa |
| 5 | 54 | 118 | $\phi_5 = 30°$, $c_5 = 50$ kPa |
| Slope face | 76 | 060 | |
| Upper surface | 15 | 070 | |
| Tension crack | 80 | 060 | |

Case (i) corresponds to the simplified analysis using the friction-only charts for a dry, static slope that gave a factor of safety of 1.1. With the tension crack half-filled with water and the seismic coefficient applied, the factor of safety drops to 0.76 (Case (iii)). For the load conditions in Case (iii), it is necessary to install a bolting force of 27.2 MN in order to raise the factor of safety to 1.5 (Case (iv)). In Case (iv), the bolting force is installed in the opposite direction to the line of intersection ($\alpha_T = 242°$) and at an angle of 8° above the horizontal ($\psi_T = -8°$)—this orientation is optimal as defined by equations (7.15) and (7.16). If the bolts are installed at 10° below the horizontal to facilitate grouting ($\psi_T = 10°$) and with a trend of 200°, then the required bolting force to produce a factor of safety of 1.5 increases to 38.3 MN (Case (v)). This result illustrates the advantage of installing anchors at, or close to, the optimal orientation.

Case (vi) illustrates that a small amount of cohesion can be most effective in improving the factor of safety because the cohesion acts over large surface areas to produce a significant resisting force.

# Chapter 8

# Circular failure

## 8.1 Introduction

Although this book is concerned primarily with the stability of rock slopes containing well-defined sets of discontinuities, it is also necessary to design cuts in weak materials such as highly weathered or closely fractured rock, and rock fills. In such materials, failure occurs along a surface that approaches a circular shape (Figure 8.1), and this chapter is devoted to a discussion on the stability analysis of these materials.

In a review of the historical development of slope stability theories, Golder (1972) traced the subject back almost 300 years. Much of the development of circular failure analysis methods was carried out in the 1950s and 1960s, and these techniques have since been used to prepare computer programs that have the versatility to accommodate a wide range of geologic, geometric, ground water and external loading conditions. This chapter discusses the principles of the theoretical work, and demonstrates their application in design charts and in the results of computer analyses. During the past half century, a vast body of literature on the subject of circular failure has accumulated, and no attempt will be made to summarize the material in this chapter. Standard soil mechanics text books such as those by Taylor (1937), Terzaghi (1943) and Lambe and Whitman (1969), and papers by Skempton (1948), Bishop (1955), Janbu (1954), Morgenstern and Price (1965), Nonveiller (1965), Peck (1967), Spencer (1967, 1969) and Duncan (1996) all contain excellent discussions on the stability of soil slopes.

The approach adopted in this chapter is to present a series of slope stability charts for circular failure. These charts enable the user to carry out a rapid check on the factor of safety of a slope, or upon the sensitivity of the factor of safety to changes in ground water conditions, slope angle and material strength properties. These charts should only be used for the analysis of circular failure in slope materials that are homogenous and where the conditions apply that were assumed in deriving the charts (see Section 8.4). More comprehensive methods of analysis are presented in Section 8.6. These methods can be used, for example, where the material properties vary within the slope, or where part of the slide surface is at a soil/rock interface and the shape of the slide surface differs significantly from a simple circular arc.

This chapter primarily addresses the stability of slopes in two dimensions, and assumes that the slope can be modeled as a unit slice through an infinitely long slope, under plane-strain conditions. Section 8.6.5 discusses three-dimensional circular failure analysis, and Section 10.3.1 discusses the influence of the radius of curvature of the slope on stability.

## 8.2 Conditions for circular failure and methods of analysis

In the previous chapters, it has been assumed that the failure of rock slopes is controlled by geological features such as bedding planes and joints that divide the rock into a discontinuous

*Figure 8.1* Circular failure in highly weathered, granitic rock (on Highway 1, near Devil's Slide, Pacifica, California).

mass. Under these conditions, one or more of the discontinuities normally defines the slide surface. However, in the case of a closely fractured or highly weathered rock, a strongly defined structural pattern no longer exists, and the slide surface is free to find the line of least resistance through the slope. Observations of slope failures in these materials suggest that this slide surface generally takes the form of a circle, and most stability theories are based upon this observation. Figure 8.1 shows a typical circular failure in a highly weathered rock slope above a highway. The conditions under which circular failure will occur arise when the individual particles in a soil or rock mass are very small compared with the size of the slope. Hence, broken rock in a fill will tend to behave as a "soil" and fail in a circular mode when the slope dimensions are substantially greater than the dimensions of the rock fragments. Similarly, soil consisting of sand, silt and smaller particle sizes will exhibit circular slide surfaces, even in slopes only a few meters in height. Highly altered and weathered rocks, as well as rock with closely spaced, randomly oriented discontinuities such as some rapidly cooled

basalts, will also tend to fail in this manner. It is appropriate to design slopes in these materials on the assumption that a circular failure process will develop.

### 8.2.1  Shape of slide surface

The actual shape of the "circular" slide surface is influenced by the geological conditions in the slope. For example, in a homogenous weak or weathered rock mass, or a rock fill, the failure is likely to form as a shallow, large radius surface extending from a tension crack close behind the crest to the toe of the slope (Figure 8.2(a)). This contrasts with failures in high cohesion, low friction materials such as clays where the surface may be deeper with a smaller radius that may exit beyond the toe of the slope. Figure 8.2(b) shows an example of conditions in which the shape of the slide surface is modified by the slope geology. Here the circular surface in the upper, weathered rock is truncated by the shallow dipping, stronger rock near the base. Stability analyses of both types of surface can be carried out using circular failure methods, although for the latter case it is

(a)

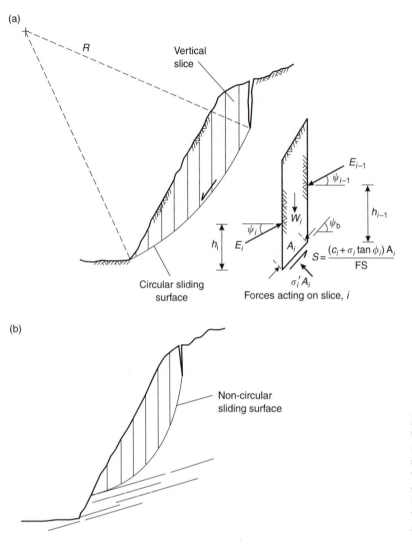

Circular sliding
surface

Forces acting on slice, $i$

$$S = \frac{(c_i + \sigma_i \tan \phi_i) A_i}{FS}$$

(b)

Non-circular
sliding surface

*Figure 8.2* The shape of
typical sliding surfaces:
(a) large radius circular
surface in homogeneous,
weak material, with the detail
of forces on slice;
(b) non-circular surface in
weak, surficial material with
stronger rock at base.

necessary to use a procedure that allows the shape
of the surface to be defined.

For each combination of slope parameters there
will be a slide surface for which the factor of
safety is a minimum—this is usually termed the
"critical surface." The procedure to find the
critical surface is to run a large number of analyses in which the center co-ordinates and the
radius of the circle are varied until the surface
with the lowest factor of safety is found. This
is an essential part of circular slope stability
analysis.

### 8.2.2   Stability analysis procedure

The stability analysis of circular failure is carried
out using the limit equilibrium procedure similar
to that described in earlier chapters for plane and
wedge failures. This procedure involves comparing the available shear strength along the sliding
surface with the force required to maintain the
slope in equilibrium.

The application of this procedure to circular failures involves division of the slope into a
series of slices that are usually vertical, but may

be inclined to coincide with certain geological features. The base of each slice is inclined at angle $\psi_b$ and has an area $A$. In the simplest case, the forces acting on the base of each slice are the shear resistance $S$ due to the shear strength of the rock (cohesion $c$; friction angle $\phi$), and forces $E$ (dip angle $\psi$; height $h$ above base) acting on the sides of the slice (see detail Figure 8.2(a)).

The analysis procedure is to consider equilibrium conditions slice by slice, and if a condition of equilibrium is satisfied for each slice, then it is also satisfied for the entire sliding mass. The number of equations of equilibrium available depends on the number of slices $N$, and the number of equilibrium conditions that are used. The number of equations available is $2N$ if only force equilibrium is satisfied, and $3N$ if both force and moment equilibrium are satisfied. If only force equilibrium is satisfied, the number of unknowns is $(3N - 1)$, while, if both force and moment equilibria are satisfied, the number of unknowns is $(5N - 2)$. Usually between 10 and 40 slices are required to realistically model the slope, and therefore, the number of unknowns exceeds the number of equations. The excess of unknowns over equations is $(N - 1)$ for force equilibrium analysis, and $(2N - 2)$ for analyses that satisfy all conditions of equilibrium. Thus, the analyses are statically indeterminate and assumptions are required to make up the imbalance between equations and unknowns (Duncan, 1996).

The various limit equilibrium analysis procedures either make assumptions to make up the balance between known and unknowns, or they do not satisfy all the conditions of equilibrium. For example, the Spencer Method assumes that the inclination of the side forces is the same for every slice, while the Fellenius and Bishop methods do not satisfy all conditions of equilibrium.

The factor of safety of the circular failure based on limit equilibrium analysis is defined as

$$FS = \frac{\text{shear strength available to resist sliding } (c + \sigma \tan \phi)}{\text{shear stress required for equilibrium on slip surface}(\tau_e)} \tag{8.1}$$

and rearranging this equation, we have

$$\tau_e = \frac{c + \sigma \tan \phi}{FS} \tag{8.2}$$

The method of solution for the factor of safety is to use an iterative process in which an initial estimate is made for FS, and this is refined with each iteration.

The influence of various normal stress distributions upon the factor of safety of soil slopes has been examined by Frohlich (1955) who found that a lower bound for all factors of safety that satisfy statics is given by the assumption that the normal stress is concentrated at a single point on the slide surface. Similarly, the upper bound is obtained by assuming that the normal load is concentrated at the two ends of the slide surface.

The unreal nature of these stress distributions is of no consequence since the object of the exercise, up to this point, is simply to determine the extremes between which the actual factor of safety of the slope must lie. In an example considered by Lambe and Whitman (1969), the upper and lower bounds for the factor of safety of a particular slope corresponded to 1.62 and 1.27, respectively. Analysis of the same problem by Bishop's simplified method of slices gives a factor of safety of 1.30, which suggests that the actual factor of safety may lie reasonably close to the lower bound solution.

Further evidence that the lower bound solution is also a meaningful practical solution is provided by an examination of the analysis that assumed the slide surface has the form of a logarithmic spiral (Spencer, 1969). In this case, the factor of safety is independent of the normal stress distribution, and the upper and lower bounds coincide. Taylor (1937) compared the results from a number of logarithmic spiral analyses with results of lower bound solutions[1] and found that the difference is negligible. Based on this comparison,

---

[1] The lower bound solution discussed in this chapter is usually known as the Friction Circle Method and was used by Taylor (1937) for the derivation of his stability charts.

Taylor concluded that the lower bound solution provides a value of the factor of safety that is sufficiently accurate for most practical problems involving simple circular failure of homogeneous slopes.

The basic principles of these methods of analyses are discussed in Section 8.6.

## 8.3   Derivation of circular failure charts

This section describes the use of a series of charts that can be used to determine rapidly the factor of safety of circular failures. These charts have been developed by running many thousands of circular analyses from which a number of dimensionless parameters were derived that relate the factor of safety to the material unit weight, friction angle and cohesion, and the slope height and face angle. It has been found that these charts give a reliable estimate for the factor of safety, provided that the conditions in the slope meet the assumptions used in developing the charts. In fact, the accuracy in calculating the factor of safety from the charts is usually greater than the accuracy in determining the shear strength of the rock mass.

Use of the stability charts presented in this chapter requires that the conditions in the slope meet the following assumptions:

(a)   The material forming the slope is homogeneous, with uniform shear strength properties along the slide surface.

(b)   The shear strength $\tau$ of the material is characterized by cohesion: $c$ and a friction angle $\phi$, that are related by the equation $\tau = c + \sigma \tan \phi$ (see Section 1.4).

(c)   Failure occurs on a circular slide surface, which passes through the toe of the slope.[2]

(d)   A vertical tension crack occurs in the upper surface or in the face of the slope.

---

2 Terzaghi (1943: 170), shows that the toe failure assumed for this analysis gives the lowest factor of safety provided that $\phi > 5°$. The $\phi = 0$ analysis, involving failure below the toe of the slope through the base material has been discussed by Skempton (1948) and by Bishop and Bjerrum (1960) and is applicable to failures which occur during or after the rapid construction of a slope.

(e)   The locations of the tension crack and of the slide surface are such that the factor of safety of the slope is a minimum for the slope geometry and ground water conditions considered.

(f)   Ground water conditions vary from a dry slope to a fully saturated slope under heavy recharge; these conditions are defined in Figure 8.4.

(g)   Circular failure charts are optimized for a rock mass density of $18.9 \, \text{kN/m}^3$. Densities higher than this give high factors of safety, densities lower than this give low factors of safety. Detailed circular analysis may be required for slopes in which the material density is significantly different from $18.9 \, \text{kN/m}^3$.

The charts presented in this chapter correspond to the lower bound solution for the factor of safety, obtained by assuming that the normal load is concentrated on a single point on the slide surface. These charts differ from those published by Taylor in that they include the influence of a critical tension crack and of ground water.

### 8.3.1   Ground water flow assumptions

In order to calculate the forces due to water pressures acting on the slide surface and in the tension crack, it is necessary to assume a set of ground water flow patterns that coincide as closely as possible with conditions that are believed to exist in the field.

In the analysis of rock slope failures discussed in Chapters 6, 7 and 9, it is assumed that most of the water flow takes place in discontinuities in the rock and that the rock itself is practically impermeable. In the case of slopes in soil or waste rock, the permeability of the mass of material is generally several orders of magnitude higher than that of intact rock and, hence, a general flow pattern will develop in the material behind the slope.

Figure 5.10(a) shows that, within the rock mass, the equipotentials are approximately perpendicular to the phreatic surface. Consequently, the flow lines will be approximately parallel to the

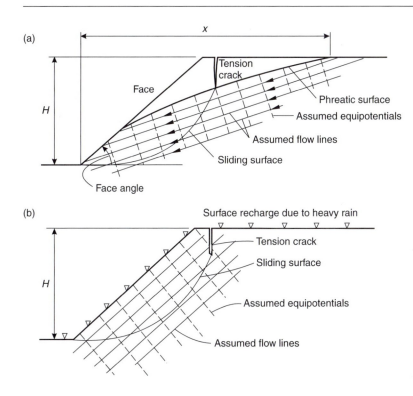

(a)

Tension crack

Face

Phreatic surface

Assumed equipotentials

Assumed flow lines

Sliding surface

Face angle

(b)

Surface recharge due to heavy rain

Tension crack

Sliding surface

Assumed equipotentials

Assumed flow lines

*Figure 8.3* Definition of ground water flow patterns used in circular failure analysis of slopes in weak and closely fractured rock: (a) ground water flow pattern under steady state drawdown conditions where the phreatic surface coincides with the ground surface at a distance $x$ behind the toe of the slope. The distance $x$ is measured in multiples of the slope height $H$; (b) ground water flow pattern in a saturated slope subjected to surface recharge by heavy rain.

phreatic surface for the condition of steady-state drawdown. Figure 8.3 shows that this approximation has been used for the analysis of the water pressure distribution in a slope under conditions of normal drawdown. Note that the phreatic surface is assumed to coincide with the ground surface at a distance $x$, measured in multiples of the slope height, behind the toe of the slope. This may correspond to the position of a surface water source, or be the point where the phreatic surface is judged to intersect the ground surface.

The phreatic surface itself has been obtained, for the range of the slope angles and values of $x$ considered, by solution of the equations proposed by L. Casagrande (1934), and discussed in the textbook by Taylor (1937). For the case of a saturated slope subjected to heavy surface recharge, the equipotentials and the associated flow lines used in the stability analysis are based upon the work of Han (1972). This work involved the use of an electrical resistance analogue method to study ground water flow patterns in slopes comprised of isotropic materials.

Figure 8.4 shows five ground water conditions ranging from fully drained to saturated, based on the models shown in Figure 8.3. For conditions 2, 3 and 4, the position of the ground water table is defined by the ratio $x/H$. These five ground water conditions are used in conjunction with the circular failure charts discussed in Section 8.4.

### 8.3.2 *Production of circular failure charts*

The circular failure charts presented in this chapter were produced by running a search routine to find the most critical combination of slide surface and tension crack for each of a wide range of slope geometries and ground water conditions. Provision was made for the tension crack to be located in either the upper surface, or in the face of the slope. Detailed checks were carried out in the region surrounding the toe of the slope where the curvature of the equipotentials results in local flow which differs from that illustrated in Figure 8.3(a).

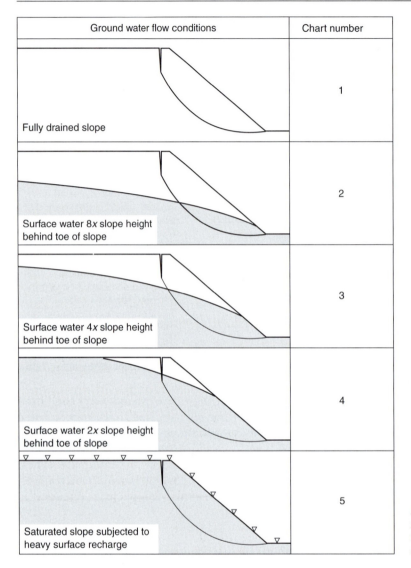

| Ground water flow conditions | Chart number |
|---|---|
| Fully drained slope | 1 |
| Surface water 8x slope height behind toe of slope | 2 |
| Surface water 4x slope height behind toe of slope | 3 |
| Surface water 2x slope height behind toe of slope | 4 |
| Saturated slope subjected to heavy surface recharge | 5 |

*Figure 8.4* Ground water flow models used with circular failure analysis charts—Figures 8.6–8.10.

The charts are numbered 1–5 (Figures 8.6–8.10) to correspond with the ground water conditions defined in Figure 8.4.

### 8.3.3  *Use of the circular failure charts*

In order to use the charts to determine the factor of safety of a slope, the steps outlined here and shown in Figure 8.5 should be followed.

*Step 1*:  Decide upon the ground water conditions which are believed to exist in the slope and choose the chart which is closest to these conditions, using Figure 8.4.

*Step 2*:  Select rock strength parameters applicable to the material forming the slope.

*Step 3*:  Calculate the value of the dimensionless ratio $c/(\gamma H \tan \phi)$ and find this value on the outer circular scale of the chart.

*Step 4*:  Follow the radial line from the value found in step 3 to its intersection with the curve which corresponds to the slope angle.

*Step 5:* Find the corresponding value of tan $\phi$/FS or $c/(\gamma H \text{FS})$, depending upon which is more convenient, and calculate the factor of safety.

Consider the following example:

A 15.2-m high cut with a face angle of 40° is to be excavated in overburden soil with a density $\gamma = 15.7\,\text{kN/m}^3$, a cohesion of 38 kPa and a friction angle of 30°. Find the factor of safety of the slope, assuming that there is a surface water source 61 m behind the toe of the slope.

The ground water conditions indicate the use of chart number 3 ($61/15.2 \sim 4$). The value of $c/(\gamma H \tan \phi) = 0.28$ and the corresponding value of tan $\phi$/FS, for a 40° slope, is 0.32. Hence, the factor of safety of the slope of 1.80.

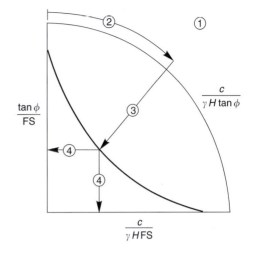

*Figure 8.5* Sequence of steps involved in using circular failure charts to find the factor of safety of a slope.

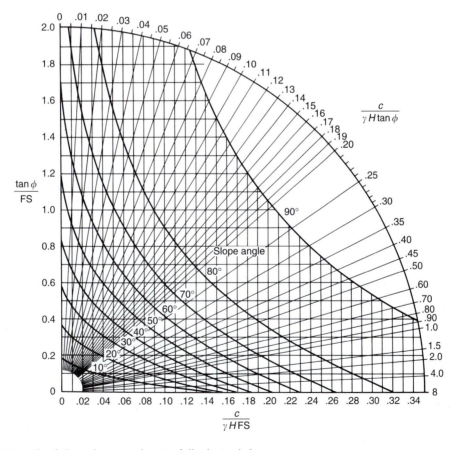

*Figure 8.6* Circular failure chart number 1—fully drained slope.

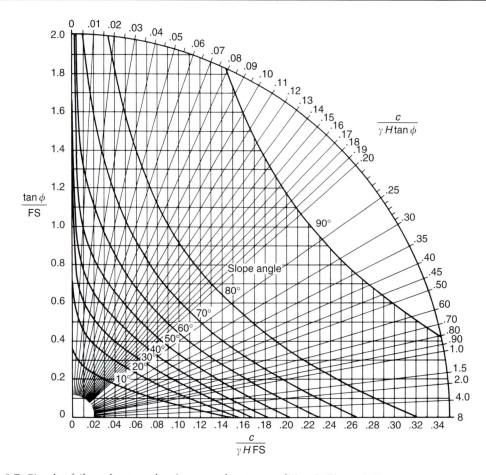

*Figure 8.7* Circular failure chart number 2—ground water condition 2 (Figure 8.5).

Because of the speed and simplicity of using these charts, they are ideal for checking the sensitivity of the factor of safety of a slope to a wide range of conditions. For example, if the cohesion were to be halved to 20 kPa and the ground water pressure increased to that represented by chart number 2, the factor of safety drops to 1.28.

## 8.4   Location of critical slide surface and tension crack

During the production of the circular failure charts presented in this chapter, the locations of both the critical slide surface and the critical tension crack for limiting equilibrium (FS = 1) were determined for each slope analyzed. These locations are presented, in the form of charts, in Figures 8.11 and 8.12.

It was found that, once ground water is present in the slope, the locations of the critical circle and the tension crack are not particularly sensitive to the position of the phreatic surface and hence only one case, that for chart number 3, has been plotted. It will be noted that the location of the critical circle center given in Figure 8.12 differs significantly from that for the drained slope plotted in Figure 8.11.

These charts are useful for the construction of drawings of potential slides and for estimating the friction angle when back-analyzing existing

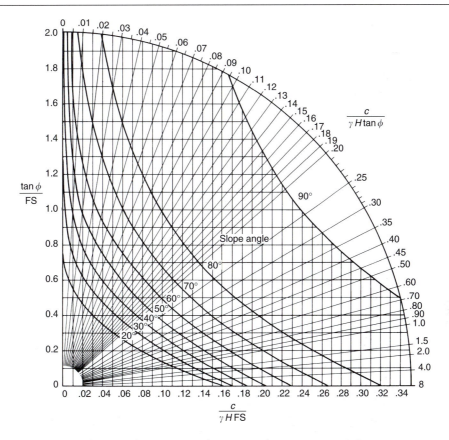

*Figure 8.8* Circular failure chart number 3—ground water condition 3 (Figure 8.4).

circular slides. They also provide a start in locating the critical slide surface when carrying out more sophisticated circular failure analysis.

As an example of the application of these charts, consider the case of a drained slope having a face angle of 30° in a soil with a friction angle of 20°. Figure 8.11 shows that the critical slide circle center is located at $X = 0.2H$ and $Y = 1.85H$ and that the critical tension crack is at a distance $b = 0.1H$ behind the crest of the slope. These dimensions are shown in Figure 8.13.

## 8.5  Examples of circular failure analysis

The following two examples illustrate the use of the circular failure charts for the study of the stability of slope in highly weathered rock.

### 8.5.1  *Example 1—China clay pit slope*

Ley (1972) investigated the stability of a China clay pit slope which was considered to be potentially unstable, and that a circular failure was the likely type of instability. The slope profile is illustrated in Figure 8.14 and the input data used for the analysis is included in this figure. The material, a heavily kaolinized granite, was tested in direct shear to determine the friction angle and cohesion.

Two piezometers in the slope and a known water source some distance behind the slope enabled an estimate to be made of the position of the phreatic surface as shown in Figure 8.14. From Figure 8.14, chart number 2 corresponds most closely to these ground water conditions.

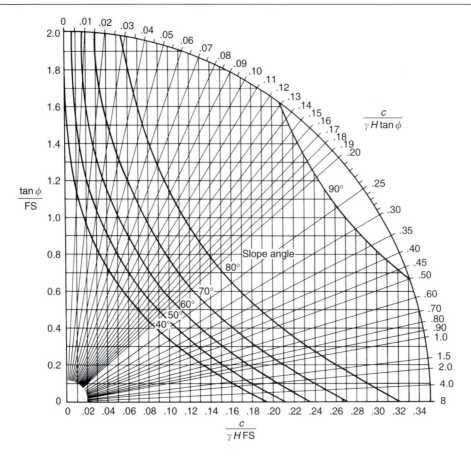

*Figure 8.9* Circular failure chart number 4—ground water condition 4 (Figure 8.4).

From the information given in Figure 8.14, the value of the ratio $c/(\gamma H \tan \phi) = 0.0056$, and the corresponding value of $\tan \phi/FS$ from chart number 2, is 0.76. Hence, the factor of safety of the slope is 1.01. A number of trial calculations using Janbu's method (Janbu *et al.*, 1956) for the critical slide circle shown in Figure 8.14, found a factor of safety of 1.03.

These factors of safety indicated that the stability of the slope was inadequate under the assumed conditions, and steps were taken to deal with the problem.

### 8.5.2  Example 2—highway slope

A highway plan called for a cut at an angle of 42°. The total height of the cut would be 61 m and it was required to check whether the cut would be stable. The slope was in weathered and altered material, and failure, if it occurred, would be a circular type. Insufficient time was available for ground water levels to be accurately established or for shear tests to be carried out. The stability analysis was carried out as follows:

For the condition of limiting equilibrium, FS = 1 and $\tan \phi/FS = \tan \phi$. By reversing the procedure outlined in Figure 8.5, a range of friction angles were used to find the values of the ratio $c/(\gamma H \tan \phi)$ for a face angle of 42°. The value of the cohesion $c$ which is mobilized at failure, for a given friction angle, can then be calculated. This analysis was carried out for dry slopes using chart number 1 (line *B*, Figure 8.15), and for saturated slopes using chart number 5 (line *A*, Figure 8.15).

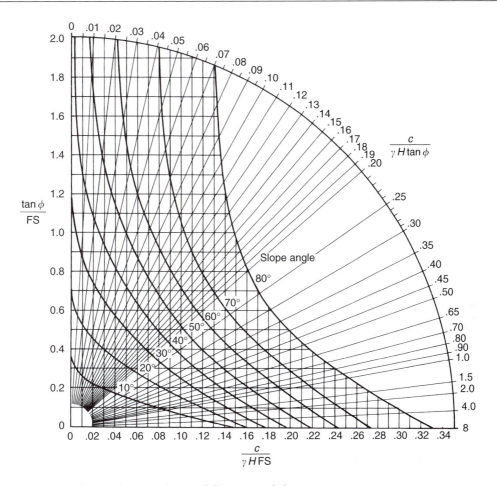

*Figure 8.10* Circular failure chart number 5—fully saturated slope.

Figure 8.15 shows the range of friction angles and cohesions that would be mobilized at failure.

The shaded circle (D) included in Figure 8.15 indicated the range of shear strengths that were considered probable for the material under consideration, based upon the data presented in Figure 4.21. This figure shows that the available shear strength may not be adequate to maintain stability in this cut, particularly when the cut is saturated. Consequently, the face angle could be reduced, or ground water conditions investigated to establish actual ground water pressures and the feasibility of drainage.

The effect of reducing the slope angle can be checked very quickly by finding the value of the

ratio $c/(\gamma H \tan \phi)$ for a flatter slope of 30°, in the same way as it was found for the 42° slope. The dashed line (C) in Figure 8.15 indicates the shear strength, which is mobilized in a dry slope with a face angle of 30°. Since the mobilized shear strength C is less than the available shear strength D, the dry slope is likely to be stable.

## 8.6  Detailed stability analysis of circular failures

The circular failure charts presented earlier in this chapter are based upon the assumption that the material forming the slope has uniform properties throughout the slope, and that failure occurs

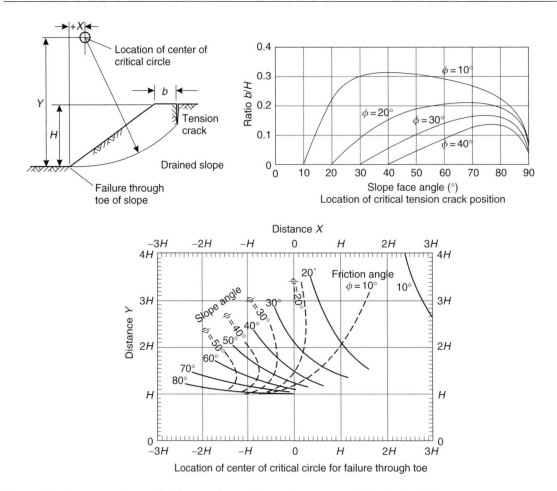

*Figure 8.11* Location of critical sliding surface and critical tension crack for drained slopes.

along a circular slide path passing through the toe of the slope. When these conditions are not satisfied, it is necessary to use one of the methods of slices published by Bishop (1955), Janbu (1954), Nonveiller (1965), Spencer (1967), Morgenstern and Price (1965) or Sarma (1979). This section describes in detail the simplified Bishop and Janbu methods of stability analysis for circular failure.

### 8.6.1 Bishop's and Janbu's method of slices

The slope and slide surface geometries, and the equations for the determination of the factor of safety by the Bishop's simplified method of slices

(1955) and the Janbu's modified method of slices (1954) are given in Figures 8.16 and 8.17 respectively. Bishop's method assumes a circular slide surface and that the side forces are horizontal; the analysis satisfies vertical forces and overall moment equilibrium. The Janbu method allows a slide surface of any shape, and assumes the side forces are horizontal and equal on all slices; the analysis satisfies vertical force equilibrium. As pointed out by Nonveiller (1965), Janbu's method gives reasonable factors of safety when applied to shallow slide surfaces (which are typical in rock with an angle of friction in excess of 30° and rockfill), but it is seriously in error

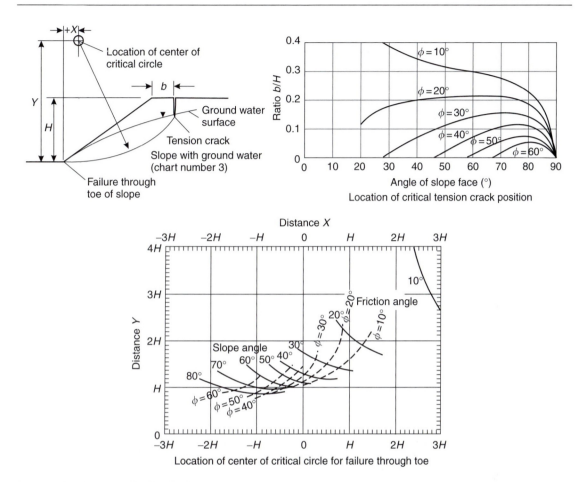

*Figure 8.12* Location of critical sliding surface and critical tension crack for slopes with ground water present.

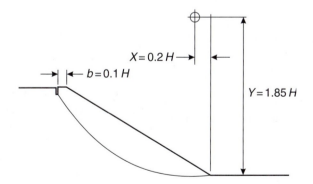

*Figure 8.13* Location of critical slide surface and critical tension crack for a drained slope at an angle of 30° in a material with a friction angle of 20°.

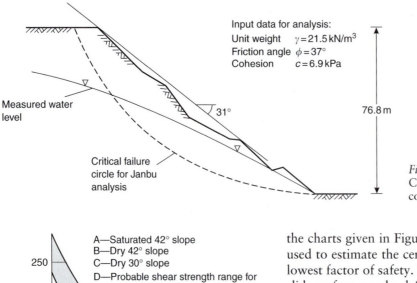

Input data for analysis:
Unit weight   $\gamma = 21.5\,\text{kN/m}^3$
Friction angle $\phi = 37°$
Cohesion   $c = 6.9\,\text{kPa}$

76.8 m

31°

Measured water
level

Critical failure
circle for Janbu
analysis

*Figure 8.14* Slope profile of China clay pit slope considered in Example 1.

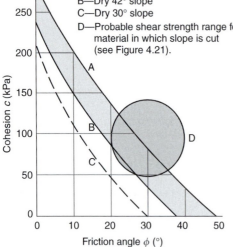

A—Saturated 42° slope
B—Dry 42° slope
C—Dry 30° slope
D—Probable shear strength range for material in which slope is cut (see Figure 4.21).

*Figure 8.15* Comparison between shear strength mobilized and shear strength available for slope considered in Example 2.

the charts given in Figures 8.11 and 8.12 can be used to estimate the center of the circle with the lowest factor of safety. In the Janbu analysis, the slide surface may be defined by known structural features or weak zones within the rock or soil mass, or it may be estimated in the same way as that for the Bishop analysis. In either case, the slide surface assumed for the first analysis may not give the lowest factor of safety, and a series of analyses are required with variations on this position to find the surface with the lowest factor of safety.

*Step 2: Slice parameters.* The sliding mass assumed in step 1 is divided into a number of slices. Generally, a minimum of five slices should be used for simple cases. For complex slope profiles, or where there are different materials in the rock or soil mass, a larger number of slices may be required in order to define adequately the problem. The parameters which have to be defined for each slice are as given here:

- base angle $\psi_b$;
- the weight of each slice $W$ is given by the product of the vertical height $h$, the unit weight $\gamma_r$ of the rock or soil and the width of the slice $\Delta x$: $W = (h\,\gamma_r\,\Delta x)$; and
- uplift water pressure $U$ on the base of each slice is given by the product of the height $h_w$ to the phreatic surface, the unit weight $\gamma_w$ of water and the width of the slice $\Delta x$, that is, $U = (h_w\,\gamma_w\,\Delta x)$.

and should not be used for deep slide surfaces in materials with low friction angles.

The procedures for using Bishop's and Janbu's methods of slices are very similar and it is convenient to discuss them together.

*Step 1: Slope and slide surface geometry.* The geometry of the slope is defined by the actual or the designed profile as seen in a vertical section through the slope. In the case of a circular failure,

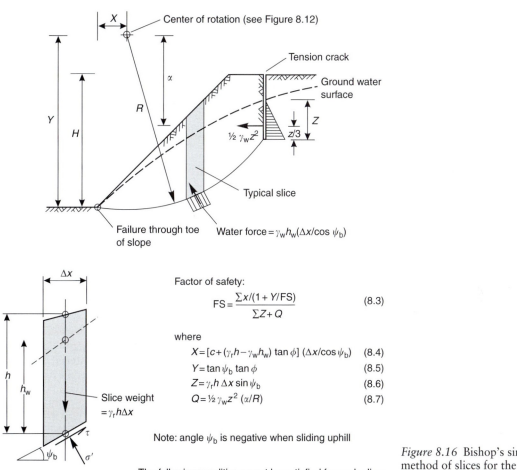

Factor of safety:

$$FS = \frac{\Sigma x/(1 + Y/FS)}{\Sigma Z + Q} \qquad (8.3)$$

where

$$X = [c + (\gamma_r h - \gamma_w h_w) \tan \phi] (\Delta x/\cos \psi_b) \qquad (8.4)$$
$$Y = \tan \psi_b \tan \phi \qquad (8.5)$$
$$Z = \gamma_r h \,\Delta x \sin \psi_b \qquad (8.6)$$
$$Q = \tfrac{1}{2} \gamma_w z^2 \, (\alpha/R) \qquad (8.7)$$

Note: angle $\psi_b$ is negative when sliding uphill

The following conditions must be satisfied for each slice:

$$(1) \; \sigma' = \frac{\gamma_r h - \gamma_w h_w - c \,(\tan \psi_b/FS)}{1 + Y/FS} \qquad (8.8)$$

$$(2) \; \cos \psi_b \,(1 + Y/FS) > 0.2 \qquad (8.9)$$

*Figure 8.16* Bishop's simplified method of slices for the analysis of non-circular failure in slopes cut into materials in which failure is defined by the Mohr–Coulomb failure criterion.

*Step 3: Shear strength parameters.* The shear strength acting on the base of each slice is required for the stability calculation. In the case of a uniform material in which the failure criterion is assumed to be that of Mohr–Coulomb (equation (1.1) in Section 1.4), the shear strength parameters $c$ and $\phi$ will be the same on the base of each slice. When the slope is cut in a number of materials, the shear strength parameters for each slice must be chosen according to the material in which it lies. When the shear strengths of the materials forming the slope are

defined by non-linear failure criterion as discussed in Section 4.5, it is necessary to determine the cohesion and friction angle for each slice at the effective normal stress for that slice (see Figure 4.23).

*Step 4: Factor of safety iteration.* When the slice and shear strength parameters have been defined, the values of $X, Y$ and $Z$ are calculated for each slice. The water force $Q$ is added to $\Sigma Z$, the sum of the components of the weight of each slice acting parallel to the slide surface. An initial estimate of FS = 1.00 for the factor of safety is

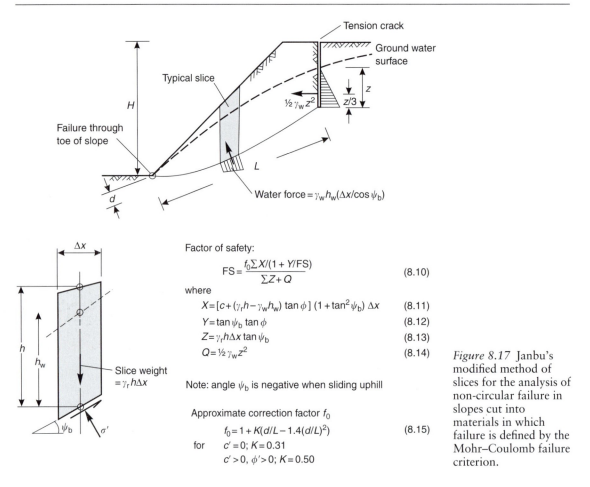

Factor of safety:

$$FS = \frac{f_0 \Sigma X/(1 + Y/FS)}{\Sigma Z + Q}$$   (8.10)

where

$X = [c + (\gamma_r h - \gamma_w h_w) \tan\phi] (1 + \tan^2\psi_b) \Delta x$   (8.11)

$Y = \tan\psi_b \tan\phi$   (8.12)

$Z = \gamma_r h \Delta x \tan\psi_b$   (8.13)

$Q = \frac{1}{2}\gamma_w z^2$   (8.14)

Note: angle $\psi_b$ is negative when sliding uphill

Approximate correction factor $f_0$

$$f_0 = 1 + K(d/L - 1.4(d/L)^2)$$   (8.15)

for   $c' = 0; K = 0.31$

$c' > 0, \phi' > 0; K = 0.50$

*Figure 8.17* Janbu's modified method of slices for the analysis of non-circular failure in slopes cut into materials in which failure is defined by the Mohr–Coulomb failure criterion.

used, and a new factor of safety is calculated from equations (8.3) and (8.10) given in Figures 8.16 and 8.17, respectively. If the difference between the calculated and the assumed factors of safety is greater than 0.001, the calculated factor of safety is used as a second estimate of FS for a new factor of safety calculation. This process is repeated until the difference between successive factors of safety is less than 0.001. For both the Bishop and the Janbu methods, approximately seven iteration cycles will be required to achieve this result for most slope and slide surface geometries.

*Step 5: Conditions and corrections.* Figure 8.16 lists two conditions (equations (8.8) and (8.9)) that must be satisfied for each slice in the Bishop analysis. The first condition ensures that the effective normal stress on the base

of each slice is always positive. If this condition is not met for any slice, the inclusion of a tension crack into the analysis should be considered. If it is impossible to satisfy this condition by readjustment of the ground water conditions or the introduction of a tension crack, the analysis as presented in Figure 8.16 should be abandoned and a more elaborate form of analysis, to be described later, should be adopted.

Condition 2 in Figure 8.16 was suggested by Whitman and Bailey (1967) and it ensures that the analysis is not invalidated by conditions which can sometimes occur near the toe of a slope in which a deep slide surface has been assumed. If this condition is not satisfied by all slices, the slice dimensions should be changed and, if this fails to resolve the problem, the analysis should be abandoned.

Figure 8.17 gives a correction factor $f_0$, which is used in calculating the factor of safety by means of the Janbu method. This factor allows for inter-slice forces resulting from the shape of the slide surface assumed in the Janbu analysis. The equation for $f_0$ given in Figure 8.17 has been derived by Hoek and Bray (1981) from the curves published in Janbu (1954).

## 8.6.2  Use of non-linear failure criterion in Bishop stability analysis

When the material in which the slope is cut obeys the Hoek–Brown non-linear failure criterion discussed in Section 4.5, the Bishop's simplified method of slices as outlined in Figure 8.18 can be used to calculate the factor of safety. The following procedure is used, once the slice parameters have been defined as described earlier for the Bishop and Janbu analyses:

1  Calculate the effective normal stress $\sigma'$ acting on the base of each slice by means of the Fellenius equation (equation (8.17) on Figure 8.18).
2  Using these values of $\sigma'$, calculate $\tan\phi$ and $c$ for each slice from equations (4.24) and (4.25).
3  Substitute these values of $\tan\phi$ and $c$ into the factor of safety equation in order to obtain the first estimate of the factor of safety.
4  Use this estimate of FS to calculate a new value of $\sigma'$ on the base of each slice, using the Bishop equation (equation (8.18) on Figure 8.18).
5  On the basis of these new values of $\sigma'$, calculate new values for $\tan\phi$ and $c$.
6  Check that conditions defined by equations (8.8) and (8.9) on Figure 8.16 are satisfied for each slice.
7  Calculate a new factor of safety for the new values of $\tan\phi$ and $c$.
8  If the difference between the first and second factors of safety is greater than 0.001, return to step 4 and repeat the analysis, using the second factor of safety as input. Repeat

this procedure until the difference between successive factors of safety is less than 0.001.

Generally, about ten iterations will be required to achieve the required accuracy in the calculated factor of safety.

## 8.6.3  Example of Bishop's and Janbu's methods of analysis

A slope is to be excavated in blocky sandstone with very closely spaced and persistent discontinuities. The slope will consist of three, 15-m high benches with two 8-m wide berms, the primary function of which are to collect surface runoff and control erosion (Figure 8.19). The bench faces will be at 75° to the horizontal, and the slope above the crest of the cut will be at an angle of 45°. The assumed position of the water table is shown on the figure. It is required to find the factor of safety of the overall slope, assuming that a circular type stability analysis is appropriate for these conditions.

The shear strength of the jointed rock mass is based on the Hoek–Brown strength criterion, as discussed in Section 4.5, which defines the strength as a curved envelope. The cohesion and friction angle for this criterion are calculated using the program ROCLAB 1.004 (RocScience, 2002a), for which the input parameters are as follows:

- Very poor quality rock mass, GSI = 20;
- Uniaxial compressive strength of intact rock (from point load testing) ≈ 150 MPa;
- Rock material constant, $m_i = 15$;
- Unit weight of rock mass, $\gamma_r = 0.025$ MN/m$^3$;
- Unit weight of water, $\gamma_w = 0.00981$ MN/m$^3$;
- For careful blasting used in excavation, disturbance factor $D = 0.7$; and
- Average slice height = 24 m (this height together with the rock mass unit weight defines the average vertical stress on the sliding surface).

Using these parameters, ROCLAB calculates, at the appropriate vertical stress level, a best fit line to the curved strength envelope to define a friction angle of 43° and a cohesion of 0.145 MPa. This is

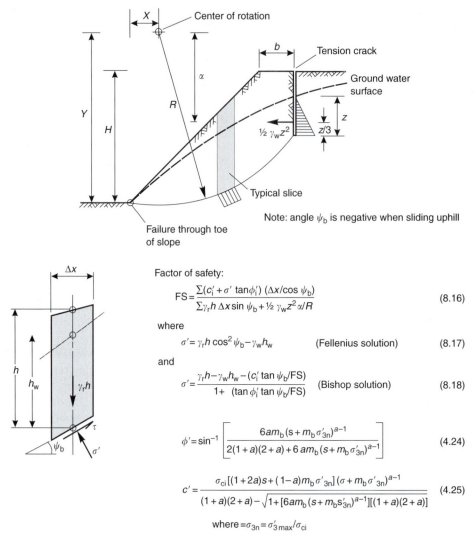

Factor of safety:

$$FS = \frac{\Sigma(c_i' + \sigma' \tan\phi_i')(\Delta x/\cos\psi_b)}{\Sigma\gamma_r h \,\Delta x\sin\psi_b + \tfrac{1}{2}\gamma_w z^2 \alpha/R} \qquad (8.16)$$

where

$$\sigma' = \gamma_r h\cos^2\psi_b - \gamma_w h_w \qquad \text{(Fellenius solution)} \qquad (8.17)$$

and

$$\sigma' = \frac{\gamma_r h - \gamma_w h_w - (c_i'\tan\psi_b/FS)}{1 + (\tan\phi_i'\tan\psi_b/FS)} \qquad \text{(Bishop solution)} \qquad (8.18)$$

$$\phi' = \sin^{-1}\left[\frac{6am_b(s+m_b\sigma_{3n}')^{a-1}}{2(1+a)(2+a)+6\,am_b(s+m_b\sigma_{3n}')^{a-1}}\right] \qquad (4.24)$$

$$c' = \frac{\sigma_{ci}[(1+2a)s+(1-a)m_b\sigma_{3n}'](\sigma+m_b\sigma_{3n}')^{a-1}}{(1+a)(2+a)-\sqrt{1+[6am_b(s+m_b s_{3n}')^{a-1}][(1+a)(2+a)]}} \qquad (4.25)$$

where $=\sigma_{3n}=\sigma_{3max}'/\sigma_{ci}$

The conditions which must be satisfied for each slice are:

(1) $\sigma' > 0$, where $\sigma'$ is calculated by Bishop's method

(2) $\cos\psi_b\,[1+(\tan\psi_b\,\tan\phi_i')/FS] > 0.2$

*Figure 8.18* Bishop's simplified method of slices for the analysis of circular failure in slope in material in which strength is defined by non-linear criterion given in Section 4.5.

the equivalent Mohr–Coulomb shear strength. In addition, the program calculates the instantaneous friction angle and cohesion corresponding to the effective normal stress on the base of each slice.

Table 8.1 shows the input parameters for the Bishop and Janbu stability analyses assuming a linear shear strength, and for the Janbu analysis assuming a non-linear shear strength. The slope is divided into eight slices, and for each slice the base angle, weight, pore pressure and width are measured. The program SLIDE (RocScience, 2002b) is then used to calculate the factors of safety for the linear and non-linear shear strengths. In the case of the non-linear strength analysis, the values of the effective normal stress on the base of

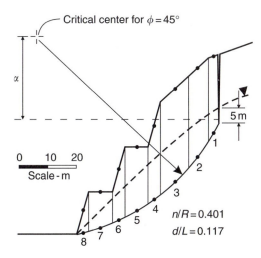

Critical center for $\phi = 45°$

$\alpha$

5 m

0   10   20

Scale - m

1
2
3
4
5
6
7
8

$n/R = 0.401$
$d/L = 0.117$

*Figure 8.19* Section of sandstone slope showing water table, slice boundaries, tension crack and the expected circular sliding surface.

the slices, and the corresponding instantaneous friction angle and cohesion are also calculated, as shown in the last three columns of Table 8.1. The calculated factors of safety estimates are

Bishop simplified method of slices for   = 1.39
  Mohr–Coulomb shear strength
Janbu modified method of slices for   = 1.26
  Mohr–Coulomb shear strength
Bishop simplified method of slices for   = 1.39
  non-linear shear strength

Note that the stability analysis of this slope using numerical analysis methods is shown in Section 10.4.1.

### 8.6.4  Circular failure stability analysis computer programs

The circular failure charts discussed in Section 8.3 provide a rapid means of carrying out stability analyses, but are limited to simple conditions as illustrated in the examples. More complex analyses can be carried out using the Bishop and Janbu methods discussed in Section 8.6.3, and the purpose of providing details on the procedures is to show the principles of the analyses.

*Table 8.1* Calculated shear strength values of slices using Mohr–Coulomb and Hoek–Brown failure criteria

| Slice parameters for all cases | | | | | Mohr–Coulomb values for Bishop and Janbu analyses | | Non-linear failure criterion values for Bishop analysis | | |
| --- | --- | --- | --- | --- | --- | --- | --- | --- | --- |
| Slice member | Angle of slice base, $\varphi$ (degrees) | Slice height (MN) | Pore pressure, $\gamma_w h_w$ (MPa) | Slice width (m) | Friction angle, $\Phi$ (degrees) | Cohesion, $c$ (MPa) | Base effective normal stress, $\sigma_n$ (MPa) | Inst. friction angle, $\phi_i$ (degrees) | Inst. cohesion, $c_i$ (MPa) |
| 1 | 25 | 1.312 | 0.017 | 6.1 | 43 | 0.145 | 0.139 | 53.8 | 0.068 |
| 2 | 29 | 1.597 | 0.047 | 6.1 | 43 | 0.145 | 0.169 | 53.8 | 0.068 |
| 3 | 34 | 2.603 | 0.071 | 6.1 | 43 | 0.145 | 0.270 | 49.8 | 0.096 |
| 4 | 39 | 2.635 | 0.087 | 6.1 | 43 | 0.145 | 0.261 | 51.3 | 0.085 |
| 5 | 44 | 3.501 | 0.095 | 6.1 | 43 | 0.145 | 0.323 | 49.0 | 0.104 |
| 6 | 50 | 3.914 | 0.087 | 6.1 | 43 | 0.145 | 0.324 | 48.6 | 0.107 |
| 7 | 57 | 3.592 | 0.047 | 6.1 | 43 | 0.145 | 0.240 | 50.3 | 0.092 |
| 8 | 65 | 2.677 | 0 | 6.1 | 43 | 0.145 | 0.109 | 54.5 | 0.064 |

There are, of course, computer programs available to carry out stability analyses of slopes, where the circular failure charts are not applicable. Important features included in these programs, which allows them to be used for a wide range of conditions, are as follows:

- Slope face can include benches and a variety of slope angles;
- Boundaries between the materials can be positioned to define layers of varying thickness and inclination, or inclusions of any shape;
- Shear strength of the materials can be defined in terms of Mohr–Coulomb or Hoek–Brown criterion;
- Ground water pressures can be defined on single or multiple water tables, or as specified pressure distributions;
- External loads, in any direction within the plane of the slope cross-section, can be positioned at their correct location on the slope. Such loads can include bridge and building foundations and bolting forces;
- Earthquake acceleration which is applied as a horizontal force in order to carry out pseudo-static stability analysis;
- The shape and position of the slide surface can be defined as a circular arc or straight line segments;
- A search routine finds the slide surface with the minimum factor of safety;
- Deterministic and probabilistic analysis methods that calculate the factor of safety and probability of failure, respectively. The probabilistic analysis requires that the design parameters be defined as distributions rather than single values;
- Error messages which identify negative stresses along the slide surface; and
- Drawing of slope showing slope geometry, material boundaries, ground water table(s) and slide surface(s).

One program that contains all these functions is the program XSTABL (Sharma, 1991). An example of the output (partial) produced by XSTABL is shown in Figure 8.20 for a benched slope excavated in sandstone, shale and siltstone above a proposed highway. For these conditions the shape of the failure surfaces are influenced by the position and thickness of the beds of the weaker material.

### 8.6.5 Three-dimensional circular failure analysis

The program XSTABL examines the stability of a unit width slice of the slope, which is a two-dimensional analysis that ignores any shear stresses on the sides of the slice (this is the same principle that is used in the plane failure analysis described in Chapter 6). While two-dimensional procedures have found to be a reliable method of analysis, there may be circumstances where three-dimensional analysis is required to define the slide surface and slope geometry more precisely. One program that provides a three-dimensional analysis is CLARA (Hungr, 1987), which divides the sliding mass into columns, rather than slices as used in the two-dimensional mode. Figure 8.21 shows an example of the CLARA analysis for a partially saturated slope in which the water table is below the bottom of the tension crack.

### 8.6.6 Numerical slope stability analysis

This chapter has been concerned solely with the limit equilibrium method of analysis in which the factor of safety is defined by the ratio of the resisting to the displacing forces on the slide surface.

An alternative method of analysis is to examine the stresses and strains within the slope as a means of assessing stability conditions. If the slope is close to failure, then a zone of high strain will develop within the slope with a shape that will be approximately coincident with the circular slide surface. If the shear strength properties are progressively reduced, there will be a sudden increase in the movement along the shear zone indicating that the slope is on the point of failure. The approximate factor of safety of the slope can be calculated from the ratio of the actual shear

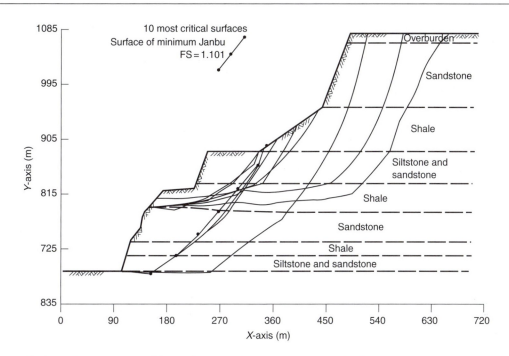

*Figure 8.20* Two-dimensional stability analysis of a highway cut using XSTABL.

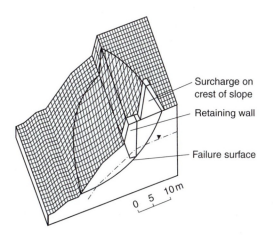

*Figure 8.21* Three-dimensional stability analysis of a slope incorporating a retaining wall and a surcharge at the crest.

## 8.7  Example Problem 8.1: circular failure analysis

### Statement

A 22-m high rock cut with a face angle of 60° has been excavated in a massive, very weak volcanic tuff. A tension crack has opened behind the crest and it is likely that the slope is on the point of failure, that is, the factor of safety is approximately 1.0. The friction angle of the material is estimated to be 30°, its density is 25 kN/m³, and the position of the water table is shown on the sketch of the slope (Figure 8.22). The rock contains no continuous joints dipping out of the face, and the most likely type of failure mode is circular failure.

strength of the rock to the shear strength at which the sudden movement occurred. This method of stability analysis is described in more detail in Section 10.3.

### Required

(a)  Carry out a back analysis of the failure to determine the limiting value of the cohesion when the factor of safety is 1.0.

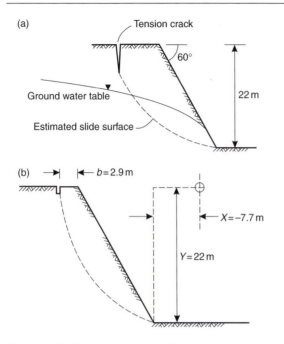

*Figure 8.22* Slope geometry for Example Problem 8.1: (a) slope geometry for circular failure with ground water table corresponding to circular failure chart number 3; (b) position of critical slide surface and critical tension crack.

(b) Using the strength parameters calculated in (a), determine the factor of safety for a completely drained slope. Would drainage of the slope be a feasible method of stabilization?

(c) Using the ground water level shown in Figure 8.22 and the strength parameters calculated in (a), calculate the reduction in slope height, that is, amount of unloading of the slope crest required to increase the factor of safety to 1.3.

(d) For the slope geometry and ground water level shown in Figure 8.22, find the coordinates of the center of the critical circle and the position of the critical tension crack.

*Solution*

(a) The ground water level shown in Figure 8.22 corresponds to ground water condition 3 in Table 8.4 in the manual, so circular failure

chart number 3 (Figure 8.8) is used in the analysis. When $\phi = 30°$ and FS $= 1.0$,

$$\tan \phi / \text{FS} = 0.58$$

The intersection of this value for $\tan \phi$/FS and the curve for a slope angle of $60°$ gives

$$\frac{c}{\gamma H \, \text{FS}} = 0.086$$

$$\therefore c = 0.086 \times 25 \times 22 \times 1.0$$

$$= 47.3 \, \text{kPa}$$

(b) If the slope were completely drained, circular failure chart 1 could be used for analysis.

$$\frac{c}{\gamma H \, \tan \phi} = \frac{47.3}{25 \times 22 \times \tan(30)}$$

$$= 0.15$$

The intersection of this inclined line with the curved line for a slope angle of $60°$ gives

$$\frac{\tan \phi}{\text{FS}} = 0.52$$

$$\therefore \text{FS} = \frac{\tan 30}{0.52}$$

$$= 1.11$$

This factor of safety is less than that usually accepted for a temporary slope, that is, FS $= 1.2$, so draining the slope would not be an effective means of stabilization.

(c) When FS $= 1.3$ and $\phi = 30°$, then $\tan \phi / \text{FS} = 0.44$.

On circular failure chart 3, the intersection of this horizontal line with the curved line for a slope angle of $60°$ gives

$$\frac{c}{\gamma H \, \text{FS}} = 0.11$$

$$\therefore H = \frac{47.3}{25 \times 1.3 \times 0.11}$$

$$= 13.2 \, \text{m}$$

This shows that the slope height must be reduced by 8.8 m to increase the factor of

# Chapter 9

# Toppling failure

## 9.1 Introduction

The failure modes discussed in the three previous chapters all relate to sliding of a rock or soil mass along an existing or induced sliding surface. This chapter discusses a different failure mode—that of toppling, which involves rotation of columns or blocks of rock about a fixed base. Similar to the plane and wedge failures, the stability analysis of toppling failures involves, first, carrying out a kinematic analysis of the structural geology to identify potential toppling conditions, and then, if this condition exists, performing a stability analysis specific to toppling failures.

One of the earliest references to toppling failures is by Muller (1968) who suggested that block rotation or toppling may have been a contributory factor in the failure of the north face of the Vaiont slide (Figure 9.1). Hofmann (1972) carried out a number of model studies under Muller's direction to investigate block rotation. Similar model studies carried out by Ashby (1971), Soto (1974) and Whyte (1973), while Cundall (1971), Byrne (1974) and Hammett (1974) who incorporated rotational failure modes into computer analysis of rock mass behavior. Figure 9.2 shows a computer model of a toppling failure in which the solid blocks are fixed and the open blocks are free to move. When the fixed blocks at the face are removed, the tallest columns of blocks topple because their center of gravity lies outside the base. The model illustrates a typical feature of toppling failures in which the tension cracks are wider at the top than at the base. This condition, which can best be observed when looking

along strike, is useful in the field identification of topples.

Papers concerning field studies of toppling failures include de Freitas and Waters (1973) who discuss slopes in Britain, and Wyllie (1980) who demonstrates stabilization measures for toppling failures related to railway operations.

Most of the discussion that follows in this chapter is based on a paper by Goodman and Bray (1976) in which a formal mathematical solution to a simple toppling problem is shown. This solution, which is reproduced here, represents a basis for designing rock slopes in which toppling is present, and has been further developed into a more general design tool (Zanbak, 1983; Adhikary *et al.*, 1997; Bobet, 1999; Sageseta *et al.*, 2001).

## 9.2 Types of toppling failure

Goodman and Bray (1976) have described a number of different types of toppling failures that may be encountered in the field, and each is discussed briefly on the following pages. The importance of distinguishing between types of toppling is that there are two distinct methods of stability analysis for toppling failures as described in the following pages—block and flexural toppling—and it is necessary to use the appropriate analysis in design.

### 9.2.1 Block toppling

As illustrated in Figure 9.3(a), block toppling occurs when, in strong rock, individual columns

*Figure 9.1* Suggested toppling mechanism of the north face of Vaiont slide (Muller, 1968).

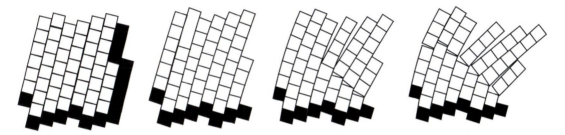

*Figure 9.2* Computer generated model of toppling failure; solid blocks are fixed in space while open blocks are free to move (Cundall, 1971).

are formed by a set of discontinuities dipping steeply into the face, and a second set of widely spaced orthogonal joints defines the column height. The short columns forming the toe of the slope are pushed forward by the loads from the longer overturning columns behind, and this sliding of the toe allows further toppling to develop higher up the slope. The base of the failure generally consists of a stepped surface rising from one cross joint to the next. Typical geological conditions in which this type of failure may occur are bedded sandstone and columnar basalt in which orthogonal jointing is well developed.

### 9.2.2 *Flexural toppling*

The process of flexural toppling is illustrated in Figure 9.3(b) that shows continuous columns of rock, separated by well developed, steeply dipping discontinuities, breaking in flexure as they bend forward. Typical geological conditions in which this type of failure may occur are thinly bedded shale and slate in which orthogonal jointing is not well developed. Generally, the basal plane of a flexural topple is not as well defined as a block topple.

Sliding, excavation or erosion of the toe of the slope allows the toppling process to start and it retrogresses back into the rock mass with the formation of deep tension cracks that become narrower with depth. The lower portion of the slope is covered with disordered fallen blocks and it is sometimes difficult to recognize a toppling failure from the bottom of the slope. Detailed examination of toppling slopes shows that the outward movement of each cantilevered column

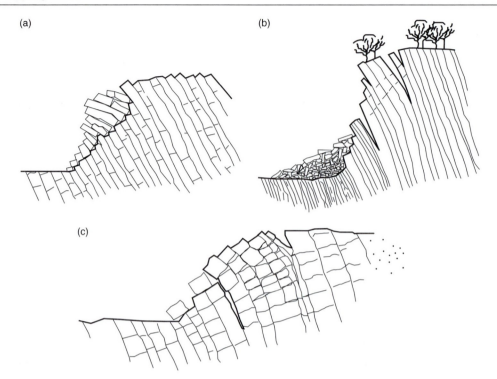

*Figure 9.3* Common classes of toppling failures: (a) block toppling of columns of rock containing widely spaced orthogonal joints; (b) flexural toppling of slabs of rock dipping steeply into face; (c) block flexure toppling characterized by pseudo-continuous flexure of long columns through accumulated motions along numerous cross-joints (Goodman and Bray 1976).

produces an interlayer slip and a portion of the upper surface of each plane is exposed in a series of back facing, or obsequent scarps, such as those illustrated in Figure 9.3(a).

### 9.2.3 *Block-flexure toppling*

As illustrated in Figure 9.3(c), block-flexure toppling is characterized by pseudo-continuous flexure along long columns that are divided by numerous cross joints. Instead of the flexural failure of continuous columns resulting in flexural toppling, toppling of columns in this case results from accumulated displacements on the cross-joints. Because of the large number of small movements in this type of topple, there are fewer tension cracks than in flexural toppling, and fewer edge-to-face contacts and voids than in block toppling.

### 9.2.4 *Secondary toppling modes*

Figure 9.4 illustrates a number of possible secondary toppling mechanisms suggested by Goodman and Bray. In general, these failures are initiated by some undercutting of the toe of the slope, either by natural agencies such as scour or weathering, or by human activities. In all cases, the primary failure mode involves sliding or physical breakdown of the rock, and toppling is induced in the upper part of the slope as a result of this primary failure (Figure 9.4(a) and (b)).

Figure 9.4(c) illustrates a common occurrence of toppling failure in horizontally bedded sandstone and shale formations. The shale is usually significantly weaker and more susceptible to weathering than the sandstone, while the sandstone often contains vertical stress relief joints. As the shale weathers, it undermines support for the

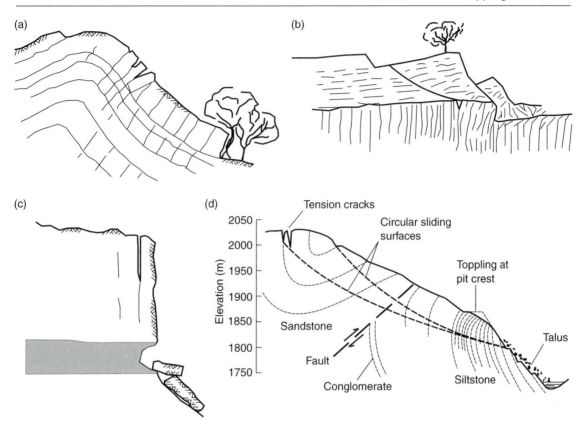

*Figure 9.4* Secondary toppling modes: (a) toppling at head of slide; (b) toppling at toe of slide with shear movement of upper slope (Goodman and Bray, 1976); (c) toppling of columns in strong upper material due to weathering of underlying weak material; (d) toppling at pit crest resulting in circular failure of upper slope (Wyllie and Munn, 1978).

sandstone and columns of sandstone, with their dimensions defined by the spacing of the vertical joints, topple from the face. At some locations the overhangs can be as wide as 5 m, and failures of substantial volumes of rock occur with little warning.

The example of the slide base toppling mode shown in Figure 9.4(d) is the failure of a pit slope in a coal mine where the beds at the crest of the pit dipped at 70° into the face, and their strike was parallel to the face. Mining of the pit slope at an angle of 50° initiated a toppling failure at the crest of the pit, which in turn resulted in a circular failure that extended to a height of 230 m above the base of the topple. Detailed monitoring of the slope showed that a total movement of about

30 m occurred on the slope above the pit, resulting in cracks opening in the crest of the mountain that were several meters wide and up to 9 m deep. Continuous movement monitoring was used to allow mining to proceed under the moving slope, and finally the slope was stabilized by back-filling the pit (Wyllie and Munn, 1979).

A further example of the toppling mechanism is illustrated in Figure 9.5 (Sjöberg, 2000). In open pit mines where the depth of the slope progressively increases, minor toppling movement may eventually develop into a substantial failure. Careful monitoring of the movement, and recognition of the toppling mechanism, can be used to anticipate when hazardous conditions are developing.

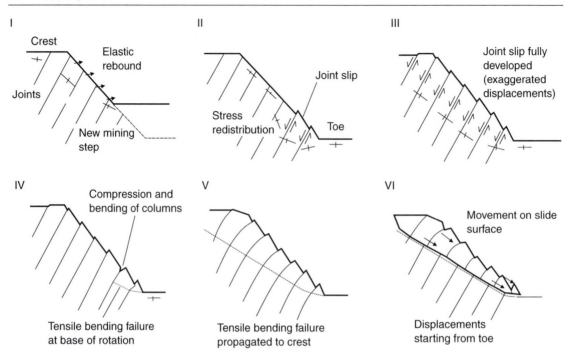

*Figure 9.5* Failure stages for large-scale toppling failure in a slope (Sjöberg, 2000).

## 9.3   Kinematics of block toppling failure

The potential for toppling can be assessed from two kinematic tests described in this section. These tests examine first the shape of the block, and second the relationship between the dip of the planes forming the slabs and the face angle. It is emphasized that these two tests are useful for identifying potential toppling conditions, but the tests cannot be used alone as a method of stability analysis.

### 9.3.1   Block shape test

The basic mechanics of the stability of a block on a plane are illustrated in Figure 9.6(a) (see also Figure 1.10). This diagram shows the conditions that differentiate stable, sliding or toppling blocks with height $y$ and width $\Delta x$ on a plane dipping at an angle $\psi_p$. If the friction angle between the base of the block and the plane is $\phi_p$, then the block will be stable against sliding when the dip of the base plane is less than the friction angle,

that is, when

$$\psi_p < \phi_p \text{ (Stable)} \qquad (9.1)$$

but will topple when the center of gravity of the block lies outside the base, that is, when

$$\Delta x/y < \tan \psi_p \text{ (Topple)} \qquad (9.2)$$

For example, for a 3 m wide block on a base plane dipping at 10°, toppling will occur if the height exceeds 17 m.

### 9.3.2   Inter-layer slip test

A requirement for toppling to occur in the mechanisms shown in Figures 9.3 and 9.5 is shear displacement on the face-to-face contacts on the top and bottom faces of the blocks. Sliding on these faces will occur if the following conditions are met (Figure 9.6(b)). The state of stress close to the slope face is uniaxial with the direction of the normal stress $\sigma$ aligned parallel to the slope

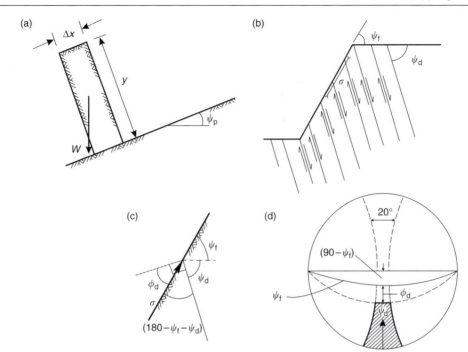

*Figure 9.6* Kinematic conditions for flexural slip preceding toppling: (a) block height/width test for toppling; (b) directions of stress and slip directions in rock slope; (c) condition for interlayer slip; (d) kinematic test defined on lower hemisphere stereographic projection.

face. When the layers slip past each other, $\sigma$ must be inclined at an angle $\phi_d$ with the normal to the layers, where $\phi_d$ is the friction angle of the sides of the blocks. If $\psi_f$ is the dip of slope face and $\psi_d$ is the dip of the planes forming the sides of the blocks, then the condition for interlayer slip is given by (Figure 9.6(c)):

$$(180 - \psi_f - \psi_d) \geq (90 - \phi_d) \qquad (9.3)$$

or

$$\psi_d \geq (90 - \psi_f) + \phi_d \qquad (9.4)$$

### 9.3.3 Block alignment test

The other kinematic condition for toppling is that the planes forming the blocks should strike approximately parallel to the slope face so that each layer is free to topple with little constraint from adjacent layers. Observations of topples in the field shows that instability is possible where the dip direction of the planes forming sides of the blocks, $\alpha_d$ is within about 10° of the dip direction of the slope face $\alpha_f$, or

$$|(\alpha_f - \alpha_d)| < 10° \qquad (9.5)$$

The two conditions defining kinematic stability of topples given by equations (9.4) and (9.5) can be depicted on the stereonet (Figure 9.6(d)). On the stereonet, toppling is possible for planes for which the poles lie within the shaded area, provided also that the base friction properties and shape of the blocks meet the conditions given by equations (9.1) and (9.2), respectively.

## 9.4 Limit equilibrium analysis of toppling on a stepped base

The method of toppling analysis described in this section utilizes the same principles of limiting

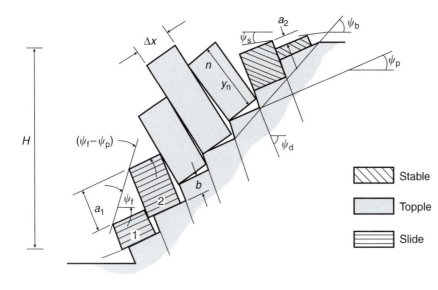

*Figure 9.7* Model for limiting equilibrium analysis of toppling on a stepped base (Goodman and Bray, 1976).

equilibrium that have been used throughout this book. While this method of analysis is limited to a few simple cases of toppling failure, it provides a basic understanding of the factors that are important in toppling, and allows stabilization options to be evaluated. The stability analysis involves an iterative process in which the dimensions of all the blocks and the forces acting on them are calculated, and then stability of each is examined, starting at the uppermost block. Each block will either be stable, toppling or sliding, and the overall slope is considered unstable if the lowermost block is either sliding or toppling. A basic requirement of this analysis is that the friction angle on the base of each block is greater than the dip angle of the base so that sliding on the base plane does not occur in the absence of any external force acting on the block (see equation (9.1)).

The limit equilibrium method of analysis is ideally suited to incorporating external forces acting on the slope to simulate a wide variety of actual conditions that may exist in the field. For example, if the lower block or blocks are unstable, then tensioned anchors with a specified tensile strength and plunge can be installed in these blocks to prevent movement. Also, ground motion due to earthquakes can be simulated by

a pseudo-static force acting on each block (see Section 6.5.4), water forces can act on the base and sides of each block, and loads produced by bridge foundations can be added to any specified block (Wyllie, 1999).

As an alternative to the detailed analysis described in this section, Zanbak (1983) developed a series of design charts that can be used to identify unstable toppling slopes, and to estimate the support force required for limiting equilibrium.

### 9.4.1  Block geometry

The first step in toppling analysis is to calculate the dimensions of each block. Consider the regular system of blocks shown in Figure 9.7 in which the blocks are rectangular with width $\Delta x$ and height $y_n$. The dip of the base of the blocks is $\psi_p$ and the dip of the orthogonal planes forming the faces of the blocks is $\psi_d (\psi_d = 90 - \psi_p)$. The slope height is $H$, and the face is excavated at angle $\psi_f$ while the upper slope above the crest is at angle $\psi_s$.

*Angle of base plane ($\psi_b$).*   The base of the toppling blocks is a stepped surface with an overall dip of $\psi_b$ (Figure 9.7). Note that there is no

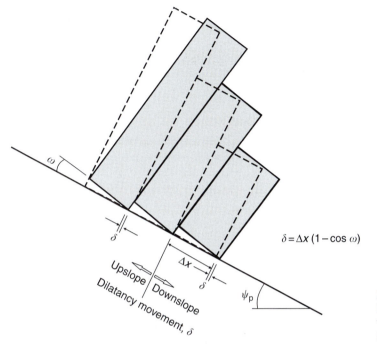

$$\delta = \Delta x\,(1 - \cos\omega)$$

*Figure 9.8* Dilatancy of toppling blocks with base plane coincident with normal to dip of blocks (Zanbak, 1983).

explicit means of determining a value of the parameter $\psi_b$. However, it is necessary to use an appropriate value for $\psi_b$ in the analysis because this has a significant effect on the stability of the slope. That is, as the base angle become flatter, the lengths of the blocks increase and there is a greater tendency of the taller blocks to topple resulting in decreased stability of the slope. If the base angle is coincident with the base of the blocks (i.e. $\psi_b = \psi_p$), then the geometry of toppling requires dilatancy $\delta$ of the blocks along the base plane and shearing on the faces of the blocks (Figure 9.8). However, if the base is stepped (i.e. $\psi_b > \psi_p$), then each block can topple without dilatancy, provided there is displacement on the face-to-face contacts (Figure 9.7). It is expected that more energy is required to dilate the rock mass than to develop shear along existing discontinuities, and so a stepped base is more likely than a planar base. Examination of base friction, centrifugal and numerical models (Goodman and Bray, 1976; Pritchard and Savigny, 1990, 1991; Adhikary *et al.*, 1997) show that base planes tend to be stepped, and the approximate dip angle is

in the range

$$\psi_b \approx (\psi_p + 10°)\ \text{to}\ (\psi_p + 30°) \tag{9.6}$$

It is considered that an appropriate stability analysis procedure for situations where the value of $\psi_b$ is unknown is to carry out a sensitivity analysis within the range given by equation (9.6) and find the value that gives the least stable condition.

Based on the slope geometry shown in Figure 9.7, the number of blocks $n$ making up the system is given by

$$n = \frac{H}{\Delta x}\left[\operatorname{cosec}(\psi_b) + \left(\frac{\cot(\psi_b) - \cot(\psi_f)}{\sin(\psi_b - \psi_f)}\right)\sin(\psi_s)\right] \tag{9.7}$$

The blocks are numbered from the toe of the slope upwards, with the lowest block being 1 and the upper block being $n$. In this idealized model, the height $y_n$ of the $n$th block in a position below the crest of the slope is

$$y_n = n\,(a_1 - b) \tag{9.8}$$

while above the crest

$$y_n = y_{n-1} - a_2 - b \tag{9.9}$$

The three constants $a_1$, $a_2$ and $b$ that are defined by the block and slope geometry and are given by

$$a_1 = \Delta x \tan(\psi_f - \psi_p) \tag{9.10}$$
$$a_2 = \Delta x \tan(\psi_p - \psi_s) \tag{9.11}$$
$$b = \Delta x \tan(\psi_b - \psi_p) \tag{9.12}$$

### 9.4.2  Block stability

Figure 9.7 shows the stability of a system of blocks subject to toppling, in which it is possible to distinguish three separate groups of blocks according to their mode of behavior:

(a)  A set of stable blocks in the upper part of the slope, where the friction angle of the base of the blocks is greater than the dip of this plane (i.e. $\phi_p > \psi_p$), and the height is limited so the center of gravity lies inside the base ($y/\Delta x < \cot \psi_p$).
(b)  An intermediate set of toppling blocks where the center of gravity lies outside the base.
(c)  A set of blocks in the toe region, which are pushed by the toppling blocks above. Depending on the slope and block geometries, the toe blocks may be stable, topple or slide.

Figure 9.9 demonstrates the terms used to define the dimensions of the blocks, and the position and direction of all the forces acting on the blocks during both toppling and sliding. Figure 9.9(a) shows a typical block ($n$) with the normal and shear forces developed on the base ($R_n$, $S_n$), and on the interfaces with adjacent blocks ($P_n$, $Q_n$, $P_{n-1}$, $Q_{n-1}$). When the block is one of the toppling set, the points of application of all forces are known, as shown in Figure 9.9(b). The points of application of the normal forces

$P_n$ are $M_n$ and $L_n$ on the upper and lower faces respectively of the block, and are given by the following.

If the $n$th block is below the slope crest, then

$$M_n = y_n \tag{9.13}$$
$$L_n = y_n - a_1 \tag{9.14}$$

If the $n$th block is the crest block, then

$$M_n = y_n - a_2 \tag{9.15}$$
$$L_n = y_n - a_1 \tag{9.16}$$

If the $n$th block is above the slope crest, then

$$M_n = y_n - a_2 \tag{9.17}$$
$$L_n = y_n \tag{9.18}$$

For an irregular array of blocks, $y_n$, $L_n$ and $M_n$ can be determined graphically.

When sliding and toppling occurs, frictional forces are generated on the bases and sides of the blocks. In many geological environments, the friction angles on these two surfaces are likely to be different. For example, in a steeply dipping sedimentary sequence comprising sandstone beds separated by thin seams of shale, the shale will form the sides of the blocks, while joints in the sandstone will form the bases of the blocks. For these conditions, the friction angle of the sides of the blocks ($\phi_d$) will be lower than friction angle on the bases ($\phi_p$). These two friction angles can be incorporated into the limit equilibrium analysis as follows.

For limiting friction on the sides of the block:

$$Q_n = P_n \tan \phi_d \tag{9.19}$$
$$Q_{n-1} = P_{n-1} \tan \phi_d \tag{9.20}$$

By resolving perpendicular and parallel to the base of a block with weight $W_n$, the normal and shear forces acting on the base of block $n$ are,

(a)

(b)

(c)

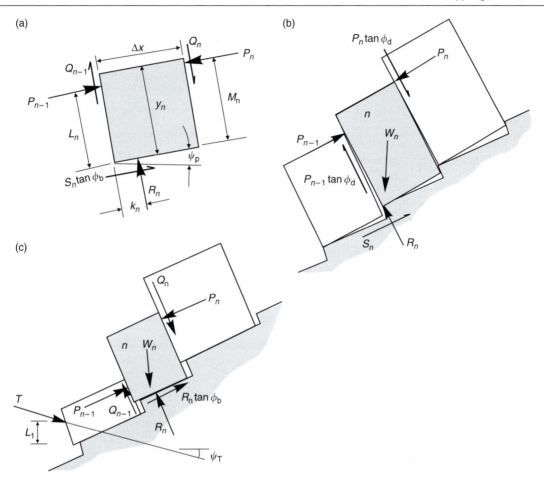

*Figure 9.9* Limiting equilibrium conditions for toppling and sliding of *n*th block: (a) forces acting on *n*th block; (b) toppling of *n*th block; (c) sliding of *n*th block (Goodman and Bray, 1976).

respectively,

$$R_n = W_n \cos \psi_p + (P_n - P_{n-1}) \tan \phi_d \quad (9.21)$$

$$S_n = W_n \sin \psi_p + (P_n - P_{n-1}) \quad (9.22)$$

Considering rotational equilibrium, it is found that the force $P_{n-1}$ that is just sufficient to prevent toppling has the value

$$P_{n-1,t} = [P_n(M_n - \Delta x \tan \phi_d) + (W_n/2)$$
$$(y_n \sin \psi_p - \Delta x \cos \psi_p)]/L_n \quad (9.23)$$

When the block under consideration is one of the sliding set (Figure 9.9(c)),

$$S_n = R_n \tan \phi_p \quad (9.24)$$

However, the magnitudes of the forces $Q_{n-1}$, $P_{n-1}$ and $R_n$ applied to the sides and base of the block, and their points of application $L_n$ and $K_n$, are unknown. Although the problem is indeterminate, the force $P_{n-1}$ required to prevent sliding of block $n$ can be determined if it is assumed that $Q_{n-1} = (\tan \phi_d \cdot P_{n-1})$. Then the shear force just sufficient to prevent sliding has the value

$$P_{n-1,s} = P_n - \frac{W_n(\cos \psi_p \tan \phi_p - \sin \psi_p)}{(1 - \tan \phi_p \tan \phi_d)}$$

$$(9.25)$$

### 9.4.3   Calculation procedure for toppling stability of a system of blocks

The calculation procedure for examining toppling stability of a slope comprising a system of blocks dipping steeply into the faces is as follows:

(i)   The dimensions of each block and the number of blocks are defined using equations (9.7)–(9.12).

(ii)   Values for the friction angles on the sides and base of the blocks ($\phi_d$ and $\phi_p$) are assigned based on laboratory testing, or inspection. The friction angle on the base should be greater than the dip of the base to prevent sliding (i.e. $\phi_p > \psi_p$).

(iii)   Starting with the top block, equation (9.2) is used to identify if toppling will occur, that is, when $y/\Delta x > \cot \psi_p$. For the upper toppling block, equations (9.23) and (9.25) are used to calculate the lateral forces required to prevent toppling and sliding, respectively.

(iv)   Let $n_1$ be the uppermost block of the toppling set.

(v)   Starting with block $n_1$, determine the lateral forces $P_{n-1,t}$ required to prevent toppling, and $P_{n-1,s}$ to prevent sliding. If $P_{n-1,t} > P_{n-1,s}$, the block is on the point of toppling and $P_{n-1}$ is set equal to $P_{n-1,t}$, or if $P_{n-1,s} > P_{n-1,t}$, the block is on the point of sliding and $P_{n-1}$ is set equal to $P_{n-1,s}$.

In addition, a check is made that there is a normal force $R$ on the base of the block, and that sliding does not occur on the base, that is

$$R_n > 0 \quad \text{and} \quad (|S_n| > R_n \tan \phi_p)$$

(vi)   The next lower block ($n_1 - 1$) and all the lower blocks are treated in succession using the same procedure. It may be found that a relatively short block that does not satisfy equation (9.2) for toppling, may still topple if the moment applied by the thrust force on the upper face is great enough to satisfy the condition stated in (v) above. If the condition $P_{n-1,t} > P_{n-1,s}$ is met for all blocks, then toppling extends down to block 1 and sliding does not occur.

(vii)   Eventually a block may be reached for which $P_{n-1,s} > P_{n-1,t}$. This establishes block $n_2$, and for this and all lower blocks, the critical state is one of sliding. The stability of the sliding blocks is checked using equation (9.24), with the block being unstable if ($S_n = R_n \tan \phi_b$). If block 1 is stable against both sliding and toppling (i.e. $P_0 < 0$), then the overall slope is considered to be stable. If block 1 either topples or slides (i.e. $P_0 > 0$), then the overall slope is considered to be unstable.

### 9.4.4   Cable force required to stabilize a slope

If the calculation process described in Section 9.4.3 shows that block 1 is unstable, then a tensioned cable can be installed through this block and anchored in stable rock beneath the zone of toppling to prevent movement. The design parameters for anchoring are the bolt tension, the plunge of the anchor and its position on block 1 (Figure 9.9(c)).

Suppose that an anchor is installed at a plunge angle $\psi_T$ through block 1 at a distance $L_1$ above its base. The anchor tension required to prevent toppling of block 1 is

$$T_t = \frac{W_1/2(y_1 \sin \psi_p - \Delta x \cos \psi_p) + P_1(y_1 - \Delta x \tan \phi_d)}{L_1 \cos(\psi_p + \psi_T)}$$

$$(9.26)$$

while the required anchor tension to prevent sliding of block 1 is

$$T_s = \frac{P_1(1 - \tan \phi_p \tan \phi_d) - W_1(\tan \phi_p \cos \psi_p - \sin \psi_p)}{\tan \phi_p \sin(\psi_p + \psi_T) + \cos(\psi_p + \psi_T)}$$

$$(9.27)$$

When the force T is applied to block 1, the normal and shear force on the base of the block are, respectively,

$$R_1 = P_1 \tan \phi_d + T \sin(\psi_p + \psi_T) + W_1 \cos \psi_p \tag{9.28}$$

$$S_1 = P_1 - T \cos(\psi_p + \psi_T) + W_1 \sin \psi_p \tag{9.29}$$

The stability analysis for a slope with a tensioned anchor in block 1 is identical to that described in Section 9.4.3, apart from the calculations relating to block 1. The required tension is the greater of $T_t$ and $T_s$ defined by equations (9.26) and (9.27).

### 9.4.5 Factor of safety for limiting equilibrium analysis of toppling failures

For both reinforced and unreinforced slopes, the factor of safety can be calculated by finding the friction angle for limiting equilibrium. The procedure is first to carry out the limiting equilibrium stability analysis as described in Section 9.4.3 using the estimated values for the friction angles. If block 1 is unstable, then one or both of the friction angles are increased by increments until the value of $P_0$ is very small. Conversely, if block 1 is stable, then the friction angles are reduced until $P_0$ is very small. These values of the friction angles are those required for limiting equilibrium.

The limiting equilibrium friction angles are termed the required friction angles, while the actual friction angles of the block surfaces are termed the available friction angles. The factor of safety for toppling can be defined by dividing the tangent of the friction angle believed to apply to the rock layers ($\tan \phi_{available}$), by the tangent of the friction angle required for equilibrium ($\tan \phi_{required}$).

$$FS = \frac{\tan \phi_{available}}{\tan \phi_{required}} \tag{9.30}$$

The actual factor of safety of a toppling slope depends on the details of the geometry of the toppling blocks. Figure 9.7 shows that once a column overturns by a small amount, there are edge-to-face contacts between the blocks, and the friction required to prevent further rotation increases. Hence, a slope just at limiting equilibrium is meta-stable. However, rotation equal to $2(\psi_b - \psi_p)$ will convert the edge-to-face contacts along the sides of the columns into continuous face contacts and the friction angle required to prevent further rotation will drop sharply, possibly even below that required for initial equilibrium. The choice of factor of safety, therefore, depends on whether or not some deformation can be tolerated.

The restoration of continuous face-to-face contact of toppled columns of rock is probably an important arrest mechanism in large-scale toppling failures. In many cases in the field, large surface displacements and tension crack formation can be observed and yet the volumes of rock that fall from the face are small.

### 9.4.6 Example of limit equilibrium analysis of toppling

The following is an example of the application of the Goodman and Bray limit equilibrium analysis to calculate the factor of safety and required bolting force of the toppling failure illustrated in Figure 9.10(a).

A rock face 92.5 m high ($H$) is cut at an angle of 56.6° ($\psi_f$) in a layered rock mass dipping at 60° into the face ($\psi_d = 60°$); the width of each block is 10 m ($\Delta x$). The angle of the slope above the crest of the cut is 4° ($\psi_s$), and the base of the blocks is stepped 1 m at every block (atn (1/10) = 5.7°, and $\psi_b = (5.7 + \psi_p) = 35.7°$). Based on this geometry, there are 16 blocks formed between the toe and crest of the slope (equation 9.7); block 10 is at the crest. Using equations (9.10)–(9.12), the constants are $a_1 = 5.0$ m, $a_2 = 5.2$ m and $b = 1.0$ m. These constants are used to calculate the height $y_n$ of each block, and the height to width ratio $y_n/\Delta x$ as shown on the table in Figure 9.10(b).

The friction angles on the faces and bases of the blocks are equal and have a value of 38.15° ($\phi_{available}$). The unit weight of the rock is

(a)

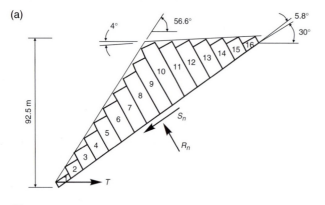

(b)

| n | $y_n$ | $y_n/\Delta x$ | $M_n$ | $L_n$ | $P_{n\cdot t}$ | $P_{n\cdot s}$ | $P_n$ | $R_n$ | $S_n$ | $S_n/R_n$ | Mode |
|----|-------|---------|-------|-------|--------|---------|--------|--------|--------|---------|---------|
| 16 | 4.0 | 0.4 | | | 0 | 0 | 0 | 866 | 500 | 0.577 | |
| 15 | 10.0 | 1.0 | | | 0 | 0 | 0 | 2165 | 1250 | 0.577 | STABLE |
| 14 | 16.0 | 1.6 | | | 0 | 0 | 0 | 3463 | 2000 | 0.577 | |
| 13 | 22.0 | 2.2 | 17 | 22 | 0 | 0 | 0 | 4533.4 | 2457.5 | 0.542 | |
| 12 | 28.0 | 2.8 | 23 | 28 | 292.5 | −2588.7 | 292.5 | 5643.3 | 2966.8 | 0.526 | T |
| 11 | 34.0 | 3.4 | 29 | 34 | 825.7 | −3003.2 | 825.7 | 6787.6 | 3520.0 | 0.519 | O |
| 10 | 40.0 | 4.0 | 35 | 35 | 1556.0 | −3175.0 | 1556.0 | 7662.1 | 3729.3 | 0.487 | P |
| 9 | 36.0 | 3.6 | 36 | 31 | 2826.7 | −3150.8 | 2826.7 | 6933.8 | 3404.6 | 0.491 | P |
| 8 | 32.0 | 3.2 | 32 | 27 | 3922.1 | −1409.4 | 3922.1 | 6399.8 | 3327.3 | 0.520 | L |
| 7 | 28.0 | 2.8 | 28 | 23 | 4594.8 | 156.8 | 4594.8 | 5872.0 | 3257.8 | 0.555 | I |
| 6 | 24.0 | 2.4 | 24 | 19 | 4837.0 | 1300.1 | 4837.0 | 5352.9 | 3199.5 | 0.598 | N |
| 5 | 20.0 | 2.0 | 20 | 15 | 4637.5 | 2013.0 | 4637.5 | 4848.1 | 3159.4 | 0.652 | G |
| 4 | 16.0 | 1.6 | 16 | 11 | 3978.1 | 2284.1 | 3978.1 | 4369.4 | 3152.5 | 0.722 | |
| 3 | 12.0 | 1.2 | 12 | 7 | 2825.6 | 2095.4 | 2825.6 | 3707.3 | 2912.1 | 0.7855 | |
| 2 | 8.0 | 0.8 | 8 | 3 | 1103.1 | 1413.5 | 1413.5 | 2471.4 | 1941.3 | 0.7855 | SLIDING |
| 1 | 4.0 | 0.4 | 4 | − | −1485.1 | 472.2 | 472.2 | 1237.1 | 971.8 | 0.7855 | |

(c)

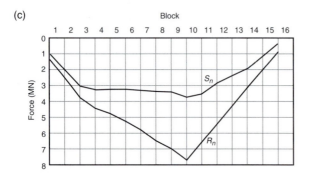

*Figure 9.10* Limited equilibrium analysis of a toppling slope: (a) slope geometry; (b) table listing block dimensions, calculated forces and stability mode; (c) distribution of normal (*R*) and shear (*S*) forces on base of blocks (Goodman and Bray, 1976).

$25 \, \text{kN/m}^3$. It is assumed that the slope is dry, and that there are no external forces acting.

The stability analysis is started by examining the toppling/sliding mode of each block, starting at the crest. Since the friction angle on the base

of the blocks is 38.15° and the dip of the base is 30°, the upper blocks are stable against sliding. Equation (9.2) is then used to assess the toppling mode. Since $\cot \psi_p = 1.73$, blocks 16, 15 and 14 are stable, because for each the ratio $y_n/\Delta x$ is less than 1.73. That is, these three blocks are short and their center of gravity lies inside the base.

For block 13, the ratio $y_n/\Delta x$ has the value 2.2, which is greater than 1.73 and the block topples. Therefore, $P_{13}$ is equal to 0 and $P_{12}$ is calculated as the greater of $P_{12,t}$ and $P_{12,s}$ given by equations (9.23) and (9.25) respectively. This calculation procedure is used to examine the stability of each block in turn progressing down the slope. As shown in the table of forces in Figure 9.10(b), $P_{n-1,t}$ is the larger of the two forces until a value of $n = 3$, whereupon $P_{n-1,s}$ is larger. Thus blocks 4 to 13 constitute the potential toppling zone, and blocks 1 to 3 constitute a sliding zone.

The factor of safety of this slope can be found by increasing the friction angles until the base blocks are just stable. It is found that the required friction angle for limit equilibrium conditions is $39°$, so the factor of safety as given by equation (9.30) is 0.97 (tan 38.15/ tan 39). The analysis also shows that the required tension in an anchor installed horizontally in block 1 to just stabilize the toe blocks is 500 kN per meter length of slope. This compares with the maximum value of $P$ (in block 5) equal to 4837 kN/m.

If $\tan \phi$ is reduced to 0.650, it will be found that blocks 1 to 4 in the toe region will slide while blocks 5 to 13 will topple. The tension in an anchor installed horizontally through block 1, required to restore equilibrium, is found to be 2013 kN/m of slope crest. This is not a large number, demonstrating that support of the "keystone" is remarkably effective in increasing the degree of stability. Conversely, removing or weakening the keystone of a toppling slope that is near failure can have serious consequences.

When the distribution of $P$ forces has been defined in the toppling region, the forces $R_n$ and $S_n$ on the base of the blocks can be calculated using equations (9.21) and (9.22). Assuming $[Q_{n-1} = P_{n-1} \tan \phi_s]$, the forces $R_n$ and $S_n$ can also be calculated for the sliding region. Figure 9.10(c) shows the distribution of these forces throughout the slope. The conditions defined by $R_n > 0$ and $|S_n| < R_n \tan \phi_p$ are satisfied everywhere.

### 9.4.7 Application of external forces to toppling slopes

There may be circumstances where there are external forces acting on the slope and it is necessary to investigate their effect on stability. Examples of external forces include water forces acting on the sides and bases of the blocks, earthquake ground motion simulated as a horizontal force acting on each block (see Section 6.5.4), and point loads produced by bridge piers located on a specific block(s). Another external force that has been considered in the worked example in Section 9.4.6 are rock anchors that are secured in stable ground beneath the toppling mass and then tensioned against the face.

A feature of limit equilibrium analysis is that any number of forces can be added to the analysis, provided that their magnitude, direction and point of application are known. Figure 9.11 shows a portion of a toppling slope in which there is a sloping water table. The forces acting on block $n$ include the force $Q$ inclined at an angle $\psi_Q$ below the horizontal, and three water forces $V_1$, $V_2$ and $V_3$, as well as the forces $P_n$ and $P_{n-1}$ produced by the blocks above and below. By resolving all these forces normal and parallel to the base of the blocks, it is possible to modify equations (9.23) and (9.25) as follows. Considering rotational equilibrium, the force $P_{n-1,t}$ that is just sufficient to prevent toppling of block $n$ has the value:

$$
\begin{aligned}
P_{n-1,t} = \{ & P_n (M_n - \Delta x \tan \phi_d) \\
& + W_n/2 (y_n \sin \psi_p - \Delta x \cos \psi_p) \\
& + V_1 y_w/3 + \gamma_w \Delta x^2/6 \\
& \times \cos \psi_p (z_w + 2y_w) - V_3 z_w/3 \\
& + Q[-\sin(\psi_Q - \psi_p)\Delta x/2 \\
& + \cos(\psi_Q - \psi_p) y_n] \} L_n^{-1} \qquad (9.31)
\end{aligned}
$$

Assuming that the blocks are in a state of limiting equilibrium, the force just sufficient to prevent

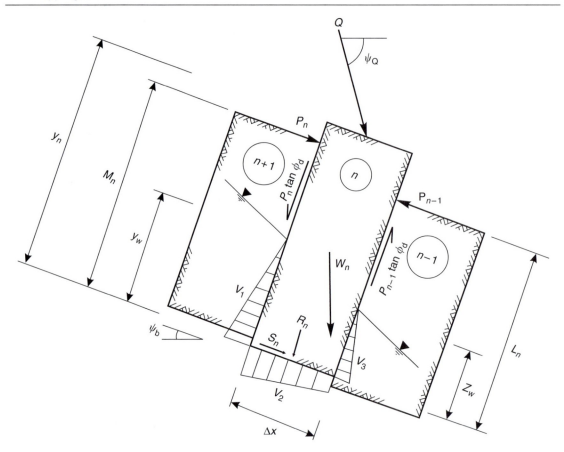

*Figure 9.11* Toppling block with external forces.

sliding of block $n$ has the value

$$P_{n-1,s} = P_n + \{-W(\cos\psi_p \tan\phi_p - \sin\psi_p)$$
$$+ V_1 - V_2 \tan\phi_p - V_3$$
$$+ Q[-\sin(\psi_Q - \psi_p)\tan\phi_p$$
$$+ \cos(\psi_Q - \psi_p)]\}$$
$$\times (1 - \tan\phi_p \tan\phi_d)^{-1} \qquad (9.32)$$

where

$$V_1 = \tfrac{1}{2}\gamma_w \cos\psi_p \cdot y_w^2;$$
$$V_2 = \tfrac{1}{2}\gamma_w \cos\psi_p(y_w + z_w)\Delta x$$
$$V_3 = \tfrac{1}{2}\gamma_w \cos\psi_p z_w^2 \qquad (9.33)$$

The limit equilibrium stability analysis then proceeds as before using the modified versions of the equations for $P_{n-1,t}$ and $P_{n-1,s}$.

## 9.5   Stability analysis of flexural toppling

Figure 9.3(b) shows a typical flexural toppling failure in which the slabs of rock flex and maintain fact-to-face contact. The mechanism of flexural toppling is different from the block toppling mechanism described in Section 9.4. Therefore, it is not appropriate to use limit equilibrium stability analysis for design of toppling slopes. Techniques that have been used to study the stability of flexural toppling include base friction models (Goodman, 1976), centrifuges (Adhikary *et al.*, 1997) and numerical modeling (Pritchard

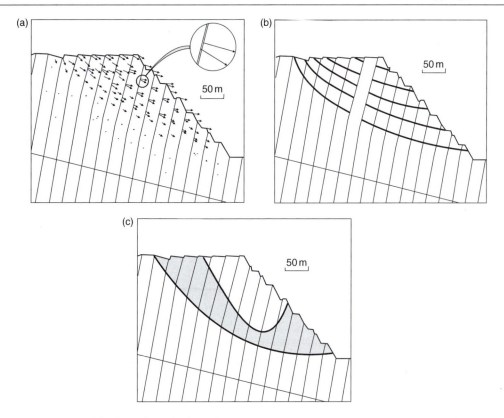

*Figure 9.12* UDEC model of toppling pit slope: (a) pure flexural toppling deformation with grid point velocity vectors; (b) contours of horizontal displacement for toppling slopes; (c) area of failed nodes due to flexure (Pritchard and Savigny, 1990).

and Savigny, 1990, 1991). All these models show the common features of this failure mechanism including interlayer shearing, obsequent scarps at the crest, opening of tension cracks that decrease in width with depth, and a limiting dip angle $\psi_b$ for the base of toppling. As discussed in Section 9.4.1, dip angle $\psi_b$ is steeper than the plane $\psi_p$ (normal to the dip of the slabs) by about 10–30°.

The centrifuge modeling by Adhikary *et al.* has been used to develop a series of design charts that relate stability to the slope face angle, the dip of the blocks into the face and the ratio of the slope height to the width of the slabs. Another input parameter is the tensile strength of the rock, because bending of the slabs induces tensile cracking in their upper face. The design charts provide information, for example, on the allowable face angle for specific geological conditions and slope height.

Alternatively, computer simulations of block movement provide a means of studying a wide range of geometric and material properties. One of the most suitable computer programs for these simulations is UDEC (*U*niversal *D*istinct *E*lement *C*ode), which has been developed by Itasca Consulting Group in Minnesota (Itasca, 2000). Figure 9.12 shows the results of an analysis carried out on an open pit mine slope (Pritchard and Savigny, 1990). The main features of UDEC analysis for studying toppling slopes are that it

- incorporates a number of materials each with differing strength properties;

- recognizes the existence of contacts or interfaces between discrete bodies, such as slabs of rocks formed by discontinuities dipping steeply into the slope face;
- calculates the motion along contacts by assigning a finite normal stiffness along the discontinuities that separate the columns of rock. The normal stiffness of a discontinuity is defined as the normal closure that occurs on the application of a normal stress and can be measured from a direct shear test (see Figure 4.17);
- assumes deformable blocks that undergo bending and tensile failure;
- allows finite displacements and rotations of the toppling blocks, including complete detachment, and recognizes new contacts automatically as the calculation progresses;
- uses an explicit "time"-marching scheme to solve the equation of motion directly. This allows modeling of progressive failure, or the amount of creep exhibited by a series of toppling blocks for a chosen slope condition, such as excavation at the toe of the slope. Note that the time step in the analysis is not actual time but a simulation of progressive movement; and
- allows the user to investigate different stabilization measures, such as installing rock bolts or installing drain holes, to determine which scenario has the most effect on block movements.

Because of the large number of input parameters that are used in UDEC and the power of the analysis, the most reliable results are obtained if the model can be calibrated against an existing toppling failure in similar geological conditions to those in the design slope. The ideal situation is in mining operations where the development of the topple can be simulated by UDEC as the pit is deepened and movement is monitored. This allows the model to be progressively updated with new data. Chapter 10 discusses numerical modeling of slopes in more detail.

The application of kinematic stability tests and reinforcement design for a flexural toppling failure is described by Davies and Smith (1993). The toppling occurred in siltstones in which the beds were very closely spaced and dipped at between 90° and 70° into the face. Excavation for a bridge abutment resulted in a series of tension cracks along the crest, and stabilization of the slope required the installation of tensioned rock bolts and excavation to reduce the slope angle.

## 9.6  Example Problem 9.1: toppling failure analysis

*Statement*

Consider a 6 m high slope with an overhanging face at an angle of 75° There is a fault, dipping at an angle of 15° out of the face, at the toe of the slope that is weathering and undercutting the face. A tension crack, which is wider at the top than at the bottom, has developed 1.8 m behind the crest of the slope indicating that the face is marginally stable (Figure 9.13). The friction angle $\phi$ of the fault is 20° and the cohesion $c$ is 25 kPa. The slope is dry.

*Required*

(a)  Calculate the factor of safety of the block against sliding if the density of the rock is 23.5 kN/m$^3$.

(b)  Is the block stable against toppling as defined by the relation:

$$\Delta x/y > \tan \psi_{\mathrm{p}}\text{---stable?}$$

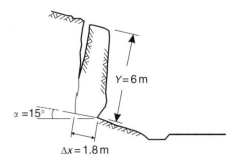

*Figure 9.13* Toppling block illustrating Example Problem 9.1.

(c) How much more undercutting of the fault must occur before toppling failure takes place?

(d) What stabilization measures would be appropriate for this slope?

*Solution*

(a) The factor of safety against sliding is determined by the methods described in Chapter 6; the equation for a dry slope is

$$FS = \frac{cA + W \cos \psi_p \cdot \tan \phi_p}{W \sin \psi_p}$$

$$= ((25 \times 1.8) + (254 \times \cos 15 \times \tan 20))/(254 \times \sin 15)$$

$$\approx 2.0$$

where

$A$ = base area of block

$= 1.8 \, \text{m}^2/\text{m}$

$W$ = weight of block/m

$= 23.5 \times 1.8 \times 6$

$= 254 \, \text{kN/m}$

(b) From the dimensions given on Figure 9.13, the following values are obtained to test stability conditions:

$$\Delta x/y = 0.3$$

$$\tan 15 = 0.27$$

The block is stable against toppling because $0.3 > 0.27$.

(c) If weathering results in the width of the base of the block being reduced by a further 0.2 m, toppling is likely to occur because: $\Delta x/y = (1.8 - 0.2)/6 \approx 0.27$.

(d) Stabilization measures which could be used on this slope include the following:

- Prevention of ground water infiltration to limit build-up of water pressure both in the tension crack and on the fault at the toe.
- Application of reinforced shotcrete to the fault to prevent further weathering.
- Trim blasting to reduce the slope angle and the dimension $y$, if this can be achieved without destabilizing the block.

# Chapter 10

# Numerical analysis

## Dr Loren Lorig and Pedro Varona[1]

## 10.1 Introduction

The previous four chapters discussed limit equilibrium methods of slope stability analysis for rock bounded by specified slide planes. In contrast, this chapter discusses numerical analysis methods to calculate the factor of safety without pre-defining slide planes. These methods are more recent developments than limit equilibrium methods and, at present (2003), are used predominately in open pit mining and landslides studies, where interest often focuses on slope displacements rather than on the relative magnitude of resisting and displacing forces.

Numerical models are computer programs that attempt to represent the mechanical response of a rock mass subjected to a set of initial conditions such as *in situ* stresses and water levels, boundary conditions and induced changes such as slope excavation. The result of a numerical model simulation typically is either equilibrium or collapse. If an equilibrium result is obtained, the resultant stresses and displacements at any point in the rock mass can be compared with measured values. If a collapse result is obtained, the predicted mode of failure is demonstrated.

Numerical models divide the rock mass into zones. Each zone is assigned a material model and properties. The material models are idealized stress/strain relations that describe how the material behaves. The simplest model is a linear elastic model, which uses the elastic properties (Young's modulus and Poisson's ratio) of the material. Elastic–plastic models use strength parameters to limit the shear stress that a zone may sustain.[2]

The zones may be connected together, termed a continuum model, or separated by discontinuities, termed a discontinuum model. Discontinuum models allow slip and separation at explicitly located surfaces within the model.

Numerical models tend to be general purpose in nature—that is, they are capable of solving a wide variety of problems. While it is often desirable to have a general-purpose tool available, it requires that each problem be constructed individually. The zones must be arranged by the user to fit the limits of the geomechanical units and/or the slope geometry. Hence, numerical models often require more time to set up and run than special-purpose tools such as limit equilibrium methods.

There are several reasons why numerical models are used for slope stability studies.

- Numerical models can be extrapolated confidently outside their databases in comparison to empirical methods in which the failure mode is explicitly defined.
- Numerical analysis can incorporate key geologic features such as faults and ground water providing more realistic approximations of behavior of real slopes than analytic models.

---

1 Itasca Consulting Group, Inc., Minneapolis, Minnesota 55401 USA.

2 In numerical analysis the terms "elements" and "zones" are used interchangeably. However, the term element is used more commonly in finite element analysis, and the term zone in finite difference analysis.

In comparison, non-numerical analysis methods such as analytic, physical or limit equilibrium may be unsuitable for some sites or tend to oversimplify the conditions, possibly leading to overly conservative solutions.

- Numerical analysis can help to explain observed physical behavior.
- Numerical analysis can evaluate multiple possibilities of geological models, failure modes and design options.

Many limit equilibrium programs exist to determine factors of safety for slopes. These execute very rapidly, and in the case of the method of slices for circular failure, use an approximate scheme in which a number of assumptions are made, including the location and angle of inter-slice forces (see Section 8.2). Several assumed slide surfaces are tested, and the one giving the lowest factor of safety is chosen. Equilibrium is satisfied only on an idealized set of surfaces. With numerical models, a "full" solution of the coupled stress/displacement, equilibrium and constitutive equations is made. Given a set of properties, the system is found either to be stable or unstable. By performing a series of simulations with various properties, the factor of safety can be found corresponding to the point of stability.

The numerical analysis is much slower, but much more general. Only since the late 1990s, with the advent of faster computers, has it become a practical alternative to the limit equilibrium method. Even so, while limit equilibrium solutions may require just a few seconds, numerical solutions to large complex problems can take an hour or more, particularly when discontinuum behavior is involved. The third section of this chapter presents typical safety factor analyses for the most common discontinuum failure modes in rock slopes.

For slopes, the factor of safety often is defined as the ratio of the actual shear strength to the minimum shear strength required to prevent failure. A logical way to compute the factor of safety with a finite element or finite difference program is to reduce the shear strength until collapse occurs. The factor of safety is the ratio of the rock's actual strength to the reduced shear strength at failure. This shear-strength reduction technique was used first with finite elements by Zienkiewicz *et al.* (1975) to compute the safety factor of a slope composed of multiple materials.

To perform slope stability analysis with the shear strength reduction technique, simulations are run for a series of increasing trial factors of safety ($f$). Actual shear strength properties, cohesion ($c$) and friction angle ($\phi$), are reduced for each trial according to the equations

$$c_{\text{trial}} = \left(\frac{1}{f}\right) c \tag{10.1}$$

$$\phi_{\text{trial}} = \arctan\left(\frac{1}{f}\right) \tan\phi \tag{10.2}$$

If multiple materials and/or joints are present, the reduction is made simultaneously for all materials. The trial factor of safety is increased gradually until the slope fails. At failure, the factor of safety equals the trial factor of safety (i.e. $f$ = FS). Dawson *et al.* (1999) show that the shear strength reduction factors of safety are generally within a few percent of limit analysis solutions when an associated flow rule, in which the friction angle and dilation angle are equal, is used.

The shear strength reduction technique has two main advantages over limit equilibrium slope stability analyses. First, the critical slide surface is found automatically, and it is not necessary to specify the shape of the slide surface (e.g. circular, log spiral, piecewise linear) in advance. In general, the failure surface geometry for slopes is more complex than simple circles or segmented surfaces. Second, numerical methods automatically satisfy translational and rotational equilibrium, whereas not all limit equilibrium methods do satisfy equilibrium. Consequently, the shear strength reduction technique usually will determine a safety factor equal to or slightly less than limit equilibrium methods. Itasca Consulting Group (2002) gives a detailed comparison of four limit equilibrium methods and one numerical method for six different slope stability cases.

*Table 10.1* Comparison of numerical and limit equilibrium analysis methods

| Analysis result | Numerical solution | Limit equilibrium |
|---|---|---|
| Equilibrium | Satisfied everywhere | Satisfied only for specific objects, such as slices |
| Stresses | Computed everywhere using field equations | Computed approximately on certain surfaces |
| Deformation | Part of the solution | Not considered |
| Failure | Yield condition satisfied everywhere; slide surfaces develop "automatically" as conditions dictate | Failure allowed only on certain pre-defined surfaces; no check on yield condition elsewhere |
| Kinematics | The "mechanisms" that develop satisfy kinematic constraints | A single kinematic condition is specified according to the particular geologic conditions |

A summary of the differences between a numerical solution and the limit equilibrium method is shown in the Table 10.1.

## 10.2  Numerical models

All rock slopes involve discontinuities. Representation of these discontinuities in numerical models differs depending on the type of model. There are two basic types of models: discontinuum models and continuum models. Discontinuities in discontinuum models are represented explicitly—that is, the discontinuities have a specific orientation and location. Discontinuities in continuum models are represented implicitly, with the intention that the behavior of the continuum model is substantially equivalent to the real jointed rock mass being represented.

Discontinuum codes start with a method designed specifically to model discontinua and treat continuum behavior as a special case. Discontinuum codes generally are referred to as Discrete Element codes. A Discrete Element code will typically embody an efficient algorithm for detecting and classifying contacts, and maintain a data structure and memory allocation scheme that can handle many hundreds or thousands of discontinuities. The discontinuities divide the problem domain into blocks that may be either rigid or deformable; continuum behavior is assumed within deformable blocks. The most widely used discrete element codes for slope stability studies are UDEC (*Universal Distinct Element Code*; Itasca Consulting Group, 2000) and 3DEC (*3-Dimensional Distinct Element Code*; Itasca Consulting Group, 2003). Of fundamental importance in discontinuum codes is the representation of joint or discontinuity behavior. Commonly used relations for representing joint behavior are discussed later in this section.

Continuum codes assume material is continuous throughout the body. Discontinuities are treated as special cases by introducing interfaces between continuum bodies. Finite element codes such as PHASE$^2$ (Rocscience, 2002c) and its predecessor PHASES (*Plastic Hybrid Analysis of Stress for Estimation of Support*) and finite difference codes such as FLAC (*Fast Lagrangian Analysis of Continua*; Itasca Consulting Group, 2001) cannot handle general interaction geometry (e.g. many intersecting joints). Their efficiency may degenerate drastically when connections are broken repeatedly. Typical continuum-based models may have less than ten non-intersecting discontinuities. Of fundamental importance to continuum codes and deformable blocks in discrete element codes is representation of the rock mass behavior. Continuum relations used to represent rock mass behavior are discussed later in this section.

Finite element programs are probably more familiar, but the finite difference method is perhaps the oldest numerical technique used to solve sets of differential equations. Both finite element and finite difference methods produce a set of algebraic equations to solve. While the methods used to derive the equations are different, the resulting equations are the same. Finite difference programs generally use an "explicit" time-marching scheme to solve the equations, whereas finite element methods usually solve systems of equations in matrix form.

Although a static solution to a problem is usually of interest, the dynamic equations of motion are typically included in the formulation of finite difference programs. One reason for doing this is to ensure that the numerical scheme is stable when the physical system being modeled is unstable. With non-linear materials, there is always the possibility of physical instability—for example, the failure of a slope. In real life, some of the strain energy is converted to kinetic energy. Explicit finite-difference programs model this process directly, because inertial terms are included. In contrast, programs that do not include inertial terms must use some numerical procedure to treat physical instabilities. Even if the procedure is successful at preventing numerical instability, the *path* taken may not be realistic. The consequence of including the full law of motion in finite difference programs is that the user must have some physical feel for what is happening. Explicit finite-difference programs are not black boxes that will "give the solution." The behavior of the numerical system must be interpreted.

FLAC and UDEC are two-dimensional finite-difference programs developed specifically for geomechanical analysis. These codes can simulate varying loading and water conditions, and have several pre-defined material models for representing rock mass continuum behavior. Both codes are unique in their ability to handle highly non-linear and unstable problems. The three-dimensional equivalents of these codes are FLAC3D (*F*ast *L*agrangian *A*nalysis of *C*ontinua in 3 *D*imensions; Itasca Consulting Group, 2002) and 3DEC (Itasca Consulting Group, 2003).

### 10.2.1   *Joint material models*

The material model used most commonly to represent joints is a linear-elastic–perfectly-plastic model. The limiting shear strength is defined by the usual Mohr–Coulomb parameters of friction angle and cohesion (see Section 4.2). A peak and residual shear strength relation can also be specified for the joints. The residual strength is used after the joint has failed in shear at the peak strength. The elastic behavior of the joints is specified by joint normal and shear stiffnesses, which may be linear or piece-wise linear.

### 10.2.2   *Rock mass material models*

It is impossible to model all discontinuities in a large slope, although it may be possible to model the discontinuities for a limited number of benches. Therefore, in large slopes much of the rock mass must be represented by an equivalent continuum in which the effect of the discontinuities is to reduce the intact rock elastic properties and strength to those of the rock mass. This is true whether or not a discontinuum model is used. As mentioned in the introduction to this chapter, numerical models divide the rock mass into zones. Each zone is assigned a material model and material properties. The material models are stress/strain relations that describe how the material behaves. The simplest model is a linear elastic model that uses only the elastic properties (Young's modulus and Poisson's ratio) of the material. Linear elastic–perfectly plastic stress–strain relations are the most commonly used rock mass material models. These models typically use Mohr–Coulomb strength parameters to limit the shear stress that a zone may sustain. The tensile strength is limited by the specified tensile strength, which in many analyses is taken to be 10% of the rock mass cohesion. Using this model, the rock mass behaves in an isotropic manner. Strength anisotropy can be introduced through a ubiquitous joint model, which limits the shear strength according to a Mohr–Coulomb criterion in a specified direction. The direction often corresponds to a predominant jointing orientation.

A more complete equivalent-continuum model that includes the effects of joint orientation and spacing is a micropolar (Cosserat) plasticity model. The Cosserat theory incorporates a local rotation of material points as an independent parameter, in addition to the translation assumed in the classical continuum, and couple stresses (moments per unit area) in addition to the classical stresses (forces per unit area). This model, as implemented in FLAC, is described in the context of slope stability by Dawson and Cundall (1996). The approach has the advantage of using a continuum model while still preserving the ability to consider realistic joint spacing explicitly. The model has not yet (as of 2003) been incorporated into any publicly available code.

The most common failure criterion for rock masses is the Hoek–Brown failure criterion (see Section 4.5). The Hoek–Brown failure criterion is an empirical relation that characterizes the stress conditions that lead to failure in intact rock and rock masses. It has been used successfully in design approaches that use limit equilibrium solutions. It also has been used indirectly in numerical models by finding equivalent Mohr–Coulomb shear strength parameters that provide a failure surface tangent to the Hoek–Brown failure criterion for specific confining stresses, or ranges of confining stresses. The tangent Mohr–Coulomb parameters are then used in traditional Mohr–Coulomb type constitutive relations and the parameters may or may not be updated during analyses. The procedure is awkward and time-consuming, and consequently there has been little direct use of the Hoek–Brown failure criterion in numerical solution schemes that require full constitutive models. Such models solve for displacements, as well as stresses, and can continue the solution after failure has occurred in some locations. In particular, it is necessary to develop a "flow rule," which supplies a relation between the components of strain rate at failure. There have been several attempts to develop a full constitutive model from the Hoek–Brown criterion: for example, Pan and Hudson (1988), Carter et al. (1993) and Shah (1992). These formulations assume that the flow rule has some fixed relation

to the failure criterion and that the flow rule is isotropic, whereas the Hoek–Brown criterion is not. Recently, Cundall et al. (2003) has proposed a scheme that does not use a fixed form of the flow rule, but rather one that depends on the stress level, and possibly some measure of damage.

Real rock masses often appear to exhibit progressive failure—that is, the failure appears to progress over time. Progressive failure is a complex process that is understood poorly and difficult to model. It may involve one or more of the following component mechanisms:

- Gradual accumulation of strain on principal structures and/or within the rock mass;
- Increases in pore pressure with time; and
- Creep, which is time-dependent deformation of material under constant load.

Each of these components is discussed briefly later in the context of slope behavior.

Gradual accumulation of strain on principal structures within the rock mass usually results from excavation, and "time" is related to the excavation sequence. In order to study the progressive failure effects due to excavation, one must either introduce characteristics of the post-peak or post-failure behavior of the rock mass into a strain-softening model or introduce similar characteristics into the explicit discontinuities. In practice, there are at least two difficulties associated with strain-softening rock mass models. The first is estimating the post-peak strength and the strain over which the strength reduces. There appear to be no empirical guidelines for estimating the required parameters. This means that the properties must be estimated through calibration. The second difficulty is that, for a simulation in which the response depends on shear localization and in which material softening is used, the results will depend on the zone sizes. However, it is quite straightforward to compensate for this form of mesh-dependence. In order to do this, consider a displacement applied to the boundary of a body. If the strain localizes inside the body, the applied displacement appears as a jump across the localized band. The thickness of the band contracts until it is equal to the minimum allowed by the grid, that is a fixed number of zone widths. Thus, the strain in the band is

$$\varepsilon = u/n\Delta z \qquad (10.3)$$

where $n$ is a fixed number, $u$ is the displacement jump, and $\Delta z$ is the zone width.

If the softening slope is linear, the change in a property value $\Delta p$ is proportional to strain, the change in property value with displacement is:

$$\frac{\Delta p}{\Delta u} = \frac{s}{n \cdot \Delta z} \qquad (10.4)$$

where $s$ is the softening slope.

In order to obtain mesh-independent results, a scaled softening slope $s$ can be input, such that

$$s = s'\Delta z \qquad (10.5)$$

where $s'$ is constant.

In this case, $(\Delta p/\Delta u)$ is independent of $\Delta z$. If the softening slope is defined by the critical strain, $\varepsilon^s_{crit}$, then

$$\varepsilon^s_{crit} \propto \frac{1}{\Delta z} \qquad (10.6)$$

For example, if the zone size is doubled, the critical strain must be halved for comparable results.

Strain-softening models for discontinuities are much more common than similar relations for rock masses. Strain-softening relations for discontinuities are built into UDEC and 3DEC, and can be incorporated into interfaces in FLAC and FLAC3D via a built-in programming language such as FISH functions. Strain-softening models require special attention when computing safety factors. If a strain-softening constitutive model is used, the softening logic should be turned off during the shear strength reduction process or the factor of safety will be underestimated. When the slope is excavated, some zones will have exceeded their peak strength, and some amount of softening will have taken place. During the

strength reduction process, these zones should be considered as a new material with lower strength, but no further softening should be allowed due to the plastic strains associated to the gradual reduction of strength.

Increases in pore pressure with time are not common in rock slopes for mines. More commonly, the pore pressures reduce due to deepening of the pit and/or drainage. However, there are cases in which the pore pressures do increase with time. In such cases, the slope may appear to fail progressively.

Creep, which is time-dependent deformation of material under constant load, is not commonly considered in the context of slope stability. It is much more common in underground excavations. Several material models are available to study creep behavior in rock slopes. These include classical viscoelastic models, power law models, and the Burger-creep viscoplastic model. Application of a creep model to the study of slope behavior at Chuquicamata mine in Chile is discussed later in this chapter (see Section 10.5.2).

## 10.3 Modeling issues

Modeling requires that the real problem be idealized, or simplified, in order to fit the constraints imposed by factors such as available material models and computer capacity. Analysis of rock mass response involves different scales. It is impossible—and undesirable—to include all features, and details of rock mass response mechanisms, into one model. In addition, many of the details of rock mass behavior are unknown and unknowable; therefore, the approach to modeling is not as straightforward as it is, say, in other branches of mechanics. This section discusses the basic issues that must be resolved when setting up a numerical model.

### 10.3.1 Two-dimensional analysis versus three-dimensional analysis

The first step in creating a model is to decide whether to perform two-dimensional or three-dimensional analyses. Prior to 2003, three-dimensional analyses were uncommon, but advances in personal computers have permitted three-dimensional analyses to be performed routinely. Strictly speaking, three-dimensional analyses are recommended/required in the following:

1   The direction of principal geologic structures does not strike within 20–30° of the strike of the slope.
2   The axis of material anisotropy does not strike within 20–30° of the slope.
3   The directions of principal stresses are not neither parallel nor perpendicular to the slope.
4   The distribution of geomechanical units varies along the strike of the slope.
5   The slope geometry in plan cannot be represented by two-dimensional analysis, which assumes axisymmetric or plain strain.

Despite the forgoing, most design analysis for slopes assumes a two-dimensional geometry comprising a unit slice through an infinitely long slope, under plane strain conditions. In other words, the radii of both the toe and crest are assumed to be infinite. This is not the condition encountered in practice—particularly in open pit mining where the radii of curvature can have an important effect on safe slope angles. Concave slopes are believed to be more stable than plain strain slopes due to the lateral restraint provided by material on either side of a potential failure in a concave slope.

Despite its potential importance in slope stability, very little has been done to quantify this effect. Jenike and Yen (1961) presented the results of limit theory analysis of axisymmetric slopes in a rigid, perfectly plastic material. However, Hoek and Brown (1981) concluded that the analysis assumptions were not applicable to rock slope design.

Piteau and Jennings (1970) studied the influence of curvature in plan on the stability of slopes in four diamond mines in South Africa. As a result of caving from below the surface, slopes were all at incipient failure with a safety factor of 1. The average slope height was 100 m. Piteau and Jennings (1970) found that the average slope angle for slopes with radius of curvature of 60 m was 39.5° as compared to 27.3° for slopes with a radius of curvature of 300 m.

Hoek and Bray (1981) summarize their experience with the stabilizing effects of slope curvature as follows. When the radius of curvature of a concave slope is less than the height of the slope, the slope angle can be 10° steeper than the angle suggested by conventional stability analysis. As the radius of curvature increases to a value greater than the slope height, the correction should be decreased. For radii of curvature in excess of twice the slope height, the slope angle given by a conventional stability analysis should be used.

To better quantify the effects of slope curvature on stability, a series of generic analyses were performed. All analyses assumed a 500 m high dry slope with a 45° face angle excavated in an isotropic homogeneous material with a density of $2600 \text{ kg/m}^3$. Initial *in situ* stresses are assumed to be lithostatic, and the excavation was made in 40 m decrements beginning from the ground surface. For these conditions, pairs of friction angle and cohesion values were selected to produce a factor of safety of 1.3 using circular failure chart number 1 (see Section 8.3). A factor of safety of 1.3 is a value that is frequently used in the design of slopes for open pit mines. The actual values used are shown in Table 10.2.

A series of analyses was performed using FLAC for different radius of curvature for both concave and convex slopes. For concave slopes, the radius of curvature is defined as the distance between

*Table 10.2* Janbu's Lambda coefficient for various combinations of friction angle and cohesion

| Friction angle | Cohesion (MPa) | $\lambda = \gamma H \tan \phi / c$ |
| --- | --- | --- |
| 45 | 0.22 | 59 |
| 35 | 0.66 | 14 |
| 25 | 1.18 | 5 |
| 15 | 1.8 | 2 |

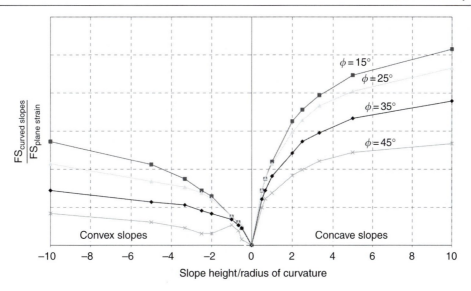

$\phi = 15°$

$\phi = 25°$

$\phi = 35°$

$\phi = 45°$

$\dfrac{FS_{curved\ slopes}}{FS_{plane\ strain}}$

Convex slopes

Concave slopes

−10   −8   −6   −4   −2   0   2   4   6   8   10

Slope height/radius of curvature

*Figure 10.1* Results of FLAC axisymmetric analyses showing effect on factor of safety of slope curvature.

the axis of revolution and the toe of the slope. For the convex slopes, the radius of curvature is defined as the distance between the axis of revolution and the crest of the slope—not the toe. Under both definitions, cones have a radius of curvature of zero.

Figure 10.1 shows the results with $FS/FS_{plane\ strain}$ versus height/radius of curvature $(H/R_c)$, which is positive for concave and negative for convex slopes. The figure shows that the factor of safety always increases as the radius of curvature decreases, but the increase is faster for concave slopes. One unexpected result is that as the friction angle increases, the effect of curvature decreases. One possible explanation is that as Janbu's lambda coefficient $(\lambda = \gamma H \tan \phi / c)$ increases, the slide surface is shallower with only a skin for purely frictional material. This, makes the slope less sensitive to the confining effect in concave slopes, and to the ratio of active/passive wedges for the convex ones.

One reason that designers are reluctant to take advantage of the beneficial effects of concave slope curvature is that the presence of discontinuities can often negate the effects. However, for massive rock slopes, or slopes with relatively short joint trace lengths, the

beneficial effects of slope curvature should not be ignored—particularly in open pit mines, where the economic benefits of steepening slopes can be significant. The same is true for convex slopes, which are also more stable than plane strain slopes. This goes against observed experience in rock slopes. If the slide surface is defined in terms of active (top) and passive (bottom) wedges, the ratio of the surface (and weight) of the passive wedge to the active wedge in a convex slope is greater than the plane strain condition. However, this only applies to a homogeneous Mohr–Coulomb material that might be found, for example, in waste dumps. The reason why "noses" in rock slopes are usually less stable may be related to the fact that they are more exposed to structurally controlled failures.

### 10.3.2 *Continuum versus discontinuum models*

The next step is to decide whether to use a continuum code or a discontinuum code. This decision is seldom straightforward. There appear to be no ready-made rules for determining which type of analysis to perform. All slope stability problems involve discontinuities at one scale or another. However, useful analyses, particularly of global stability, have been made by assuming that the rock mass can be represented as an equivalent continuum. Therefore, many analyses begin with continuum models. If the slope under consideration is unstable without structure, there is no point in going to discontinuum models. If, on the other hand, a continuum model appears to be reasonably stable, explicit incorporation of principal structures should give a more accurate estimation of slope behavior.

Selection of joint geometry for input to a model is a crucial step in discontinuum analyses. Typically, only a very small percentage of joints can actually be included in a model in order to create models of reasonable size for practical analysis. Thus, the joint geometry data must be filtered to select only those joints that are most critical to the mechanical response. This is done by identifying those that are most susceptible to slip and/or separation for the prescribed loading condition. This may involve determining whether sufficient kinematic freedom is provided, especially in the case of toppling, and calibrating the analysis by comparing observed behavior to model response.

### 10.3.3  Selecting appropriate zone size

The next step in the process is to select an appropriate zone size. The finite difference zones assume that the stresses and strains within each zone do not differ with position within the zone—in other words, the zones are the lowest-order elements possible. In order to capture stress and strain gradients within the slope adequately, it is necessary to use relatively fine discretizations. By experience, the authors have found that at least 20 (and preferably 30) zones are required over the slope height of interest. As discussed later, if flexural toppling is involved, a minimum of four zones across the rock column are required. Finite element programs using higher-order elements likely would require less zones than the constant strain/constant stress elements common in finite difference codes.

### 10.3.4  Initial conditions

Initial conditions are those conditions that existed prior to mining. The initial conditions of importance at mine sites are the *in situ* stress field and the ground water conditions. The role of stresses has been traditionally ignored in slope analyses. There are several possible reasons for this:

- Limit equilibrium analyses, which are widely used for stability analyses, cannot include the effect of stresses in their analyses. Nevertheless, limit equilibrium analyses are thought to provide reasonable estimates of stability in many cases, particularly where structure is absent, such as soil slopes.
- Most stability analyses have traditionally been performed for soils, where the range of possible *in situ* stresses is more limited than for rocks. Furthermore, many soil analyses have been performed for constructed embankments such as dams, where *in situ* stresses do not exist.
- Most slope failures are gravity driven, and the effects of *in situ* stress are thought to be minimal.
- *In situ* stresses in rock masses are not routinely measured for slopes, and their effects are largely unknown.

One particular advantage of stress analysis programs such as numerical models is their ability to include pre-mining initial stress states in stability analyses and to evaluate their importance.

In order to evaluate the effects of *in situ* stress state on stability, five cases were run using a simple model similar to the model shown in Figure 10.2. For each of the five cases, the slope angle was 60°, the slope height was 400 m, the material density was 2450 kg/m³, the friction angle was 32°, and the cohesion was 0.92 MPa. The results of FLAC analyses are shown in Table 10.3.

In general, it is impossible to say what effect the initial stress state will have on any particular problem, as behavior depends on factors

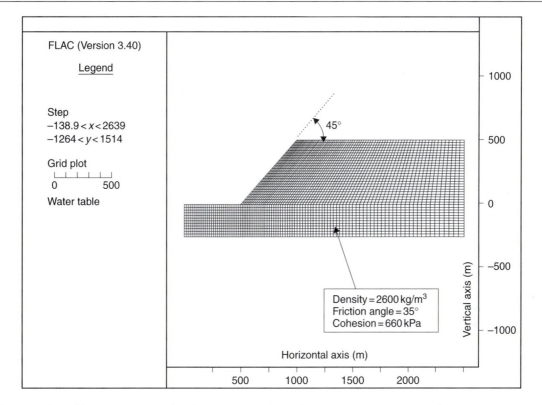

*Figure 10.2* Problem geometry used to determine the effect of *in situ* stresses on slope stability.

*Table 10.3* Effect of *in situ* stress on slope stability [x—horizontal in-plane direction; y—vertical in-plane direction; z—out-of-plane direction]

| In-plane horizontal stress | Out-of-plane horizontal stress | Factor of safety |
|---|---|---|
| $\sigma_{xx} = \sigma_{yy}$ | $\sigma_{zz} = \sigma_{yy}$ | 1.30 |
| $\sigma_{xx} = 2.0\,\sigma_{yy}$ | $\sigma_{zz} = 2.0\,\sigma_{yy}$ | 1.30 |
| $\sigma_{xx} = 0.5\,\sigma_{yy}$ | $\sigma_{zz} = 0.5\,\sigma_{yy}$ | 1.28 |
| $\sigma_{xx} = 2.0\,\sigma_{yy}$ | $\sigma_{zz} = 0.5\,\sigma_{yy}$ | 1.30 |
| $\sigma_{xx} = 0.5\,\sigma_{yy}$ | $\sigma_{zz} = 2.0\,\sigma_{yy}$ | 1.28 |

such as orientation of major structures, rock mass strength and water conditions. However, some observations on the effects of *in situ* stress on stability can be made:

• *The larger the initial horizontal stresses, the larger the horizontal elastic displacements.* This is not much help, as elastic displacements are not particularly important in slope studies.

• *Initial horizontal stresses in the plane of analysis that are less than the vertical stresses tend to slightly decrease stability and reduce the depth of significant shearing with respect to a hydrostatic stress state.* This observation may seem counter-intuitive; smaller horizontal stresses would be expected to increase stability. The explanation lies in the fact that the lower horizontal stresses actually provide slightly decreased normal stress on potential shearing surfaces and/or joints within the slope. This observation was confirmed in a UDEC analysis of a slope in Peru where *in situ* horizontal stresses lower than the vertical stress led to deeper levels of joint shearing in toppling structures compared to cases involving horizontal stresses that were equal to or greater than the vertical stress.

• It is important to note that the regional topography may limit the possible stress states, particularly at elevations above regional valley floors. Three-dimensional models have been very useful in the past in addressing some regional stress issues.

### 10.3.5 Boundary conditions

Boundaries are either real or artificial. Real boundaries in slope stability problems correspond to the natural or excavated ground surface that is usually stress free. Artificial boundaries do not exist in reality. All problems in geomechanics, including slope stability problems, require that the infinite extent of a real problem domain be artificially truncated to include only the immediate area of interest. Figure 10.3 shows typical recommendations for locations of the artificial far-field boundaries in slope stability problems. Artificial boundaries can be of two types: prescribed displacement, or prescribed stress. Prescribed displacement boundaries inhibit displacement in either the vertical direction or horizontal direction, or both. Prescribed displacement boundaries are used to represent the condition at the base of the model and toe of the slope.

Displacement at the base of the model is always fixed in both the vertical and horizontal directions to inhibit rotation of the model. Two assumptions can be made regarding the displacement boundaries near the toe of any slope. One assumption is that the displacements near the toe are inhibited only in the horizontal direction. This is the mechanically correct condition for a problem that is perfectly symmetric with respect to the plane or axis representing the toe boundary. Strictly speaking, this condition only occurs in slopes of infinite length, which are modeled in two-dimensions assuming plane strain, or in slopes that are axially symmetric in which the pit is a perfect cone. In reality, these conditions are rarely satisfied. Therefore, some models are extended laterally to avoid the need to specify any boundary condition at the toe of the slope. It is important to note that difficulties with the boundary condition near the slope toe are usually a result of the two-dimensional assumption. In three-dimensional models, this difficulty generally does not exist.

The far-field boundary location and condition must also be specified in any numerical model for slope stability analyses. The general notion is to select the far-field location so that it does not significantly influence the results. If this criterion is met, whether the boundary is prescribed-displacement or prescribed-stress is not important. In most slope stability studies, a prescribed-displacement boundary is used. The authors have used a prescribed-stress boundary in a few cases and found no significant differences with respect to the results from a prescribed-displacement boundary. The magnitude of the horizontal stress for the prescribed-stress boundary must match the assumptions regarding the initial stress state in order for the model to be in equilibrium. However, following any change in the model, such as an excavation increment, the prescribed-stress boundary causes the far-field boundary to displace toward the excavation while maintaining its original stress value. For this reason, a prescribed-stress boundary is also referred to as a "following" stress, or constant stress boundary, because the stress does not change and follows the displacement of the boundary. However, following stresses are most likely where slopes are cut into areas where the

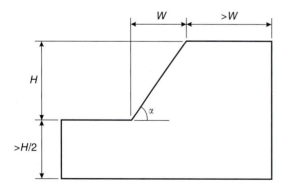

*Figure 10.3* Typical recommendations for locations of artificial far-field boundaries in slope stability analyses.

topography rises behind the slope. Even where slopes are excavated into an inclined topography, the stresses would flow around the excavation to some extent, depending on the effective width of the excavation perpendicular to the downhill topographic direction.

A summary of the effects of boundary conditions on analysis results is as follows:

• A fixed boundary causes both stresses and displacements to be underestimated, whereas a stress boundary does the opposite.

• The two types of boundary condition "bracket" the true solution, so that it is possible to conduct tests with smaller models to obtain a reasonable estimate of the true solution by averaging the two results.

A final point to be kept in mind is that all open pit slope stability problems are three-dimensional in reality. This means that the stresses acting in and around the pit are free to flow both beneath and around the sides of the pit. Therefore, it is likely that, unless there are very low strength faults parallel to the analysis plane, a constant stress or following stress boundary will over-predict the stresses acting horizontally.

### 10.3.6 Incorporating water pressure

The effect of water pressure in reducing effective stresses and, hence, slope stability is well understood. However, the effect of various assumptions regarding specification of pore pressure distributions in slopes is not as well understood. Two methods are commonly used to specify pore pressure distributions within slopes. The most rigorous method is to perform a complete flow analysis, and use the resultant pore pressures in the stability analyses. A less rigorous, but more common method is to specify a water table, and the resulting pore pressures are given by the product of the vertical depth below the water table, the water density and gravity. In this sense, the water table approach is equivalent to specifying a piezometric surface. Both methods use similar phreatic surfaces. However, the water table method under-predicts actual pore pressure

concentrations near the toe of a slope, and slightly over-predicts the pore pressure behind the toe by ignoring the inclination of equipotential lines.

Seepage forces must also be considered in the analysis. The hydraulic gradient is the difference in water pressure that exists between two points at the same elevation, and results from seepage forces (or drag) as water moves through a porous medium. Flow analysis automatically accounts for seepage forces.

To evaluate the error resulting from specifying a water table without doing a flow analysis, two identical problems were run. In one case, a flow analysis was performed to determine the pore pressures. In the second case, the pressures were determined using only a piezometric surface that was assumed to be the phreatic surface taken from the flow analysis. The material properties and geometry for both cases are shown in Figure 10.2. The right-hand boundary was extended to allow the far-field phreatic surface to coincide with the ground surface at a horizontal distance of 2 km behind the toe. Hydraulic conductivity within the model was assumed to be homogeneous and isotropic. The error caused by specifying the water table can be seen in Figure 10.4. The largest errors, under prediction of up to 45%, are found just below the toe, while over prediction errors in pore pressure values behind the slope are generally less than 5%. The errors near the phreatic surface are insignificant, as they result from the relatively small pore pressures just below the phreatic surface where small errors in small values result in large relative errors.

For a phreatic surface at the ground surface at a distance of 2 km, a factor of safety of 1.1 is predicted using circular failure chart number 3 (refer to Section 8.3). The factor of safety determined by FLAC was approximately 1.15 for both cases. The FLAC analyses give similar safety factors because the distribution of pore pressures in the area behind the slope where failure occurs is very similar for the two cases. The conclusion drawn here is that there is no significant difference in predicted stability between a complete flow analysis and simply specifying a piezometric surface. However, it is not clear if this conclusion

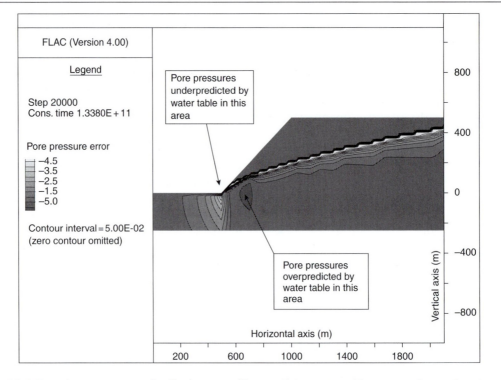

*Figure 10.4* Error in pore pressure distribution caused by specifying water table compared to performing a flow analysis.

can be extrapolated to other cases involving, for example, anisotropic flow.

### 10.3.7 Excavation sequence

Simulating excavations in numerical models poses no conceptual difficulties. However, the amount of effort required to construct a model depends directly on the number of excavation stages simulated. Therefore, most practical analyses seek to reduce the number of excavation stages. The most accurate solution is obtained using the largest number of excavation steps, because the real load path for any zone in the slope will be followed closely. In theory, it is impossible to prove that the final solution is independent of the load path followed. However, for many slopes, stability seems to depend mostly on slope conditions, such as geometry and pore pressure distribution at the time of analysis, and very little on the load path taken to get there.

A reasonable approach regarding the number of excavation stages has evolved over the years. Using this approach, only one, two or three excavation stages are modeled. For each stage, two calculation steps are taken. In the first step, the model is run elastically to remove any inertial effects caused by sudden removal of a large amount of material. Second, the model is run allowing plastic behavior to develop. Following this approach, reasonable solutions to a large number of slope stability problems have been obtained.

### 10.3.8 Interpretation of results

As noted in the introduction, finite difference programs are not black boxes that "give the solution." The behavior of the numerical system and results from finite difference models must be interpreted in much the same way as slope movement data are interpreted. Finite difference programs record displacements and velocities at nominated points within the rock mass. During the analysis, the recorded values can be examined to see if they are increasing, remaining steady, or decreasing. Increasing displacements and velocities indicate an unstable situation; steady displacements and decreasing velocities indicate a stable situation. In addition, velocity and displacement vectors for every point in the model can be plotted. Fields of constant velocity and displacement indicate failure.

The authors have found that velocities below 1e−6 indicate stability in FLAC and FLAC3D; conversely, velocities above 1e−5 indicate instability. Note that no units are given for velocities. This is because the velocities are not real, due to the damping and mass scaling used to achieve static solutions. While the displacements are real, the velocities are not, and there is no information on the "time" the displacement occurs.

It is also possible to examine the failure (plasticity) state of points within the model, where failure is defined as failure in tension or shear. Care must be used in examining the failure state indicators. For example, local overstressing at the base of toppling columns can appear to form a deep-seated slip surface when, in reality, it is just compressive failure of the columns. Therefore, the failure (plasticity) indicators must be reviewed in the context of overall behavior before any definitive conclusions can be drawn.

## 10.4 Typical stability analysis

In this section, typical stability analyses for a variety of failure modes are discussed. The objective of this section is to show how numerical models can be used to simulate slope behavior, and compute safety factors for typical problems. Modeling issues important in each of the following failure modes are discussed:

- Rock mass failure;
- Plane failure—daylighting and non-daylighting;
- Wedge failure—daylighting and non-daylighting;

- Toppling failure—block and flexural; and
- Flexural buckling failure.

The two-dimensional distinct element code, UDEC, was used for most of the analyses, and the characteristics of the slopes that were modeled are as follows:

| | |
|---|---|
| Slope height | 260 m |
| Slope angle | 55° |
| Water pressure | none/dry |
| Density | 2660 kg/m$^3$ |
| | (26.1 kN/m$^3$) |
| Rock mass friction angle | 43° |
| Rock mass cohesion | 675 kPa |
| Rock mass tension | 0 |
| Rock mass bulk modulus | 6.3 GPa |
| Rock mass shear modulus | 3.6 GPa |
| Joint friction angle | 40° |
| Dilation angle | 0° |

A maximum zone size of 15 m was used except where noted. In all cases, the factor of safety was estimated by simultaneously reducing the rock mass properties and the joint friction until failure occurs using the procedure shown in equations (10.1) and (10.2). The safety factor was assumed to be the reciprocal of the reduction required to produce failure. For example, if the strengths must be reduced by 25% (i.e. 75% of their "real" strength) in order to achieve failure, the safety factor is 1.33.

### 10.4.1 Rock mass failure

Numerical analysis of slopes involving purely rock mass failure is studied most efficiently using continuum codes such as PHASE$^2$, FLAC or FLAC3D. As mentioned in the previous section, discontinuities are not considered explicitly in continuum models; rather, they are assumed to be smeared throughout the rock mass. Assuming that rock mass shear strength properties can be estimated reasonably, the analysis is straightforward. The process for initially estimating the rock mass properties is often based on empirical relations as described, for example, by Hoek and

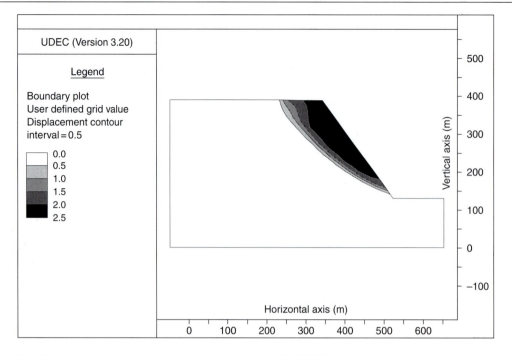

*Figure 10.5* Rock mass failure mode for slope determined with UDEC.

Brown (1997). These initial properties are then modified, as necessary, through the calibration process.

Failure modes involve mainly shearing through the rock mass. For homogeneous slopes where the slide surface is often approximately circular, intersecting the toe of the slope and becoming nearly vertical near the ground surface. The failure mode for the parameters listed earlier is shown in Figure 10.5. The calculated safety factor is 1.64.

The following is a comparison of a slope stability analysis carried out using limit equilibrium circular failure analysis (Bishop method) and numerical stability analysis. In Chapter 8, the stability of a benched slope in strong, but closely fractured, sandstone including a water table and tension crack is described (see Figure 8.19). The rock mass is classified as a Hoek–Brown material with strength parameters:

$m_i = 0.13$
$\text{GSI} = 20$

$\sigma_c = 150\,\text{MPa}$
Disturbance factor, $D = 0.7$

The tensile strength is estimated to be 0.012 MPa. For the Bishop's analysis method, the Mohr–Coulomb strength is estimated by fitting a straight line to the curved Hoek–Brown failure envelope at the normal stress level estimated from the slope geometry. Using this procedure, friction angle and cohesion were

$\phi = 43°$

$c = 0.145\,\text{MPa}$

The mass density of the rock mass and water were $2550\,\text{kg/m}^3$ ($25.0\,\text{kN/m}^3$) and $1000\,\text{kg/m}^3$ ($9.81\,\text{kN/m}^3$) respectively. The phreatic surface is located as shown in Figure 8.19. Based upon these parameters, the Bishop method produces a location for the circular slide surface and tension crack, as shown in Figure 8.19, and a factor of safety of 1.39.

In using FLAC to analyze the stability of the slope in Figure 8.19, the slide surface can evolve during the calculation in a way that is representative of the natural evolution of the physical slide surface in the slope. It is not necessary to make an estimate for the location of the circular slide surface when beginning an analysis, as it is with limit equilibrium methods. FLAC will find the slide surface and failure mechanism by simulating the material behavior directly. A reasonably fine grid should be selected to ensure that the slide surface will be well defined as it develops. It is best to use the finest grid possible when studying problems involving localized failure. Here, a zone size of 2 m was used.

The FLAC analysis showed a factor of safety of 1.26, with the slide surface closely resembling that produced from the Bishop solution (Figure 10.6). However, the tensile failure extends farther up the slope in the FLAC solution. It is important to recognize that the limit equilibrium solution only identifies the onset of failure, whereas the

FLAC solution includes the effect of stress redistribution and progressive failure after movement has been initiated. In this problem, tensile failure continues up the slope as a result of the tensile softening. The resulting factor of safety allows for this weakening effect.

### 10.4.2 Plane failure—daylighting and non-daylighting

Failure modes that involve rigid blocks sliding on planar joints that daylight in the slope face are most efficiently solved using analytical methods. For comparison purposes, a UDEC analysis is performed for blocks dipping at 35° out of the slope. The joints are assumed to have a cohesion of 100 kPa and a friction angle of 40°. The resulting safety factor is 1.32, which agrees with the analytic value given by equation (6.4) in Chapter 6, assuming that no tension crack forms. The plane failure mode in the UDEC analysis is shown in Figure 10.7.

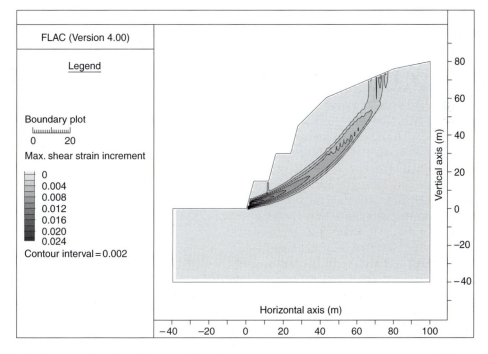

*Figure 10.6* Failure mode and tension crack location determined with FLAC for slope in closely fractured sandstone slope (refer to Figure 8.19).

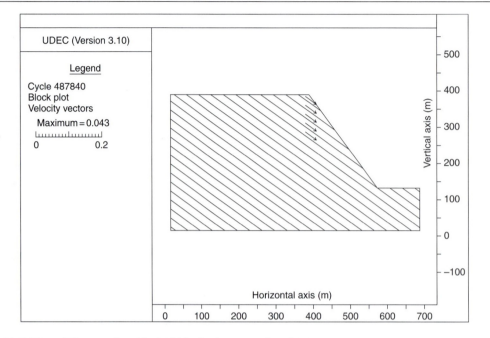

*Figure 10.7* Plane failure mode with rigid blocks determined with UDEC.

If a tension crack does form, then the factor of safety is slightly reduced. Deformable blocks with elastic–plastic behavior are required to form tension cracks within the UDEC analysis. When deformable zones are used, the resultant safety factor is 1.27, similar to the value of 1.3 given by the analytic solution. The difference may be that the analytic solution assumes a vertical tension crack, whereas the UDEC analysis indicates that the tension crack curves where it meets the sliding plane (see Figure 10.8).

Similar analyses can be performed for non-daylighting failure planes. In this case, failure involves sliding on discontinuities and shearing through the rock mass at the toe of the slope, as shown in Figure 10.9. Here, the cohesionless sliding planes dip at 70° and are spaced 20 m apart. The resultant safety factor is about 1.5.

### 10.4.3  Wedge failure—daylighting and non-daylighting

Analyses involving wedge failures are similar to those involving plane failures, except that the analyses must be performed in three dimensions. As with plane failure, sliding analysis of daylighting rigid blocks is best solved using analytic methods, as described in Chapter 7. Analyses involving formation of tension cracks and/or non-daylighting wedges require numerical analysis. Candidate codes include FLAC3D and 3DEC. The plasticity formulation in FLAC3D uses a mixed discretization technique and presently provides a better solution than 3DEC in cases where rock mass failure dominates. On the other hand, setting up problems involving more than one sliding plane in FLAC3D is more difficult and time consuming than similar problems in 3DEC.

### 10.4.4  Toppling failure—block and flexural

Toppling failure modes involve rotation and thus usually are difficult to solve using limit equilibrium methods. As the name implies, block toppling involves free rotation of individual blocks (Figure 9.3(a)), whereas flexural toppling involves bending of rock columns or plates (Figure 9.3(b)).

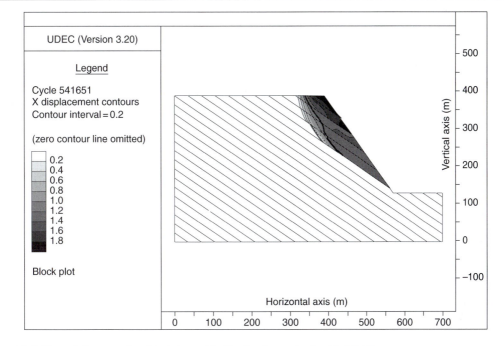

*Figure 10.8* Plane failure mode with deformable blocks determined with UDEC.

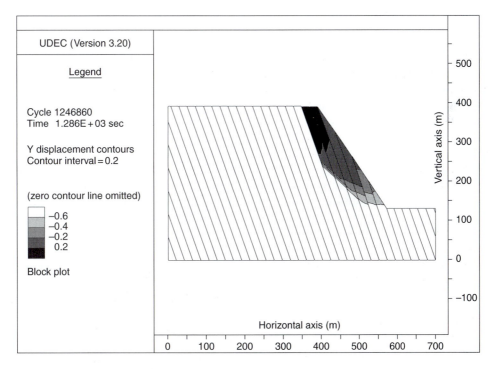

*Figure 10.9* Non-daylighting plane failure mode determined with UDEC.

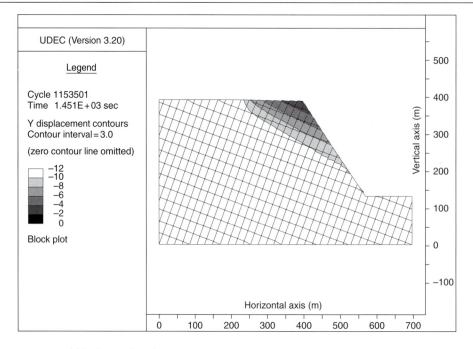

*Figure 10.10* Forward block toppling failure mode determined with UDEC.

Block toppling occurs where narrow slabs are formed by joints dipping steeply into the face, combined with flatter cross-joints (see Section 9.4). The cross-joints provide release surfaces for rotation of the blocks. In the most common form of block toppling, the blocks, driven by self-weight, rotate forward out of the slope. However, backward or reverse toppling can also occur when joints parallel to the slope face and flatter cross-joints are particularly weak. In cases of both forward and backward toppling, stability depends on the location of the center of gravity of the blocks relative to their base.

Figure 10.10 shows the results of an analysis involving forward block toppling. The steep joint set dips at 70° with a spacing of 20 m. The cross-joints are perpendicular and are spaced at 30 m. The resultant safety factor is 1.13. Figure 10.11 shows the result of an analysis involving backward block toppling. In this case, the face-parallel joints are spaced at 10 m, and the horizontal joints are spaced at 40 m. The factor of safety for this failure mode is 1.7.

Flexural toppling occurs when there is one dominant, closely spaced, set of joints dipping steeply into the face, with insufficient cross-jointing to permit free rotation of blocks. The columns bend out of the slope like cantilever beams. Figure 10.12 shows the results of analysis with joints spaced at 20 m. The factor of safety is 1.3, with the safety factor being reduced as the joint spacing decreases. Problems involving flexural toppling require finer zoning than problems involving block toppling. Because flexural toppling involves high stress gradients across any rock column, it is necessary to provide sufficient zones to represent accurately the stress gradients due to bending. In the modeling of centrifuge tests reported by Adhikary and Guo (2000), UDEC modeling required four zones across each column, resulting in a model with nearly 20,000 three-noded triangular zones. In contrast, a finite element model with Cosserat plasticity elements required only about 1200, eight-noded isoparametric quadrilateral elements. Both models produced good agreement with the laboratory results (see also Section 9.5).

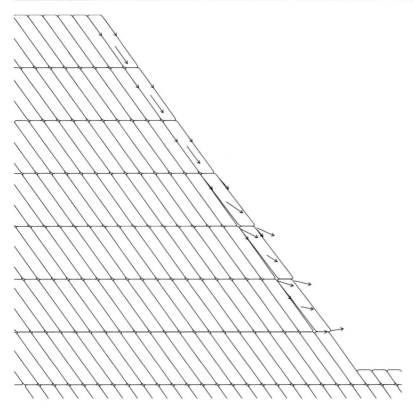

*Figure 10.11* Reverse (backward) block toppling failure mode determined with UDEC; arrows show movement vectors.

### 10.4.5  *Flexural buckling failure*

Buckling failures (see Figure 10.13) are also difficult to reproduce in numerical models because of the large number of zones required to represent the high stress gradients involved in buckling. One of the most complete studies on the topic of numerical analysis of buckling in rock slopes is given by Adhikary *et al.* (2001), who provide design charts based on numerical analysis using the proprietary finite element program AFENA (Carter and Balaam, 1995) and a Cosserat material model to simulate behavior of foliated rock.

## 10.5  Special topics

### 10.5.1  *Reinforcement*

Reinforcement is often used to stabilize civil slopes, and occasionally critical mine slopes.

Three different types of reinforcement can be represented in numerical models:

- fully grouted rock bolts (local reinforcement);
- cable bolts; and
- end-anchored rock bolts.

The basic formulation for each type of reinforcement is discussed briefly.

The local reinforcement formulation considers only the local effect of reinforcement where it passes through existing discontinuities. This condition immediately implies that some form of discontinuous behavior is being modeled in the rock mass. The formulation results from observations of laboratory tests of fully grouted untensioned reinforcement in good quality rock with one discontinuity, which indicate that strains in the reinforcement are concentrated across the discontinuity (Bjurstrom, 1974; Pells, 1974; Spang and Egger, 1990). This behavior can be achieved

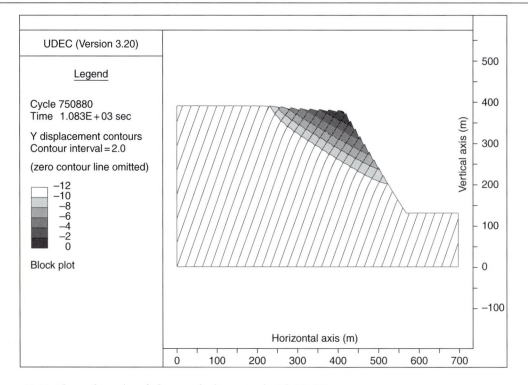

*Figure 10.12* Flexural toppling failure mode determined with UDEC.

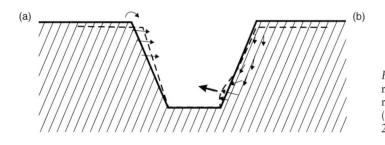

*Figure 10.13* A schematic representation of slopes in a foliated rock mass: (a) flexural toppling; and (b) flexural buckling (Adhikary *et al.*, 2001).

in the computational model by calculating, for each zone, the forces generated by deformation of an "active length" of the element where it crosses a discontinuity (see Figure 6.9). This formulation exploits simple force–displacement relations to describe both the shear and axial behaviors of reinforcement across discontinuities. Large shear displacements are accommodated by considering the simple geometric changes that develop locally in the reinforcement near a discontinuity. Although the local reinforcement model can be used with either rigid blocks or deformable

blocks, the representation is most applicable to cases in which deformation of individual rock blocks may be neglected in comparison with deformation of the reinforcing system. In such cases, attention may be focused reasonably on the effect of reinforcement near discontinuities. The original description of a local reinforcement model is given by Lorig (1985).

In assessing the support provided by rock reinforcement, two components of restraint should be considered. First, the reinforcement provides local restraint where it crosses

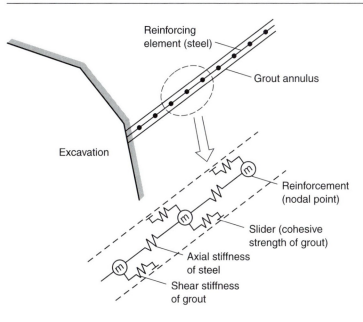

Reinforcing
element (steel)

Grout annulus

Excavation

Reinforcement
(nodal point)

Slider (cohesive
strength of grout)

Axial stiffness
of steel

Shear stiffness
of grout

*Figure 10.14* Conceptual mechanical representation of fully bonded reinforcement, accounting for shear behavior of the grout annulus.

discontinuities. Second, there is restraint to intact rock due to inelastic deformation in the failed region surrounding an excavation. Such situations arise in modeling inelastic deformations associated with failed rock and/or reinforcement systems such as cable bolts, in which the cement or resin grout bonding agent may fail in shear over some length of the reinforcement. Cable elements allow the modeling of a shearing resistance along their length, as provided by the shear resistance generated by the bond between the grout and either the cable or the rock. The cable is assumed to be divided into a number of segments of length $L$, with nodal points located at each segment end. The mass of each segment is lumped at the nodal points, as shown in Figure 10.14. Shearing resistance is represented by spring/slider connections between the structural nodes and the rock in which the nodes are located.

End-anchored rock bolts are the simplest to model. They simply supply axial restraint to the portions of the model in which they are anchored. The axial stiffness $K$, is given by

$$K = \frac{AE}{L} \qquad (10.7)$$

where $A$ is the cross-sectional area of the bolt, $E$, the modulus of the steel and $L$ the distance between the anchoring points

### 10.5.2   Time-dependent behavior

The issue of time-dependent behavior is discussed in reference to behavior of the west wall of Chuquicamata mine, which experiences large on-going displacements of the order of 2–4 m per year. The slope behavior is affected by the presence of a pervasive fault and an adjacent zone of sheared rock near the toe of the slope (Figure 10.15). Deformation of these materials is expressed in toppling further upslope. Previous analyses attempted to estimate safety factors for the slope using UDEC. However, difficulties in identifying both a clear point of failure and a failure mode suggested that other criteria should be considered in assessing the acceptability of west-wall slope designs. Slope displacement and displacement rates were considered as other criteria. However, these criteria required use of material models that could represent time-dependent behavior. Such models were not available in programs used to study discontinuum slope behavior. The modeling described

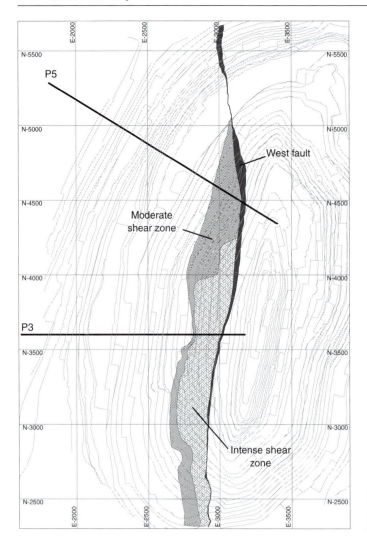

*Figure 10.15* Plan of Chuquicamata open pit showing shear zone (modeled as a time-dependent material), and Profiles P3 and P5.

here demonstrates that the time-dependent behavior of the west wall can be reasonably simulated when the sheared zone is represented by a two-component power-law creep model combined with a Mohr–Coulomb elasto-plastic model. Measured slope movements and changes in displacement rates over a period of six years are compared to model predictions for two profiles (see Figure 10.16).

Profile P3 is an east–west section located at mine coordinate N3600; it is a good section for calibration of behavior of the west wall for two reasons. First, the location of P3 is near the middle of the west wall and therefore is representative of conditions in this wall. Second, its orientation is perpendicular to the west wall and the geology, allowing representative two-dimensional analysis. Profile P5 is a good section for calibration because mining with steep slope angles within the shear zone led to a slope failure in February 2002. Both profiles have good historical information about slope movement from prism monitoring, as described in the next section.

Records of slope movement were available from monitoring records. The prism locations for

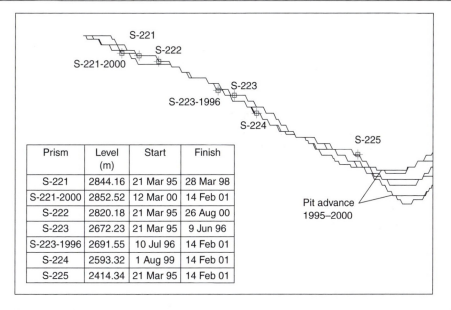

| Prism | Level (m) | Start | Finish |
|---|---|---|---|
| S-221 | 2844.16 | 21 Mar 95 | 28 Mar 98 |
| S-221-2000 | 2852.52 | 12 Mar 00 | 14 Feb 01 |
| S-222 | 2820.18 | 21 Mar 95 | 26 Aug 00 |
| S-223 | 2672.23 | 21 Mar 95 | 9 Jun 96 |
| S-223-1996 | 2691.55 | 10 Jul 96 | 14 Feb 01 |
| S-224 | 2593.32 | 1 Aug 99 | 14 Feb 01 |
| S-225 | 2414.34 | 21 Mar 95 | 14 Feb 01 |

*Figure 10.16* Location of movement monitoring prisms in Profile P3 (see Figure 10.15 for location of Profile P3).

Profile P3 are shown in Figure 10.16, which also shows the position of the pit at the end of years 1995–2000. The prism records for both profiles show the following important characteristics:

- horizontal displacements greater than vertical displacements, which is characteristic of toppling behavior;
- decreasing displacement rates from mid-1995 to the end of 1999; and
- increasing displacement rates starting near the end of 1999 in Profile P3 and the end of 2000 in Profile P5; these periods correspond to the times when the shear zone was being mined.

UDEC models for Profiles P3 and P5 are shown in Figures 10.17 and 10.18, respectively, and have the following features.

- Rock mass behavior for all units except the shear zone is represented by an elasto-plastic model, with a bilinear Mohr–Coulomb failure surface. The bilinear model approximates a Hoek–Brown failure surface, and is easier to use than the non-linear Hoek–Brown failure envelope.
- Faults and other major discontinuities were included explicitly in the models. Predominate jointing structure was included implicitly through a ubiquitous joint model in Granodiorita Fortuna, which is located upslope from the sheared zone.
- Water pressures were taken from MINEDW (a three-dimensional finite element developed by Hydrologic Consultants Inc.), and transferred to the UDEC model at yearly intervals.
- Lithologic units were obtained from Chuquicamata's block model and imported into the UDEC model using a recently developed transfer algorithm.
- Hydrostatic initial *in situ* stresses were assumed. Initial *in situ* stresses with deviatoric components would induce creep under initial pre-mining conditions, a condition that is not believed to be correct.
- Small deformation logic was used to avoid problems with poor zone geometry resulting from large deformations within the shear zone.

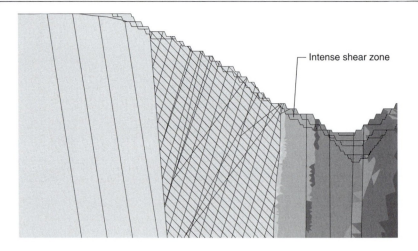

*Figure 10.17* UDEC model for Profile P3 with lithology, discontinuities and annual pit geometries.

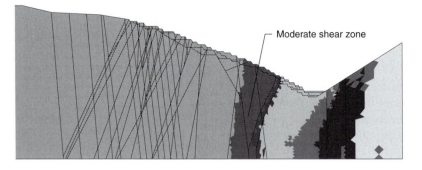

*Figure 10.18* UDEC model of Profile P5 with lithology, discontinuities and annual pit geometries (see Figure 10.15 for location of Profile P5).

Creep behavior was believed to be concentrated within the sheared zone located just to the west of the West Fault. In the model discussed here, the behavior of the sheared rock was represented using a viscoplastic model that combined the behavior of the viscoelastic two-component Norton Power Law model and the Mohr–Coulomb elasto-plastic model. The standard form of the Norton Power Law (Norton, 1929) is

$$\varepsilon_{cr} = A\sigma^n \qquad (10.8)$$

$$\sigma = \left(\frac{3}{2}\right)^{1/2} \left(\sigma_{ij}^d \sigma_{ij}^d\right)^{1/2} \qquad (10.9)$$

where $\varepsilon_{cr}$ is the creep rate, $\sigma_{ij}^d$ is the deviatoric part of $\sigma_{ij}$, and $A$ and $n$ are material properties that were found by calibration.

Modeling was performed for conditions representative of the years 1996 through 2002. Initially, the model was brought to equilibrium under conditions representative of January 1996. At this point, the creep model was turned on and run for one year of simulated time. For each subsequent year, new water pressures and slope geometry were introduced, and the model was run for another year of simulated time.

Calibration was performed by adjusting the power law parameters until reasonable agreement was reached between the prism records and

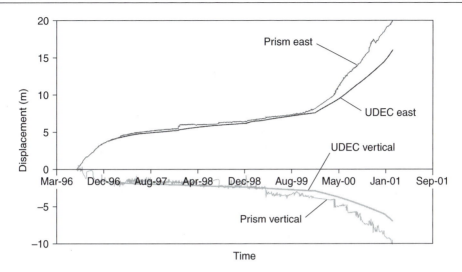

*Figure 10.19* Comparison of movement record for prism S-223 records with UDEC results for Profile P3; $A = 1e$–23 and $n = 2.5$ (equations (10.8) and (10.9)).

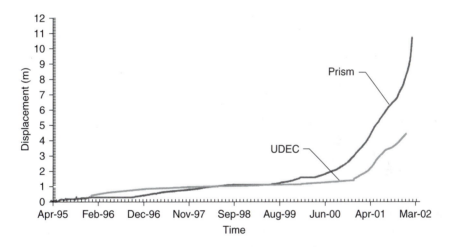

*Figure 10.20* Comparison of actual prism movement record with UDEC results for Profile P5; $A = 1e$–24 and $n = 2.5$ (equations (10.8) and (10.9)).

the numerical results. Representative results are shown in Figures 10.19 and 10.20 for P3 and P5, respectively. The sharp increase in displacement P5 resulted in slope failure in the upper portion of the slope.

In the analyses reported here, it has been assumed that creep behavior initiates as soon as deviatoric stresses are present, and the state of stress is not hydrostatic. However, it is more

likely that creep behavior starts after a threshold deviatoric stress is reached. Evidence for this can be seen by examining the pre-mining *in situ* stress state, which has been shown through measurements to include deviatoric stresses. There was no evidence of creep behavior in the pre-mining condition. Thus, it can be concluded that a threshold deviatoric stress exists below which no creep behavior occurs.

### 10.5.3 Dynamic analysis

Traditional approaches to dynamic analysis are based on a pseudo-static approach in which the effects of an earthquake are represented by constant horizontal and/or vertical accelerations. The first explicit application of the pseudo-static approach to the seismic slope stability has been attributed to Terzaghi (1950). The application of horizontal and/or vertical accelerations can be made in limit equilibrium methods and numerical methods alike. The results of pseudo-static analyses depend on the value of the seismic coefficient as discussed in Section 6.5.4. Difficulty in assigning appropriate pseudo-static coefficients and in interpretation of pseudo-static safety factors, coupled with the advance of numerical models has provided an alternative to the use of the pseudo-static approach for seismic slope stability analyses. Numerical methods, in addition to the Newmark method discussed in Section 6.5.5, allow permanent slope deformations resulting from seismic excitation to be computed.

Both finite-element and finite-difference approaches can be used to compute permanent deformations. Typical analyses involve application of a seismic record to the base of a model and propagating the wave through the model. Small amounts of damping are sometimes applied to account for real energy losses that are not represented by either the joint behavior or the rock mass behavior.

Although there are no documented cases of large-scale failures of open pits under seismic loads, there are many instances of failure of natural slopes during earthquakes (see Section 6.5.1). In open pits, smaller-scale failures comprising rock fall and bench-scale structurally controlled failures may occur under severe shaking. Where such failures are an operational hazard, mitigation can usually be provided by suitable catch bench configurations.

# Chapter 11

# Blasting

## 11.1  Introduction

Excavation of rock slopes usually involves blasting, and it is appropriate that the subject receives attention in this book on rock slope engineering. The fragmentation of rock by explosives is a major subject in its own right and the fundamentals are dealt with in a number of excellent textbooks and handbooks (Langefors and Kihlstrom, 1973; Hemphill, 1981; CIL, 1984; Du Pont, 1984; FHWA, 1985; Atlas Powder Co., 1987; Persson *et al.*, 1993; ISEE, 1998; Oriard, 2002).

The responsibility for the design and implementation of blasting operations varies with the type of project. On mines, there will usually be a department responsible for all aspects of blasting, possibly with some assistance from technical representatives of the explosive supplier. This approach is suited to the circumstances where blasting is carried out frequently, and there is good experience of local conditions. This situation allows the blast designs to be adjusted to accommodate such factors as variations in geology and optimization of equipment operations. The primary requirements of blasting in open pit mines are to produce a muck pile that is fragmented to suit operation of the excavating and hauling equipment. Also, times for equipment moves before and after the blast are minimized if flyrock is controlled. A further requirement of blasting is to control damage to the rock and minimize slope instability when excavating at final faces. Production blasting methods are discussed in Section 11.3.

In contrast to mining operations, on civil projects blasting is usually the responsibility of the contractor, with the principle duty of the owner's representative being to check that the desired results are produced. That is, the work is carried out under a performance-type contract in which the required results are specified, but the methods of achieving these are left to the contractor. This situation requires that the owner understands blasting methods so that the procedures and results can be reviewed and, if necessary, modifications discussed with the contractor. The owner should also ensure that accurate records are kept of each blast as required by most legislation governing blasting. The records are also useful in relating the results obtained to the methods used, and for cost control purposes.

Rock excavation for civil construction often requires the formation of cut faces that will be stable for many years, and as steep as possible to minimize excavation volume and land use. While these two requirements are contradictory, the stability of cuts will be enhanced, and the maximum safe slope angle increased, by using a blasting method that does the least possible damage to the rock behind the final face. Section 11.4 describes methods of minimizing blasting damage that are included in the general term "controlled blasting."

When blasting in urban or industrial areas, precautions are required to control damage to residences and other sensitive structures. Section 11.5 describes methods of controlling structural damage due to blast vibrations, as well as minimizing hazards of flyrock, air blast and noise.

## 11.2 Mechanism of rock fracturing by explosives

The mechanism by which rock is fractured by explosives is fundamental to the design of blasting patterns, whether for production or controlled blasting. It also relates to the damage to surrounding structures and disturbance to people living in the vicinity. The following is a description of this mechanism (FHWA, 1991; Hagan, 1992; Persson et al., 1993; Oriard, 2002).

When an explosive is detonated, it is converted within a few thousandths of a second into a high temperature and high pressure gas. When confined in a blast hole, this very rapid reaction produces pressures, that can reach 18 000 atm, to be exerted against the blast hole wall. This energy is transmitted into the surrounding rock mass in the form of a compressive strain wave that travels at a velocity of 2000–6000 m/s.

As the strain wave enters the rock surrounding the blast hole, the material for a distance of one to two charge radii (in hard rock, more in soft rock) is crushed by compression (Figure 11.1(a)). As the compressive wave front expands, the stress level quickly decays below the dynamic compressive strength of the rock, and beyond this pulverized zone the rock is subjected to intense radial compression that causes tangential tensile stresses to develop. Where these stresses exceed the dynamic tensile breaking strength of the rock, radial fractures form. The extent of these fractures depends on the energy available in the explosive and the strength properties of the rock, and can equal 40–50 times the blast hole diameter. As the compressive wave passes through the rock, concentric shells of rock undergo radial expansion resulting in tangential relief-of-load fractures in the immediate vicinity of the blast hole.

These concentric fractures follow cylindrical surfaces, and are subsequently created nearer and nearer to the free face. When the compressive wave reaches a free face, it is reflected as a tensile strain wave. If the reflected tensile wave is sufficiently strong, "spalling" occurs progressively from any effective free face back towards the blast hole. This causes unloading of the

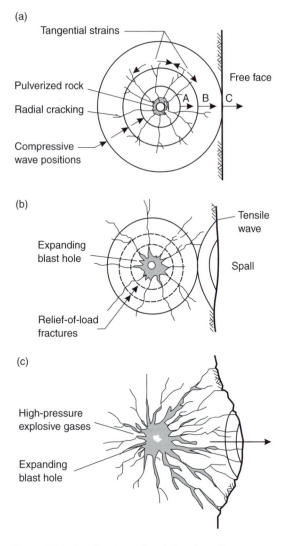

Figure 11.1 Mechanism of rock breakage by explosives.

rock mass, producing an extension of previously formed radial cracks (Figure 11.1(b)). Rock is much weaker in tension than compression, so the reflected strain wave is particularly effective in fracturing rock.

The process of fracture formation due to strain wave energy typically occurs throughout the burden within 1 or 2 ms after detonation, whereas the build-up of explosive gases takes in the order of 10 ms. As the rock is unloaded due to radial expansion and reflection of the compressive wave, it is now possible for the expanding gases to wedge open the strain wave-generated cracks and begin to expel the rock mass (Figure 11.1(c)). This stage is characterized by the formation of a dome around the blast hole. As wedging action takes place due to the heaving and pushing effect of the expanding gases, considerably more fracturing occurs due to shear failure as the rock mass is expelled in the direction of the free face. In highly fissured rocks, fragmentation and muck pile looseness are caused mostly by expanding gases.

The fragmentation achieved by the process described in the previous paragraph is highly dependent upon the confinement of the explosive, the coupling of charges within the blast holes, the burden distance and the sequencing of the blast. That is, if confinement of the charge by stemming is inadequate, some energy will be lost from the blast holes, and inadequate explosive/rock coupling results in poor transmission of strain energy to the rock mass. Also, excessive burdens result in choking and poor movement of the rock, whereas inadequate burden results in waste of explosive energy and excessive throw of blasted rock. The best results are produced when effective delaying of individual blast holes ensures maximum development and utilization of free faces by reducing the effective burden. This provides freedom for the rock to move toward the free face and reduces damage to the surrounding rock (see Section 11.3).

To prevent damage to rock behind the face, the zone of crushed rock and radial cracking around the holes in the final row is controlled by reducing the explosive energy, and decoupling the charge in the holes (see Section 11.4, Controlled blasting). As the shock wave travels beyond the limit of rock breakage and into the surrounding rock, it sets up vibrations both within the rock and at the ground surface. Structures located close to the blast, and through which these vibration waves pass, may be damaged by twisting and rocking motion induced by the ground motion. Damage can be controlled by reducing the explosive weight detonated per delay (see Section 11.5).

## 11.3 Production blasting

The basic economics of rock excavation using explosives are shown in Figure 11.2 (Harries and Mercer, 1975). The production of a well-fragmented and loosely packed muck pile that has not been scattered around the excavation area, facilitates loading and hauling operations. This condition is at the minimum total cost point on the graph. However, close to the final face, drilling and blasting costs will increase because more closely spaced and carefully loaded holes will be required to limit damage to the rock. Conversely, the production of riprap will involve the use of holes with a spacing greater than the largest block size required.

In order to achieve the optimum results of blasting under all conditions, a thorough understanding of the following parameters is required:

1  type, weight, distribution of explosive;
2  nature of the rock;
3  bench height;
4  blast hole diameter;

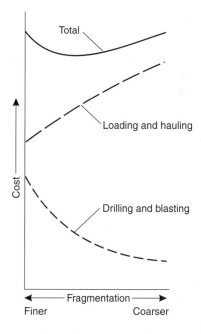

*Figure 11.2* Effect of fragmentation on the cost of drilling, blasting, loading and hauling.

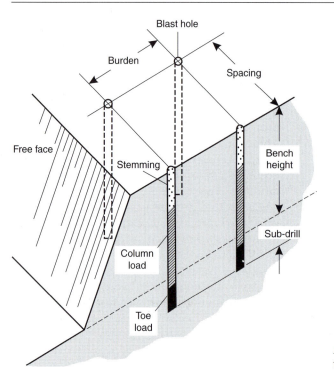

*Figure 11.3* Definition of bench blasting terms.

5   burden;
6   spacing;
7   subdrill depth;
8   stemming;
9   initiation sequence for detonation of explosives; and
10  powder factor.

Factors 3–8 are illustrated in Figure 11.3, and this section describes procedures for calculating the parameters involved in designing production blasts. This discussion is based on work by Dr C. J. Konya (FHWA, 1991). It should be noted that the equations provided in the following sections defining blasting parameters are guidelines only and will need to be modified, as necessary, to suit local site conditions.

## 11.3.1 Explosive properties

The strength of an explosive is a measure of the work done by a certain weight or volume of explosive. This strength can be expressed in absolute units, or as a ratio relative to a standard explosive. Usually the bulk strength of explosives is related to the strength of ANFO that is assigned an arbitrary bulk strength of 100. ANFO is the term used for the most widely used explosive comprising ammonium nitrate prills (0.5 mm diameter spheres) and 5.5% fuel oil.

One measure of the strength of an explosive is its velocity of detonation (VOD); the higher the velocity the greater the shattering effect. However, explosive strength, density and degree of confinement are also factors that should be considered in selecting an explosive for a specific purpose. Table 11.1 lists the velocity of detonation, specific gravity and water resistance of different classes of explosives.

Explosive strength is defined by weight and bulk strengths. Weight strengths are useful when comparing blast designs in which explosives of different strengths are used, and when comparing the cost of explosives because explosives are sold by weight. The relative bulk (or volume) strength (RBS) is related to the weight strength

*Table 11.1* Typical properties of explosives products

| Explosive type | Density (g/cc) | VOD (m/s) | Relative bulk strength* (ANFO = 100) | Water resistance |
|---|---|---|---|---|
| Packaged, detonator-sensitive emulsions | 1.12–1.2 | 4600–5200 | 115–170 | Excellent |
| Packaged, booster-sensitive emulsions | 1.24–1.26 | 4300–5050 | 125–155 | Excellent |
| Watergels | 1.20 | 4785 | 129 | Excellent |
| Dynamites | 1.2–1.42 | 3350–5600 | 170–130 | Good to excellent |
| Wall control dynamites | 0.75–1.3 | 1650–2600 | 76–114 | Good to poor |
| Boosters | 1.34–1.6 | 5600–7900 | 167–280 | Excellent |
| ANFO | 0.84 | 4000 | 100 | None |
| Bulk emulsions | 1.25 | 5200–5500 | 120–150 | Excellent |

Note

* *Relative of bulk strength* (RBS)—is a comparison of theoretical chemical energy per unit volume of an explosive to ANFO that has been assigned an RBS of 100.

by the specific gravity, and this value is important in calculating the volume of blast hole required to contain a given amount of explosive energy. A higher bulk strength requires less blast hole capacity to contain a required charge.

The sensitivity of an explosive is a characteristic that determines the method by which a charge is detonated, the minimum diameter of the charge and the safety with which the explosive can be handled. Highly sensitive explosives will detonate when used in smaller diameter charges, and can be detonated with a relatively low strength detonator. As the sensitivity of the explosive is decreased, the diameter of the charge and the energy of the booster/detonator must be increased.

Table 11.1 provides information on typical properties of the main classes of explosives. Each class of explosive has a set of characteristics suitable to specific applications and conditions such as the size of the blast hole, the presence of water and the need to control flyrock and noise. For example, ANFO and bulk emulsions are commonly used for large-scale blasts in open pits and quarries, while watergels and dynamites are used in smaller construction projects. Also, as shown in Figure 11.3, it is necessary when using ANFO as the main explosive, to use a higher strength explosive in the lower end of the hole ("toe load"). The function of the toe load is to

both ensure complete detonation of the ANFO, and to break the rock in the floor of the bench where it is most highly confined.

### 11.3.2  Bench height

Bench heights are usually determined by the geometry of the site, with single benches being used where the excavation depth is up to about 8 m. On larger construction projects and in open pit mines and quarries, multi-benches operations are conducted. For these operations, the selection of the optimum bench height to maximize the overall cost efficiency of drilling and blasting requires the correct combination of drilling and loading equipment. Furthermore, regulations may limit the bench height, in relation to the maximum reach of the excavating equipment, to minimize the risk of damage or injury in the event of collapse of the face. The following are some of the factors that should be considered in the selection of the bench height:

(a)  Optimum blast hole diameter increases with bench height. In general, an increase in blast hole diameter results in a decrease in drilling costs.

(b)  For vertical blast holes and sloping bench face, the front row toe burden may become excessive as the bench height increases. Where small diameter blast holes are drilled in high benches, blast holes may need to be angled, at least in the front row.

(c) Drilling accuracy becomes more critical in higher benches. Where precise alignment of holes on the final face is required, the maximum bench height is normally limited to 8 or 9 m.

### 11.3.3 Burden

The influence of the effective burden (the distance between rows of holes and the nearest free face) on fragmentation is related to the mechanism of rock fracture described in Section 11.2. The blast is most efficient when the shock wave is reflected in tension from a free face so that the rock is broken and displaced to form a well-fragmented muck pile. This efficiency depends to a large extent on having the correct burden. Too small a burden will allow the radial cracks to extend to the free face resulting in venting of the explosion gases with consequent loss of efficiency and the generation of flyrock and air blast problems. Too large a burden, where the shock wave is not reflected from the free face, will choke the blast resulting in poor fragmentation and a general loss of efficiency.

The relationship between the bench height $H$ and the burden $B$ can be expressed in terms of the "stiffness ratio," $H/B$. If this ratio is low such that the burden is about equal to the bench height, then the blast will be highly confined resulting in severe backbreak, airblast, flyrock and vibration. In contrast, if the $H/B >\sim 4$, there is little confinement and the explosive gases will be vented at the free face also resulting in airblast and flyrock. It is found that a stiffness ratio of 3–4 produces good results, or

$$B = 0.33 \times H \text{ to } 0.25 \times H \tag{11.1}$$

The burden distance calculated from equation (11.1) depends not only upon the blast hole pattern, but also upon the sequence of firing. As illustrated in Figure 11.4(a), a square blast hole

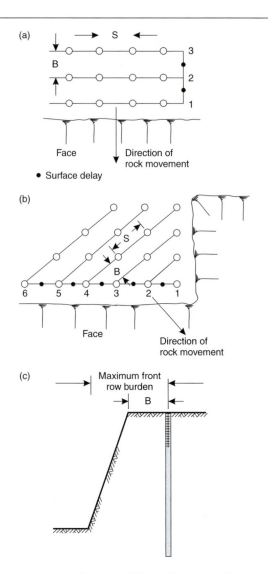

Figure 11.4 Definition of blast hole spacing (S) and burden (B): (a) burden and spacing for a square blasting pattern; (b) burden and spacing for an *en echelon* blasting pattern; (c) effect of face angle on front row burden.

pattern which is fired row by row from the face gives an effective burden equal to the spacing between successive rows parallel to the face. On the other hand, an identical pattern of blast holes fired *en echelon* results in different burdens and spacings, and a spacing to burden ratio greater than 1 (Figure 11.4(b)).

An important factor in designing a blast is the choice of the front row burden. Once this row has been detonated and effectively broken, new free faces are created for the next row, until the last row is fired. If vertical blast holes are used and the bench face is inclined, the front row burden will increase with depth (Figure 11.4(c)). Allowance can be made for this variation by using a higher energy bottom load in the front row of holes. Alternatively, the blast hole can be inclined to give a more uniform burden. When the free face is uneven, the use of easer holes to reduce the burden to acceptable limits is advisable.

For multiple row blasts, the rows towards the back of the blast are progressively more confined, and consequently the degree of fragmentation may diminish. This effect can be corrected for by decreasing the burden of the third and subsequent rows by a factor of 0.9.

### 11.3.4 Blast hole diameter

Blast hole diameters on construction projects may range from about 40 mm for hand-held drills, to 100 mm for "air-trac" drills and 200 mm for "track drills". All these drills are rotary percussive and are powered with compressed air. In open pit mines, electric powered rotary drills are commonly used with which holes up to 600 mm are drilled with roller tri-cone bits (ADI, 1996).

Persson (1975) shows that the cost of drilling and blasting decreases as the hole size increases. This is because the hole volume increases with the square of hole diameter so that the same volume of explosive can be loaded into fewer holes. This cost saving is offset by the greater shattering of the rock that is produced by the more highly concentrated explosive, which can result in less stable slopes, and larger rock fragments that the excavating equipment may not be able to handle.

Once the burden $B$ (units: m) has been set to provide an appropriate stiffness ratio (equation (11.1)), the diameter of the explosive $d_{ex}$ (units: mm) can be determined as follows:

$$d_{ex} \approx \frac{B \times 1000}{(24\gamma_{ex}/\gamma_r) + 18} \quad (11.2)$$

where $\gamma_{ex}$ and rock $\gamma_r$ are the unit weights of the explosive and rock, respectively.

Equation (11.2) can be used where there is a correlation between the energy of the explosive and its unit weight. However, emulsion slurry explosives have a range of energies with a near constant unit weight, and for these conditions it is appropriate to calculate the burden using the relative bulk strength (RBS) compared to ANFO (RBS = 100). The blast hole diameter taking into account the RBS of the explosive is given by

$$d_{ex} \approx \frac{B \times 1000}{8(RBS/\gamma_r)^{0.33}} \quad (11.3)$$

### 11.3.5 Nature of the rock

The nature and degree of heterogeneity of the rock mass is very important in blast design. That is, discontinuities such as joints, bedding planes, faults, and soft seams can allow the explosive's energy to be wastefully dissipated rather than perform the work intended. In some cases, the discontinuities can dominate the fracture pattern produced by the explosive, and the influence of the structural geology often overshadows that of the rock's mechanical and physical properties. Best fragmentation is usually obtained where the face is parallel to the major discontinuity set.

Heave energy of the explosive is important in highly fissured rock. The explosion gases jet into, wedge open, and extend the pre-existing cracks. Therefore, the overall degree of fragmentation tends to be controlled by the structural geology. For example, closely spaced joints and bedding planes result in increased fragmentation because few new fracture surfaces need be created in the blast. For these conditions, longer stemming columns and correspondingly lower powder factors or energy factors can be used, and low-density, low-velocity explosives (e.g. ANFO) are preferred to higher-velocity explosives that cause excessive fragmentation immediately around the charge. Satisfactory results are achieved when the charges provide sufficient heave energy to displace the rock into a loose, readily excavated muck pile, without scattering the rock around the site.

The effects of structural geology on blast design can be quantified by applying two correction factors to the calculated burden distance. These factors relate to both the orientation of any persistent discontinuities relative to the face and fracture characteristics, as shown in Tables 11.2 and 11.3 respectively. The correction factors are applied to the calculated burden distance as follows:

$$B' = k_\psi \cdot k_s \cdot B \qquad (11.4)$$

### 11.3.6  Sub-drill depth

Sub-drilling or drilling to a depth below the required grade is necessary in order to break the rock at bench level. Poor fragmentation at this level will form a series of hard "toes" and an irregular bench floor resulting in high operating costs for loading and hauling equipment. However, excessive sub-drilling can result in unnecessary drilling and explosive costs.

*Table 11.2*  Correction factors for dip of structure

| Orientation of structure | Correction factor, $k_\psi$ |
| --- | --- |
| Structure dipping steeply out of face | 1.18 |
| Structure dipping steeply into face | 0.95 |
| Other orientation of structure | 1.00 |

*Table 11.3*  Correction factors for discontinuity characteristics

| Structural characteristics | Correction factor, $k_s$ |
| --- | --- |
| Closely jointed, closely spaced weakly cemented seams | 1.30 |
| Thin, well-cemented layers with tight joints | 1.10 |
| Massive, intact rock | 0.95 |

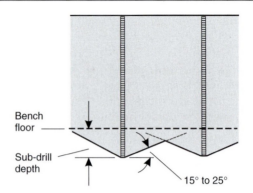

*Figure 11.5*  Rock breakage at the bottom of a blast hole with the use of sub-drilling.

Breakage of the rock usually projects from the base of the toe load in the form of an inverted cone with sides inclined at 15–25° to the horizontal, depending upon the strength and structure of the rock (Figure 11.5). In multi-row blasting, the breakage cones link up to give a reasonably even transition from broken to undamaged rock. Experience has shown that a sub-drill depth of 0.2–0.5 times the burden is usually adequate for effective digging to grade. Where benches are to be formed on the final face, it is advisable to eliminate the sub-drilling in the back rows to help maintain stability of the bench crest.

### 11.3.7  Stemming

The use of stemming to fill the upper portion of the hole above the charge contains the explosive gases and directs the explosive effort into the rock mass. Stemming material comprising well graded, angular gravel is more effective than drill cuttings that are more easily ejected from the hole. The optimum size of the stemming material increases with the diameter of the blast hole, and the average size of the stemming particles should be about 0.05 times the diameter of the blast hole.

The effects of stemming length on blast results are similar to those of burden distance discussed previously. That is, a short stemming length will allow the explosive gases to vent, generating flyrock and airblast problems and reducing the effectiveness of the blast, while too great a stemming length will give poor fragmentation of the rock above the column load.

The common stemming length is about 0.7 times the burden, which is adequate to keep material from ejecting prematurely from the hole. If unacceptably large blocks are obtained from the top of the bench, even when the minimum stemming column consistent with flyrock and airblast problems is used, fragmentation can be improved by locating a small "pocket" charge centrally within the stemming (Hagan, 1975).

### 11.3.8 Hole spacing

When cracks are opened parallel to the free face as a result of the reflected tensile strain wave, gas pressure entering these cracks exerts an outward force that fragments the rock and heaves it on to the muck pile. Obviously, the lateral extent to which the gas can penetrate is limited by the size of the crack and the volume of gas available, and a stage will be reached when the force generated is no longer large enough to fragment and move the rock. If the effect of a single blast hole is reinforced by holes on either side, the total force acting on the strip of burden material will be evened out and uniform fragmentation of this rock will result.

Figure 11.6 illustrates drill hole patterns with a variety of burden/spacing ratios. While the square pattern is the easiest to layout, in some conditions better fragmentation is obtained when the spacing is greater than the burden. For a series of delayed holes, the spacing $S$ can be calculated from the following two equations:

For a stiffness ratio $H/B$ between 1 and 4,

$$S = \frac{(H + 7B)}{8} \tag{11.5}$$

and for a stiffness ratio $H/B$ greater than 4,

$$S = 1.4 \times B \tag{11.6}$$

### 11.3.9 Hole detonation sequence

A typical blast for a construction project or open pit mine may contain as many as 100 blast holes,

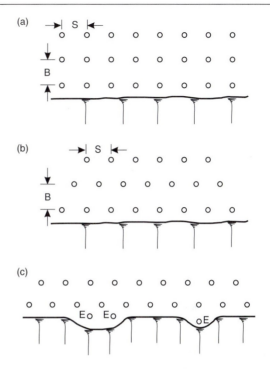

Figure 11.6 Typical blast hole patterns used in production blasting: (a) square pattern with burden/spacing ratio 1:1; (b) staggered pattern with burden/spacing ratio 1:1.15; (c) easer holes (E) to assist movement of front row burden.

which in total contain several thousand kilograms of explosive. Simultaneous detonation of this quantity of explosive would not only produce very poorly fragmented rock, but would also damage the rock in the walls of the excavation and create large vibrations in nearby structures. In order to overcome this situation, the blast is broken down into a number of sequential detonations by delays. When the front row is detonated and moves away from the rock mass to create a new free face, it is important that time be allowed for this new face to be established before the next row is detonated. Figure 11.7 show examples of detonation sequences. Row-to-row blasts are parallel to the free face, with the row closest to the face being detonated first in the sequence (Figure 11.7(a)). The V cut shown in Figure 11.7(b), where the rows are inclined to the face, is used to open a new free face, and when

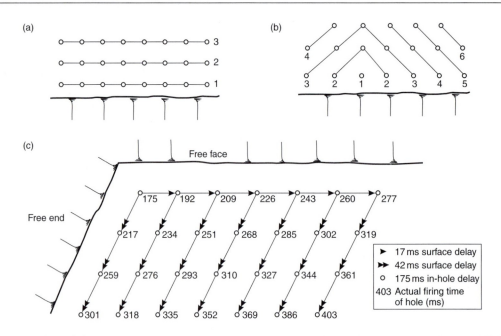

*Figure 11.7* Typical detonation sequences: (a) square "row-by-row" detonation sequence; (b) square "V" detonation sequence; (c) hole-by-hole detonation using both surface and in-hole non-electric delays (W. Forsyth).

blasting in strongly jointed rock where near vertical joints strike across the bench at an angle to the face.

In many cases, blasting results can be improved by introducing hole-by-hole firing, where every blast hole is initiated in sequence at a unique time (Figure 11.7(c)). Where appropriate delays are selected, hole-by-hole initiation exploits the positive benefits of blast hole interaction while avoiding most of the negative effects. This can lead to finer fragmentation, looser muckpiles, less overbreak, lower ground vibration, and better control over the position and profile of the final muckpile.

Hole-by-hole firing can be achieved by using in-hole detonators. However, the available range of commercial in-hole delays is limited and, hence hole-by-hole initiation is usually achieved by using a surface delay system to control blast hole sequencing. If long inter-row or inter-hole delays are required, a combination of surface and in-hole delays will avoid downline cutoffs caused by ground movement during the blast. For the detonation sequence shown in Figure 11.7(c),

there is an identical in-hole delay of 175 ms in each hole, together with surface delays of 17 ms along the free face, and 42 ms delays between the rows. The diagram shows the actual firing times of each hole using this delay arrangement.

The required delay interval is related to distance between holes by the following two relationships.

For row-to-row detonation:

$$\text{Time delay between rows (units: ms)} \approx (10\text{--}13) \times (\text{burden}) \ (\text{units: m}) \tag{11.7a}$$

For example, for a 5 m burden the delay between rows is 50–65 ms.

For hole-to-hole detonation:

$$\text{Time delay between holes (units: ms)} \approx \frac{(\text{delay constant})}{\times (\text{hole spacing}) \ (\text{units: m})} \tag{11.7b}$$

*Table 11.4* Delay constant–rock type relationship for hole-to-hole delay

| Rock type | Delay constant (ms/m) |
| --- | --- |
| Sand, loam, marl, coal | 6–7 |
| Soft limestone, shale | 5–6 |
| Compact limestone and marble, granite, basalt, quartzite, gneiss, gabbro | 4–6 |
| Diabase, diabase porphyrites, compact gneiss and micaschist, magnetite | 3–4 |

Values for the delay constant depend on the rock type as shown in Table 11.4. For example, when blasting granite with a hole-to-hole spacing of 6 m, the delay interval would be about 30 ms.

These two relationships for calculating delay times take into account both the time required to displace the broken rock and establish a new free face, and the natural scatter that occurs in the actual firing times of delays. The error in actual firing time compared to the rated firing time may be as high as 15%, and such errors may result in holes firing out of sequence, especially if the delay interval is short. The development of electronic delay detonators provides a higher degree of precision in firing times compared to chemical delay elements. A further advantage of electronic detonators is the ability, with some products, to program the delay interval in the field to suit site conditions (McKinstry *et al.*, 2002; Watson, 2002).

### 11.3.10 *Fragmentation*

The objective of selecting the appropriate combination of design parameters, as discussed on the preceding pages, is to achieve a desired result for the blast. These objectives may include a specified size range of rock fragments, or a final face with minimal blast damage, or noise and ground vibration levels within specified limits.

The basic design parameter for production blasting, where the objective is to produce a certain degree of fragmentation, is the "powder factor"—the weight of explosive required to break a unit volume of rock, for example, $kg/m^3$. The powder factor is derived from the procedures discussed in this section to calculate the blast hole diameter and depth, the hole pattern and the amount and type of explosive in each hole. That is, the weight of explosive and the volume of rock are given by

Weight of explosive per hole, $W_{ex}$

= (diameter of explosive)

× (unit weight of explosive)

× (bench height − stemming length

+ subdrill depth)

and

Volume of rock per hole, $V$

= (bench height) × (burden) × (spacing)

$$\text{Powder factor} = \frac{W_{ex}}{V} \qquad (11.8)$$

The effect of the powder factor on fragmentation is shown in Figure 11.8 where the average fragment size is related to the powder factor for a range of burdens. These graphs, which are based

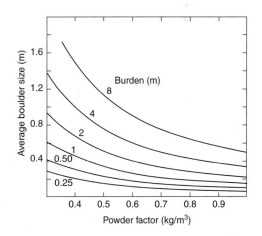

*Figure 11.8* Relationship between average boulder size $L$, powder factor $q$ and burden $B$ in bench blasting (Persson *et al.*, 1993).

on theoretical equations developed by Langefors and Kihlstrom (1973) and Persson *et al.* (1993) together with extensive field testing, can be used to check on the likely results for a given blast design and assess the possible effects of design modifications.

### 11.3.11 *Evaluation of a blast*

Once the dust has settled and the fumes have dispersed after a blast, an inspection of the area should be carried out. The main features of a satisfactory blast are as follows (Figure 11.9):

- The front row should have moved out evenly but not too far—excessive throw is unnecessary and expensive to clean up. The heights of most benches are designed for efficient loader operation and low muckpiles, due to excessive front row movement, results in low loader productivity.

- The main charge should have lifted evenly and cratering should, at worst, be an occasional occurrence. Flat or wrinkled areas are indicative of misfires or poor delaying.
- The back of the blast should be characterized by a drop, indicating a good forward movement of the free face. Tension cracks should be visible in front of the final excavation lines, although excessive cracking behind the final excavation line represents damage to the slopes and waste of explosive.

The quality of blast has a significant effect on components of the rock excavation cost such as secondary drilling and blasting of oversize boulders, loading rate, the condition of the haul roads, and loader and truck maintenance. For example, oversized fragments, hard toes, tight areas and low muck piles (caused by excessive throw) have the most significant detrimental

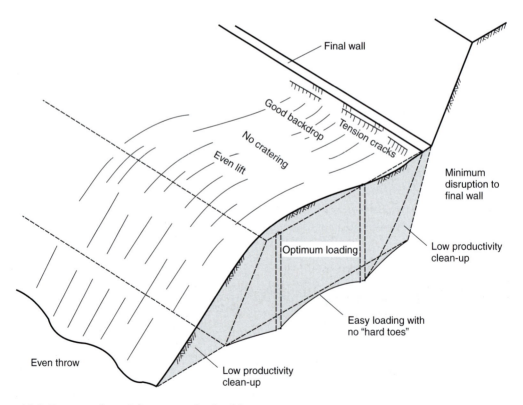

*Figure 11.9* Features of a satisfactory production blast.

effect on the excavation rates. Therefore, careful evaluation of the blast to determine how improvements could be made to the design is usually worthwhile.

## 11.4   Controlled blasting to improve stability

Slope instability is often related to blast damage to the rock behind the face. Blast-induced instability is usually surficial, extending possibly 5–10 m behind the face for open pit scale blasts, that can result in rock falls occurring over time as water and ice open cracks and loosen blocks. It is also possible that the blast damage can cause larger-scale instability where, for example, the slope contains persistent bedding planes dipping out of the face. The explosive gases can travel along, and open, the beds resulting in displacement of substantial blocks of rock.

Control of blast damage to final walls can be limited by implementing one or both of the following procedures. First, the production blast should be designed to limit rock fracturing behind the final wall, and second, controlled blasting methods such as line drilling, pre-shearing, and cushion blasting can be used to define final faces precisely (Hagan and Bulow, 2000). With respect to production blasting, the following precautions help to avoid excessive backbreak:

(a)   Choke blasting into excessive burden or broken muck piles should be avoided.
(b)   The front row charge should be adequately designed to move the front row burden.
(c)   Adequate delays and timing intervals should be used for good movement towards free faces and the creation of new free faces for following rows.
(d)   Delays should be used to control the maximum instantaneous charge.
(e)   Back row holes, together with reduced charge "buffer holes," should be drilled at an optimum distance from the final face to facilitate excavation and yet minimize damage to the wall. The length of the stemming in the buffer holes may also need to be adjusted depending on the degree of fracture along the crest of the bench.

### 11.4.1   Pre-shearing and cushion blasting

On permanent slopes for many civil projects, even small slope failures are not acceptable, and the use of controlled blasting to limit damage to the final wall is often required; an example of controlled blasting is shown in Figure 11.10. The principle behind these methods is that closely spaced,

*Figure 11.10* Example of controlled blasting for rock cut on highway project (strong, highly folded gneiss, I-26/US23, near Mars Hill, North Carolina) (courtesy: North Carolina Department of Transportation).

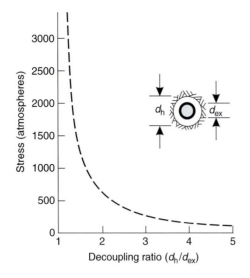

*Figure 11.11* Stress level for decoupled blast holes (FHWA, 1991).

parallel holes drilled on the final face are loaded with a light explosive charge that has a diameter smaller than that of the hole. The effect of an air-gap around the explosive provides a cushion that significantly diminishes the shock wave that is transmitted to the rock. If the decoupling ratio, that is the ratio of hole diameter to the explosive diameter is greater than about 2, then the pressure of the shock wave will be about 10–20% of that produced by an explosive tightly packed in the hole (Figure 11.11). This pressure is not sufficient to produce crushing of the rock around the hole (see Figure 11.1), but radial fractures form preferentially between the holes to create a clean break on the plane of the holes. It is found that it is not necessary to fire the holes on the final line on the same delay, and that the same results are obtained if every hole is fired on a separate delay (Oriard, 2002).

The following is a discussion on various methods of controlled blasting, and their advantages and disadvantages. The three basic methods of controlled blasting are *line drilling, cushion or trim blasting* and *pre-shear blasting*. Line drilling involves drilling holes precisely along the required break line at a spacing of two to four holes diameters, and then leaving a number of unloaded holes between the loaded holes. Line drilling is only used where very precise wall control is needed, such as corners in excavations. Cushion and pre-shear blasting are the most commonly used methods, with the main difference between the two being that in cushion blasting the final row holes are detonated last in the sequence, while in pre-shearing the final line holes are detonated first in the sequence. The following are some of the factors that should be considered in selecting either cushion or pre-shear blasting:

(a) *Burden*—Pre-shearing should only be used where the burden is adequate to contain the explosive energy that is concentrated along the shear line. For narrow burdens, the energy may be sufficient to displace the entire mass of rock between the shear line and the face (Oriard, 2002). As a guideline for the use of pre-shearing, the burden should at least be equal to the bench height, and preferably greater.

(b) *Discontinuities*—In closely jointed/sheared rock, the highly confined gases generated along the shear line in pre-shearing may vent into the cracks resulting in damage to the rock. In cushion blasting, the rock is somewhat less confined, and more stable slopes may be produced.

(c) *Vibration*—The shock wave generated by highly confined pre-shearing may be greater than that of cushion blasting. As noted earlier in this section, it is not necessary to detonate the shear line holes on a single delay, so employing hole-by-hole delays can limit ground motion when vibrations must be closely controlled.

A general comment on the design of controlled blasts is that it is often necessary to carry out a number of trail blasts at the start of a project, and when the rock conditions change, to determine the optimum hole layout and explosive charge. This requires flexibility on the part of the contractor, and the use of end-product rather than method specifications.

The cost savings achieved by controlled blasting cannot be measured directly. However, it is generally accepted that, for permanent slopes on many civil projects, these savings are greater than the extra cost of drilling closely spaced, carefully aligned holes and loading them with special charges. The savings are the result of being able to excavate steeper slopes, and reduce excavation volume and land take. It is also found that less time is spent scaling loose rock from the face after the blast, and the resulting face is more stable and requires less maintenance during its operational life. From an aesthetic point of view, steep cuts have smaller exposed areas than flat slopes, although the traces of the final line drill holes on the face may be considered objectionable.

### 11.4.2  Drilling

The maximum depth that can be successfully excavated by cushion or pre-shear blasting depends on the accuracy of the hole alignment. Deviations of more than about 150 mm from the plane of the holes generally give poor results due to the uneven distribution of explosive on the shear plane, and the creation of an irregular face. While holes up to 27 m deep have been successfully cushion blasted, the depths of final line holes are usually limited to about 8–10 m. Drill hole alignment can be enhanced with the use of high rigidity drill steel, button bits and limiting the down-hole pressure on the bit.

The penetration rates of the drill should also be considered when determining the depth to be cushion blasted. If, for example, the penetration beyond a given depth becomes excessively slow, it may be more economical to carry out the excavation in a series of benches in order to keep penetration rates and drilling costs at acceptable levels. Also, when laying out final line drill holes in a benched excavation, allowance should be made for a minimum 0.3 m offset per bench since it is not possible to position the drill flush to the wall of the upper bench. This situation results in the overall slope of a multi-bench excavation being flatter than the bench face angle, and this difference should be allowed for in laying out the final line holes (Figure 11.12).

When cushion blasting around curved areas or corners, closer spacings are required than when

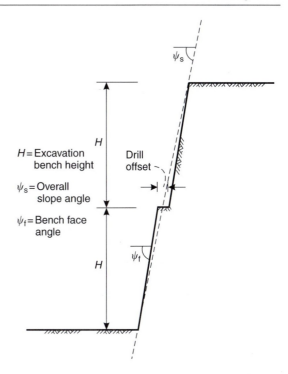

$H$ = Excavation bench height

$\psi_s$ = Overall slope angle

$\psi_f$ = Bench face angle

*Figure 11.12* Alternative explosive placements for controlled blasting (adapted from ISEE, 1998).

blasting a straight section. Also, unloaded guide holes can be used to advantage when blasting non-linear faces (Wyllie, 1999).

In unconsolidated sedimentary formations where it is difficult to hold a smooth wall, unloaded guide holes between cushion holes may be used. Generally, small diameter guide holes are employed to reduce drilling costs. Where only the top of the formation is weathered, the guide holes need be drilled only to that depth and not the full depth of the cushion holes.

### 11.4.3  Explosive load

The required explosive load in the final line holes can be obtained by a combination of steps. First, the charge diameter should be smaller than the hole so that the decoupling ratio is at least 2 (see Figure 11.11). Second, an explosive with a low velocity of detonation should be used that will not shatter the rock. Third, the charge should be distributed along the hole so that there is

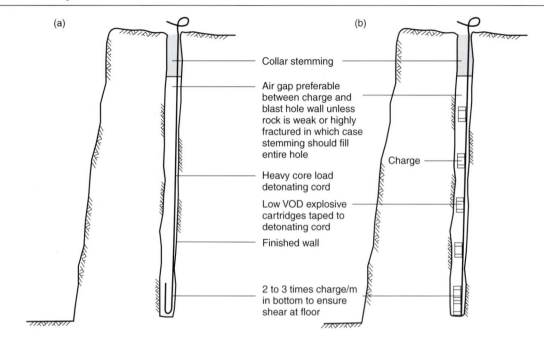

*Figure 11.13* Layout of final line blast holes on multi-bench excavation taking into account drill off-sets.

reasonably uniform explosive load on the face. The required charge distribution can be achieved using either a continuous column of a explosive packaged in a small diameter polyethylene tube (Figure 11.13(a)), or explosive cartridges (or portions of cartridges) are spaced up the hole. Methods of spacing the cartridges include taping them to detonating cord (Figure 11.13(b)), using wooden spacers, or placing them, at the required distance apart, in "C" shaped plastic tubes. It is preferable that the explosive not touch the rock in the walls of the hole, which can be achieved using sleeves to center the explosive in the hole. To promote shearing at the bottom of the hole, a bottom charge two to three times that used in the upper portion of the hole is generally employed.

The approximate explosive load per meter of blast hole $l_{ex}$ that will produce sufficient pressure to cause splitting to occur, but not damage the rock behind the final face, can be approximated by

$$l_{ex} = \frac{(d_h)^2}{12,100} \text{ (kg/m, for } d_h \text{ in mm)} \quad (11.9a)$$

or

$$l_{ex} = \frac{(d_h)^2}{28} \text{ (lb/ft, for } d_h \text{ in inches)} \quad (11.9b)$$

where $d_h$ is the hole diameter.

### 11.4.4   Stemming

Similar to production holes, the upper part of final line holes is unloaded and stemmed with angular gravel to contain the explosive gases in the hole. For hole diameters up to about 100 mm, the stemming length is in the range of 0.6–1.0 m, and varies with the formation being shot. In homogeneous formations, only the top of the hole is stemmed so that air gap around the charge serves as a protective "cushion". However, when stemming is not used around the charges, the explosive gases can find weak zones in the formation and tend to vent before the desired shear between holes is obtained. Similarly, the gases may find areas of weakness back into the finished wall and produce overbreak. Therefore, in weak and highly fractured, or faulted rock, complete stemming between and around individual charges may be desirable.

### 11.4.5 Spacing and burden

The spacing between blast holes on the final line differs slightly between pre-shearing and cushion blasting, as given by the following relationships:

Pre-shearing: Spacing

$$\approx (10\text{--}12) \times \text{(hole diameter)} \qquad (11.10a)$$

Cushion blasting: Spacing

$$\approx (16) \times \text{(hole diameter)} \qquad (11.10b)$$

For pre-shearing the burden is effectively infinite, but as discussed in Section 11.4.1, it should be at least equal the bench height. For cushion blasting, the burden should be larger than the spacing so that the fractures preferentially link between holes along the final wall and do not extend into the burden. The burden is given by

Cushion blasting: Burden

$$\geq (1.3) \times \text{(hole spacing)} \qquad (11.11)$$

### 11.4.6 Hole detonation sequence

As discussed in Section 11.4.1, the main difference between pre-shearing and cushion blasting is the detonation sequence. In pre-shearing, the final row holes are detonated first in the sequence, and in cushion blasting, the final row holes are detonated last in the sequence. Furthermore, satisfactory results are obtained by detonating each hole along the final line on separate delays, and it is not necessary to use a single delay for the full length of the final wall blast.

Figure 11.14 shows a possible blast hole layout and detonation sequence for pre-shearing a through-cut. This excavation is suitable for pre-shearing because the burden is infinite and there is no possibility for prematurely displacing the burden. The shear line holes on either side of the cut are detonated first, followed by the production blast as a 'V' cut. Theoretically, the length of a pre-shear shot is unlimited. In practice, however, shooting far in advance of primary excavation can be troublesome if the rock characteristics

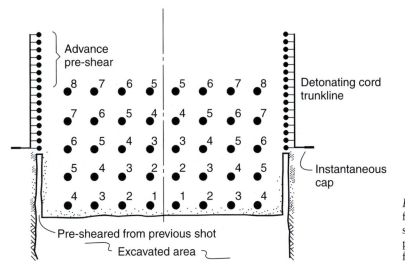

*Figure 11.14* Blasting procedure for through-cut showing delay sequence for pre-shearing during production blasting (adapted from ISEE, 1998).

change and the load causes excessive shatter in the weaker areas. By carrying the pre-shear only one-half shot in advance of the primary blasting, the knowledge gained from the primary blasts regarding the rock can be applied to subsequent pre-shear shots.

## 11.5   Blast damage and its control

Blasting in urban areas must often be controlled to minimize the risk of damage to structures, and disturbance to people living and working in the vicinity. Three types of damage that can be caused by blasting include (Figure 11.15):

(a) *Ground vibrations*—structural or cosmetic damage resulting from ground vibration induced by the shockwave spreading out from the blast area.
(b) *Flyrock*—impact damage by rock ejected from the blast.
(c) *Airblast and noise*—damage due to over-pressure generated in the atmosphere.

The basic mechanism causing damage is the excess energy of the shock wave, generated by the explosive detonation, as it spreads out from the immediate blast area. As the shock wave spreads out, its energy diminishes both due to the energy consumed in breaking and deforming the rock, and because it occupies a progressively larger volume of rock with time. At distances where there is insufficient energy to break the

rock, vibrations will be set up that can be large enough to damage structures. Furthermore, if the explosive gases are not adequately confined by the burden, the shock wave released at the face can generate both flyrock that is ejected from the blast, and considerable noise.

When designing a blast in an urban area, one must take into consideration not only the potential for damage in the vicinity of the blast, but also possible disturbance to people at a considerable distance from the site. Disturbance to people living outside the potential damage zone can give rise to complaints and possibly spurious damage claims. This section provides information on allowable vibration and air blast levels, and discusses methods of preventing both damage to structures and disturbance to people.

On most urban construction projects, blasting is only one of the many possible sources of vibration. Figure 11.16 shows how the peak-particle velocity produced by various types of construction equipment compares with the vibrations produced by detonation of 0.45 kg of dynamite. This chart represents approximate values, and actual vibration levels will vary from site to site. Detonation of an explosive charge produces a short duration, transient vibration compared to other sources, such as heavy machinery which produce steady-state (or pseudo-steady) vibrations. Generally, the steady-state vibrations are more disturbing to people than transient vibrations, even if the latter have a higher peak particle velocity. Also, vibrations produced by the steady-state sources can damage structures close to the source, so in some circumstances the effects of non-blasting vibrations should be considered.

### 11.5.1   Damage from ground vibration

The following is a discussion of the properties of ground vibrations, and how these properties relate to damage to structures that are strained by these motions.

When an explosive charge is detonated near a free surface, the elastic response of the rock to the shock wave is the generation of two body waves and one surface wave. The faster of the

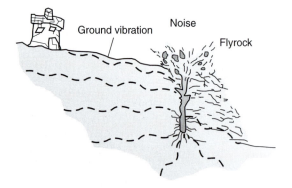

*Figure 11.15* Causes of blast damage.

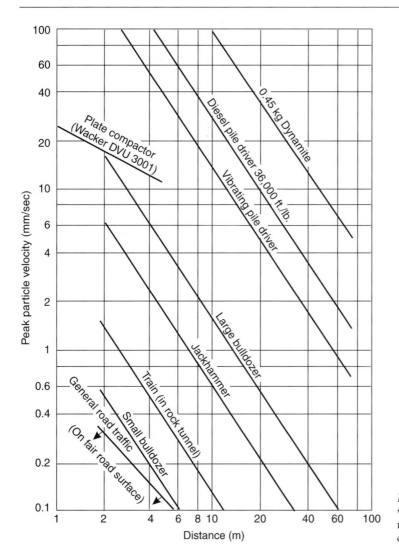

*Figure 11.16* Peak particle velocities produced by construction machinery compared to explosive charge (adapted from Wiss, 1981).

two body waves propagated within the rock is a compressive, or *P*, wave, while the slower type is a shear, or *S*, wave. The surface wave, or *R* wave is slower than either the *P* or *S* wave; it is named after Raleigh who proved its existence. In terms of vibration damage, the *R* wave is the most important since it propagates along the ground surface, and because its amplitude decays more slowly with distance traveled than the *P* or *S* waves.

The wide variations in geometric and geological conditions on typical blasting sites preclude

the solution of ground vibration magnitudes by means of elastodynamic equations. Therefore, the most reliable predictions are given by empirical relationships developed from observations of actual blasts.

Of the three most easily measured properties of the stress waves, that is, acceleration, velocity and displacement, it is generally agreed that velocity can be most readily correlated with damage to structures. The stress wave has three components—vertical, horizontal and radial, and it is necessary to measure all three components and use the greatest, termed the Peak Particle Velocity (PPV), to assess damage potential. The difference between the particle velocity of a stress wave, and the velocity of propagation of the wave can be explained as follows. As the wave passes through the ground, each particle of the rock and soil undergoes an elliptical motion, and it is the velocity of this oscillating motion (possibly up to 0.5 m/s) that is measured in assessing blast damage. In contrast, the velocity of propagation of the wave is in the range 300–6000 m/s, and this has no direct bearing on damage.

Ground motion can be described as a sinusoidal wave in which the variation of the particle velocity $v$ with time $t$ is given by (Figure 11.17):

$$v = A \sin(\omega t) \tag{11.12}$$

where $A$ is the amplitude of the wave, and $\omega$ is the angular velocity. The magnitude of the angular velocity given by

$$\omega = 2\pi f = 2\pi \frac{1}{T} \tag{11.13}$$

where $f$ is of the frequency (vibrations per second, or Hertz) and $T$ is the period (time for one complete cycle). The wavelength $L$ of the vibration is the distance from crest to crest of one full cycle and is related to the period $T$ and the velocity of propagation $V$ by

$$L = VT \tag{11.14}$$

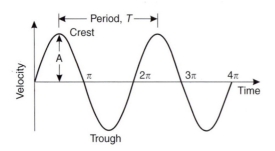

Figure 11.17 Sinusoidal wave motion for typical ground vibrations.

If the particle velocity $v$ has been measured, then the displacement $\delta$ can be found by integration, and the acceleration $a$ by differentiation as follows:

$$\delta = \frac{v}{\omega} \quad \text{and} \quad a = \omega v \ (\text{m/s}^2)$$

or

$$a = \frac{\omega v}{9.81} \ (\text{g/ms}^2) \tag{11.15}$$

The most reliable relationship between blast geometrics and ground vibration is that relating particle velocity to *scaled distance*. The scaled distance is defined by the function $R/\sqrt{W}$, where $R$ (m) is the radial distance from the point of detonation, and $W$ (kg) is the mass of explosive detonated per delay. Field tests have established that the maximum particle velocity, $V$ (mm/s) is related to the scaled distance by following attenuation relationship (Oriard, 1971):

$$V = k \left( \frac{R}{\sqrt{W}} \right)^\beta \tag{11.16}$$

where $k$ and $\beta$ are constants that have to be determined by measurements on each particular blasting site. Equation (11.16) plots as a straight line on log–log paper, where the value of $k$ is given by the PPV intercept at a scaled distance of unity, and the constant $\beta$ is given by the slope of the line. An example of such a plot is given in Figure 11.18.

In order to obtain data from the preparation of a plot, such as that in Figure 11.19, it is necessary to make vibration measurements with a suitable monitoring instrument. Table 11.5 shows typical specifications for a seismograph suitable for measuring blast vibrations, as well as vibrations produced by a wide range of construction equipment such as pile drivers. Of importance for monitoring non-blasting applications is the useful frequency range of the equipment; for the Instantel DS677, this range is 2–250 Hz, which means that vibrations with frequencies outside this range will not be detected. Some of the features of instruments currently available (2003) are measurement of both ground vibration—velocity,

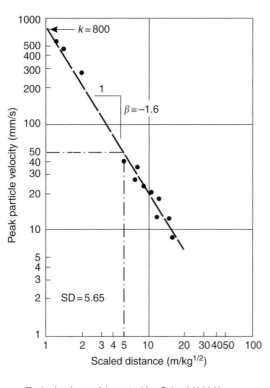

Typical values of k quoted by Oriard (2002)

k = 1130  (160)—average values
  = 1700  (242)—typical upper bound (90% bound)
  = 4270  (605)—high confinement, coupling and
            rock strength (99% bound).

units:  ⌐                   ⌐ units: in./s, ft, lb
mm/s, m, kg

*Figure 11.18* Hypothetical plot of measured particle velocity versus scaled distance from blast to determine attenuation constants k and β.

acceleration, displacement and frequency in vertical, longitudinal and transverse axes, and air pressure. In addition, the instruments incorporate a trigger that starts recording when a pre-set vibration level or air pressure is detected. The results are digitally recorded so the data can be downloaded to a computer for storage and further analysis.

Measurement of ground vibrations involves installing geophones on the ground close to the structure of interest, or on the structure itself.

It is important that the geophone be properly coupled to the ground or structure. The International Society of Rock Mechanics (ISRM, 1991) suggests that the method of mounting is a function of the particle acceleration of the wave train being monitored. When vertical accelerations are less than $0.2g$, the geophone may be placed on a horizontal surface without being anchored in place. When the maximum particle accelerations are between $0.2g$ and $1.0g$, the geophones should be completely buried when monitoring in soil, or firmly attached to rock, asphalt or concrete. Appropriate methods of attaching a geophone to these surfaces include double-sided tape, epoxy or quick setting cement. If these methods are unsatisfactory or if maximum particle accelerations exceed $1.0g$, then only cement or bolts are appropriate to secure the geophone to a hard surface. Note that weighting the geophone with a sandbag, for example, is not effective because the bag will move by the same amount as the geophone. In all cases, the geophone should be level and aligned with the longitudinal axis along the radial line to the blast.

*Vibration damage thresholds.* Much work has been carried out to estimate threshold vibration levels for damage to many different types of structures (Siskind *et al.*, 1976, 1980; Stagg *et al.*, 1984). These peak particle velocity levels, which are listed in Table 11.6, have been established from many observations in the field and are now used with confidence as a basis for design of blasts where ground vibrations must be controlled.

The damage criterion most frequently used in urban areas is a peak particle velocity of 50 mm/s, which is the level below which the risk of damage to most residential structures is very slight. However, for poorly constructed buildings, and old buildings of historic interest, allowable vibration levels may be as low as 10 mm/s. The required limit should be determined from the structural condition of the building.

Figure 11.19 shows the relationship between the distance of a structure from the blast, the explosive weight detonated per delay and the expected peak particle velocity at the structure.

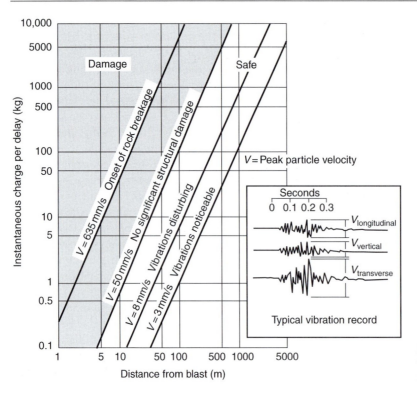

Figure 11.19 Typical blast vibration control diagram for residential structures.

These graphs have been drawn up using the relationship given in equation (11.16) for values of $k = 1600$ and $\beta = -1.5$. It is intended for use as a guideline in the assessment of blast damage for residential structures. If the blast design and this graph indicate that the vibration level is close to the damage threshold, then it is usually wise to carry out trial blasts and measure the vibration levels produced. These data can be used to produce a graph similar to that shown in Figure 11.18, from which the values of the constants $k$ and $\beta$ for the site can be determined. The constants can be used to draw up a blast design based on the calculated allowable charge weight per delay. It has been found that the values of $k$ and $\beta$ will vary considerably from site to site, so vibration measurements are useful in critical situations unless conservative restrictions are placed on allowable explosive weights per delay.

Figure 11.19 shows that 100 kg of explosive detonated per delay may cause minor cracking of plaster in houses at distances less than 100 m from the blast, while the vibrations will be noticeable at distances up to about 850 m. Halving of the mass of explosive detonated per delay to 50 kg will reduce these distances to 70 m and 600 m respectively. Thus, the use of delays to limit the weight of explosive detonated per delay is the most effective method of controlling both damage and reactions of the public to the blasting operations.

*Effect of vibration frequency on ground vibrations.* The frequency of the vibration is also of importance in assessing damage potential. If the principle frequency, that is the frequency of greatest amplitude pulse, is approximately equal to the natural frequency of the structure, then there is a greater risk of damage than if the principle and natural frequencies are significantly different (Dowding, 1985). The natural frequency of two-storey residential buildings is in the range of 5–20 Hz, and the natural frequency diminishes with increasing height of the structure. The principal frequency of a blast will vary with such

*Table 11.5* Instantel DS677 technical specifications

| Ranges | All channels are autoranging. Seismic (three channels): (0–250 mm/s)[a] |
|---|---|
| | Air pressure (one channel): (up to 140 dB peak (200 kPa) |
| Trigger | Seismic: 0.50–50.85 mm/s |
| levels | Air pressure: 92–129 dB (0.8–56.4 kPa) |
| Resolution | Seismic: 0.1245 mm/s |
| | Air pressure: 1 dB (0.02 Pa) |
| Frequency | All channels 2–250 Hz, ±3 dB |
| response | (independent of record time) |
| Recording | Standard: 1–7 s in steps of 1 s |
| times | Option: 1–10 s in steps of 1 s |
| | Additional 0.25 s pre-trigger in all records |
| Acceleration | Computed up to 30 $g$ with a resolution of 0.013 $g$ |
| | (0.01 displayed) |
| Displacement | Computed to 38 mm |
| | Metric resolution 0.000127 mm, 0.001 displayed |

Note
a  Measurement units (Imperial or Metric) are user selectable in the field. Air pressure values are rms weighted.

*Table 11.6* Peak particle velocity threshold damage levels

| Velocity (mm/s) | Effect/damage |
|---|---|
| 3–5 | Vibrations perceptible to humans. |
| 10 | Approximate limit for poorly constructed and historic buildings. |
| 33–50 | Vibrations objectionable to humans. |
| 50 | Limit below which risk of damage to structures is very slight (less than 5%). |
| 125 | Minor damage, cracking of plaster, serious complaints. |
| 230 | Cracks in concrete blocks. |

factors as the type of blast, the distance between the blast and the structure, and the material through which the ground vibrations travel. Typical construction blasts produce vibrations with principal frequencies in the range of about 50–200 Hz. It is found that large quarry andmine blasts produce vibrations with lower principal frequencies than construction blasts, and that principal frequencies decrease with increasing distance from the blast due to frequency attenuation.

Figure 11.20 shows the relationship between peak particle velocity, vibration frequency and approximate damage thresholds for residential structures. This diagram demonstrates that with increasing frequency, the allowable PPV also increases.

*Effect of geology on ground vibrations.* It has been found that blast vibrations are modified by the presence of overburden at the measurement location. In general, vibrations measured on overburden have a lower frequency and higher amplitude than those measured on rock at the same distance from the blast. A consequence of this is that if the particle velocity is approximately the same at two locations, the lower frequency of the vibrations in overburden will make the blast vibrations more readily felt by humans.

*Vibrations in uncured concrete.* On some construction projects there may be a need to carry out blasting operations close to uncured concrete. Under these circumstances, explosive charge weights per delay should be designed to keep ground vibrations within limits that are determined by the age of the concrete, the distance of the concrete from the blast and the type of structure (Oriard and Coulson, 1980; Oriard, 2002). Table 11.7 shows an approximate relationship

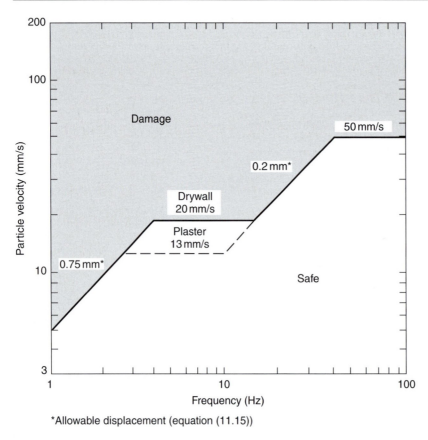

*Figure 11.20* Allowable vibration levels for residential structures due to blasting (Siskind *et al.*, 1980).

*Allowable displacement (equation (11.15))

*Table 11.7* Relationship between age of concrete and allowable peak particle velocity (Oriard, 2002)

| Concrete age from batching | Allowable PPV mm/s (in./s) |
| --- | --- |
| 0–4 h | 100 (4) × DF |
| 4 h to 1 day | 150 (6) × DF |
| 1–3 days | 225 (9) × DF |
| 3–7 days | 300 (12) × DF |
| 7–10 days | 375 (5) × DF |
| More than 10 days | 500 (20) × DF |

| Distance factor, DF | Distance from blast, m (ft) |
| --- | --- |
| 1.0 | 0–15 (0–50) |
| 0.8 | 15–46 (50–150) |
| 0.7 | 46–76 (150–250) |
| 0.6 | >76 (>250) |

between allowable peak particle velocity levels and the concrete age for mass concrete. At ages less than four hours, the concrete has not yet set and ground vibration levels are permissible, with gradually increasing levels allowed as the concrete sets.

Table 11.7 also shows that vibration levels must be reduced with increasing distance, as indicated by the distance factor (DF). Concrete can withstand higher vibration levels at higher frequencies, because at low frequencies greater deflections will be induced in the structure. This is of particular concern for structural walls of freshly poured concrete. Vibration frequencies decrease as the distance from the blast increases because there is an attenuation of frequency with distance. The result of this frequency attenuation is that, at equal curing times, higher vibration levels are permitted at closer distances.

In critical conditions it is recommended that vibration measurements and strength tests be conducted to confirm the performance of the concrete and the relationships given in Table 11.7.

*Electronic equipment and machinery.* Some types of electronic/electrical equipment are sensitive to vibrations. Studies have been done on computer disk drives, telecommunication equipment such as relay stations and fiber optic cables, as well as electrical equipment such as older model power transformers that have mercury cut-out switches. Vibrations from blasting, pile driving, or other construction activities can interfere with the operation of this equipment, and in the absence of guidelines from the manufacturer on allowable vibration levels, it may be necessary to conduct carefully calibrated test blasts.

*Human response to blast vibrations.* Humans are very sensitive to vibrations and can feel the effects of a blast well outside the potential damage zone. Figure 11.21 shows the relationship between peak particle velocity, frequency and the possible human response to vibrations. This indicates that low frequency vibrations are more readily felt than high frequency vibrations. The frequency of blast vibrations is usually in the range of 50–200 Hz.

*Control of vibrations.* The magnitude of blast vibrations at a particular location is dependent upon the distance from the blast and the charge weight per delay. Of the blast design factors discussed in Section 11.4, the most important are the use of delays and the correct detonation sequence so that each hole, or row of holes, breaks toward a free face.

To control vibration levels at a particular distance from the blast, it is necessary to limit the explosive charge detonated per delay according to the relationship given in equation (11.16). Calculation of the allowable charge weight per delay, from either trial blasts or design charts, will determine how many holes can be detonated on a single delay. If the charge weight in a single hole

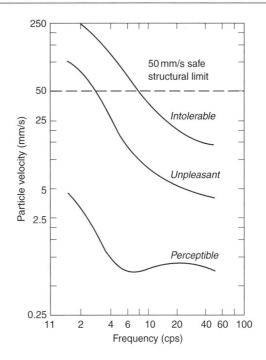

*Figure 11.21* Human response to blast vibrations related to particle velocity and frequency (adapted from Wiss, 1981).

is more than that allowable, then either shorter holes must be drilled, or a decked charge could be used. In a decked charge, the explosive load is separated with stemming material, and each charge is detonated on a separate delay. The minimum delay interval between charges or holes in order to limit the risk of constructive interference of vibrations produced by each charge is about 15–20 ms.

*Pre-blast surveys.* At locations where there is a potential for damage to structures due to blast vibrations, it is usual to carry pre-blast surveys on all structures within the potential damage zone. These surveys should record, with photographs and/or video tape where appropriate, all pre-existing cracks, other structural damage and settlement problems. The Office of Surface Mining (OSM, 2001) has drawn up a standardized method of recording structural damage which ensures that the survey is systematic and

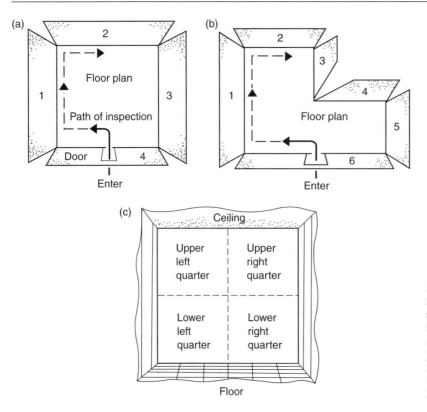

*Figure 11.22* Method of making building damage surveys: (a) wall identification procedure; (b) multi-wall identification procedure; (c) detailed wall identification procedure (Office of Surface Mining, 2001).

thorough (Figure 11.22). In addition to the building survey, a public relations program informing people of the blasting operations, and carefully documented vibration measurements will usually minimize complaints and spurious damage claims.

### 11.5.2  Control of flyrock

When the front row burden is inadequate or when the stemming column is too short to contain the explosive gases, a crater is formed and rock ejected from the crater may be thrown a considerable distance (Figure 11.23). This figure also shows that flyrock can be caused by poor drill alignment, and by geologic conditions that allow venting of the explosive gases along discontinuities in the rock mass.

In practice, the complete control of flyrock is difficult, even if the blast is designed with the recommended stemming and burden dimensions. Therefore, in areas where there is a possibility of damage to structures, blasting mats should be used to control flyrock. Blasting mats consist of rubber tires or strips of conveyor belting chained together. When there is a possibility that the mat could be displaced by the explosive energy, they should be weighted with soil, or anchored to the bedrock.

### 11.5.3  Control of air blast and noise

These two problems are taken together because they both arise from the same cause. Air blast, which occurs close to the blast itself, can cause structural damage such as the breaking of windows. Noise, into which the air blast degenerates with distance from the blast, can cause discomfort and give rise to complaints from those living close to the blasting operations.

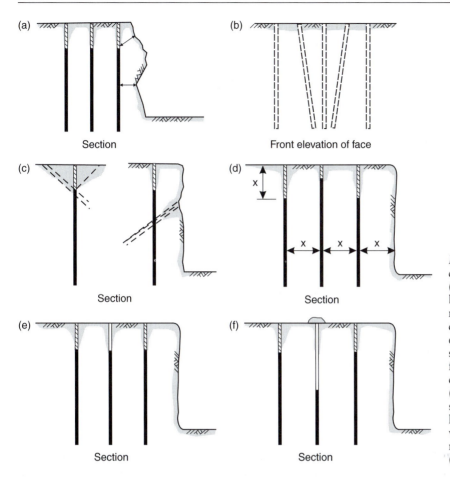

*Figure 11.23* Common causes of flyrock: (a) inadequate front row burden; (b) hole misalignment resulting in concentration of explosives; (c) weak seams vent gas to rock face; (d) holes loaded close to bench surface; (e) some holes with no stemming; (f) blocked holes loaded with fixed weight of explosive or number of cartridges (after CIL, 1984).

Factors contributing to the development of air blast and noise include overcharged blast holes, poor stemming, uncovered detonating cord, venting of explosive gases along cracks in the rock extending to the face, and the use of inadequate burdens giving rise to cratering. In fact, many of the hole layout and charging conditions shown in Figure 11.23 can result in airblast in addition to flyrock.

The propagation of the pressure wave depends upon atmospheric conditions including temperature, wind and the pressure–altitude relationship. Cloud cover can also cause reflection of the pressure wave back to ground level at some distance from the blast. Figure 11.24 gives an indication of how the propagation of the shockwave is affected by the variation of temperature with altitude. This shows that air blast problems can be most severe during temperature inversions.

Figure 11.25 gives a useful guide to the response of structures and humans to sound pressure level (Ladegaard-Pedersen and Dally, 1975). The maximum safe air blast levels recommended by the US Bureau of Mines is 136 dB for pressure measurements made using a linear peak weighting network. The relationship between decibels and pressure $P$ (kPa) is given by the following equation:

$$dB = 20 \log_{10} \left( \frac{P}{P_0} \right) \tag{11.17}$$

where $P_0$ is the over-pressure of the lowest sound that can be heard, about $2 \times 10^{-5}$ kPa.

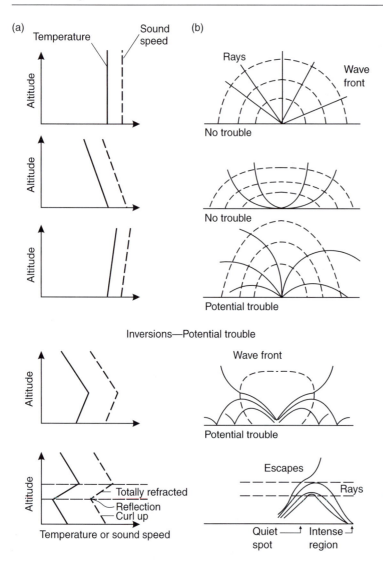

*Figure 11.24* Effect of atmospheric conditions on air blast: (a) variation of temperature and sound speed with altitude; (b) corresponding pattern of sound rays and wave front (Baker, 1973).

The decrease of sound pressure with distance can be predicted by means of cube root scaling. The scaling factor with distance $K_R$ is given by:

$$K_R = \frac{R}{\sqrt[3]{W}} \qquad (11.18)$$

where $R$ is the radial distance from the explosion and $W$ is the weight of charge detonated per delay.

Figure 11.26 gives the results in the original English units of pressure measurements carried out by the US Bureau of Mines in a number of quarries. The burden $B$, was varied and the length of stemming was 2.6 ft per inch (0.31 m stemming per cm) diameter of borehole. For example, if a 1000 lb (454 kg) charge is detonated with a burden of 10 ft (3.1 m), then the over-pressure at a distance of 500 ft (152 m), is found as follows:

$$\frac{R}{\sqrt[3]{W}} = \frac{500}{\sqrt[3]{1000}} = 50$$

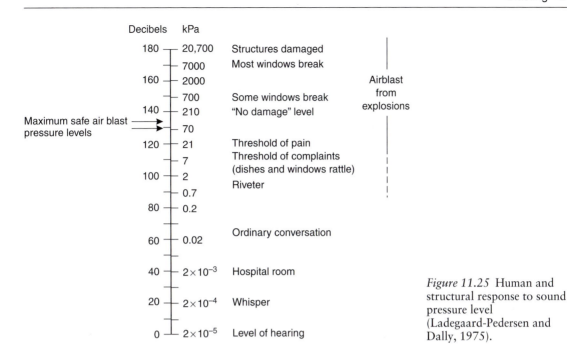

Decibels    kPa

| 180 | 20,700 | Structures damaged |
|  | 7000 | Most windows break |
| 160 | 2000 | |
|  | 700 | Some windows break |
| 140 | 210 | "No damage" level |

Maximum safe air blast pressure levels ➤ 70

| 120 | 21 | Threshold of pain |
|  | 7 | Threshold of complaints |
|  |  | (dishes and windows rattle) |
| 100 | 2 | |
|  |  | Riveter |
|  | 0.7 | |
| 80 | 0.2 | |
| 60 | 0.02 | Ordinary conversation |
| 40 | $2\times10^{-3}$ | Hospital room |
| 20 | $2\times10^{-4}$ | Whisper |
| 0 | $2\times10^{-5}$ | Level of hearing |

Airblast from explosions

*Figure 11.25* Human and structural response to sound pressure level (Ladegaard-Pedersen and Dally, 1975).

and

$$\frac{B}{\sqrt[3]{W}} = \frac{10}{\sqrt[3]{1000}} = 1$$

From Figure 11.26, over-pressure equals about 0.015 psi (0.1 kPa), or 74 db.

These calculations are related to the air blast produced by the explosive charge itself. However, a significant component of the air blast is produced by detonating cord and a reduction in noise can be achieved by covering the detonating cord with sand. Alternatively, a detonating system such as Nonel can be used, which comprises a fine plastic tube that propagates the shock wave with little noise.

## 11.6  Example Problem 11.1: blast design

### Statement

A 6 m high rock bench is to be excavated by blasting. The rock contains thin, well-cemented layers that dip steeply out of the face, and the specific gravity of the rock is 2.6. The available explosive has a specific gravity of 1.3. The broken rock will be excavated by a front-end loader with a maximum vertical reach of 5 m.

### Required

(a)  Determine a suitable blast hole pattern, that is, the burden, spacing, and the diameter of the explosive.

(b)  Determine the depth of subgrade drilling, the length of the stemming and the explosive load per hole.

(c)  Calculate the powder factor (kg/m³).

### Solution

(a)  The bench can be blasted in a single lift because most percussion drills can drill to a depth of 6 m with good directional control and penetration rate, and it would not be dangerous for the loader to dig a 6 m high muck pile.

For a stiffness ratio of 0.3 and a bench height of 6 m, the required burden distance

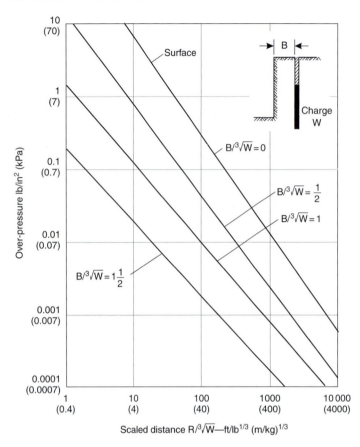

*Figure 11.26* Over-pressure as a function of scaled distance for bench blasting (Ladegaard-Pedersen and Dally, 1975).

is 1.8 m (see equation (11.1)). The adjusted burden to account for the rock condition is 2.3 m, using equation (11.4) with $k_\psi = 1.18$ and $k_s = 1.1$.

The explosive diameter, calculated from equation (11.2), is 78 mm.

The spacing between holes, calculated from equation (11.5), is 2.8 m.

(b) The depth of subgrade drilling is 0.7 m, based on a subgrade depth equal to 0.3 of the burden.

The length of the stemming is 1.6 m, based on a stemming length equal to 0.7 of the burden.

The length of the explosive column is 5.1 m, based on a bench height of 6 m, a subgrade depth of 0.7 m and a stemming length of 1.6 m. For this explosive length, a specific

gravity of 1.3 and a diameter of 78 mm, the weight of explosive per hole is 31.7 kg.

(c) The volume of rock to be broken per hole is 38.6 m³, for a bench height of 6 m, a burden of 2.3 m and a spacing of 2.8 m.

The powder factor is 0.8 kg/m³. With reference to Figure 11.8, the average boulder size of the blasted rock will be about 0.4 m, which can be readily loaded with a front-end loader.

## 11.7   Example Problem 11.2: controlled blasting design

### Statement

A 6 m high slope has been previously excavated for a highway by blasting, and it is required that the face be trimmed back by 3 m. It is necessary that controlled blasting be used for this trimming operation so that there is minimal overbreak and the new face is stable.

### Required

(a) Determine the most appropriate type of controlled blasting for this operation.
(b) If the explosive available has a diameter of 25 mm, calculate the blast hole diameter, explosive charge (kg/m of hole) and hole spacing.
(c) If the explosive has a specific gravity of 1.1, determine how the explosive can be distributed in the hole to achieve the required charge.
(d) Assess if it is necessary for a second row of blast holes to be drilled between the present face and the final line. If a second row is necessary, determine how far should this row be from the final line, and what detonation sequence should be used.

### Solution

(a) Cushion blasting should be used to remove the 3 m thick slice of rock. In highway construction, it is rarely necessary to use line drilling because it is expensive and is only used where very high quality slopes are required. Pre-shearing would be used only where the burden is at least equal to the bench height.
(b) For an explosive diameter of 25 mm, a 50 mm diameter hole would produce a decoupling ratio of 2. The required explosive charge per meter of blast hole is 0.21 kg/m, from equation (11.9a).

   The spacing between holes would be 0.8 m, from equation (11.10b).
(c) The weight of explosive for a 25 mm diameter cartridge with a specific gravity of 1.1 is 0.54 kg/m. To produce an explosive charge of 0.21 kg/m, a possible distribution of this explosive up the hole would

be to have cartridge length of 200 mm, with 300 mm long spacers between each cartridge.
(d) From equation (11.11), the required burden is at least 1 m. Since the total burden on the cushion blast is 3 m, it would be necessary to drill a row or holes about 1.5 m behind the face. The detonation sequence would be to fire the front row at least 20 ms before the final row, based on equation (11.7a).

## 11.8 Example Problem 11.3: blast damage control

### Statement

A historic building is located 140 m from the blast site and a hospital is located at a distance of 1 km.

### Required

(a) Determine the maximum allowable charge weight per delay to minimize the risk of damage to the historic building.
(b) Determine if the ground vibrations would be disturbing to patients in the hospital.

### Solution

(a) Allowable charge weights per delay are determined from damage threshold vibration levels for different structures listed in Table 11.6 and from equation (11.16).

   If $k = 1600$ and $\beta = -1.5$ and the threshold for damage to the historic building is 10 mm/s, then at $R = 140$ m, the allowable instantaneous charge, $W$ is 23 kg/delay.
(b) Figure 11.21 shows that vibrations are objectionable to humans when the peak particle velocity exceeds about 33–50 mm/s. For a charge weight per delay of 23 kg, equation (11.16) shows that the vibration levels at the hospital would be about 0.5 mm/s, so they are unlikely to be even perceptible by the patients (perceptible threshold is about 3–5 mm/s).

# Chapter 12

# Stabilization of rock slopes

## 12.1 Introduction

In mountainous terrain, the operation of highways and railways, power generation and transmission facilities, and the safety of residential and commercial developments often require stable slopes and control of rock falls. This applies to both excavated and natural slopes. In contrast, open pit mines tolerate a certain degree of slope instability unless there is a hazard to the miners or a significant loss of production. For example, minor failures of benches usually have little effect on operations unless the fall lands on a haul road and results in tire or equipment damage. In the event of a large-scale slope failure in an open pit mine, often the only economic and feasible stabilization measure is drainage, which may involve long horizontal drains, pumped wells or drainage adits (see Section 12.4.6). A more common means of managing large-scale slope instability is to monitor the movement so that mining can continue beneath the moving slope. Procedures for monitoring movement and interpreting the results are discussed in Chapter 13.

This chapter is concerned mainly with civil slopes because the high cost of failures means that stabilization programs are often economically justified. For example, on highways, even minor falls can cause damage to vehicles, injury or death to drivers and passengers, and possibly discharge of toxic substances where transport vehicles are damaged. Also, substantial slope failures on transportation systems can severely disrupt traffic, usually resulting in both direct and indirect economic losses. For railroads and toll highways, closures result in a direct loss of revenue. Figure 12.1 shows a rock slide that occurred from a height of about 300 m above the road and closed both the road and an adjacent railway.

While the cost of a slide, such as that shown in Figure 12.1 is substantial, the cost of even a single vehicle accident can be significant. For example, costs may be incurred for hospitalization of the driver and passengers, for repair to the vehicle, and in some cases for legal charges and compensation payments. Often there are additional costs for stabilization of the slope that will involve both engineering and contracting charges, usually carried out at premium rates because of the emergency nature of the work.

Many transportation systems were constructed over a century ago in the case of railroads, and decades ago in the case of many highways. At that time, the blasting techniques that were often used in construction caused significant damage to the rock. Furthermore, since the time of construction deterioration of stability conditions is likely due to weathering of the rock, and loosening of the surficial blocks by ice and water, and by the growth of tree roots. All these effects can result in on-going instability that may justify remediation programs.

For urban developments in mountainous terrain, hazards that can threaten or even destroy structures include rolling boulders and landslides. The most effective protection against these conditions is initial hazard mapping, and then zoning

*Figure 12.1* Highway closure caused by rock fall in very strong, blocky granite from a height of about 300 m.

unsafe areas to preclude development where mitigation cannot be carried out.

In order to minimize the cost of falls, rock slope stabilization programs are often a preferred alternative to relocation or abandonment of the facility. Such programs involve a number of inter-related issues including geotechnical and environmental engineering, safety, construction methods and costs, and contracting procedures. Methods for the design of stabilization measures for rock slopes are described in this chapter, and in other references such as Brawner and Wyllie (1975); Fookes and Sweeney (1976); Piteau and Peckover (1978); Wyllie (1991); Schuster (1992); Federal Highway Administration (FHWA) (1993, 1998); Transportation Research Board (TRB) (1996) and Morris and Wood (1999). These procedures have been used extensively since the 1970s and can, therefore, be used with confidence for a wide range of geological conditions. However, as described in this chapter, it is essential that appropriate method(s) be used for the particular conditions at each site.

The first part of this chapter discusses the cause of rock falls, and the planning and management of stabilization programs. For systems with a large number of rock slopes, these programs usually involve making an inventory of rock fall hazards and stability conditions, and maintaining these records in a database and linked GIS map, and preparing a prioritized stabilization schedule. The remainder of the chapter discusses stabilization measures, categorized according to rock reinforcement, rock removal and rock fall protection.

## 12.2 Causes of rock falls

The State of California made a comprehensive study of rock falls that occurred on the state highway system to assess both the causes of the rock falls and the effectiveness of the various remedial measures that have been implemented (McCauley *et al.*, 1985). With the diverse topography and climate within California, their records provide a useful guideline on the stability conditions of rock slopes and the causes of falls. Table 12.1 show the results of a study of a total of 308 rock falls on California highways in which 14 different causes of instability were identified.

Of the 14 causes of rock falls, 6 are directly related to water, namely rain, freeze–thaw, snow-melt, channeled runoff, differential erosion, and springs and seeps. There is also one cause that is indirectly related to rainfall—the growth of tree roots in cracks that can open fractures and loosen blocks of rock on the face. These seven causes of rock falls together account for 68% of the total falls. These statistics are confirmed by the authors' experience in the analysis of rock fall records over a 25-year period on a major railroad in western Canada in which approximately 70% of the events occurred during the winter. The weather conditions during the winter included heavy rainfall, prolonged periods of freezing temperatures, and daily freeze–thaw cycles in the fall and spring. The results of a similar study carried out by Peckover (1975) are shown in Figure 12.2. They clearly show that the majority of rock falls occurred between October and March, the wettest and coldest time of the year in western Canada. Also in this geographical area, studies have been conducted on the relationship between the frequency and volume of rock slides (Hungr et al., 1999). The study showed that for falls with volumes less than $1\,m^3$, there were as many as 50 falls per year, whereas falls with volumes of $10,000\,m^3$ occurred every 10–50 years approximately.

The other major cause of rock falls in the California study is the particular geologic conditions at each site, namely fractured rock, adverse planar fractures (fractures dipping out of slope face), and soil decomposition. These three causes represented 17% of the falls, and the total rock falls caused by water and geologic factors accounted for 85% of the falls. These statistics demonstrate that water and geology are the most important factors influencing rock slope stability.

It appears that the study in California was carried out during a time that there were no significant earthquakes, because these events frequently trigger rock falls, and cause displacement

*Table 12.1* Causes of rock falls on highways in California

| Cause of rock fall | Percentage of falls |
| --- | --- |
| Rain | 30 |
| Freeze–thaw | 21 |
| Fractured rock | 12 |
| Wind | 12 |
| Snowmelt | 8 |
| Channeled runoff | 7 |
| Adverse planar fracture | 5 |
| Burrowing animals | 2 |
| Differential erosion | 1 |
| Tree roots | 0.6 |
| Springs or seeps | 0.6 |
| Wild animals | 0.3 |
| Truck vibrations | 0.3 |
| Soil decomposition | 0.3 |

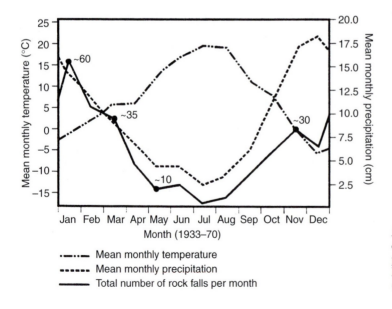

Mean monthly temperature (°C)

Mean monthly precipitation (cm)

Month (1933–70)

·—··— Mean monthly temperature
······ Mean monthly precipitation
——— Total number of rock falls per month

*Figure 12.2* Correlation of number of rock falls with temperature and precipitation on railway lines in Fraser Canyon, British Columbia (Peckover 1975).

and failure of landslides (Van Velsor and Walkinshaw, 1991; Jibson and Harp, 1995). Section 6.5 discusses methods to incorporate seismic ground motion in slope stability analyses.

## 12.3   Rock slope stabilization programs

On transportation systems in mountainous terrain, there may be hundreds of rock slopes with a variety of rock fall hazards resulting in a significant cost to the operator. Under these circumstances, a long-term, multi-year stabilization program is often justified; this section describes the steps involved in implementing such a program.

### 12.3.1   Planning stabilization programs

When implementing a program to stabilize a large number of slopes, the best use of available funds is often made by setting up a systematic program that identifies and rates the most hazardous sites. Annual stabilization work can then be scheduled, with the most hazardous sites having the highest priority. Table 12.2 shows an example of how such a program may be structured.

The objective of the program shown in Table 12.2 is to be proactive in identifying and stabilizing slopes before rock falls and accidents occur. This requires a careful examination of each site to identify the potential hazard, and estimate the likely benefit of the stabilization work. In

contrast, a reactive program places the emphasis in areas where rock falls and accidents have already occurred, and where the hazard may then be diminished.

An effective proactive approach to stabilization requires a consistent, long-term program under the direction of a team experienced in both the engineering and construction aspects of this work. Another important component of this work is to keep accurate records, with photographs, of slope conditions, rock falls and stabilization work. This information will document the location of hazardous areas and determine the long-term effectiveness of the program in reducing the incidence of rock falls. These records can be most conveniently handled using database programs that readily allow updating and retrieval of records.

### 12.3.2   Rock slope inventory systems

The relative rock fall hazard at a site as compared to other sites can be used in selecting priorities. Early work on this topic by Brawner and Wyllie (1975) and Wyllie (1987), was adapted by Pierson *et al.* (1990) into a process for the rational management of rock slopes on highways, which has been named the Rock Fall Hazard Rating System (RHRS). The first step in this process is to make an inventory of the stability conditions of each slope so that they can be ranked according to their rock fall hazard (Steps 1 and 2 in Table 12.2).

The rock fall areas identified in the inventory are ranked by scoring the categories shown in

*Table 12.2* Rock slope stabilization for transportation systems

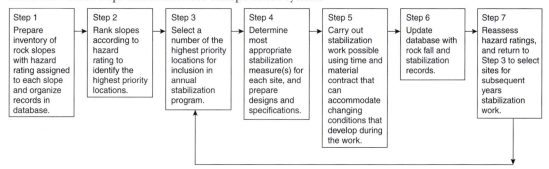

*Table 12.3* Summary sheet of the rock fall hazard rating system (Wyllie, 1987; Pierson *et al.*, 1990)

| Category | Rating criteria and score | | | |
|---|---|---|---|---|
| | *Points 3* | *Points 9* | *Points 27* | *Points 81* |
| (a) Slope height (m) | 7.5 m | 15 m | 23 m | 30 m |
| (b) Ditch effectiveness | Good catchment | Moderate catchment | Limited catchment | No catchment |
| (c) Average vehicle risk (% of time) | 25% of the time | 50% of the time | 75% of the time | 100% of the time |
| (d) Percentage of decision sight distance (% of design value) | Adequate sight distance, 100% of design value | Moderate sight distance, 80% of design value | Limited sight distance, 60% of design value | Very limited sight distance 40% of design value |
| (e) Roadway width including paved shoulders (m) | 13.5 m | 11 m | 8.5 m | 6 m |
| (f) *Geologic character* Case 1 Structural condition | Discontinuous joints, favorable orientation | Discontinuous joints, random orientation | Continuous joints, adverse orientation | Continuous joints, adverse orientation |
| Rock friction | Rough, irregular | Undulating | Planar | Clay infilling, or slickensided |
| Case 2 Structural condition | Few differential erosion features | Occasional erosion features | Many erosion features | Major erosion features |
| Difference in erosion rates | Small difference | Moderate difference | Large difference | Extreme difference |
| (g) Block size ___ Quantity of rock fall event | 0.3 m ___ 3 m$^3$ | 0.6 m ___ 6 m$^3$ | 1.0 m ___ 9 m$^3$ | 1.2 m ___ 12 m$^3$ |
| (h) Climate and presence of water on slope | Low to moderate precipitation; no freezing periods, no water on slope | Moderate precipitation, or short freezing periods, or intermittent water on slope | High precipitation or long freezing periods, or continual water on slope | High precipitation and long freezing periods, or continual water on slope and long freezing periods |
| (i) Rock fall history | Few falls | Occasional falls | Many falls | Constant falls |

Table 12.3. These categories represent the significant elements of a rock slope that contribute to the overall hazard. The four columns correspond to logical breaks in the hazard represented by each category. The criteria scores increase exponentially from 3 to 81 points, and represent a continuum of points from 1 to 100. An exponential system allows for a rapid increase in score which distinguishes the more hazardous sites. Using a continuum of points allows flexibility in evaluating the relative impact of conditions that are variable by nature. Some categories require a subjective evaluation while others can be directly measured and then scored.

### 12.3.3  *Hazard rating criteria*

The following is a brief description of each of the categories that are used to rate the rock fall hazard along a highway (refer to Table 12.3).

(a) *Slope height*—Vertical height of the slope measured from the highest point from which rock fall is expected. If falls originate from the natural slope above the cut, the cut height plus the additional slope height (vertical distance) is used.

(b) *Ditch effectiveness*—effectiveness of a ditch is measured by its ability to prevent falling rock from reaching the traveled way. In estimating the ditch effectiveness, four factors are to be considered: (1) slope height and angle; (2) ditch width, depth and shape; (3) anticipated block size and quantity of rock fall; and (4) effect on rock fall trajectories of slope irregularities (launching features). A launching feature can negate the benefits expected from a fallout area. The ditch effectiveness can be assessed both by comparing the dimensions with those recommended in the ditch design chart shown in Figure 12.21 (Ritchie, 1963), and from information provided by maintenance personnel.

(c) *Average Vehicle Risk (AVR)*—AVR represents the percentage of time a vehicle will be present in the rock fall section. The percentage is obtained from the average daily traffic count (vehicles per day, ADT), the length of the rock fall hazard area (*L*, km) and the posted speed limit (*S*, km/h) by the following relationship:

$$AVR\ (\%) = \frac{(ADT/(24\,h/d))L}{S} \times 100\%$$

(12.1)

For example, if the length of the slope is 0.2 km in an area where the posted speed is 90 kph and the average daily traffic count is 7000 vehicles per day, the average vehicle risk is 65% and the corresponding hazard score is 18. A rating of 100% means that on average at least one vehicle can be expected to be under the slope at all times, and the hazard score is 81.

(d) *Percentage of decision sight distance (DSD)*—The DSD is used to determine the

*Table 12.4* Decision site distance to avoid obstacles

| Posted speed limit, kph (mph) | Decision site distance, m (ft) |
|---|---|
| 48 (30) | 137 (450) |
| 64 (40) | 183 (600) |
| 80 (50) | 229 (750) |
| 97 (60) | 305 (1000) |
| 113 (70) | 335 (1100) |

length of roadway (in m) needed to make a complex or instantaneous decision. The DSD is critical when obstacles on the road are difficult to perceive, or when unexpected or unusual maneuvers are required. Sight distance is the shortest distance along a roadway that an object is continuously visible to the driver. Throughout a rock fall section, the sight distance can change appreciably. Horizontal and vertical highway curves, together with obstructions such as rock outcrops and roadside vegetation can severely limit the available sight distance. The relationship between DSD and the posted speed limit used in the inventory system has been modified from AASHTO's Policy on Geometric Design of Highways and Streets (1984) as shown in Table 12.4.

The actual site distance is related to the DSD by equation (12.2) as follows:

$$DSD\ (\%) = \frac{Actual\ site\ distance}{Desision\ site\ distance} \times 100\%$$

(12.2)

For example, if the actual site distance is restricted by the road curvature to 120 m in a zone with a posted speed limit of 80 kph, then the DSD is 52%. Based on the charts provided in the RHRS manual, the score for this condition is 42.

(e) *Roadway width*—It is the dimension that represents the available maneuvering room to avoid a rock fall, measured perpendicular to the highway centerline from edge of pavement to edge of pavement. The minimum width is measured when the roadway width is not constant.

(f)  *Geologic character*—Geologic conditions that cause rock fall generally fit into two cases. *Case 1* is for slopes where joints, bedding planes or other discontinuities are the dominant structural features of a rock slope. *Case 2* is for slopes where differential erosion forming overhangs or over-steepened slopes is the dominant condition that controls rock fall. The case which best fits the slope should be used when doing the evaluation. If both situations are present, both are scored but only the worst case (highest score) is used in the rating.

### Geologic character—Case 1

*Structural condition*—Adverse discontinuities are those with orientations that promote plane, wedge or toppling failures.

*Rock friction*—Friction on a discontinuity is governed by the characteristics of the rock material and any infilling, as well as the surface roughness (see Chapter 4, Section 4.2.4).

### Geologic character—Case 2

*Structural condition*—Differential erosion or over-steepening is the dominant condition that leads to rock fall. Erosion features include over-steepened slopes, unsupported rock units or exposed resistant rocks.

*Difference in erosion rates*—Different rates of erosion within a slope directly relate to the potential for a future rock fall event. The score should reflect how quickly erosion is occurring; the size of rocks, blocks or units being exposed; the frequency of falls; and the amount of material released during a rock fall.

(g)  *Block size or volume of rock fall per event*— Type of event most likely to occur, related to the spacings and continuous lengths of the discontinuity sets. The score should also take into account any tendency of the blocks of rock to break up as they fall down the slope.

(h)  *Climate and presence of water on slope*— Water and freeze–thaw cycles contribute to both the weathering and movement of rock materials. If water is known to flow continually or intermittently on the slope, it is rated accordingly. This rating could be based on the relative precipitation over the region in which the ratings are being made, and incorporate the influence of freeze–thaw cycles.

(i)  *Rock fall history*—Historical information is an important check on the potential for future rock falls. Development of a database of rock falls allows more accurate conclusions to be made of the rock fall potential.

### 12.3.4  Database analysis of slope inventory

It is common practice to enter the results of the slope inventory into a computer database. The database can be used both to analyze the data contained in the inventory and to facilitate updating the inventory with new information on rock falls and construction work. The following are some examples of database analysis:

- Rank slopes in order of increasing point score to identify the most hazardous sites.
- Correlate rock fall frequency with such factors as weather conditions, rock type, and slope location.
- Assess severity of rock falls from analysis of delay hours or road closures caused by falls.
- Assess effectiveness of stabilization work from annual number of rock falls.

### 12.3.5  Selection of high priority sites

It has been found that, when managing on-going stabilization programs with durations of possibly several decades and involving many hundreds of rock slopes, there is a need to put in place a rational process for selecting high priority sites.

This becomes necessary because slope stability conditions deteriorate over time, and it is not possible to re-rate every slope, every year, according to the scoring system shown in Table 12.3. However, it is possible to inspect all the higher priority slopes on an annual basis to assess stability, and from this assessment determine whether stabilization is required and within what time frame. This involves assigning each slope an "Inspection Rating" and a corresponding "Required Action" (see Table 12.5). The filled boxes in the table indicate allowable Actions for each of the Ratings. For example, for an Urgent slope the permissible actions are to limit service and work at the site within one month, or to carry out a follow-up inspection to assess stability conditions in more detail. However, for either an Urgent or Priority slope it is not permissible to assign "No Action" to the site.

The following are examples of criteria that could be used to assign Inspection Ratings, using a combination of measurement, the rating scores given in Table 12.5, and subjective observations of stability:

- *Urgent*—Obvious recent movement or rock falls, kinematically feasible block with dimensions large enough to be a hazard; weather conditions are detrimental to stability. Failure possible within next few months.
- *Priority*—Likely movement since last inspection of block, large enough to be a hazard; failure possible within next two years approximately.

- *Observe*—Possible recent movement, but no imminent instability. Check specific stability conditions in next inspection.
- *OK*—no evidence of slope movement.

It has been found that there are two primary benefits in assigning a Required Action for every slope. First, this forces the inspector to make a decision on the urgency for mitigation, and second, it automatically draws up a list of work sites for the current year and the next two years. This list becomes the basic planning tool for the on-going program.

### 12.3.6  Selection of stabilization measures

This section provides some guidelines on selecting the method, or methods, of stabilization that are most appropriate for the topographical, geological and operational conditions at the site. Methods of slope stabilization fall into three categories:

(a)  Reinforcement;
(b)  Rock removal; and
(c)  Protection.

Figure 12.3 includes 16 of the more common stabilization measures divided into these categories. The following are examples of the factors that will influence the selection of appropriate stabilization methods. Where the slope is steep and the toe is close to the highway or railway, there will be no space to excavate a catch ditch or

*Table 12.5* Inspection ratings and corresponding actions

| Inspection Rating | Required Actions | | | | |
|---|---|---|---|---|---|
| | Limit service; work within 1 month | Work in current year | Follow-up inspection | Work in 1–2 years | No action |
| Urgent | × | | × | | |
| Priority | | × | × | × | |
| Observe | | | | | × |
| Okay | | | | | × |

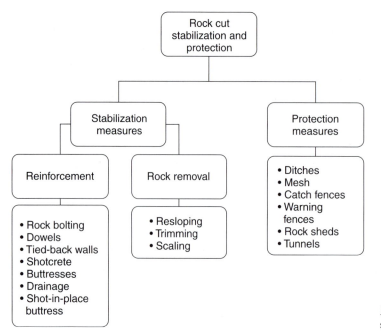

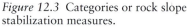

*Figure 12.3* Categories or rock slope stabilization measures.

construct a barrier. Therefore, alternative stabilization measures may be to remove loose rock, secure it in place with bolts, or to drape mesh on the slope. It is generally preferable to remove loose rock and eliminate the hazard, but only if this will form a stable face and not undermine other potentially loose rock on the face. If the source of the rock falls is a zone of boulders in an erodible soil matrix that cannot be stabilized by bolting of effectively scaled, then a combination ditch–containment structure may be more suitable. If there is limited space at the toe of the slope for this work, there may be no alternative but to relocate or realign the facility.

When selecting and designing stabilization measures that are appropriate for a site, geotechnical, construction and environmental issues must be considered. The geotechnical issues—geology, rock strength, ground water, and stability analysis—are discussed in previous chapters. Construction and environmental issues, which can affect the costs and schedule of the work, must be addressed during the design phase of the project. Issues that are frequently important

are equipment access, available work time during traffic closures, and disposal of waste rock and soil.

Another factor to consider in the selection of stabilization measures is the optimum level of work. For example, a minor scaling project will remove the loosest rock on the slope face, but, if the rock is susceptible to weathering, this work may have to be repeated every three to five years. Alternatively, a more comprehensive program can be carried out using shotcrete and bolting, in addition to scaling. Although the initial costs of this second program would be higher, it would be effective for a longer period, perhaps for 20–30 years. Alternative stabilization programs such as these, including the alternative of doing no work, can be compared using decision analysis. Decision analysis is a systematic procedure for evaluating alternative courses of action taking into account the likely range of construction costs and design life of the stabilization work, as well as the probability and costs of rock falls occurring and causing accidents (Wyllie, 1980; Roberds, 1991; Roberds *et al.*, 2002).

The following is a brief discussion of some construction issues that may have a significant influence on stabilization work.

*Blasting.*   Damage to rock faces by excessively heavy blasting is a frequent cause of instability in the years following excavation of a slope. Methods of controlled blasting, such as pre-shearing and trim blasting as described in Chapter 11, can be used to excavate a slope to a specified line with minimal damage to the rock behind the face.

*Topography.*   If there is a steep slope above the crest of a cut, then stabilization work that involves laying back the cut will have the effect of increasing the height of the cut. This increase in the cut height will require a larger catch ditch, and may result in additional stability problems, especially if there is a substantial layer of soil or weathered rock at the surface.

*Construction access.*   Determine the type of equipment that is likely to be required to carry out the work, and how this equipment will be used at the site. For example, if it is planned to excavate a substantial volume of rock in order to lay back a slope, then it is likely that airtrac drills and excavators will have to work on the slope. In steep terrain, it may be found that the construction of an access road for this equipment is costly and causes additional instability. Furthermore, a cut width of at least 5 m is required to provide sufficient working width for this equipment. Also, if stabilization work is planned using large diameter rock bolts, then it is essential that suitable drilling equipment can access the site. For example, on steep faces, holes with a diameter larger than about 100 mm will have to be drilled with heavy equipment supported from a crane. Where it is not possible to use such heavy drilling equipment, it would be necessary to drill smaller diameter holes with hand-held equipment, and use a larger number of smaller size bolts.

*Construction costs.*   Cost estimates for stabilization work must take into account both the costs of the work on the slope, and indirect costs such as mobilization, traffic control, waste disposal, and environmental studies as discussed next. A significant cost issue on active transportation routes is the use of cranes to access the slope. If the work is done from a platform suspended from a crane located on the road, this may block two to three lanes of traffic. In contrast, traffic closures can be minimized by having the construction crews work off ropes secured behind the crest of the slope.

*Waste disposal.*   The least expensive method of disposing of waste rock produced by excavation and scaling operations in mountainous terrain is dumping rock down the slope below the site. However, disposing of waste rock in this manner has a number of drawbacks. First, a steeply sloping pile of loose rock may be a visual scar on the hillside which can be difficult to vegetate. Second, the waste rock may become unstable if not adequately drained or keyed into the existing slope; if it fails, the material may move a considerable distance and endanger facilities located down-slope. Third, where the site is located in a river valley, the dumped rock may fall in the river and have a deleterious effect on fish populations. In order to minimize these impacts, it is sometimes required that the excavated rock be hauled to designated, stable waste sites.

Another problem that may need to be addressed in the disposal of waste rock is acid-water drainage. In areas of North Carolina and Tennessee, for example, some argillite and schist formations contain iron-disulfides; percolation of water through fills constructed with this rock produces low pH, acidic runoff. One method that has been used to control this condition is to mix the rock with lime to neutralize the acid potential and then to place the blended material in the center of the fill (Byerly and Middleton, 1981). Sometimes it is necessary to encase the rock–lime mixture in an impervious plastic membrane.

*Aesthetics.*   A series of steep, high rock cuts above a highway may have a significant visual impact when viewed both by the road user and the local population. In scenic areas, it may be desirable to incorporate appropriate landscaping measures in the design of the rock cuts in order to minimize their visual impact (Norrish and Lowell, 1988). Examples of aesthetic treatments of rock

faces include designing blasts to produce an irregular face with no traces of the blast holes, to
recess the heads of rock bolts, and to color and
sculpt shotcrete so that it has the appearance
of rock.

*Dust, noise, ground vibration.* Many rock
stabilization operations can produce considerable
noise and dust, and blasting has the additional
risk of ground vibrations (see Section 11.5.1).
Prior to letting the contract, consideration should
be given to the acceptable ground vibration levels
for the site conditions, so that the necessary steps
can be taken to limit their effects.

*Biological and botanical effects.* On some
projects steps may have to be taken to limit
disturbance to wildlife and vegetation. Typical
precautions that can be taken are to schedule
work outside of specified "windows" of animal

activity, and to relocate protected plants outside
the work area.

## 12.4   Stabilization by rock reinforcement

Figure 12.4 shows a number of reinforcement
techniques that may be implemented to secure
potentially loose rock on the face of a rock cut.
The common feature of all these techniques is that
they minimize relaxation and loosening of the
rock mass that may take place as a result of excavation. Once relaxation has been allowed to take
place, there is a loss of interlock between the
blocks of rock and a significant decrease in the
shear strength. Figure 4.13 illustrates the effect
of installing rock bolts to maintain the interlock
on high roughness angle, second-order asperities. Once relaxation has taken place, it is not

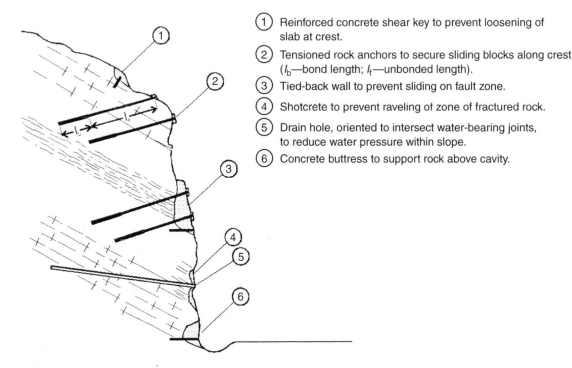

① Reinforced concrete shear key to prevent loosening of slab at crest.

② Tensioned rock anchors to secure sliding blocks along crest ($l_b$—bond length; $l_t$—unbonded length).

③ Tied-back wall to prevent sliding on fault zone.

④ Shotcrete to prevent raveling of zone of fractured rock.

⑤ Drain hole, oriented to intersect water-bearing joints, to reduce water pressure within slope.

⑥ Concrete buttress to support rock above cavity.

*Figure 12.4* Rock slope reinforcement methods (TRB, 1996).

possible to reverse the process. For this reason, reinforcement of rock slopes is most effective if it is installed prior to excavation—a process known as pre-reinforcement.

### 12.4.1  Shear keys

Reinforced shear keys provide support for blocks of rock up to about a meter thick, as well as zones of loose and weathered rock at the crest of the slope (Figure 12.4, Item 1). Shear keys are used where the support required is limited by the size of the blocks, and to prevent raveling and loosening of closely fractured, weak rock. If rock bolts were to be installed in this rock, the raveling would soon expose the head of the bolt resulting in loss of support.

Shear keys comprise lengths of reinforcing steel about 25–32 mm diameter and about 1000 mm long fully grouted into holes about 500–750 mm deep drilled into stable rock. The holes are located close to the toe of the rock to be supported, and are spaced about 500–1000 mm apart, depending on the support required. Lengths of reinforcing bars, about 6–8 mm diameter, are then placed horizontally and secured to the vertical bars. Finally, the reinforcing steel is fully encapsulated in shotcrete, or concrete poured in intimate contact with the rock.

The support provided by the shear key is equal to the shear strength of the vertical steel bars, and possibly the cohesion of the rock-concrete surface. The shear key acts as a resisting force in the limit equilibrium equations (see Section 6.3), and if the magnitude of this shear force is $R_k$, then the factor of safety for a block with weight $W$ is

$$FS = \frac{W \cos \psi_p \tan \phi + R_k}{W \sin \psi_p} \qquad (12.3)$$

where $\psi_p$ is the dip of the base of the block and $\phi$ is the friction angle on the base of the rock block (assuming a dry slope). The factor of safety calculated by equation (12.3) could be for a unit length of the slope, or a specified length, depending on how forces $W$ and $R_k$ are defined.

Shear keys on a much larger scale have been used for the stabilization of dam foundations and abutments (Moore and Imrie, 1982). A tunnel was driven along a distinctly defined shear zone, with the excavation extending into sound rock on either side of the tunnel. The tunnel was then filled with concrete to create a high strength inclusion along the sliding plane.

### 12.4.2  Rock anchors

Typical applications of rock anchors, as shown in Figure 12.4, items 2 and 3, are to prevent sliding of blocks or wedges of rock on discontinuities dipping out of the face. It is important to note that the primary function of rock anchors is to modify the normal and shear forces acting on the sliding planes, rather than to rely on the shear strength of steel where the anchor crosses this plane. In this chapter, the term "rock anchor" refers to both rigid bars and flexible cables that can be used in bundles; the design principles and construction methods are similar for both materials.

Rock anchors may be fully grouted and untensioned, or anchored at the distal end and tensioned. The different applications of untensioned, pre-reinforcement bolts and tensioned anchors are shown in Figure 12.5 (see also Figure 4.13). Pre-reinforcement of an excavation may be achieved by installing fully grouted but untensioned bolts (dowels) at the crest of the cut prior to excavation. The fully bonded dowels prevent loss of interlock of the rock mass because the grouted bolts are sufficiently stiff to prevent movement on the discontinuities (Moore and Imrie, 1982; Spang and Egger, 1990). However, where blocks have moved and relaxed, it is generally necessary to install tensioned anchors to prevent further displacement and loss of interlock. The advantages of untensioned bolts are their lower cost and quicker installation compared to tensioned anchors.

Tensioned rock anchors are installed across potential slide surfaces and bonded in sound rock beyond the surface. The application of a tensile force in the anchor, which is transmitted into the

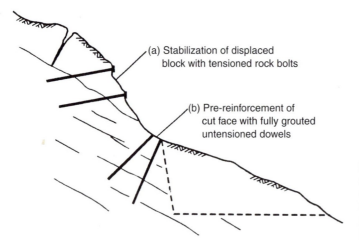

(a) Stabilization of displaced block with tensioned rock bolts

(b) Pre-reinforcement of cut face with fully grouted untensioned dowels

*Figure 12.5* Reinforcement of a rock slope: (a) tensioned rock bolts in a displaced block; (b) fully grouted, untensioned dowels installed prior to excavation to pre-reinforce the rock (TRB, 1996).

rock by a reaction plate at the rock surface, produces compression in the rock mass, and modifies the normal and shear stresses on the slide surface. Chapters 6, 7 and 9 each contain design information on the procedures for calculating both the anchor force and anchor orientation required to produce a specified factor of safety; as discussed in Section 6.4, there is an optimum anchor orientation that minimizes the required force.

Once the anchor force and hole orientation requirements have been determined, the following nine steps are involved in an anchor installation (Littlejohn and Bruce, 1977; FHWA, 1982; BSI, 1989; Xanthakos, 1991; PTI, 1996; Wyllie, 1999).

*Step 1: Drilling*—Determine drill hole diameter and length that can be drilled at the site based on available equipment and the access for this equipment.

*Step 2: Bolt materials and dimensions*—Select anchor materials and dimensions that are compatible with hole diameter and the required anchoring force.

*Step 3: Corrosion*—Assess the corrosivity of the site, and apply an appropriate level of corrosion protection to the anchors.

*Step 4: Bond type*—Select either cement or resin grout or a mechanical anchor to secure the distal end of the anchor in the hole. Factors influencing this decision include the hole diameter, tensile load, anchor length, rock strength and speed of installation.

*Step 5: Bond length*—Based on the bonding type, hole diameter, anchor tension and rock strength, calculate the required bond length.

*Step 6: Total anchor length*—Calculate the total anchor length, which is the total of the bond length and free stressing length. The free stressing length should extend from the rock surface to the top of the bond zone, with the top of the bond zone being below the potential sliding plane.

*Step 7: Anchor pattern*—Layout anchor pattern so that they are approximately evenly spaced on the face and produce the required overall anchor force.

*Step 8: Waterproofing drill holes*—Check that there are no discontinuities in the bond zone into which grout could leak, and seal the hole if necessary by grouting and redrilling.

*Step 9: Testing*—Set up a testing procedure that will verify that the bonded length can sustain the design load, and that the full length of the free stressing length is being tensioned.

Each of these nine steps is discussed in more detail as follows.

*Step 1: Drilling*

The diameter of the drill hole is partially determined by the available drilling equipment, but must also meet certain design requirements. The hole diameter should be large enough to allow the anchor to be inserted in the hole without driving or hammering, and allow full embedment in a continuous column of grout. A hole diameter significantly larger than the anchor will not materially improve the design and will result in unnecessary drilling costs and possibly excessive grout shrinkage. As a guideline, the diameter of the drill hole should be about 1.5–2 times the diameter of the full anchor assembly, with corrosion protection, if any.

*Percussion drilling.* Holes for rock anchors are usually drilled with percussion equipment that utilizes a combination of impact and rotation of a tungsten carbide drill bit to crush the rock and advance the hole. The cuttings are removed by compressed air that is pumped down a hole in the center of the rods and is exhausted up the annulus between the rods and the wall of the hole. Percussion drills are either pneumatic or hydraulic powered, and the hammer is either at the surface or down the hole (DTH drill). The advantages of percussion drills are their high penetration rates, good availability and the slightly rough wall that is produced. Precautions that must be taken include minimizing hole deviation by controlling the down pressure on the rods, and avoid loosing the drill string in zones of weathered and broken rock.

Where holes are to be drilled through an upper layer of soil, or intermediate zones of weathered rock in which collapse of the hole is possible, equipment is available that installs casing as the hole is advanced. Equipment manufactured by Tubex[1] uses a bit that expands, when torque is applied, to ream out the hole to a diameter slightly larger than the casing (Figure 12.6). At

1 Manufacturer's name are given as example only, and are not intended as endorsements of their products.

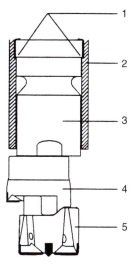

*Figure 12.6* Tubex drill bit for advancing casing through soil and weathered rock (courtesy: Sandvik Drilling) 1, Shoulder; 2, Bit tube; 3, Guide; 4, Reamer; 5, Pilot bit.

the completion of drilling, the drill rods and contracted bit can be withdrawn inside the casing. The maximum hole diameter for Tubex drills is 356 mm. Drills manufactured by Klemm and Barber advance casing during drilling by applying thrust and torque to the casing, which is independent of the thrust and torque on the drill rods.

For holes drilled with hand-held percussion drills, the limits for efficient operation are a maximum hole diameter of about 60 mm and a maximum length is about 6 m. For track-mounted percussion drills the hole diameters range between about 75 and 150 mm, and the maximum hole length for top hammer drills is about 60 m, with the main limitation being excessive hole deviation. For DTH drills the maximum hole length is several hundred meters. For hole diameters larger than about 150 mm in hard rock, there is a substantial increase in the size of the drilling equipment, and this equipment is usually used in vertical holes rather than near-horizontal hole.

*Rotary drilling.* For drilling in weak rock such as chalk and some shales it is possible to use rotary drilling methods that include augers, drag bits and tri-cone bits; drill hole diameters range from 150 to 600 mm. These methods generally require that the hole be self-supporting, although when using hollow-stem augers, bentonite or cement grout can be circulated in the hole to stabilize the walls.

### Step 2: Anchor materials and dimensions

Anchors are available as either deformed steel bars, or 7-wire strand cables. Figures 12.7 and 12.8 show typical features of these two types of anchor, both of which incorporate an optional corrosion protection system.

*Bar anchors.* Most bars are manufactured with a continuous, coarse thread that is resistant to damage, and allows the bars to be cut to any length to suit site conditions. Common steel grades used for thread bars are 517/690 MPa and 835/1030 MPa: yield stress/ultimate stress, with a modulus of elasticity of 204.5 GPa. Bar diameters range from 19 mm to 57 mm and lengths of bar can be joined by threaded couplers. It is usual that only a single bar is installed in each hole, rather than groups of bars. If a tension force is applied to the bar, the head of the bar is secured with a reaction plate, washer and threaded nut.

Another type of bar anchor is a self-drilling product that comprises a hollow core drill steel with a continuous coil thread, and a disposable bit. The anchor is used most commonly when drilling through broken rock and soil seams where the hole tends to collapse as soon as the drill steel is removed. When using this type of anchor, the drill steel is left in the hole when drilling is complete, following which cement grout is pumped down the center hole to fill the annual space and encapsulate the anchor. It is also possible to use an adaptor with the drill that allows grout to be circulated down the hole while drilling; this approach may be used where compressed air circulation is not effective in removing the cuttings. Where the application of the anchor is reinforcement of fractured rock masses, rather than anchoring of defined blocks, then it is appropriate to install fully grouted, untensioned anchors. However, it is possible to

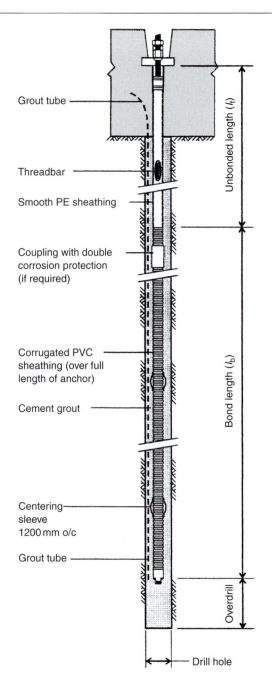

*Figure 12.7* Typical threadbar rock anchor with double corrosion protection system comprising grouted corrugated plastic sleeve over full length of anchor, and smooth sheath on unbonded length (Class I corrosion protection) (courtesy: DSI Anchor Systems).

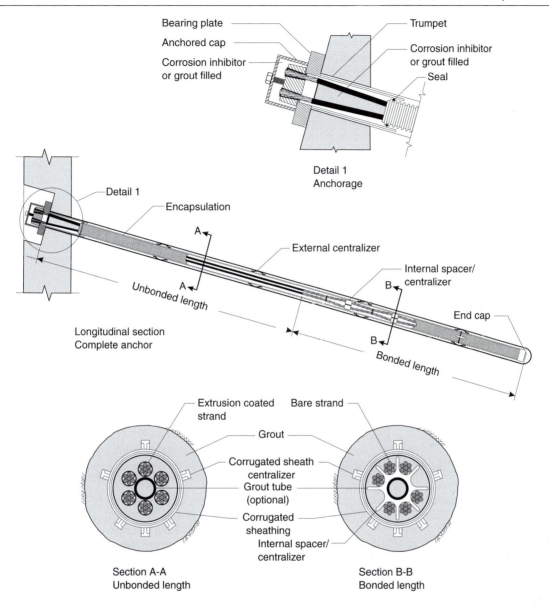

*Figure 12.8* Typical multi-strand cable anchor with corrosion protection system comprising grouted corrugated plastic sleeve on bond length, and smooth greased sheath on unbonded length (courtesy: Lang Tendons Inc.).

install tensioned anchors by driving a smooth casing over the grouted bar to the depth of the top of the bond zone. The grout above the bond zone is washed out as the casing is driven to create an unbonded length. Some trade names of self-drilling anchors are MAI and IBO, and they are available in diameters ranging from 25 mm to 51 mm, with ultimate strengths of 200 kN to 800 kN respectively.

*Strand anchors.*   Wire strand is manufactured by twisting together seven, 5 mm diameter steel wires to form a strand with a diameter of 12 mm.

Each strand has an ultimate tensile strength of 260 kN, and anchors with higher capacities can be produced by assembling individual strands into bundles; bundles as large as 94 strands have been used in improving the seismic stability of concrete dams. For slope stabilization requiring shallow dip holes, the largest bundle may be about 12 strands. The strands are flexible which facilitates handling in the field, but they cannot be coupled. When a tension is applied to strand, the end exposed at the surface is secured with a pair of tapered wedges that grip the strand and fit tightly into tapered holes in the reaction plate (Figure 12.8, detail 1).

### Step 3: Corrosion protection

Corrosion protection for steel bar and strand anchors should be considered for all projects, including temporary installations if the site conditions are corrosive (King, 1977; Baxter, 1997). Even if anchors are not subject to corrosion at the time of installation, conditions may change in the future that must be accounted for in design. The following list describes conditions that will usually create a corrosive environment for steel anchors (Hanna, 1982; PTI, 1996):

- soils and rocks that contain chlorides;
- seasonal changes in the ground water table;
- marine environments where they are exposed to sea water that contains chlorides and sulfates;
- fully saturated clays with high sulfate content;
- anchorages that pass through different ground types which possess different chemical characteristics;
- stray direct electrical current that develops galvanic action between the steel and the surrounding rock;
- peat bogs; and
- cinder, ash or slag fills; organic fills containing humic acid; acid mine or industrial waste.

Corrosion potential is also related to the soil resistivity by the magnitude of the current that can flow between the soil and the steel. In general, the corrosion potential decreases with increasing

*Table 12.6* Parameter limits for corrosiveness of ground water and soil (PTI, 1996; TRB, 2002)

|  | Non-aggressive | Aggressive |
|---|---|---|
| *Properties of groundwater* | | |
| pH | 6.5–5.5 | <5.5 |
| Lime-dissolving ($CO_2$), mg/l | 15–30 | >30 |
| Ammonium ($NH_4^+$), mg/l | 15–30 | >30 |
| Magnesium ($Mg^{2+}$), mg/l | 100–300 | >300 |
| Sulphate ($SO_4^{2-}$), mg/l | 200–600 | >600 |
| *Properties of Soil* | | |
| Resistivity ($\Omega$), ohm/cm | 2000–5000 | <2000 |
| pH | 5–10 | <5 |

resistivity of the soil, as follows:

$$\text{organic soil} > \text{clay} > \text{silt} > \text{sand} > \text{gravel}$$

Table 12.6 lists the properties of ground water and soil with respect to the site conditions being non-aggressive or aggressive for corrosion of steel anchors.

Where aggressive conditions exist, a corrosion protection system is usually used, which should meet the following requirements for long-term reliability:

- There will be no break down, cracking or dissolution of the protection system during the service life of the anchor.
- The fabrication of the protection system can be carried out either in the plant or on site in such a manner that the quality of the system can be verified.
- The installation and stressing of the anchor can be carried out without damage to the protection system.
- The materials used in the protection system are inert with respect to both the steel anchor and the surrounding environment.

The Post Tensioning Institute (PTI, 1996) categorizes corrosion protection systems as Class I and Class II. *Class I* protection is used for permanent anchors in aggressive environments, or in non-aggressive environments where the consequences of failure are significant. Both the bond and unbonded lengths of the tendon or bar are protected with either cement grout-filled encapsulation or an epoxy coating; the head of the anchor is also protected. *Class II* protection is used for temporary anchors in non-aggressive environments; protection is limited to grout on the bond length, a sheath on the unbonded length, and protection of the head if exposed. Figures 12.7 and 12.8 show typical Class I corrosion protection systems for bar and strand anchors respectively.

Based on these categories of corrosion, a decision tree has been developed to assess the vulnerability of rock anchors to corrosion and loss of anchorage capacity (Figure 12.9) (TRB, 2002). High strength steel (ultimate tensile strength $\sigma_{ult} > 1000$ MPa) is vulnerable to attack from hydrogen embrittlement and corrosion stress cracking. Generally, high strength steel is used to manufacture wire strand elements ($\sigma_{ult} \approx 1700-1900$ MPa), and strand anchors are more vulnerable than bar anchors because of the larger surface area of steel.

It is also possible to estimate the service life of anchors based on the rate of corrosion by calculating the loss of element thickness over time. The service life $t$ in years is given by

$$\ln(t) = \frac{\ln(X) - \ln(K)}{n} \qquad (12.4)$$

where $X$ is the loss of thickness or radius ($\mu$m), and $K$ and $n$ are constants (Table 12.7). The loss of thickness $X$ is computed from the original radius $r_o$, and the critical radius $r_{crit}$ that is the radius at which the yield stress is reached, at constant load, due to the loss of cross-section compared to the original cross-section $A_o$, i.e.

$$r_{crit} = \sqrt{\frac{0.6A_o}{\pi}} \qquad (12.5)$$

and

$$X = (r_o - r_{crit}) \qquad (12.6)$$

Approximate values for $K$ are 35 for normal conditions, 50 for aggressive conditions, and 340 for very aggressive conditions, as defined in Table 12.6. Equation (12.5) assumes that the working stress equals 0.6 times the yield stress.

Methods of protecting steel against corrosion include galvanizing, applying an epoxy coating, or encapsulating the steel in cement. Cement is commonly used for corrosion protection, primarily because it creates a high pH environment that protects the steel by forming a surface layer of hydrous ferrous oxide. In addition, cement grout is inexpensive, simple to install, has sufficient strength for most applications, and a long service life. Because of the brittle nature of grout and its tendency to crack, particularly when loaded in tension or bending, it is usual that the protection system comprise a combination of grout and a plastic (high density polyethylene, HDPE) sleeve. In this way, the grout produces the high pH environment around the steel, while the plastic sleeve provides protection against cracking. In order to minimize the formation of shrinkage cracks that reduce corrosion resistance of the grout, it is usual to use non-shrink grouts for all components of the installation. Figures 12.7 and 12.8 show examples of three-layer corrosion protection systems in which the steel is encapsulated in a grout-filled HDPE sheath, and the outer annulus, between the sheath and the rock, formed by the centering sleeves, is filled with a second grout layer.

For anchors with unbonded lengths, it is particularly important that the head be protected from both corrosion and damage. This is because loss of the nut or wedges, or fracturing of the rock under the reaction plate, will result in loss of tension in the anchor even if the remainder of the anchor is entirely intact.

*Step 4: Bond type*

Tensioned anchors comprise two portions—a bond length and an unbonded length (Figures 12.7 and 12.8). In the bond length, the bar or strand is bonded by one of a variety of means to the surrounding rock. In the unbonded length, the bar or

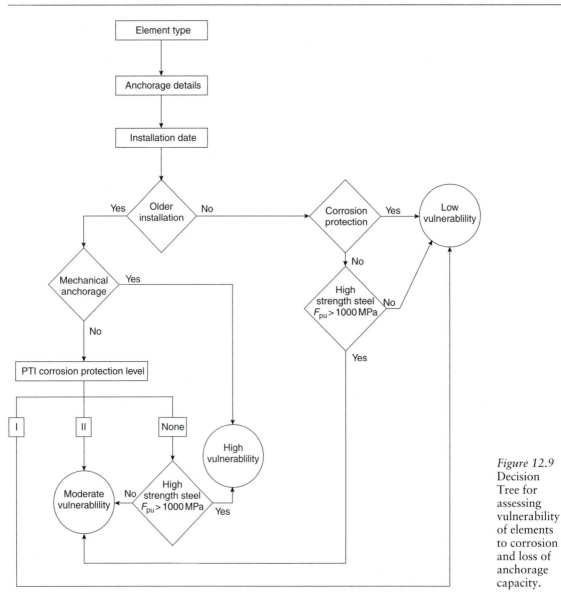

*Figure 12.9* Decision Tree for assessing vulnerability of elements to corrosion and loss of anchorage capacity.

*Table 12.7* Values of constants $K$ and $n$ for corrosion rate calculations

| Parameter | Normal<br>$\Omega = 2000$–$5000$;[a] pH $= 5$–$10$ | Aggressive<br>$\Omega = 700$–$2000$; pH $= 5$–$10$ | Very aggressive<br>$\Omega = {<}700$; pH $= {<}5$ |
| --- | --- | --- | --- |
| $K\,(\mu m)$ | 35 | 50 | 340 |
| $n$ | 1.0 | 1.0 | 1.0 |

Note

a  $\Omega$ is soil resistivity (ohm/cm).

strand is unbonded and is free to strain as tension is applied. Figure 12.4 shows that the bond zone is located in stable rock below the potential sliding plane so that when the anchor is tensioned, stresses are applied to this plane to increase the factor of safety (see Section 6.4).

Methods of securing the distal end of an anchor in the drill hole include resin, mechanical, and cement grout anchors. The selection of the appropriate anchor will depend on such factors as the required capacity of the anchor, speed of installation, strength of the rock in the anchor zone, access to the site for drilling and tensioning equipment, and the level of corrosion protection required. The following is a brief discussion of each of these anchorage methods.

*Resin anchors.* These comprise a plastic cartridge about 25 mm in diameter and 200 mm long that contains a liquid resin and a hardener that set when mixed together (Figure 12.10). Setting times vary from about 1 minute to as much as 90 minutes, depending on the reagents used. The setting time is also dependent on the temperature, with fast-setting resin hardening in about 4 minutes at a temperature of $-5°C$, and in about 25 s at $35°C$.

*Figure 12.10* Resin cartridges for anchoring rock bolts (TRB, 1996).

The installation method consists of inserting a sufficient number of cartridges into the drill hole to fill the annular space around the bar. It is important that the hole diameter, in relation to the bar size, be within specified tolerances so that complete mixing of the resin is achieved when the bar is spun. This usually precludes the use of coupled anchors because the hole diameter to accommodate the coupling will be too large for complete resin mixing. The bar is spun as it is driven through the cartridges to mix the resin and form a rigid solid anchorage. The required speed of rotation is about 60 revolutions per minute, and spinning is continued for about 30 s after the bar has reached the end of the hole. It is preferable that threaded bar be rotated in the direction that augers the resin into the hole, particularly in up-holes.

The maximum bolt length is limited to about 12 m because most drills cannot rotate longer bars at sufficient speed to mix the resin. It is possible to install a tensioned, resin-grouted bolt by using a fast-setting (about 2 minutes) resin for the anchor, and a slower setting (30 minutes) resin for the remainder of the bar. The bolt is tensioned between the times that the fast and slow resins set.

The primary advantage of resin anchorage is the simplicity and speed of installation, with support of the slope being provided within minutes of spinning the bolt. The disadvantages are the limited length and tension capacity ($\sim 400\,kN$) of the bolt, and the fact that only rigid bars can be used. Furthermore, the resin is not as effective as cement grout for corrosion protection of the steel. Unlike cement grout, resin does not provide the high pH protective layer against corrosion, and it cannot be verified that the cartridges completely encapsulate the steel.

*Mechanical anchors.* These comprise a pair of steel platens that are pressed against the walls of the drill hole. The anchor is expanded by driving or torquing a steel wedge between the platens.

The advantage of mechanical anchors is that installation is rapid, although not as rapid as resin anchors, and tensioning can be carried out as soon as the anchor has been set. Grouting can then be carried out using a grout tube attached to the bar, or through the center hole in the case of the bolt manufactured by the Williams Form Hardware and Rockbolt Co. The disadvantages of mechanical anchors are that they can be used only in medium to strong rock in which the anchor will grip, and the maximum working tensile load is about 200 kN. Mechanical anchors for permanent installations must always be fully grouted because the wedge will creep and corrode in time, resulting in loss of support.

*Cement grout.* It is the most common method of anchoring long-service-life rock anchors because the materials are inexpensive, it provides corrosion protection, and installation is simple. Cement grout anchorage can be used in a wide range of rock and soil conditions, and the cement provides corrosion protection. Figures 12.7 and 12.8 show typical installations with cement anchorage and centering sleeves to ensure complete encapsulation of the steel. The grout mix usually comprises non-shrink, unsanded cement and water at a water:cement ratio in the range of 0.4–0.45. This ratio will produce a grout that can be pumped down a small diameter grout tube, yet produce a high strength, continuous grout column with minimal bleed of water from the mix. Admixtures are sometimes added to the grout to reduce bleeding, and increase the viscosity of the grout. In down holes, grout is always placed with a grout tube extending to the distal end of the hole in order to displace air and water in the hole.

## Step 5: Bond length

For cement and resin grout anchored bolts, the stress distribution along the bond length is highly non-uniform; the highest stress is concentrated in the proximal end of the bond zone, and ideally the distal end of the bond is unstressed (Farmer, 1975; Aydan, 1989). However, it is found, as a simplification, that the required length of the bond zone can be calculated assuming that the shear stress at the rock–grout interface is uniformly distributed along the anchor. Based on this assumption, the allowable shear stress $\tau_a$ is given by equation (12.7):

$$\tau_a = \frac{T}{\pi d_h l_b} \tag{12.7}$$

or, the design bond length $l_b$ is

$$l_b = \frac{T}{\pi d_h \tau_a} \tag{12.8}$$

where $T$ is the design tension force and $d_h$ is the hole diameter. Values of $\tau_a$ can be estimated from the uniaxial compressive strength ($\sigma_i$) of the rock in the anchor zone according to the following relationship (Littlejohn and Bruce, 1977):

$$\tau_a = \frac{\sigma_i}{30} \tag{12.9}$$

Approximate ranges of allowable bond stress ($\tau_a$) related to rock strength and rock type are presented in Table 12.8. It is important to note that the allowable shear stress values listed in Table 12.8 incorporate a factor of safety of about 3, so these values can be used with confidence in design.

## Step 6: Total anchor length

The total length of a tensioned anchor is the sum of the bond length as determined in Steps 4 and 5, and the unbonded length (see Figure 12.4). The unbonded length extends from the proximal end of the bond zone to the head of the bolt, and there are three components to this length, as follows. First, the distal end of the unbonded length must be beyond the potential sliding surface so that the tensile force applied to the anchor is transferred into the rock at the sliding surface. If the location of this surface is precisely known, then the distal end of the unbonded length could be 1–2 m below the sliding surface, while if the sliding surface is a zone rather than a plane, then this distance should be increased accordingly. The second component of the length extends from the sliding surface to the rock surface, and this length will depend on the slope geometry. The third length component

*Table 12.8* Allowable rock–grout bond stresses in cement grout anchorages (PTI, 1996; Wyllie, 1999)

| Rock description | Compressive strength range (MPa) | Allowable bond stress (MPa) |
|---|---|---|
| Strong rock | >100 | 1.05–1.40 |
| Medium rock | 50–100 | 0.7–1.05 |
| Weak rock | 20–50 | 0.35–0.7 |
| *Rock type* | | |
| Granite, basalt | | 0.55–1.0 |
| Dolomitic limestone | | 0.45–0.70 |
| Soft limestone | | 0.35–0.50 |
| Slates, strong shales | | 0.30–0.45 |
| Weak shales | | 0.05–0.30 |
| Sandstone | | 0.30–0.60 |
| Concrete | | 0.45–0.90 |

is the distance from the rock surface to the head of the anchor where the bearing plate and nut are located. For strong rock the bearing plate can bear directly on the rock (Figure 12.4, item 2), whereas in conditions where the stress under the bearing plate could crush the rock, a reinforced concrete or shotcrete reaction pad would be required (Figure 12.4, item 3).

### Step 7: Anchor pattern

The layout of the anchors on the face should be such that there is a reasonably uniform stress applied to the sliding plane. This will require that the horizontal and vertical spacing be about equal. Also, the anchors should not be too close to the toe where the thickness of rock above the slide plane is limited, or close to the crest where the anchor may pass through a tension crack. For a plane failure where the support force $T$ is calculated per unit length of slope, then the required vertical spacing $S_v$ for an installation comprising $n$ horizontal rows is given by

$$S_v = \frac{B \cdot n}{T} \qquad (12.10)$$

where $B$ is the design tension force in each bolt.

### Step 8: Waterproofing drill hole

If the drill hole intersects open discontinuities in the bond length into which there could be significant leakage of grout, it will be necessary to seal these discontinuities before installing the anchor. The potential for grout leakage into the rock can be checked by filling the hole with water and applying an excess pressure of 35 kPa. If, after allowing time for some saturation of the rock mass around the hole, the water leakage over a 10 minute period exceeds 9.5 l, then there is potential that grout in the bond zone will flow into the rock before it has time to set PTI (1996). Under these conditions, the hole is sealed with a low fluid or sanded grout, and then is re-drilled after a setting time of about 15–24 h; if the grout is allowed to set fully, it is possible that the drill will wander from the original alignment and intersect the ungrouted discontinuity. A second water inflow test is then conducted. The procedure for testing, grouting and re-drilling is repeated until the hole is sealed.

### Step 9: Testing

Where tensioned rock anchors are installed, a procedure is required to check that the anchor can sustain the full design load at the required depth, and that there will be no loss of load with time. A suitable testing procedure has been drawn up by the Post Tensioning Institute (1996) that comprises the following four types of tests:

(a) Performance test;
(b) Proof test;
(c) Creep test; and
(d) Lift-off test.

The performance and proof tests consist of a cyclic testing sequence, in which the deflection of the head of the anchor is measured as the anchor is tensioned (Figure 12.11). The design load should not exceed 60% of the ultimate strength of the steel, and the maximum test load is usually 133% of the design load, which should not exceed 80% of the ultimate strength of the steel. As a guideline, performance tests are usually carried out on the first two to three anchors and on 2% of the remaining anchors, while proof tests are carried out on the remainder of the anchors. The testing sequences are as follows, where AL is an alignment load to take slack out of the anchor assembly and $P$ is the design load (Figure 12.12(a)):

*Performance test*:

AL, $0.25P$

AL, $0.25P, 0.5P$

AL, $0.25P, 0.5P, 0.75P$

AL, $0.25P, 0.5P, 0.75P, 1.0P$

AL, $0.25P, 0.5P, 0.75P, 1.0P, 1.2P,$

AL, $0.25P, 0.5P, 0.75P, 1.0P, 1.2P,$

    $1.33P$—hold for creep test[*]

AL, $P$—lock off anchor, carry out lift-off test.

*Proof test*:

AL, $0.25P, 0.5P, 0.75P, 1.0P, 1.2P,$

    $1.33P$—hold for creep test[*]

$P$—lock off anchor, carry out lift-off test.

[*]*Creep test*—elongation measurements are made at 1, 2, 3, 4, 5, 6 and 10 minutes. If the total creep exceeds 1 mm between 1 and 10 minutes, the load is maintained for an additional 50 minutes with elongation measurements made at 20, 30, 40, 50 and 60 minutes.

The usual method of tensioning rock bolts is to use a hollow-core hydraulic jack that allows the applied load to be precisely measured, as well as cycling the load and holding it constant for the creep test. It is important that the hydraulic jack be calibrated before each project to ensure that the indicated load is accurate. The deflection of

*Figure 12.11* Test set-up for a tensioned multi-strand cable anchor comprising hydraulic jack with pressure gauge to measure load, and dial gauge on independent mount to measure anchor elongation. (Photograph by W. Capaul.)

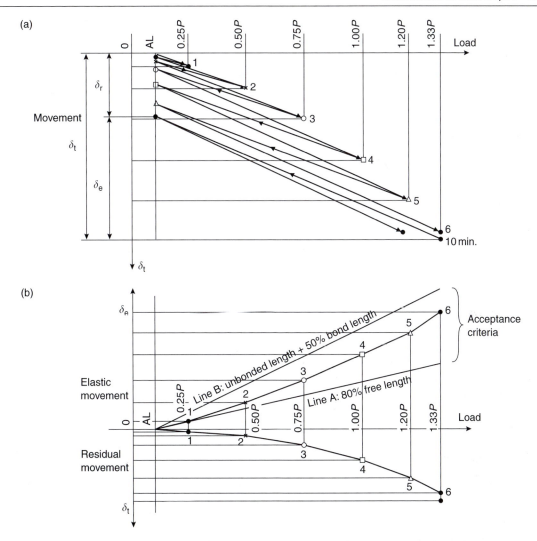

*Figure 12.12* Results of performance test for tensioned anchor: (a) cyclic load/movement measurements; (b) load/elastic movement plot (PTI, 1996).

the anchor head is usually measured with a dial gauge, to an accuracy of about 0.05 mm, with the dial gauge mounted on a stable reference point that is independent of movement of the anchor. Figure 12.11 shows a typical test arrangement for tensioning a cable anchor comprising a hydraulic jack, and the dial gauge set up on tripod.

The purpose of the performance and creep tests is to ensure that the anchor can sustain a constant load greater than the design load, and that

the load in the anchor is transmitted into the rock at the location of the potential slide surface. The creep test is carried out by holding the maximum test load constant for a period up to 10 minutes, and checks that there is no significant loss of load with time. The creep test also removes some of the initial creep in the anchor. The lift-off test checks that the tension applied during the testing sequence has been permanently transferred to the anchor. The Post Tensioning Institute (PTI)

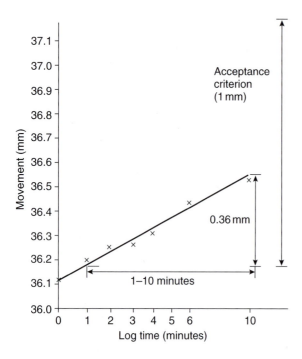

*Figure 12.13* Results of creep test showing measured elongation over 10 minutes test period compared with acceptance criteria of 1 mm elongation.

provides acceptance criteria for each of the four tests, and it is necessary that each anchor meets all the acceptance criteria.

The results of a performance test shown in Figure 12.12(a) are used to calculate the elastic elongation $\delta_e$ of the head of the anchor. The total elongation of the anchor during each loading cycle comprises elastic elongation of the steel and residual $\delta_r$ (or permanent) elongation due to minor cracking of the grout and slippage in the bond zone. Figure 12.12(a) shows how the elastic and residual deformations are calculated for each load cycle. Values for $\delta_e$ and $\delta_r$ at each test load, together with the PTI load–elongation acceptance criteria, are then plotted on a separate graph (Figure 12.12(b)). For both performance and proof tests, the four acceptance criteria for tensioned anchors are as follows:

*First*, the total elastic elongation is greater than 80% of the theoretical elongation of the unbonded length—this ensures that the load applied at the head is being transmitted to the bond length.

*Second*, the total elastic elongation is less than the theoretical elongation of the unbonded length plus 50% of the bond length—this ensures that load in the bond length is concentrated in the upper part of the bond and there is no significant shedding of load to the distal end.

*Third*, for the creep test, the total elongation of the anchor head during the period of 1–10 minutes is not greater than 1 mm (Figure 12.13), or if this is not met, is less than 2 mm during the period of 6–60 minutes. If necessary, the duration of the creep test can be extended until the movement is less than 2 mm for one logarithmic cycle of time.

*Fourth*, the lift-off load is within 5% of the designed lock-off load—this checks that there has been no loss of load during the operation of setting the nut or wedges, and releasing the pressure on the tensioning jack.

The working shear strength at the steel–grout interface of a grouted deformed bar is usually greater than the working strength at the rock–grout interface. For this reason, the required anchor length is typically determined from the stress level developed at the rock–grout interface.

### 12.4.3 Reaction wall

Figure 12.4, item 3 shows an example where there is potential for a sliding type failure in closely fractured rock. If tensioned rock bolts are used to support this portion of the slope, the fractured rock may degrade and ravel from under the reaction plates of the anchors, and eventually the tension in the bolts will be lost. In these circumstances, a reinforced concrete wall can be constructed to cover the area of fractured rock, and then the holes for the rock anchors can be drilled through sleeves in the wall. Finally, the anchors are installed and tensioned against the face of the wall. The wall acts as both a protection against raveling of the rock, and a large reaction plate for the rock anchors. Where necessary, reinforced shotcrete can be substituted for concrete.

Since the purpose of the wall is to distribute the anchor loads into rock, the reinforcing for the wall should be designed such that there is no cracking of the concrete under the concentrated loads of the anchor heads. It is also important that there are drain holes through the concrete to prevent build-up of water pressure behind the wall.

### 12.4.4 Shotcrete

Shotcrete is a pneumatically applied, fine-aggregate mortar that is usually placed in a 50–100 mm layer, and is often reinforced for improved tensile and shear strength (American Concrete Institute, 1995). Zones and beds of closely fractured or degradable rock may be protected by applying a layer of shotcrete to the rock face (Figure 12.4, item 4). The shotcrete will control both the fall of small blocks of rock, and progressive raveling that could eventually produce unstable overhangs. However, shotcrete provides little support against sliding for the overall slope; its primary function is surface protection. Another component of a shotcrete installation is the provision of drain holes to prevent build-up of water pressures behind the face.

*Reinforcement.* For permanent applications, shotcrete should be reinforced to reduce the risk of cracking and spalling. The two common methods of reinforcing are welded-wire mesh, or steel or polypropylene fibers. Welded-wire mesh is fabricated from light gauge ($\sim$3.5 mm diameter) wire on 100 mm centers, and is attached to the rock face on about 1–2 m centers with steel pins, complete with washers and nuts, grouted into the rock face. The mesh must be close to the rock surface, and fully encased in shotcrete, taking care that there are no voids behind the mesh. On irregular surfaces it can be difficult to attach the mesh closely to the rock. In these circumstances, the mesh can be installed between two layers of shotcrete, with the first layer creating a smoother surface to which the mesh can be more readily attached.

An alternative to mesh reinforcement is to use steel or polypropylene fibers that are a component of the shotcrete mix and form a reinforcement mat throughout the shotcrete layer (Morgan *et al.*, 1989, 1999). The steel fibers are manufactured from high strength carbon steel with a length of 30–38 mm and diameter of 0.5 mm. To resist pullout, the fibers have deformed ends or are crimped. The proportion of steel fibers in the shotcrete mix is about $60 \, \text{kg/m}^3$, while comparable strengths are obtained for mixes containing 6 kg of polypropylene fibers per cubic meter of shotcrete. The principal function of fibers is to significantly increase the shear, tensile and post-crack strengths of the shotcrete compared to non-reinforced shotcrete; shotcrete will tend to be loaded in shear and tension when blocks of fractured rock loosen behind the face.

The disadvantages of steel fibers are their tendency to rust at cracks in the shotcrete, and the hazard of the "pin cushion" effect where persons come in contact with the face; polypropylene fibers overcome both these disadvantages.

*Mix design.*    Shotcrete mixes comprise cement and aggregate (10–2.5 mm aggregate and sand), together with admixtures (superplasticizers) to provide high early strengths. The properties of shotcrete are enhanced by the use of micro-silica that is added to the mix as a partial replacement for cement (USBM, 1984). Silica fume is an ultra fine powder with a particle size approximately equal to that of smoke. When added to shotcrete, silica fume reduces rebound, allows thicknesses of up to 500 mm to be applied in a single pass, and covers surfaces on which there is running water. There is also an increase in the long-term strength in most cases.

Shotcrete can be applied as either a wet-mix or a dry-mix. For wet-mix shotcrete the components, including water, are mixed at a ready-mix concrete plant and the shotcrete is delivered to the site by ready-mix truck. This approach is suitable for sites with good road access and the need for large quantities. For dry-mix shotcrete the dry components are mixed at the plant and then placed in 1 m$^3$ bags that have a valve in the bottom (Figure 12.14). At the site, the bags are discharged into the hopper on the pump and

a pre-moisturizer adds 4% water to the mix. The mix is then pumped to the face where additional water is added through a ring valve at the nozzle. The advantages of the dry-mix process are its use in locations with difficult access, and where small quantities are being applied at a time. It is also useful to be able to adjust the quantity of water in areas where there is varying amounts of seepage on the face.

Typical mixes for dry-mix and wet-mix silica fume, steel fiber reinforced shotcrete are shown in Table 12.9 (Morgan *et al.*, 1989).

*Shotcrete strength.*    The strength of shotcrete is defined by three parameters that correspond to the types of loading conditions to which shotcrete may be subjected when applied to a slope. Typical values for these parameters are as follows:

(a)  Compressive strength of 20 MPa at 3 days and 30 MPa at 7 days;
(b)  First crack flexural strength of 4.5 MPa at 7 days; and
(c)  Toughness indices of $I_5 = 4$ and $I_{10} = 6$.

*Figure 12.14* Dry-mix shotcrete process using bagged mix feeding a pump and pre-moisturizer.

*Table 12.9* Typical shotcrete mixes

| Material | Dry-mix (kg/m³) | Shotcrete (% dry materials) | Wet-mix (kg/m³) | Shotcrete (% dry materials) |
|---|---|---|---|---|
| Cement, Type I | 400 | 18.3 | 420 | 18.3 |
| Silica fume | 50 | 2.3 | 40 | 1.7 |
| 10 mm coarse aggregate | 500 | 22.9 | 480 | 20.9 |
| Sand | 1170 | 53.7 | 1120 | 48.7 |
| Steel fibers | 60 | 2.8 | 60 | 2.6 |
| Water reduced | — | — | 21 | 0.09 |
| Superplasticizer | — | — | 61 | 0.04 |
| Air entraining admixture | — | — | if required | if required |
| Water | 170ᵃ | — | 180 | 7.8 |
| Total wet mass | 2350 | 100 | 2300 | 100 |

Note

a Total water from pre-moisturizer and added at nozzle (based on saturated surface dry aggregate concept).

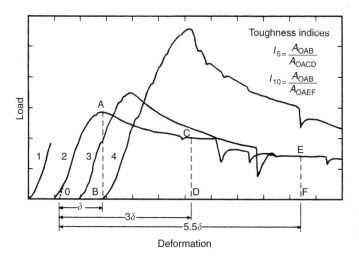

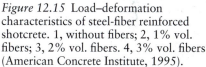

Toughness indices

$$I_5 = \frac{A_{OAB}}{A_{OACD}}$$

$$I_{10} = \frac{A_{OAB}}{A_{OAEF}}$$

*Figure 12.15* Load–deformation characteristics of steel-fiber reinforced shotcrete. 1, without fibers; 2, 1% vol. fibers; 3, 2% vol. fibers. 4, 3% vol. fibers (American Concrete Institute, 1995).

The flexural strength and toughness indices are determined by cutting a beam with dimensions of 100 mm square in section and 350 mm long from a panel shot in the field, and testing the beam in bending. The test measures the deformation beyond the peak strength, and the method of calculating the $I_5$ and $I_{10}$ toughness indices from these measurements is shown in Figure 12.15.

*Surface preparation.* The effectiveness of shotcrete is influenced by the condition of the rock surface to which it is applied—the surface should be free of loose and broken rock, soil, vegetation and ice. The surface should also be damp to improve the adhesion between the rock and the shotcrete, and the air temperature should be above 5°C for the first seven days when the shotcrete is setting. Drain holes should be drilled through the shotcrete to prevent build-up of water pressure behind the face; the drain holes are usually about 0.5 m deep, and located on 1–2 m centers. In massive rock the drain holes should be drilled before the shotcrete is applied, and located to intersect discontinuities that carry water. The holes are temporarily plugged with wooden pegs or rags while applying the shotcrete.

*Aesthetics.* A requirement on some civil projects is that shotcreted faces should have a natural appearance. That is, the shotcrete should be colored to match the natural rock color, and the face sculpted to show a pattern of "discontinuities." This work is obviously costly, but the final appearance can be a very realistic replica of a rock face.

### 12.4.5 *Buttresses*

Where a rock fall or weathering has formed a cavity in the slope face, it may be necessary to construct a concrete buttress in the cavity to prevent further falls (Figure 12.4, item 6). The buttress fulfills two functions: first, to retain and protect areas of weak rock, and second, to support the overhang. Buttresses should be designed so that the direction of thrust from the rock supports the buttress in compression. In this way, bending moments and overturning forces are eliminated and there is no need for heavy reinforcement of the concrete, or tiebacks anchored in the rock.

If the buttress is to prevent relaxation of the rock, it should be founded on a clean, sound rock surface. If this surface is not at right angles to the direction of thrust, then the buttress should be anchored to the base using steel pins to prevent sliding. Also, the top of the buttress should be poured so that it is in contact with the underside of the overhang. In order to meet this second requirement, it may be necessary to place the last pour through a hole drilled downward into the cavity from the rock face, and to use a non-shrink agent in the mix.

### 12.4.6 *Drainage*

As shown in Table 12.1, ground water in rock slopes is often a primary or contributory cause of instability, and a reduction in water pressures usually improves stability. This improvement can be quantified using the design procedures discussed in Chapters 6–10. Methods of controlling water pressure include limiting surface infiltration, and drilling horizontal drain holes or driving adits at the toe of the slope to create outlets for

the water (Figure 12.16). The selection of the most appropriate method for the site will depend on such factors as the intensity of the rainfall or snow melt, the permeability of the rock and the dimensions of the slope.

*Surface infiltration.* In climates that experience intense rainfall that can rapidly saturate the slope and cause surface erosion, it is beneficial for stability to construct drains both behind the crest and on benches on the face to intercept the water (Government of Hong Kong, 2000). These drains are lined with masonry or concrete to prevent the collected water from infiltrating the slope, and are dimensioned to carry the expected peak design flows (see Figure 1.1(a)). The drains are also interconnected so that the water is discharged to the storm drain system or nearby water courses. Where the drains are on steep gradients, it is sometimes necessary to incorporate energy dissipation protrusions in the base of the drain to limit flow velocities. In climates with high rainfall there is usually rapid vegetation growth, and periodic maintenance will be required to keep the drains clear.

*Horizontal drain holes.* An effective means of reducing the water pressure in many rock slopes is to drill a series of drain holes (inclined upwards at about 5°) into the face. Since most of the ground water is contained in discontinuities, the holes should be aligned so that they intersect the discontinuities that are carrying the water. For the conditions shown in Figure 12.4, the drain holes are drilled at a shallow angle to intersect the more persistent discontinuities that dip out of the face. If the holes were drilled at a steeper angle, parallel to these discontinuities, then the drainage would be less effective.

There are no widely used formulae from which to calculate the required spacing of drill holes, but as a guideline, holes are usually drilled on a spacing of about 3–10 m, to a depth of about one-half to one-third of the slope height. The holes are often lined with perforated casing, with the perforations sized to minimize infiltration of fines that are washed from fracture infillings. Another aspect of the design of drain holes is the disposal

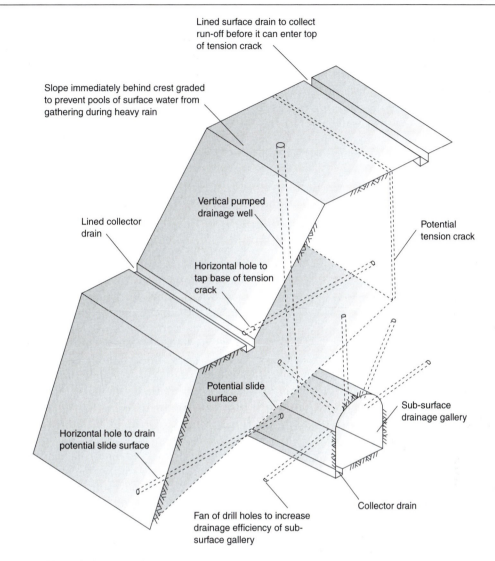

Lined surface drain to collect
run-off before it can enter top
of tension crack

Slope immediately behind crest graded
to prevent pools of surface water from
gathering during heavy rain

Vertical pumped
drainage well

Lined collector
drain

Potential
tension crack

Horizontal hole to
tap base of tension
crack

Potential slide
surface

Sub-surface
drainage gallery

Horizontal hole to drain
potential slide surface

Collector drain

Fan of drill holes to increase
drainage efficiency of sub-
surface gallery

*Figure 12.16* Slope drainage methods.

of the seepage water. If this water is allowed to infiltrate the toe of the slope, it may result in degradation of low-strength materials, or produce additional stability problems downstream of the drains. Depending on site conditions, it may be necessary to collect all the seepage water in a manifold and dispose of it at some distance from the slope.

Drain holes can be drilled to depths of several hundred meters, sometimes using drilling equipment that installs the perforated casing as the drill advances to prevent caving. Also, it is common to drill a fan of holes from a single set up to minimize drill moves (Cedergren, 1989).

*Drainage adits.*   For large slides, it may not be possible to reduce significantly the water pressure in the slope with relatively small drain holes. In these circumstances, a drainage tunnel may be driven into the toe of the slide from which a series of drain holes are drilled up into the saturated rock. For example, the Downie Slide in British Columbia has an area of about 7 km$^2$ and a thickness of about 250 m. Stability of the slope was of concern when the toe was flooded by the construction of a dam. A series of drainage tunnels with a total length of 2.5 km were driven at an elevation just above the high water level of the reservoir. From these tunnels, a total of 13,500 m of drain holes was drilled to reduce the ground water pressures within the slope. These drainage measures have been effective in reducing the water level in the slide by as much as 120 m, and reducing the rate of movement from 10 mm/year to about 2 mm/year (Forster, 1986). In a mining application, ground water control measures for the Chuquicamata pit in Chile include a 1200 m long drainage adit in the south wall, and a number of pumped wells (Flores and Karzulovic, 2000).

Methods of estimating the influence of a drainage tunnel on ground water in a slope include empirical procedures (Heuer, 1995), theoretical models of ground water flow in homogeneous rock (Goodman et al., 1965), and three-dimensional numerical modeling (McDonald and Harbaugh, 1988). In all cases, the flow and drawdown values will be estimates because of the complex and uncertain relationship between ground water flow and structural geology, and the difficulty of obtaining representative permeability values.

Empirical procedures for calculating inflow quantities are based on actual flow rates measured in tunnels. Based on these data, a relationship has been developed between the normalized steady-state inflow intensity (l/min/m tunnel length/m head) and the rock mass conductivity determined from packer tests (Heuer, 1995). The flow quantities can be calculated for both vertical recharge where the tunnel passes under an aquifer, and radial flow for a tunnel in an infinite rock mass. This empirical relationship has been developed because it has been found the actual flows can be one-eighth of the calculated theoretical values based on measured conductivities.

Approximate inflow quantities can also be estimated by modeling the drainage adit as an infinitely long tunnel in a homogeneous, isotropic porous medium, with the pressure head on the surface of the tunnel assumed to be atmospheric. If flow occurs under steady-state conditions such that there is no drainage of the slope and the head above the tunnel $H_0$ is constant with time, the approximate rate of ground water flow $Q_0$ per unit length of tunnel is given

$$Q_0 = \frac{2\pi K H_0}{2.3 \log(2H_0/r)} \qquad (12.11)$$

where $r$ is the radius of the tunnel driven in homogeneous material with hydraulic conductivity $K$. For rock formations with low porosity and low specific storage it is likely that transient conditions will develop where the head diminishes with time as the slope drains.

An important aspect of slope drainage is to install piezometers to monitor the effect of drainage measures on the water pressure in the slope. For example, one drain hole with a high flow may only be draining a small, permeable zone in the slope and monitoring may show that more holes would be required to lower the water table throughout the slope. Conversely, in low permeability rock, monitoring may show that a small seepage quantity that evaporates as it reaches the surface is sufficient to reduce the water pressure and significantly improve stability conditions.

### 12.4.7 "Shot-in-place" buttress

On landslides where the slide surface is a well-defined geological feature such as a continuous bedding surface, stabilization may be achieved by blasting this surface to produce a "shot-in-place" buttress (Aycock, 1981; Moore, 1986). The effect of the blasting is to disturb the rock surface and effectively increase its roughness, which increases the total friction angle. If the total friction angle is greater than the dip of the slide surface, then sliding may be halted. Fracturing and dilation of the rock may also help reduce water pressures on the slide surface.

The method of blasting involves drilling a pattern of holes through the slide surface and placing an explosive charge at this level that is just sufficient to break the rock. This technique requires that the drilling begins while it is still safe for the drills to access the slope, and before the rock becomes too broken for the drills to operate. Obviously, this stabilization technique should be used with a great deal of caution because of the potential for exacerbating stability conditions, and probably should only be used in emergency situation when there are no suitable alternatives.

## 12.5   Stabilization by rock removal

Stabilization of rock slopes can be accomplished by the removal of potentially unstable rock;

Figure 12.17 illustrates typical removal methods including

- resloping zones of unstable rock;
- trim blasting of overhangs;
- scaling of individual blocks of rock.

This section describes these methods, and the circumstances where removal should and should not be used. In general, rock removal is a preferred method of stabilization because the work will eliminate the hazard, and no future maintenance will be required. However, removal should only be used where it is certain that the new face will be stable, and there is no risk of undermining the upper part of the slope. Area 4 on Figure 12.17 is an example of where rock removal should be carried out with care. It would be safe to remove

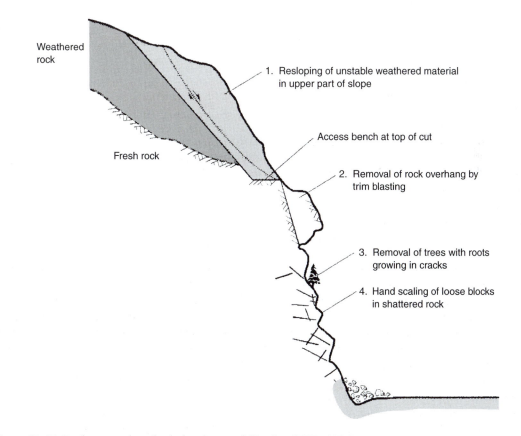

*Figure 12.17* Rock removal methods for slope stabilization (TRB, 1996).

the outermost loose rock, provided that the fracturing was caused by blasting and only extended to a shallow depth. However, if the rock mass is deeply fractured, continued scaling will soon develop a cavity that will undermine the upper part of the slope.

Removal of loose rock on the face of a slope is not effective where the rock is highly degradable, such as shale. In these circumstances, exposure of a new face will just start a new cycle of weathering and instability. For this condition, more appropriate stabilization methods would be protection of the face with shotcrete and rock bolts, or a tied-back wall.

### 12.5.1  Resloping and unloading

Where overburden or weathered rock occurs in the upper portion of a cut, it is often necessary to cut this material at an angle flatter than the more competent rock below (Figure 12.17, item 1). The design procedure for resloping and unloading starts with back analysis of the unstable slope. By setting the factor of safety of the unstable slope to 1.0, it is possible to calculate the rock mass strength parameters (see Section 4.4). This information can then be used to calculate the required reduced slope angle and/or height that will produce the required factor of safety.

Another condition that should be taken account of during design is weathering of the rock some years after construction, at which time resloping may be difficult to carry out. A bench can be left at the toe of the soil or weathered rock to provide a catchment area for minor slope failures and provide equipment access. Where a slide has developed, it may be necessary to unload the crest of the cut to reduce its height and diminish the driving force.

Resloping and unloading is usually carried out by excavating equipment such as excavators and bulldozers. Consequently, the cut width must be designed to accommodate suitable excavating equipment on the slope with no danger of collapse of the weak material while equipment is working; this width would usually be at least 5 m. Safety for equipment access precludes the

excavation of "sliver" cuts in which the toe of the new cut coincides with that of the old cut.

### 12.5.2  Trimming

Failure or weathering of a rock slope may form an overhang on the face (Figure 12.17, item 2), which could be a hazard if it were to fail. In these circumstances, removal of the overhang by trim blasting may be the most appropriate stabilization measure. Section 11.4 discusses methods of controlled blasting that are applicable to situations where it is required to trim blast small volumes of rock with minimal damage to the rock behind the trim line.

Where the burden on a trim blast is limited, flyrock may be thrown a considerable distance because there is little rock to contain the explosive energy. In these circumstances appropriate precautions such as the use of blasting mats would be required to protect any nearby structures and power lines. Blasting mats are fabricated from rubber tires or conveyor belts chained or wired together.

### 12.5.3  Scaling

Scaling describes the removal of loose rock, soil and vegetation on the face of a slope using hand tools such as scaling bars, shovels and chain saws. On steep slopes workers are usually supported by ropes, anchored at the crest of the slope (Figure 12.18). A suitable type of rope for these conditions is a steel-core, hemp rope that is highly resistant to cuts and abrasion. The scalers work their way down the face to ensure there is no loose rock above them.

A staging suspended from a crane is an alternative to using ropes for the scalers to access the face. The crane is located at the toe of the slope if there is no access to the crest of the slope. The disadvantages of using a crane, rather than ropes, are the expense of the crane, and on highway projects, the extended outriggers can occupy several lanes of the highway with consequent disruption to traffic. Also, scaling from a staging suspended from crane can be less safe than using ropes

*Figure 12.18* High scaler suspended on rope and belt while removing loose rock on steep rock slope (Thompson River Canyon, British Columbia, Canada) (TRB, 1996).

because the scalers are not able to direct the crane operator to move quickly in the event of a rock fall from the face above them.

An important component of a scaling operation in wet climates is the removal of trees and vegetation growing on the face, and to a distance of several meters behind the crest of the slope. Tree roots growing in fractures on the rock face can force open the fractures and eventually cause rock falls. Also, movement of the trees by the wind produces leverage by the roots on loose blocks. The general loosening of the rock on the face by tree roots also permits increased infiltration of water which, in temperate climates, will freeze and expand and cause further opening of the cracks. As shown in Table 12.1, approximately 0.6% of the rock falls on the California highway system can be attributed to root growth.

### 12.5.4 Rock removal operations

Where rock removal operations are carried out above active highways or railroads, or in urban areas, particular care must be taken to prevent injury or damage from falling rock. This will usually require that all traffic be stopped while rock

removal is in progress, and until the slope has been made safe and the road has been cleared of debris. Where there are pipelines or cables buried at the toe of the slope, it may be necessary to protect them, as well as pavement surfaces or rail track, from the impact of falling rock. Adequate protection can usually be provided by placing a cover of sand and gravel to a depth of about 1.5–2 m. For particularly sensitive structures, additional protection can be provided by rubber blast mats.

### 12.6 Protection measures against rock falls

An effective method of minimizing the hazard of rock falls is to let the falls occur and control the distance and direction in which they travel. Methods of rock fall control and protection of facilities at the toe of the slope include catchment ditches and barriers, wire mesh fences, mesh hung on the face of the slope and rock sheds. A common feature of all these protection structures is their energy-absorbing characteristics in which the rock fall is either stopped over some distance, or is deflected away from the facility that is being protected. As described in this section, it is possible by the use of appropriate techniques, to control rocks with dimensions up to about 2 m, falling from heights of several hundred meters, and impacting with energies as high as 1 MJ. Rigid structures, such as reinforced concrete walls or fences with stiff attachments to fixed supports, are rarely appropriate for stopping rock falls.

## 12.6.1  Rock fall modeling

Selection and design of effective protection measures require the ability to predict rock fall behavior. An early study of rock falls was made by Ritchie (1963) who drew up empirical ditch design charts related to the slope dimensions (see Section 10.6.2). Since the 1980s, the prediction of rock fall behavior was enhanced by the development of a number of computer programs that simulate the behavior of rock falls as they roll and bounce down slope faces (Piteau, 1980; Wu, 1984; Descoeudres and Zimmerman, 1987; Spang, 1987; Hungr and Evans, 1988; Pfeiffer and Bowen, 1989; Pfeiffer *et al.*, 1990; Azzoni and de Freitas, 1995).

Figure 12.19 shows an example of the output from the rock fall simulation program *RocFall* (Rocscience, 2004). The cross-section shows the trajectories of 20 rock falls, one of which rolls out of the ditch. Figures 12.19(b) and (c) show respectively the maximum bounce heights and total kinetic energy at intervals down the slope. The input for the program comprises the slope and ditch geometry, the irregularity (roughness) of the face, the restitution coefficients of the slope materials, the mass and shape of the block, and the start location and velocity. The degree of variation in the shape of the ground surface is modeled by randomly varying the surface roughness for each of a large number of runs, which in turn produces a range of trajectories.

The results of analyses such as those shown in Figure 12.19, together with geological data on block sizes and shapes, can be used to estimate the dimensions of a ditch, or the optimum position, required height and energy capacity of a fence or barrier. In some cases, it may also be necessary to

verify the design by constructing a test structure. Sections 12.6.2–12.6.4 describe types of ditches, fences and barriers, and the conditions in which they can be used.

*Benched Slopes.*  The excavation of intermediate benches on rock cuts usually increases the rock fall hazard, and is therefore not recommended for most conditions. Benches can be a hazard where the crests of the benches fail due to blast damage, and the failed benches leave irregular protrusions on the face. Rock falls striking these protrusions tend to bounce away from the face and land a considerable distance from the base. Where the narrow benches fill with debris, they will not be effective in catching rock falls. It is rarely possible to remove this debris because of the hazard to equipment working on narrow, discontinuous benches.

There are, however two situations where benched slopes are a benefit to stability. First, in horizontally bedded sandstone/shale/coal sequences the locations and vertical spacing of the benches is often determined by the lithology. Benches are placed at the top of the least resistant beds, such as coal or clay shale, which weather quicker (Wright, 1997). With this configuration, the more resistant lithology is not undermined as the shale weathers (Figure 12.20). The width of intermediate benches may vary from 6 to 8 m, and the face angle depends on the durability of the rock. For example, shales with a slake durability index of 50–79 are cut at angles of 43° (1.33H:1V) and heights up to 9 m, while massive sandstone and limestone may be excavated at a face angles as steep as 87° (1/20H:1V) and heights up to 15 m. Figure 12.20 also shows a bench at the toe of the overburden slope to contain minor sloughing and provide access for cleaning.

A second application for benched slopes is in tropical areas with deeply weathered rock and intense periods of rain. In these conditions, lined drainage ditches on each bench and down the slope face are essential to collect runoff and prevent scour and erosion of the weak rock (Government of Hong Kong, 2000).

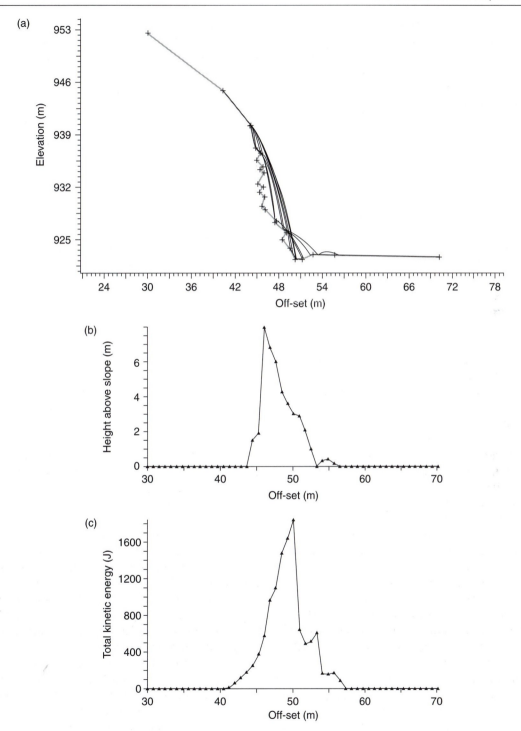

*Figure 12.19* Example of analysis of rock fall behavior: (a) trajectories of 20 rock falls; (b) variation in vertical bounce heights along the slope; (c) variation in total kinetic energy along the slope.

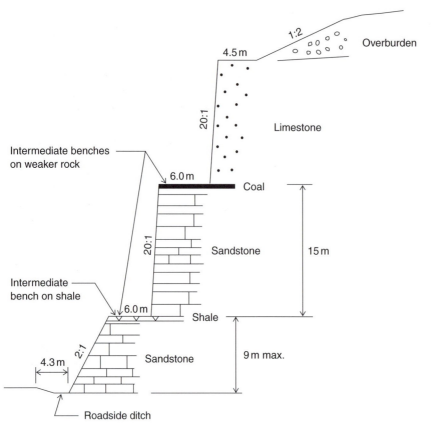

Figure 12.20 Configuration of benched cut in horizontally bedded shale and sandstone, with weaker coal and shale formations located at toe of cut faces.

## 12.6.2  Ditches

Catch ditches at the toe of slopes are often a cost-effective means of stopping rock falls, provided there is adequate space at the toe of the slope (Wyllie and Wood, 1981). The required dimensions of the ditch, as defined by the depth and width, are related to the height and face angle of the slope; a ditch design chart developed from field tests is shown in Figure 12.21 (Ritchie, 1963). The figure shows the effect of slope angle on the path that rock falls tend to follow, and how this influences ditch design. For slopes steeper than about 75°, the rocks tend to stay close to the face and land near the toe of the slope. For slope angles between about 55° and 75°, falling rocks tend to bounce and spin with the result that they can land a considerable distance from the base; consequently, a wide ditch is required. For slope

angles between about 40° and 55°, rocks will tend to roll down the face and into the ditch.

To up-date the work carried out by Ritchie, a comprehensive study of rock fall behavior and the capacity of catchment areas has been carried out by the Oregon Department of Transportation (2001). This study examined rock fall from heights of 12, 18 and 24 m on slopes with five increments of face angles ranging from vertical to 45° (1V:1H). The catchment areas at the toe of the slope were planar surfaces with inclinations of 76° (1/4H:1V), 80° (1/6H:1V) and horizontal to simulate unobstructed highway shoulders. The tests observed both the impact distance from the toe and the roll-out distance. The report includes design charts that show, for all combinations of slope geometry, the relationship between the percent rock retained and the width of the catchment area.

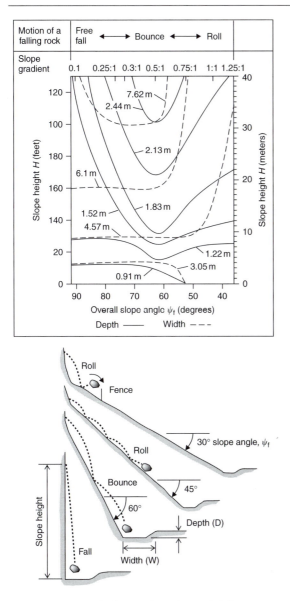

*Figure 12.21* Ditch design chart for rock fall catchment (Ritchie, 1963).

### 12.6.3  Barriers

A variety of barriers can be constructed either to enhance the performance of excavated ditches, or to form catchment zones at the toe of slopes (Andrew, 1992a). The required type of barrier and its dimensions depend on the energy of the falling blocks, the slope dimensions and the availability of construction materials. A requirement of all barriers is flexibility upon impact. Barriers absorb impact energy by deforming, and systems with high impact energy capacity are both flexible, and are constructed with materials that can withstand the impact of sharp rocks without significant damage. The following is a brief description of some commonly used barriers.

*Gabions and concrete blocks.* Gabions or concrete blocks are effective protection barriers for falling rock with diameters up to about 0.75 m. Figure 12.22(a) shows an example of a ditch with two layers of gabions along the outer edge forming a 1.5 m high barrier.

The function of a barrier is to form a "ditch" with a vertical facing the slope face that traps rolling rock. Barriers are particularly useful at the toe of flatter slopes where falling rock rolls and spins down the face but does not bounce significantly. Such rocks may land in a ditch at the toe of the slope but can roll up the sloping outer side; a vertical barrier will help to trap such falls.

Gabions are rock-filled, wire mesh baskets, typically measuring 0.91 m by 0.91 m in cross-section, that are often constructed on-site with local waste rock. Advantages of gabions are the ease of construction on steep hillsides and where the foundation is irregular, and their capacity to sustain considerable impact from falling rock. However, gabions are not immune to damage by impacts of rock and maintenance equipment, and repair costs can become significant. Barriers constructed with pre-cast concrete with similar dimensions as gabions are also used on transportation systems for rock fall containment. Although concrete blocks are somewhat less resilient than gabions, they have the advantages of wide availability and rapid installation. In order for concrete blocks to be effective, flexibility must be provided by allowing movement at the joints between the blocks. In contrast, mass concrete walls are much less flexible and tend to shatter on impact.

*Geofabric–soil barriers.* Various barriers have been constructed using geofabric and soil layers,

*Figure 12.22* Rock fall containment structures: (a) rock catch ditch with 1.5 m high gabion along outer edge (Fraser River Canyon, British Columbia); (b) barrier constructed with MSE wall and wire rope fence on top of wall (Interstate 40 near Asheville, North Carolina) (Courtesy: North Carolina Department of Transportation).

each about 0.6 m thick, built up to form a barrier, which may be as high as 4 m (Threadgold and McNichol, 1985) (Figure 12.22(b)). By wrapping the fabric around each layer it is possible to construct a barrier with vertical front and back faces; the face subject to impact can be protected from damage with such materials as railway ties, gabions and rubber tires (Figures 12.23(a) and (b)). The capacity of a barrier of this type to stop rock falls depends on its mass in relation to the impact energy, the shear resistance at the base and the capacity to deform without failing. The deformation may be both elastic deformation of the barrier components, and shear displacement at the fabric layers or on the base. A disadvantage of barriers such as those shown in Figure 12.23 is that a considerable space is required for both the barrier and the catchment area behind it.

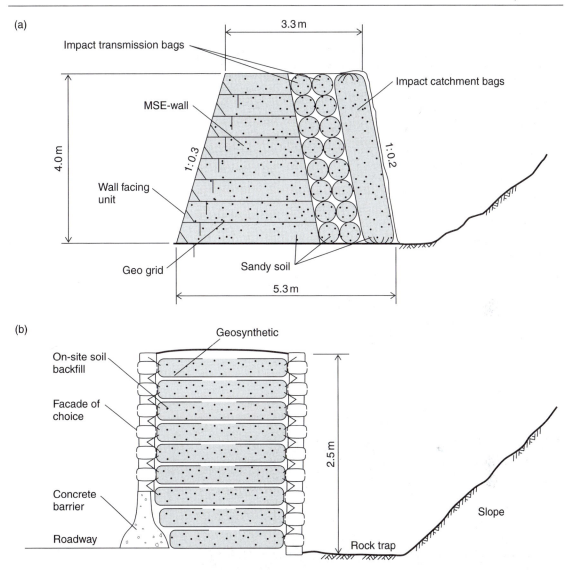

*Figure 12.23* Rock fall barriers constructed with soil and geofabric, and a variety of facings: (a) a 4 m high Wall with impact energy capacity of 5000 kJ (Protec, 2002); (b) a 2.5 m high wall with energy capacity of 950 kJ (Barrett and White, 1991).

Extensive testing of prototype barriers by the Colorado Department of Transportation has shown that limited shear displacement occurs on the fabric layers, and that they can withstand high energy impacts without significant damage (Barrett and White, 1991). Also, a 4 m high geofabric and soil barriersuccessfully withstood impact from boulders with volumes of up to 13 m$^3$ and impact energies of 5000 kJ on Niijima Island in Japan (Protec Engineering, 2002), and a similar 1.8 m wide geofabric barrier stopped rock impacts delivering 950 kJ of energy.

### 12.6.4 Rock catch fences and attenuators

During the 1980s, various fences and nets suitable for installation on steep rock faces, in ditches and on talus run-out zones were developed and thoroughly tested (Smith and Duffy, 1990; Barrett and White, 1991; Duffy and Haller, 1993). Nets are also being used in open pit mines for rock fall control (Brawner and Kalejta, 2002). A design suitable for a particular site depends on the topography, anticipated impact loads, bounce height and local availability of materials. A common feature of all these designs is their ability to withstand impact energy from rock falls due to their construction without any rigid components. When a rock impacts a net, there is deformation of the mesh which then engages energy absorbing components over an extended time of collision. This deformation significantly increases the capacity of these components to stop rolling rock and allows the use of light, low cost elements in construction.

*Wire-rope nets.* Nets with energy absorption capacity ranging from 40 to 2000 kJ have been developed as proprietary systems by a number of manufacturers (Geobrugg Corporation and Isofer Industries). The components of these nets are a series of steel I-beam posts on about 6 m centers, anchored to the foundation with grouted bolts, and guy cables anchored on the slope. Additional flexibility is provided by incorporating friction brakes on the cable supporting the nets and the guy cables. Friction brakes are loops of wire in a steel pipe that are activated during high energy events to help dissipate the impact forces (Figure 12.24). It has also been found that nets are effective in containing debris flows because the water rapidly drains from the debris material and its mobility is diminished (California Polytechnical State University, 1996).

The mesh is a two-layer system comprising a 50 mm chain link mesh, and either woven steel wire-rope mesh or interlocking steel rings. The

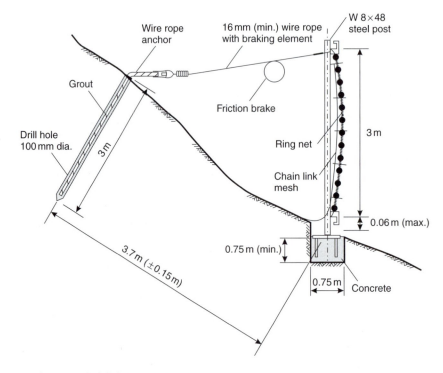

*Figure 12.24* Geobrugg rock fall fence (TRB, 1996).

woven wire-rope net is constructed typically with 8 mm diameter wire rope in a diagonal pattern on 100–200 mm centers. The wire rope and net dimensions will vary with expected impact energies and block sizes. An important feature of the wire-rope net is the method of fixing the intersection points of the wire rope with high strength crimped fasteners. The mesh is attached to the posts by lacing it on a continuous perimeter wire rope that is attached to brackets at the top and bottom of each post.

As an alternative to the woven wire mesh, ring nets are fabricated with 0.31 m diameter rings, each of which is interlocked with four adjacent rings. The rings are fabricated from 3 mm diameter high tensile steel wire, and the number of wires in each ring varies between 5 and 19 depending on the design energy capacity of the net.

*Rock fall attenuators.*   Where rocks fall down a narrow gully or chute bounded by stable rock walls, it is possible to install a variety of fences that slow down and absorb the energy of rock falls (Andrew, 1992b). The general method of construction is to install an anchor in each rock face to support a wire rope from which the fence, spanning the gully, is suspended. For rock falls with dimensions up to about 200 mm it is possible to use chain link mesh draped down the chute from the support rope; wire-rope mesh or ring nets can be used for larger blocks. Falling rocks are gradually brought to a halt as they bounce and roll under the mesh.

Maintenance requirements and worker safety of fence systems should be considered in design. A properly designed system should not need frequent repairs if the impacts are within the tolerances of design energies. However, cleaning of accumulated rock is necessary for any system. Typically, fixed barriers such as geofabric walls require room behind them for cleaning operations. In contrast, woven wire rope and ring nets do not have this requirement because of their modular design, allowing the nets to be cleaned from the front by removing or lifting each panel in turn.

### 12.6.5  Draped mesh

Wire mesh hung on the face of a rock slope can be an effective method of containing rock falls close to the face and preventing them from bouncing on to the road (Ciarla, 1986). Because the mesh absorbs some of the energy of the falling rock, the required dimensions of the ditch at the base of this slope are considerably reduced from those shown in Figure 12.21. Chain link mesh is a suitable method for controlling rock falls with dimensions less than about 0.6–1 m, and woven wire rope or ring nets are suitable for rock with dimensions up to about 1.3 m. For installations covering a high slope where the weight of the lightweight mesh may exceed its strength, the mesh can be reinforced with lengths of wire rope. In all cases, the upper edge of the mesh or net should be placed close to the source of the rock fall so the blocks have little momentum when they impact the mesh.

The mesh is not anchored at the bottom of the slope or at intermediate points. The freely hanging mesh permits rocks to work their way down to the ditch, rather than accumulating behind the mesh; the weight of such accumulations can fail the mesh.

### 12.6.6  Warning fences

Fences and warning signals that are triggered by falling rock are often used to protect railroads, and occasionally highways. The warning fence consists of a series of posts and cantilever cross-arms, which support rows of wires spaced about 0.5 m apart. The wires are connected to a signal system that shows a red light if a wire is broken. The signal light is located far enough from the rock slope that the traffic has time to stop, and then to proceed with caution before it reaches the rock fall location. Warning systems can also be incorporated into rock fall fences (Section 12.6.4), so that a second level of protection is provided in the event of a large fall that exceeds the energy capacity of the fence.

Warning fences are most applicable on transportation systems where traffic is light enough to accommodate occasional closures of the line. However, the use of warning fences as a protection measure has a number of disadvantages. The signal lights must be located a considerable distance from the slope, and falls may occur after the traffic has passed the light. Also, false alarms can be caused by minor falls of rock or ice, and maintenance costs can be significant.

### 12.6.7   Rock sheds and tunnels

In areas of extreme rock fall hazard where stabilization of the slope would be very costly, construction of a rock shed or even relocation of the highway into tunnels may be justified. Figure 12.25 shows two alternate configurations for sheds depending on the path of the falling rock. Where the rock falls have a steep trajectory, the shed has a flat roof covered with a layer of energy absorbing material such as gravel (Figure 12.25(a)). Sheds are constructed with reinforced concrete or steel, designed to withstand the worst case impact loading at the edge of the roof. The design should also consider the stability under impact loading of the foundations for the outer columns that are often located at the crest of steep slopes. Figure 12.25(b) shows three sheds with sloping roofs that are designed to deflect rolling rock over the railway. Because these sheds do not sustain direct impact they are of much lighter construction than that in Figure 12.25(a), and there is no protective layer on the roof.

Extensive research on the design of rock sheds has been carried out in Japan where tens of kilometers of sheds have been constructed to protect both railways and highways (Yoshida *et al.*, 1991; Ishikawa, 1999). Much of the research has involved full-scale testing in which boulders have been dropped on prototype sheds that are fully instrumented to measure deceleration in the boulder, and the induced stresses and strains in the major structural components. Objectives of the tests are to determine the effectiveness of

*Figure 12.25* Typical rock shed construction: (a) reinforced concrete structures with horizontal roof covered with layer of gravel (Photograph courtesy: Dr H. Yoshida, Kanazawa, Japan); (b) sheds constructed with timber and reinforced concrete with sloping roofs that deflect rock falls over the railway (White Canyon, Thompson River, British Columbia) (Courtesy: Canadian National Railway).

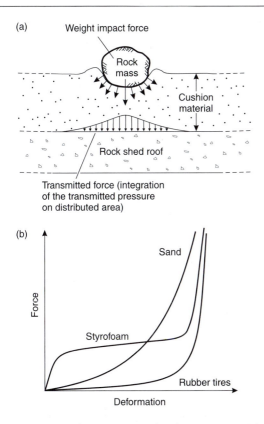

*Figure 12.26* Characteristics of cushioning materials:
(a) definition of weight impact force and transmitted
impact force due to rock fall impact on cushion;
(b) relationship between force and deformation for
impact loading of gravel, styrofoam and rubber tires
(Yoshida *et al.*, 1991).

various cushioning materials in absorbing and
dispersing the impact energy, and to assess the
influence of the flexibility of the structure on the
maximum impact that can be sustained without
damage.

A critical feature of shed design is the weight
and energy absorption characteristics of the cushioning material. Ideally the cushion should both
absorb energy by compression, and disperse the
point impact energy so that the energy transmitted into the structure occurs over a large
area. Furthermore, the cushion should remain
intact after impact so it does not need to be
replaced. The effectiveness of the material can be
expressed as the difference between the "weight
impact force" induced by boulder impact, and
the "transmitted force" that is absorbed by the
structure (Figure 12.26(a)). Gravel is the most
commonly used cushioning material because it is
inexpensive and widely available. However, the
disadvantage of gravel is its weight, and there
is a point where the gravel layer is so thick
that its weight exceeds the rock fall impact loading. Rubber tires have also been used, but it
is found that they are highly compressible with
little energy absorption. A viable alternative to
gravel is reinforced Styrofoam that is an effective
energy absorbing material with low unit weight,
which allows for some saving in the dimensions of the structure (Mamaghani *et al.*, 1999).
The disadvantage of Styrofoam is its cost compared to gravel, so the cost benefit of its use
should be carefully evaluated. Figure 12.26(b)
shows typical force–deformation characteristics
of gravel, Styrofoam and rubber tires (Yoshida,
2000).

In locations at which it is impractical to construct a rock shed or stabilize the slope by other
means, it may be necessary to drive a tunnel to
bypass the hazard zone. For example, a railway
in British Columbia drove a 1200 m long tunnel
to avoid a section of track located on a narrow bench between a steep, unstable rock cliff
above a 400 m deep lake. Major rock falls were a
hazard to train operations and had caused track
closures lasting as long as two weeks (Leighton,
1990).

# Chapter 13

# Movement monitoring

## 13.1 Introduction

Many rock slopes move to varying degrees during the course of their operational lives. Such movement indicates that the slope is in a quasi-stable state, but this condition may continue for many years, or even centuries, without failure occurring. However, in other cases, initial minor slope movement may be a precursor for accelerating movement followed by collapse of the slope. Because of the unpredictability of slope behavior, movement monitoring programs can be of value in managing slope hazards, and they provide information that is useful for the design of remedial work.

Slope movement is most common in open pit mines, and many mines continue to operate safely for years with moving slopes that are carefully monitored to warn of deteriorating stability conditions. Other slopes that undergo long-term movement are landslides that may creep for hundreds of years resulting in accumulative movement of tens of meters. Such movement may comprise an approximately uniform creep rate, on which may be superimposed short periods of more rapid movement resulting from such events as earthquakes, unusually high precipitation periods and human activities. Human activities that can be detrimental to slope stability include excavations of the base, and changing the ground water conditions by dam filling or irrigation.

This chapter describes common methods of monitoring movement of rock slopes, and interpretation of the results. It is considered that monitoring programs are most appropriate for actively mined slopes such as open pit mines and quarries which have a limited operational life and where a carefully managed, on-going survey operation can be set up. The survey will be able to identify accelerating movement of the slope and take measures to minimize the risk by moving operations away from the active slide. Figure 13.1 shows an example of an open pit slope where careful monitoring identified the increasing rate of movement, which allowed the actual collapse to be photographed. There are several well-documented cases of slope monitoring at open pits where mining continued for several months below the moving slope. Eventually the rate of movement increased rapidly indicating that stability conditions were deteriorating and operations were halted shortly before the slope failed (Kennedy and Neimeyer, 1970; Brawner et al., 1975; Wyllie and Munn, 1979; Broadbent and Zavodni, 1982).

Monitoring may also be suitable for large landslides that threaten facilities such as reservoirs, transportation systems and residential areas. The weaknesses of such programs are that they may have to be maintained for long periods and may involve sophisticated monitoring and telemetry, which will be costly. Also, it may be difficult to identify deteriorating stability conditions that will clearly show there is a need to evacuate the site. It is considered that where there is a significant risk to lives and property, remediation is preferred to long-term monitoring.

(a)

(b)

(c)

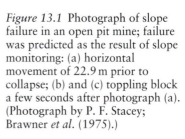

*Figure 13.1* Photograph of slope failure in an open pit mine; failure was predicted as the result of slope monitoring: (a) horizontal movement of 22.9 m prior to collapse; (b) and (c) toppling block a few seconds after photograph (a). (Photograph by P. F. Stacey; Brawner *et al.* (1975).)

## 13.2 Types of slope movement

In setting up a movement monitoring program it is useful to have an understanding of the type of movement that is occurring. This information can be used to select appropriate instrumentation for the site, and assist in interpretation of the results. For example, if the slope were undergoing a toppling failure, then crack width monitors at the crest would provide direct measurement of horizontal movement. In comparison, if an inclinometer were to be installed, it may not be certain that it extended to a depth below the zone of movement, which would result in erroneous readings. Furthermore, the type of movement is related to the failure mechanism and this information can be used to ensure that an appropriate type of stability analysis is used. That is, outward and downward movement at the crest and bulging at the toe would indicate a plane or circular failure, whereas horizontal movement at the crest only would be more indicative of a toppling failure.

The following is a discussion on common types of slope movement, and their implications for slope stability.

### 13.2.1 Initial response

When a slope is first excavated or exposed, there is a period of initial response as a result of elastic rebound, relaxation and/or dilation of the rock mass due to changes in stress induced by the excavation (Zavodni, 2000). This initial response will occur most commonly in open pit mines where the excavation rate is relatively rapid. In comparison, the expose of slopes by the retreat of glaciation and the gradual steepening of slopes due to river erosion at the toe will occur over time periods that may be orders of magnitude longer. However, the cumulative strain of such slopes can be considerable. Elastic rebound strain takes place without the development of a definite sliding surface, and is likely the result of dilation and shear of existing discontinuities.

Martin (1993) reports on the initial response measurements of three open pit mines, which showed that total displacement varied from 150 mm in a strong massive rock mass at Palabora in South Africa to more than 500 mm in highly fractured and altered rock at the Goldstrike Mine in Nevada. The rates of movement during initial response periods decreased with time and eventually showed no movement. Based on the monitoring carried out at Palabora, the following relationship has been established between the rate of movement $V$ (mm/day) and the time $t$ (days):

$$V = A\,e^{-bt} \tag{13.1}$$

where $A$ and $b$ are constants that are a function of the rock mass properties, the slope height and angle, the mining rate, external influences and the ultimate failure mechanism. The reported values of $A$ range from 0.113 to 2.449, while values for $b$ range from 0.0004 to 0.00294.

The critical property of the relationship shown in equation (13.1) is that the rate of movement decreases with time, indicating that the slope is not at risk from failure.

Another characteristic of initial response type of movement is that it can occur within a large volume of rock. For example, during the steepening of the 150 m deep Berkeley Pit from a slope angle of 45° to an angle of 60°, movement measurements in two adits showed that rebound occurred at a distance of up to 120 m behind the face at the toe of the slope (Zavodni, 2000). This rebound and relaxation mechanism has been modeled using the FLAC and UDEC codes (Itasca Group, MN) with the objective of predicting such behavior on similar pits.

### 13.2.2 Regressive and progressive movement

Following a period of initial response and then possible stability, slope "failure" would be indicated by the presence of tension cracks at, or near the crest of the slope. The development of such cracks is evidence that the movement of the slope has exceeded the elastic limit of the rock mass. However, it is possible that mining can safely continue under these conditions with the implementation of a monitoring system. Eventually, an

(a)

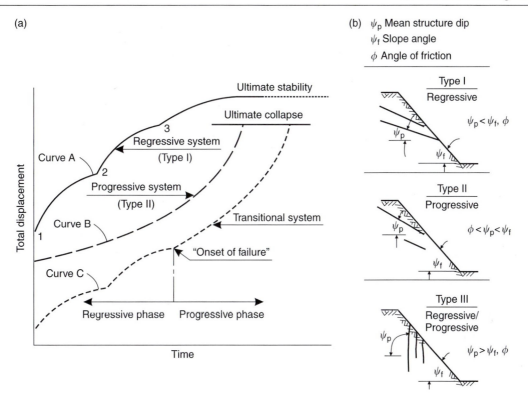

(b)   $\psi_p$ Mean structure dip
$\psi_f$ Slope angle
$\phi$ Angle of friction

*Figure 13.2* Types of slope movement: (a) typical repressive and progressive displacement curves; (b) structural geological conditions corresponding to types of slope movement (Broadbent and Zavodni, 1982).

"operational slope failure" may develop, which can be described as a condition where the rate of displacement exceeds the rate at which the slide material can be safety mined (Call, 1982).

A means of identifying either plastic strain of the rock mass or operational failure is to distinguish between regressive and progressive time–displacement curves (Figure 13.2). A regressive failure (curve A) is one that shows short-term decelerating displacement cycles if disturbing events external to the slope, such as blasting or water pressure, are removed. Conversely, a progressive failure (curve B) is one that displaces at an increasing rate, with the increase in rate often being algebraic to the point of collapse, unless stabilization measures are implemented. Correct interpretation of the curves is valuable in understanding the slope failure mechanism, and in predicting the future performance of the slope.

Figure 13.2 also shows geological conditions that are commonly associated with these types of time–displacement curves. Where the slope contains discontinuities that dip out of the face, but at a shallow angle that is flatter than the friction angle of these surfaces (Type I), then it is usual that some external stimuli such as blasting or water pressures will be required to initiate movement. The onset of movement indicates that the factor of safety of the slope has dropped just below 1.0, but with a reduction of the external stimuli, the factor of safety will increase and the rate of movement will begin to reduce. In the case of water pressures causing movement, the opening of tension cracks and dilation of the rock mass may temporarily result in the water pressures diminishing, but as pressures gradually build up, another cycle of movement may start. Another condition associated with regressive movement is stick-slip behavior, which is related to the difference between the static and dynamic coefficients of friction on rock surfaces (Jaeger and Cook, 1976).

Operations can be continued below slopes experiencing regressive movement, but it is necessary that the mining be conducted for short periods with frequent pullbacks, with care being taken to identify the transition to a progressive failure (Zavodni, 2000). As shown in Figure 13.2, geological conditions that may be associated with progressive failure are discontinuities that dip out of the face at a steeper angle than the friction angle (Type II). Also, a slide surface on which the shear strength gradually diminishes with displacement may experience progressive failure. The duration of the progressive stage of a failure has varied from 4 days to 45 days, with no obvious correlation between the time and the site conditions (Zavodni and Broadbent, 1980). However, more rapid failure would be expected where there is a well-defined slide surface.

As shown by curve C in Figure 13.2, a regressive failure may transition into a progressive failure and rapidly lead to collapse. Causes of this change in behavior can include where mining daylights a sliding surface, break up of the rock at the toe of the slope, an increase in water pressure, or continued mining causing the slope to accelerate beyond recovery. It is obviously important to recognize the onset of progressive failure, which will require a diligent monitoring program and careful analysis of the results.

### 13.2.3  Long-term creep

In contrast to the rapid excavation, and the consequent large scale, relatively fast movements that take place in open pit mines, mountain slopes may creep over periods of hundreds of years. Long-term creep may occur where there is no defined failure surface, such as a toppling failure (Type III, Figure 13.2), or where the change in slope geometry is very slow, for example, due to stress relief following glacial retreat or erosion at the toe by a river. Other causes of such long-term movement are historical

earthquakes that each cause displacement, and climatic changes that result in periods of high precipitation and increased water pressures in the slope. The Downie and Dutchman's Ridge Slides in British Columbia, which experienced tens of meters of ancient, downslope creep prior to reservoir filling at the base, are both examples of long-term creep (Moore and Imrie, 1993; Moore et al., 1997).

The authors have examined several dozen landslides in western North America where a series of tension cracks at the crest indicate that tens of meters of movement has occurred. In most of these cases, there is no evidence of recent movement because the rock surfaces are weathered and there is undisturbed soil and vegetation filling the cracks. It is possible that very slow creep is occurring, but no long-term monitoring program was available to determine if this was occurring. In one case in Alaska, comparison of historic photographs in the local museum showed no substantive change in the appearance of the slope over a period of 120 years. From these observations, it has been concluded that the presence of tension cracks does not necessarily indicate that there is risk of imminent collapse. However, the hazard may be significant if there is evidence of recent movement such as disturbance to the soil and movement of blocks of rock, or there is a proposed change to the forces acting on the slope, because of excavation at the toe, for example.

### 13.3  Surface monitoring methods

This section describes common procedures for making surface measurements of slope movement. In general, monitoring of the surface of a slide is likely to be less costly to set up and maintain than sub-surface measurements that will require drilling holes to install the instruments. However, surface measurements can only be used where the surface movement accurately represents the overall movement of the slope. For example, it would not be appropriate to make surface measurements where loose blocks of rock on the surface were toppling and rotating independently of the main slide movement. Other factors to consider in the selection of a monitoring system include the time available to set up the instruments, the rate of movement and safe access to the site.

Options for monitoring equipment include automatically collecting measurements at pre-set intervals on data loggers, and using telemetry to transmit these results to another location for analysis and plotting. These systems can also incorporate alarms that are triggered if pre-set movement thresholds are exceeded (Baker, 1991). An important aspect of such automated systems is the cost of installation, and particularly maintenance. These costs usually limit their use to high hazard locations, and for temporary situations while longer-term stabilization is implemented.

### 13.3.1   Crack width monitors

Since tension cracks are an almost universal feature of slope movement, crack width measurements are often a reliable and inexpensive means of monitoring movement. Figure 13.3 shows two methods of measuring crack widths. The simplest procedure is to install a pair of pins on either side of the crack and measure the distance between them with a steel tape (Figure 13.3(a)). If there are two pins on either side of the crack, then the diagonal distance can also be measured to check the transverse displacement. The maximum practical distance between the pins is probably 2 m.

Figure 13.3(b) shows a wire extensometer that can be used to measure the total movement across a series of cracks over a distance of as much as 20 m. The measurement station is located on stable ground beyond the cracks, and the cable extends to a pin located on the crest of the slope. The cable is tensioned by the weight, and movement is measured by the position of the steel block threaded on the cable. If the movement exceeds the length of the steel rule, the cable can be extended by moving the counterweight and resetting the steel block to the left end of the rule. The wire extensometer can also incorporate a warning system comprising a second steel block threaded on the cable that is set at a selected distance from a trip switch. If the movement exceeds this pre-set

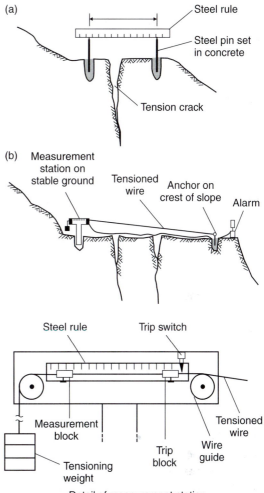

*Figure 13.3* Measurement of tension crack width: (a) measurement of distance between steel pins; (b) wire extensometer with trip switch to warn of excessive movement (Wyllie and Munn, 1979).

limit, the trip switch is triggered and an alarm is activated. As movement occurs it is necessary to reset the position of the front block, with the distance from the trip switch being determined by the rate of movement. The selection of an appropriate distance from the trip switch is important in order that the alarm provide a warning of deteriorating stability conditions, while not triggering false alarms that result in operators loosing confidence in the value of the monitoring.

The main limitations of crack width monitoring are that the upslope pin or reference point must be on stable ground, and that it is necessary that people access the crest of the slide to make the measurements. This work could be hazardous where the slope is moving rapidly. These limitations can be overcome to some degree by automating the system using vibrating wire strain gauges and data loggers to automatically read the distance and record the measurements.

### 13.3.2　Surveying

On large slides where access to the slope is hazardous and/or there is a need to make frequent and precise measurements and rapidly analyze the results, surveying using EDM (electronic distance measurement) equipment is the most suitable monitoring method (Vamosi and Berube, 1987; ACG, 1998). There are usually three components of a survey system (Figure 13.4). First, one or several reference points are required on stable ground, but that can be viewed from the instrument stations closer to the slide. Second, a number of instrument stations are set up on reasonably stable ground at locations from which the slide is visible. If the co-ordinate positions of the movement stations are to be measured, then the instrument stations should be arranged such that they form an approximately equilateral triangle. Third, a series of stations are set up on, and possibly just outside the slide area, which are then located relative to the instrument stations. It is preferable that the measurement direction be in the likely direction of movement so that the distance readings approximate the actual slide movement. For example, in Figure 13.4(a), it is preferable to measure stations on the north portion of the slide from instrument station 1, and those on the south side from instrument station 2. The stations on the slide can be reflectors used on heavy equipment, or survey prisms, depending on the sight distance and the accuracy required.

The survey arrangement shown in Figure 13.4 can be used to measure at any desired frequency or level of accuracy. For example, for slow moving slides the readings may be made every

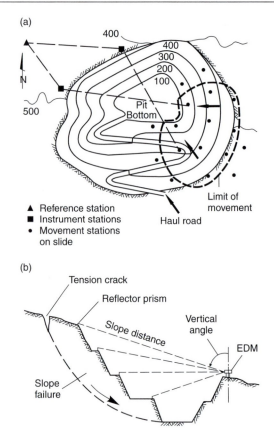

(a)

▲ Reference station
■ Instrument stations
● Movement stations on slide

(b)

*Figure 13.4* Survey system to remotely measure slope movement: (a) typical arrangement of reference, instrument and monitoring stations; (b) measurement of vertical angle and distance to determine vertical displacement (Wyllie and Munn, 1979).

few weeks or months, while for a rapidly moving slide above an active mining operation, an automated system can be set up that takes a series of readings at pre-set intervals, and records and plots the results. Also, quick checks of stability can be made by making distance measurements only, and these can be followed up with triangulation measurements to determine the co-ordinates of each station at less frequent intervals. Figure 13.4(b) shows that measurement of the vertical angle and the slope distance allows the vertical displacement to be measured, which is of value in determining the mechanism of failure (see Section 13.5).

### 13.3.3 Laser imaging

An advance on monitoring individual stations on a slide is laser imaging that involves making a precise three-dimensional map of the entire face (Spacial Data Services, 2002). The system involves directing the laser at the slope, selecting the area to be scanned and the density of the scan, and then the laser rapidly and automatically makes a large number of closely spaced scans to cover the area. The result is a dense, accurate three-dimensional point cloud that can be processed to produce contour map. By making a series of such maps over time from the same reference point, the position of the face can be compared between each scan, and the location and magnitude of the movement measured.

### 13.3.4 Tiltmeters

It is possible to measure the tilt of a feature to a resolution of about 10 arc seconds using a tilt-meter. These measurements involve bolting or gluing a base plate to the rock face on which the tiltmeter is precisely mounted. The instrument can either be permanently mounted on the face so that readings can be made at any time, or can be located on the mounting plate just when readings are being made.

The advantage of tiltmeters is that rapid and precise measurements can be made of the tilt, from which an assumed movement can be calculated. The disadvantages are that the instrument is costly, and it may be difficult to find a small portion of the rock face, the movement of which is representative of the slope movement. It is considered that the primary application of tiltmeters is on structures such as dams and retaining walls rather than rock slopes.

### 13.3.5 Global positioning system

The global positioning system (GPS) may be a suitable method of monitoring slope movement where the slide covers a large area and extreme precision is not required. Stations can be set up on the slide and their co-ordinates measured at any desired frequency with the GPS unit. Greater

accuracy can be achieved by setting up a base station on stable ground outside the slide area, and accurately determining its position. The GPS readings on the slide are then referenced to the co-ordinates of the base station (differential GPS).

The advantages of GPS monitoring are the low cost and ease of set up, but the disadvantages are that the accuracy is limited by the built-in error for civilian users, and in steep terrain there may be an insufficient number of satellites visible to obtain readings.

### 13.3.6 Synthetic aperture radar

A technique for precise monitoring of movement over large areas is to use radar satellite remote sensing techniques. This technique is known as Interferometric Synthetic Aperture Radar (SAR) and involves capturing a radar image of the ground surface, which is then compared with images taken at a different time to obtain the relative ground movement. Significant features of this technique are that the image can cover an area a large as $2500 \, km^2$, relative movements can be measured in the range of 5–25 mm, and the measurements are independent of the weather, cloud cover and daylight (www.terrainsar.com, 2002).

These attributes mean that SAR is ideally suited to precise movement monitoring of large areas over long time periods, with no need to set up reference points on the ground. However, some limitations of the technique are that the frequency of the measurements are governed by the interval between satellite orbits over the site, which presently (2003) is about once every 24–35 days, and the processing of the data can take another 35–40 days. Also, movement is most accurately monitored in the vertical direction.

## 13.4 Sub-surface monitoring methods

Sub-surface measurement of slope movement is often a useful component of a monitoring program in order to provide a more complete picture of the slope behavior. In cases where surface monitoring is not feasible, then sub-surface measurements will be the only measurements available.

The main purpose of these measurements is to locate the slide surface or surfaces, and monitor the rate of movement; in some cases the holes are used for monitoring both movement and water pressures.

### 13.4.1   Borehole probes

One of the simplest sub-surface monitoring methods is the borehole probe comprising a length of reinforcing steel about 2 m long that is lowered down the drill hole on a length of rope. If the hole intersects a moving slide plane, the hole will be displaced at this level and it will no longer be possible to pull the bar past this point. Similarly, a probe can be lowered down the hole, and in this way both the top and bottom of the slide plane can be located.

The advantages of the probe are the low cost and simplicity, but it will provide little information on the rate of movement.

### 13.4.2   Time–domain reflectometry

Time–domain reflectometry is another means of locating a sliding surface, which can also monitor the rate of movement (Kane and Beck, 1996). This method involves grouting into a borehole a co-axial cable comprising inner and outer metallic conductors separated by an insulating material. When a voltage pulse waveform is sent down the cable, it will be reflected at any point where there is a change in the distance between the conductors. The reflection occurs because the change in distance alters the characteristic impedance of the cable. Movement of a sliding plane that causes a crimp or kink in the cable will be sufficient to change the impedance, and the instrumentation can detect the location of the movement.

The primary advantages of time–domain reflectometry are that the cable is inexpensive so that it can be sacrificed in a rapidly moving slide. Also, the readings can be made in a few minutes from a remote location either by extending the cable to a safe location off the slide, or by telemetry. The ability to make remote readings can achieve significant savings compared to inclinometers (see

Section 13.4.3) because of the reduced travel time, and the readout box directly shows the movement without the need to download and plot the results.

### 13.4.3   Inclinometers

Inclinometers are instruments ideally suited to long-term, precise monitoring of the position of a borehole over its entire length. By making a series of readings over time, it is also possible to monitor the rate of movement. The components of the inclinometer are a plastic casing with four longitudinal grooves cut in the inside wall, and a probe that is lowered down the casing on an electrical cable with graduated depth markings (Figure 13.5(a)). The probe contains two accelerometers, aligned so that they measure the tilt of the probe in two mutually perpendicular directions. The probe is also equipped with a pair of wheels that run in the grooves in the casing and maintain the rotational stability of the probe.

The first requirement of accurate monitoring is to extend the borehole below the depth of movement so that readings made from the end of the hole are referenced to a stable base. Precautions are also needed during installation of the casing to maintain the vertical alignment of the grooves and prevent spiraling. Readings are made by lowering a probe to the end of the hole and then raising it in increments equal to the length of the wheelbase $L$ of the probe. At each depth increment the tilt $\psi$ is measured. Figure 13.5(b) shows the procedure for calculating the displacement ($L \sin \psi$) for each increment, and the total displacement at the top of the hole $\Sigma(L \sin \psi)$. A check of the results is usually made by rotating the probe by 180° and taking a second set of readings. Another precaution is to allow time during the readings for the probe to reach temperature equilibrium in the hole.

## 13.5   Data interpretation

Interpretation of the movement data is an essential part of monitoring operation in order to identify quickly acceleration or deceleration of the slope that indicates deteriorating or

(a)

(b)

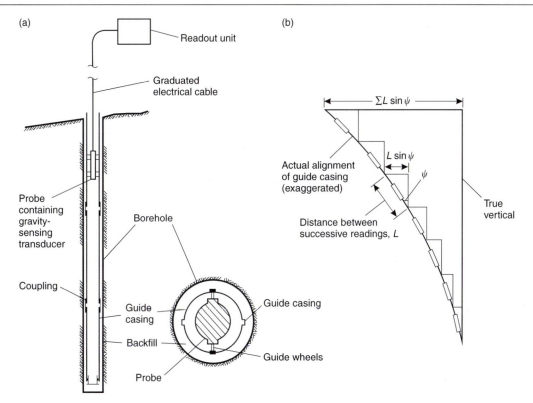

*Figure 13.5* Inclinometer for measuring borehole deflection: (a) arrangement of grooved casing and inclinometer probe; (b) principle of calculating deflection from tilt measurement (Dunnicliff, 1993).

improving stability conditions respectively. This allows appropriate action to be taken with respect to the safety and economics of the operation. The importance of updating the plots as the readings are made is that failures have occurred within days of cracks first being observed (Stacey, 1996). Unfortunately, there are instances of careful monitoring measurements being recorded, but because they were not plotted, acceleration of the slope that was a clear precursor to failure was not recognized.

This section describes a number of procedures for interpreting monitoring results to provide information on both stability conditions and the mechanism of failure. With respect to the mechanism of failure, this information is useful in designing stabilization measures, which require that the appropriate method of analysis be used, such as plane or toppling.

### 13.5.1   *Time–movement and time–velocity plots*

The monitoring program, whether carried out by surveying, crack width gauges, GPS, satellite scans or inclinometers will provide readings of movement against time. Plots of this data are fundamental to understanding the mechanism of the slope movement, and possibly predicting the time of failure. The following is a discussion of a monitoring program in an open pit coal mine where a movement monitoring program was used to safely mine below a moving slope for most of the life of the pit (Wyllie and Munn, 1979).

Figure 13.6(a) shows a cross-section of the final pit and the slope above the pit, as well as the lithology and geological structure of this slope. Soon after mining commenced at the 1870 m elevation in March 1974, a toppling failure was initiated

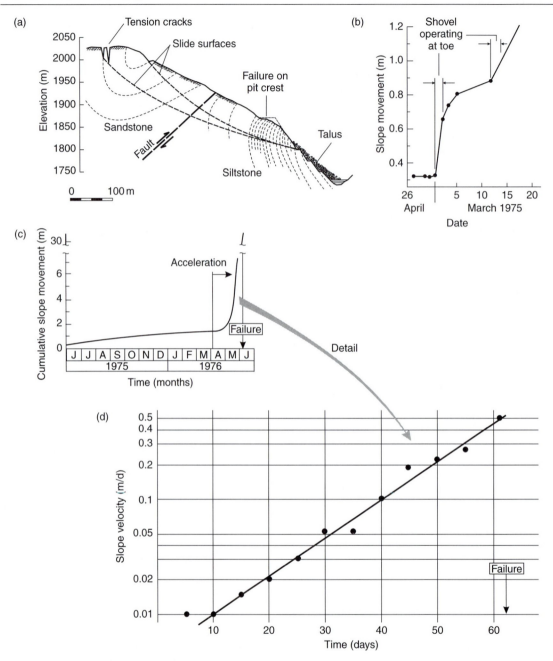

*Figure 13.6* Movement monitoring at open pit coal mine: (a) cross-section of pit and hillside showing geology and extent of slope failure; (b) regressive slope movement when mining at 1840 m level; (c) slope movement over 13 months leading to slope failure; (d) slope velocity over two months prior to failure (Wyllie and Munn, 1979).

in the overturned siltstone beds at the crest of the pit. When mining on the 1840 m bench, a series of cracks formed on the 1860 m bench and a movement monitoring program was set up in February 1975 using a combination of wire extensometers (Figure 13.3(b)) and surveying of prisms. This monitoring system was used to control the mining operation with the objective of mining back to the final wall so that the coal could eventually be mined to the bottom of the pit. Figure 13.6(b) shows the sensitivity of the slope movement to mining at the toe of the toppling slope, and typical regressive behavior as soon as the shovel was pulled back. This experience was used to establish the criterion, based on hourly movement readings, that mining would be halted as soon as the rate of movement reached 25 mm per hour. When this rate reduced to 15 mm per day over a period of about 10 days, mining recommenced. Using this control procedure, mining continued towards the final depth of about 1700 m with the slope moving at an average rate of 6 mm per day.

In April 1976, the slope started to accelerate, and over the next two months total movement of about 30 m occurred on the hillside above the pit and the maximum velocity reached nearly a meter per day (Figures 13.6(c) and (d)). The acceleration on the slope movement plots gave an adequate warning of deterioration stability conditions and mining was abandoned. The area with the greatest movement was on the toppling beds along the crest of the pit, and in early June 1976 two separate slope failures occurred with a total volume of 570,000 m$^3$. After the failures, the monitoring system was re-established which showed that the rate of movement was gradually decreasing, and after a month it was decided to restart mining at the bottom of the pit. This decision was also based on borehole probe measurements, which showed that the circular slide surfaces, associated with the toppling at the pit crest, daylighted in the upper part of the pit slope (Figure 13.6(a)). Therefore, mining at the base of the pit would have little effect on stability.

The type of movement monitoring data shown in Figures 13.6(c) and (d) has been analyzed to help predict the time of failure once the progressive stage of slope movement has developed (Zavodni and Broadbent, 1980). Figure 13.7 shows the semi-log time–velocity plot in feet per day preceding the slope failure at the Liberty Pit. On this plot it is possible to identify the velocities at the start $V_0$ and the mid-point $V_{mp}$ of progressive stage of movement. A constant $K$ is defined as

$$K = \frac{V_{mp}}{V_0} \tag{13.2}$$

Study of six carefully documented slope failures shows that the average value of $K$ is $-7.21$, with a standard deviation of 2.11. For example, Figure 13.6(d) shows a $K$ value of about $-7$ ($-0.07/0.01$).

The general equation for a semi-log straight line graph has the form

$$V = C\,e^{St} \tag{13.3}$$

where $V$ is the velocity, $C$ is the intercept of the line on the time axis, $e$ is the base of the natural logarithm, $S$ is the slope of the line and $t$ is the time. Therefore, the velocity at any time is given by

$$V = V_0\,e^{St} \tag{13.4}$$

Combining equations (13.2) and (13.3) gives the following relationship for the velocity at collapse $V_{col}$:

$$V_{col} = K^2\,V_0 \tag{13.5}$$

The use of equation (13.4) in conjunction with a time–velocity plot allows an estimation to be made of the time of collapse. For example, from Figure 13.6(d) where $K = -7$ and $V_0 = 0.01$ m/day, the value of $V_{col}$ is 0.49 m/day. Extrapolation of the velocity–time line shows that this rate will occur at about 61 days, which is very close to the actual day of collapse.

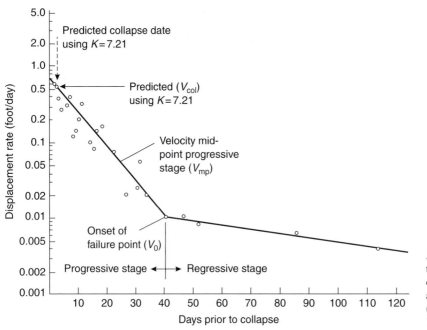

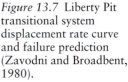

*Figure 13.7* Liberty Pit transitional system displacement rate curve and failure prediction (Zavodni and Broadbent, 1980).

It is likely that the rate at which collapse occurs depends to some degree on the geological conditions on the sliding plane. For example, failure is likely to occur faster if sliding is occurring on a well-defined structural feature such as a fault that daylights on the face, compared to that shown in Figure 13.6(a) where the slide plane developed by fracture through intact rock. The reason for this is that in the case of a fault, the shear strength will diminish from peak to residual with relatively little movement compared to that of failure through the rock mass.

### 13.5.2  Slope failure mechanisms

Figure 13.8 shows a number of methods of analyzing movement monitoring results that may help to identify the mechanism of slope failure. This information can be useful in applying the appropriate method of stability analysis and in the design of stabilization measures.

Figure 13.8(a) shows a combined displacement and velocity plot which shows that the acceleration of the slope stopped after day 5. This change in behavior is clearly evident on the velocity plot where the velocity is constant after day 5. In comparison, on the movement plot the change in gradient is not so obvious. This slope movement would be typical of regressive type instability.

Figure 13.8(b) shows the magnitude and dips of movement vectors for survey stations on the crest, mid-height and toe of the slide. The dip angles approximately equal the dip of the underlying failure surface, and in this instance indicate that a circular failure is taking place in which the sliding surface is steep near the crest and near-horizontal near the base. This information would also show the location of the toe of the slide, which may not be toe of the slope, as was the case for the slide shown in Figure 13.6(a). Figure 13.8(c) shows a movement vector for a typical toppling failure in which the stations located on the overturning beds at the crest may move upwards by small amount, while there is little movement below the crest.

Figure 13.8(d) shows contours of slope velocity plotted on a plane of the pit. These plots show both the extent of the slide, and the area(s) of most rapid movement. Such plots, when regularly updated, can be useful in identifying an increase

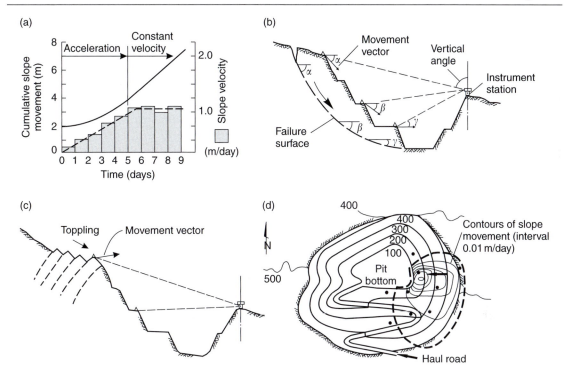

*Figure 13.8* Interpretation of movement monitoring data: (a) displacement and velocity plots show onset of regressive movement; (b) movement vectors showing circular failure mechanism; (c) movement vectors showing toppling failure mechanism; (d) slope velocity contours show extent of slope movement (Wyllie and Munn, 1979).

in the dimensions of the slide, and/or a change in the most rapidly moving area. This information will assist in the planning of mining operations, for example, to complete mining in the south-east corner of the pit before failure occurs. Also, if the haul road is on a relatively slowly moving part of the slide, this may allow time to develop new access to the pit.

# Chapter 14

# Civil engineering applications

## 14.1 Introduction

When a slope above an important civil engineering structure is found to be unstable, an urgent decision is commonly required on effective and economical remedial measures. Evidence of potential instability includes open tension cracks behind the crest, movement at the toe, failures of limited extent in part of the slope, or failure of an adjacent slope in similar geology. Whatever the cause, once doubt has been cast upon the stability of an important slope, it is essential that its overall stability should be investigated and, if necessary, appropriate remedial measures implemented. This chapter describes five rock slopes on civil engineering projects in a variety of geological and climatic conditions, and the slope stabilization measures that were implemented. For each example, information is provided on the geology, rock strength and ground water conditions, as well as the stability analysis, design of the remedial work and construction issues.

The purpose of these case studies is to describe the application of the investigation and design techniques described in previous chapters of the book.

## 14.2 Case Study I—Hong Kong: choice of remedial measures for plane failure

### 14.2.1 Site description

A 60 m high cut had an overall face angle of 50°, made up of three, 20 m high benches with face angles of 70° (Figure 14.1). A small slide

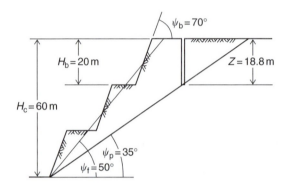

*Figure 14.1* Geometry assumed for two-dimensional plane failure analysis of the slope in Case Study I.

in a nearby slope has caused attention to be focused on this particular cut and concern has been expressed that a major slide could occur resulting in serious damage to an important civil engineering structure at the foot of the cut. An assessment was required of the short- and the long-term stability of the cut, and recommendations for appropriate remedial measures, should these prove necessary. No previous geological or engineering studies had been carried out on this cut, and no boreholes were known to exist in the area. The site was in an area of high rainfall intensity and low seismicity. A horizontal seismic coefficient, $a_H$ of $0.08g$ had been suggested as the maximum to which this cut was likely to be subjected.

### 14.2.2 Geology

The cut was in slightly weathered granite containing several sets of steeply dipping joints,

*Table 14.1* Orientation of slope and joint sets shown in Figures 14.1 and 14.2

| Feature | Dip (°) | Dip direction (°) |
|---|---|---|
| Overall slope face | 50 | 200 |
| Individual benches | 70 | 200 |
| Sheet joint | 35 | 190 |
| Joint set *J*1 | 80 | 233 |
| Joint set *J*2 | 80 | 040 |
| Joint set *J*3 | 70 | 325 |

as well as sheet jointing that dipped at 35° and formed the natural slopes in the area. Faced with this problem and having no geological or engineering data from which to work, the first task was to obtain a representative sample of structural geology to establish the most likely failure mode. Time would not allow a drilling program to be mounted. Consequently, the collection of structural data had to be based upon surface mapping, which was reasonable because of the extensive rock exposure in the cut face and natural slopes.

The structural mapping identified the geometrical and structural geology features listed in Table 14.1.

### 14.2.3  Rock shear strength

Because no information was available on the shear strength of the sheet joints forming the potential sliding surface, the strength values used in design were estimated from previous experience of the stability of slopes in granite. Figure 4.21 is a summary of shear strength values developed primarily from back analysis of slope failures; point '11' most closely represented the strength of the rock at the site. Based on this experience, it was considered that even heavily kaolinized granites exhibit friction values in the range of 35–45° because of the angular nature of the mineral grains. The cohesion of these surfaces was likely to be variable depending on the degree of weathering of the surface and the persistence of the joints; a cohesion range of 50–200 kPa was selected.

### 14.2.4  Ground water

There were no boreholes in the slope so the subsurface ground water conditions were unknown. However, since the site was in an area that experienced periods of intense rainfall, it was expected that significant transient ground water pressures would develop in the slope following these events.

### 14.2.5  Stability analysis

The stereoplot of the data in Table 14.1 is shown in Figure 14.2, including a friction circle of 35°. Note that, although the three joint sets provided a number of steep release surfaces, which would allow blocks to separate from the rock mass, none of their lines of intersection, which are circled in Figure 14.2, fall within the zone designated as potentially unstable (refer to Figure 7.3(b)). On the other hand, the great circle representing the sheet joints passes through the zone of potential instability. Furthermore, the dip direction of the sheet joints is close to that of the cut face, so the most likely failure mode was a plane slide on the sheet joints in the direction indicated in Figure 14.2.

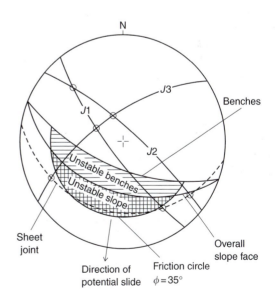

*Figure 14.2* Stereoplot of geometric and geological data for slope shown in Figure 14.1.

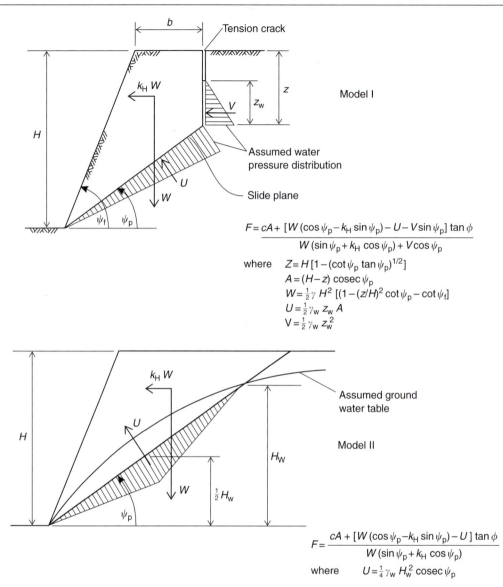

*Figure 14.3* Theoretical models of plane slope failures for Case Study I.

The stability check carried out in Figure 14.2 suggested that both the overall cut and the individual benches were potentially unstable, and it was therefore clearly necessary to carry out further analysis of both.

The two steeply dipping joint sets $J1$ and $J2$ were oriented approximately parallel to the slope face, and there was a strong possibility

of a tension crack forming on these discontinuities behind the crest of the cut. One possible failure mode was that illustrated as Model I in Figure 14.3; this theoretical model assumed that a tension crack occurred in the dry state in the most critical position (refer to Figure 6.6), and that this crack filled to depth $z_w$ with water during a period of exceptionally heavy rain.

A simultaneous earthquake subjected the slope to ground motion that was simulated with a horizontal seismic coefficient $k_H$ of 0.08, generating a force of $k_H W$, where $W$ was the weight of the sliding block. The factor of safety of this slope with the inclusion of a pseudo-static horizontal earthquake loading is given by the equations in Figure 14.3 (refer to Section 6.5.4, pseudo-static stability analysis).

To allow for the possible presence of substantial sub-surface water, an alternative theoretical model was proposed. This is illustrated as Model II in Figure 14.3 and, again this model includes the pseudo-static earthquake loading.

Having decided upon the most likely failure mode and having proposed one or more theoretical models to represent this failure mode, a range of possible slope parameter values was substituted into the factor of safety equations to determine the sensitivity of the slope to the different conditions to which it was likely to be subjected. Table 14.2 summarizes the input data. The factors of safety of the slopes were calculated by substituting these values into the equations on Figure 14.3 as follows:

Overall Cut Model I

$$FS = \frac{80.2c + (18{,}143 - 393z_w - 2.81z_w^2)\tan\phi}{14{,}995 + 4.02z_w^2}$$

Table 14.2 Input data for Case Study I plane stability analysis

| Parameter | Parameter value |
| --- | --- |
| Cut height | $H_c = 60\,\text{m}$ |
| Overall slope angle | $\psi_f = 50°$ |
| Bench face angle | $\psi_b = 70°$ |
| Bench height | $H_b = 20\,\text{m}$ |
| Failure plane angle | $\psi_p = 35°$ |
| Distance to tension crack (slope) | $b_s = 15.4\,\text{m}$ |
| Distance to tension crack (bench) | $b_b = 2.8\,\text{m}$ |
| Rock density | $\gamma_r = 25.5\,\text{kN/m}^3$ |
| Water density | $\gamma_w = 9.81\,\text{kN/m}^3$ |
| Seismic coefficient | $k_H = 0.08$ |

Overall Cut Model II

$$FS = \frac{104.6c + (20{,}907 - 4.28H_w^2)\tan\phi}{17{,}279}$$

Individual benches Model I

$$FS = \frac{17.6c + (2815 - 86.3z_w - 2.81z_w^2)\tan\phi}{2327 + 4.02z_w^2}$$

Individual benches Model II

$$FS = \frac{34.9c + (4197 - 4.28H_w^2)\tan\phi}{3469}$$

One of the most useful studies of the factor of safety equations was to find the shear strength which would have to be mobilized for failure (i.e. FS = 1.0). These analyses examined the overall cut and the individual benches for a range of water pressures. Figure 14.4 gives the results of the study and the numbered curves on this plot represent the following conditions:

Curve 1   Overall Cut, Model I, dry, $z_w = 0$.
Curve 2   Overall Cut, Model I, saturated, $z_w = z = 14\,\text{m}$.
Curve 3   Overall Cut, Model II, dry, $H_w = 0$.
Curve 4   Overall Cut, Model II, saturated, $H_w = 60\,\text{m}$.
Curve 5   Individual bench, Model I, dry, $z_w = 0$.
Curve 6   Individual bench, Model II, saturated, $z_w = z = 9.9\,\text{m}$.
Curve 7   Individual bench, Model II, dry, $H_w = 0$.
Curve 8   Individual bench, Model II, saturated, $H_w = H = 20\,\text{m}$.

The reader may feel that a consideration of all these possibilities is unnecessary, but it is only coincidental that, because of the geometry of this particular cut, the shear strength values found happen to fall reasonably close together. In other cases, one of the conditions may be very much more critical than the others, and it would take considerable experience to detect this condition

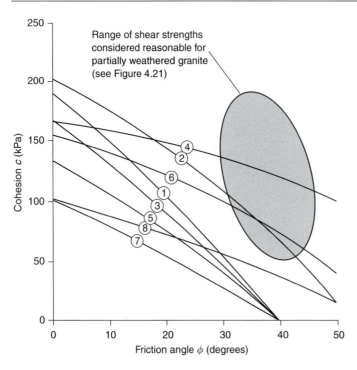

*Figure 14.4* Shear strength mobilized for failure of slope considered in Case Study I (Hoek and Bray, 1977).

without going through the calculations required to produce Figure 14.4.

The elliptical area in Figure 14.4 surrounds the range of shear strengths considered reasonable for partially weathered granite. As discussed in Section 14.2.3, these values are based on the plot given in Figure 4.21. Figure 14.4 shows that when the cut is fully saturated and subject to earthquake loading (lines 2, 4 and 6), the likely available shear strength along the sliding surfaces would be exceeded by the driving forces acting on the sliding surface, and failure would be possible. Considering the rate of weathering of granite in tropical environments over the operational life of the slope, with a consequent reduction in available cohesive strength, these results indicated that the cut was unsafe and that the steps should be taken to increase its stability.

Four basic methods for improving the stability of the cut were considered:

(a)   Reduction of cut height;
(b)   Reduction of cut face angle;
(c)   Drainage; and
(d)   Reinforcement with tensioned anchors.

In order to compare the effectiveness of these different methods, it was assumed that the sheet joint surface had a cohesive strength of 100 kPa and a friction angle of 35°. The increase in factor of safety for a reduction in slope height, slope angle and water level was found by altering one of the variables at a time in the equations on Figure 14.3. The influence of reinforcing the cut was obtained by modifying these equations to include a bolting force as shown in equation (6.22).

Model I: FS

$$= \frac{cA + (W(\cos \psi_p - k_H \sin \psi_p) - U - V \sin \psi_p + T \sin(\psi_T + \psi_p)) \tan \phi}{W(\sin \psi_p + k_H \cos \psi_p) + V \cos \psi_p - T \cos(\psi_T + \psi_p)}$$

(14.1)

Model II: FS

$$= \frac{cA + (W(\cos \psi_p - k_H \sin \psi_p) - U + T \sin(\psi_T + \psi_p)) \tan \phi}{W(\sin \psi_p + k_H \cos \psi_p) - T \cos(\psi_T + \psi_p)}$$

(14.2)

where $T$ is total reinforcing force (kN/m) applied by the anchors, and $\psi_T$ is the plunge, or

(a)

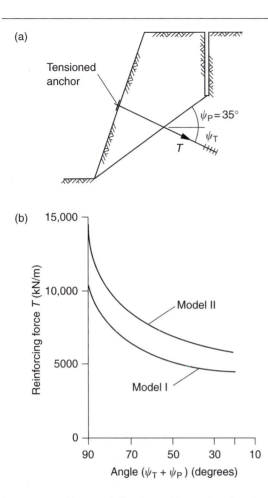

Tensioned
anchor

$\psi_P = 35°$

$\psi_T$

$T$

(b)

15,000

Reinforcing force $T$ (kN/m)

10,000

Model II

5000

Model I

0

90   70   50   30   10

Angle ($\psi_T + \psi_P$) (degrees)

*Figure 14.5* Slope stabilization with tensioned rock anchors: (a) orientation of tensioned anchors; (b) total reinforcing force required for a factor of safety of 1.5.

inclination of this force below the horizontal (Figure 14.5(a)).

Figure 14.6 compares the different methods that were considered for increasing the stability of the overall cut. In each case, the change is expressed as a percentage of the total range of each variable: $H = 60$ m, $\psi_f = 50°$, $z_w/z = 1$, $H_w = 60$ m. However, the variation of the reinforcing force is expressed as a percentage of the weight of the wedge of rock being supported. In calculating the effect of the reinforcement, it was assumed that the anchors are installed horizontally, that is $\psi_T = 0°$. The influence of the anchor

inclination $\psi_T$ on the reinforcing load required to produce a factor of safety of 1.5 is shown in Figure 14.5(b). This shows that the required bolting force can be approximately halved by installing the bolts horizontally ($\psi_T = 0°$, or $\psi_T + \psi_p = 35°$), rather than normal to the plane ($\psi_T = 55°$, or $\psi_T + \psi_p = 90°$). As discussed in Section 6.4.1, the generally optimum angle for tensioned rock anchors is given by equation (6.23). In practice, cement grouted anchors are installed at about 10–15° below the horizontal to facilitate grouting.

### 14.2.6   Stabilization options

The following is a discussion on the stabilization options analyzed in Figure 14.6.

*Reduce height.* Curves 1 and 2 show that reduction in cut height is not an effective solution to the problem. In order to achieve the required factor of safety of 1.5, the slope height would have to be reduced by 50%. If this solution were to be adopted, it would be more practical to excavate the entire slope since most of the volume of rock to be excavated is contained in the upper half of the slope.

*Reduce face angle.* Reducing the angle of the cut face would be very effective stabilization measure as shown by line 3. The required factor of safety of 1.5 is achieved for a reduction of less than 25% of the slope angle. That is, the slope angle should be reduced from 50° to 37.5°. This finding is generally true and a reduction in the face angle is often an effective remedial measure. In the case of slopes under construction, using a flatter slope is always a prime choice for improving stability. However, a practical consideration is the difficulty of excavating a "sliver" cut because of the limited access for equipment on the narrow, lower part of the cut.

Curve 4 (reduction of face angle for slope without tension crack) is an anomaly and demonstrates that calculations can sometimes produce unrealistic results. The reduction in factor of safety shown by this curve is a result of the reduction in the weight of the sliding block as the

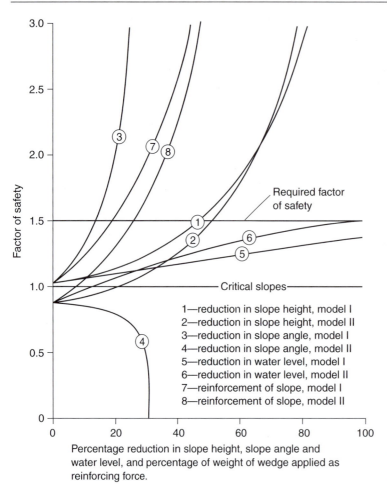

*Figure 14.6* Comparison between alternative methods of increasing stability of overall slope considered in Case Study I.

face angle is reduced. Since the water pressure on the sliding surface remains constant, the effective stress acting on the sliding surface decreases and hence the frictional component of the resisting force decreases. When a very thin sliver of rock remains, the water pressure will "float" it off the slope. The problem with this analysis lies in the assumption that the block is completely impermeable and that the water remains trapped beneath the sliding surface. In fact, the block would break up long before it floated and hence the water pressure acting on the sliding surface would be dissipated.

*Drainage.* Curves 5 and 6 show that drainage would not be an effective stabilization option for both slope models. In neither case is a factor of safety of 1.5 achieved. This is something of a surprise since drainage is usually one of the most cost-effective drainage measures. The reasons for the poor performance of drainage in this case are due to the combination of the slope geometry and the shear strength of the failure surface.

*Anchoring.* Curves 7 and 8 show that reinforcing the cut by means of tensioned anchors with a force equal to 5000 kN per meter of slope length would achieve a factor of safety of 1.5, assuming the anchors are installed just below the horizontal. In other words, reinforcement of a 100 m length of slope would require the installation of 500 anchors, each with a capacity of 1 MN.

The two most attractive options for long-term remediation were reinforcement using tensioned cables or bar anchors, or reduction of the slope face angle. Reinforcement was rejected because of the high cost, and the uncertainty of long-term corrosion resistance of the steel anchors. The option finally selected was to reduce the face angle to 35° by excavating the entire block down to the sheet joints forming the sliding surface. This effectively removed the problem. Since good quality aggregate is always needed in Hong Kong, it was decided to work the slope as a quarry. It took several years to organize this activity and during this time, the water levels in the slope were monitored with piezometers. Although the road was closed twice during this period, no major problems occurred and the slope was finally excavated back to the sliding plane.

## 14.3   Case Study II—Cable anchoring of plane failure

### 14.3.1   Site description

A potential rock fall hazard had developed on a 38 m high, near-vertical rock face located above a two-lane highway (Figure 14.7). A stabilization program was required that could be implemented with minimal interruption to traffic. The rock falls could vary from substantial failures with volumes of several hundred cubic meters formed by widely spaced, persistent joints, to falls of crushed and fractured rock with dimensions of tens of centimeters. The rock falls were a hazard to traffic because of the curved alignment and limited sight distance, together with the 2 m wide ditch between the toe of the rock cut

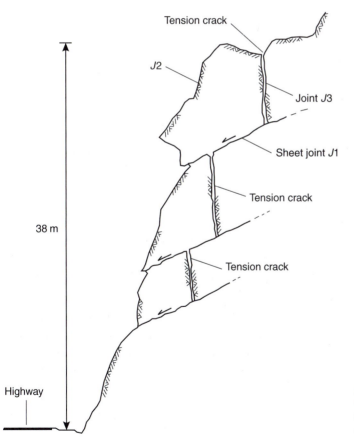

*Figure 14.7* Cross-section of the slope in Case Study II showing movement along sheet joints and location of tension cracks.

and the highway shoulder with limited rock fall containment capacity.

The evidence of instability was a series of tension cracks that had opened as the result of down-slope movement on the sheet joints. The movement had created a layer of crushed rock on each of the sheet joints.

Cross-sections of the slope were developed using a reflectorless EDM (electronic distance measuring), and surface mapping involving rappelling down the face was used to collect structural geology data. The positions of the critical joints were marked with reference points painted on the face, the co-ordinates of which were picked up by the survey. This information was used to determine accurately the shape and dimensions of the major blocks, and the positions of major sliding planes. It was decided that diamond drilling would not be required to obtain geological data because there was excellent exposure of the rock in the face.

### 14.3.2 Geology

The cut had been excavated in a very strong, coarse-grained, fresh, blocky granite containing four sets of joints that were generally orthogonally oriented. The predominant structural geology features were two sets of joints dipping out of the face—sheet joints dipping at an angle of about 20–30°, and a second set (J2) dipping at 45–65°. A third set (J3) dipped steeply into the face, and a fourth set (J4) also steeply dipping, was oriented at right angles to the face (Figure 14.8). Figures 14.8(a) and (b) show respectively the contoured and great circle stereo plots of the surface mapping data. The sheet joints had continuous lengths of several tens of meters and the spacings of all the joints were in the range of 5–8 m.

The cross-section of the slope (Figure 14.7) shows the shape and dimensions of the blocks formed by the joint sets. The blocks were sliding on the sheet joints with joint set J3 forming a series of tension cracks behind the face, while set J4 formed release surfaces at the sides of the blocks. The mapping located tension cracks that were up to 150 mm wide, as well as sheared rock

on the sheeting joints at the base of the each major block. The substantial volumes of the blocks were the result of the persistence and wide spacing of the discontinuities. Since the dip directions of the slope face and the sheet joints were within 20° of each other, this geometry formed a plane failure as illustrated in Figures 2.16 and 2.18.

### 14.3.3 Rock shear strength

The blocks shown on Figure 14.7 were sliding on the continuous sheet joints because the rock was very strong and there is no possibility of fracture taking place through intact rock. Therefore, stability of the blocks was partially dependent on the shear strength of the sheet joints, which were smooth, planar or slightly undulating, and there was generally no infilling apart from slight weathering of the surfaces. For these conditions where the joints had no infilling, the cohesion was zero and the shear strength comprised only friction.

The total friction angle, comprising the friction ($\phi_r$) of the granite and surface roughness ($i$) of the sheet joints, was determined as follows. Block samples of rock containing open, but undisturbed, sheet joints were collected at the site and 100 mm square test pieces were cut from the block. Direct shear tests were then conducted to determine the friction angle of the granite; each sample was tested four times using normal stresses $\sigma$ of 150, 300, 400 and 600 kPa (reference Figure 4.16). These normal stress test values were based on the likely stress acting on the lower sheet joint, calculated from

$$\sigma = \gamma_r H \cos \psi_p \qquad (14.3)$$

For a rock unit weight ($\gamma_r$) of 26 kN/m$^3$, a rock thickness ($H$) of 25 m on a plane dipping ($\psi_p$) at 25°, the normal stress equals 600 kPa.

The direct shear tests showed that the peak friction angle ($\phi_{peak}$) for the initial test at $\sigma = 150$ kPa was 47°, but at higher stresses this diminished as the result of shearing on the sliding surface to a residual angle ($\phi_{residual}$) of 36° (Figure 14.9). Because of the displacement that

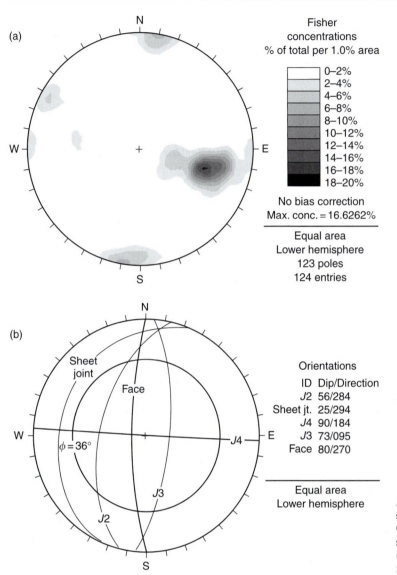

(a)

Fisher
concentrations
% of total per 1.0% area

| | |
|---|---|
| | 0–2% |
| | 2–4% |
| | 4–6% |
| | 6–8% |
| | 8–10% |
| | 10–12% |
| | 12–14% |
| | 14–16% |
| | 16–18% |
| | 18–20% |

No bias correction
Max. conc. = 16.6262%

Equal area
Lower hemisphere
123 poles
124 entries

(b)

Orientations

| ID | Dip/Direction |
|---|---|
| J2 | 56/284 |
| Sheet jt. | 25/294 |
| J4 | 90/184 |
| J3 | 73/095 |
| Face | 80/270 |

Equal area
Lower hemisphere

Figure 14.8 Stereonets of structural geology of slope in Case Study II: (a) contoured plot showing pole concentrations; (b) great circles of joint sets, slope face and friction circle.

had already taken place along the *in situ* sheet joints, it was considered appropriate to use the residual friction angle in design.

Careful examination of the rock along the sheared sheet joints showed that the rock was crushed and there was little intact rock contact. Therefore it was decided that it would not be appropriate to include a roughness component to friction angle, and a friction angle of 36° used in design.

### 14.3.4 Ground water

The site was located in an area with high precipitation in the form of both rain and snow. Although there were no piezometers to measure water pressure in the slope, the level of the water table was assessed from observations of seepage from sheet joint exposed at the base of the lowest block. It was expected that the water table would generally be low because of the dilated nature of the rock

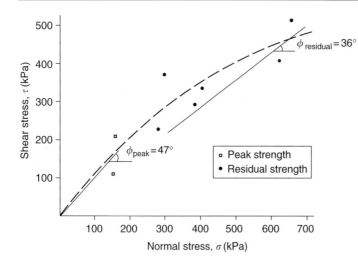

*Figure 14.9* Results of direct shear tests on sheet joints in the granite for Case Study II.

mass would promote drainage. However, during heavy precipitation events, it was likely that high, transient water pressures would develop and this was accounted for in design.

It was assumed for design that water would accumulate in the tension crack to depth $z_w$, and that water forces would be generated both in the tension crack ($V$) and along the sliding plane ($U$) (Figure 14.10).

### 14.3.5   Earthquakes

The site was located in seismically active area, and it was assumed that the actual ground motions would be made up of both horizontal and vertical components that could be in phase. These ground motions were incorporated in the design by using both horizontal ($k_H$) and vertical ($k_V$) seismic coefficients as follows:

$$k_H = 0.15; \text{ and } k_V = 0.67 \times k_H = 0.1$$

The seismic ground motions were incorporated into the slope design assuming that the acceleration would act as two pseudo-static forces.

### 14.3.6   Stability analysis

The nominal, static factor of safety of individual blocks sliding on the sheet joints dipping at 25°

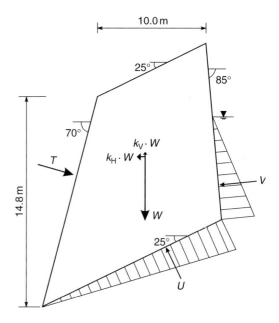

*Figure 14.10* Cross-section of block used in design to model the assemblage of rock blocks in the slope for Case Study II.

was about 1.5 ($\tan \phi / \tan \psi_p = \tan 36 / \tan 25 = 1.5$). However, the shear movement along the sheet joints and the corresponding pattern of tension cracks behind the face shown in Figure 14.7 indicated that, under certain conditions, the factor of safety diminished to approximately 1.0.

It was considered that the cause of the movement was a combination of water pressures and ice jacking on the joints, seismic ground motions over geologic time and blast damage during construction. Also, failure could have been progressive in which movement of one block would drag the adjacent block(s), and as movement occurred crushing of rock asperities along the sliding surfaces reduced the friction angle.

The stability of the sliding blocks was studied using a plane stability model in which it was assumed that the cross-section was uniform at right angles to the slope face, and that sliding took place on a single plane dipping out of the face. In order to apply this model to the actual slope, a simplifying assumption was made in which the three blocks were replaced by a single equivalent block that had the same weight as the total of the three blocks and the same stability characteristics.

The shape and dimensions of the equivalent single block were defined by the following parameters (Figure 14.10):

Sliding plane, dip $\psi_p = 25°$; tension crack, dip $\psi_t = 85°$; slope face, dip $\psi_f = 70°$; upper slope, dip $\psi_s = 25°$; height of face, $H = 18\,\text{m}$; distance of tension crack behind crest, $b = 10\,\text{m}$.

Stability analysis of this block showed that the factor of safety was approximately 1.0 when the water in the tension crack was about 1 m deep, and a pseudo-static seismic coefficient of $0.15g$ was applied. The static factor of safety for these conditions was 1.53, and reduced to 1.15 when the water level in the tension crack was 50% of the crack depth ($z_w = 7.8\,\text{m}$).

### 14.3.7 Stabilization method

Two alternative stabilization methods were considered for the slope. Either, to remove the unstable rock by blasting and then, if necessary bolt the new face, or reinforce the existing slope by installing tensioned anchors. The factors considered in the selection were the need to maintain

traffic on the highway during construction, and the long-term reliability of the stabilized slope.

The prime advantage of the blasting operation was that this would have been a long-term solution. In comparison, the service life of the rock anchors would be limited to decades due to corrosion of the steel and degradation of the rock under the head. However, the disadvantage of the blasting operation was that removal of the rock in small blasts required for the maintenance of traffic on the highway might have destabilized the lower blocks resulting in a large-scale slope failure. Alternatively, removal of all the loose rock in a single blast would have required several days of work to clear the road of broken rock, and to scale and bolt the new face. Bolting of the new face would probably have been necessary because the sheet joints would still daylight in the face and form a new series of potentially unstable blocks.

It was decided that the preferred stabilization option was to reinforce the slope by installing a series of tensioned rock anchors extending through the sheet joints into sound rock. The advantages of this alternative were that the work could proceed with minimal disruption to traffic, and there would be little uncertainty as to the condition of the reinforced slope.

The rock anchoring system was designed using the slope model shown in Figure 14.10. For static conditions and the tension crack half-filled with water ($z_w = 7.8\,\text{m}$), it was calculated that an anchoring force of 550 kN per meter length of slope was necessary to increase the static factor of safety to 1.5. With the application of the pseudo-static seismic coefficients, the factor of safety was approximately 1.0, which was considered satisfactory taking into account the conservatism of this method of analysis. The anchors were installed at an angle of 15° below the horizontal, which was required for efficient drilling and grouting of the anchors. The factor of safety of 1.5 was selected to account for some uncertainty in the mechanism of instability, and the possibility that there may have been additional loose blocks behind those that could be observed at the face.

The arrangement of anchors on the face was dictated by the requirements to reinforce each

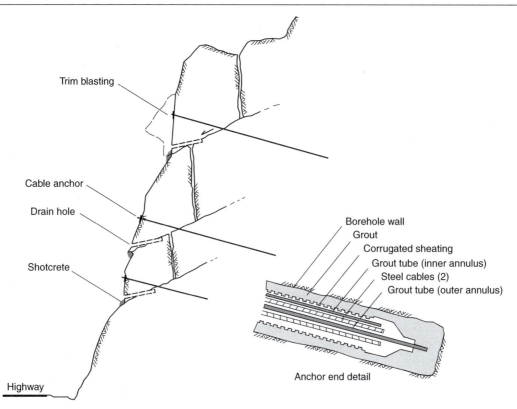

*Figure 14.11* Cross-section of stabilized slope for Case Study II showing layout of cable anchors, and the trim blast, shotcrete and drain holes; detail shows lower end of cable anchors with arrangement of grout tubes.

of the three blocks, to intersect the sheet joints and to locate the bond zone for the anchors in sound rock (Figure 14.11). Because of the limited area on the face in which anchors could be installed, it was necessary to minimize the number of anchors. This was achieved using steel strand cables, because of their higher tensile strength compared to rigid bars. A further advantage of the cables was that they could be installed in a hole drilled with a light rig that would be set up on the slope without the support of a heavy crane that would block traffic. Also, the installation would be facilitated because cable bundles were lighter than bars, and could be installed as a single length without the use of couplings.

Details of the anchor design that met these design and construction requirements were as follows:

Working tensile load of 2-strand, 15 mm diameter, 7-wire strand anchor at 50% of ultimate tensile strength = 248 kN;

For three rows of anchors arranged as shown on Figure 14.11, the total support force = 744 kN ($3 \times 248 = 744$). Therefore the required horizontal spacing between the vertical rows:

Spacing

$$= \frac{\text{supplied anchor force by three rows of anchors}}{\text{required anchor force for factor of safety of 1.5}}$$

$$= \frac{744 \, \text{kN}}{550 \, \text{kN/m}}$$

$$\sim 1.5 \, \text{m}$$

The bond length ($l_b$) for the anchors was calculated assuming that the shear stress developed by the tension in the anchor ($T$) was uniformly distributed at the rock–grout peripheral surface of the drill hole (diameter, $d_h = 80\,mm$). For the strong granitic rock in the bond zone the allowable shear strength ($\tau_a$) of the rock–grout bond was estimated to be 1000 kPa (PTI, 1996). The bond length was calculated as follows:

$$\text{Bond length} = \frac{T}{\pi \times d_h \tau_a}$$

$$= \frac{248}{\pi_x 0.080 \times 1000}$$

$$\sim 1\,m$$

The actual bond length used for the anchors was 2 m to allow for loss of grout in fracture zones in the rock where the bond zones were located, and to ensure that the steel–grout bond strength was not exceeded (Wyllie, 1999).

In addition to the cable anchors, which were required to prevent large-scale instability, the following stabilization measures were implemented to minimize the risk of surficial rock falls that could be a hazard to traffic (Figure 14.11):

- Trim blasting was used to remove the overhang on the face of the upper block. This rock was fractured and marginally stable, and it would not have been safe to set up the drill on this face and then drill the anchor holes through it.
- The seams of fractured rock along each of the sheet joints were first scaled by hand to remove the loose, surficial rock, and then steel fiber reinforced shotcrete was applied to prevent further loosening of the blocks of rock.
- Drain holes, 4 m long on 3 m centers were drilled through the shotcrete to intersect the sheet joints and prevent build up of water pressure in the slope.

### 14.3.8 Construction issues

The following is a brief description of a number of issues that were addressed during construction to accommodate the site conditions actually encountered.

- Drilling was carried out with a down-the-hole hammer drill, without the use of casing. Particular care had to be taken to keep the hole open and avoid the loss of the hammer when drilling through the broken rock on the sheet joints.
- The thrust and rotation components for the drill were mounted on a frame that was bolted to the rock face, with a crane only being used to move the equipment between holes. This arrangement allowed drilling to proceed with minimal disruption to highway traffic.
- Grouting of the anchor holes to the surface was generally not possible because the grout often flowed into open fractures behind the face. In order to ensure that the 2 m long bond zones were fully grouted, the lower portion of each hole was filled with water and a well sounder was used to monitor the water level. Where seepage into fractures occurred, the holes were sealed with cement grout and then redrilled, following which a further water test was carried out.
- Corrosion protection of the anchors was provided with a corrugated plastic sheath that encased the steel cables, with cement grout filling the annular spaces inside and outside the sheath. In order to facilitate handling of the cable assemblies on the steep rock face, the grouting was only carried out once the anchors had been installed in the hole. This involved two grout tubes and a two-stage grouting process as follows. First, grout was pumped down the tube contained within the plastic sheath to fill the sheath and encapsulate the cables. Second, grout was pumped down the tube sealed into the end cap of the sheath to fill the annular space between the sheath and the borehole wall.

- Testing of the anchors to check the load capacity of the bond zone was carried out using the procedures discussed in Section 12.4.2 (PTI, 1996).

## 14.4 Case Study III—Stability of wedge in bridge abutment

### 14.4.1 Site description

This case study describes the stability analysis of a bridge abutment in which the geological structure formed a wedge in the steep rock face on which the abutment was founded (Figure 14.12). The analysis involved defining the shape and dimensions of the wedge, the shear strength of the two sliding planes, and the magnitude and orientation of a number of external forces. The stability of the wedge was examined under a combination of load conditions, and the anchoring force was calculated to produce a factor of safety against sliding of at least 1.5.

The site was located in an area subject to both high precipitation and seismic ground motion. The bridge was a tensioned cable structure with the cables attached to a concrete reaction block located on a bench cut into the rock face. The cables exerted an outward force on the abutment ($15°$ below the horizontal) along the axis of the bridge. The structural geology of the site comprised bedding and two sets of faults that together formed wedge-shaped blocks in the slope below the abutment. The stability of the slope was examined using the wedge stability analysis method to determine the static and dynamic factors of safety, with and without rock anchors. Figure 14.12 is a sketch of the abutment showing the shape of the wedge and the orientations of the bridge force ($Q$). The anchors were installed in the upper surface of the abutment, inclined at an angle of $45°$ below the horizontal, and oriented at $180°$ from the direction of the line of intersection. On Figure 14.12, the five planes forming the wedge are numbered according to the system shown on Figure 7.18(a).

### 14.4.2 Geology

The rock was slightly weathered, strong, massive sandstone with the bedding dipping at an angle

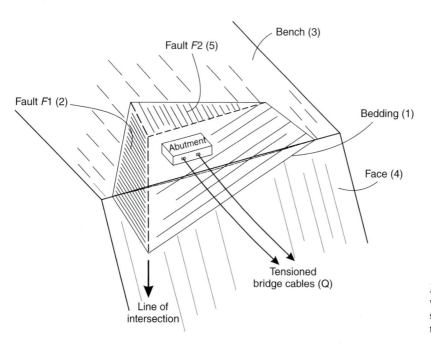

*Figure 14.12* View of wedge in bridge abutment showing fire planes forming the wedge in Case Study III.

of 22° to the west (orientation 22/270). The site investigation identified a persistent bedding plane at a depth of 16 m below the bench level that contained a weak shale interbed. This plane formed the flatter of the two sliding planes forming the wedge block. There were also two sets of faults in the slope with orientations 80/150 (*F*1) and 85/055 (*F*2). The faults were planar and contained crushed rock and fault gouge, and were likely to have continuous lengths of tens of meters. Fault *F*1 formed the second sliding plane, on the left side of the wedge (Figure 14.12). Fault *F*2 formed the tension crack at the back of the wedge, and was located at a distance of 12 m behind the slope crest, measured along the outcrop of fault *F*1.

Figure 14.13 is a stereonet showing the orientations of the great circles of the three discontinuity sets, and the slope face (orientation 78/220), and upper bench (orientation 02/230).

### 14.4.3   *Rock strength*

The stability analysis required shear strength values for both the *F*1 fault and the bedding. The fault was likely to be a continuous plane over the

length of the wedge, for which the shear strength of the crushed rock and gouge would comprise predominately friction with no significant cohesion. The shear strength of the bedding plane was that of the shale interbed. The shear strength of both materials was determined by laboratory testing using a direct shear test machine (see Figure 4.16).

The direct shear tests carried out on fault infilling showed friction angles averaging 25° with zero cohesion, and for the shale the friction angle was 20° and the cohesion was 50 kPa. Although both the fault and the bedding were undulating, it was considered that the effective roughness of these surfaces would not be incorporated in the friction angle because shearing was likely to take place entirely within the weaker infilling, and not on the rock surfaces.

### 14.4.4   *Ground water*

This area was subject to periods of intense rain that was likely to flood the bench at the crest of the slope. Based on these conditions it was assumed for the analysis that maximum water pressures would be developed on the planes forming the wedge.

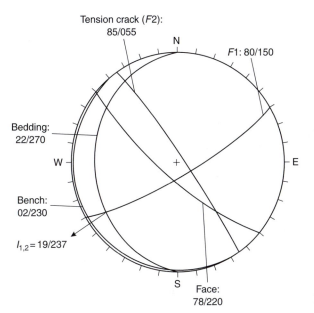

*Figure 14.13* Stereonet of five planes forming wedge in bridge abutment shown in Figure 14.12.

### 14.4.5   Seismicity

The seismic coefficient for the site was 0.1. The stability analysis used the pseudo-static method in which the product of the seismic coefficient, the gravity acceleration and the weight of the wedge was assumed to produce a horizontal force acting out of the slope along the line of intersection of the wedge.

### 14.4.6   External forces

The external forces acting on the wedge comprised water forces on planes 1, 2 and 5, the seismic force, the bridge load and the rock anchors. Figure 14.14 shows the external forces in plan and section views.

The water forces were the product of the areas of planes 1 and 2 and the water pressure distribution. The seismic force was the product of the horizontal seismic coefficient and the weight of the wedge. The analysis procedure was to run the stability analysis to determine the weight of the wedge (volume multiplied by rock unit weight), from which the seismic force was calculated.

For the bridge, the structural load on the abutment due to the tensioned cables had a magnitude of 30 MN, and trend and plunge values of 210° and 15°, respectively. The trend coincided with the bridge axis that was not at right angles to the rock face, and the plunge coincided with the sag angle of the catenary created by the sag in the cables.

The rock anchors were installed in the upper surface of the bench and extended through the bedding plane into stable rock to apply normal and shear (up-dip) forces to the bedding plane.

### 14.4.7   Stability analysis

The stability of the abutment was analyzed using the comprehensive wedge analysis procedure described in Appendix III, and the computer program SWEDGE version 4.01 by Rocscience (2001). The input data required for this analysis comprised the shape and dimensions of the wedge, the rock properties and the external forces acting on the wedge. Values of these input parameters, and the calculated results, are listed on the next page.

(i)   *Wedge shape and dimensions*

The shape of the wedge was defined by five surfaces with orientations as shown in Figure 14.13.

(a)   Plane 1 (bedding):        22°/270°
(b)   Plane 2 (fault F1):        80°/150°
(c)   Plane 3
        (upper slope):            02°/230°

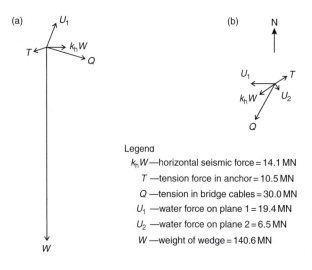

Legend
$k_h W$ —horizontal seismic force = 14.1 MN
$T$ —tension force in anchor = 10.5 MN
$Q$ —tension in bridge cables = 30.0 MN
$U_1$ —water force on plane 1 = 19.4 MN
$U_2$ —water force on plane 2 = 6.5 MN
$W$ —weight of wedge = 140.6 MN

*Figure 14.14* Sketch showing magnitude and orientation of external forces on wedge: (a) section view along line of intersection; (b) plan view.

(d)  Plane 4 (face):          78°/220°
(e)  Plane 5
      (tension crack,
      fault $F2$):            85°/055°

The orientation of the line of intersection between planes 1 and 2 was calculated to be

(a)  Line of intersection:  18.6°/237°

The dimensions of the wedge were defined by two length parameters:

- Height, $H1$ (vertical height from line of intersection to crest):   16 m;
- Length, $L$ (length along plane 1 from crest to tension crack):   25 m.

(ii)  *Rock properties*
The rock properties comprised the shear strengths of planes 1 and 2, and the rock unit weight:

- Bedding with shale interbed: $c_1 = 50$ kPa, $\phi_1 = 20°$;
- Fault $F1$: $c_2 = 0$ kPa, $\phi_2 = 35°$;
- Unit weight of rock, $\gamma_r = 0.026$ MN/m$^3$; and
- Unit weight of water, $\gamma_w = 0.01$ MN/m$^3$.

(iii)  *External forces*
The magnitude and orientation of the external forces were as follows.

- Water forces acted normal to each plane and were calculated to have the following values, for fully saturated conditions:

$U_1 = 19.73$ MN;

$U_2 = 6.44$ MN; and

$U_5 = 1.55$ MN.

- The wedge weight acted vertically and was calculated (from the wedge volume and the rock unit weight) to have magnitude:

$W = 143.35$ MN

- The horizontal component of the seismic force acted in the direction along the line of intersection and had magnitude

$k_H W = 0.1W$
$= 14.1$ MN oriented at 0°/237°

- The bridge force, $Q$ acted along the center line of the bridge at an angle of 15° below the horizontal:

$Q = 30$ MN oriented at 15°/210°

- The factor of safety of the abutment with no reinforcement provided by tensioned anchors was as follows:

(a)  FS = 2.58—dry, static, $Q = 0$
(b)  FS = 2.25—saturated, static, $Q = 0$
(c)  FS = 1.73—saturated, $k_H = 0.1$, $Q = 0$
(d)  FS = 1.32—saturated, static, $Q = 30$ MN
(e)  FS = 1.10—saturated, $k_H = 0.1$, $Q = 30$ MN

- It was considered that the factors of safety for load conditions (d) and (e) were inadequate for a structure critical to the operation of the facility, and that the minimum required static and seismic factors of safety should be 1.5 and 1.25, respectively. These factors of safety were achieved, with the bridge load applied, by the installation of tensioned anchors (tension load $T$), which gave the following results:

(a)  FS = 1.54—saturated, static, $T = 10.5$ MN, $\psi_T = 15°, \alpha_T = 056°$ (parallel to the line of intersection); and
(b)  FS = 1.26—saturated, $k_H = 0.1$, $T = 10.5$ MN, $\psi_T = 15°$, $\alpha_T = 056°$.

- It was found that the factor of safety for the reinforced wedge could be optimized by varying the orientation of the anchors. If the trend of the anchors was between the trends of the line of intersection and the bridge load (i.e. $\alpha_T = 035°$), it was possible to reduce the anchor force required to achieve the required factor of safety to 8.75 MN.

- It is noted that the discussion in this case study only addressed the stability of the wedge, and did not discuss the method of attaching the tensioned bridge cables to the rock wedge. Also, it is assumed that all the external forces acted through the center of gravity of the wedge so that no moments were generated.

## 14.5 Case Study IV—Circular failure analysis of excavation for rock fall ditch

### 14.5.1 Site description

As the result of a series of rock falls from a rock face above a railway, a program was undertaken to improve stability conditions (Figure 14.15).

The initial stabilization work involved selective scaling and bolting of the face, but it was found that this only provided an improvement for one or two years before new rock falls occurred as the rock weathered and blocks loosened on joint surfaces. Rock falls were a potential hazard because the curved alignment and stopping distance of as much as 2 km meant that trains could not be brought to a halt if a rock fall was observed. In order to provide long-term protection against rock falls, it was decided to excavate the face to create a ditch that was wide enough to contain substantial falls from the new face. This work involved a drilling and blasting operation to cut back the face to a face angle of 75°, and constructing a gabion wall along the outer edge of the ditch that acted as an energy absorbing barrier to contain rock falls (Wyllie and Wood, 1981).

The railway and highway were located on benches cut into a rock slope above a river, and there were steep rock faces above and below the upper bench on which the railway was located; a 30 m length of the track was supported by a masonry retaining wall (Figure 14.15). The

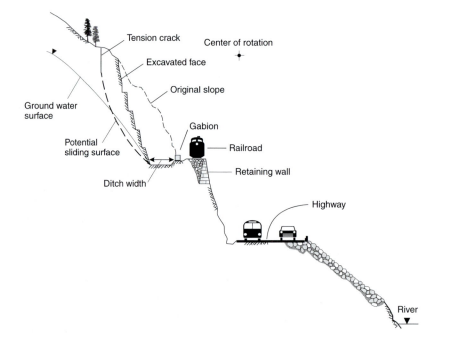

*Figure 14.15* Geometry of slope above railway in Case Study IV. Sketch shows dimensions of ditch after excavation of slope, and shape of potential circular sliding surface through rock mass.

original cut above the railway was about 30 m high at a face angle of 60°, and the 2 m wide ditch at the toe of the slope was not adequate to contain rock falls. Blasting had been used to excavate the slope, and there was moderate blast damage to the rock in the face.

The site was in a climate with moderate precipitation that experienced long periods of freezing temperatures during the winter. Formation of ice in fractures in the rock behind the face could loosen blocks of rock resulting in the occurrence of rock falls with little warning; rock falls tended to occur in the spring when the ice started to melt.

### 14.5.2 Geology

The cut was in medium strong, slightly to moderately weathered volcanic tuff containing joints spaced at about 0.5–2 m, and lengths up to 3 m. There was one consistent set of joints that had a near vertical dip and a strike at about 45° to the strike of the cut face. However, the orientations of the other joints were variable over short distances. Many of the joints had calcite infillings that had a low cohesive strength.

Because of the variable orientations and limited persistence of the joints throughout the length of the cut, there was little structurally controlled instability on the overall rock face.

### 14.5.3 Ground water

Because of the low precipitation in the area, it was assumed that the ground water level in the slope would have little influence on stability.

### 14.5.4 Rock shear strength

An important design issue for the project was the stability of the overall cut face above the railway, and whether it could be cut back safely to create a rock fall ditch. The rock strength relevant to this design was that of the rock mass because potential failure surfaces would pass partially through intact rock, and partially along any low persistence joints oriented approximately parallel to this surface. It was not possible to test samples with diameters of several meters that would be representative of the rock mass, or to determine

the proportions of intact rock and joint plane that would form the sliding surface in the slope. Therefore, two empirical methods as described in the next paragraph were used to estimate the cohesion and friction angle of the rock mass.

The first method of estimating the rock mass strength was to carry out a back analysis of the existing 30 m high cut above the railway, which involved the following steps. First, there was no evidence of instability of the overall slope, which had been standing for over 100 years, or natural slopes in the same rock type. These slopes had probably been subject in the past to earthquakes and occasional periods of high water pressure. Therefore, a factor of safety in the range of 1.5–2.0 was assumed for the existing slope. Second, since there was no geological structure that would form a sliding surface, it was likely that instability would take the form of a shallow circular failure, as described in Chapter 8. Third, as discussed in Section 14.3.3, the water table was in the lower part of the slope and it was appropriate to use Chart Number 2 (Figure 8.7) to perform stability analyses. Fourth, for blocky rock with no significant clay on the joint surfaces, a friction angle of 35° was estimated; the rock unit weight was 26 kN/m³. Using these data, for the 30 m high slope at a face angle of 60°, it was possible to use the circular failure design chart to calculate the rock mass cohesion as approximately 150 kPa (for FS = 1.75; $\tan\phi$/FS = 0.40; $c/\gamma H$ FS = 0.11). Figure 4.21 was used as an additional guideline in selecting shear strength values.

As a comparison with the back analysis method of determining rock mass strength, the Hoek–Brown strength criterion (see Section 4.5), was used to calculate a friction angle of 38° and a cohesion of about 180 kPa (input parameters: $\sigma_{ci}$ = 40 MPa; GSI = 45; $m_i$ = 10; $D$ = 0.9) based on the program ROCLAB version 1.007 (Rocscience, 2002a).

The two sets of strength values are reasonably close, but the difference illustrates the uncertainty in determining rock mass strengths, and the need to carry out sensitivity analyses to evaluate the possible influence on this range in strengths on stability.

### 14.5.5  Ditch and slope design

The two principle design issues for the project were the dimensions of the ditch to contain rock falls, and the stability of the slope excavated to create the ditch.

*Ditch.* The required depth and width of the ditch to contain rock falls is related to both the height and slope angle of the cut face as illustrated in Figure 12.21 (Ritchie, 1963). These design recommendations show that the required ditch dimensions are reduced for a proposed face angle of 75°, compared to the existing 60° face. Another factor in the ditch design was the face angle of the outside face of the ditch. If this face is steep and constructed with energy absorbing material, then rocks that land in the base of the ditch are likely to be contained. However, if the outer face has a gentle slope, they may roll out of the ditch.

For a 30 m high rock face at an angle of 75°, the required ditch dimensions were a depth of 2 m and a base width of 7 m. In order to reduce the excavation volume, the ditch was excavated to a depth of 1 m, and a 1 m high gabion wall was placed along the outer side of the excavation to create a vertical, energy absorbing barrier.

*Slope stability.* The stability of the excavated slope was examined using Circular Chart No. 2. The proposed excavation would increase the face angle from 60° to 75° without increasing the height of 30 m significantly, and the rock mass strength and the ground water conditions in the new slope would be identical to those in the existing slope. Chart number No. 2 showed that the factor of safety of the new slope was about 1.3 ($c/(\gamma H \tan\phi) = 0.275; \tan\phi/FS \approx 0.2$). Figure 14.15 shows the approximate location of the potential tension crack, and sliding surface with the minimum factor of safety, determined using Figure 8.11 ($X = -0.9H; Y = H; b/H = 0.15$).

### 14.5.6  Construction issues

The excavation was by drill and blast methods because the rock was too strong to be broken by rippers. The following are some of the issues that were addressed during construction:

The blasting was carried out in 4.6 m lifts using vertical holes. The "step-out" required at the start of each bench to allow clearance for the head of the drill was 1.2 m, so the overall slope angle was 75°. The production holes were 63 mm diameter on a 1.5 m square pattern and the powder factor was 0.3 kg/m$^3$.

Controlled blasting was used on the final face to minimize the blast damage to the rock behind the face. The final line holes were spaced at 0.6 m and charged with de-coupled, low velocity explosive at a load factor of 0.3 kg/m of hole length. The final line holes were detonated last in the sequence (cushion blasting) because the limited burden precluded pre-shear blasting.

The detonation sequence of the rows in the blast was at right angles to the face in order to limit the throw of blasted rock on to the railway and highway, and minimize closure times.

The track was protected from the impact of falling rock by placing a 1 m thick layer of gravel on the track before each blast. This could be quickly removed to allow operations of the train.

Near the bottom of the cut it was necessary to protect from blast damage the masonry retaining wall supporting the track. This was achieved by controlling the explosive weight per delay so that the peak particle velocity of the vibrations in the wall did not exceed 100 mm/s.

## 14.6  Case Study V—Stabilization of toppling failure

### 14.6.1  Site description

A rock slope above a railway was about 25 m high, and the rock forming the slope was a blocky granite in which a toppling failure was occurring (Wyllie, 1980). Movement of the upper toppling block was crushing the rock at the base and

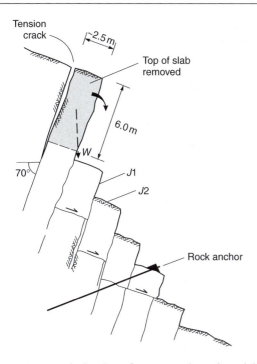

*Figure 14.16* Idealized configuration of toppling slabs in Case Study V showing excavation and bolting.

causing rock falls that were a hazard to railway operations (Figure 14.16). The site was in a high precipitation climate, with a moderate risk of seismic ground motions. Stabilization measures were undertaken to limit the rock fall hazard and to prevent additional toppling motion.

## 14.6.2 Geology

The granite at the site was fresh and very strong, and contained three well-defined sets of joints with orthogonal orientations. The most prominent set ($J1$) dipped at about 70°, with the strike at right angles to the railway alignment. The second set ($J2$) had the same strike but dipped at about 20°, while the third set ($J3$) was near vertical with the strike parallel to the track. The spacing of the joints was between 2 and 3 m, and the persistence of the $J1$ joint set was in the range of 10–40 m. The joints were planar but rough, and contained no infilling. Figures 14.16 and 14.17 show a sketch of the slope and the dimensions of the blocks formed by the jointing.

## 14.6.3 Rock strength

The compressive strength of the granite was in the range of 50–100 MPa, and it was estimated that the friction angle of the joints was between 40° and 45° with no cohesion. These values were determined by inspection because of the limited time available to assess the site and plan a stabilization program.

## 14.6.4 Ground water

The site experienced periods of heavy rainfall and rapid snow melt, so it was expected that transient high water pressures would develop in the lower part of the slope. In the upper part of the slope, water pressures were unlikely because water would not collect in the tension cracks exposed in the face.

## 14.6.5 Stability conditions

The uniform spacing and orientation of the $J1$ joints formed a series of slabs in the slope that were approximately 2.5 m wide and had vertical heights of as much as 20 m. The slabs dipped at about 70° so the center of gravity of the slab lay outside the base when the height exceeded about 6 m; this was a necessary condition for toppling (see Figure 1.10). As shown in Figure 14.17, the upper slab had an exposed face about 7 m high and toppling of this slab had opened a tension crack about 200 mm wide along the $J1$ joint set. As the upper block toppled, it generated thrust forces on the lower slabs. The short length of these lower slabs meant that their centers of gravity were well inside their bases so toppling did not occur. However, the thrust was great enough to cause the lower blocks to slide on the $J2$ joint set. This set dipped at 20° and had a friction angle of about 40°; limit equilibrium analysis of the sliding blocks showed that the thrust force required to cause sliding was equal to about 50% of the weight of the block. This shear displacement caused some fracturing and crushing of the rock that was the source of the rock falls.

The mechanism of instability at the site was essentially identical to the theoretical toppling mechanism discussed in Chapter 9 and shown in

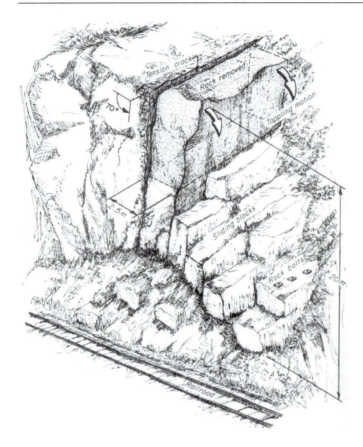

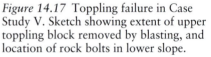

*Figure 14.17* Toppling failure in Case Study V. Sketch showing extent of upper toppling block removed by blasting, and location of rock bolts in lower slope.

Figure 9.7. That is, the tall, upper slabs toppled and caused the lower, shorter slabs to slide. Possible stabilization options for these conditions included reducing the height of the toppling slabs so that the center of gravity lay inside the base, or installing a support force in the sliding slabs at the base. These two measures were adopted, with the combined effect of reducing the tendency for the upper slabs to topple, and preventing movement of the lower slabs.

### 14.6.6  *Stabilization method*

The following three stabilization measures were undertaken to reduce the rock fall hazard and to improve the long-term stability of the slope:

- Scaling was carried out on the face above the railway to remove loose rock. This work

included the removal of all trees growing in open cracks in the rock because these had contributed to the loosening of the blocks of rock on the face.

- A row of bolts was installed through one of the lower slabs. This work was done prior to excavation at the crest in order to prevent any further movement due to blasting vibrations.

- Blasting was used to remove the upper 6 m of the top slab. The blasting was carried out in stages in order to limit blast vibrations in the lower slope and allow additional bolts to be installed if further movement occurred. The blasting pattern comprised 6 m long holes on about 0.6 m centers, with three rows being detonated on each blast. A light explosive charge of $0.4 \, \text{kg/m}^3$ was used, with spacers between the sticks of explosive in the blast holes.

Chapter 15

# Mining applications

Alan F. Stewart, P. Mark Hawley, Nick D. Rose
and Brent W. Gilmore*

## 15.1 Introduction

Rock slope engineering of open pit mines requires careful application and adaptation of the full range of tools that have been presented in earlier chapters of this book. Each ore body and host rock mass is unique, and comprises distinctive mineralogical assemblages and rock types. In many instances, stratigraphy may be complexly deformed by geologic forces. Geologic and geomechanical characteristics, such as lithology, mineralogy, alteration, rock strength, *in situ* stress, geologic structure and fabric, and ground water conditions may vary widely between different deposits, and even within a given deposit. The challenge for the slope designer is first to determine which of these characteristics are important in terms of stability. The next step is to plan and execute focused investigations to obtain the information required to define the key stability parameters. Stability analyses are then conducted, and results are used in conjunction with experience and judgment to develop slope design criteria for use by mine planners and operators.

In open pit mining, the optimum slope design is usually one that maximizes overall slope angles and minimizes the amount of waste stripping. At the same time, it must effectively manage the risk of overall slope instability, and provide for safe and efficient movement of personnel, equipment and materials during mining operations. The general methodology for designing open pit

mine slopes is described in this chapter by way of four hypothetical examples. These examples represent a range of mine design and rock mechanics issues in a variety of geologic environments.

Most open pit mines are developed using benches that are designed to contain and control rock falls and small failures. The geometry of the pit and slopes is defined by the shape of the ore body, the height and width of the benches, and the locations of haul roads and stepouts; Figure 1.5 illustrates a typical pit slope geometry. As discussed in the following examples, inter-ramp slopes are defined as slope sections comprised of multiple benches between haul roads or stepouts. Haul roads are necessary to provide access to the ore and waste, and stepouts may be required for reasons of stability or to accommodate the shape of the ore body. Overall slopes incorporate inter-ramp slopes as well as haul roads and stepouts, and extend from the crest to the toe of the pit wall.

## 15.2 Example 1—porphyry deposits

This example describes a preliminary slope design investigation conducted as part of a feasibility study for a new porphyry copper deposit. Preliminary mine plans indicated a maximum open pit depth of 250 m. No mining activity had occurred in the deposit, and no previous design studies had been conducted, other than exploration drilling, mapping and sampling related to ore reserve definition.

A geotechnical investigation program was conducted that incorporated site reconnaissance, structural mapping of available outcrops,

* Piteau Associates Engineering Ltd, North Vancouver, BC, Canada.

geomechanical logging of drill cores, and a testing program involving point load index testing of core, and direct shear testing of selected discontinuities. In addition, six geotechnical coreholes were drilled to obtain oriented core. Piezometers were targeted for various holes throughout the property to monitor ground water levels and obtain an indication of potential pit dewatering requirements.

### 15.2.1 Design issues

The proposed pit would have a modest overall depth of 250 m, and would be excavated in a competent rock mass with a consistent, pervasive set of joints and faults related to the genesis of the deposit. Open pit slope design was expected to be controlled by the stability of individual benches, and the need to optimize bench geometry to minimize waste stripping. Due to the combination of moderate overall slope height and a competent rock mass, inter-ramp and overall slope stability were not significant concerns.

### 15.2.2 Engineering geology

The porphyritic intrusion was dacitic in composition, hosted by tertiary andesites and andesite breccias, and was hydrothermally altered with a distinctive alteration zonation ranging from potassic to phyllic to propylitic. In terms of rock mass competency, the potassic alteration increased the overall competency of the rock, whereas the phyllic alteration significantly weakened the rock and reduced discontinuity shear strength. Propylitic alteration appeared to have had little influence on overall rock competency.

Results of the structural mapping and core orientation indicated a pattern of radial and tangential jointing and faulting that appeared to be centered around the intrusive core. The radial joint set (Set 1) dipped sub-vertically and with a strike approximately radial to the center of the intrusive complex. These structures were probably related to the original intrusion and facilitated development of the hydrothermal

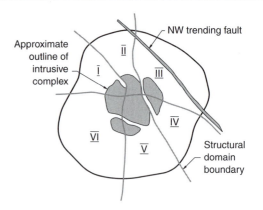

*Figure 15.1* Distribution of structural domains.

system that deposited the ore. The strike of the tangential set (Set 2) was approximately normal to Set 1 and dipped at 45–60° towards the center. Set 2 was probably formed during collapse of the hydrothermal system. Peak orientations of these two principal sets varied depending on their position in relation to the intrusive center.

Based on the distribution of discontinuity orientations, the deposit was divided into six structural domains distributed radially around the deposit, as illustrated in Figure 15.1. Within each structural domain the geologic structural fabric was expected to be reasonably consistent. Figure 15.2 is a stereonet that shows the distribution of discontinuities in Structural Domain I.

Regionally, northwest trending sub-vertical faults were present throughout the area. In particular, a large fault zone with a width of about 10 m was interpreted to intersect the northeast corner of the proposed pit.

### 15.2.3 Rock strength and competency

Field estimates of hardness (ISRM, 1981b) obtained during geomechanical logging of the drill core were correlated with point load index results. Both of these measures of rock strength indicated a moderately hard rock mass, with unconfined compressive strengths (UCS) ranging from about 40 to 100 MPa. Local zones of phyllic alteration had an average UCS as low as about 5 MPa.

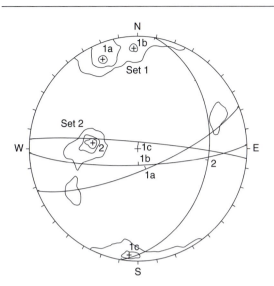

*Figure 15.2* Stereonet of discontinuities in Structural Domain I.

Laboratory direct shear testing of selected joints collected from the drill core indicated friction angles of between about 30° and 42°, depending on the type and intensity of alteration present. Results also indicated little or no cohesion. For faults and fault gouge, the average friction angle was about 20° with negligible cohesion.

Geomechanical core logging data, including RQD, joint spacing, joint condition and hardness, were compiled, and average Rock Mass Ratings (RMR) were determined according to Bieniawski (1976). For purposes of rock mass characterization, ground water conditions were assumed to be dry. The average RMR was 65 (good quality rock mass) for all core, and ranged from approximately 35 (poor quality rock mass) for phyllically altered rocks to about 85 (very good quality rock mass) for potassically altered rocks.

### 15.2.4  Hydrogeology

Initial monitoring of several piezometers installed in exploration drill holes indicated low piezometric pressures in most areas of the proposed pit. However, water levels appeared slightly elevated in the northeast, probably in response to the large regional fault zone described above that may have been acting as an aquitard to ground water flow. Localized horizontal drain holes, targeting areas such as this fault zone, and in-pit sumps would probably be sufficient to manage expected ground water volumes. Additional hydrogeological assessments would be required as the pit developed.

### 15.2.5  Slope stability analyses and slope design

It is usually impractical and uneconomic to design open pit slopes such that no failures occur. Therefore, a more pragmatic approach is to design the pit with benches, and excavate the slopes under controlled conditions such that any failures that do occur are caught and effectively controlled on berms.

Initially, slope stability analysis involved assessment of possible failure modes relating to structural discontinuities (i.e. joints and faults) that could result in shallow failure of individual benches, or large-scale failure involving multiple benches or overall slopes. Subsequent analyses were conducted to assess the potential for deep-seated rotational rock mass failure of the ultimate pit slopes, based on preliminary inter-ramp slope angles developed from the bench designs.

As noted earlier, the rock mass was divided into six structural domains arranged in pie-shaped segments about the center of the intrusive complex (Figure 15.1). Based on the preliminary mine plan, the rock mass was further subdivided into design sectors, or zones with consistent geologic structure as well as uniform pit slope orientation. Within each design sector, kinematic assessments were conducted to determine possible failure modes that could occur (see Figure 2.21). Two basic failure modes were considered: wedge failures and plane failures. Figure 15.3 is a stereonet that shows kinematically possible failure modes identified in a typical design sector in Structural Domain I. Limit equilibrium stability analyses, utilizing discontinuity shear strengths determined from laboratory direct shear testing, were then

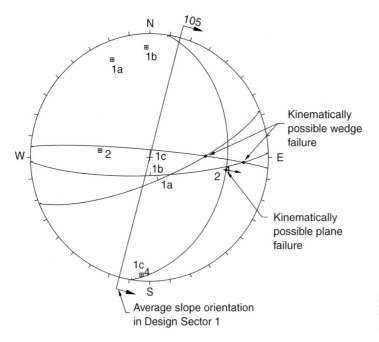

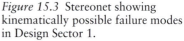

Average slope orientation
in Design Sector 1

*Figure 15.3* Stereonet showing
kinematically possible failure modes
in Design Sector 1.

conducted for each failure mode to determine
which failure modes were critical to design. Critical failure modes were defined as kinematically
possible failures with factors of safety less than or
equal to 1.2. In addition, the dip direction of critical plane failures was less than about 30° oblique
to the slope, and the trend of the line of intersection of critical wedge failures was less than about
45° oblique to the slope.

Surface mapping and general reconnaissance
showed that joints were likely to persist throughout the rock mass, and to have an average continuity of about 10–15 m. Consequently, they
were expected to have a significant impact on
breakback of individual benches, but to have limited importance in terms of overall slope stability.
Faults, although not as prevalent, were much
more continuous and could impact inter-ramp
and overall slopes as well as individual benches.
Based on an assessment of the various critical
failure modes, associated factors of safety and
degree of development of the joint and fault sets
involved, the apparent dip or plunge considered
to control bench stability was determined for each
design sector. It was expected that the blasted and

excavated bench face angles would range from
57° to 62° ("breakback angle").

Bench height is usually determined by the size
of drilling and excavation equipment, and other
mine planning considerations. In this example,
a bench height increment of 15 m was chosen
for feasibility assessments. In the more competent rocks, 30 m high double benches were
considered appropriate. Double benches typically allow steeper inter-ramp and overall slopes
to be developed, although the size of potential failures increases and wider catchment berms
are generally required. In the less competent
rocks, single benches were considered appropriate to control raveling and rock falls, as
well as bench-scale wedges and plane failures.
Bench heights, minimum berm widths, and the
apparent dip or plunge considered to control
bench stability determined earlier were used
to determine maximum inter-ramp slope angles
for each design sector. Minimum berm widths
of 8 and 10 m were recommended for single
and double benches, respectively. Recommended inter-ramp slope design criteria ranged from
38° to 42° for single benches developed in zones

of intense phyllic alteration, to 45° to 49° for double benches developed in competent potassic and propylitic altered rocks. Results of deep-seated limit equilibrium stability assessments of the overall slopes indicated adequate stability for the proposed maximum slope heights and recommended inter-ramp slope angles.

## 15.3   Example 2—stratigraphically controlled deposits

The process for designing slopes in structurally complex, stratigraphically controlled deposits is demonstrated in the following example using a hypothetical open pit coal mine developed in intensely folded and thrust-faulted sedimentary strata. While this example was developed based on the authors' experience at several mines in the Canadian Rocky Mountains and Foothills in British Columbia and Alberta, the concepts can be applied to other sedimentary, strataform or stratabound deposits.

### 15.3.1   Design issues

Layered ore deposits may be tilted, folded and/or faulted, such as the coal measures of Western Canada, the iron ore deposits of Brazil, and a variety of other deposits hosted in bedded sedimentary, foliated metamorphic or layered volcanic rocks. These deposits often present special issues for pit slope design. For example, the orientation of bedding or foliation frequently controls wall stability and slope design, and ore horizons may be narrow, resulting in project economics that may be very sensitive to stripping. Also, the structural geology is often complex and can vary significantly over short distances. Stratigraphy may also be complicated by thrust and normal faulting that can both follow and cross-cut strata, resulting in apparent stratigraphic thickening, thinning or truncating. It is often difficult or impractical to understand fully the geologic complexity of these types of deposits in advance of mining. As a result, material changes in the interpretation may occur during mining as strata are exposed and mapped. Consequently, design criteria need to be flexible

and readily adaptable to both subtle and dramatic changes in geologic interpretation.

### 15.3.2   Engineering geology

In this example of an open pit coal mine, the bottom of the stratigraphic sequence was characterized by a thick sequence of interbedded Jurassic marine shales and siltstones (Domain 1). These were overlain by Cretaceous terrestrial siltstones, sandstones and minor mudstones (Domain 2), which in turn underlayed Cretaceous coal measure rocks comprising interbedded coal, carbonaceous mudstones, siltstones and sandstones (Domain 3). The footwall of the lowest coal seam comprised a relatively massive, thick sandstone unit. Figure 15.4 shows a typical geologic cross-section through the deposit.

The strata had been deformed into a fold sequence comprising a synclinal core flanked by overturned anticlines. Thrust faults had developed approximately parallel to the axial planes of the folds, and had thickened the coal sequence in the core of the syncline.

The stereographic projections in Figure 15.5 illustrate the main discontinuity sets, as determined by outcrop mapping. The most prominent discontinuity set was bedding joints (Set A), and although the dip of this set varied widely, the strike was relatively constant. Peak orientations generally fell on a great circle, which was consistent with cylindrical folding (note the inferred fold axis shown on Figure 15.5(a)). In addition to bedding joints, two other discontinuity sets were apparent:

- Set B: strike approximately perpendicular to bedding, and with sub-vertical dip; and
- Set C: strike approximately parallel to bedding, and dip about normal to bedding.

Collectively these three discontinuity sets formed an approximately orthogonal system, which is typical of folded sedimentary rocks. The primary orientation of regional thrust faulting is also indicated on Figure 15.5(b).

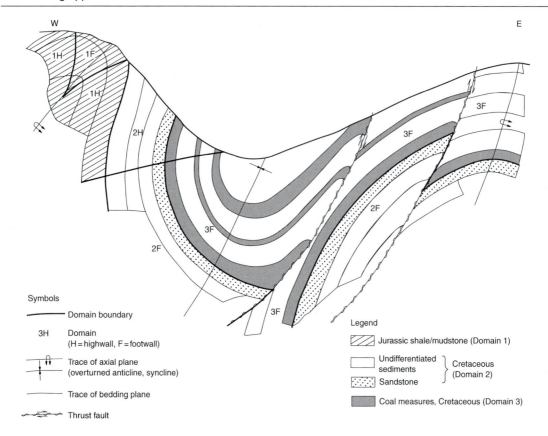

*Figure 15.4* Example 2—typical geologic cross-section of coal formation (modified after Hawley and Stewart (1986)).

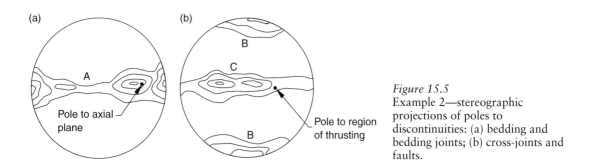

*Figure 15.5* Example 2—stereographic projections of poles to discontinuities: (a) bedding and bedding joints; (b) cross-joints and faults.

### 15.3.3  Rock strength and competency

Estimates of intact rock strength, discontinuity shear strength and general rock mass competency were developed from geomechanical core logging, point load testing, and laboratory unconfined compressive strength and direct shear testing.

The marine shales and siltstones that form the base of the sedimentary sequence were thinly bedded, fissile, fair quality rocks. They had low durability and tended to slake and degrade when exposed. These rocks were highly anisotropic with UCS ranging from about 35 MPa along bedding to about 80 MPa across bedding. Bedding joints were closely spaced (<0.3 m), and RMR values typically ranged from 40 to 50 (i.e. fair quality rock mass).

The Cretaceous siltstones and sandstones that formed the footwall of the coal measures were more massive and competent than the underlying Jurassic rocks. Bedding joint spacing was about 1 m, UCS was typically greater than about 150 MPa and RMR was greater than about 60 (i.e. good quality rock mass).

The competency of the coal measure rocks was extremely variable. At the low end were sheared coal seams with UCS of about 14 MPa or less, and RMR of about 30 (i.e. poor quality rock mass). Carbonaceous shales and mudstones were slightly more competent with UCS of about 25 MPa and RMR of about 40. Interseam siltstones and sandstones were the most competent, with strengths similar to the sedimentary rocks in the immediate footwall of the coal measures.

The shear strength of the discontinuities also varied widely, depending on the discontinuity type, lithology and infilling materials. Faults, shears and bedding joints in coal had a nominal friction angle of about 23° and negligible cohesion. Carbonaceous bedding and cross-joints had a nominal shear strength of about $\phi = 25°, c = 15$ kPa, while non-carbonaceous bedding and cross-joints had a nominal shear strength of about $\phi = 36°, c = 60$ kPa.

### 15.3.4  Hydrogeology

The ground water flow system was anisotropic, with high hydraulic conductivity in the plane of bedding compared to that across bedding. Coal seams and fractured sandstone and siltstone units tended to act as aquifers, and shale/mudstone units tended to act as aquitards. The principal direction of ground water flow was parallel to the plunging axes of the folds. Because topography tended to mimic the gross fold structure, artesian conditions could exist in the toes of excavated footwall slopes. Horizontal drain

holes were required to control potentially adverse piezometric pressures in footwall slopes. Highwall slopes were typically moderately to well drained, and enhanced depressurization was not normally required for these walls.

### 15.3.5  Structural domains

Based on stratigraphic and competency considerations, the rock mass was first subdivided into three structural domains: the Jurassic shales and siltstones (Domain 1), the footwall siltstones and sandstones (Domain 2), and the coal measures (Domain 3). Each domain was further subdivided based on the orientation of bedding with respect to proposed slope orientations. Footwall domains (F) were defined as domains where bedding strikes parallel to the proposed slope and dips in the same direction as the slope. Highwall domains (H) were defined as domains where bedding strikes parallel to the proposed slope and dips into the slope. Domains are shown on Figure 15.4.

### 15.3.6  Kinematic analyses

Kinematic assessments were conducted for each domain using stereographic projection techniques described in Chapter 2 to determine possible failure modes. These analyses confirmed that possible failure modes were highly dependent on the orientation (both strike and dip) of the slope with respect to bedding. Some examples of kinematically possible failure modes that were considered are illustrated schematically in Figure 15.6.

For footwall domains, the key failure modes that controlled stability all involved sliding along bedding discontinuities. Simple plane failure may have occurred where the slope undercut bedding (Figure 15.6(a)), or bedding was offset by faulting (Figure 15.6(b)). More complex failure modes may also have occurred, such as bilinear failure involving shearing through the toe of the slope (Figure 15.6(c)), ploughing failure where a driving slab forces a key block to rotate out of the toe of the slope (Figure 15.6(d)), or bucking failure (Figure 15.6(e)).

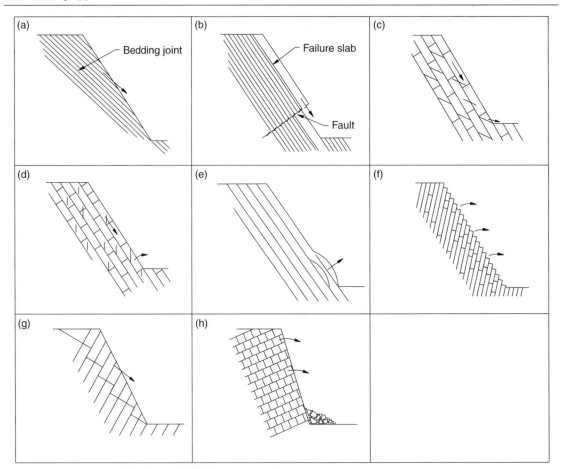

*Figure 15.6* Example 2—kinematically possible failure modes.

For highwall domains, the key failure modes that controlled stability included toppling on bedding (Figure 15.6(f)), stepped-path plane failure involving sliding along cross-joints with release on bedding joints (Figure 15.6(g)), and raveling (i.e. rock falls involving individual detached rock blocks) (Figure 15.6(h)).

### 15.3.7 *Stability analyses*

Stability analyses were conducted for each of the primary modes of failure in each domain using limit equilibrium techniques. Failure models were developed to assess the sensitivity of stability to variations in the geometry of the slope, bedding

orientation, bedding joint spacing, rock mass competency, discontinuity shear strength and ground water conditions. The analyses techniques used for simple plane, wedge and toppling failure were similar to those presented in Chapters 6, 7 and 9. More complex failure modes, such as bilinear slab, ploughing and buckling failure, were analyzed using limit equilibrium methods similar to those described by Hawley *et al.* (1986).

Analyses results for footwall domains were presented in the form of stability curves that related the dip of bedding to slope or bench height for a given factor of safety. As illustrated schematically in Figure 15.7, multiple curves were developed for each mode to assess sensitivity to

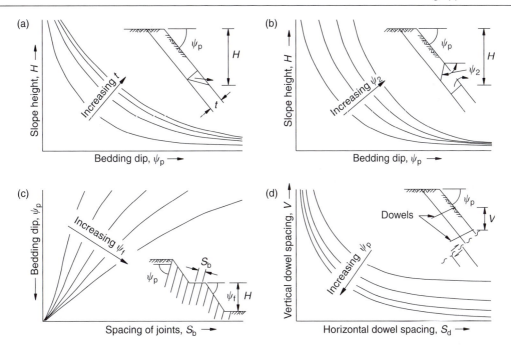

*Figure 15.7* Schematic illustration of stability analysis results: (a) plane failure; (b) ploughing failure; (c) toppling failure; (d) slab failure with artificial support (modified after Hawley and Stewart (1986)).

variations in key parameters, such as the spacing of bedding joints, or the dip of cross-joints, and to assess the cost/benefit of artificial support.

For highwall domains, analysis results for potential plane, wedge and stepped path failures were presented in terms of expected breakback angles using a similar approach as described in Example 1. Analyses results for potential toppling failure were presented in the form of stability curves that relate bedding joint dip and spacing to stable bench face angle (see Figure 15.7(c)).

### 15.3.8  Slope design concepts

To provide the mine planners with flexible design criteria that could be easily adapted to changing geologic conditions, a series of slope design concepts were developed. Each concept consisted of a basic slope type, and specific slope design criteria. Each concept was applicable within a given domain over a specified range of geologic conditions. Table 15.1 summarizes the various slope design concepts, associated basic slope types, their range of applicability, and critical failure modes that control slope design and pertinent comments.

In developing the slope design concepts, some basic slope parameters first had to be defined in consultation with the mine planners. These included fixed criteria, such as bench height increment and minimum catch berm width, which were based on the size of the mining equipment and regulatory requirements, and more subjective considerations, such as the overall design factor of safety and acceptable level of risk.

In some cases, more than one slope design concept was applicable. For example, artificial support was an alternative that provided a steeper slope design than a conventional approach. Alternative slope design concepts provided the mine planners with additional flexibility. The decision as to which alternative to adopt was based on specific cost/benefit analyses, operational convenience or other criteria.

*Table 15.1* Slope design concepts

| Slope design concept | Basic slope type | Bedding orientation | Illustration | Critical failure modes | Applicability | Design criteria |
|---|---|---|---|---|---|---|
| F-I | Benched footwall slope; bedding undercut. | Bedding dips shallowly out of the slope. | | Stepped planar failure on bedding. | Domains where bedding joints are discontinuous or bedding dip is flatter than the friction angle. | Excavate benched slope. Benches designed to limit the size of potential stepped failures and provide catchment for small failures and raveling debris. |
| F-II | Unbenched footwall slope; bedding not undercut. | Bedding dips shallowly to moderately out of the slope. | | Planar failure on bedding. | Domains where bedding joints are continuous or bedding dip is steeper than the friction angle, but not steep enough to initiate buckling, ploughing, bilinear or other slab-type failures. | Excavate slope parallel to bedding. Do not undercut bedding. |
| F-III | Benched footwall slope; bedding not undercut. | Bedding dips moderately to steeply out of the slope. | | Buckling, ploughing, bilinear or other slab-type failures. | Domains where bedding joints are continuous and bedding dip is significantly steeper than the friction angle. | Excavate bench faces parallel to bedding. Do not undercut bedding. Bench height designed to limit potential for development of slab-type failures. Bench width designed to provide catchment for small failures and raveling debris. |
| F-IV | Unbenched, supported footwall slope; bedding not undercut. | | | Buckling, ploughing, bilinear or other slab-type failures. | Domains where bedding joints are continuous and bedding dip is significantly steeper than the friction angle. | Excavate slope parallel to bedding. Apply artificial support to prevent development of major slab-type failures. |
| H-I | Benched, unsupported highwall slope. | Bedding dips steeply into slope. | | Toppling; raveling. | Domains where bedding joints are continuous and closely spaced. | Excavate slope using single benches. Flat bench face angle designed to limit potential for toppling. Minimal bench width designed to provide catchment for raveling debris. |
| H-II | Benched, supported highwall slope. | | | Toppling; raveling. | Domains where bedding joints are continuous and closely spaced. | Excavate benched slope. Artificial support designed to limit potential for toppling, maximize bench height and/or bench face angle and/or increase available bench width to contain small slab-type failures and raveling debris. |
| H-III | Benched, unsupported highwall slope. | Bedding dips shallowly to moderately into slope. | | Planer, stepped planar, wedges or stepped wedges on cross-joints; raveling. | Domains not subject to other kinematically possible failure modes. | Excavate benched slope. Benches designed to limit the size of potential planar, wedge and stepped failures and provide catchment for small failures and raveling debris. |

Source: Adapted after Hawley and Stewart (1986).

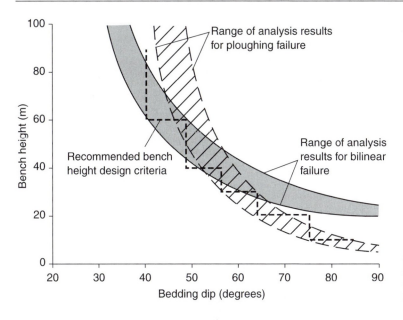

*Figure 15.8* Example 2—typical footwall bench height design criteria (modified after Hawley and Stewart (1986)).

Specific design criteria were developed for the slope design concept in each domain based on the results of the stability and sensitivity analyses. Critical failure modes were determined for each basic slope type, and analyses results were used to define ranges of acceptable slope and bench geometries. For footwall domains, the results of plane, bilinear and ploughing failure analyses were used to define allowable unbenched slope heights based on the dip of bedding (e.g. Figure 15.8). For highwall domains, toppling failure analyses were used to define the ranges of bedding dip where toppling failure controlled stability, and to assess appropriate slope geometries to prevent toppling. For highwall domains not subject to toppling, design criteria were based on predicted breakback and minimum catch bench widths required to control small wedge and plane failures, and raveling.

### 15.3.9 *Preliminary design*

A preliminary slope design was prepared based on the slope design concepts described before. Detailed geotechnical sections were constructed at regular intervals normal to the proposed slopes.

On each section, a provisional pit bottom and slope toe were determined in consultation with mine planners. Based on the domain and orientation of bedding in the toe of the slope, an appropriate slope design concept was selected and applied. This slope design concept was projected upwards for as far as conditions remained appropriate. When a point was reached where the conditions were no longer applicable, a new slope design concept was chosen. This process was repeated until the full wall height was developed and the pit crest was reached on each geotechnical section. Figure 15.9 is an example of how this iterative process was applied to the typical cross-section given in Figure 15.4.

To achieve a practical overall slope design, it was necessary to blend the slope geometry between sections. Bench heights and berm widths had to be modified locally to deal with local rolls in the bedding, the occurrence of faults and other geologic complexities. Once the preliminary design was completed, an assessment of the potential for overall or deep-seated slope instability was conducted, and slope geometries were modified as required to meet minimum overall slope stability objectives.

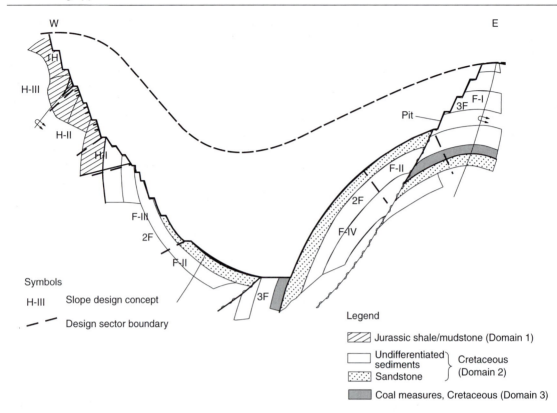

*Figure 15.9* Example 2—slope design concepts applied to typical geologic cross-section (modified after Hawley and Stewart (1986)).

## 15.4   Example 3—deep-seated deformation in a weak rock mass

Weak rock mass conditions can occur in many types of ore deposits, especially where ore deposition is associated with alteration or complex structural zones. The lithologies associated with these conditions can be considered to represent a wide range of geological environments including: (i) highly fractured plutonic rocks (e.g. copper porphyry deposits); (ii) metasedimentary or metavolcanic rocks (e.g. shear hosted gold deposits); or (iii) mafic volcanic rocks (e.g. asbestos deposits). This example is a generalized case history of combined experience at four operating mines with open pit slopes ranging from 300 to 500 m high. The main similarity between these projects is the presence of a weak rock mass associated

with a near-vertical regional fault or shear zone, exposed in the lower portion of one of the pit walls, that defines a boundary to the ore body.

Overall, these rock masses are variably altered, structurally complex and exhibit high ground water pressures. Slope depressurization is difficult due to structural compartmentalization of ground water and low rock mass conductivity.

### 15.4.1   Design and operational issues

Large-scale pit slopes may be prone to deep-seated deformation due to stress concentrations in the highly deformable weak rock mass in the toe of the slope, or complex modes of failure such as squeezing or toppling extending to a considerable depth behind the face. These conditions often require a number of analytical and empirical approaches to be applied in design. However, limitations may exist in being able to predict, adequately, initial slope performance. Consequently, early mining phases may require conservative slope angles to provide experience from which future slope performance can be assessed. Once experience is gained, deterministic, probabilistic, empirical and numerical modeling assessments can be calibrated against slope performance, allowing ultimate pit slope designs to be optimized.

Deep-seated deformation can result in slope movements of tens of meters per year. Therefore, a comprehensive slope movement monitoring system is required to provide advanced warning of increased slope movement rates. This typically includes a network of reflective survey prisms, wire extensometers and borehole inclinometers in critical areas. Contingency planning is also required to build flexibility into the mine designs, such that mitigation measures can be implemented to remediate areas of instability, if necessary.

Depending on the critical nature of the pit slopes, the location of important mine infrastructure and the flexibility of the mine plan (i.e. single versus dual, or multiple, ramp access), deformation analysis using a discontinuum modeling approach such as UDEC (see Chapter 10) may be carried out. Deformation analysis requires a high level of understanding of the slope deformation controls, as well as detailed slope monitoring and ground water information. With adequate calibration, these models can provide predictions of possible slope behavior, allowing movement threshold criteria and contingency plans to be developed.

### 15.4.2  Engineering geology

The engineering geology of the slope is shown on the cross-section in Figure 15.10. The geology was based on detailed pit mapping and core logging, and the structural geology interpretation was based on oriented core drilling and projections of structural mapping from the existing pit.

A 50 m wide regional fault zone dipped at approximately 80° into the lower pit slope, with a strike approximately parallel to the slope face.

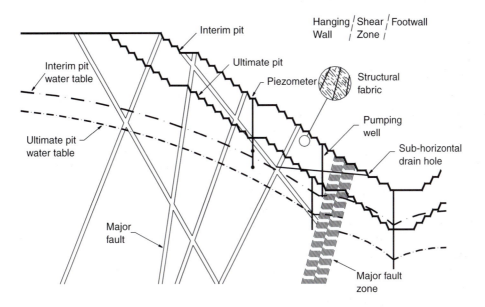

*Figure 15.10* Example 4—engineering geology cross-section of open pit slope prone to deep-seated deformation.

The rock units shown on Figure 15.10 were termed Hanging Wall, Footwall and Shear Zone rocks relative to the fault. Sympathetic faults and joints related to the major fault zone were aligned parallel to the slope azimuth and dipped between 65° and 80° into the wall. The combined influence of these features created the potential for deep-seated toppling. A second structural set consisted of faults and joints that dipped toward the open pit at 45–65° (see detail of structural fabric). Pervasive joints of this set controlled the geometry of the bench faces, but were non-daylighting on the flatter inter-ramp and overall slopes.

### 15.4.3   Rock strength and rock mass competency

In general, rocks were weakest in the faults and Shear Zone, and strongest in the Hanging Wall and Footwall. Shear strengths of discontinuity surfaces and fault gouge were based on direct shear testing, as well as back analysis of existing failures. Faults and joints had friction angles of 23° and 30°, respectively, and cohesion ranged between 0 and 50 kPa for both discontinuity types.

Typical ranges of intact rock strength and Hoek–Brown "disturbed" rock mass strengths are shown in Table 15.2, with average parameters in brackets. Equivalent Mohr–Coulomb strength parameters were estimated using a normal stress of 1 MPa, which was considered to represent average stress conditions at the inter-ramp scale.

### 15.4.4   Hydrogeology and slope depressurization measures

The hydrogeology of the rock mass was structurally compartmentalized by steeply dipping faults that acted as structural barriers to ground water flow. Overall, the conductivity of the rock mass was low due to alteration associated with the ore body and main structural zones. Even if some natural depressurization did occur as the slope was mined, perched ground water conditions could occur, leading to significant residual piezometric pressures in the slope.

Pit slope depressurization measures typically consisted of sub-horizontal (slightly upwards inclined) drain holes drilled to depths of 200–300 m (Figure 15.10). In rock masses with steeply dipping, low conductivity structures, sub-horizontal drain holes provided a cost-effective means of slope depressurization. Advanced depressurization with drain holes that were long enough to penetrate behind the next mining phase provide considerable improvements in stability, especially when consolidation of low shear strength materials was achieved. Other practical methods of slope depressurization included vertical pumping wells and vertical drains. Underground drainage galleries, which may be justified in cases where water pressures have

*Table 15.2* Summary of rock mass strength parameters

| Rock type | Rock Mass Rating (RMR) | Unconfined compressive strength (MPa) | Intact rock constant, $m_i$ | Friction angle, $\phi(°)$ | Cohesion, $c$ (kPa) |
|---|---|---|---|---|---|
| Hanging Wall | 35–45 (40) | 25–40 (35) | 15–25 (20) | 32 | 300 |
| Shear Zone | 25–30 (25) | 15–25 (25) | 15 | 17 23[a] | 190 50[a] |
| Footwall | 40–60 (50) | 25–75 (50) | 15–25 (20) | 40 | 400 |

Note
a  Strength from back analysis and laboratory direct shear testing.

a very significant influence on stability, were considered too costly for this application.

### 15.4.5 *Slope stability analyses*

Limit equilibrium rock mass analyses of kinematically possible failure modes were used to evaluate inter-ramp and overall slope stability. Back analyses of previous instabilities and as-built slopes were carried out to establish appropriate material strength parameters for forward analyses of proposed slope designs. These assessments were complemented by development of empirical slope height–angle relationships to compare stable versus unstable slope geometries. Sensitivity analyses were carried out to identify critical inter-ramp and overall slope heights at various slope angles. Parametric assessments were also carried out to assess the sensitivity of the factor of safety to variations in slope conditions such as ground water pressures. Once preliminary slope design parameters and initial mine plans were developed, stability analyses were carried out on specific geotechnical cross-sections to verify the inter-ramp and overall slope designs.

Figure 15.11 shows a typical stability analysis model that incorporates the major geotechnical units and ground water projections for the ultimate pit. In the Footwall rocks, Hoek–Brown non-linear strengths were used in the model. In the Hanging Wall, strength anisotropy was accounted for by using joint strengths for dips of 45–65° toward the pit, and Mohr–Coulomb strengths for the remaining Hanging Wall rock mass (Table 15.2). For the Fault and Shear Zone materials, Mohr–Coulomb discontinuity shear strengths were used due to the soil-like nature of these materials. The inter-ramp slope geometries were represented by straight-line segments connecting the inter-ramp slopes at the mid-bench level. This simplified the model geometry and prevented the breakthrough of shear surfaces on the bench faces, reducing the potential for computational problems. A minimum factor of safety of 1.2 was determined for a non-circular analysis of the overall slope. This minimum factor of safety would not be encountered until the final stages of mining, and therefore was considered acceptable for the overall slope design.

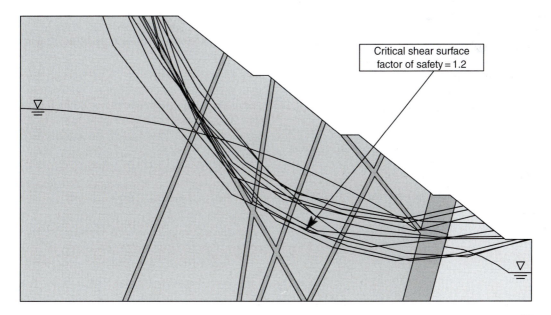

*Figure 15.11* Example 4—non-circular limit equilibrium analysis results for the ultimate pit using SLIDE™.

### 15.4.6  Slope design and operational management

The geometry of the 15 m high single benches was controlled by plane and wedge failures involving pervasive jointing dipping at 45–65°. The average breakback angle of the bench faces was 54°. For a minimum design catch berm width of 7.6 m, this defined an upper bound allowable inter-ramp slope angle of 39°. Double benching was not considered advisable in this case due to the hazards associated with 30 m high, bench-scale failures.

Based on the results of deep-seated stability analyses, a 38° inter-ramp slope angle was adopted with 35 m wide stepouts or ramps placed at maximum inter-ramp slope heights of 120 m. The inter-ramp slope angle corresponding to the "angle of repose" (38°) was also chosen to control raveling and rock falls associated with deep-seated squeezing and toppling slope deformation. The ramps and stepouts both provided operational flexibility if instability was encountered, and the de-coupled or re-distributed stresses in the step-outs had the effect of reducing overall slope displacements. The resulting overall slope angle was 34° at a height of 450 m.

Based on the possible mode and magnitudes of slope deformation, contingency plans were incorporated to maximize flexibility in the mine design and manage slope deformations. These included, but were not limited to

- adjustments to the mining rate;
- dozing and backfilling of ramp crests;
- waste rock buttressing at the toe of unstable areas;
- temporary splitting of mining phases, thus allowing slope depressurization measures (e.g. drain holes) to be installed;
- offloading of the pit crest; and
- provision of secondary (dual) access.

Ongoing slope management included detailed assessment of slope monitoring trends to predict periods of peak velocity or failure. Remedial measures were implemented when slope movement exceeded threshold criteria, or exhibited potential for progressive failure.

## 15.5  Example 4—overall slope design in a competent rock mass

This example is based on experience with various competent rock masses, and is illustrated by a hypothetical case history of a 500 m deep open pit mine that had been operating for a number of years with few slope stability or operational problems of any consequence. The geometries of the 30 m high double benches and inter-ramp slopes were designed and excavated to control plane and wedge failures involving steeply dipping bench-scale, and larger discontinuities. The existing pit had inter-ramp and overall slope angles of 55° and 50°, respectively. It was planned to increase the pit depth to 700 m, and there was concern regarding the stability of the proposed slopes with respect to deep-seated slope deformation.

### 15.5.1  Design aspects and issues

The following issues were considered during assessment of the proposed pit slopes. First, study of the engineering geology showed that the majority of the rock mass was strong, with favorably oriented discontinuities. Limit equilibrium stability analyses for the initial pit slope design, completed many years earlier for a 500 m deep open pit, determined that the inter-ramp and overall slope angles were controlled by bench stability and geometry, and not by multi-bench or overall stability. There were no major geologic structures or combinations of major structures that appeared to control stability. In addition, the strength of the rock mass was sufficiently high that deep-seated slope deformation was not a concern for the 500 m slope height. However, a study was required of the consistency of the engineering geology data to the final proposed pit depth.

The second issue was the actual performance of the pit walls with respect to the original slope design criteria. In this regard, the existing pit slopes were documented by measuring the bench face angles, berm widths and amount of crest breakback. This information provided valuable data on both the various geological structures and their influence on bench stability for the range of slope orientations, and the suitability of the original slope design parameters.

A third issue was the *in situ* stress environment, and its influence on the potential for deep-seated deformation that could influence the stability of the overall slopes.

Fortunately, due to the extended length of time that the mine had already been operating, and the ongoing data collection program, many of the parameters that were required for the study were reasonably well understood. For those parameters that were not well defined, sensitivity analyses were conducted to help evaluate a range of possible conditions.

### 15.5.2    Engineering geology

The bedrock comprised a series of near-vertical mafic intrusions of gabbro, peridotite and serpentinite within a granitic host rock. Occasional narrow (<10 m wide), sub-vertical northwest/southeast trending diabase dykes cut through the entire assemblage. The majority of the rock was essentially fresh and unaltered, except for an approximately 50 m surficial layer of more weathered rock. An east–west striking, sub-vertical to steeply south dipping regional fault zone intersected the floor of the pit and was projected to be encountered near the toe of the ultimate north pit wall. The fault zone ranged up to about 15 m thick and was characterized as a "zone of breakage," with little or no soft fault gouge. A cross-section through the north pit wall is illustrated in Figure 15.12.

Information on the structural geology was obtained both in the pit, and below the pit bottom to the final proposed depth. This investigation involved mapping the pit walls to characterize the orientation and distribution of the discontinuities, and drilling a number of diamond drill holes with oriented core. The mapping, supported by the core orientation measurements, showed that the geologic structure was dominated by two persistent fault and joint sets, with an additional four moderately to weakly developed joint sets of limited persistence. All of these structural sets appeared to rotate with the pit wall, such that their relationship with the orientation of the pit walls was approximately constant. One of the persistent fault and joint sets dipped at 35–40° into the wall with a strike approximately parallel to the slope, while the second set had an average dip of 65–80° out of the slope. The average spacing of the persistent structures was estimated to be 25–45 m. Three of the remaining discontinuity sets had a strike oblique into the slope at an average dip of at least 70° and a maximum persistence of about 30 m. The fourth joint set had a dip of less than 10° and an average persistence of only 15 m.

### 15.5.3    Rock strength and competency

Both laboratory testing of intact samples and estimates of strength conducted during mapping of the pit walls indicated that the various rock types were all strong, with uniaxial compressive strengths ranging from 95 to 180 MPa. Laboratory direct shear testing of natural discontinuities showed that joints in all rock types had negligible cohesion, and peak and residual friction angles that ranged from 30° to 35° and 26° to 29°, respectively. Faults had peak and residual friction angles of 24° and 17°, respectively, and no cohesion.

Characterization of the various portions of the rock mass was conducted using established empirical classification systems. All of the rocks in the mine area were considered to be of good to very good quality, having RMR values in the range of 75–85. In addition, limited triaxial testing of the primary rock types was conducted. Rock quality and strength data were used to estimate peak and residual rock mass strengths using the Hoek–Brown strength criterion (see Section 5.4.2).

### 15.5.4    Hydrogeology

The hydrogeologic regime was based on the interpreted bedrock geology, piezometer testing

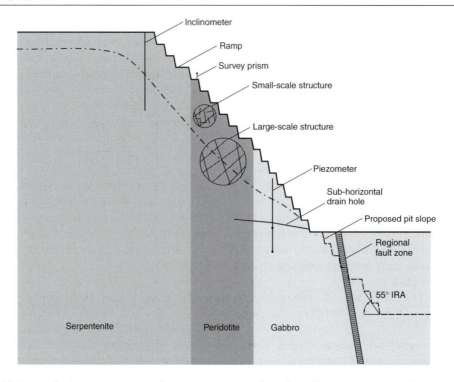

Serpentenite
Peridotite
Gabbro

*Figure 15.12* Example 4—engineering geology cross-section of pit slope illustrating proposed pit deepening.

and monitoring, and seepage observations within the open pit. Most of the rock mass in the mine area was interpreted to have a low hydraulic conductivity, typically less than about $10^{-9}$ m/s. However, conductivity along the diabase dyke contacts and in the vicinity of the continuous faults appeared to be one to two orders of magnitude higher. Weathered bedrock within the upper 50 m of the ground surface was estimated to have a hydraulic conductivity that was similar to, or slightly greater than, that of the dykes and faults. While it was evident that most of the seepage exited the pit walls within about 60 m of the pit bottom, it also appeared that the seepage was compartmentalized in some areas, with local pockets of seepage being evident across the pit walls.

Two hundred meter long sub-horizontal drain holes had proven to be effective in depressurizing the pit walls as the pit was deepened. The drain holes had typically targeted the faults and dyke contacts.

### 15.5.5 *Slope performance*

Evaluating the performance of the existing pit slopes provided important information in the assessment of the proposed deepening of the pit. It was determined from slope documentation that, with few exceptions, the slopes had performed as expected. The safety berms had generally provided sufficient catchment room for rock fall and raveling material, and the occasional slope failure. Prism monitoring, which had been carried out for many years, indicated that the slopes were not experiencing undue movement. All slope movement appeared to reflect normal initial response or slope relaxation. In addition, final wall controlled blasting had caused minimal damage to the integrity of the rock mass.

A review of the history of the pit slopes with respect to the nature and size of any incidents of instability was also carried out. While it was noted that instability had been experienced from time to time, all of the slope failures were less than 30 m high, except for one double bench failure (i.e. 60 m high). Localized measures, which included the use of waste rock buttresses, scaling and a minor amount of doweling and anchoring, were implemented to remediate the various areas of instability.

### 15.5.6   Slope stability analyses

Analysis of the geologic structure was first carried out to investigate the variation of structural orientations with depth for the fault and joint sets in each structural domain. These analyses showed that the orientation, distribution and nature of geologic structural populations throughout the pit had not changed appreciably since the original slope design study. In addition, little variation in peak orientations seemed to be occurring with depth. Based on the updated structural geology, which included information to a depth of approximately 700 m, kinematic and stability analyses of possible failure modes were conducted. In these analyses, emphasis was placed on the data from the lower portion of the pit wall to the proposed pit bottom. Not surprisingly, considering the consistency of the structural populations with depth and the positive performance of the pit slopes to that point, these assessments yielded favorable results. Based solely on limit equilibrium analyses of potential planar, wedge and toppling failures, it was shown that the previously designed bench, inter-ramp and overall slope designs could be continued.

To develop a more comprehensive understanding of slope deformation and to evaluate the potential for deep-seated instability, numerical modeling of the critical pit slopes was conducted. Preliminary assessments were conducted using finite element analysis of stress conditions with the computer program Phase$^2$ (Rocscience, 2002c). More detailed assessments were conducted using UDEC (see Chapter 10). The model incorporated the two continuous fault sets noted before (see Figure 15.12 for the structural model input into UDEC), along with the rock mass strength parameters. Sensitivity analyses were conducted with respect to the length and spacing of the two fault sets, ground water and *in situ* stress. Calibration of the model was conducted by comparing the monitored slope displacements with the model response. After a number of iterations, a good correlation between the two was obtained for both horizontal and vertical displacements. Predictive modeling of the proposed deepened pit was then carried out. To investigate the positive influence of confinement of the rock mass in the area of the proposed pit bottom, where the pit walls had a relatively limited radius of curvature, three-dimensional effects were also checked numerically. For the range of parameters encompassed by the sensitivity analyses, modeling results indicated that the rock mass was sufficiently competent that deepening of the open pit to 700 m should not adversely affect the overall stability of the pit walls. However, the results also indicated that a certain level of depressurization of the pit walls would be required as the pit was deepened.

### 15.5.7   Implementation and ongoing evaluation

Notwithstanding the positive results of the stability analyses, it is most important in any slope design study to monitor the ongoing behavior of the pit walls. This is particularly critical in situations where pit slopes are expanding the bounds of previous experience in a given rock mass. In this case, continued monitoring of the prisms and borehole inclinometers was planned so the results could be compared with the movements predicted by the modeling. Should monitoring results indicate that slope movement was beginning to outpace predicted movements, further analyses and possibly remedial measures may have been warranted.

Since the analyses indicated that the pit walls should be depressurized as mining progressed to depth, an aggressive deep drain hole program was recommended. Piezometer installation was also recommended at a number of locations to monitor the depressurization over time. To maintain the rock mass in as competent state as possible, and to minimize the potential for rock falls and other modes of instability, the continued use of controlled blasting practices on the final walls was strongly recommended.

## 15.6 Conclusions

The approaches to open pit slope design illustrated in the first two examples described in this chapter have been successfully implemented on numerous projects worldwide over the last 25 years. They rely predominantly on limit equilibrium stability analysis techniques that are well established and widely used. Early design criteria that were based largely on analytical studies have been confirmed, refined and updated based on observed slope performance. Refinements in the underlying analytical tools continue to improve

our understanding of the failure modes and sensitivity of stability to the key parameters. One of the main benefits of these approaches is their inherent flexibility and adaptability to changing pit geometry, geology and ground water conditions.

The latter two examples introduced additional degrees of complexity in which potential failure modes could not be adequately described or analyzed using simple limit equilibrium techniques alone. These examples describe the application of sophisticated stability analysis models that require extensive calibration and mature engineering judgment. Regardless of the approach employed, the reliability of the underlying geologic structural and engineering geology models of the rock mass are critical to the successful implementation of any slope design.

# Appendix I

# Stereonets for hand plotting of structural geology data

## I.1 Introduction

Analysis of the orientation of structural geology data involves first, plotting poles representing the dip and dip direction of each discontinuity. This plot will help to identify discontinuity sets, for which both the average orientation and the scatter (dispersion) can be calculated. The second step in the analysis is to plot great circles representing the average orientation of each set, major discontinuities such as faults, and the dip and dip direction of the cut face. Hand plotting of structural data can be carried out on the stereonets provided in this appendix. Further details of the plotting procedures are provided in Chapter 2, Section 2.5.

## I.2 Plotting poles

Poles can be plotted on the polar stereonet (Figure I.1) on which the dip direction is indicated on the periphery of the circle, and the dip is measured along radial lines with zero degrees at the center. It should be noted that the stereonet shown on Figure I.1 is the lower hemisphere plot in which the dip direction scale starts at the bottom of the circle and increases in a clockwise direction, with the north arrow corresponding to the dip direction of 180°. The reason for setting up the scale in this manner is that if the field readings, as measured with a structural compass, are plotted directly on the stereonet, the poles are correctly plotted on the lower hemisphere plot.

The procedure for plotting poles is to lay a sheet of tracing paper on the printed polar net and mark the north direction and each quadrant position around the edge of the outer circle. A mark is then made to show the pole that represents the orientation of each discontinuity as defined by its dip and dip direction. Poles for shallow dipping discontinuities lie close to the center of the circle, and poles of steeply dipping discontinuities lie close to the periphery of the circle.

## I.3 Contouring pole concentrations

Concentrations of pole orientations can be identified using a counting net such as that shown in Figure I.2. The Kalsbeek net is made up of mutually overlapping hexagons, each with an area of 1/100 of the full area of the stereonet. Contouring is performed by overlaying the counting net on the pole plot and counting the number of poles in each hexagon; this number is marked on the net. These numbers of poles are converted into percentages by dividing each by the total number of poles and multiplying by 100. Once a percentage is written in each hexagon, contours can be developed by interpolation.

## I.4 Plotting great circles

Great circles are plotted on the equatorial net (Figure I.3), but they cannot be plotted directly on this net because the true dip can only be scaled off the horizontal axis. The plotting procedure for

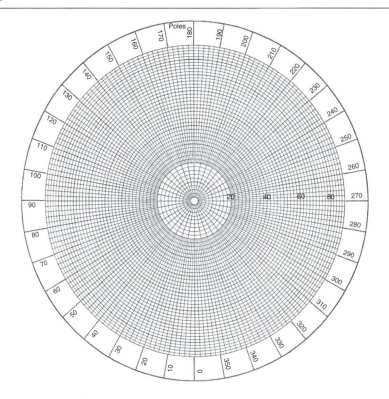

*Figure I.1* Equal-area polar net for plotting poles.

great circles consists of the following steps:

1   Lay a piece of tracing paper on the net with a thumbtack through the center point so that the tracing paper can be rotated on the net.
2   Mark the north direction of the net on the tracing paper.
3   Locate the dip direction of the plane on the scale around the circumference of the net and mark this point on the tracing paper. Note that the dip direction scale on the equatorial net for plotting great circles starts at the north point at the top of the circle and increases in a clockwise direction.
4   Rotate the tracing paper until the dip direction mark coincides with one of the horizontal axes of the net, that is, the 90° or 180° points of the dip direction scale.
5   Locate the arc on the net corresponding to the dip of the plane and trace this arc on

to the paper. Note that a horizontal plane has a great circle at the circumference of the net, and a vertical plane is represented by a straight line passing through the center of the net.
6   Rotate the tracing paper so that the two north points coincide and the great circle is oriented correctly.

## I.5   Lines of intersection

The intersection of two planes is a straight line, which defines the direction of sliding of a wedge formed by these two planes. The procedure for determining the orientation of the line of intersection between two planes is:

1   Locate the line of intersection between the two planes, which is represented by the point at which the two great circles intersect.

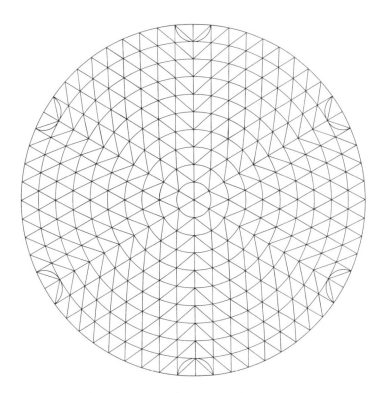

*Figure I.2* Kalsbeek counting net for contouring pole concentrations.

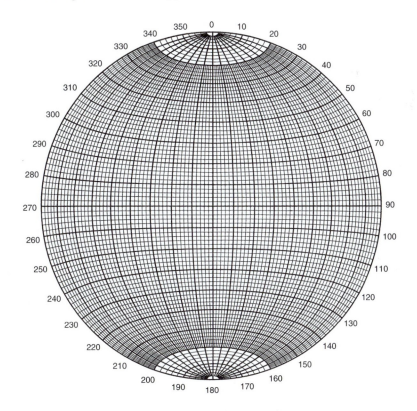

*Figure I.3* Equal-area equatorial net for plotting poles and great circles.

# Appendix II

# Quantitative description of discontinuities in rock masses

## II.1  Introduction

This appendix provides details of the parameters used in geological mapping and diamond drilling for the quantitative description of rock masses. The information provided is based entirely on the procedures drawn up by the International Society of Rock Mechanics (ISRM, 1981a), and which are discussed in more detail in Sections 4.2 and 4.3 of this book. The objectives of using the ISRM procedures for geological mapping and drill core logging are as follows. First, these procedures are quantitative so that each parameter is measured and the results can be used either directly, or interpreted, in design. Second, the use of standardized procedures allows different personnel to work to the same standards, and to produce comparable information.

The following is a description of the parameters that describe the rock mass, together with tables listing values used to quantify these parameters. Also provided are mapping forms that can be used to record both geological mapping and oriented core logging. Further information on geological characterization and methods of data collection are discussed in Chapter 4.

## II.2  Rock mass characterization parameters

Figure II.1 illustrates the parameters that characterize the rock mass, and Figure II.2 shows how they can be divided into six classes related to the rock material and its strength, the discontinuity characteristics, infilling properties, the dimensions and shape of the blocks of rock, and ground water conditions. Each of the parameters is discussed in this appendix.

### II.2.1  Rock material description

#### A  Rock type

The value of including the rock type in describing a rock mass is that this defines the process by which the rock was formed. For example, sedimentary rocks such as sandstone usually contain well-ordered sets of discontinuities because they are laid down in layers, and are medium to low strength because they have usually only been subject to moderate heating and compression. Also, the rock type gives an indication of the properties of the rock mass from general experience of their engineering performance. For example, granite tends to be strong and massive and resistant to weathering in comparison to shale which is often weak and fissile, and can weather rapidly when exposed to wetting and drying cycles.

Table II.1 shows a procedure for defining the rock type. This procedure involves identifying three primary characteristics of rock as follows:

1  Color, as well as whether light or dark minerals predominate;
2  Texture or fabric ranging from crystalline, granular or glassy; and
3  Grain size that can range from clay particles to gravel (Table II.2).

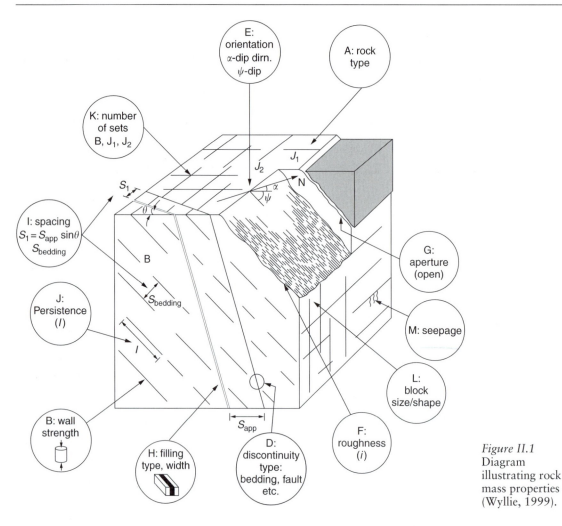

*Figure II.1*
Diagram
illustrating rock
mass properties
(Wyllie, 1999).

## B   Rock strength

The compressive strength of the rock comprising the discontinuity surfaces is an important component of shear strength and deformability, especially if the surfaces are in direct rock-to-rock contact as in the case of unfilled joints. Slight shear displacement of individual joints caused by shear stresses within the rock mass, often results in small asperity contact areas. Where the concentrated stresses locally approach or exceed the compression strength of the rock wall materials, asperity damage occurs. The surface strength is quantified in the determination of shear strength as the Joint Compressive Strength (JCS) as discussed in Section 3.4.2(b). Table II.3 defines ranges of rock material strength with a corresponding grade (R6 etc.) related to simple field identification procedures.

## C   Weathering

• Rock masses are frequently weathered near ground level, and are sometimes altered by hydrothermal processes. The weathering (and alteration) is generally more pronounced on

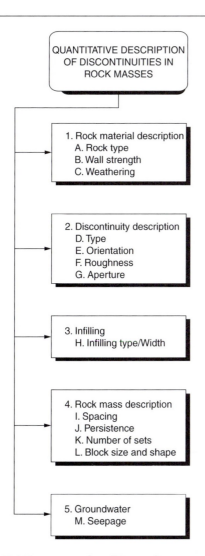

*Figure II.2* Parameters describing rock mass characteristics.

the rock exposed on the discontinuity surfaces than in the interior of rock blocks because water flow occurs in the discontinuities. This results in the rock strength on the discontinuity surfaces being less than that of the fresher rock found in the interior of the rock blocks. A description of the state of weathering or alteration both for the rock material and for the rock mass is therefore, an essential part of the description of the rock mass.

- There are two main results of weathering: one dominated by mechanical disintegration, the other by chemical decomposition including solution. Generally, both mechanical and chemical effects act together, but, depending on climatic regime, one or other may be dominant. Mechanical weathering results in opening of discontinuities, the formation of new discontinuities by rock fracture, the opening of grain boundaries, and the fracture or cleavage of individual mineral grains. Chemical weathering results in discoloration of the rock and leads to the eventual decomposition of silicate minerals to clay minerals; some minerals, notably quartz, resist this action and may survive unchanged. Solution is an aspect of chemical weathering, which is particularly important in the case of carbonate and saline minerals.
- The relatively thin "skin" of surface rock that affects shear strength and deformability can be tested by means of simple index tests. The apparent uniaxial compression strength can be estimated both from Schmidt hammer tests and from scratch and geological hammer tests, since the latter have been approximately calibrated against a large body of test data as shown in Table II.3.
- Mineral coatings will affect the shear strength of discontinuities to a marked degree, if the surfaces are planar and smooth. The type of mineral coatings should be described where possible. Samples should be taken when in doubt.

Table II.4 defines grades of rock weathering.

### II.2.2  Discontinuity description

#### D   Discontinuity type

- The discontinuity type is useful in the description of the rock mass because each type has properties that influence the behavior of the rock mass. For example, faults can have lengths of several kilometers and contain low strength gouge, while joints lengths

*Table II.1* Rock type classification

| | Detrital Sedimentary (BEDDED) | Detrital — carbonate (BEDDED) | Pyroclastic (BEDDED) | Chemical Organic (BEDDED) | Metamorphic FOLIATED | Metamorphic MASSIVE | Igneous MASSIVE — Acid rocks | Igneous MASSIVE — Intermediate rocks | Igneous MASSIVE — Basic rocks | Igneous MASSIVE — Ultra-basic rocks |
|---|---|---|---|---|---|---|---|---|---|---|
| **Genetic Group** | | | | | | | | | | |
| **Usual Structure** | BEDDED | BEDDED | BEDDED | BEDDED | FOLIATED | MASSIVE | MASSIVE | | | |
| **COMPOSITION** | Grains of rock, quartz, feldspar and minerals | At least 50% of grains are of carbonate | At least 50% of grains are of fine-grained volcanic rock | | Quartz, feldspars, micas, acicular dark minerals | | Light coloured minerals are quartz, feldspar, mica and feldspar-like minerals | | | Dark minerals |
| **Very coarse grained** (Grain size 60) | Grains are of rock fragments / Rounded grains: CONGLOMERATE | CALCIRUDITE | Rounded grains AGGLOMERATE / Angular grains VOLCANIC BRECCIA | SALINE ROCKS / Halite / Anhydrite / Gypsum | MIGMATITE / GNEISS Alternate layers of granular and flakey minerals | HORNFELS / MARBLE / GRANULITE | PEGMATITE | PEGMATITE | | PYROXENITE and PERIDOTITE |
| **Coarse grained** (Grain size 2) — RUDACEOUS | Angular grains: BRECCIA | | | | | | | | | |
| **Medium grained** — ARENACEOUS | SANDSTONE: Grains are mainly mineral fragments / QUARTZ SANDSTONE: 95% quartz, voids empty or cemented / ARKOSE: 75% quartz, up to 25% feldspar: voids empty of cemented / ARGILLARCEOUS SANDSTONE: 75% quartz, 15% + fine detrital material | CALCARENITE — LIMESTONE (undifferentiated) | TUFF | CHERT | SCHIST / PHYLLITE | QUARTZITE / AMPHIBOLITE | GRANITE / MICRO-GRANITE | DIORITE / MICRO-DIORITE | GABBRO / DOLERITE | SERPENTINE |
| **Fine grained** (0.06 / 0.002) — ARGILLACEOUS or LUTACEOUS | MUDSTONE SHALE: fissile mudstone / SILTSTONE 50% fine-grained particles / CLAYSTONE 50% very fine-grained particles / CALCAREOUS MUDSTONE | CALCISILTITE | Fine-grained TUFF | FLINT / COAL OTHERS | SLATE / MYLONITE | | RHYOLITE | ANDESITE | BASALT | |
| **Very fine grained** | | CALCILUTITE | Very fine-grained TUFF | | | | | | | |
| **GLASSY** | | | | | | | OBSIDEIAN and PITCHSTONE | | TACHYLYTE | |

Note: Numbers can be used to identify rock types on data sheets (see Appendix III).
*Reference: Geological Society Engineering Group Working Party (1977).*

*Table II.2* Grain size scale

| Description | Grain size |
|---|---|
| Boulders | 200–600 mm (7.9–23.6 in) |
| Cobbles | 60–200 mm (2.4–7.9 in) |
| Coarse gravel | 20–60 mm (0.8–0.24 in) |
| Medium gravel | 6–20 mm (0.2–0.8 in) |
| Fine gravel | 2–6 mm (0.1–0.2 in) |
| Coarse sand | 0.6–2 mm (0.02–0.1 in) |
| Medium sand | 0.2–0.6 mm (0.008–0.02 in) |
| Fine sand | 0.06–0.2 mm (0.002–0.008 in) |
| Silt, clay | <0.06 mm (<0.002 in) |

*Table II.3* Classification of rock material strengths

| Grade | Description | Field identification | Approximate compressive (MPa) | Range of strength (psi) |
|---|---|---|---|---|
| R6 | Extremely strong rock | Specimen can only be chipped with geological hammer. | >250 | >36,000 |
| R5 | Very strong rock | Specimen requires many blows of geological hammer to fracture it. | 100–250 | 15,000–36,000 |
| R4 | Strong rock | Specimen requires more than one blow with a geological hammer to fracture it. | 50–100 | 7000–15,000 |
| R3 | Medium weak rock | Cannot be scraped or peeled with a pocket knife; specimen can be fractured with single firm blow of geological hammer. | 25–50 | 3500–7000 |
| R2 | Weak rock | Can be peeled with a pocket knife; shallow indentations made by firm blow with point of geological hammer. | 5–25 | 725–3500 |
| R1 | Very weak rock | Crumbles under firm blows with point of geological hammer; can be peeled by a pocket knife. | 1–5 | 150–725 |
| R0 | Extremely weak rock | Indented by thumbnail. | 0.25–1 | 35–150 |
| S6 | Hard clay | Indented with difficulty by thumbnail. | >0.5 | >70 |
| S5 | Very stiff clay | Readily indented by thumbnail. | 0.25–0.5 | 35–70 |
| S4 | Stiff clay | Readily indented by thumb but penetrated only with great difficulty. | 0.1–0.25 | 15–35 |
| S3 | Firm clay | Can be penetrated several inches by thumb with moderate effort. | 0.05–0.1 | 7–15 |
| S2 | Soft clay | Easily penetrated several inches by thumb. | 0.025–0.05 | 4–7 |
| S1 | Very soft clay | Easily penetrated several inches by fist. | <0.025 | <4 |

*Table II.4* Weathering and alteration grades

| Grade | Term | Description |
|-------|------|-------------|
| I | Fresh | No visible sign of rock material weathering; perhaps slight discoloration on major discontinuity surfaces. |
| II | Slightly weathered | Discoloration indicates weathering of rock material and discontinuity surfaces. All the rock material may be discolored by weathering and may be somewhat weaker externally than in its fresh condition. |
| III | Moderately weathered | Less than half of the rock material is decomposed and/or disintegrated to a soil. Fresh or discolored rock is present either as a continuous framework or as corestones. |
| IV | Highly weathered | More than half of the rock material is decomposed and/or disintegrated to a soil. Fresh or discolored rock is present either as a discontinuous framework or as corestones. |
| V | Completely weathered | All rock material is decomposed and/or disintegrated to soil. The original mass structure is still largely intact. |
| VI | Residual soil | All rock material is converted to soil. The mass structure and material fabric are destroyed. There is a large change in volume, but the soil has not been significantly transported. |

usually do not exceed a few meters and they often contain no infilling. Section 3.3.3 describes the characteristics of the most common types of discontinuities, which include faults, bedding, foliation, joints, cleavage and schistosity.

### E   Discontinuity orientation

- The orientation of a discontinuity in space is described by the dip of the line of steepest declination measured from horizontal, and by the dip direction measured clockwise from true north. Example: dip ($\psi$)/dip direction ($\alpha$) (45°/025°).
- The orientation of discontinuities relative to an engineering structure largely controls the possibility of unstable conditions or excessive deformations developing. The importance of orientation increases when other conditions for deformation are present, such as low shear strength and a sufficient number of

discontinuities or joint sets for sliding to occur.
- The mutual orientation of discontinuities will determine the shape of the individual blocks comprising the rock mass.

### F   Roughness

- The roughness of a discontinuity surface is a potentially important component of its shear strength, especially in the case of undisplaced and interlocked features (e.g. unfilled joints). The importance of surface roughness declines as aperture, or infilling thickness, or the degree of previous displacement increases.
- The roughness can be characterized by waviness, and the unevenness or asperities. Waviness describes large-scale undulations, which, if interlocked and in contact, cause dilation during shear displacement since they are too large to be sheared off. Unevenness or asperities describe small-scale roughness.

Asperities will tend to be damaged during shear displacement if the ratio of the rock strength on the discontinuity surface to the normal stress level is low, in which case there will be little dilation on these small-scale features.

- In practice, both waviness and asperities can be measured in the field, while asperities can be measured as a component of a direct shear test.
- Roughness can be sampled by linear profiles taken parallel to the direction of sliding, that is, parallel to the dip (dip vector). In cases where sliding is controlled by two intersecting discontinuity planes, the direction of potential sliding is parallel to the line of intersection of the planes.
- The purpose of all roughness sampling is for estimating or calculating shear strength and dilation. Presently available methods of interpreting roughness profiles and estimating shear strength include measuring the $i$ value (or inclination) of the irregularities, or the Joint Roughness Coefficient (JRC) of the surface (Figure II.3). The contribution of the surface roughness to the total friction angle

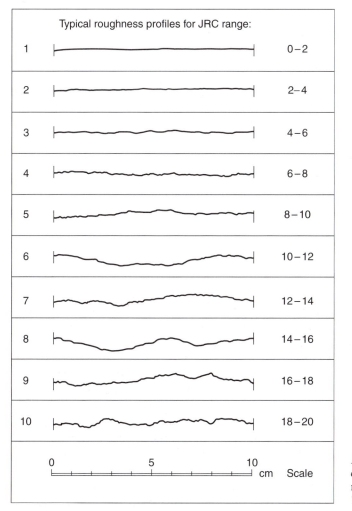

Typical roughness profiles for JRC range:

| 1 | 0–2 |
| 2 | 2–4 |
| 3 | 4–6 |
| 4 | 6–8 |
| 5 | 8–10 |
| 6 | 10–12 |
| 7 | 12–14 |
| 8 | 14–16 |
| 9 | 16–18 |
| 10 | 18–20 |

0        5        10
                          cm    Scale

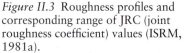

*Figure II.3* Roughness profiles and corresponding range of JRC (joint roughness coefficient) values (ISRM, 1981a).

of a surface is discussed in more detail in Section 3.4.3.

Descriptive terms that can be used to define roughness are a combination of small-scale features (several centimeters dimensions): *rough, smooth, slickensided,* and larger-scale features (several meters dimensions): *stepped, undulating, planar.* These terms can be combined to describe decreasing levels of roughness shown in Table II.5.

## G  Aperture

- Aperture is the perpendicular distance separating the adjacent rock surfaces of an open discontinuity, in which the intervening space is air or water filled. Aperture is thereby distinguished from the width of a filled discontinuity. Discontinuities that have been filled (e.g. with clay) also come under this category if the filling material has been washed out locally.

*Table II.5* Descriptive terms for roughness

| | |
|---|---|
| I | Rough, stepped |
| II | Smooth, stepped |
| III | Slickensided, stepped |
| IV | Rough, undulating |
| V | Smooth, undulating |
| VI | Slickensided, undulating |
| VII | Rough, planar |
| VIII | Smooth, planar |
| IX | Slickensided, planar |

- Large aperture can result from shear displacement of discontinuities having appreciable roughness and waviness, from tensile opening, from outwash of infillings, and from solution. Steeply dipping discontinuities that have opened in tension as a result of valley erosion or glacial retreat may have very large apertures.

- In most sub-surface rock masses, apertures will probably be less than half a millimeter, compared to the tens, hundreds or even thousands of millimeters width of some of the outwash or extension varieties. Unless discontinuities are exceptionally smooth and planar, it will not be of great significance to the shear strength that a "closed" feature is 0.1 mm wide or 1.0 mm wide. However, hydraulic conductivity is influenced by minor changes in aperture.

- Unfortunately, visual observation of small apertures is inherently unreliable since, with the possible exceptions of drilled holes and bored tunnels, visible apertures are bound to be disturbed by blasting or surface weathering effects. Aperture can be measured indirectly by hydraulic conductivity testing.

- Apertures are recorded from the point of view of both their loosening and conducting capacity. Joint water pressure, inflow of water and outflow of storage products (both liquid and gas) will all be affected by aperture.

Apertures can be described by the terms listed in Table II.6.

*Table II.6* Aperture dimensions

| Aperture | Description | |
|---|---|---|
| <0.1 mm | Very tight | |
| 0.1–0.25 mm | Tight | "Closed" features |
| 0.25–0.5 mm | Partly open | |
| 0.5–2.5 mm | Open | |
| 2.5–10 mm | Moderately wide | "Gapped" features |
| >10 mm | Wide | |
| 1–10 cm | Very wide | |
| 10–100 cm | Extremely wide | "Open" features |
| >1 m | Cavernous | |

## II.2.3  Infilling description

### H  Infilling type and width

- Infilling is the term for material separating the adjacent rock surfaces of discontinuities, e.g. calcite, chlorite, clay, silt, fault gouge, breccia, etc. The perpendicular distance between the adjacent rock surfaces is termed the *width* of the filled discontinuity, as opposed to the *aperture* of a gapped or open feature.
- Due to the variety of occurrences, filled discontinuities display a wide range of physical behavior, in particular as regards their shear strength deformability and conductivity. Short-term and long-term behavior may be quite different such that it is easy to be misled by favorable short-term conditions.
- The wide range of physical behavior depends on many factors of which the following are probably the most important:

  - Mineralogy of filling material (Table II.1);
  - Grading or particle size (Table II.2);
  - Over-consolidation ratio;
  - Water content and conductivity (Table II.11);
  - Previous shear displacement;
  - Surface roughness (Figure II.3 and Table II.5);
  - Width (Table II.6); and
  - Fracturing or crushing of surface rock.

- Every attempt should be made to record these factors, using quantitative descriptions where possible, together with sketches and/or color photographs of the most important occurrences. Certain index tests are suggested for a closer investigation of major discontinuities considered to be a threat to stability. In special cases, the results of these field descriptions may warrant the recommendation for large-scale *in situ* testing, possibly in the case of slopes containing a critical structural feature above an important facility.

## II.2.4  Rock mass description

### I  Spacing

- The spacing of adjacent discontinuities largely controls the size of individual blocks of intact rock. Several closely spaced sets tend to give conditions of low rock mass cohesion, whereas those that are widely spaced are much more likely to yield interlocking conditions. These effects depend upon the persistence of the individual discontinuities.
- In exceptional cases, a close spacing may change the mode of failure of a rock mass from plane or wedge to circular or even to flow (e.g. a "sugar cube" shear zone in quartzite). With exceptionally close spacing the orientation is of little consequence as failure may occur through rotation or rolling of the small rock pieces.
- As in the case of orientation, the importance of spacing increases when other conditions for deformation are present, that is, low shear strength and a sufficient number of discontinuities or joint sets for sliding to occur.
- The spacing of individual discontinuities and associated sets has a strong influence on the mass conductivity and seepage characteristics. In general, the hydraulic conductivity of any given set will be inversely proportional to the spacing, if individual joint apertures are comparable.

Spacing can be described by the terms listed in Table II.7.

*Table II.7* Spacing dimensions

| Description | Spacing (mm) |
| --- | --- |
| Extremely close spacing | <20 |
| Very close spacing | 20–60 |
| Close spacing | 60–200 |
| Moderate spacing | 200–600 |
| Wide spacing | 600–2000 |
| Very wide spacing | 2000–6000 |
| Extremely wide spacing | >6000 |

## J Persistence

- Persistence implies the areal extent or size of a discontinuity within a plane. It can be crudely quantified by observing the discontinuity trace lengths on the surface of exposures. It is one of the most important rock mass parameters, but one of the most difficult to quantify.
- The discontinuities of one particular set will often be more continuous than those of the other sets. The minor sets will therefore tend to terminate against the primary features, or they may terminate in solid rock.
- In the case of rock slopes, it is of the greatest importance to attempt to assess the degree of persistence of those discontinuities that are unfavorably orientated for stability. The degree to which discontinuities persist beneath adjacent rock blocks without terminating in solid rock or terminating against other discontinuities determines the degree to which failure of intact rock would be involved in eventual failure. Perhaps more likely, it determines the degree to which "down-stepping" would have to occur between adjacent discontinuities for a slip surface to develop. Persistence is also of the greatest importance to tension crack development behind the crest of a slope.
- Frequently, rock exposures are small compared to the area or length of persistent discontinuities, and the real persistence can only be guessed. Less frequently, it may be possible to record the dip length and the strike length of exposed discontinuities and thereby estimate their persistence along a given plane through the rock mass using probability theory. However, the difficulties and uncertainties involved in the field measurements will be considerable for most rock exposures.

Persistence can be described by the terms listed in Table II.8.

## K Number of sets

- The mechanical behavior of a rock mass and its appearance will be influenced by the number of sets of discontinuities that intersect one

Table II.8 Persistence dimensions

| Very low persistence | <1 m |
| Low persistence | 1–3 m |
| Medium persistence | 3–10 m |
| High persistence | 10–20 m |
| Very high persistence | >20 m |

another. The mechanical behavior is especially affected since the number of sets determines the extent to which the rock mass can deform without involving failure of the intact rock. The number of sets also affects the appearance of the rock mass due to the loosening and displacement of blocks in both natural and excavated faces (Figure II.4).

- The number of sets of discontinuities may be an important feature of rock slope stability, in addition to the orientation of discontinuities relative to the face. A rock mass containing a number of closely spaced joint sets may change the potential mode of slope failure from translational or toppling to rotational/circular.
- In the case of tunnel stability, three or more sets will generally constitute a three-dimensional block structure having a considerably more "degrees of freedom" for deformation than a rock mass with less than three sets. For example, a strongly foliated phyllite with just one closely spaced joint set may give equally good tunneling conditions as a massive granite with three widely spaced joint sets. The amount of overbreak in a tunnel will usually be strongly dependent on the number of sets.

The number of joint sets occurring locally (e.g. along the length of a tunnel) can be described according to the following scheme:

I    massive, occasional random joints;
II   one joint set;
III  one joint set plus random;
IV  two joint sets;
V   two joint sets plus random;
VI  three joint sets;

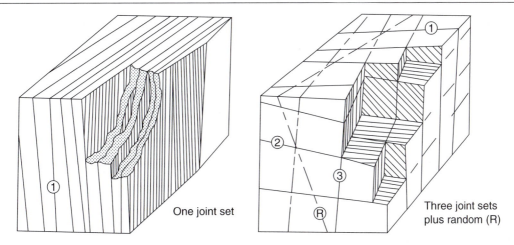

One joint set

Three joint sets
plus random (R)

*Figure II.4* Examples illustrating the effect of the number of joint sets on the mechanical behavior and appearance of rock masses (ISRM, 1981a).

VII    three joint sets plus random;
VIII   four or more joint sets; and
IX     crushed rock, earth-like.

Major individual discontinuities should be recorded on an individual basis.

*L   Block size and shape*

- Block size is an important indicator of rock mass behavior. Block dimensions are determined by discontinuity spacing, by the number of sets, and by the persistence of the discontinuities delineating potential blocks.
- The number of sets and the orientation determine the shape of the resulting blocks, which can take the approximate form of cubes, rhombohedra, tetrahedrons, sheets, etc. However, regular geometric shapes are the exception rather than the rule since the joints in any one set are seldom consistently parallel. Jointing in sedimentary rocks usually produces the most regular block shapes.
- The combined properties of block size and interblock shear strength determine the mechanical behavior of the rock mass under given stress conditions. Rock masses composed of large blocks tend to be less deformable, and in the case of underground construction,

develop favorable arching and interlocking. In the case of slopes, a small block size may cause the potential mode of failure to resemble that of soil, (i.e. circular/rotational) instead of the translational or toppling modes of failure usually associated with discontinuous rock masses. In exceptional cases, "block" size may be so small that flow occurs, as with a "sugar-cube" shear zones in quartzite.

- Rock quarrying and blasting efficiency are related to the *in situ* block size. It may be helpful to think in terms of a block size distribution for the rock mass, in much the same way that soils are categorized by a distribution of particle sizes.
- Block size can be described either by means of the average dimension of typical blocks (block size index $I_b$), or by the total number of joints intersecting a unit volume of the rock mass (volumetric joint count $J_v$).

Table II.9 lists descriptive terms give an impression of the corresponding block size.

Values of $J_v > 60$ would represent crushed rock, typical of a clay-free crushed zone.

*Rock masses.* Rock masses can be described by the following adjectives to give an impression of block size and shape (Figure II.5).

(i)   *massive*—few joints or very wide spacing
(ii)  *blocky*—approximately equidimensional
(iii) *tabular*—one dimension considerably smaller than the other two

(iv)  *columnar*—one dimension considerably larger than the other two
(v)   *irregular*—wide variations of block size and shape
(vi)  *crushed*—heavily jointed to "sugar cube"

*Table II.9* Block dimensions

| Description | $J_v$ (joints/m³) |
|---|---|
| Very large blocks | <1.0 |
| Large blocks | 1–3 |
| Medium-sized blocks | 3–10 |
| Small blocks | 10–30 |
| Very small blocks | >30 |

### II.2.5   Ground water

M   *Seepage*

- Water seepage through rock masses results mainly from flow through water conducting discontinuities ("secondary" hydraulic conductivity). In the case of certain sedimentary

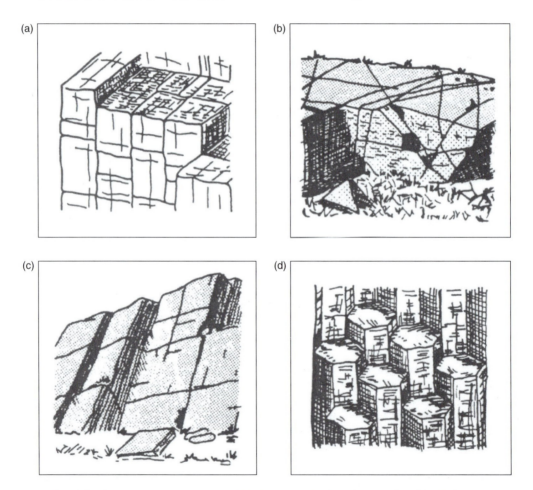

*Figure II.5* Sketches of rock masses illustrating block shape: (a) blocky; (b) irregular; (c) tabular; and (d) columnar (ISRM, 1981a).

rocks, such as poorly indurated sandstone, the "primary" hydraulic conductivity of the rock material may be significant such that a proportion of the total seepage occurs through the pores. The rate of seepage is proportional to the local hydraulic gradient and to the relevant directional conductivity, proportionality being dependent on laminar flow. High velocity flow through open discontinuities may result in increased head losses due to turbulence.

- The prediction of ground water levels, likely seepage paths, and approximate water pressures may often give advance warning of stability or construction difficulties. The field description of rock masses must inevitably precede any recommendation for field conductivity tests, so these factors should be carefully assessed at early stages of the investigation.

- Irregular ground water levels and perched water tables may be encountered in rock masses that are partitioned by persistent impermeable features such as dykes, clay-filled discontinuities or low conductivity beds. The prediction of these potential flow barriers and associated irregular water tables is of considerable importance, especially for projects where such barriers might be penetrated at depth by tunneling, resulting in high pressure inflows.

- Water seepage caused by drainage into an excavation may have far-reaching consequences in cases where a sinking ground water level would cause settlement of nearby structures founded on overlying clay deposits.

- The approximate description of the local hydrogeology should be supplemented with detailed observations of seepage from individual discontinuities or particular sets, according to their relative importance to stability. A short comment concerning recent precipitation in the area, if known, will be helpful in the interpretation of these observations. Additional data concerning ground water trends, and rainfall and temperature records will be useful supplementary information.

- In the case of rock slopes, the preliminary design estimates will be based on assumed values of effective normal stress. If, as a result of field observations, one has to conclude that pessimistic assumptions of water pressure are justified, such as a tension crack full of water and a rock mass that does not drain readily, then this will clearly influence the slope design. So also will the field observation of rock slopes where high water pressures can develop due to seasonal freezing of the face that blocks drainage paths.

Seepage from individual unfilled and filled discontinuities or from specific sets exposed in a tunnel or in a surface exposure, can be assessed according to the descriptive terms in Tables II.10 and II.11.

In the case of an excavation that acts as a drain for the rock mass, such as a tunnel, it is helpful if the flow into individual sections of the structure are described. This should ideally be performed immediately after excavation since ground water levels, or the rock mass storage, may be depleted

*Table II.10* Seepage quantities in unfilled discontinuities

| Seepage rating | Description |
| --- | --- |
| I | The discontinuity is very tight and dry, water flow along it does not appear possible. |
| II | The discontinuity is dry with no evidence of water flow. |
| III | The discontinuity flow is dry but shows evidence of water flow, that is, rust staining. |
| IV | The discontinuity is damp but no free water is present. |
| V | The discontinuity shows seepage, occasional drops of water, but no continuous flow. |
| VI | The discontinuity shows a continuous flow of water—estimate l/min and describe pressure, that is, low, medium, high. |

*Table II.11*  Seepage quantities in filled discontinuities

| Seepage rating | Description |
|---|---|
| I | The filling materials are heavily consolidated and dry, significant flow appears unlikely due to very low permeability. |
| II | The filling materials are damp, but no free water is present. |
| III | The filling materials are wet, occasional drops of water. |
| IV | The filling materials show signs of outwash, continuous flow of water—estimate l/min. |
| V | The filling materials are washed out locally, considerable water flow along out-wash channels—estimate l/min and describe pressure that is low, medium, high. |
| VI | The filling materials are washed out completely, very high water pressures experienced, especially on first exposure—estimate l/min and describe pressure. |

*Table II.12*  Seepage quantities in tunnels

*Rock mass (e.g. tunnel wall)*

| Seepage rating | Description |
|---|---|
| I | Dry walls and roof, no detectable seepage. |
| II | Minor seepage, specify dripping discontinuities. |
| III | Medium inflow, specify discontinuities with continuous flow (estimate l/min /10 m length of excavation). |
| IV | Major inflow, specify discontinuities with strong flows (estimate l/min /10 m length of excavation). |
| V | Exceptionally high inflow, specify source of exceptional flows (estimate l/min /10 m length of excavation). |

rapidly. Descriptions of seepage quantities are given in Table II.12.

- A field assessment of the likely effectiveness of surface drains, inclined drill holes, or drainage galleries should be made in the case of major rock slopes. This assessment will depend on the orientation, spacing and apertures of the relevant discontinuities.
- The potential influence of frost and ice on the seepage paths through the rock mass should be assessed. Observations of seepage from the surface trace of discontinuities may be misleading in freezing temperatures. The possibility of ice-blocked drainage paths should

be assessed from the points of view of surface deterioration of a rock excavation, and of overall stability.

## II.3   Field mapping sheets

The two mapping sheets included with this appendix provide a means of recording the qualitative geological data described in this appendix.

*Sheet 1—Rock mass description sheet* describes the rock material in terms of its color, grain size and strength, the rock mass in terms of the block shape, size, weathering and the number of discontinuity sets and their spacing.

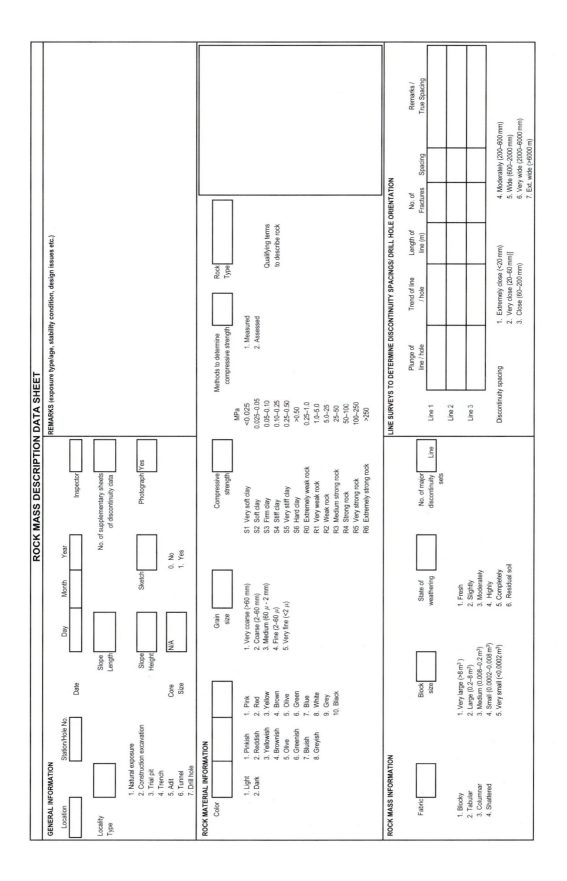

# ROCK MASS DESCRIPTION DATA SHEET

**GENERAL INFORMATION**

Location 

Station/Hole No. 

Date 

Day Month Year 

Inspector 

Locality 

Type
1. Natural exposure
2. Construction excavation
3. Trial pit
4. Trench
5. Adit
6. Tunnel
7. Drill hole

Slope Length 

Slope Height 

Core Size 

N/A 

No. of supplementary sheets of discontinuity data 

Sketch 

Photograph Yes 
0. No
1. Yes

**REMARKS** (exposure type/age, stability condition, design issues etc.)

Rock Type 

Methods to determine compressive strength 
1. Measured
2. Assessed

Qualifying terms to describe rock

**ROCK MATERIAL INFORMATION**

Color 

1. Light
2. Dark

1. Pinkish
2. Reddish
3. Yellowish
4. Brownish
5. Olive
6. Greenish
7. Bluish
8. Greyish

1. Pink
2. Red
3. Yellow
4. Brown
5. Olive
6. Green
7. Blue
8. White
9. Grey
10. Black

Grain size 
1. Very coarse (>60 mm)
2. Coarse (2–60 mm)
3. Medium (60 $\mu$ – 2 mm)
4. Fine (2–60 $\mu$)
5. Very fine (<2 $\mu$)

Compressive strength 

MPa
S1 Very soft clay — <0.025
S2 Soft clay — 0.025–0.05
S3 Firm clay — 0.05–0.10
S4 Stiff clay — 0.10–0.25
S5 Very stiff clay — 0.25–0.50
S6 Hard clay — >0.50
R0 Extremely weak rock — 0.25–1.0
R1 Very weak rock — 1.0–5.0
R2 Weak rock — 5.0–25
R3 Medium strong rock — 25–50
R4 Strong rock — 50–100
R5 Very strong rock — 100–250
R6 Extremely strong rock — >250

**ROCK MASS INFORMATION**

Fabric 
1. Blocky
2. Tabular
3. Columnar
4. Shattered

Block size 
1. Very large (>8 m³)
2. Large (0.2–8 m³)
3. Medium (0.008–0.2 m³)
4. Small (0.0002–0.008 m³)
5. Very small (<0.0002 m³)

State of weathering 
1. Fresh
2. Slightly
3. Moderately
4. Highly
5. Completely
6. Residual soil

No. of major discontinuity sets 

Line 

**LINE SURVEYS TO DETERMINE DISCONTINUITY SPACINGS/ DRILL HOLE ORIENTATION**

| | Plunge of line / hole | Trend of line / hole | Length of line (m) | No. of Fractures | Spacing | Remarks / True Spacing |
|---|---|---|---|---|---|---|
| Line 1 | | | | | | |
| Line 2 | | | | | | |
| Line 3 | | | | | | |

Discontinuity spacing
1. Extremely close (<20 mm)
2. Very close (20–60 mm)]
3. Close (60–200 mm)
4. Moderately (200–600 mm)
5. Wide (600–2000 mm)
6. Very wide (2000–6000 mm)
7. Ext. wide (>6000 m)

# DISCONTINUITY SURVEY DATA SHEET

## GENERAL INFORMATION

Location ☐   Station / Hole No. ☐

Date   Day ☐   Month ☐   Year ☐

Inspector ☐

Discontinuity data sheet no. ☐   of ☐

## NATURE AND ORIENTATION OF DISCONTINUITY

| Chainage or Depth | Type | Dip | Dip Direction | Persistence | Termination | Aperture/ Width | Nature of Filling | Strength of Filling | Surface Roughness | Surface Shape | Waviness Wavelength | Waviness Amplitude | JRC | Water Flow | Spacing | Remarks |
|---|---|---|---|---|---|---|---|---|---|---|---|---|---|---|---|---|
| | | | | | | | | | | | | | | | | |
| | | | | | | | | | | | | | | | | |
| | | | | | | | | | | | | | | | | |
| | | | | | | | | | | | | | | | | |
| | | | | | | | | | | | | | | | | |
| | | | | | | | | | | | | | | | | |
| | | | | | | | | | | | | | | | | |
| | | | | | | | | | | | | | | | | |
| | | | | | | | | | | | | | | | | |

**Type**
0. Fault zone
1. Fault
2. Joint
3. Cleavage
4. Schistosity
5. Shear
6. Fissure
7. Tension Crack
8. Foliation
9. Bedding

**Persistence**
1. Very low persistence   <1 m
2. Low persistence   1–3 m
3. Medium persistence   3–10 m
4. High persistence   10–20 m
5. Very high persistence   >20 m

**Aperture/width**
1. Very tight (<0.1 mm)
2. Tight (0.1–0.25 mm)
3. Partly open (0.25–0.5 mm)
4. Open (0.5–2.5 mm)
5. Moderately wide (2.5–10 mm)
6. Wide (>10 mm)
7. Very wide (1–10 mm)
8. Extremely wide (10–100 cm)
9. Cavernous (>1 m)

**Termination**
0. Neither end visible
1. One end visible
2. Both ends visible

**Surface shape**
1. Stepped
2. Undulating
3. Planar

**Nature of filling**
1. Clean
2. Surface staining
3. Non-cohesive
4. Inactive clay or clay matrix
5. Swelling clay or clay matrix
6. Cemented
7. Chlorite, talc or gypsum
8. Other — specify

**Surface roughness**
1. Rough
2. Smooth
3. Polished
4. Slickensided

**Compressive strength of infilling**

| | | MPa |
|---|---|---|
| S1 | Very soft clay | <0.025 |
| S2 | Soft clay | 0.025–0.05 |
| S3 | Firm clay | 0.05–0.10 |
| S4 | Stiff clay | 0.10–0.25 |
| S5 | Very stiff clay | 0.25–0.50 |
| S6 | Hard clay | >0.50 |
| R0 | Extremely weak rock | 0.25–1.0 |
| R1 | Very weak rock | 1.0–5.0 |
| R2 | Weak rock | 5.0–25 |
| R3 | Medium strong rock | 25–50 |
| R4 | Strong rock | 50–100 |
| R5 | Very strong rock | 100–250 |
| R6 | Extremely strong rock | >250 |

**Spacing**
1. Extremely close spacing   <20 mm
2. Very close spacing   20–60 mm
3. Close spacing   60–200 mm
4. Moderate spacing   200–600 mm
5. Wide spacing   600–2000 mm
6. Very wide spacing   2000–6000 mm
7. Extremely wide spacing

**Water flow (open)**
0. Discontinuity is very light and dry, water flow along it does not appear possible.
1. The discontinuity is dry with no evidence of water flow.
2. The discontinuity is dry but shows evidence of water flow. i.e. rust staining, etc.
3. The discontinuity is damp but no free water is present.
4. The discontinuity shows seepage, occasional drops of water, but no continuous flow.
5. The discontinuity shows a continuous flow of water (Estimate l/min and describe pressure, i.e. low medium, high).

**Water flow (filled)**
6. The filling materials are heavily consolidated and dry; significant flow appears unlikely due to very low permeability.
7. The filling materials are damp, but no free water is present.
8. The filling materials are wet; occasional drops of water.
9. The filling materials show signs of outwash, continuous flow of water (estimate litres/minute).
10. The filling materials are washed out locally; considerable water flow along out-wash channels (estimate litres/minute and describe pressure, i.e. low, medium, high).

# Appendix III

# Comprehensive solution wedge stability

## III.1  Introduction

This appendix presents the equations and procedure to calculate the factor of safety for a wedge failure as discussed in Chapter 7. This comprehensive solution includes the wedge geometry defined by five surfaces, including a sloped upper surface and a tension crack, water pressures, different shear strengths on each slide plane, and up to two external forces (Figure III.1). External forces that may act on a wedge include tensioned anchor support, foundation loads and earthquake motion. The forces are vectors defined by their magnitude, and their plunge and trend. If necessary, several force vectors can be combined to meet the two force limit. It is assumed that all forces act through the center of gravity of the wedge so no moments are generated, and there is no rotational slip or toppling.

## III.2  Analysis methods

The equations presented in this appendix are identical to those in appendix 2 of *Rock Slope Engineering*, third edition (Hoek and Bray, 1981). These equations have been found to be versatile and capable of calculating the stability of a wide range of geometric and geotechnical conditions. The equations form the basis of the wedge stability analysis programs SWEDGE (Rocscience, 2001) and ROCKPACK III (Watts, 2001). However, two limitations to the analysis are discussed in Section III.3.

As an alternative to the comprehensive analysis presented in this appendix, there are two

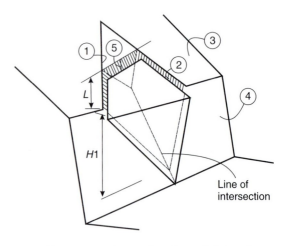

*Figure III.1* Dimensions and surfaces defining size and shape of wedge.

shorter analyses that can be used for a more limited set of input parameters. In Section 7.3, a calculation procedure is presented for a wedge formed by planes 1, 2, 3 and 4 shown in Figure III.1, but with no tension crack. The shear strength is defined by different cohesions and friction angles on planes 1 and 2, and the water pressure condition assumed is that the slope is saturated. However, no external forces can be incorporated in the analysis.

A second rapid calculation method is presented in the first part of appendix 2 in *Rock Slope Engineering*, third edition. This analysis also does not incorporate a tension crack or external forces, but does include two sets of shear strength parameters and water pressure.

## III.3  Analysis limitations

For the comprehensive stability analysis presented in this appendix there is one geometric limitation related to the relative inclinations of plane 3 and the line of intersection, and a specific procedure for modifying water pressures. The following is a discussion of these two limitations.

*Wedge geometry.* For wedges with steep upper slopes (plane 3), and a line of intersection that has a shallower dip than the upper slope (i.e. $\psi_3 > \psi_i$), there is no intersection between the plane and the line; the program will terminate with the error message "Tension crack invalid" (see equations (III.50) to (III.53)). The reason for this error message is that the calculation procedure is to first calculate the dimensions of the overall wedge from the slope face to the apex (intersection of the line of intersection with plane 3). Then the dimensions of a wedge between the tension crack and the apex are calculated. Finally, the dimensions of the wedge between the face and the tension crack are found by subtracting the overall wedge from the upper wedge (see equations (III.54) to (III.57)).

However, for the wedge geometry where ($\psi_3 > \psi_i$), a wedge can still be formed if a tension crack (plane 5) is present, and it is possible to calculate a factor of safety using a different set of equations. Programs that can investigate the stability wedges with this geometry include YAWC (Kielhorn, 1998) and (PanTechnica, 2002).

*Water pressure.* The analysis incorporates the average values of the water pressure on the sliding planes ($u_1$ and $u_2$), and on the tension crack ($u_5$). These values are calculated assuming that the wedge is fully saturated. That is, the water table is coincident with the upper surface of the slope (plane 3), and that the pressure drops to zero where planes 1 and 2 intersect the slope face (plane 4). These pressure distributions are simulated as follows. Where no tension crack exists, the water pressures on planes 1 and 2 are given by $u_1 = u_2 = \gamma_w H_w/6$, where $H_w$ is the vertical height of the wedge defined by the two ends of the line of intersection. The second method

allows for the presence of a tension crack and gives $u_1 = u_2 = u_5 = \gamma_w H_{5w}/3$, where $H_{5w}$ is the depth of the bottom vertex of the tension crack below the upper ground surface. The water forces are then calculated as the product of these pressures and the areas of the respective planes.

To calculate stability of a partially saturated wedge, the reduced pressures are simulated by reducing the unit weight of the water, $\gamma_w$. That is, if it is estimated that the tension crack is one-third filled with water, then a unit weight of $\gamma_w/3$ is used as the input parameter. It is considered that this approach is adequate for most purposes because water levels in slopes are variable and difficult to determine precisely.

## III.4  Scope of solution

This solution is for computation of the factor of safety for translational slip of a tetrahedral wedge formed in a rock slope by two intersecting discontinuities (planes 1 and 2), the upper ground surface (plane 3), the slope face (plane 4), and a tension crack (plane 5 (Figure III.1)). The solution allows for water pressures on the two slide planes and in the tension crack, and for different strength parameters on the two slide planes. Plane 3 may have a different dip direction to that of plane 4. The influence of an external load $E$ and a cable tension $T$ are included in the analysis, and supplementary sections are provided for the examination of the minimum factor of safety for a given external load, and for minimizing the anchoring force required for a given factor of safety.

The solution allows for the following conditions:

(a) interchange of planes 1 and 2;
(b) the possibility of one of the planes overlying the other;
(c) the situation where the crest overhangs the toe of the slope (in which case $\eta = -1$); and
(d) the possibility of contact being lost on either plane.

## III.5 Notation

The wedge geometry is illustrated in Figure III.1; the following input data are required:

$\psi, \alpha$ = dip and dip direction of plane, or plunge and trend of force

$H1$ = slope height referred to plane 1

$L$ = distance of tension crack from crest, measured along the trace of plane 1

$u$ = average water pressure on planes 1 and 2

$c$ = cohesion of each slide plane

$\phi$ = angle of friction of each slide plane

$\gamma$ = unit weight of rock

$\gamma_w$ = unit weight of water

$T$ = anchor tension

$E$ = external load

$\eta$ = $-1$ if face is overhanging, and $+1$ if face does not overhang

Other terms used in the solution are as follows:

$FS$ = factor of safety against sliding along the line of intersection, or on plane 1 or plane 2

$A$ = area of sliding plane or tension crack

$W$ = weight of wedge

$V$ = water thrust on tension crack (plane 5)

$\left.\begin{array}{l} N_a = \text{total normal force of plane 1} \\ S_a = \text{shear force on plane 1} \\ Q_a = \text{shear resistance on plane 1} \\ FS_1 = \text{factor of safety} \end{array}\right\}$ when contact is maintained on plane 1 only

$\left.\begin{array}{l} N_b = \text{total normal force on plane 2} \\ S_b = \text{shear force on plane 2} \\ Q_b = \text{shear resistance on plane 2} \\ FS_2 = \text{factor of safety} \end{array}\right\}$ when contact is maintained on plane 2 only

$\left.\begin{array}{l} N_1, N_2 = \text{effective normal reactions} \\ S = \text{total shear force on planes 1 and 2} \\ Q = \text{total shear resistance on planes 1 and 2} \\ FS_3 = \text{factor of safety} \end{array}\right\}$ when contact is maintained on both planes 1 and 2

$N_1', N_2', S'$, etc. = values of $N_1, N_2, S$ etc. when $T = 0$

$N_1'', N_2'' S''$, etc. = values of $N_1, N_2, S$ etc. when $E = 0$

$\vec{a}$ = unit normal vector for plane 1

$\vec{b}$ = unit normal vector for plane 2

$\vec{d}$ = unit normal vector for plane 3

$\vec{f}$ = unit normal vector for plane 4

$\vec{f_5}$ = unit normal vector for plane 5

$\vec{g}$ = vector in the direction of intersection line of 1, 4

$\vec{g_5}$ = vector in the direction of intersection line of 1, 5

$\vec{i}$ = vector in the direction of intersection line of 1, 2

$\vec{j}$ = vector in the direction of intersection line of 3, 4

$\vec{j_5}$ = vector in the direction of intersection line of 3, 5

$\vec{k}$ = vector in plane 2 normal to $\vec{i}$

$\vec{l}$ = vector in plane 1 normal to $\vec{i}$

$R$ = magnitude of vector $\vec{i}$

$G$ = square of magnitude of vector $\vec{g}$

$G_5$ = square of magnitude of vector $\vec{g_5}$

*Note*: The computed value of $V$ is negative when the tension crack dips away from the toe of the slope, but this does not indicate a tensile force.

## III.6 Sequence of calculations

1 *Calculation of factor of safety when the forces T and E are either zero or completely specified in magnitude and direction.*

(a) Components of unit vectors in directions of normals to planes 1–5, and of forces $T$ and $E$.

$(a_x, a_y, a_z)$

$$= (\sin \psi_1 \sin \alpha_1, \sin \psi_1 \cos \alpha_1, \cos \psi_1) \tag{III.1}$$

$(b_x, b_y, b_z)$

$$= (\sin \psi_2 \sin \alpha_2, \sin \psi_2 \cos \alpha_2, \cos \psi_2) \tag{III.2}$$

$(d_x, d_y, d_z)$

$$= (\sin \psi_3 \sin \alpha_3, \sin \psi_3 \cos \alpha_3, \cos \psi_3) \tag{III.3}$$

$(f_x, f_y, f_z)$

$$= (\sin \psi_4 \sin \alpha_4, \sin \psi_4 \cos \alpha_4, \cos \psi_4) \tag{III.4}$$

$(f_{5x}, f_{5y}, f_{5z})$

$$= (\sin \psi_5 \sin \alpha_5, \sin \psi_5 \cos \alpha_5, \cos \psi_5) \tag{III.5}$$

$(t_x, t_y, t_z)$

$$= (\cos \psi_t \sin \alpha_t, \cos \psi_t \cos \alpha_t, - \sin \psi_t) \tag{III.6}$$

$(e_x, e_y, e_z)$

$$= (\cos \psi_e \sin \alpha_e, \cos \psi_e \cos \alpha_e, - \sin \psi_e) \tag{III.7}$$

(b)  Components of vectors in the direction of the lines of intersection of various planes.

$(g_x, g_y, g_z)$

$$= (f_y a_z - f_z a_y), (f_z a_x - f_x a_z),$$
$$(f_x a_y - f_y a_x) \tag{III.8}$$

$(g_{5x}, g_{5y}, g_{5z})$

$$= (f_{5y} a_z - f_{5z} a_y), (f_{5z} a_x - f_{5x} a_z),$$
$$(f_{5x} a_y - f_{5y} a_x) \tag{III.9}$$

$(i_x, i_y, i_z)$

$$= (b_y a_z - b_z a_y), (b_z a_x - b_x a_z),$$
$$(b_x a_y - b_y a_x) \tag{III.10}$$

$(j_x, j_y, j_z)$

$$= (f_y d_z - f_z d_y), (f_z d_x - f_x d_z),$$
$$(f_x d_y - f_y d_x) \tag{III.11}$$

$(j_{5x}, j_{5y}, j_{5z})$

$$= (f_{5y} d_z - f_{5z} d_y), (f_{5z} d_x - f_{5x} d_z),$$
$$(f_{5x} d_y - f_{5y} d_x) \tag{III.12}$$

$(k_x, k_y, k_z)$

$$= (i_y b_z - i_z b_y), (i_z b_x - i_x b_z),$$
$$(i_x b_y - i_y b_x) \tag{III.13}$$

$(l_x, l_y, l_z)$

$$= (a_y i_z - a_z i_y), (a_z i_x - a_x i_z),$$
$$(a_x i_y - a_y i_x) \tag{III.14}$$

(c)  Numbers proportional to cosines of various angles.

$$m = g_x d_x + g_y d_y + g_z d_z \tag{III.15}$$
$$m_5 = g_{5x} d_x + g_{5y} d_y + g_{5z} d_z \tag{III.16}$$
$$n = b_x j_x + b_y j_y + b_z j_z \tag{III.17}$$
$$n_5 = b_x j_{5x} + b_y j_{5y} + b_z j_{5z} \tag{III.18}$$
$$p = i_x d_x + i_y d_y + i_z d_z \tag{III.19}$$
$$q = b_x g_x + b_y g_y + b_z g_z \tag{III.20}$$
$$g_5 = b_x g_{5x} + b_y g_{5y} + b_z g_{5z} \tag{III.21}$$
$$r = a_x b_x + a_y b_y + a_z b_z \tag{III.22}$$
$$s = a_x t_x + a_y t_y + a_z t_z \tag{III.23}$$
$$v = b_x t_x + b_y t_y + b_z t_z \tag{III.24}$$
$$w = i_x t_x + i_y t_y + i_z t_z \tag{III.25}$$
$$s_e = a_x e_x + a_y e_y + a_z e_z \tag{III.26}$$
$$v_e = b_x e_x + b_y e_y + b_z e_z \tag{III.27}$$
$$w_e = i_x e_x + i_y e_y + i_z e_z \tag{III.28}$$
$$s_5 = a_x f_{5x} + a_y f_{5y} + a_z f_{5z} \tag{III.29}$$
$$v_5 = b_x f_{5x} + b_y f_{5y} + b_z f_{5z} \tag{III.30}$$
$$w_5 = i_x f_{5x} + i_y f_{5y} + i_z f_{5z} \tag{III.31}$$
$$\lambda = i_x g_x + i_y g_y + i_z g_z \tag{III.32}$$
$$\lambda_5 = i_x g_{5x} + i_y g_{5y} + i_z g_{5z} \tag{III.33}$$
$$\varepsilon = f_x f_{5x} + f_y f_{5y} + f_z f_{5z} \tag{III.34}$$

(d)   Miscellaneous factors.

$$R = \sqrt{1 - r^2} \tag{III.35}$$

$$= \frac{1}{R^2} \cdot \frac{nq}{|nq|} \tag{III.36}$$

$$\mu = \frac{1}{R^2} \cdot \frac{mq}{|mq|} \tag{III.37}$$

$$\upsilon = \frac{1}{R} \cdot \frac{p}{|p|} \tag{III.38}$$

$$G = g_x^2 + g_y^2 + g_z^2 \tag{III.39}$$

$$G_5 = g_{5x}^2 + g_{5y}^2 + g_{5z}^2 \tag{III.40}$$

$$M = (Gp^2 - 2mp\lambda + m^2 R^2)^{1/2} \tag{III.41}$$

$$M_5 = (G_5 p^2 - 2m_5 p\lambda_5 + m_5^2 R^2)^{1/2} \tag{III.42}$$

$$h = \frac{H1}{|g_z|} \tag{III.43}$$

$$h_5 = \frac{Mh - |p|L}{M_5} \tag{III.44}$$

$$B = [\tan^2 \phi_1 + \tan^2 \phi_2 - 2(\mu r / \rho)$$
$$\times \tan \phi_1 \tan \phi_2] / R^2 \tag{III.45}$$

(e)   Plunge and trend of line respectively of line of intersection of planes 1 and 2:

$$\psi_i = \arcsin(\upsilon i_z) \tag{III.46}$$

$$\alpha_i = \arctan\left(\frac{-\upsilon i_x}{-\upsilon i_y}\right) \tag{III.47}$$

The term $-\upsilon$ should not be cancelled out in equation (III.47) since this is required to determine the correct quadrant when calculating values for dip direction, $\alpha_i$.

(f)   Check on wedge geometry.

No wedge is formed, terminate computation
$$\begin{cases} \text{if } p\,i_z < 0, \text{ or} & \text{(III.48)} \\ \text{if } n\,q\,i_z < 0 & \text{(III.49)} \end{cases}$$

Tension crack invalid, terminate computation
$$\begin{cases} \text{if } \epsilon\,\eta\,q_5 i_z < 0, \text{ or} & \text{(III.50)} \\ \text{if } h_5 < 0, \text{ or} & \text{(III.51)} \\ \text{if } \left[|\frac{m_5\,h_5}{m\,h}|\right] > 1, \text{ or} & \text{(III.52)} \\ \text{if } \left[|\frac{n\,q_5\,m_5\,h_5}{n_5\,q\,m\,h}|\right] > 1 & \text{(III.53)} \end{cases}$$

(g)   Areas of faces and weight of wedge.

$$A_1 = \frac{|mq|h^2| - |m_5 q_5|h_5^2}{2|p|} \tag{III.54}$$

$$A_2 = \frac{(|q|m^2 h^2 / |n| - |q_5|m_5^2 h_5^2 / |n_5|)}{|2p|} \tag{III.55}$$

$$A_5 = \frac{|m_5 q_5|h_5^2}{2|n_5|} \tag{III.56}$$

$$W = \frac{\gamma \left(q^2 m^2 h^3 / |n| - q_5^2 m_5^2 h_5^3 / |n_5|\right)}{6|p|} \tag{III.57}$$

(h)   Water pressure.

(i)   With no tension crack

$$u_1 = u_2 = \frac{\gamma_w h |m_5|}{6|p|} \tag{III.58}$$

(ii)   With tension crack

$$u_1 = u_2 = u_5 = \frac{\gamma_w h_5 |m_5|}{3d_z} \tag{III.59}$$

$$V = u_5 A_5 \eta \left(\frac{\varepsilon}{|\varepsilon|}\right) \tag{III.60}$$

(i)  Effective normal reactions on planes 1 and 2 assuming contact on both planes.

$$N_1 = \rho\{W\,k_z + T(r\,v - s)$$
$$+ E(r\,v_e - s_e) + V(r\,v_5 - s_5)\}$$
$$- u_1\,A_1 \qquad (\text{III}.61)$$

$$N_2 = \mu\{W\,l_z + T(r\,s - v)$$
$$+ E(r\,s_e - v_e) + V(r\,s_5 - v_5)\}$$
$$- u_2\,A_2 \qquad (\text{III}.62)$$

(j)  Factor of safety when $N_1 < 0$ and $N_2 < 0$ (contact is lost on both planes).

$$FS = 0 \qquad (\text{III}.63)$$

(k)  If $N_1 > 0$ and $N_2 < 0$, contact is maintained on plane 1 only and the factor of safety is calculated as follows:

$$N_a = Wa_z - Ts - Es_e - Vs_5 - u_1A_1r$$
$$(\text{III}.64)$$

$$S_x = (Tt_x + Ee_x + N_a a_x + Vf_{5x} + u_1A_1b_x)$$
$$(\text{III}.65)$$

$$S_y = (Tt_y + Ee_y + N_a a_y + Vf_{5y} + u_1A_1b_y)$$
$$(\text{III}.66)$$

$$S_z = (Tt_z + Ee_z + N_a a_z$$
$$+ Vf_{5z} + u_1A_1b_z) + W \qquad (\text{III}.67)$$

$$S_a = (S_x^2 + S_y^2 + S_z^2)^{1/2} \qquad (\text{III}.68)$$

$$Q_a = (N_a - u_1A_1)\tan\phi_1 + c_1A_1 \qquad (\text{III}.69)$$

$$FS_1 = \left(\frac{Q_a}{S_a}\right) \qquad (\text{III}.70)$$

(l)  If $N_1 < 0$ and $N_2 > 0$, contact is maintained on plane 2 only and the factor of safety is calculated as follows:

$$N_b = (Wb_z - Tv - Ev_e - Vv_5 - u_2A_2r)$$
$$(\text{III}.71)$$

$$S_x = (Tt_x + Ee_x + N_b b_x + Vf_{5x} + u_2A_2a_x)$$
$$(\text{III}.72)$$

$$S_y = (Tt_y + Ee_y + N_b b_y + Vf_{5y} + u_2A_2a_y)$$
$$(\text{III}.73)$$

$$S_z = (Tt_z + Ee_z + N_b b_z + Vf_{5z}$$
$$+ u_2A_2a_z) + W \qquad (\text{III}.74)$$

$$S_b = (S_x^2 + S_y^2 + S_z^2)^{1/2} \qquad (\text{III}.75)$$

$$Q_b = (N_b - u_2A_2)\tan\phi_2 + c_2A_2 \qquad (\text{III}.76)$$

$$FS_2 = \left(\frac{Q_b}{S_b}\right) \qquad (\text{III}.77)$$

(m)  If $N_1 > 0$ and $N_2 > 0$, contact is maintained on both planes and the factor of safety is calculated as follows:

$$S = v(Wi_z - Tw - Ew_e - Vw_5)$$
$$(\text{III}.78)$$

$$Q = N_1\tan\phi_1 + N_2\tan\phi_2$$
$$+ c_1A_1 + c_2A_2 \qquad (\text{III}.79)$$

$$FS_3 = \left(\frac{Q}{S}\right) \qquad (\text{III}.80)$$

2  *Minimum factor of safety produced when load E of given magnitude is applied in the worst direction.*

(a)  Evaluate $N_1'', N_2'', S'', Q'', FS_3''$ by use of equations (III.61), (III.62), (III.78), (III.79) and (III.80) with $E = 0$.

(b)  If $N_1'' < 0$ and $N_2'' < 0$, even before $E$ is applied. Then $FS = 0$, terminate computation.

(c)  $$D = \{(N_1'')^2 + (N_2'')^2 + 2\left(\frac{mn}{|mn|}\right)N_1''N_2''r\}^{1/2}$$
$$(\text{III}.81)$$

$$\psi_e = \arcsin\left\{\left(-\frac{1}{G}\left(\frac{m}{|m|}\right)\cdot N_1''a_z\right.\right.$$
$$\left.\left. + \frac{n}{|n|}\cdot N_2''b_z\right)\right\} \qquad (\text{III}.82)$$

$$\alpha_e = \arctan\left\{\frac{\frac{m}{|m|}.N_1''a_x + \frac{n}{|n|}.N_2''b_x}{\frac{m}{|m|}.N_1''a_y + \frac{n}{|n|}.N_2''b_y}\right\} \qquad (\text{III}.83)$$

If $E > D$, and $E$ is applied in the direction $\psi_e, \alpha_e$, or within a certain range encompassing this direction, then contact is lost on both planes and FS = 0. Terminate calculation.

(d) If $N_1'' > 0$ and $N_2'' < 0$, assume contact on plane 1 only after application of $E$. Determine $S_x'', S_y'', S_z'', S_a'', Q_a'', FS_1''$ from equations (III.65) to (III.70) with $E = 0$. If $FS_1'' < 1$, terminate computation. If $FS_1'' > 1$:

$$FS_1 = \frac{S_a'' Q_a'' - E\{(Q_a'')^2 + ((S_a'')^2 - E^2)\tan^2\phi_1\}^{1/2}}{(S_a'')^2 - E^2}$$

(III.84)

$$\psi_{e1} = \arcsin\left(\frac{S_z''}{S_a''}\right) - \arctan\left(\frac{\tan\phi_1}{(FS_1)}\right)$$

(III.85)

$$\alpha_{e1} = \arctan\left(\frac{S_x''}{S_a''}\right) + 180°$$

(III.86)

(e) If $N_1'' < 0$ and $N_2'' > 0$, assume contact on plane 2 only after application of $E$. Determine $S_x'', S_y'', S_z'', S_b'', Q_b'', FS_2''$ from equations (III.72) to (III.77) with $E = 0$. If $FS_2'' < 1$, terminate computation. If $FS_2'' > 1$:

$$FS_2 = \frac{S_b'' Q_b'' - E\{(Q_b'')^2 + ((S_b'')^2 - E^2)\tan^2\phi_2\}^{1/2}}{(S_b'')^2 - E^2}$$

(III.87)

$$\psi_{e2} = \arcsin\left(\frac{S_z''}{S_b''}\right) - \arctan\left(\frac{\tan\phi_2}{(FS_2)}\right)$$

(III.88)

$$\alpha_{e2} = \arctan\left(\frac{S_x''}{S_y''}\right) + 180°$$

(III.89)

(f) If $N_1'' > 0$ and $N_2'' > 0$, assume contact on both planes after application of E. If $FS_3'' < 1$, terminate computation.

If $FS_3'' > 1$:

$$FS_3 = \frac{S'' Q'' - E\{(Q'')^2 + B((S'')^2 - E^2)\}^{1/2}}{(S'')^2 - E^2}$$

(III.90)

$$\chi = \sqrt{B + (FS_3)^2}$$

(III.91)

$$e_x = -\frac{((FS_3)vi_x - \rho k_x \tan\phi_1 - \mu l_x \tan\phi_2)}{\chi}$$

(III.92)

$$e_y = -\frac{((FS_3)vi_y - \rho k_y \tan\phi_1 - \mu l_y \tan\phi_2)}{\chi}$$

(III.93)

$$e_z = -\frac{((FS_3)vi_z - \rho k_z \tan\phi_1 - \mu l_z \tan\phi_2)}{\chi}$$

(III.94)

$$\psi_{e3} = \arcsin(-e_z)$$

(III.95)

$$\alpha_{e3} = \arctan\left(\frac{e_x}{e_y}\right)$$

(III.96)

Compute $s_e$ and $v_e$ using equations (III.26) and (III.27)

$$N_1 = N_1'' + E\rho(r\, v_e - s_e)$$

(III.97)

$$N_2 = N_2'' + E\mu(r\, s_e - v_e)$$

(III.98)

Check that $N_1 \geqq 0$ and $N_2 \geqq 0$

3  *Minimum cable or bolt tension $T_{\min}$ required to raise the factor of safety to some specified value FS.*

(a) Evaluate $N_1', N_2', S', Q'$ by means of equations (III.61), (III.62), (III.78), (III.79) with $T = 0$.

(b) If $N_2' < 0$, contact is lost on plane 2 when $T = 0$. Assume contact on plane 1 only, after application on $T$. Evaluate $S_x', S_y', S_z', S_a'$ and $Q_a'$ using equations (III.65) to (III.69) with $T = 0$.

$$T_1 = \frac{((FS)S_a' - Q_a')}{\sqrt{(FS)^2 + \tan^2\phi_1}}$$

(III.99)

$$\psi_{t1} = \arctan\left(\frac{\tan\phi_1}{(FS)}\right) - \arcsin\left(\frac{S'_z}{S'_a}\right)$$

(III.100)

$$\alpha_{t1} = \arctan\left(\frac{S'_x}{S'_y}\right)$$

(III.101)

(a)  If $N'_1 < 0$, contact is lost on plane 1 when $T = 0$. Assume contact on plane 2 only, after application of $T$. Evaluate $S'_x, S'_y, S'_z, S'_b$ and $Q'_b$ using equations (III.72) to (III.76) with $T = 0$.

$$T_2 = \frac{((FS)S'_b - Q'_b)}{\sqrt{(FS)^2 + \tan^2\phi_2}}$$

(III.102)

$$\psi_{t2} = \arctan\left(\frac{\tan\phi_2}{(FS)}\right) - \arcsin\left(\frac{S'_z}{S'_b}\right)$$

(III.103)

$$\alpha_{t2} = \arctan\left(\frac{S'_x}{S'_y}\right)$$

(III.104)

(a)  All cases. No restrictions on values of $N'_1$ and $N'_2$. Assume contact on both planes after application of $T$.

$$\chi = \sqrt{((FS)^2 + B)}$$

(III.105)

$$T_3 = \frac{((FS)S' - Q')}{\chi}$$

(III.106)

$$t_x = \frac{((FS)vi_x - \rho k_x \tan\phi_1 - \mu l_x \tan\phi_2)}{\chi}$$

(III.107)

$$t_y = \frac{((FS)vi_y - \rho k_y \tan\phi_1 - \mu l_y \tan\phi_2)}{\chi}$$

(III.108)

$$t_z = \frac{((FS)vi_z - \rho k_z \tan\phi_1 - \mu l_z \tan\phi_2)}{\chi}$$

(III.109)

$$\psi_{t3} = \arcsin(-t_z)$$

(III.110)

$$\alpha_{t3} = \arctan\left(\frac{t_x}{t_y}\right)$$

(III.111)

Compute $s$ and $v$ using equations (III.23) and (III.24).

$$N_1 = N'_1 + T_3\rho(rv - s)$$

(III.112)

$$N_2 = N'_2 + T_3\mu(rs - v)$$

(III.113)

If $N_1 < 0$ or $N_2 < 0$, ignore the results of this section.
If $N'_1 > 0$ and $N'_2 > 0$, $T_{min} = T_3$
If $N'_1 > 0$ and $N'_2 < 0$, $T_{min}$ = smallest of $T_1, T_3$
If $N'_1 < 0$ and $N'_2 > 0$, $T_{min}$ = smallest of $T_2, T_3$
If $N'_1 < 0$ and $N'_2 < 0$, $T_{min}$ = smallest of $T_1, T_2, T_3$

**Example** *Calculate the factor of safety for the following wedge:*

| Plane | 1 | 2 | 3 | 4 | 5 |
|---|---|---|---|---|---|
| $\psi$ | 45 | 70 | 12 | 65 | 70 |
| $\alpha$ | 105 | 235 | 195 | 185 | 165 |

$\eta = +1$
$H1 = 100\,\text{ft}, L = 40\,\text{ft}, c_1 = 500\,\text{lb/ft}^2,$
$c_2 = 1000\,\text{lb/ft}^2$
$\phi_1 = 20°, \phi_2 = 30°, \gamma = 160\,\text{lb/ft}^3.$

(1a)  $T = 0, E = 0, u_1 = u_2 = u_5$

$u_5$ calculated from equation (III.59).

$(a_x, a_y, a_z) = (0.68301, -0.18301, 0.70711)$
$(b_x, b_y, b_z) = (-0.76975, -0.53899, 0.34202)$
$(d_x, d_y, d_z) = (-0.05381, -0.20083, 0.97815)$
$(f_x, f_y, f_z) = (-0.07899, -0.90286, 0.42262)$
$(f_{5x}, f_{5y}, f_{5z}) = (0.24321, -0.90767, 0.34202)$
$(g_x, g_y, g_z) = (-0.56107, 0.34451, 0.63112)$
$(g_{5x}, g_{5y}, g_{5z}) = (-0.57923, 0.061627, 0.57544)$
$(i_x, i_y, i_z) = (-0.31853, 0.77790, 0.50901)$
$(j_x, j_y, j_z) = (-0.79826, 0.05452, -0.03272)$
$(j_{5x}, j_{5y}, j_{5z}) = (-0.81915, -0.25630, -0.09769)$
$(k_x, k_y, k_z) = (0.54041, -0.28287, 0.77047)$
$(l_x, l_y, l_z) = (-0.64321, -0.57289, 0.47302)$

$m = 0.57833$

$m_5 = 0.58166$

$n = 0.57388$

$n_5 = 0.73527$

$p = 0.35880$

$q = 0.46206$

$q_5 = 0.60945$

$r = -0.18526$

$s_5 = 0.57407$

$v_5 = 0.41899$

$w_5 = -0.60945$

$\lambda = 0.76796$

$\lambda_5 = 0.52535$

$\varepsilon = 0.94483$

$R = 0.98269$

$\rho = 1.03554$

$\mu = 1.03554$

$\nu = 1.01762$

$G = 0.83180$

$G_5 = 0.67044$

$M = 0.33371$

$M_5 = 0.44017$

$h = 158.45$

$h_5 = 87.521$

$B = 0.56299$

$\psi_i = 31.20°$

$\alpha_i = 157.73°$

$\left. \begin{array}{l} pi_z > 0 \\ \\ nqi_z > 0 \end{array} \right\}$ Wedge is formed

$\left. \begin{array}{l} \varepsilon\eta qs i_z > 0 \\ h_5 > 0 \\ \frac{|m_5 h_5|}{|mh|} = 0.5554 < 1 \\ \frac{|nq_5 m_5 h_5|}{|n_5 qmh|} = 0.57191 < 1 \end{array} \right\}$ Tension crack valid

$A_1 = 5565.01\text{ft}^2$

$A_2 = 6428.1\text{ft}^2$

$A_5 = 1846.6\text{ft}^2$

$W = 2.8272 \times 10^7\,\text{lb}$

$u_1 = u_2 = u_5 = 1084.3\,\text{lb/ft}^2$;

$V = 2.0023 \times 10^6\,\text{lb}$

$\left. \begin{array}{l} N_1 = 1.5171 \times 10^7\,\text{lb} \\ N_2 = 5.7892 \times 10^6\,\text{lb} \end{array} \right\}$ Both positive therefore contact on planes 1 and 2.

$S = 1.5886 \times 10^7\,\text{lb}$

$Q = 1.8075 \times 10^7\,\text{lb}$

FS = 1.1378—*Factor of Safety*

(1b)  $T = 0, E = 0$, dry slope, $u_1 = u_2 = u_5 = 0$.

As in (1a) except as follows:

$\left. \begin{array}{l} V = 0 \\ N_1 = 2.2565 \times 10^7\,\text{lb} \\ N_2 = 1.3853 \times 10^7\,\text{lb} \end{array} \right\}$ Both positive, therefore contact on both planes 1 and 2.

$S = 1.4644 \times 10^7\,\text{lb}$

$Q = 2.5422 \times 10^7\,\text{lb}$

$FS_3 = 1.7360$—*Factor of Safety*

(2)  As in (1b), except $E = 8 \times 10^6$ lb. Find the value of $FS_{min}$.

Values of $N_1'', N_2'', S'', Q'', FS_3''$ as given in (1b).

$N_1'' > 0, N_2'' > 0, FS_3'' > 1$, continue calculation.

$B = 0.56299$

$FS_3 = 1.04$—$FS_{min}$ *(minimum factor of safety)*

$\chi = 1.2798$

$e_x = 0.12128$

$e_y = -0.99226$

$e_z = 0.028243$

$\psi_{e3} = -1.62°$—*plunge of force (upwards)*

$\alpha_{e3} = 173.03°$—*trend of force*

$\left. \begin{array}{l} N_1 = 1.9517 \times 10^7\,\text{lb} \\ N_2 = 9.6793 \times 10^6\,\text{lb} \end{array} \right\}$ Both positive therefore contact maintained on both planes.

(3)  As in (1a) except that the minimum cable tension $T_{min}$ required to increase the factor of safety to 1.5 is to be determined

$N_1', N_2', S'$ and $Q'$—as given in (1a)

$\chi = 1.6772$

$T_3 = 3.4307 \times 10^6$ lb—$T_{min}$ *(minimum cable tension)*

$t_x = -0.18205$

$t_y = 0.97574$

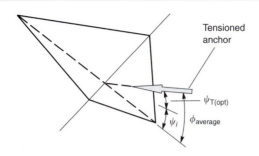

*Figure III.2* Optimum anchor orientation for reinforcement of a wedge.

$$t_z = 0.12148$$

$\psi_{t3} = -6.98°$—*plunge of cable (upwards)*

$\alpha_{t3} = 349.43°$—*trend of cable*

Note that the optimum plunge and trend of the anchor are approximately:

$$\psi_{t3} = \tfrac{1}{2}(\phi_1 + \phi_2) - \psi_i$$

$$\approx 25 - 31.2$$

$$\approx -6.2° \text{ (upwards)}$$

$$\alpha_{t3} \approx \alpha_i \pm 180°$$

$$\approx 157.73 + 180$$

$$\approx 337.73°$$

That is, the best direction in which to install an anchor to reinforce a wedge is

*The anchor should be aligned with the line of intersection of the two planes, viewed from the bottom of the slope, and it should be inclined at the average friction angle to the line of intersection (Figure III.2).*

# Conversion factors

| Imperial unit | SI unit | SI unit symbol | Conversion factor (imperial to SI) | Conversion factor (SI to imperial) |
|---|---|---|---|---|
| *Length* | | | | |
| Mile | kilometer | km | 1 mile = 1.609 km | 1 km = 0.6214 mile |
| Foot | meter | m | 1 ft = 0.3048 m | 1 m = 3.2808 ft |
| | millimeter | mm | 1 ft = 304.80 mm | 1 mm = 0.003 281 ft |
| Inch | millimeter | mm | 1 in = 25.40 mm | 1 mm = 0.039 37 in |
| *Area* | | | | |
| Square mile | square kilometer | $km^2$ | $1 \text{ mile}^2 = 2.590 \text{ km}^2$ | $1 \text{ km}^2 = 0.3861 \text{ mile}^2$ |
| Acre | hectare | ha | $1 \text{ mile}^2 = 259.0 \text{ ha}$ | $1 \text{ ha} = 0.003 861 \text{ mile}^2$ |
| | hectare | ha | 1 acre = 0.4047 ha | 1 ha = 2.4710 acre |
| | square meter | $m^2$ | $1 \text{ acre} = 4047 \text{ m}^2$ | $1 \text{ m}^2 = 0.000 247 1 \text{ acre}$ |
| Square foot | square meter | $m^2$ | $1 \text{ ft}^2 = 0.092 90 \text{ m}^2$ | $1 \text{ m}^2 = 10.7643 \text{ ft}^2$ |
| Square inch | square millimeter | $mm^2$ | $1 \text{ in}^2 = 645.2 \text{ mm}^2$ | $1 \text{ mm}^2 = 0.001 550 \text{ in}^2$ |
| *Volume* | | | | |
| Cubic yard | cubic meter | $m^3$ | $1 \text{ yd}^3 = 0.7646 \text{ m}^3$ | $1 \text{ m}^3 = 1.3080 \text{ yd}^3$ |
| Cubic foot | cubic meter | $m^3$ | $1 \text{ ft}^3 = 0.028 32 \text{ m}^3$ | $1 \text{ m}^3 = 35.3150 \text{ ft}^3$ |
| | liter | l | $1 \text{ ft}^3 = 28.32 \text{ l}$ | $1 \text{ liter} = 0.035 31 \text{ ft}^3$ |
| Cubic inch | cubic millimeter | $mm^3$ | $1 \text{ in}^3 = 16 387 \text{ mm}^3$ | $1 \text{ mm}^3 = 61.024 \times 10^{-6} \text{ in}^3$ |
| | cubic centimeter | $cm^3$ | $1 \text{ in}^3 = 16.387 \text{ cm}^3$ | $1 \text{ cm}^3 = 0.061 02 \text{ in}^3$ |
| | liter | l | $1 \text{ in}^3 = 0.016 39 \text{ l}$ | $1 \text{ liter} = 61.02 \text{ in}^3$ |
| Imperial gallon | cubic meter | $m^3$ | $1 \text{ gal} = 0.004 56 \text{ m}^3$ | $1 \text{ m}^3 = 220.0 \text{ gal}$ |
| | liter | l | 1 gal = 4.546 l | 1 liter = 0.220 gal |
| Pint | liter | l | 1 pt = 0.568 l | 1 liter = 1.7606 pt |
| US gallon | cubic meter | $m^3$ | $1 \text{ US gal} = 0.0038 \text{ m}^3$ | $1 \text{ m}^3 = 263.2 \text{ US gal}$ |
| | liter | l | 1 US gal = 3.8 l | 1 liter = 0.264 US gal |
| *Mass* | | | | |
| Ton | tonne | t | 1 ton = 0.9072 tonne | 1 tonne = 1.1023 ton |
| ton (2000 lb) (US) | kilogram | kg | 1 ton = 907.19 kg | 1 kg = 0.001 102 ton |
| ton (2240 lb) (UK) | | | 1 ton = 1016.1 kg | 1 kg = 0.000 984 ton |
| Kip | kilogram | kg | 1 kip = 453.59 kg | 1 kg = 0.002 204 6 kip |
| Pound | kilogram | kg | 1 lb = 0.4536 kg | 1 kg = 2.204 6 lb |

(*continued*)

Continued

| Imperial unit | SI unit | SI unit symbol | Conversion factor (imperial to SI) | Conversion factor (SI to imperial) |
|---|---|---|---|---|
| *Mass density* | | | | |
| ton per cubic yard (2000 lb) (US) | kilogram per cubic meter | $kg/m^3$ | $1\,ton/yd^3 = 1186.49\,kg/m^3$ | $1\,kg/m^3 = 0.000\,842\,8\,ton/yd^3$ (US) |
| | tonne per cubic meter | $t/m^3$ | $1\,ton/yd^3 = 1.1865\,t/m^3$ | $1\,t/m^3 = 0.8428\,ton/yd^3$ (US) |
| ton per cubic yard (2240 lb) (UK) | kilogram per cubic meter | $kg/cm^3$ | $1\,ton/yd^3 = 1328.9\,kg/m^3$ | $1\,kg/cm^3 = 0.000\,75\,ton/yd^3$ (UK) |
| pound per cubic foot | | | $1\,lb/ft^3 = 16.02\,kg/m^3$ | $1\,kg/cm^3 = 0.062\,42\,lb/ft^3$ |
| | tonne per cubic meter | $t/m^3$ | $1\,lb/ft^3 = 0.01602\,t/m^3$ | $1\,t/m^3 = 62.42\,lb/ft^3$ |
| pound per cubic inch | gram per cubic centimeter | $g/cm^3$ | $1\,lb/in^3 = 27.68\,g/cm^3$ | $1\,g/cm^3 = 0.036\,13\,lb/in^3$ |
| | tonne per cubic meter | $t/m^3$ | $1\,lb/in^3 = 27.68\,t/m^3$ | $1\,t/m^3 = 0.036\,13\,lb/in^3$ |
| *Force* | | | | |
| ton force (2000 lb) (US) | kilonewton | kN | $1\,tonf = 8.896\,kN$ | $1\,kN = 0.1124\,tonf$ (US) |
| ton force (2240 lb) (UK) | | | $1\,tonf = 9.964\,KN$ | $1\,kN = 0.1004\,tonf$ (UK) |
| kip force | kilonewton | kN | $1\,kipf = 4.448\,kN$ | $1\,kN = 0.2248\,kipf$ |
| pound force | newton | N | $1lbf = 4.448\,N$ | $1\,N = 0.2248\,lbf$ |
| tonf/ft (2000 lb) (US) | kilonewton per meter | kN/m | $1\,tonf/ft = 29.186\,kN/m$ | $1\,kN/m = 0.034\,26\,tonf/ft$ (US) |
| tonf/ft (2240 lb) (UK) | kilonewton per meter | | $1\,tonf/ft = 32.68\,kN/m$ | $1\,kN/m = 0.0306\,tonf/ft$ (UK) |
| pound force per foot | newton per meter | N/m | $1\,lbf/ft = 14.59\,N/m$ | $1\,N/m = 0.068\,53\,lbf/ft$ |
| *Hydraulic conductivity* | | | | |
| centimeter per second | meter per second | m/s | $1\,cm/s = 0.01\,m/s$ | $1\,m/s = 100\,cm/s$ |
| foot per year | meter per second | m/s | $1\,ft/yr = 0.9665 \times 10^{-8}\,m/s$ | $1\,m/s = 1.0346 \times 10^8\,ft/yr$ |
| foot per second | meter per second | m/s | $1\,ft/s = 0.3048\,m/s$ | $1\,m/s = 3.2808\,ft/s$ |
| *Flow rate* | | | | |
| cubic foot per minute | cubic meter per second | $m^3/s$ | $1\,ft^3/min = 0.000\,471\,9\,m^3/s$ | $1\,m^3/s = 2119.093\,ft^3/min$ |
| | liter per second | l/s | $1\,ft^3/min = 0.4719\,l/s$ | $1\,l/s = 2.1191\,ft^3/min$ |

*(continued)*

Continued

| Imperial unit | SI unit | SI unit symbol | Conversion factor (imperial to SI) | Conversion factor (SI to imperial) |
|---|---|---|---|---|
| cubic foot per second | cubic meter per second | $m^3/s$ | $1\,ft^3/s = 0.028\,32\,m^3/s$ | $1\,m^3/s = 35.315\,ft^3/s$ |
| | liter per second | l/s | $1\,ft^3/s = 28.32\,l/s$ | $1\,l/s = 0.035\,31\,ft^3/s$ |
| gallon per minute | liter per second | l/s | $1\,gal/min = 0.075\,77\,l/s$ | $1\,l/s = 13.2\,gal/min$ |
| *Pressure, stress* | | | | |
| ton force per square foot (2000 lb) (US) | kilopascal | kPa | $1\,tonf/ft^2 = 95.76\,kPa$ | $1\,kPa = 0.01044\,ton\,f/ft^2$ (US) |
| ton force per square foot (2240 lb) (UK) | | | $1\,tonf/ft^2 = 107.3\,kPa$ | $1\,kPa = 0.00932\,ton/ft^2$ (UK) |
| pound force per square foot | pascal | Pa | $1\,lbf/ft^2 = 47.88\,Pa$ | $1\,Pa = 0.020\,89\,lbf/ft^2$ |
| | kilopascal | kPa | $1\,lbft/ft^2 = 0.047\,88\,kPa$ | $1\,kPa = 20.89\,lbf/ft^2$ |
| pound force per square inch | pascal | Pa | $1\,lbf/in^2 = 6895\,Pa$ | $1\,Pa = 0.000\,1450\,lbf/in^2$ |
| | kilopascal | kPa | $1\,lbf/in^2 = 6.895\,kPa$ | $1\,kPa = 0.1450\,lbf/in^2$ |
| *Weight density*[a] | | | | |
| pound force per cubic foot | kilonewton per cubic meter | $kN/m^3$ | $1\,lbf/ft^3 = 0.157\,kN/m^3$ | $1\,kN/m^3 = 6.37\,lbf/ft^3$ |
| *Energy* | | | | |
| Foot lbf | joules | J | $1\,ft\,lbf = 1.355\,J$ | $1\,J = 0.7376\,ft\,lbf$ |

Note
a  Assuming a gravitational acceleration of $9.807\,m/s^2$.

# References

Abrahamson, N. A. (2000) State of the practice of seismic hazard evaluation. *Proc. Geoeng 2000*, Melbourne, Australia, 659–85.

Adhikary, D. P. and Guo, H. (2000) An orthotropic Cosserat elasto-plastic model for layered rocks. *J. Rock Mech. Rock Engng.*, 35(3), 161–170.

Adhikary, D. P., Dyskin, A. V., Jewell, R. J. and Stewart, D. P. (1997) A study of the mechanism of flexural toppling failures of rock slopes. *J. Rock Mech. Rock Engng*, 30(2), 75–93.

Adhikary, D. P., Mühlhaus, H.-B. and Dyskin, A. V. (2001) A numerical study of flexural buckling of foliated rock slopes. *Int. J. Num. Methods Geomech.*, 25, 871–84.

American Association of State Highway and Transportation Officials (AASHTO) (1984) *A Policy on Geometric Design of Highways and Streets.* American Association of State of Highway and Transportation Officials, Washington, DC.

American Association of State Highway and Transportation Officials (AASHTO) (1996) *Standard Specifications for Highway Bridges*, 16th edn, AASHTO, Washington, DC.

American Concrete Institute (ACI) (1995) *Specifications for Materials, Proportioning and Application of Shotcrete.* ACI Report 506.2-95, Revised 1995.

Andrew, R. D. (1992a) Restricting rock falls. ASCE, *Civil Engineering*, Washington, DC, October, pp. 66–7.

Andrew, R. D. (1992b) Selection of rock fall mitigation techniques based on Colorado Rock fall simulation program. *Transportation Research Record*, 1343, TRB, National Research Council, Washington, DC, pp. 20–22.

Ashby, J. (1971) Sliding and toppling modes of failure in models and jointed rock slopes. *MSc. Thesis.* London University, Imperial College.

Athanasiou-Grivas, D. (1979) Probabilistic evaluation of safety of soil structures. *ASCE, J. Geotech. Engng*, 105 (GT9), 109–15.

Athanasiou-Grivas, D. (1980) A reliability approach to the design of geotechnical systems. Rensselaer Polytechnic Institute Research Paper, *Transportation Research Board Conference*, Washington, DC.

Atkinson, L. C. (2000) The role and mitigation of groundwater in slope stability. *Slope Stability in Surface Mines*, ch. 9. SME, Littleton, CO, pp. 89–96.

Atlas Powder Company (1987) *Explosives and Rock Blasting.* Atlas Powder Company, Dallas, TX.

Australian Center for Geomechanics (ACG) (1998) *Integrated Monitoring Systems for Open Pit Wall Deformation.* MERIWA Project M236, Report ACG: 1005–98.

Australian Drilling Industry (ADI) (1996) *Drilling: Manual of Methods, Applications and Management*, 4th edn. Australian Drilling Industry Training Committee, CRC Press LLC, Boca Raton, FL, 615 pp.

Aycock, J. H. (1981) Construction problems involving shale in a geologically complex environment—State Route 32, Grainger County, Tennessee. *Proc. 32nd Highway Geology Symp.*, Gatlinburg, TN.

Aydan, O. (1989) *The Stabilization of Rock Engineering Structures by Rock Bolts.* Doctorate of Engng Thesis, Dept of Geotechnical Engng, Nagoya University, Japan.

Azzoni, A. and de Freitas, M. H. (1995) Experimentally gained parameters decisive for rock fall analysis. *Rock Mech. Rock Engng*, 28(2), 111–24.

Baecher, G. B., Lanney, N. A. and Einstein, H. (1977) Statistical description of rock properties and sampling. *Proc. 18th US Symp. Rock Mech.* Johnson Publishing Co., Keystone, CO.

Baker, D. G. (1991) Wahleach power tunnel monitoring. *Field Measurements in Geotechnics.* Balkema, Rotterdam, pp. 467–79.

Baker, W. E. (1973) *Explosives in Air.* University of Texas Press, Austin, TX.

Balmer, G. (1952) A general analytical solution for Mohr's envelope. *Am. Soc. Test. Mat.*, 52, 1260–71.

Bandis, S. C. (1993) Engineering properties and characterization of rock discontinuities. In: *Comprehensive Rock Engineering: Principles, Practice and Projects* (ed. J. A. Hudson) Vol. 1, Pergamon Press, Oxford, pp. 155–83.

Barrett, R. K. and White, J. L. (1991) Rock fall prediction and control. *Proc. National Symp. on Highway and Railway Slope Maintenance*, Assoc. of Eng. Geol., Chicago, pp. 23–40.

Barton, N. R. (1971) A model study of the behavior of excavated slopes. *PhD Thesis*, University of London, Imperial College, 520 pp.

Barton, N. R. (1973) Review of a new shear strength criterion for rock joints. *Engng Geol.*, Elsevier, 7, 287–322.

Barton, N. R. (1974) *A Review of the Shear Strength of Filled Discontinuities in Rock*. Norwegian Geotechnical Institute, Pub. No. 105.

Barton, N. R. and Bandis, S. (1983) Effects of block size on the shear behaviour of jointed rock. *Issues in Rock Mechanics—Proc. 23rd US Symp. on Rock Mechanics*, Berkeley, CA, Soc. Mining Eng. of AIME, 739–60.

Baxter, D. A. (1997) Rockbolt corrosion under scrutiny. *Tunnels and Tunneling Int.*, July, pp. 35–8.

Bieniawski, Z. T. (1976) Rock mass classification in rock engineering. In: *Exploration for Rock Engineering, Proc. Symp.* (ed. Z. T. Bieniawski) Vol. 1, Cape Town, Balkema, pp. 97–106.

Bishop, A. W. (1955) The use of the slip circle in the stability analysis of earth slopes. *Geotechnique*, 5, 7–17.

Bishop, A. W. and Bjerrum, L. (1960) The relevance of the triaxial test to the solution of stability problems. *Proc. ASCE Conf Shear Strength of Cohesive Soils*, Boulder, CO, pp. 437–501.

Bjurstrom, S. (1974) Shear strength on hard rock joints reinforced by grouted untensioned bolts. In: *Proc. 3rd International Congress on Rock Mechanics*. Vol. II: Part B, National Academy of Sciences, Washington, DC, pp. 1194–9.

Black, W. H., Smith, H. R. and Patton, F. D. (1986) Multi-level ground water monitoring with the MP System. *Proc. NWWA-AGU Conf. on Surface and Borehole Geophysical Methods and Groundwater Instrumentation*, Denver, CO, pp. 41–61.

Bobet, A. (1999) Analytical solutions for toppling failure (Technical Note). *Int. J. Rock Mech. Min. Sci.*, 36, 971–80.

Brawner, C. O., Stacey, P. F. and Stark, R. (1975) A successful application of mining with pitwall movement. *Proc. Canadian Institute of Mining, Annual Western Meeting*, Edmonton, October, 20 pp.

Brawner, C. O. and Kalejta, J. (2002) Rock fall control in surface mining with cable ring net fences. *Soc. Mining Eng., Proc. Annual Meeting*, Phoenix, AZ, February, 10 pp.

Brawner, C. O. and Wyllie, D. C. (1975) Rock slope stability on railway projects. *Proc. Am. Railway Engng Assoc.*, Regional Meeting, Vancouver, BC.

British Standards Institute (BSI) (1989) *British Standard Code of Practice for Ground Anchorages, BS 8081: 1989*. BSI, 2 Park Street, London, W1A 2BS, 176 pp.

Broadbent, C. D. and Zavodni, Z. M. (1982) Influence of rock structure on stability. *Stability in Surface Mining*, Vol. 3, Ch. 2. Soc. of Mining Engineers, Denver, CO.

Brown, E. T. (1970) Strength of models of rock with intermittent joints. *J. Soil Mech. Fdns Div.*, ASCE 96, SM6, 1935–49.

Byerly, D. W. and Middleton, L. M. (1981) Evaluation of the acid drainage potential of certain Precambrian rocks in the Blue Ridge Province. *32nd Annual Highway Geology Symp.*, Gatlinburg, TN, pp. 174–85.

Byrne, R. J. (1974) Physical and numerical models in rock and soil slope stability. *PhD Thesis*. James Cook University of North Queensland, Australia.

CIL (1983) *Blaster's Handbook*. Canadian Industries Limited, Montréal, Québec.

CIL (1984) Technical Literature, Canadian Industries Limited, Toronto, Canada.

California Polytechnical State University (1996) *Response of the Geobrugg cable net system to debris flow loading*. Dept Civil and Environmental Engng, San Luis Obispo, CA, 68 pp.

Call, R. D. (1982) Monitoring pit slope behaviour. *Stability in Surface Mining*, Vol. 3, Ch. 9. Soc. of Mining Engineers, Denver, CO.

Call, R. D., Saverly, J. P. and Pakalnis, R. (1982) A simple core orientation device. In: *Stability in Surface Mining* (ed. C. O. Brawner), SME, AIME, New York, pp. 465–81.

Canada Department of Energy, Mines and Resources (1978) *Pit Slope Manual*. DEMR, Ottawa, Canada.

Canadian Geotechnical Society (1992) *Canadian Foundation Engineering Manual*. BiTech Publishers Ltd, Vancouver, Canada.

Canadian Standards Association (1988) *Design of Highway Bridges*. CAN/CSA-56-88, Rexdale, Ontario.

Carter, J. P. and Balaam, N. G. (1995) *AFENA Users' Manual, Version 5*. University of Sydney, Centre for Geotechnical Research.

Carter, T. G., Carvalho, J. L. and Swan, G. (1993) Towards practical application of ground reaction curves. In: *Innovative Mine Design for the 21st Century* (eds W. F. Bawden and J. F. Archibald), Rotterdam, Balkema, pp. 151–71.

Casagrande, L. (1934) Näherungsverfahren zur Ermittlung der Sickerung in geschütteten Dämmen auf underchläassiger Sohle. *Die Bautechnik*, Heft 15.

Caterpillar Tractor Co. (2001) *Caterpillar Performance Handbook, edition 32*. Caterpillar Tractor Co., Peoria, IL.

CDMG (1997) *Guidelines for Evaluating and Mitigating Seismic Hazards in California*. California Div. of Mines and Geology, Special Publication 117, www/consrv.ca.gov/dmg/pubs/sp/117/

Cedergren, H. R. (1989) *Seepage, Drainage and Flow Nets*, 3rd edn. John Wiley & Sons, New York, USA, 465 pp.

Chen, Z. (1995a) Keynote Lecture: Recent developments in slope stability analysis. *Proc. 8th Int. Congress on Rock Mechanics*, Vol. 3, Tokyo, Japan, pp. 1041–8.

Chen, Z. editor in chief (1995b) *Transactions of the Stability Analysis and Software for Steep Slopes in China. Vol. 3.1: Rock Classification, Statistics of Database of Failed and Natural Slopes*. China Inst. of Water Resources and Hydroelectric Power Research (in Chinese).

Cheng, Y. and Liu, S. (1990) Power caverns of the Mingtan Pumped Storage Project, Taiwan. In *Comprehensive Rock Engineering* (ed. J. A. Hudson), Pergamon Press, Oxford, Vol. 5, pp. 111–32.

Christensen Boyles Corp. (2000) *Diamond Drill Products—Field Specifications*. CBC, Salt Lake City, UT.

Ciarla, M. (1986) Wire netting for rock fall protection. *Proc. 37th Ann. Highway Geology Symp.*, Helena, Montana, Montana Department of Highways, pp. 10–118.

Cluff, L. S., Hansen, W. R., Taylor, C. L., Weaver, K. D., Brogan, G. E., Idress, I. M., McClure, F. E. and Bayley, J. A. (1972) Site evaluation in seismically active regions—an interdisciplinary team approach. *Proc. Int. Conf. Microzonation for Safety, Construction, Research and Application*, Seattle, WA, Vol. 2, pp. 9-57–9-87.

Coates, D. F., Gyenge, M. and Stubbins, J. B. (1965) Slope stability studies at Knob Lake. *Proc. Rock Mechanics Symp.*, Toronto, pp. 35–46.

Colog Inc. (1995) *Borehole Image Processing System (BIP)*, Golden, CO, and Raax Co. Ltd., Australia.

Coulomb, C. A. (1773) Sur une application des règles de Maximis et Minimis a quelques problèmes de statique relatifs à l'Architechture. *Acad. Roy. des Sciences Memoires de math. et de physique par divers savans*, 7, 343–82.

Cruden, D. M. (1977) Describing the size of discontinuities. *Int. J. Rock Mech. Min. Sci. & Geomech. Abstr.*, 14, 133–7.

Cruden, D. M. (1997) Estimating the risks from landslides using historical data. *Proc. Int. Workshop on Landslide Risk Assessment* (eds D. M. Cruden and R. Fell), Honolulu, HI, Balkema, Rotterdam, 177–84.

CSIRO (2001) SIROJOINT Geological Mapping Software. *CSIRO Mining and Exploration*, Pullenvale, Queensland, Australia.

Cundall, P.(1971) A computer model for simulating progressive, large scale movements in blocky rock systems. *Proc. Int. Symp. on Rock Fracture*. Nancy, France, Paper 11–8.

Cundall, P. A., Carranza-Torres, C. and Hart, R. D. (2003) A new constitutive model based on the Hoek–Brown criterion. Presented at *FLAC and Numerical Modeling in Geomechanics*, Sudbury, Canada, October.

Davies, J. N. and Smith, P. L. P. (1993) Flexural toppling of siltstones during a temporary excavation for a bridge foundation in North Devon. *Comprehensive Rock Engineering*, Pergamon Press, Oxford, UK, 5, Ch. 31, 759–75.

Davis, G. H. and Reynolds, S. J. (1996) *Structural Geology of Rocks and Regions*, 2nd edn. John Wiley & Sons, New York, 776 pp.

Davis, S. N. (1969) Porosity and permeability of natural materials. In: *Flow through Porous Media* (ed. R. de Weist) Academic Press, London, pp. 54–89.

Davis, S. N. and De Wiest, R. J. M. (1966) *Hydrogeology*, John Wiley & Sons, New York and London.

Dawson, E. M. and Cundall, P. A. (1996) Slope stability using micropolar plasticity. In: *Rock Mechanics Tools and Techniques* (ed. M. Aubertin et al.) Rotterdam, Balkema, pp. 551–8.

Dawson, E. M., Roth, W. H. and Drescher, A. (1999) Slope stability analysis by strength reduction, *Géotechnique*, 49(6), 835–840.

Deere, D. U. and Miller, R. P. (1966) *Engineering Classification and Index Properties of Intact Rock.* Technical Report No. AFWL-TR-65-116, Air Force Weapons Laboratory, Kirkland Air Force Base, New Mexico.

Dershowitz, W. S. and Einstein, H. H. (1988) Characterizing rock joint geometry with joint system models. *Rock Mech. Rock Engng*, 20(1), 21–51.

Dershowitz, W. S. and Schrauf, T. S. (1987) Discrete fracture flow modeling with the JINX package. *Proc. 28th US Symp. Rock Mechanics*, Tucson, pp. 433–9.

Dershowitz, W. S, Lee, G., Geier, J., Hitchcock, S. and LaPointe, P. (1994) *FRACMAN Interactive Discrete Feature Data Analysis, Geometric Modeling, and Exploration Simulation.* User documentation V. 2.4, Golder Associates Inc., Redmond, Washington.

Descoeudres, F. and Zimmerman, T. (1987) Three-dimensional calculation of rock falls. *Proc. Int. Conf. Rock Mech.*, Montreal, Canada.

Dowding, C. H. (1985) *Blast Vibration Monitoring and Control.* Prentice-Hall, Englewood Cliffs, NJ.

Du Pont De Memours & Co. Inc. (1984) *Blaster's Handbook.* Du Pont, Wilmington, DE.

Duffy, J. D. and Haller, B. (1993) Field tests of flexible rock fall barriers. *Proc. Int. Conf. on Transportation Facilities through Difficult Terrain*, Aspen, Colorado, Balkema, Rotterdam, Netherlands, pp. 465–73.

Duncan, J. M. (1996) Landslides: *Investigation and Mitigation*, Transportation Research Board, Special Report 247, Washington, DC, Ch. 13, Soil Slope Stability Analysis, pp. 337–71.

Dunnicliff, J. (1993) *Geotechnical Instrumentation for Monitoring Field Performance*, 2nd edn, John Wiley & Sons, New York, 577 pp.

Durn, J. and Douglas, L. H. (1999) Do rock slopes designed with empirical rock mass strength stand up? *9th Cong. Int. Soc. Rock Mech.*, Paris, 87–90.

Einstein, H. H. (1993) Modern developments in discontinuity analysis. *Comprehensive Rock Engineering*, Pergamon Press, Oxford, 3, Ch. 9, 193–213.

Einstein, H. H., Veneziano, D., Baecher, G. B. and O'Reilly, K. J. (1983) The effect of discontinuity persistence on slope stability. *Int. J. Rock Mech. Min. Sci. & Geomech. Abstr.*, 20, 227–36.

Erban, P. J. and Gill, K. (1988) Consideration of the interaction between dam and bedrock in a coupled machanic-hydraulic FE-program. *Rock Mech. Rock Engng*, 21(2), 99–118.

European Committee for Standardization (1995) *Eurocode 1: Basis of Design and Actions on Structures—Part 1, Basis of Design.* Central Secretariat, Brussels.

Farmer, I. W. (1975) Stress distribution along a resin grouted anchor. *Int. J. Rock Mech & Geomech. Abstracts.*, 12, 347–51.

Fecker, E. and Rengers, N. (1971) Measurement of large scale roughness of rock planes by means of profilometer and geological compass. *Proc. Symp. on Rock Fracture*, Nancy, France, Paper 1–18.

Federal Highway Administration (FHWA) (1982) *Tiebacks.* Publication No. FHWA/RD-82/047, Washington, DC.

Federal Highway Administration (FHWA) (1991) *Rock Blasting and Overbreak Control.* FHWA, US Department of Transportation Contract No. DTFW 61-90-R-00058.

Federal Highway Administration (FHWA) (1993) *Rockfall Hazard Mitigation Methods.* Publication No. FHWA SA-95-085, Washington, DC.

Federal Highway Administration (FHWA) (1998) *Rock Slopes.* Publication No. FHWA-HI-99-007, FHWA, Washington, DC.

Fell, R. (1994) Landslide risk assessment and acceptable risk. *Can. Geotech. J.*, 31, 261–72.

Fleming, R. W., Spencer, G. S. and Banks, D. C. (1970) Empirical study of the behaviour of clay shale slopes. *US Army Nuclear Cratering Group Technical Report, No. 15.*

Flores, G. and Karzulovic, A. (2000) The role of the geotechnical group in an open pit: Chuquicamata Mine, Chile. *Slope Stability in Surface Mining*, SME, Littleton, CO, 141–52.

Fookes, P. G. and Sweeney, M. (1976) Stabilization and control of local rock falls and degrading rock slopes. *Quart. J. Engng Geol.*, 9, 37–55.

Forster, J. W. (1986) Geological problems overcome at Revelstoke, part two. *Water Power and Dam Construction*, August.

Frankel, F., Mueller, C., Bernard, T., Perkins, D., Leyendecker, E. V., Dickman, N., Hanson, S. and Hopper, M. (1996) *Interim National Hazards Map: Documentation.* Draft Report, US Geological Survey, Denver, CO.

Franklin, A. G. and Chan, F. K. (1977) Earthquake resistance of earth and rock-fill dams. Report 5: Permanent displacement of earth embankments by Newmark sliding block analysis. US Army Engineer Waterways Experiment Station, Vicksburg, MS, Miscellaneous Paper S-71-17, 59 pp.

Freeze, R. A. and Cherry, J. A. (1979) *Groundwater.* Prentice Hall, New Jersey, USA, 604 pp.

Freitas, M. H. and Watters, R. J. (1973) Some field examples of toppling failure. *Géotechnique*, 23(4), 495–514.

Frohlich, O. K. (1955) General theory of the stability of slopes. *Géotechnique*, 5, 37–47.

Geological Society Engineering Group Working Party (1977) The logging of rock cores for engineering purposes. *Quart. J. Engng Geol.*, 3, 1–24.

Glass, C. E. (2000) The influence of seismic events on slope stability. *Slope Stability in Surface Mining*, Soc. Mining, Metallurgy and Exploration, Littleton, CO, 97–105.

Golder, H. Q. (1972) The stability of natural and man-made slopes in soil and rock. *Geotechnical Practice for Stability in Open Pit Mining*. (eds C. O. Brawner and V. Milligan), AIME, New York, 79–85.

Goodman, R. E. (1964) The resolution of stresses in rock using stereographic projection. *Int. J. Rock Mech. Mining Sci.*, 1, 93–103.

Goodman, R. E. (1970) The deformability of joints. In *Determination of the in situ Modulus of Deformation of Rock*. Am. Soc. Testing and Materials, Spec. Tech. Publication, No. 477, 174–96.

Goodman, R. E. (1976) *Methods of Geological Engineering in Discontinuous Rocks*. West Publishing Co., St Paul, MN, 472 pp.

Goodman, R. E. (1980) *Introduction to Rock Mechanics*. John Wiley and Sons, New York.

Goodman, R. E. and Bray, J. (1976) Toppling of rock slopes. *ASCE, Proc. Specialty Conf. on Rock Eng. for Foundations and Slopes*, Boulder, CO, 2, 201–34.

Goodman, R. E. and Seed, H. B. (1966) Earthquake induced displacements of sand embankments. *ASCE* Vol. 92, SM2, pp. 125–46.

Goodman, R. E. and Shi, G. (1985) *Block Theory and its Application to Rock Engineering*. Prentice Hall, Englewood Cliffs, NJ.

Goodman, R. E., Moye, D. G., van Schalkwyk, A. and Javandel, I. (1965) Ground water inflows during tunnel driving. *Engng Geol.*, 70, 396–8.

Griffiths, D. H. and King, R. F. (1988) *Applied Geophysics for Geologists and Engineers*, 2nd edn. Pergamon Press, Oxford, UK.

Haar, M. E. (1962) *Ground Water and Seepage*. McGraw Hill Co., New York.

Hagan, T. N. (1975) Blasting physics—what the operator can use in 1975. *Proc. Aust. Inst. Mining and Metall.*, Annual Conf., Adelaide, Part B, 369–86.

Hagan, T. N. (1992) Personal communication, Blasting Ltd., Queensland, Australia.

Hagan, T. N. and Bulow, B. (2000) Blast designs to protect pit walls. *Slope Stability in Surface Mining*, Soc. Min. Metallurgy and Exploration, Denver, CO, pp. 125–30.

Haines, A. and Terbrugge, P. J. (1991) Preliminary estimate of rock slope stability using rock mass classification. *7th Cong. Int. Soc. of Rock Mech.*, Aachen, Germany, pp. 887–92.

Hamel, J. V. (1970) The Pima Mine slide, Pima County, Arizona. *Geol. Soc. America*, Abstracts with Programs, 2(5), p. 335.

Hamel, J. V. (1971a) The slide at Brilliant cut. *Proc. 13th Symp. Rock Mechanics*, Urbana, IL, pp. 487–510.

Hamel, J. V. (1971b) Kimberley pit slope failure. *Proc. 4th Pan-American Conf. on Soil Mechanics and Foundation Engineering*, Puerto Rico, 2, 117–27.

Hammett, R. D. (1974) A study of the behaviour of discontinuous rock masses. *PhD Thesis*. James Cook University of North Queensland, Australia.

Han, C. (1972) The technique for obtaining equipotential lines of ground water flow in slopes using electrically conducting paper. *MSc. Thesis*, London University (Imperial College).

Hanna, T. H. (1982) *Foundations in Tension—Ground Anchors*. Trans. Tech. Publications/McGraw Hill Book Co., Clausthal-Zellerfeld, West Germany.

Harp, E. L. and Noble, M. A. (1993) An engineering rock classification to evaluate seismic rock fall susceptibility and its application to the Wasatch Front. *Bull. Assoc. Eng. Geologists.*, XXX(3), 293–319.

Harp, E. L. and Wilson, R. C. (1995) Shaking intensity thresholds for rock falls and slides: evidence from the 1987 Whittier Narrows and Superstition Hills earthquake strong motion records. *Bull. Seismological Soc. Am.*, 85(6), 1739–57.

Harp, E. L. and Jibson, R. W. (2002) Anomalous concentrations of seismically triggered rock falls in Pacoima Canyon: are they caused by highly susceptible slopes or local amplification of seismic shaking. *Bull. Seismological Soc. Am.*, 92(8), 3180–9.

Harp, E. L., Jibson, R. W., Kayen, R. E., Keffer, D. S., Sherrod, B. L., Collins, B. D., Moss, R. E. S. and Sitar, N. (2003) Landslides and liquefaction triggered by the M 7.9 Denali Fault earthquake of 3 November, 2002. GSA Today (Geological Society of America), August, 4–10.

Harr, M. E. (1977) *Mechanics of Particulate Matter—A Probabilistic Approach*. McGraw-Hill, New York, 543 pp.

Harries, G. and Mercer, J. K. (1975) The science of blasting and its use to minimize costs. Proc. Austr. Inst. Mining and Metall. Annual Conf. Adelaide, Part b, 387–99.

Hawley, P. M. and Stewart, A. F. (1986) Design of open pit coal mine slopes: an integrated approach. *Proc. Int. Symp. on Geotechnical Stability in Surface Mining*. Calgary, pp. 69–77. © Swets & Zeitlinger.

Hawley, P. M., Martin, D. C. and Acott, C. P. (1986) Failure mechanics and design considerations for footwall slopes. *CIM Bulletin*, Vol. 79, No. 896, 47–53.

Hemphill, G. B. (1981) *Blasting Operations*. McGraw Hill Inc., New York.

Hencher, S. R. and Richards, L. R. (1989) Laboratory direct shear testing of rock discontinuities. *Ground Engineering*, March, 24–31.

Hendron, A. J. and Patton, F. D. (1985) The Vaiont slide: a geotechnical analysis based on new geological observations of the failure surface. *Waterways Experiment Station Technical Report*, US Army Corps of Engineers, Vicksburg, MS, Vol. 1, 104 pp.

Heuer, R. E. (1995) Estimating ground water flow in tunnels. *Proc. Rapid Excavation and Tunneling Conf.*, San Francisco, pp. 41–80.

Hocking, G. (1976) A method for distinguishing between single and double plane sliding of tetrahedral wedges. *Int. J. Rock Mech. Mining Sci.*, 13, 225–6.

Hoek, E. (1968) Brittle failure of rock. In: *Rock Mechanics in Engineering Practice* (eds K. G. Stagg and O. C. Zienkiewicz), John Wiley & Sons, London, pp. 99–124.

Hoek, E. (1970) Estimating the stability of excavated slopes in opencast mines. *Trans. Inst. Mining and Metallurgy*, London, 79, A109–32.

Hoek, E. (1974) Progressive caving induced by mining an inclined ore body. *Trans. Inst. Mining and Metallurgy*, London, 83, A133–39.

Hoek, E. (1983) Strength of jointed rock masses, 23rd. Rankine Lecture. *Géotechnique* 33(3), 187–223.

Hoek, E. (1990) Estimating Mohr–Coulomb friction and cohesion values from the Hoek–Brown failure criterion. *Int. J. Rock Mech. Mining Sci. & Geomech. Abstr.* 12(3), 227–29.

Hoek, E. (1994) Strength of rock and rock masses, *ISRM News Journal*, 2(2), 4–16.

Hoek, E. and Bray, J. (1977) *Rock Slope Engineering*, 1st edn, IMM, London.

Hoek, E. and Bray, J. (1981) *Rock Slope Engineering*, 3rd edn, Inst. Mining and Metallurgy, London, UK.

Hoek, E. and Brown, E. T. (1980a) Empirical strength criterion for rock masses. *J. Geotech. Engng Div.*, ASCE 106 (GT9), 1013–35.

Hoek, E. and Brown, E. T. (1980b) *Underground Excavations in Rock*, London, Inst. Mining Metallurgy, London, UK.

Hoek, E. and Brown, E. T. (1988) The Hoek–Brown failure criterion—a 1988 update. *Proc. 15th Canadian Rock Mech. Symp.* (ed. J.C. Curran), pp. 31–8. Toronto, Dept Civil Engineering, University of Toronto.

Hoek, E. and Brown, E. T. (1997) Practical estimates or rock mass strength. *Int. J. Rock Mech. Min. Sci. & Geomech. Abstr.*, 34(8), 1165–86.

Hoek, E. and Marinos, P. (2000) Predicting tunnel squeezing. *Tunnels and Tunnelling Int.* Part 1—November 2000, Part 2—December 2000.

Hoek, E. and Richards, L. R. (1974) *Rock Slope Design Review*. Golder Associates Report to the Principal Govt. Highway Engineer, Hong Kong, 150 pp.

Hoek, E., Bray, J. and Boyd, J. (1973) The stability of a rock slope containing a wedge resting on two intersecting discontinuities. *Quart. J. Engng Geol.*, 6(1) 22–35.

Hoek, E., Wood D. and Shah S. (1992) A modified Hoek–Brown criterion for jointed rock masses. *Proc. Rock Characterization, Symp. Int. Soc. Rock Mech.: Eurock '92*, (ed. J. A. Hudson), Brit. Geotech. Soc., London, pp. 209–14.

Hoek, E., Kaiser P. K. and Bawden W. F. (1995) *Support of Underground Excavations in Hard Rock*. Rotterdam, Balkema.

Hoek, E., Marinos, P. and Benissi, M. (1998) Applicability of the Geological Strength Index (GSI) classification for very weak and sheared rock masses. The case of the Athens Schist Formation. *Bull. Engng Geol. Env.*, 57(2), 151–60.

Hoek, E., Carranza-Torres, C. and Corkum, B. (2002) Hoek–Brown failure criterion—2002 edition. *Proc. North Am. Rock Mech. Soc. Meeting*, Toronto, Canada, July, 267–73.

Hofmann, H. (1972) "Kinematische Modellstudien zum Boschungs-problem in regalmassig geklüfteten Medien." Veröffentlichungen des Institutes für Bodenmechanik und Felsmechanik. Kalsruhe, Hetf 54.

Hong Kong Geotechnical Engineering Office (2000) *Highway Slope Manual*. Civil Engineering Department, Govt. Hong Kong, Special Administrative Region, 114 pp.

Hudson, J. A. and Priest, S. D. (1979) Discontinuities and rock mass geometry. *Int. J. Rock Mech. Min. Sci. & Geomech. Abstr.*, 16, 336–62.

Hudson, J. A. and Priest, S. D. (1983) Discontinuity frequency in rock masses. *Int. J. Rock Mech. Min. Sci. & Geomech. Abstr.*, 20, 73–89.

Huitt, J. L. (1956) Fluid flow in a simulated fracture. *J. Am. Inst. Chem. Eng.*, 2, 259–64.

Hungr, O. (1987) An extension of Bishop's simplified method of slope stability to three dimensions. *Géotechnique*, 37, 113–17.

Hungr, O. and Evans, S. G. (1988) Engineering evaluation of fragmental rock fall hazards. *Proc. 5th Int. Symp. on Landslides*, Lausanne, July, pp. 685–90.

Hungr, O., Evans, S. G. and Hazzard, J. (1999) Magnitude and frequency of rock falls and rock slides along the main transportation corridors of southwestern British Columbia. *Canadian Geotech. J.*, 36, 224–38.

Hutchinson, J. N. (1970) Field and laboratory studies of a fall in upper chalk cliffs at Joss Bay, Isle of Thanet. *Proc. Roscoe Memorial Symp.*, Cambridge.

Hynes, M. E. and Franklin, A. G. (1984) Rationalizing the seismic coefficient method. *Miscellaneous Paper GL-84-13*, US Army Engineer Waterways Experiment Station, Vicksburg, Mississippi, p. 34.

IAEG Commission on Landslides (1990) Suggested nomenclature for landslides. *Bull. Int. Assoc. Eng. Geol.*, 41, 13–16.

International Society of Explosive Engineers (ISEE) (1998) *Blasters' Handbook*, 17th edn Int. Soc. of Explosive Eng., Cleveland, OH, 742 pp.

International Society for Rock Mechanics (ISRM) (1981a) *Suggested Methods for the Quantitative Description of Discontinuities in Rock Masses* (ed. E. T. Brown). Pergamon Press, Oxford, UK, 211 pp.

International Society of Rock Mechanics (ISRM) (1981b) *Rock Characterization, Testing and Monitoring; ISRM Suggested Method*. Pergamon Press, Oxford, UK.

International Society of Rock Mechanics (ISRM) (1981c) Basic geological description of rock masses. *Int. J. Rock Mech. Min. Sci. & Geomech. Abstr.*, 18, 85–110.

International Society of Rock Mechanics (1985) Suggested methods for determining point load strength. *Int. J. Rock Mech.*, 22 (2), 53–60.

International Society of Rock Mechanics (1991) Suggested methods of blast vibration monitoring. Dowding, C. H., coordinator. *Int. J. Rock Mech. Min. Sci. & Geomech. Abstr.*, Pergamon Press, 129 (2), 143–56.

Ishikawa, N. (1999) Recent progress on rock shed studies in Japan. *Proc. Joint Japan–Swiss Sci. Seminar on Impact Loading by Rock Falls and Design of Protection Measures*, Japan Soc. Civil Engng, Kanazawa, Japan, pp. 1–6.

Itasca Consulting Group Inc. (2000) *UDEC (Universal Distinct Element Code), Version 3.1* Minneapolis, MN.

Itasca Consulting Group Inc. (2001) *FLAC (Fast Lagrangian Analysis of Continua), Version 4.0*, Minneapolis, MN.

Itasca Consulting Group Inc. (2002) *FLAC3D (Fast Lagrangian Analysis of Continua in 3 Dimensions), Version 2.1*, Minneapolis, MN.

Itasca Consulting Group Inc. (2003) *3DEC (Three-Dimensional Distinct Element Code), Version 3.0*, Minneapolis, MN.

Jacob, C. E. (1950). Flow of ground water. In: *Engineering Hydraulics* (ed. H. Rouse). John Wiley and Sons, New York, pp. 321–86.

Jaegar, J. C. (1970) The behaviour of closely jointed rock. *Proc. 11th Symp. Rock Mech.*, Berkeley, CA, pp. 57–68.

Jaeger, J. C. and Cook, N. G. W. (1976) *Fundamentals of Rock Mechanics*, 2nd edn. Chapman and Hall, London, UK, 585 pp.

Janbu, N. (1954) Application of composite slide circles for stability analysis. *Proc. European Conference on Stability of Earth Slopes*. Stockholm, 3, pp. 43–9.

Janbu, N., Bjerrum, L. and Kjaernsli, B. (1956) *Soil Mechanics Applied to Some Engineering Problems* (in Norwegian with English summary). Norwegian Geotech. Inst., Publication 16.

Jenike, A. W. and Yen, B. C. (1961) Slope stability in axial symmetry. In: *Proc. 5th Rock Mechanics Symposium (University of Minnesota, 1961)*, pp. 689–711 Pergamon, London.

Jennings, J. E. (1970) A mathematical theory for the calculation of the stability of open cast mines. *Proc. Symp. on the Theoretical Background to the Planning of Open Pit Mines*, Johannesburg, pp. 87–102.

Jibson, R. W. (1993) Predicting earthquake-induced landslide displacements using Newark's sliding block analysis. *Transportation Research Record 1411*, Transportation Research Board, Washington, DC, pp. 9–17.

Jibson, R. W. (2003) Personal communication.

Jibson, R. W. and Harp, E. L., (1995) Inventory of Landslides Triggered by the 1994 Northridge, California Earthquake. *Dept of the Interior, USGS*, Open–File 95-213, 17 pp.

Jibson, R. W., Harp, E. L., and Michael, J. A. (1998) A method for producing digital probabilistic seismic landslide hazard map: an Example from the Los Angeles, California area. *Dept. Interior, USGS*, Open–File Report 98-113, 17 pp.

John, K. W. (1970) Engineering analysis of three-dimensional stability problems utilizing the reference hemisphere. *Proc. 2nd Int. Cong. Int. Soc. Rock Mech.*, Belgrade, 2, 314–21.

Kane, W. F. and Beck, T. J. (1996) Rapid slope monitoring. *Civil Engineering*, ASCE, Washington, DC, June, 56–8.

Keefer, D. L. (1984) Landslides caused by earthquakes. *Geol. Soc. of America Bull.*, 95, 406.21.

Keefer, D. L. (1992) The susceptibility of rock slopes to earthquake-induced failure. *Proc. 35th Annual Meeting of the Assoc. of Eng. Geologists* (ed. Martin L. Stout), Long Beach, CA, pp. 529–38.

Kennedy, B. A. and Neimeyer, K. E. (1970) Slope monitoring systems used in the prediction of a major slope failure at the Chuquicamata Mine, Chile. *Proc. of Symp. On Planning Open Pit Mines*, Johannesburg, South Africa, pp. 215–25.

Kielhorn, W. (1999) Another wedge calculator. Computer software, kielhorn@infomatch.com

Kiersch, G. A. (1963). Vaiont Reservoir Disaster. *Civil Engng*, 34(3), 32–9.

Kikuchi, K., Kuroda, H. and Mito, Y. (1987) Stochastic estimation and modeling of rock joint distribution based on statistical sampling. *6th Int. Congress on Rock Mech.*, Montreal, Balkema, pp. 425–8.

King, R. A. (1977) A review of soil corrosiveness with particular reference to reinforced earth. *Transport and Road Research Laboratory*, Crowthorne, UK, Supplementary Report No. 316.

Kobayashi, Y., Harp, E. L. and. Hagawa, T. (1990) Simulation of rock falls triggered by earthquakes. *Rock Mech. Rock Engng*, 23(1), 1–20.

Kreyszig. E. (1976) *Advanced Engineering Mathematics*. John Wiley and Sons, New York, pp. 770–6.

Kulatilake, P. H. S. (1988) State of the art in stochastic joint geometry modeling. *Proc. 29th US Symp. Rock Mech.* (eds P. A. Cundall, J. Sterling and A. M. Starfield), Balkema, Rotterdam, pp. 215–29.

Kulatilake, P. H. S. and Wu, T. H. (1984) Estimation of the mean length of discontinuities. *Rock Mech. Rock Engng*, 17(4), 215–32.

Ladegaard-Pedersen, A. and Dally, J. W. (1975) *A Review of Factors Affecting Damage in Blasting*.

Report to the National Science Foundation. Mech. Engng Dept, Univ. of Maryland, 170 pp.

Lambe, W. T. and Whitman, R. V. (1969). *Soil Mechanics*. Wiley, New York.

Langefors, U. and Kihlstrom, B. (1973). *The Modern Technique of Rock Blasting*. John Wiley and Sons, New York, 2nd edn.

Lau, J. S. O. (1983) The determination of true orientations of fractures in rock cores. *Can. Geotech. J.*, 20, 221–7.

Leighton, J. C. (1990) New tunnel at Shalath Bluff on BC Rail's Squamish Subdivision. *Proc. 8th Annual Meeting of the Tunnelling Association of Canada*, Vancouver, BC, October, Bitech Publishers Ltd., pp. 255–66.

Ley, G. M. M. (1972) *The Properties of Hydrothermally Altered Granite and their Application to Slope Stability in Open Cast Mining*. MSc. Thesis, London University, Imperial College.

Leyshon, P. R. and Lisle, R. J. (1996) *Stereographic Projection Techniques in Structural Geology*. Butterworth and Heinemann, Oxford, UK, 104 pp.

Lin, J.-S. and Whitman, R. V. (1986) Earthquake induced displacement of sliding blocks. *J. Geotech. Engng Div.*, ASCE, Vol. 112, No.1 Jan. 1986.

Ling, H. I. and Cheng, A. H.-D. (1997) Rock sliding induced by seismic forces. *Int. J. Rock Mech. Mining Sci.* 34(6), 1021–9.

Littlejohn, G. S. and Bruce, D. A. (1977) *Rock Anchors—State of the Art*. Foundation Publications Ltd., Brentwood, Essex, UK.

Londe, P. (1965) Une method d'analyse a trois dimensions de la stabilite d'une rive rocheuse. *Annales des Ponts et Chaussees*, Paris, 37.60.

Londe, P., Vigier, G. and Vormeringer, R. (1969) Stability of rock slopes—a three-dimensional study. *J. Soil Mech. Fndn Engng Div.* ASCE, 95 (SM1), 235–62.

Londe, P., Vigier, G. and Vormeringer, R. (1970) Stability of rock slopes—graphical methods. *J. Soil Mech. Fndn Engng Div.* ASCE, 96 (SM4), 1411–34.

Lorig, L. J. (1985) A simple numerical representation of fully bonded passive rock reinforcement for hard rocks, *Computers & Geotechnics*, 1, 79–97.

Lorig, L. and Varona, P. (2001) Practical slope-stability analysis using finite-difference codes. In: *Slope Stability in Surface Mining* (eds W. A. Hustrulid, M. J. McCarter and D. J. A. Van Zyl). Society for Mining, Metallurgy and Exploration, Inc., Littleton, pp. 115–24.

Louis, C. (1969) A study of ground water flow in jointed rock and its influence on the stability of rock masses. Doctorate thesis, Univ. of Karlsruhe (in German). English translation: *Imperial College Rock Mech. Research Report No. 10*, 50 pp.

McCauley, M. L., Works, B. W. and Naramore, S. A. (1985) *Rockfall Mitigation*. Report FHWA/CA/TL-85/12. FHWA, US Department of Transportation.

McClay, K. R. (1987) *The Mapping of Geological Structures*, John Wiley & Sons, Sussex, UK.

McDonald, M. and Harbaugh, A. (1988) A modular three-dimensional finite-difference ground water flow model. *US Geological Survey Tech. Water Resources Inv.*, Bk. 6, Ch. A1.

McGuffey, V., Athanasiou-Grivas, D., Iori, J. and Kyfor Z. (1980) *Probabilistic Embankment Design—A Case Study*. Transportation Research Board, Washington, DC.

McKinstry, R., Floyd, J. and Bartley, D. (2002) Electronic detonator performance evaluation at Barrick Goldstrike Mines Inc. *J. Explosives Engng*, Int. Soc. Explosives Eng., Cincinnati, OH, May/June, pp. 12–21.

McMahon, B. K. (1982) *Probabilistic Design in Geotechnical Engineering*. Australian Mineral Foundation, AMF Course 187/82, Sydney.

Mahtab, M. A. and Yegulalp, T. M. (1982) A rejection criterion for definition of clusters in orientation data. *Proc. 22nd Symp. on Rock Mech.*, Berkeley, CA, Soc. Min. Eng., American Inst. Mining, Metallurgical and Petroleum Engineers. pp. 116–24.

Maini, Y. N. (1971) In situ parameters in jointed rock—their measurement and interpretation. PhD Thesis, University of London.

Mamaghani, I. H. P., Yoshida, H. and Obata, Y. (1999) Reinforced expanded polystyrene Styrofoam covering rock sheds under impact of falling rock. *Proc. Joint Japan–Swiss Sci. Seminar on Impact Loading by Rock Falls and Design of Protection Measures*, Japan Soc. Civil Eng., Kanazawa, Japan, pp. 79–89.

Marinos, P. and Hoek, E. (2000). GSI—a geologically friendly tool for rock mass strength estimation. *Proc. GeoEng 2000 Conference*, Melbourne.

Marinos, P., and Hoek, E. (2001) Estimating the geotechnical properties of heterogeneous rock masses such as flysch. Accepted for publication in the *Bull. Int. Assoc. of Engng Geologists*.

Markland, J. T. (1972) A useful technique for estimating the stability of rock slopes when the rigid wedge sliding type of failure is expected. *Imperial College Rock Mechanics Research Report No. 19*, 10 pp.

Marsal, R. J. (1967) Large scale testing of rock fill materials. *J. Soil Mech. Fdns. Div., ASCE*, 93, SM2, 27–44.

Marsal, R. J. (1973) Mechanical properties of rock fill. In: *Embankment Dam Engineering, Casagrande Volume*, Wiley and Sons, New York, pp. 109–200.

Martin, D. C. (1993) *Time-dependent deformation of rock slopes*. PhD Thesis, University of London, August, 1993.

Mearz, N. H., Franklin, J. A. and Bennett, C. P. (1990) Joint roughness measurements using shadow profilometry. *Int. J. Rock Mech. Min. Sci. & Geomech. Abstr.*, 27(5), 329–43.

Meyerhof, G. G. (1984) Safety factors and limit states analysis in geotechnical engineering. *Can. Geotech. J.*, 21, 1–7.

Middlebrook, T. A. (1942) Fort Peck slide. *Proc. ASCE*, Vol. 107, Paper 2144, p. 723.

Ministry of Construction, Japan (1983) *Reference Manual on Erosion Control Works* (in Japanese), Erosion Control Department, Japan, 386 pp.

Mohr, O. (1900) Welche Umstände bedingen die Elastizitätsgrenze und den Bruch eines Materials? *Z. Ver. dt. Ing.*, 44, 1524–30; 1572–77.

Moore, H. (1986) Construction of a shot-in-place rock buttress for landslide stabilization. *Proc. 37th Highway Geology Symp.*, Helena, Montana, 21 pp.

Moore, D. P. and Imrie, A. S. (1982) Rock slope stabilization at Revelstoke Dam site. *Trans. 14th Int. Cong. on Large Dams*, ICOLD, Paris, 2, pp. 365–85.

Moore, D. P. and Imrie, A. S. (1993) Stabilization at Dutchman's Ridge. *Proc. 6th Int. Symp. on Landslides*, Christchurch, NZ, Balkema, Vol. 3, 6 pp.

Moore, D. P., Imrie, A. S. and Enegren, E. G. (1997) Evaluation and management of Revelstoke reservoir slopes. *Int. Commission on Large Dams, Proc. 19th Congress*, Florence, Q74, R1, 1–23.

Morgan, D. R., McAskill, N., Richardson, B. W. and Zellers, R. C. (1989) A comparative study of plain, polypropylene fiber, steel fiber, and wire mesh reinforced shotcretes. Transportation Research Board, Annual Meeting, Washington, DC, 32 pp. (plus appendices).

Morgan, D. R., Heere, R., McAskill, N. and Chan, C. (1999) Comparative evaluation of system ductility of mesh and fibre reinforced shotcretes. *Proc. Conf. on Shotcrete for Underground Support VIII*, Engineering Foundation (New York) Campos do Jordao, Brazil, 23 pp.

Morgenstern, N. R. (1971) The influence of ground water on stability. *Proc. 1st. Symp. on Stability in Open Pit Mining*, Vancouver, Canada, AIME. New York, 65.82.

Morgenstern, N. R. and Price, V. E. (1965) The analysis of the stability of general slide surfaces. *Geotechnique*. 15, 79–93.

Morris, A. J. and Wood, D. F. (1999) Rock slope engineering and management process on the Canadian pacific Railway. Proc. 50th Highway Geology Symposium, Roanoke, VA.

Morriss, P. (1984) *Notes on the Probabilistic Design of Rock Slopes*. Australian Mineral Foundation, notes for course on Rock Slope Engineering, Adelaide, April.

Muller, L. (1968) New considerations of the Vaiont slide. *Felsmechanik und engenieurgeologie*, 6 (1), 1–91.

National Highway Institute (NHI) (1998) *Geotechnical Earthquake Engineering*. Publication No. FHWA HI-99-012, Washington, DC, 265 pp.

Newmark, N. M. (1965) Effects of earthquakes on dams and embankments. *Geotechnique*, 15(2), 139–60.

Nonveiller, E. (1965) The stability analysis of slopes with a slide surface of general shape. *Proc. 6th Int. Conf. Soil Mech. Foundation Engng*. Montreal. 2, pp. 522.

Norrish, N. I. and Lowell, S. M. (1988) Aesthetic and safety issues for highway rock slope design. *Proc. 39th Annual Highway Geology Symp.*, Park City, Utah.

Norton, F. H. (1929) *Creep of Steel at High Temperatures*. McGraw-Hill, New York.

Office of Surface Mining (OSM) (2001) Use of explosives: preblasting surveys. *US Dept of the Interior, Surface Mining Law Regulations*, Subchapter K, 30 CRF, Section 816.62, Washington, DC.

Oregon Department of Transportation (2001) *Rock Fall Catchment Area Design Guide*. ODOT Research Group Report SPR-3(032), Salem, OR, 77 pp. with appendices.

Oriard, L. L. (1971) Blasting effects and their control in open pit mining. *Proc. Second Int. Conf. on Stability in Open Pit Mining*, Vancouver, AIME, New York, pp. 197–222.

Oriard, L. L. (2002) *Explosives Engineering, Construction Vibrations and Geotechnology*. Int. Soc. Explosives Engineers, Cleveland, OH, 680 pp.

Oriard, L. L. and Coulson, J. H. (1980) *Blast Vibration Criteria for Mass Concrete. Minimizing Detrimental Construction Vibrations*. ASCE, Preprint 80–175, pp. 103–23.

Pahl, P. J. (1981) Estimating the mean length of discontinuity traces. *Int. J. Rock Mech. Min. Sci. & Geomech. Abstr.*, 18, 221–8.

Pan, X. D. and Hudson, J. A. (1988) A simplified three dimensional Hoek–Brown yield criterion. In: *Rock Mechanics and Power Plants*, Rotterdam, Balkema, pp. 95–103.

PanTechnica Corp. (2002) *KbSlope Slope Stability Program for KeyBlock Analysis*. PanTechnica Corporation, Caska, Minnesota, www.pantechnica.com/

Patton, F. D. (1966) Multiple modes of shear failure in rock. *Proc. 1st. Int. Congress on Rock Mech.*, Lisbon, 1, 509–13.

Patton, F. D. and Deere, D. U. (1971) Geologic factors controlling slope stability in open pit mines. *Proc. 1st. Symp. on Stability in Open Pit Mining*, Vancouver, Canada, AIME. New York, 23–48.

Paulding, B. W. Jr. (1970) Coefficient of friction of natural rock surfaces. *Proc. ASCE J. Soil Mech. Foundation Div.*, Vol. 96 (SM2), 385–94.

Peck, R. B. (1967) Stability of natural slopes. *Proc. ASCE*, 93 (SM 4), pp. 403–17.

Peckover, F. L. (1975) Treatment of rock falls on railway lines. *American Railway Engineering Association*, Bulletin 653, Washington, DC, pp. 471–503.

Pells, P. J. N. (1974) The behaviour of fully bonded rock bolts. In: *Advances in Rock Mechanics*. Vol 2: Part B, pp. 1212–17 National Academy of Sciences, Washington, DC.

Pentz, D. L. (1981) Slope stability analysis techniques incorporating uncertainty in the critical parameters. *Third Int. Conf. on Stability in Open Pit Mining*, Vancouver, Canada.

Persson, P. A. (1975) Bench drilling—an important first step in the rock fragmentation process. *Atlas Copco Bench Drilling Symposium*, Stockholm.

Persson, P.A., Holmburg, R. and Lee, J. (1993) *Rock Blasting and Explosive Engineering*. CRC Press, Boca Raton FL.

Peterson, J. E., Sullivan, J. T. and Tater, G. A. (1982) The use of computer enhanced satellite imagery for geologic reconnaissance of dam sites. *ICOLD, 14th Cong. on Large Dams*, Rio de Janeiro, Q53, R26, Vol. II, 449–71.

Pfeiffer, T. J. and Bowen, T. D. (1989) Computer simulation of rock falls. *Bull. Assoc. Eng. Geol.*, XXVI (1), 135–46.

Pfeiffer, T. J., Higgins, J. D. and Turner, A. K. (1990) Computer aided rock fall hazard analysis. *Proc. Sixth Int. Congress, Int. Assoc. of Engineering Geology*, Amsterdam. Balkema, Rotterdam, Netherlands, pp. 93–103.

Phillips, F. C. (1971) *The Use of Stereographic Projections in Structural Geology*. Edward Arnold, London, UK, 90 pp.

Pierce, M., Brandshaug, T. and Ward, M. (2001) Slope stability assessment at the Main Cresson Mine. In: *Slope Stability in Surface Mining* (eds W. A. Hustralid, M. J. McCarter and D. J. A. Van Zyl). Littleton: Soc. Mining, Metallurgy and Exploration, Inc., 239–50.

Pierson, L., Davis, S. A. and Van Vickle, R. (1990) *The Rock Fall Hazard Rating System, Implementation Manual*. Technical Report #FHWA-OR-EG-90-01, Washington, DC.

Piteau, D. R. (1980) Slope stability analysis for rock fall problems: the computer rock fall model for simulating rock fall distributions. *Rock Slope Engineering, Part D. Federal Highway Administration Reference Manual FHWA-TS-79-208*: Department of Transportation, Washington, DC.

Piteau, D. R. and Jennings, J. E. (1970) The effects of plan geometry on the stability of natural slopes in rock in the Kimberley area of South Africa. In: *Proceedings of the 2nd Congress of the International Society of Rock Mechanics (Belgrade)*. Vol 3: Paper 7–4.

Piteau, D. R. and Peckover, F. L. (1978) Engineering of rock slopes. Landslides analysis and control, Special Report 176, Chapter 9, National Academy of Sciences, Washington, DC, pp. 192–234.

Post Tensioning Institute (PTI) (1996) *Recommendations for Prestressed Rock and Soil Anchors, 2nd edn*. Phoenix, Az, 70 pp.

Priest, S. D. and Hudson, J. A. (1976) Discontinuity spacings in rock. *Int. J. Rock Mech. Min. Sci. & Geomech. Abstr.*, 13, 135–48.

Priest, S. D. and Hudson, J. A. (1981) Estimation of discontinuity spacing and trace length using scanline surveys. *Int. J. Rock Mech. Min. Sci. & Geomech. Abstr.*, 18, 183–97.

Pritchard, M. A. and Savigny, K. W. (1990) Numerical modelling of toppling. *Can. Geotech. J.*, 27, 823–34.

Pritchard, M. A. and Savigny, K. W. (1991) The Heather Hill landslide: an example of a large scale toppling failure in a natural slope. *Can. Geotech. J.*, 28, 410–22.

Protec Engineering (2002) Rock fall caused by earthquake and construction of GeoRock Wall in Niijima Island, Japan. http://www.proteng.co.jp

Pyke, R. (1999) Selection of seismic coefficients for use in pseudo-static slope stability analysis. http://www.tagasoft.com/opinion/article2.hmtl, 3 pp.

Rengers, N. (1971) Roughness and friction properties of separation planes in rock. *Thesis*, Tech. Hochschule Fredericiana, Karlsruhe, Inst. Bodenmech. Felsmech. Veröff, 47, 129 pp.

Ritchie, A. M. (1963) Evaluation of rock fall and its control. *Highway Research Record 17*, Highway Research Board, NRC, Washington, DC, pp. 13–28.

Roberds, W. J. (1984) Risk-based decision making in geotechnical engineering: overview of case studies. *Engineering Foundation Conf. on Risk-based Decision Making in Water Resources*. Santa Barbara, CA.

Roberds, W. J. (1986) Applications of decision theory to hazardous waste disposal. *ASCE Specialty Conf. GEOTECH IV*, Boston, MA.

Roberds, W. J. (1990) Methods of developing defensible subjective probability assessments. *Transportation Research Board*, Annual Meeting, Washington, DC.

Roberds, W. J. (1991) Methodology for optimizing rock slope preventative maintenance programs. *ASCE, Geotechnical Engineering Congress*, Boulder, CO, Geotechnical Special Publication 27, pp. 634–45.

Roberds, W. J., Ho, K. K. S. and Leroi, E. (2002) Quantitative risk assessment of landslides. *Transportation Research Record 1786*, Paper No. 02-3900, pp. 69–75, Transportation Research Board, Washington, DC.

Roberts, D. and Hoek, E. (1972) A study of the stability of a disused limestone quarry face in the Mendip Hills, England. *Proc. 1st. Int. Conf. on Stability in Open Pit Mining*, Vancouver, Canada. Published by AIME, New York, pp. 239–56.

Rocscience (2001) *SWEDGE—Probabilistic Analysis of the Geometry and Stability of Surface Wedges*. Rocscience Ltd., Toronto, Canada, www.rocscience.com/

Rocscience Ltd. (2002a) *ROCLAB Software for Calculating Hoek–Brown Rock Mass Strength*. Toronto, Ontario, www.rocscience.com/

Rocscience Ltd. (2002b) *SLIDE—2D Slope Stability Analysis for Rock and Soil Slopes*. Toronto, Ontario, www.rocscience.com/

Rocscience, I. (2002c) *PHASE$^2$ Version 5* (Toronto, Rocscience).

Rocscience (2003) *ROC PLANE—Planar Sliding Stability Analysis for Rock Slopes*. Toronto, Ontario, www.rocscience.com/

Rocscience (2004) *Roc Fall—Statistical Analysis of Rock falls*. Toronto, Ontario, www.rocscience.com/

Rohrbaugh, J. (1979) Improving the quality of group judgment: social judgment analysis and the Delphi technique. *Organizational Behaviour and Human Performance*, 24, 73–92.

Ross-Brown, D. R. (1973) *Slope Design in Open Cast Mines*. PhD Thesis, London University, 250 pp.

Sageseta, C., Sánchez, J. M. and Cañizal, J. (2001) A general solution for the required anchor force in rock slopes with toppling failure. *Int. J. Rock Mech. Min. Sci.*, 38, 421–35.

Salmon, G. M. and Hartford, N. D. (1995) Risk analysis for dam safety. *Int. Water Power and Dam Construction*, 21, 38–9.

Sarma, S. K. (1975) Seismic stability of earth dams and embankments. *Geotechnique* 25 (4), 743–61.

Sarma, S. K. (1979) Stability analysis of embankments and slopes. *J. Geotech. Engng Div.*, ASCE, 105 (GT12) 1511–24.

Savely, J. P. (1987) Probabilistic analysis of intensely fractured rock masses. *Sixth International Congress on Rock Mechanics*, Montreal, 509–14.

Scheidegger, A. E. (1960) *The Physics of Flow Through Porous Media*. Macmillan, New York.

Schuster, R. L. (1992) Recent advances in slope stabilization. Keynote Paper, Session G3, *Proc. 6th Int. Symp. on Landslides*, Auckland, Balkema, Rotterdam, Netherlands.

Seed, H. B. (1979) Considerations in the earthquake-resistant design of earth and rockfill dams. *Geotechnique*, 29(3), 215–63.

Shah, S. (1992) *A Study of the Behaviour of Jointed Rock Masses*, PhD Thesis, University of Toronto.

Sharma, S. (1991) XSTABL, an integrated slope stability analysis method for personal computers, Version 4.00. *Interactive Software Designs Inc.*, Moscow, Idaho, USA.

Sharp, J. C. (1970) Fluid flow through fractured media. PhD Thesis, University of London.

Siskind, D. D., Stachura, V. J. and Raddiffe, K. S. (1976) *Noise and Vibrations in Residential Structures from Quarry Production Blasting*. US Bureau of Mines, Report of Investigations 8168.

Siskind, D. E., Staff, M. S., Kopp, J. W. and Dowding, C. H. (1980). *Structure Response and Damage Produced by Ground Vibrations from Surface Blasting*. US Bureau of Mines, Report of Investigations 8507.

Sjöberg, J. (1999) *Analysis of Large Scale Rock Slopes*. Doctoral thesis 1999:01, Division of Rock mechanics, Luleå University of Technology.

Sjöberg, J. (2000) Failure mechanism for high slopes in hard rock. *Slope Stability in Surface Mining*, Society of Mining, Metallurgy and Exploration, Littleton, CO, pp. 71–80.

Sjöberg, J., Sharp, J. C. and Malorey, D. J. (2001) Slope stability at Aznalcóllar. In: *Slope Stability in Surface Mining* (eds W. A. Hustralid, M. J. McCarter and D. J. A. Van Zyl), Society for Mining, Metallurgy and Exploration, Inc., Littleton, CO, 183–202.

Skempton, A. W. (1948) The $\phi = 0$ analysis for stability and its theoretical basis. *Proc. 2nd Int. Conf. Soil Mech. Foundation Engng*, Rotterdam, Vol. 1, pp. 72.

Skempton, A. W. and Hutchinson, J. N. (1969) Stability of natural slopes and embankment foundations. State of the art report. Proc. *7th Int. Conf. on Soil Mechanics*, Mexico, Vol. 1, pp. 291–340.

Smith, D. D. and Duffy J. D. (1990) *Field Tests and Evaluation of Rock Fall Restraining Nets*. Division of Transportation Materials and Research, Engineering Geology Branch, California Department of Transportation, Sacramento, CA.

Snow, D. T. (1968) Rock fracture spacings, openings and porosities. *J. Soil Mech. Fndn. Dir.*, Proc. ASCE, 94, 73–91.

Sonmez, H. and Ulusay, R. (1999) Modifications to the geological strength index (GSI) and their applicability to the stability of slopes. *Int. J. Rock Mech. Min. Sci.*, 36(6), 743–60.

Soto, C. (1974) *A Comparative Study of Slope Modelling Techniques for Fractured Ground*. MSc. Thesis. London University, Imperial College.

Spacial Data Services Inc. (2002) Cyrax Laser Scanning. Canada. //www.sds3dscan.com/

Spang, K. and Egger, P. (1990) Action of fully-grouted bolts in joined rock for fractured ground. *J. Rock Mech. Rock Engng.*, 23, 210–99.

Spang, R. M. (1987) Protection against rock fall—stepchild in the design of rock slopes. *Proc. Int. Conf. Rock Mech.*, Montreal, Canada, ISRM, Lisbon, Portugal, pp. 551–7.

Spencer, E. (1967) A method of analysis of the stability of embankments assuming parallel inter-slice forces. *Geotechnique*, 17, 11–26.

Spencer, E. (1969) Circular and logarithmic spiral slide surfaces. *J. Soil Mech. Foundation Div. ASCE.* 95(SM 1), 227–234.

Stacey, P. F. (1996) Second workshop on large scale slope stability. Las Vegas, Sept. 13 (no proceedings).

Stagg, M. S., Siskind, D. E., Stevens, M. G. and Dowding, C. H. (1984) *Effects of Repeated Blasting on a Wood Frame House.* US Bureau of Mines, Report of Investigations 8896.

Starfield, A. M. and Cundall, P. A. (1988) Towards a methodology for rock slope modelling. *Int. J. Rock Mechanics, Mining Sci. & Geomech. Abstr.*, 25(3), 99–106.

Stauffer, M. R. (1966) An empirical-statistical study of three-dimensional fabric diagrams as used in structural analysis. *Can. J. Earth Sci.*, 3, 473–98.

Stewart, A. F., Wessels, F. and Bird, S. (2000) Design, implementation and assessment of open-pit slopes at Palabora over the last 29 years. In: *Slope Stability in Surface Mining* (eds W. A. Hustralid, M. J. McCarter and D. J. A. Van Zyl), Society for Mining, Metallurgy and Exploration, Inc., Littleton, CO, pp. 177–81.

Taylor, D. W. (1937) *Stability of Earth Slopes.* J. Boston Soc. Civil Engineers, 24, 197 pages.

Terzaghi, K. (1943) *Theoretical Soil Mechanics.* John Wiley, New York.

Terzaghi, K. (1950) *Mechanisms of Landslides.* Engineering Geology (Berkley) Volume (Geological Society of America).

Terzaghi, K. (1962) Stability of steep slopes on hard unweathered rock. *Geotechnique*, 1–20.

Terzaghi, K. and Peck R. (1967). *Soil Mechanics in Engineering Practice.* John Wiley and Sons, New York, N. Y.

Terzaghi, R. (1965) Sources of errors in joint surveys. *Geotechnique*, 15, 287–304.

Theis, C. V. (1935) The relation of the lowering of the piezometric surface, and the rate and duration of discharge of a well using ground water storage. *Trans. Amer. Geophysical Union*, 16, 519–24.

Threadgold, L. and McNichol, D. P. (1985) *Design and construction of polymer grid boulder barriers to protect a large public housing site for Hong Kong Housing Authority.* Polymer Grid Reinforcement, Thomas Telford, London, UK.

Todd, D. K. (1959) *Ground Water Hydrology.* John Wiley and Sons, New York, pp. 47–9 and 78–114.

Transportation Research Board (TRB) (1996) *Landslides, Investigation and Mitigation.* National Research Council, Special Report 247, Ch. 1, Washington DC, 673 pp.

Transportation Research Board (TRB) (1999) Geotechnical Related Development and Implementation of Load and Resistance Factor Design (LRFD) Methods. *NCHRP Synthesis No. 276*, Washington, DC, 69 pp.

Transportation Research Board (TRB) (2002) *Evaluation of Metal Tensioned Systems in Geotechnical Applications.* NCHRP Project No. 24–13, Washington, DC, 102 pp. plus figures and appendices.

Trollope, D. H. (1980) The Vaiont slope failure. *Rock Mechanics*, 13(2), 71–88.

Tse, R. and Cruden, D. M. (1979) Estimating joint roughness coefficients. *Int. J. Rock Mech. Min. Sci. & Geomech. Abstr*, 16, 303–7.

Ucar, R. (1986) Determination of shear failure envelope in rock masses. *J. Geotech. Eng. Div. ASCE*, 112(3), 303–15.

United States Bureau of Mines (USBM) (1984) *Selected Pneumatic Gunites for Use in Underground Mines: A Comparative Engineering Analysis.* USBM, Dept. of the Interior, Information Circular 8984.

University of Utah, (1984) Flooding and landslides in Utah—an economic impact analysis. *University of Utah Bureau of Economic and Business Research*, Utah Dept. of Community and Economic Development, and Utah Office of Planning and Budget, Salt Lake City, 123 pp.

USEPA (1993) Technical manual: solid waste disposal facility criteria. *United States Environmental Protection Agency*, EPA/530/R-93/017, Washington, DC.

Vamosi, S. and Berube, M. (1987) Is Parliament Hill moving? *Canadian Dept. Energy Mines and Resources*, Geos Magazine, 4, 18–22.

Van Velsor, J. E. and Walkinshaw, J. L. (1992) Accelerated movement of a large coastal landslide following the October 17, 1989 Loma Prieta earthquake in California. *Transportation Research Record 1343*, Transportation Research Board, Washington, DC, pp. 63–71.

Watson, J. (2002) ISEE (2002) Electronic blast initiation—a practical users guide. *J. Explosives Eng.*, Int. Soc. Explosives Eng., Cincinnati, OH, May/June, pp. 6–10.

Watts, C. F. Associates (2001) *ROCKPACK III for the Analysis of Rock Slope Stability.* cwatts@runet.edu

Wei, Z. Q., Egger, P. and Descoeudres, F. (1995) Permeability predictions for jointed rock masses. *Int.*

*J. Rock Mech. and Min. Sciences*, Pergamon Press, 32 (3), 251–61.

Whitman, R. V. (1984) Evaluating calculated risk in geotechnical engineering. *J. Geotech. Engng, ASCE*, 110, 145–88.

Whitman, R. V. and Bailey, W. A. (1967) The use of computers in slope stability analysis. *J. Soil Mech. Fndn. Eng.*, ASCE, 93, SM4, 475–98.

Whyte, R. J. (1973) *A Study of Progressive hanging wall caving at Chambishi copper mine in Zambia using the base friction model concept.* MSc. Thesis. London University, Imperial College.

Wiss, J. F. (1981) Construction vibrations: state-of-the-art. *Proc. Am. Soc. Civil Engng, Geotech. Eng. Div.*, Vol. 107. No. GT2, February, pp. 167–80.

Wittke, W. W. (1965) Method to analyze the stability of rock slopes with and without additional loading (in German). *Felsmechanick und Ingenieurgeolgie.* Supp. II. Vol. 30, 52–79. English translation in *Imperial College Rock Mechanics Research Report No. 6*, July, 1971.

Wright, E. M. (1997) State of the art of rock cut design in eastern Kentucky. *Proc. Highway Geology Symp.*, Knoxville, TN, pp. 167–73.

Wu, S.-S. (1984) Rock fall evaluation by computer simulation. *Transportation Research Board*, Washington, Transportation Research Record, No. 1031.

Wu, T. H., Ali, E. M. and Pinnaduwa, H. S. W. (1981) *Stability of slopes in shale and colluvium.* Ohio Dept. of Transportation and Federal Highway Administration, Prom. No. EES 576. Research Report prepared by Ohio State University, Dept. Civil Engng.

www.terrainsar.com (2002) Webpage describing features of Synthetic Aperture Radar.

Wyllie, D. C. (1980) Toppling rock slope failures, examples of analysis and stabilization. *Rock Mech.*, 13, 89–98.

Wyllie, D. C. (1987) Rock slope inventory system. *Proc. Federal Highway Administration Rock Fall Mitigation Seminar*, FHWA, Region 10, Portland, Oregon.

Wyllie, D. C. (1991) Rock slope stabilization and protection measures. Assoc. Eng. Geologists, *National Symp. on Highway and Railway Slope Stability*, Chicago.

Wyllie, D. C. (1999) *Foundations on Rock, 2nd edn*, Taylor and Francis, London, UK, 401 pp.

Wyllie, D. C. and Munn, F. J. (1979) Use of movement monitoring to minimize production losses due to pit slope failure. *Proc. 1st Int. Symp. on Stability in Coal Mining*, Vancouver, Canada, Miller Freeman Publications, pp. 75–94.

Wyllie, D. C. and Wood, D. F. (1981) Preventative rock blasting protects track. *Railway Track and Structures*, Chicago, IL, Sept., 34–40.

Wyllie, D. C., McCammon, N. R. and Brumund, W. F. (1979) Use of risk analysis in planning slope stabilization programs on transportation routes. *Transportation Research Board*, Research Record 749, Washington DC.

Xanthakos, P. P. (1991) *Ground Anchorages and Anchored Structures.* John Wiley & Sons Inc., New York, 686 pp.

Yoshida, H. (2000) Personal communication.

Yoshida, H., Ushiro, T., Masuya, H. and Fujii, T. (1991) An evaluation of impulsive design load of rock sheds taking into account slope properties (in Japanese). *J. Struct. Eng.*, 37A (March), 1603–16.

Youd, T. L. (1978) Major cause of earthquake damage is ground movement. *Civil Engng, ASCE*, April, 47–51.

Youngs, R. R., Day, S. M. and Stevens, J. L. (1988) Near field ground motions on rock for large subduction earthquakes. *Earthquake Engineering and Soil Dynamics II—Recent Advances in Ground-Motion Evaluation*, ASCE Geotechnical Special Publication No. 20, pp. 445–62.

Yu, X. and Vayassde, B. (1991) Joint profiles and their roughness parameters. Technical note, *Int. J. Rock Mech. Min. Sci. & Geomech. Abstr.*, 16(4), 333–6.

Zanbak, C. (1983) Design charts for rock slope susceptible to toppling. *ASCE, J. Geotech. Engng*, 109 (8), 1039–62.

Zavodni, Z. M. (2000) Time-dependent movements of open pit slopes. *Slope Stability in Surface Mining.* Soc. Mining, Metallurgy and Exploration, Littleton CO, Ch. 8, pp. 81–7.

Zavodni, Z. M. and Broadbent, C. D. (1980) Slope failure kinematics. *Canadian Institute of Mining Bulletin*, 73 (816).

Zhang, X., Powrie, W., Harness, R. and Wang, S. (1999) Estimation of permeability for the rock mass around the ship locks at the Three Gorges Project, China. *Int. J. Rock Mech. Min. Sci.*, 36, 381–97.

Zienkiewicz, O. C., Humpheson, C. and Lewis, R. W. (1975) Associated and non-associated visco-plasticity and plasticity in soil mechanics, *Géotechnique*, 25(4), 671–89.

# Index